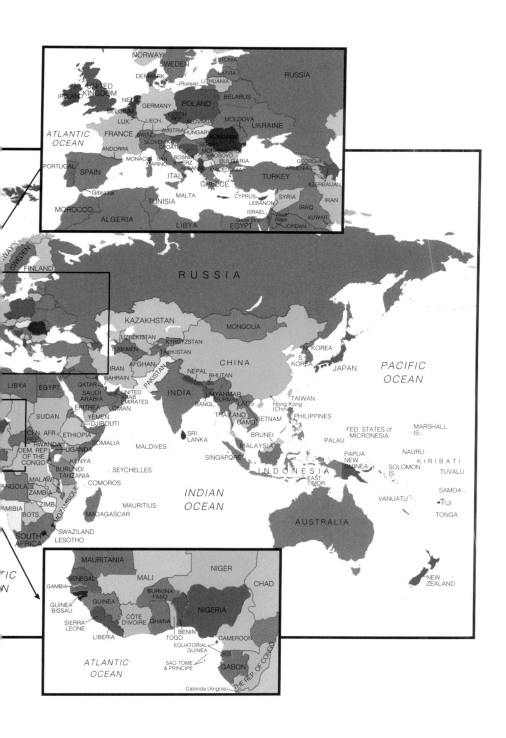

WORLD POLITICS

WORLD POLITICS

The Menu for Choice

NINTH EDITION

Bruce Russett
Yale University

Harvey Starr
University of South Carolina

David Kinsella
Portland State University

WADSWORTH
CENGAGE Learning

Australia • Brazil • Japan • Korea • Mexico • Singapore
• Spain • United Kingdom • United States

WADSWORTH
CENGAGE Learning

**World Politics: The Menu for Choice,
Ninth Edition**

Bruce Russett

Harvey Starr

David Kinsella

Executive Editor: Carolyn Merrill

Development Editor: David Estrin

Assistant Editor: Katherine Hayes

Editorial Assistant: Nathan Gamache

Technology Project Manager: Caitlin Holroyd

Senior Marketing Manager: Amy Whitaker

Marketing Coordinator: Josh Hendrick

Marketing Communications Manager:
    Heather Baxley

Content Project Manager: Alison Eigel Zade

Art Director: Linda Helcher

Production Technology Analyst: Jamison MacLachlan

Print Buyer: Rebecca Cross

Rights Acquisition Account Manager - Text:
    Roberta Broyer

Rights Acquisition Account Manager - Image:
    Leitha Etheridge-Sims

Production Service: Lori Hazzard Macmillan
    Publishing Solutions

Photo Research: Pre-Press PMG

Cover Designer: Jen2 Design

Cover Image: Felix Clouzot/ The Image Bank/
    Getty Images

Compositor: Macmillan Publishing Solutions

For product information and technology assistance contact us at
Cengage Learning Customer & Sales Support, 1-800-354-9706
For permission to use material from this text or product submit all requests online at **www.cengage.com/permissions**
Further permissions questions can be e-mailed to
permissionrequest@cengage.com

Library of Congress Control Number: 2008938609

Student Edition:
ISBN-13: 978-0-495-41068-3
ISBN-10: 0-495-41068-3

Wadsworth
20 Channel Center Street
Boston, MA 02210
USA

Cengage Learning products are represented in Canada by Nelson Education, Ltd.

For your course and learning solutions, visit **www.cengage.com.**
Purchase any of our products at your local college store or at our preferred online store **www.ichapters.com.**

Printed in Canada
1 2 3 4 5 6 7 12 11 10 09 08

BRIEF CONTENTS

CONTENTS

PREFACE

World politics is a fascinating subject. It is also a vast and complex subject. Students of world politics are asked to master, in varying degrees, history, current affairs, political and economic theory, principles of social science research, and ethics. Through eight editions, this book has been providing students with the tools they need to get started on their journey, and this newest edition aims to do the same for students whose journeys are starting in the second decade of a new century.

World politics is constantly changing, and no one can hope to absorb fully these changes as they are occurring. We believe that a broad and self-conscious theoretical orientation remains the best resource for comprehending and coping with change, now and in the years ahead. Thus, this book includes a substantial component of theory, from both older and newer sources. The study of world politics is also constantly changing. In recent decades we have altered the ways we think about the subject; standards of concept formation, of logic, and of evidence are markedly different from what they were, and even now they are in a state of flux. Advances in the study of world politics can be consolidated only when we have the pedagogical skills and tools to educate the next generation. The consolidation we have tried for in *World Politics* is inclusive rather than exclusive. We have sought to synthesize the best of older traditions with newer approaches.

Students must learn something about how theory is constructed and tested, so we deal to some extent with the social scientific method, providing some "how to" material and guidelines for recognizing well-executed research. We stress the importance of cause-and-effect statements, encourage a respect for evidence, and help students recognize the type of statements for which evidence is not altogether relevant. To succeed in a rapidly changing world as active citizens rather than passive objects of historical forces, students must develop a good set of basic concepts and questions, a penchant for analysis, a healthy bit of skepticism regarding "conventional wisdom," and some tolerance for ambiguity when our understanding is, at best, incomplete.

We also provide a great deal of historical and contemporary factual material about world politics. One kind of fact is, simply, information about what is, and what has been, "out there" in the world. History and information about the contemporary world system are essential, so the book includes material on the characteristics of the major participants in world politics and the scope and function of major international institutions. We always introduce or punctuate our theoretical discussions with details on how the "real world" seems to work or has worked in the past. To supplement the wealth of factual material in text, we provide two appendixes: a chronology of major events from the Napoleonic Wars to the present, and a set of comparative data on the characteristics of modern nation-states.

Another kind of fact is the evidence needed to support or refute major theoretical statements about world politics. We have tried to give the students some sense of the volume and quality of evidence relevant to various statements. When we feel that the evidence is reasonably solid, we have tried to document it. When we consider the evidence sparse or ambiguous, we have tried to indicate that, too. We also give references to the theoretical and empirical literature, so that students—and instructors—will not have to take our statements on faith. At the same time, we have tried not to burden students with excessive technical detail or pedantry.

We feel strongly that the study of world politics should concern itself with values, not just theories and facts—with how the world should work as well as how it does work. In world politics there are often both winners and losers. There is nothing natural or inevitable about who wins and who loses. Rather, these outcomes are products of the choices made by state leaders and by ordinary citizens. Students need guidance on how choices can be made, or perhaps avoided, while at the same time taking into account the consequences in terms of peace, security, equity, justice, and respect. These are values that many of us—maybe most of us, to varying degrees—hold dear. All choices involve ethics, and serious reflection on such matters is an important component of the study of world politics.

PLAN OF THE BOOK

Part I of the book explores the analytical dimensions of world politics, introducing the students to the modern study of world politics, as organized according to the six levels of analysis we find useful: world system, interstate relations, society, government, roles, and the individual. It also introduces and develops one of our unifying themes—reflected in the book's subtitle, *The Menu for Choice*—that actors' decisions are constrained by the set of options presented by both global and domestic conditions. In Part I we discuss and illustrate how influences at various levels affect the process of policy making and choice.

The analytic themes developed in Part I are woven through the remainder of the book. Each of the remaining chapters explores a broadly defined issue area in contemporary world politics. Part II examines international conflict and cooperation, covering domestic and interstate war, armament and disarmament, international law and organization, and the causes of peace. Part III is devoted to international political economy, including the political economy of national

security and defense, economic interdependence, regional integration and globalization, and the North–South development gap. Part IV of the book is oriented
toward the future, with a chapter on global ecology and the capacity of the planet
to sustain a burgeoning human population, plus a concluding chapter that examines three scenarios for world politics in the twenty-first century.

We have found that certain key theories and concepts help to frame what can
often appear to first-time students of world politics as a jumble of facts, concepts,
and disagreements about the way the world works. Therefore, we introduce three
broad theoretical perspectives at the beginning of the book—realism, liberalism,
and radicalism—and we return to these frequently throughout the book to help
students realize that most of the major fundamental debates in world politics are
not erratic or haphazard, but usually reflect competing worldviews.

As with the two previous editions, this ninth edition includes many concepts and
examples from game theory—many more, indeed, than most other books of this
sort. Rational choice analysis is now a common approach to the study of world politics, and our teaching experience suggests that game theory can be an effective pedagogical tool for communicating key concepts and puzzles. We generally present this
material by way of a sidebar feature called "In Greater Depth." These analytical
boxes allow us to lay out the basics of the rational choice approach in the context
of examples related to the subject matter of the chapter in which they appear. By
the time students have finished the book, they will also have had an introductory
minicourse in the application of rational choice concepts to issues in world politics.
Another benefit of the sidebar feature is that it makes the book more adaptable to
different styles of instruction. If an instructor prefers that students treat this material
as optional reading—or that students bypass it altogether—this is easily done without any loss of continuity in regard to the main text.

The ninth edition of *World Politics* is thoroughly updated. For example, discussion of the following topics have been added or expanded: the analytical perspectives of constructivism and reflectivism (Chapter 2); American primacy
(Chapter 4); personal character and decision making (Chapter 7); the war on terror and the law of war (Chapter 10); international customary and criminal law
(Chapter 10); the World Trade Organization (Chapter 13); EU expansion and its
tentative steps toward political union (Chapter 14); democracy and development
(Chapter 15). As always, all figures and tables have been updated with the latest
available information, and some have been replaced with new ones that more
effectively communicate the points we are making. This edition includes some
additional maps.

WORLD POLITICS AND THE WEB

The *World Politics* website—for both students and instructors—provides a variety
of supplemental resources catered specifically to this textbook and to a first course
on world politics. These resources include a set of chapter summaries, flash cards,
chapter quizzes with feedback, and other pedagogical tools. For instructors, there
are lecture slides and an instructor's manual. The website also includes links to
other Internet addresses relevant to the topics covered in each chapter. Connect to
the book's website at www.cengage.com/politicalscience/russett/worldpolitics9e.

Readers will encounter references to Internet-based sources in this book. We have found the Internet to be an invaluable resource for the latest information about world politics, and this has allowed us to provide students with information that is as up-to-date as it can be. Mindful of the fact that web pages come and go, and of the related problem of "link rot," we endeavor to maintain a current list of websites referenced in each chapter on the *World Politics* homepage.

ACKNOWLEDGMENTS

We owe thanks to innumerable colleagues and students who have assisted us over the years as we have worked toward producing and improving this book. Rather than single out some for expressions of gratitude here, we will pass over those who in the past contributed to the formation of our thinking. Many of them, though not all, will find themselves footnoted in the text. We do want to thank explicitly those whose comments on the eighth edition assisted us as we prepared the current edition—Nicole Burtchett, Kelly Kadera, Robert Mandel, Stuart Thorson, and Ming Wan—as well as those who have read and commented on parts or all of this book in its previous editions: Francis Adams, William Avery, Andrew Bennett, Bruce Bueno de Mesquita, Steve Chan, Claudio Cioffi-Revilla, Delane Clark, David Clinton, Jonathan Crystal, Vesna Danilovic, Robert Dorf, Raymond Duvall, Nader Entesser, Michael Francis, John Freeman, Scott Sigmund Gartner, F. Gregory Gause, Guy Gosselin, Isebill Gruhn, Donald Hafner, Rober Hamburg, Robert Harkavy, Jeffrey Hart, Terrance Hopmann, Darril Hudson, Patrick James, Robert Jervis, Brian Job, Robert Keohane, Joseph Lepgold, Andrew Long, Zeev Maoz, Sean Matheson, Will Moore, Douglas Nelson, Rene Peritz, James Ray, J. Rogers, J. David Singer, Randolph Siverson, Christopher Sprecher, Patricia Stein Wrightson, Michael Stohl, Richard Stoll, William Thompson, Herbert Tillema, Michael Ward, and Dina Zinnes. Thanks also to Susan Finnemore Brennan, senior editor at W. H. Freeman and Company, publisher of the first five editions of *World Politics*, to Marilea Polk Fried at Bedford/St. Martin's, publisher of the sixth edition, and to David Tatom and Carolyn Merrill at Wadsworth, the book's home as of the seventh edition. Parts of the book represent research done with the aid of grants from the Carnegie Corporation, the Ford Foundation, the John D. and Catherine T. MacArthur Foundation, the National Science Foundation, the United States Institute of Peace, and the World Society Foundation (Switzerland). Over the course of nine editions our home universities—Yale, Indiana, South Carolina, American, and Portland State—have provided truly fine environments for research and reflection. We hope that all these people and institutions will in some degree be pleased with the outcome; any embarrassment with it must be ours alone.

Bruce Russett
Harvey Starr
David Kinsella

ABOUT THE AUTHORS

Bruce Russett (Ph.D., Yale University, 1961) is Dean Acheson Professor of International Relations and Editor of the *Journal of Conflict Resolution* since 1972. He has been president of the International Studies Association and the Peace Science Society (International), and holds an honorary doctorate from Uppsala University. He has also taught at Harvard, Columbia, MIT, and the Free University of Brussels, and was Visiting Professor of International Capital Markets Law at the University of Tokyo. In addition, he has held research appointments at the University of Michigan, University of North Carolina, the Richardson Institute in London, the Netherlands Institute for Advanced Study, and the University of Tel Aviv. He has had numerous research grants from the National Science Foundation, and from the Carnegie Corporation of New York, the Center for Global Partnership of the Japan Foundation, the Ford Foundation, the Guggenheim Foundation, the Naval War College, the U.S. Institute of Peace, and the World Society Foundation of Switzerland. His publications include twenty-six books and over 230 articles.

Harvey Starr (Ph.D., Yale University 1971) is the Dag Hammarskjld Professor in International Affairs in the Department of Political Science at the University of South Carolina. He has been president of the Peace Science Society (International), vice president of the American Political Science Association, and president of the Conflict Processes Section of the APSA. He has served as editor of *International Interactions* (1991–2000) and associate editor of the *Journal of Politics* (2001–2003). He specializes in international relations theory and method, international conflict, geopolitics, and foreign policy analysis. He has also taught at the University of Aberdeen, Scotland, and the Australian National University. He is the author or coauthor of thirteen books and monographs, and over eighty journal articles or book chapters; recent books are the edited volumes, *Necessary Conditions: Theory, Methodology, and Applications* (Rowman and Littlefield, 2002), and *Approaches, Levels and Methods of Analysis in International Relations: Crossing Boundaries* (Palgrave Macmillan, 2006).

David Kinsella (Ph.D., Yale University, 1993) is Professor of Political Science in the Mark O. Hatfield School of Government at Portland State University. He has served as Editor of *International Studies Perspectives* (2005–2009) and was former president of the International Studies Association's Midwest Region. He has also taught at American University, the University of Missouri, and Yale, and was a Mershon postdoctoral fellow at Ohio State University. His areas of research include the arms trade, international conflict processes, and international law and ethics. He is co-editor of *The Morality of War: A Reader* (Lynne Rienner, 2007) and author of several journal articles and book chapters.

I would rather understand a single cause than be king of Persia.
—Democritus of Abdera

ANALYZING WORLD POLITICS

PART

1

World Politics: Levels of Analysis, Choice, and Constraint

FOUR MOMENTOUS EVENTS

Dropping the Atomic Bomb

On August 6, 1945, the U.S. bomber *Enola Gay* dropped an atomic bomb on the Japanese city of Hiroshima. Coupled with the explosion of another bomb over Nagasaki three days later, this act precipitated the Japanese surrender and the end of World War II. Nearly 200,000 people, most of them noncombatant civilians, ultimately died from the explosions. These two bombings represented the first, and so far the only, time nuclear weapons were used against enemy targets. Exploding a bomb of this magnitude (about 4,000 times more powerful than the biggest conventional World War II explosive) marked an enormous leap in "killing ability." At the same time, it brought forth the age of nuclear deterrence in which peace among the great powers was kept, at least in part, by the awesome threat of mutual annihilation. At the time of these bombings, both scientists and statesmen realized that they were engaged in an act that would fundamentally change the future; the nuclear physicist J. Robert Oppenheimer, on watching the first test explosion a month before Hiroshima, quoted to himself the phrase from the Hindu scripture, the Bhagavad Gita, "I am become death, destroyer of worlds."

Despite the magnitude of this act and the precedents it set, there was remarkably little discussion within the U.S. government as to whether the bomb should be used in war. Questions of morality were either ignored or quickly stilled with the argument that, overall, using the bomb would save lives. The only alternative to the use of the bomb to force Japan's surrender seemed to be an American invasion of the Japanese home islands, in which tens of thousands of Americans and hundreds of thousands of Japanese casualties could be expected. U.S. Secretary of War Henry L. Stimson later wrote that the reasons for dropping the atomic bomb "have always seemed compelling and clear, and I cannot see how any person vested with such responsibilities as mine could have taken any other course or given any other advice to his chiefs." British Prime Minister Winston Churchill reported that "the decision whether or not to use the atomic bomb to compel the surrender of Japan was never even an issue. There was unanimous, automatic, unquestioned agreement."[1] How can we explain this?

Particular characteristics of President Harry Truman may have made some difference. Before President Franklin Roosevelt's death in April 1945, it was assumed that the atomic bomb would be used in combat, although Roosevelt had not entirely ruled out the possibility of first warning the enemy and demonstrating the power of the bomb in a test. However, Truman was inexperienced and uninformed about foreign affairs; when he became president he was not even aware of the atomic bomb project. He was therefore in no position to challenge the existing basic assumption about the bomb's intended use or to dissent sharply from the military and foreign policy plans that had been put into effect by the advisers he had inherited from Roosevelt. Only one adviser—Admiral William Leahy, whose opinion had already been devalued because of his prediction that the bomb would not work at all—did not accept the consensus. There was some disagreement among the nuclear scientists who had produced the bomb, but in the end the prevailing scientific opinion was that they could "propose no technical demonstration likely to bring an end to the war; we can see no acceptable alternative to direct military use."[2]

Truman was caught up in the near unanimity around him. Roosevelt, although he was more experienced and politically stronger, probably would not have behaved much differently. Bureaucratic momentum carried matters along, and it would have required either a very unusual president or an exceptionally open structure of decision making to slow it. Furthermore, the alternative seemed technically and politically dangerous. The Japanese could be warned and the bomb tested publicly in some deserted spot, but there was a risk that the bomb would not go off or not look very impressive. The enemy would be uncowed, and some advisers feared that Congress would then be in a political uproar over the fizzled demonstration and consequent American casualties suffered in an invasion. Nowhere—in the executive branch, in Congress, or in the public at large—was there much disagreement over the need to end the war as soon as possible, principally to spare American lives. Consequently, there were few moral restraints on the use of atomic weapons in this war. Certainly there had been little objection earlier to the massive, conventional bombing of civilian targets in Germany and Japan.

The basic constraints, therefore, stemmed from the international situation: A war waged against a determined opponent at a time when the moral and legal restrictions on warfare were few. Moreover, the international balance of forces likely to emerge after the war reinforced this perspective. The wartime Soviet–American alliance was deteriorating rapidly, especially in the face of severe disagreements about who should control Eastern Europe. Most American decision makers welcomed the atomic bomb as a trump card of "atomic diplomacy," which would impress the Russians with American power and encourage them to

---

[1] Henry L. Stimson, "The Decision to Use the Atomic Bomb," *Harper's* 194 (February 1947), p. 106; Winston S. Churchill, *Triumph and Tragedy* (Boston: Houghton Mifflin, 1953), p. 639.

[2] Scientific report quoted in Stimson, "The Decision to Use the Atomic Bomb," p. 101.

make concessions to the American view about how the postwar world should be organized. In addition, the Soviet Union had not yet entered the war with Japan. If the atomic bomb could force a Japanese surrender before the Russians were to attack Japan (in fact, the surrender came after that attack), then it would help limit Russian intrusions into Japanese-controlled portions of East Asia. American foreign policy decision makers largely agreed on these perceptions, as did most members of Congress and most opinion leaders in the American public.[3]

ENDING THE COLD WAR

In November 1988, British Prime Minister Margaret Thatcher proclaimed, "The cold war is over." The events that followed dramatically confirmed her judgment. The cold war, which had dominated world politics for more than forty years, enforcing political domination on hundreds of millions of people and threatening to bring war on billions, was indeed over. The basic values of the West—democratic government and free-market economics—had triumphed, and the end of the cold war was then confirmed, even initiated, by the leader of the "losing" state, Soviet President Mikhail Gorbachev.

The events came in a cascade. First, Gorbachev made limited political and economic reforms in the Soviet Union. Then free elections ousted the communist governments in most of Eastern Europe, and Gorbachev made no move to intervene on their behalf. In November 1989, the Berlin Wall was breached; by October 1990, East and West Germany were united. Gorbachev took no military or political action to save what had been the Soviet Union's most important and loyal ally. In response to demands from the new anticommunist governments, Gorbachev withdrew all Soviet military forces from Czechoslovakia and Hungary in 1991 and concluded a major arms-reduction agreement with the West. Nearly all of the formerly antagonistic North Atlantic Treaty Organization (NATO) and Warsaw Pact countries agreed to reduce their military forces, with the Soviets accepting disproportionately deeper cuts. Soviet forces assumed a defensive posture, unable to mount any threat of invading Western Europe. Even the Warsaw Pact between the USSR and its former East European satellites—the linchpin of Soviet security and control—was disbanded in 1991, as was the Council for Mutual Economic Assistance (Comecon), which had regulated trade among these countries for more than forty years. Gorbachev announced that Soviet troops would come home, without victory, from the war in Afghanistan, and he insisted that Soviet-dependent governments, such as that in Nicaragua, face the consequences of elections. At home, open dissent and secessionist movements emerged in many Soviet republics; free elections resulted in anticommunist governments in several and brought the end of the communist monopoly on power everywhere. In fact, by the end of 1991, the Soviet Union itself had dissolved as a single entity, ultimately leaving the

---

[3] A valuable study is Barton J. Bernstein, "The Atomic Bombings Reconsidered," *Foreign Affairs* 41 (January/February 1995), pp. 135–152. For the relevance of diplomacy toward the Soviet Union, see, contrastingly, Gar Alperovitz, *Atomic Diplomacy: Hiroshima and Potsdam*, 2nd ed. (London: Penguin, 1985), especially the new introduction, and McGeorge Bundy, *Danger and Survival* (New York: Vintage, 1988), chap. 2.

state of Russia and fourteen other successor states of the former Soviet Union.[4] Gorbachev twisted and turned like an adroit slalom skier, but the slope he was on seemed to be leading ever nearer to a cliff of drastic and uncontrollable economic and political change. After a reactionary coup against Gorbachev in August 1991 failed, the new president, Boris Yeltsin, forced even more radical changes.

The end of the cold war, as initiated by Gorbachev's actions, was as astonishing as it was swift. It was one of those world-shaking turns that few theories either clearly anticipate or explain well after the fact. Nevertheless, we must grope toward an understanding, and in doing so we can at least offer some possible explanations, even if we can prove little.

In one clear sense, Gorbachev's personal characteristics deserve much of the credit. Following a series of aging leaders in ill health (his predecessors, Leonid Brezhnev, Yuri Andropov, and Konstantin Chernenko, all died within a three-year period), Gorbachev was only fifty-three when he came to power. He was vigorous, a skilled politician, and committed to reforming (but not necessarily to revolutionizing) the Soviet system. His fresh perspectives, energy, drive, and intelligence were essential to the task. Previous leaders might have seen the need for some reforms but were unable or unwilling to make dramatic changes.[5]

Exclusive attention to Gorbachev's personal qualities, however, leaves much out. He changed Soviet domestic and foreign policies because they had not worked, even by standards widely accepted among communist leaders. The Soviet economy was stagnant, with per capita income showing essentially no growth since the late 1970s, and the life expectancy of Soviet citizens was dropping. The insular and centrally planned Soviet economy, dependent on heavy industry and collective farms, was increasingly unable to compete in world markets driven by technological innovation and the free flow of goods, capital, and information within and between states. The burden of military spending bore down ever more painfully on Soviet living standards, as did Soviet expenditures to prop up allies in Africa, Asia, and Central America. The USSR had overreached globally, acquiring weak clients and eroding its own security. Something had to give. But why did it give then, rather than later or sooner?

Another element was surely the increasingly assertive political and military competition the Soviet Union faced from the United States, which intensified in the decade or so before Gorbachev made his big changes. In the last years of the Jimmy Carter administration, and more dramatically in the Ronald Reagan years, the United States and its allies increased NATO's military capabilities, especially by developing and deploying high-tech weapons that exploited Western scientific advances. American military assistance to opponents of Soviet-backed regimes in Afghanistan, Angola, Cambodia, Nicaragua, and elsewhere raised the costs to the USSR of supporting those governments. Again, the Soviet Union had always been

---

[4] The collapse of the Soviet Union is well recounted by Robert V. Daniels, *The End of the Communist Revolution* (London: Routledge, 1993).

[5] For an in-depth look at the personal background and qualities of the man who saw things differently from his predecessors, see Gail Sheehy, *The Man Who Changed the World: The Lives of Mikhail S. Gorbachev* (New York: HarperCollins, 1990).

technologically behind the West and had long borne heavy costs—so why could it have not maintained itself longer? In addition, the United States was also feeling the burdens of the cold war and by 1986 was no longer increasing its own military expenditures. American care in responding to Soviet overtures—not exploiting Soviet weakness so as to risk "enraging a cornered bear"—played an important part in allowing Soviet liberalization to continue.

Yet another influence was the spread of information across international borders, and especially in both directions across what had been known as the Iron Curtain. Citizens of communist countries could now know more and more about the prosperity and political liberties enjoyed by their counterparts in the West. By the 1980s, most East Germans could regularly watch West German television, and informal personal contacts between Western and Eastern peoples were increasingly difficult to regulate. Under pressure of the human-rights provisions of the wide-ranging Helsinki Accords of 1975, communist governments increasingly chose to tolerate dissident movements. Western news agencies regularly operated in East European and Soviet cities; any violent crackdown on dissent would have been shown immediately on hundreds of millions of television screens around the globe. Technological and cultural changes around the world were making communist efforts to insulate their people from world developments ever more anachronistic, ineffective, and costly. Furthermore, relaxation of the Soviet grip in Eastern Europe interacted with relaxation at home.

All these factors—the nature of the Soviet leadership, domestic political and economic decay, international political competition, global information flows—suggest reasons why the cold war ended. But no single explanation completely marginalizes the others or explains why the end came just when it did. If Gorbachev himself was essential to the changes, then that still begs the question of why he was ready to change, even at enormous personal and national risk. Gorbachev faced opportunities and constraints; he was willing to make certain choices and was given very little latitude to make others. The reasons we list suggest a portion of the range of influences on world politics that any serious analyst must consider.

ASIAN FINANCIAL CRISIS

Beginning in the late 1980s, many middle-income countries embarked on a process of financial deregulation whereby central governments became less and less involved in such matters as setting interest rates and limiting the activities of foreign investors. Soon financial capital began pouring into these "emerging markets" in search of high returns. East Asian markets were a popular destination for foreign capital, and when nervous investors began to pull out of Mexico in 1994, causing a currency crisis and ultimately requiring a financial bailout by the United States and the International Monetary Fund (IMF), Asian markets became more popular still. Although capital flight from Mexico prompted investors to withdraw from other Latin American markets—the "tequila effect"—few investors seemed to be concerned that the truly massive financial flows into Asia might be excessive. Asian countries had been experiencing strong economic growth, and their deregulated financial sectors met with the approval of both investors and international financial institutions such as the IMF and the World Bank.

The Asian financial crisis started in Southeast Asia. During the 1990s, many Southeast Asian currencies were pegged to the U.S. dollar, meaning that when the dollar appreciated, so did the Thai baht, the Indonesian rupiah, the Malaysian ringgit, and the Philippine peso. Thailand had been experiencing slower growth and declining exports in 1996 and 1997, and the feeling among investors and currency speculators was that the Thai currency was overvalued—that is, its face value was more than its true worth—which led to the divestiture of baht-denominated assets and widespread trading of the Thai currency for dollars and yen. With the demand for bahts falling, the Thai central bank did what it could to purchase bahts in order to maintain the baht's value against the dollar, but it was quickly overwhelmed. In July 1997, Thailand was forced to let the value of its currency fall to levels determined by the financial market, and the baht plummeted.

The scenario was repeated in Indonesia in August 1997, and similar events unfolded in Malaysia and the Philippines. The financial crisis then spread to East Asia. In October, the South Korean won plunged in value, sending the world's eleventh largest economy reeling. Despite heroic efforts by the Korean central bank to prevent its currency from breaching the psychologically important barrier of 1,000 won to the dollar, what one Korean official said would "never, never, never" happen did happen in November when the won was allowed to close at 1,009. The pressure on the won reverberated. The Singapore and Taiwanese dollars also sank to new lows, whereas the value of the Hong Kong dollar remained steady only as a result of intensive intervention by Hong Kong central bankers in the currency market.

The currency crisis threatened severe economic dislocation in each of the affected countries and, in some cases, forecast economic collapse as it became clear that some major corporate institutions would not be able to meet financial obligations to their creditors, their customers, or their workers. Thailand, Indonesia, the Philippines, and even South Korea turned to the international community for help. Before long, more than $110 billion had been pledged to these countries on behalf of the IMF, the World Bank, and other sources (primarily the U.S. and Japanese governments). In return, the recipients promised to undertake various economic and financial reforms.

Within twelve months of the collapse of the baht, most Asian currencies had recovered, but the economic damage brought on by the financial crisis was stunning. During 1998, the Thai economy contracted by 10 percent, while Indonesia's shrank by 13 percent. Millions of people watched their incomes and savings dry up as assets were devalued, wages were cut, and unemployment soared. The economic crisis had a profound impact on domestic politics in Asia as well. Japan was criticized for not doing more to prevent the meltdown in Southeast Asia, and international pressure mounted for the Japanese government to stimulate its own economy and open its markets in order to assist the region's economic and financial recovery. In April 1998, Prime Minister Ryutaro Hashimoto announced an unprecedented $128 billion domestic program that consisted of major government spending and substantial tax cuts. In Korea, the financial crisis helped clinch electoral victory for longtime political outsider Kim Dae Jung. And in Indonesia, economic hardships triggered a series of violent riots that ultimately toppled President Suharto after more than three decades in office—a departure that, among other things, helped pave the way for negotiations on East Timorese independence.

There were two main explanations for the Asian financial crisis. One placed the blame on factors internal to Asian societies. Long before the crisis, many Asian governments were criticized in the West for their authoritarian political practices. Dismissing these criticisms as the West's failure to appreciate "Asian values" was relatively easy when the Asian governments had an enviable record of delivering economic prosperity to their citizens. But now the tables were turned as critics pointed to the economic downside of Asian values: poor regulation, high corporate debt, favoritism, even corruption. The multibillion-dollar financial empire controlled by the Suharto family in Indonesia stood as a potent symbol of the excesses of Asian "crony capitalism." This was essentially the IMF's perspective on the crisis, which is why the Fund insisted on economic and financial reform as a condition for its bailout. It was also the prevalent view within the U.S. government and on Wall Street.[6]

The other perspective looked instead to external factors, seeing in the crisis the classic characteristics of a financial panic. According to this explanation, although there may have been elements of cronyism and other weaknesses in the Asian economies, their macroeconomic fundamentals were basically sound. It was just that the enthusiasm with which international investors sought to profit from the so-called Asian miracle was a bit excessive, and it created a bubble of confidence. The bubble burst in summer 1997, investors panicked, and the exodus of capital from the region left currency values in the gutter. International investors participated in a self-fulfilling prophecy. It was their own actions, more than internal economic weaknesses and poor management, that undermined the economic and financial stability of the region. What made Asian economies vulnerable to investor pullout was the very openness and financial deregulation that attracted the huge influx of foreign capital in the first place. Easy come, easy go.

For those people who found more merit in this second explanation, including many policy makers in Asia and other emerging economies, a key lesson of the financial crisis was that government intervention in capital markets was ineffective. With the exception of Hong Kong, none of the Asian central banks succeeded in preventing huge devaluations of their national currencies. Thus, in the aftermath, there were calls for the re-regulation of capital flows in hopes that this would enhance the limited leverage exercised by governments when the next currency crisis comes along.

At the same time, the meltdown in Asia provided an opportunity for the IMF to expand its own role in world affairs, as it had during the Latin American debt crisis of the 1980s and Eastern Europe's transition to market capitalism in the early 1990s. This has generally pleased those who emphasized the homegrown causes of the crisis, because the IMF has spearheaded internal economic and financial reforms consistent with the Western model of free-market capitalism. The policies of the IMF during the Asian crisis were criticized by many, but the restructuring of the "international

---

[6] For the U.S. government's and Wall Street's views of the crisis, see Robert E. Rubin and Jacob Weisberg, *In an Uncertain World: Tough Choices from Wall Street to Washington* (New York: Random House, 2003), chaps. 8–9. For a critique, see Robert Wade and Frank Veneroso, "The Asian Crisis: The High Debt Model vs. the Wall Street–Treasury–IMF Complex," *New Left Review* 228 (March/April 1998), pp. 3–23.

financial architecture" to incorporate lessons learned from the Asian crisis has done nothing to diminish the IMF as an integral component.[7]

The events of 1997 and 1998 highlight some important features of contemporary international relations. In this case, the connection between domestic affairs and foreign affairs was painfully apparent. Although the free flow of capital across national boundaries was nothing new—Asian economies benefited from large capital inflows during the years before the crisis—the sheer magnitude and speed of the capital outflow in fall 1997 was remarkable and devastating. The crisis also illustrates the fusion of economics and politics, nowhere more clearly than in the social and political upheaval that followed in the wake of Indonesia's currency collapse. The student of world affairs must be attentive to international economics as well as international politics, and neither of these realms can be understood in isolation from what goes on within national boundaries.

9/11

On the morning of September 11, 2001, two passenger jets crashed into the north and south towers of the World Trade Center in New York City and a third into the Pentagon on the outskirts of Washington, D.C. A fourth jet, also headed for Washington, D.C. (the White House or the U.S. Capitol), plunged into the ground in Shanksville, Pennsylvania, after a struggle between the plane's hijackers and passengers. Almost 3,000 people were killed in the terrorist attacks, including approximately 400 emergency personnel who perished along with others when the two World Trade Center towers collapsed within forty minutes of each other; more than 2,000 people were injured. An estimated $16 billion in physical assets were destroyed, and rescue and cleanup cost more than $11 billion.[8] It was the most destructive attack in the history of modern terrorism. For the American people, who have enjoyed a history of insulation from foreign attack, the psychological impact of 9/11 was profound.

The hijackers were operatives of al Qaeda, a global terrorist network led by Osama bin Laden and dedicated to resurrecting the caliphate that once united all Muslims under Islamic law. Although bin Laden, a Saudi exile, and his associates had once received support from the United States in their fight against Soviet forces occupying Afghanistan in the 1980s, the United States became enemy number one after it established a military presence in Saudi Arabia—home to Mecca and Medina, Islam's most sacred sites—as a result of the Iraqi invasion of Kuwait and the subsequent Gulf War. More generally, bin Laden and his deputy, Ayman al-Zawahiri, inveighed against U.S. support for Israel and that nation's occupation of Palestinian land and because the United Sates had helped to prop up corrupt and

---

[7] Jeffrey E. Garten, "Lessons for the Next Financial Crisis," *Foreign Affairs* 78 (March/April 1999), pp. 76–92; Barry Eichengreen, *Toward a New International Financial Architecture: A Practical Post–Asia Agenda* (Washington, D.C.: Institute for International Economics, 1999).

[8] The cumulative loss in national income through the end of 2003 was forecast to be 5 percent of the gross domestic product (GDP), or about $500 billion; see Patrick Lenain, Marcos Bonturi, and Vincent Koen, "The Economic Consequences of Terrorism," OECD Working Paper No. 334 (July 2002), pp. 6–8.

repressive regimes in the Arab world. Although many people, including those in the administration of George W. Bush, hastened to add that the United States was targeted because of a hatred of American freedoms and the American way of life, it is unlikely that those grounds alone provided sufficient animus for al Qaeda's *jihad*, or holy war, against the United States.

Under the guidance of Khalid Sheikh Mohammed, Mohammed Atef, and bin Laden himself, planning for the "planes operation," as it was known to those involved, began to gel nearly three years before the 9/11 attack (ten strikes against targets on both coasts were originally envisioned).[9] Ironically, although the planners' grievance was at least partly a reaction to the openness of American society and the global reach of Western culture, these became essential tools of the 9/11 hijackers. After training in al Qaeda camps in Afghanistan, two of what would eventually become a group of nineteen hijackers—fifteen Saudi nationals, one Egyptian, one Lebanese, and two Emiris—arrived in Los Angeles in January 2000, soon establishing residences in San Diego. In May and June, three more operatives arrived in Newark, New Jersey, from Hamburg, Germany, where they had been students for several years (a fourth was denied a travel visa), after which they moved to Florida to attend flight school. This Hamburg contingent would subsequently pilot three of the four planes. The fourth pilot had received flight training in Arizona as early as 1997, before returning to Saudi Arabia, and more training again in 2001. Although some of their travels and activities raised eyebrows with law enforcement officials in both the United States and Germany, and should have raised many more, these Arab nationals were able to maintain low profiles in open and multicultural Western societies.

With the arrival of the remaining "muscle" hijackers, those whose job it was to storm the flight decks and keep flight crews and passengers at bay, all that was required to carry out the planned attacks was coordination and some luck. The passenger-screening procedures in place at the Boston, Newark, and Washington, D.C., airports did not prevent the hijackers from boarding the planes, and they did not prevent them from boarding with the box cutters and mace they would need to incapacitate the pilots and any interfering flight attendants or air marshals. Having undertaken a suicide mission, the hijackers' success depended in the end on intimidating the passengers, including by threatening to detonate explosives (which they did not actually have aboard), long enough to guide their fuel-laden missiles to their targets.

The coordination of simultaneous attacks was key, a capacity that al Qaeda had demonstrated in the twin bombings of the U.S. embassies in Kenya and Tanzania in 1998. Three of the planes were seized within forty minutes of each other. Airline officials concluded that a simultaneous hijacking was in progress and had barely broadcast their warnings to other aircraft when the fourth plane, which took off late, was seized. By then, both towers of the World Trade Center had been hit and the crash into the Pentagon was only minutes away. The delay

---

[9] The definitive account of the planning, execution, and reaction to the attacks is *The 9/11 Commission Report: Final Report of the National Commission on Terrorist Attacks Upon the United States* (New York: Norton, 2004). For a review of post–9/11 academic and policy literature, see Lisa Anderson, "Shock and Awe: Interpretations of the Events of September 11," *World Politics* 56 (January 2004), pp. 303–325.

and the passengers' realization that the hijackers were planning a similar suicide attack prompted a heroic counter-mutiny resulting in the failure of this fourth and final plane to reach its target. Had the passengers not acted, it is likely that the plane would have been intercepted by one of two pairs of fighter jets scrambled in response to the first hijacking. (The U.S. military did not become aware of the second hijacking until that plane hit the south tower, and it learned of the third hijacking just three minutes before the Pentagon was hit, when the closest fighters were 150 miles away.) By planning and executing near-simultaneous attacks, al Qaeda overwhelmed the U.S. air defense system.

Al Qaeda's planes operation was an example of what has been called *asymmetric warfare*: unconventional actions designed to exploit particular weaknesses of an opponent that otherwise possesses vastly superior military might. The success of the 9/11 attack was not a product of al Qaeda's material capabilities. It was the product of ingenuity, planning and organization, patience, and a fanatical devotion to the mission and cause, all of which were directed at American vulnerabilities. The masterminds counted on the ability of their operatives to infiltrate the country, establish residences there, obtain training in flight schools (and weight rooms), and even avail themselves of spiritual reinforcement through continued practice of their radicalized Islamic faith—all while maintaining access to al Qaeda's global communications and financial networks. An attack such as 9/11 simply would not have been possible in an earlier period. The ease of travel, instant communication, and the multiplicity of peoples and cultural practices tolerated by many modern societies is an ongoing consequence of the current era of globalization. Terrorist attacks by globally networked groups such as al Qaeda may be another.

This possibility led the Bush administration to launch not only a campaign against al Qaeda but also an all-out "war on terror." Terrorism was not a new problem; Osama bin Laden himself had been at the top of the list for U.S. counterterrorism operations since the mid-1990s.[10] But on matters of international security, where both problems and solutions often revolve around the actions of nation-states, nonstate entities with global reach such as al Qaeda make difficult targets. The Bush administration's war on terror purported to hold nation-states accountable for the terrorist groups they harbored or supported in other ways. When U.S. military forces overthrew the Taliban regime in Afghanistan in the months following 9/11, the purpose was to dismantle terrorist training camps and to deny al Qaeda its foremost state sponsor. There was widespread international support for the U.S. military response as an act of self-defense. The overthrow of Saddam Hussein's regime in Iraq two years later, on the other hand, was much more divisive. Although the Bush administration was unsuccessful in implicating the Iraqi government in 9/11, the Iraq War was cast as the second military campaign of the U.S. war on terror and as such won the approval of most Americans. International public opinion was decidedly against the war, however, as was the U.N. Security Council, and the invasion and occupation of Iraq opened an unparalleled fissure in North Atlantic relations.

---

[10] *The 9/11 Commission Report*, chap. 4; see also Richard A. Clarke, *Against All Enemies: Inside America's War on Terror* (New York: Free Press, 2004).

Some people believe that the 9/11 attacks will become the historical marker for the first post–cold war period in world politics, one defined mainly in terms of unchecked American power and a sustained U.S.-led campaign against global terrorism with roots in Middle Eastern politics and society. That will be for historians to decide. But from our vantage point at the beginning of the twenty-first century, predictions that the end of the cold war would usher in an era in which political violence and military conflict give way to more peaceful forms of economic competition appear now to have been mistaken, or at least premature.

LEVELS OF ANALYSIS

The preceding four events are taken from different times; involve both developed and developing countries, state and nonstate actors; and deal with military, political, and economic matters. The quality of evidence necessary for understanding the decisions that were made varies from one case to another, as does the plausibility of our speculations. Political scientists usually find it difficult to predict a single event, such as the American decision to drop the atomic bomb on Japan or the 9/11 attacks, and economists cannot predict financial meltdowns, as occurred in Asia in 1997. More often we try to understand what factors contribute to the occurrence of certain classes of events—for example, warfare, terrorism, or currency fluctuation. Thus, most analysts see their job as one of trying to detect comparable, preceding events that seem to produce similar types of behavior.

How can states and other actors existing within similar environments behave so differently? Why do actors in different environments sometimes behave similarly? To address such puzzles, we need to describe what international systems look like, how they change over time, and how they affect the behavior of the entities within them. We also need to look at the internal, or domestic, makeup of states. Doing so helps us understand the conditions under which states will cooperate or coordinate their actions with other international actors, and those under which conflicts will develop, escalate, and even lead to violence. We wish to understand what processes—cooperative or conflictual; economic, diplomatic, or military—result in what patterns of outcomes. We wish to understand the causes of the patterns we find.

In our attempts to uncover causes, or significant preceding events, we have found it useful to distinguish between levels of analysis—points on an ordered scale of size and complexity. These levels include units whose behavior we attempt to describe, predict, or explain, as well as units whose impact on individual decision makers we examine. That is, a level may refer to the actors themselves, to the states or individuals whose actions we are trying to explain, or (as in our discussions so far) to different kinds of influences on those actors. In our earlier examples, we used influences from various levels of analysis to explain decisions made by national political leaders and economic officials.

INTERNATIONAL SYSTEM AND NATION-STATE

In an influential article, J. David Singer introduced the idea of levels of analysis and discussed two broad levels: the international system and the nation-state. He highlighted a major distinction used in discerning influences on foreign policy:

(1) internal, or domestic, influences, which originate within the boundaries of the nation-state; and (2) external influences, which arise outside the state's borders.

The international system is the most comprehensive level of analysis. It permits the observer to study international relations as a whole—that is, to look at the overall global patterns of behavior among states and the level of interdependence among them. These patterns include the overall distribution of capabilities, resources, and status in world politics. The nation-state level of analysis allows us to investigate in far more detail the conditions and processes within states that affect foreign policy choices. Thus, although the international-system level provides a more comprehensive picture of patterns and generalizations, the nation-state level provides a picture of greater depth, detail, and intensity. Singer summarized the level-of-analysis problem with this set of analogies:

> In any area of scholarly inquiry, there are always several ways in which the phenomena under study may be sorted and arranged for purposes of systematic analysis. Whether in the physical or social sciences, the observer may choose to focus upon the parts or upon the whole, upon the components or upon the system. He may, for example, choose between the flowers or the garden, the rocks or the quarry, the trees or the forest, the houses or the neighborhood, the cars or the traffic jam, the delinquents or the gang, the legislators or the legislature, and so on.[11]

In international relations it is possible to study the flowers, rocks, trees, houses, cars, delinquents, legislators, or to shift the level of analysis and study the garden, quarry, forest, neighborhood, traffic jam, gang, legislature. Thus, we may choose to study international phenomena from a "macro" or a "micro" perspective: Is it the international system that accounts for the behavior of its constituent state units, or is it the states that account for variations in the international system? Do we look at the state or at its societal components, ethnic groups or classes, or specific economic interests? Do we look at the government or its constituent bureaucracies? Do we look at bureaucracies or at the individuals who make them up? Do we look at the system or its constituent parts?

The international-system level lets us see, for example, the conditions that permitted the cold war to end or several Asian currencies to collapse. Analysis at that level is concerned with questions about the impact of the distribution of military power, or about the impact of international capital mobility in the world economy. Looking at Truman or Gorbachev, their particular situations and characters, gives us a better understanding of how such conditions were perceived and interpreted and leads us to questions about the importance of the individual decision maker in policy choices. Thinking about the individual investor, about personal calculations of profit and loss, helps us understand the social psychology of financial panics that can impoverish millions of people. In all four of the cases discussed, we can see how questions are linked across levels.

---

[11] J. David Singer, "The Level-of-Analysis Problem in International Relations," in Klaus Knorr and Sidney Verba, eds.,*The International System: Theoretical Essays* (Princeton, N.J.: Princeton University Press, 1961), p. 77. See also Kenneth N. Waltz, *Man, the State, and War: A Theoretical Analysis* (New York: Columbia University Press, 1954), who refers not to levels of analysis but to "images" of international relations.

Distinguishing among various levels of analysis helps us with the different aspects of explanation and understanding. The macro perspective tells one story, explaining what has occurred because of factors emanating from the environment outside a particular decision-making unit. That unit might be understood as an individual decision maker, a bureaucracy within a government, or the government as a whole. The micro perspective tells another story, helping us understand the significance of events from the point of view of people within the units. Using different levels of analysis allows us to clarify what kinds of questions we want to ask and what kinds of questions might be answered most profitably from which perspective.[12]

SIX LEVELS OF ANALYSIS

Singer's distinction is valuable, but his two levels can be elaborated on. Analysts proposed more developed schemes, one of which identifies six levels: (1) decision-making *individuals* and their characteristics, (2) the decision makers' *roles*, (3) the structure of the *government* within which the decision makers operate, (4) the *society* the decision makers govern and within which they live, (5) the sets of *relations* that exist between the decision makers' nation-state and other international actors, and (6) the *world* system (see Figure 1.1).[13]

Individual Decision Makers   At the most disaggregated level of analysis we have individual decision makers. In what ways—education and socialization, personality traits, or physical health—does the particular foreign policy maker differ from other individuals who have held or might have held the position in the past? Explanations at this level must relate differences in the characteristics of decision makers to differences in the decisions they make—for example, what can be explained by contrasting Truman's or Gorbachev's foreign policy inexperience with the foreign policy of such experienced predecessors as Franklin Roosevelt or Leonid Brezhnev?

Sometimes we are not interested in the traits and experiences of great or dastardly national leaders but in the motivations of "typical" individuals faced with situations that require them to choose among alternative policies or courses of action. We may be able to understand a great deal about foreign policy decisions or international events by considering what any actor would do under a particular set of circumstances. Actors' preferences—for example, whether the decision makers involved in trade negotiations are more concerned with access to foreign markets or protection from foreign competition—and not their personal characteristics or experiences per se are important components of some types of explanation at this level of analysis.

---

[12] Martin Hollis and Steve Smith, *Explaining and Understanding International Relations* (Oxford: Clarendon, 1990). They note, "At each stage the 'unit' of the higher level becomes the 'system' of the lower layer" (p. 8). See also Barry Buzan, "The Level of Analysis Problem in International Relations Reconsidered," in Ken Booth and Steve Smith, eds.,*International Relations Theory Today* (University Park: Pennsylvania State University Press, 1995), pp. 198–216.

[13] This analytical scheme is adapted from the one presented in James N. Rosenau, *The Scientific Study of Foreign Policy*, rev. ed. (London: Pinter, 1980), chap. 6.

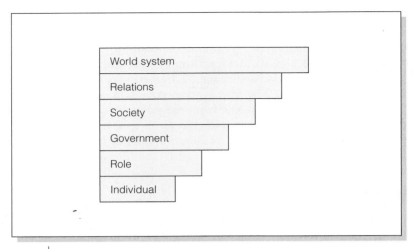

FIGURE 1.1 | LEVELS OF ANALYSIS IN WORLD POLITICS

Distinguishing among levels of analysis helps us clarify what kinds of questions we want to ask and what kinds of questions might be answered most effectively from different vantage points. Many explanations exist primarily at one level of analysis, but some may span two or more levels.

Roles of Decision Makers   Foreign policy is heavily affected by the roles individual decision makers have within the foreign policy bureaucracy. When acting on behalf of an organization, a decision maker is the focal point of innumerable pressures and constraints. We might, for example, expect an air force chief of staff to be concerned with protecting the air force as an institution—to see that it receives a fair share of budgets, equipment, and talented personnel and is assigned missions that will improve its operating capabilities without overtaxing them in hopeless causes. Any individual—military or civilian—placed in charge of an institution has a responsibility to look out for the interests of that institution. He or she must also consider the interests of other people and institutions, of course, and not pursue the organization's interests completely to the exclusion of all others. However, the person in charge knows that if he or she does not protect the organization, then no one else will. Other institutions are also protected by their own personnel pursuing organizational interests and by those at higher levels in charge of coordinating and overseeing the missions of multiple governmental agencies. Thus, the U.S. secretary of defense must arbitrate among the interests of the three military services (and the civilian defense bureaucracy), and the president must somehow reconcile the interests of the numerous competing military and nonmilitary departments within the national security establishment. As part of our examination of individual roles, we must also consider the small-group environment within which individuals sometimes function (for example, a president or prime minister in a cabinet setting) and ask how group interaction affects both perceptions and actions.

Individuals also acquire interests and perspectives from their roles in the larger society. Corporate executives, for instance, typically acquire a set of attitudes and perspectives that are not necessarily specific to the particular companies they run but are broadly shared with other executives and distinct from those of labor union officials. Soviet Communist party leaders who had shared common experiences of the Bolshevik revolution, the Western intervention after World War I, and the German invasions during two world wars, as well as the experiences of trying to hold together a multiethnic empire, had a set of shared perspectives very different from those of the post–World War II generation of Communist political leaders in Latvia, Lithuania, and Estonia.

Governmental Structure   The structure of the government in which decision makers operate represents another set of influences on decisions. A democratic system of government with frequent and truly competitive elections will pose a different set of opportunities and constraints for decision makers than will an authoritarian government. In the former, a leader generally needs to build a wider base of approval for chosen courses of action because the leader is likely to be held accountable for those policies in elections held at regular, specified intervals. In an authoritarian system, a leader can work from a narrower political base to repress opposition, even if the fear of a coup or revolt by one's opponents is present.

Subtler differences in types of government are also important. Gorbachev attempted in vain to maintain political direction over a form of government that was changing from a tightly controlled authoritarian system to a presidential system based on free elections. As the government became increasingly open, Gorbachev and other high officials had to operate under ever greater constraints, both from the public and from entrenched interest groups, having opened a Pandora's box of change, in both government and society, that ultimately could not be controlled. In Iran, although the country has had an Islamic system of government since the revolution in 1979, amendments to the constitution in 1989 strengthened the position of the popularly elected president. This change allowed for a gradual softening in Iran's relations with the West under Presidents Rafsanjani and Khatami but then a worsening of relations under President Ahmadinejad as hardliners politically outmaneuvered reformers.

Characteristics of the Society   Expanding our set of influences still further, we come to the nongovernmental characteristics of society that affect foreign policy choices. Governments in rich countries have far more material resources at their disposal than do those of poorer countries; the former can afford large quantities of modern weapons and can offer economic assistance to other states while their citizens maintain a high standard of living. Again, changing economic conditions in the Soviet Union, through its dissolution and the emergence of Russia and other successor states, provide an example of the impact of domestic factors on foreign policy. As the domestic picture worsened, the USSR and then Russia moved from its position as a reasonably wealthy superpower competitor of the United States to a new role as supplicant for aid and trade from the developed Western states.

Big countries, though they may be relatively poor, still have more resources at their disposal than do small countries. China and India can afford nuclear weapons far more readily than can Laos and Ireland. Small and poor countries are especially likely to be deeply penetrated by other countries or by nonstate actors such as multinational corporations. Different forms of economic organization may have foreign policy implications as well. Various theories highlight the role of capitalism in generating pressures on state leaders to secure access to foreign markets and resources, by military means if necessary. It is reasonable to ask, then, whether capitalist countries have been significantly more prone to war than socialist countries, and, if so, why.

Culture is another characteristic of society that may be relevant for understanding some aspects of world politics. In 2001, the Bush administration justified its war against the Taliban in Afghanistan in part by drawing attention to the plight of Afghan women and girls at the hands of the Ministry for the Promotion of Virtue and Prevention of Vice. The administration not only was claiming that the Taliban was imposing social and economic restrictions that were at odds with traditional Afghan culture, but also appealing to cultural sensitivities in the United States and in other countries where women enjoy substantially equal rights as men. One suspects that at least some of the public support for the U.S. war in Afghanistan would not have been forthcoming if not for such cultural issues.

International Relations   The behavior of states is affected by their internal characteristics and by the ongoing relationships and patterns of interaction between states. These interactions help shape the nature of influence exercised between the states—how influence is attempted, how successful it is, and what outcomes are produced as a result. A small, weak country will act differently toward a neighboring small, weak country than toward a neighboring superpower. Democracies may maintain peaceful relations with each other, but the differences between a democracy and a neighboring dictatorship may bring them into conflict. Rich and poor countries are likely to develop a relationship of dominance or dependence vis-à-vis each other that looks very different depending on which country you inhabit.

At this level of analysis, then, we are interested in what can be learned from the interactions between states that cannot be explained by the characteristics of each state individually (its society, government, or leaders). Scholars refer to such explanations as "dyadic." For example, although some believe that democracies are inherently more peaceful—because of their governmental structures or societal characteristics—others argue that democracies are only more peaceful in their relations with other democracies and that their relations with authoritarian regimes can be quite contentious and even aggressive. Theory and research in this area have focused on the dynamics unique to the interaction between democratic governments and democratically governed peoples.

The World System   Finally, it is essential to consider the larger international, regional, or global system in which decision makers operate. A system is simply a set of interacting elements. A world system with two dominant powers (elements) differs in very important ways from one with four or five powers of essentially equal strength; and both differ from a unipolar world with one predominant power. A world of two superpowers tends to focus global fears and antagonisms between those two nations and their blocs of allies; a world of several roughly equal powers produces at least the possibility of shifting alliances or coalitions to balance power without creating permanent antipathies. A unipolar world—as some people think has emerged with the end of the cold war, Russia's continued preoccupation with internal problems, and American military dominance demonstrated in the wars against Yugoslavia, Afghanistan, and Iraq—considerably reduces the possibility of effective counterbalancing alliances.

Another aspect of the larger system that we ought to consider is the global distribution of wealth and technological development. In this regard, the contemporary world is a far different place from the world of the eighteenth century. Rapid communication, swift transportation, and techniques of mass destruction have revolutionized the character of warfare and the prospects for national security. These technologies—and the enormous industrial structures, commercial relations, and financial flows supported by the wealth of the modern world—also have created a far more interdependent system than existed centuries or even decades ago. A cutback in Middle East oil production, the collapse of a major stock market, or a highly destructive terrorist incident can produce virtually instant, and often drastic, worldwide repercussions. And with the Internet, satellite television, and cellular communications, even those people who are not directly affected by such events usually become instantly aware of them and may be prompted to change their behavior.

ACTORS IN WORLD POLITICS

The six basic levels of analysis serve as a way to organize the first part of this book. In Part I we proceed systematically through these various levels, identifying some of the most important ideas or theories about how these levels affect national decision making. We focus primarily on the policies adopted by the governments of nation-states, as influenced by various entities at different levels of analysis within each state's total environment. This focus is typical of the field of study known as international relations or international politics. States usually have control over territory, dominion over the people in the territory, and a monopoly over the legitimate use of force within that territory. In many ways, the state remains the most significant single type of actor in determining conditions of war and peace, as well as the distribution of wealth and resources.

There are good reasons, nevertheless, to refer to our field of study as *world* politics (rather than *international* relations or *international* politics), thereby acknowledging the importance of actors other than nation-states. The distinction is observed in the title of this book, and we shall often refer to nonstate actors. Decision makers typically act not merely on their own behalf but also on behalf of some group or organization. One such group is the nation-state itself, for whom a president or prime minister acts, along with countless other state officials. Other entities relevant to world politics include: (1) organizations operating within a nation-state, such as lobbying groups, labor unions, or insurgencies; (2) parts of national governments, such as the British ministry of defense or the Democratic leadership of the U.S. House of Representatives; (3) intergovernmental organizations such as the United Nations or NATO; and (4) international nongovernmental organizations such as Amnesty International, the Roman Catholic Church, or al Qaeda.

Within nation-states there exist numerous subgroups based on ethnic, racial, linguistic, religious, cultural, regional, or economic identifications. The process by which states fragment and subgroups strive for independence as separate international actors (for example, the violent fragmentation of what had been Yugoslavia) or as autonomous transnational actors (for example, the Kurds, who are spread across five different nation-states) gives such groups an important place in world politics. James Rosenau includes such subgroups with all other nonstate actors in his discussion of the rise of a "multicentric" world of politics, which he claims now coexists with the "state-centric" world.[14] Depending on the circumstances, nonstate groups and individuals can be important actors in world politics. Although we give special attention to the state as actor, we must remember that the state acts within an environment that includes the multicentric world of groups and individuals pursuing their own rather than their states' interests. Levels of analysis, which focus our attention on different entities and different forms of interaction, help identify the variety of key actors in world politics.

Interdependence is a key feature of systems, including the international system. It is not too extreme to say that in a complex and interdependent system, everything affects everything else. Chaos theory, for example, suggests that small changes in initial conditions may produce large changes in the ultimate behavior of the system. One mark of a good analyst is the ability to simplify a complex reality in a way that concentrates on the most important relationships and temporarily sets aside the others. Jacob Bronowski explained:

> I believe that there are no events anywhere in the universe which are not tied to every other event in the universe. . . . But you cannot carry on science on the supposition that you are going to be able to connect every event with every other event. . . . It is, therefore, an essential part of the methodology of science to divide the world for any experiment into what we regard as relevant and what we regard, for purposes of that experiment, as irrelevant.[15]

Any simplification leaves something out. Any level of analysis ignores something significant, and another simplification—another level of analysis—will direct our attention to something different. In examining the Asian financial crisis, we did not look at the specific personality characteristics of leaders of the various countries caught up in that event. In looking at the atom bomb decision, an explanation based on Truman's role as president will be different from one based on his personality traits, and still different from an explanation based on the global distribution of power or the U.S.–Soviet relationship. But we have to start somewhere. Certain questions about national decision makers' behavior are more readily answered from one level than from another. Questions that can be answered from various levels allow for different perspectives on the same issue and may require different kinds of evidence. Microlevel information on the perceptions of individual leaders and their true preferences may, for instance, be very hard to obtain. But if one contends that nearly all leaders of poor and weak countries have the analogous

---

[14] James N. Rosenau, *Turbulence in World Politics: A Theory of Change and Continuity* (Princeton, N.J.: Princeton University Press, 1990). See also his *People Count! Networked Individuals in Global Politics* (Boulder, Colo.: Paradigm Publishers, 2008).

[15] Jacob Bronowski, *The Origins of Knowledge and Imagination* (New Haven, Conn.: Yale University Press, 1978), p. 58.

preferences in similar situations, then individualized information regarding preferences may not be needed so long as one has adequate macrolevel information at the societal level of analysis.

The choice of a level of analysis is therefore determined by one's theory and by the availability of data, but explanations from different levels need not exclude each other. They may be complementary, with each making a contribution to our overall understanding. To some degree, estimates of the relative weight of each explanation can be compiled through the techniques of data gathering and analysis typical of modern social science. Beyond that, however, we remain in the realm of speculation, intuition, and informed wisdom.

THE "MENU": CHOICE AND CONSTRAINT IN WORLD POLITICS

OPPORTUNITY AND WILLINGNESS

How can we use levels of analysis to help us understand the choices that decision makers make on behalf of key actors in world politics? At each level we have a decision-making unit and its environment. We can study what goes on inside each unit as well as the ways in which the units' behaviors are constrained by their environment. As Martin Hollis and Steve Smith put it, "Whatever the unit, its activities can be explained from without or understood from within. Every unit has a decision-making process. Those making the decisions are influenced from outside and from inside." A particular choice is a function of **opportunity**—the possibilities and constraints that the decision maker faces. When presented with opportunity, a decision maker's **willingness** to choose a course of action reflects his or her goals and motivations.[16]

Choices are constrained at multiple levels: by the decision maker's role in the governmental process; by the form and structure of the government itself; by the resources, demographic makeup, and politics of society; by the web of influence and relations connecting the decision maker's state with other world actors; and, finally, by the structure and dynamics of the world system. Each level affects the opportunities available to decision makers, the images they hold, and the ways in which they make choices. The concepts of opportunity and willingness encourage us to try to explain world politics by reference to the variety of forces constraining actors and to understand these actors' choices by reference to their motivations and beliefs.[17]

---

[16] See Benjamin A. Most and Harvey Starr, *Inquiry, Logic and International Politics* (Columbia: University of South Carolina Press, 1989), chap. 2. The quote is from Hollis and Smith, *Explaining and Understanding International Relations*, p. 42.

[17] Opportunity and willingness are similar to two other concepts used by social scientists, "structure" and "agency." See Alexander E. Wendt, "The Agent–Structure Problem in International Relations Theory," *International Organization* 41 (Summer 1987), pp. 337–370; Walter Carlsnaes, "The Agency–Structure Problem in Foreign Policy Analysis," *International Studies Quarterly* 36 (September 1992), pp. 245–270; and Gil Friedman and Harvey Starr, *Agency, Structure, and International Politics* (London: Routledge, 1997).

Opportunity   Otto von Bismarck, the nineteenth-century Prussian statesman, once remarked that politics is the art of the possible. The decision environment consists of options, risks, and potential costs and benefits. How are all these elements captured by the concept of opportunity?

First, the environment makes possible certain courses of action and not others. Napoléon could not threaten Moscow with nuclear destruction, nor could Franklin Roosevelt coerce the Japanese in 1941 with the atomic bomb—but Truman, with that opportunity at hand, had to decide whether and how to make use of it. In the eighth century, the Spanish could not draw on the resources of the New World to repel the initial Islamic invasion of Iberia because no European knew there was a world beyond what was represented by the maps of the day. The economically besieged countries trying to deal with the Great Depression of the 1930s could not call on the IMF for assistance because it did not exist.

Determining what is possible involves two considerations. First, the phenomenon—nuclear weapons, satellite communication, capitalism, democracy, human rights standards—must have been invented or discovered so that it presents a possibility to at least some actors. Second, actors must have some sense of the availability of this possibility within the system. Nuclear weapons do exist; however, most states cannot "take advantage" of them—for example, to deter an attack by a hostile state—because they have neither the wealth nor the expertise to acquire or develop such weapons. The technology needed to place telecommunications satellites in space is widely known but is not affordable to all. Though a possibility may exist, limits on resources will affect the ability to make use of it. Capitalism and democracy are economic and political arrangements that are common today, but the possibilities and constraints they present are not the same for all societies. Nor are these arrangements universally admired.

Those who make decisions on behalf of states and other actors are able to avail themselves of opportunities because they operate in a global environment that permits interaction with others and because they have access to resources allowing certain kinds of action. Lewis Fry Richardson, one of the pioneers of the scientific study of war and peace, drew a parallel between war and murder. Wondering why people in one country tended to murder each other more often than they murdered foreigners, he came to the simple conclusion that they had much less opportunity to murder foreigners because they had far fewer contacts with them.[18] Police records indicate that a person is most likely to be murdered by a close relative or a friend, presumably because constant contact and high levels of interaction provide the opportunity for murder. Similarly, Thailand and Bolivia are unlikely to fight each other because their range of interaction is too limited to allow a conflict to develop.

Willingness   The concept of willingness concerns the motivations that lead people to seize or decline opportunities. The goals, hopes, and desires of decision makers are important considerations because they may shed light on why one course of action was chosen over another. Willingness derives from calculations of the costs

---

[18] Lewis F. Richardson, *Statistics of Deadly Quarrels* (Chicago: Quadrangle Books, 1961), p. 288.

and benefits flowing from alternative courses of action and informed by perceptions of the global scene and domestic political conditions. Although it is sometimes useful to assume that these costs and benefits are assessed objectively, we must bear in mind that decision makers behave on the basis of their perceptions of the world, which in fact may be very different from the way it appears to others.

Such differences will often stand out in bold relief when decision makers attempt to implement their policies. Neville Chamberlain, the British prime minister, believed that Adolf Hitler could be appeased and so gave in to his demands at Munich in 1938, expecting that Hitler's aggressive impulses would be sated. The result, however, was further Nazi expansion. History also provides us with a picture of Hitler some years later, isolated in his Berlin bunker, moving army divisions on a map—lost divisions that were real only to him and that had no impact on the Red Army as it moved inexorably toward the German capital. The impact of the 9/11 attacks was magnified because they were perpetrated against a people who had taken their physical security for granted. The willingness of the American public to support an interventionist military policy after 9/11 was a consequence of a dramatic change in its perception of threat.

Thus, when we study different environments, we are also interested in how they affect the images of the world that decision makers hold. Willingness involves factors that affect how decision makers see the world, process information about what they see, formulate preferences, and ultimately make choices. Behavior is a product of *both opportunity and willingness;* they are *jointly necessary conditions.*[19] Successful deterrence, for example, requires both appropriate weapons— the opportunity—and the willingness to pay the political and military costs of using the weapons should deterrence fail. The development of the atomic bomb made its use a possibility, but analysts since 1945 have been studying the willingness of state leaders to use it.

THE MENU

Opportunity, willingness, and the relationships between the decision-making entity and its environment can be summarized and brought together through the analogy of a menu. The person (entity or actor) who enters a restaurant is confronted by a gastronomical environment—the menu. The menu provides a number of behavioral opportunities, not determining the diner's choice but constraining what is possible (pizza, lasagna, and linguini are possible in an Italian restaurant, but chicken chow mein and matzo ball soup generally are not). The menu also affects the probability of the diner's choice through price, portion size, specials, and the restaurant's reputation for certain dishes. In an Italian restaurant whose menu proclaims that it has served pizza since 1910 and offers more than fifty varieties at low prices, a diner is most probably going to order a pizza. The restaurant, however, offers

---

[19] Claudio Cioffi-Revilla and Harvey Starr, "Opportunity, Willingness, and Political Uncertainty: Theoretical Foundations of Politics," in Gary Goertz and Harvey Starr, eds.,*Necessary Conditions: Theory, Methodology, and Applications* (Lanham, Md.: Rowman & Littlefield, 2003), pp. 225–248.

other selections as well, and the probabilities they will be ordered are affected by how a diner sees those choices. Though the restaurant may not be known for its lasagna, which may be extraordinarily expensive, lasagna is still a possibility. A patron who is Chinese and unable to read English may order the lasagna believing that he or she is ordering pizza. A patron who is obsessed with lasagna of any quality, and for whom price is no object, may also make this selection. Knowing a patron's palate and resources, as well as the patron's perception of the menu, permits us to analyze and predict his or her choice of entrée.

The menu analogy is helpful for understanding that the opportunities presented to international actors are constrained in various ways and that these constraints affect the willingness of decision makers to act. Constraints can be external or, as is so often the case, they can be self-imposed. For nearly three decades, the academic writings of former U.S. Secretary of State Henry Kissinger have stressed the domestic and international constraints on the foreign policy decision maker. The skilled diplomat, Kissinger has emphasized, understands these constraints and learns to work within them to achieve his or her desired aims.[20] The skilled diplomat also realizes that the menu changes and is therefore on the lookout for better choices as new selections become available.

PLAN OF THE BOOK

Most of Part I will follow the levels-of-analysis framework presented in this chapter. First, however, Chapter 2 gives a brief overview of how world politics can be studied. Although we highlight the social scientific approach, we also discuss some of the limitations of this approach as voiced by critical scholars in recent years. Before moving on to discussions of the different levels of analysis, Chapter 3 discusses the various actors on the world stage. We give much attention to the development of the contemporary state system, nations, and nationalism, and we consider how the nation-state compares with other international actors.

The chapters that follow begin with the most comprehensive context or environment and work their way down to the most specific. Chapter 4 deals with the world system and how the global environment affects the behavior of international actors. Chapter 5 looks at relations among states and the ways states interact. Chapter 6 covers the domestic environment of states and the effects of societal and governmental factors on foreign policy and world politics. Finally, Chapter 7 explores the behavior of decision makers—people who are constrained by their roles and whose individual characteristics affect the way they perceive the world. Part I thus offers an understanding of the complex set of environments within which decision makers work.

Part II focuses on issues of international conflict and cooperation. Although people often think of the international arena as a realm of conflict, a remarkable amount of cooperative behavior also occurs. We therefore examine not only the

---

[20] See, for example, Henry Kissinger, *Diplomacy* (New York: Simon & Schuster, 1994), as well as his *Does America Need a Foreign Policy? Toward a Diplomacy for the 21st Century* (Darby, Penn.: Diane Publishing, 2004).

causes of conflict and war but also factors that contribute to cooperation and the willingness of states and nonstate actors to address shared problems. Along the way, we summarize the theory and research of many recent efforts, as well as older studies that have had a lasting impact on our understanding. We also refer often to historical examples of cooperative and antagonistic behavior, trying to show how current behavior is conditioned by the past experience of world history and how decision makers interpret that experience.

It is impossible to fully grasp world politics without a basic understanding of its economic dimensions, and so Part III focuses on a variety of topics in "international political economy." Matters involving international trade and finance, including the sorts of developments that set the stage for the Asian financial crisis described earlier in this chapter, fall under this rubric. The disparity in wealth between the Global North and South, the emergence of regional economic blocs, and the economic aspects of national defense are other topics we discuss in this part of the book.

Part IV considers the ecological challenges confronting the human race and the global environment. Given these new challenges to global interdependence and order, we discuss alternative ways to manage such interdependence. Finally, we speculate about the future of world politics in the new century.

THINKING ABOUT WORLD POLITICS: THEORY AND REALITY

CHAPTER 2

COMPETING PERSPECTIVES

As students of world politics, we are confronted with multiple perspectives on the key actors on the international stage, the nature of their interactions, and the most likely outcomes. We are also presented with alternative points of view concerning the most appropriate ways of acquiring information about world politics and the prospects for achieving a true understanding of the international scene. Perspectives of the first sort are sometimes referred to as *substantive theories*; they address the "substance" of world politics—*who* and *what* do we observe when we examine the international system? Perspectives of the second sort can be called *analytical approaches*; they generally address issues that preoccupy scholars and researchers—*how* do we observe and study the phenomena comprising world politics?[1] It is useful, then, to begin with an overview of international relations theory.

REALISTS, LIBERALS, AND RADICALS

World War I left leaders and ordinary people aghast. The balance of power—the relative equality of strength among all the contending major states and the willingness to shift alliances to preserve equilibrium when one state threatened to become dangerous—had provided a substantial degree of stability in Europe since the end of the Napoleonic Wars in 1815. That system was violently upset by a war that lasted four years and left 9 million soldiers dead. Many people, foremost among them U.S. President Woodrow Wilson, concluded that the balance-of-power system was fatally flawed and a new world order had to be constructed. These people became known as **idealists** because they had a vision, or ideal, of how a new and peaceful world order might be constructed, especially among democratic nations. They supported the formation of the League of Nations and other institutions of

---

[1] These perspectives are also sometimes called *metatheories*. For a useful comparative survey of the full range of international relations theory, see Fred Chernoff, *Theory and Metatheory in International Relations: Concepts and Contending Accounts* (New York: Palgrave Macmillan, 2007).

international law, hoping to build a system of collective security in which all nations would band together to defeat unjust aggression. The events leading to World War II, however, disillusioned many idealists. Democracy was overthrown in Germany, Italy, Spain, and elsewhere. The United States never joined the League, and those countries that were members of the League failed to prevent or punish blatant acts of aggression. The Western democracies did not band together against the fascists or the Nazis until it was almost too late.

After World War II, people once again vowed that global wars must be prevented. Reformers supported the creation of a new organization, the United Nations, to replace the League of Nations. Once again they emphasized the benefits of collective security and the rule of international law, which would curb countries' hostile behaviors. This time the United States did join the international organization and the members, perhaps having learned a lesson, did cooperate to a greater degree. They continued to trust in democratic forms of government, which respected individual rights, and they hoped that the spread of democracy would lead to more peaceful relations among states. These people, who drew their inspiration from the same progressive political philosophy as did the idealists after World War I, are usually called **liberals**. Their faith in human progress and social harmony was extended to the "society of states," an arena in which institutions and other linkages between states could facilitate and promote cooperation, coordination, and nonviolent modes of conflict resolution. Those linkages may need to be strengthened, but, the liberals believe, they are already much more than some distant "ideal." This perspective on world politics also goes by other names, including *liberal internationalism, liberal institutionalism,* and *transnationalism.*[2]

Realists, holding a different perspective, remained skeptical. Their insistence that the worst of World War II could have been avoided by earlier resistance to Hitler derived from what they considered a more "realistic" understanding of conflict and power in international politics. According to realists—which was the central approach to the study of international politics in the decades after World War II and continues to be very influential today—people are self-interested, even selfish, and seek to dominate others. They cannot be depended on to cooperate, and if they do cooperate, they will stop when it no longer serves their immediate interests. This is a conservative view of human relations, which the realists extended to relations between states. They consider nation-states the only consequential actors in world politics, with international organizations such as the United Nations only as important as their most powerful members wish them to be. States are assumed to be rational, unitary actors pursuing essentially the same goals of national interest regardless of their form of government or type of economic organization. Realists attach great importance to the anarchic nature of world politics. States are sovereign; they interact with one another in the absence of any higher authority. Because they must look out for their own interests in what is essentially a "self-help" system, international politics is a constant struggle for power. As much as

[2] See, for example, Andrew Moravcsik, "Taking Preferences Seriously: A Liberal Theory of International Politics," *International Organization* 51 (Autumn 1997), pp. 513–553; Michael W. Doyle, "Liberalism and World Politics," *American Political Science Review* 80 (December 1986), pp. 1151–1169.

we may wish otherwise, these are the realities of international life, and states neglect them at their own peril. The realist view of international relations is also known as the *power politics* perspective or *realpolitik*.[3]

Both realists and liberals perceive important, but incomplete, truths about world politics, and each side offers a corrective to excessive faith in one or the other position. The world is a dangerous place. We cannot reshape it as we like, and being "good" will not necessarily make a nation safe. Realism as an approach to international relations helps to explain why states fight or threaten each other, but it may be less effective in explaining much of the cooperative behavior we witness. Usually states do obey international law, not because they are particularly "good," but because it is in their interest to be law-abiding and it encourages others to obey the law as well. Nation-states work together in many ways, including in the peaceful conduct of trade and finance, the movement of people across national borders, the exchange of information, and the promotion of public health. Without this cooperation, the substantial peace and prosperity we know would be impossible. The need to explain order (and to seek order) in a dangerous world may require moving beyond realism in order to take more seriously actors other than nation-states and issues other than the pursuit of national power. Just as realism was a reaction to the idealists' naiveté and the failure to stop Nazi Germany, liberalism was and continues to be a reaction to the dangers of overemphasizing power politics and the naked pursuit of short-term advantage in a world that includes not only weapons of mass destruction but also poverty, hatred, and injustice.

A third perspective that paints a coherent picture of how the world works should be distinguished from both realism and liberalism. **Radicals**, whose views often derive insights from Marxist thought, share with realists the conviction that people are motivated largely by self-interest and are ready to dominate others, and that those who would oppress must be resisted. Like realists, radicals consider states to be very important actors in world affairs, but they also emphasize the conflicting interests of social classes. Classes (capitalists, workers, peasants) clash for control of state policy within countries, and the government pursues not some overall national interest but the interest of the dominant class. States are therefore not unitary actors. Classes exist within societies, but they also span national boundaries. Capitalists, for example, may cooperate internationally to maintain a political and economic environment that is hospitable to investment by multi-national corporations. Where realists see anarchy, radicals see a hierarchy of social classes and nation-states in which the weak are subordinated to the strong. Like realists, they see individuals as acting from a kind of rationality, but one that is often distorted by false consciousness regarding their interests—through acceptance by the weak of perspectives and values propagated by the strong. Like many liberals, radicals are dissatisfied with the global status quo and hope to transform world politics so as to make the system more equitable and just. Imperialism and wars,

---

[3] For early, and now truly classic, statements of realist thought, see Edward Hallett Carr, *The Twenty Years' Crisis, 1919–1939: An Introduction to the Study of International Relations*, 2nd ed. (New York: St. Martin's, 1946); and Hans J. Morgenthau, *Politics Among Nations: The Struggle for Power and Peace*, 5th ed. (New York: Knopf, 1973). For a contemporary statement, see John J. Mearsheimer, *The Tragedy of Great Power Politics* (New York: W. W. Norton, 2001).

they believe, have often been caused by capitalists' attempts to maintain their economic advantage, by their competition with capitalists in rival states, and by their efforts to preclude challenges to the international rules of the game upon which the global capitalist system rests. To have genuine and long-lasting peace, the most extreme adherents to this view believe that capitalism must be abolished; others advocate less extreme measures to curb its excesses. As with the other perspectives, this one gets labeled in various ways. Some refer to it as the *Marxist perspective* or as *socialism* or *socialist internationalism*.[4]

Full-blown Marxist radicalism is no longer very popular, chiefly because of the economic and political failures of communism and socialism. Although there were once many adherents to this school of thought, far fewer today consider the radical model for the organization of society to be a credible one. Nevertheless, the radical perspective still has much to offer the study of world politics. Regardless of whether one accepts the basic philosophical premises of Marxism, it provides an important antidote to complacency about contemporary world conditions. The continuing force of the radical critique is well illustrated by the demonstrations against the World Trade Organization (WTO) in Seattle in 2000 (the "Battle in Seattle"), as well as subsequent demonstrations against the WTO, the IMF, and the World Bank in other cities. Various worldviews have been represented at these headline-catching rallies, but the radical perspective has provided a core unifying set of principles for many of the organizers and supporters.[5]

These three perspectives, with their different emphases, offer different predictions and theoretical explanations about world politics, and are summarized in Table 2.1. In each case, some of the beliefs are not easily confirmed or refuted by evidence. The perspectives lead their proponents to make different assumptions, ask different questions, and adopt different levels of analysis in their explanations. But they often lead to contrasting explanations or predictions that can be tested and found to be more or less consistent with contemporary world events or the historical record. At various points in this book we will contrast explanations or predictions derived from the three perspectives.

It is fair to say that twentieth-century world politics—both theory and practice—were dominated by the realist and liberal perspectives, each ascendant at different times. Radicalism has always presented a serious alternative view, however, one adopted by many prominent scholars and, of course, world leaders. Together these three perspectives constitute "mainstream" thinking about world politics. They are more than worldviews or even schools of thought for they have also motivated the vast majority of theorizing and research on international relations. They are, in other words, the field's dominant theoretical *paradigms*.

---

[4] A classic work in the radical tradition is V. I. Lenin's *Imperialism: The Highest Stage of Capitalism* (New York: International Publishers, 1939). A contemporary statement is Immanuel Wallerstein, *World-Systems Analysis: An Introduction* (Durham, N.C.: Duke University Press, 2004).

[5] The Marxist perspective has also given rise to "critical theory," which remains a vibrant school of thought in international relations scholarship. See, for example, Robert W. Cox, *Production, Power and World Order: Social Forces in the Making of History* (New York: Columbia University Press, 1987); Andrew Linklater, *Beyond Realism and Marxism: Critical Theory and International Relations* (London: Macmillan, 1990).

TABLE 2.1	THREE THEORETICAL PERSPECTIVES ON WORLD POLITICS		
	Realism	**Liberalism**	**Radicalism**
Nature of the System	Anarchic, a self-help system. Order and stability rests on the distribution of power.	Anarchic, with elements of order and hierarchy supported by rules and laws.	Formally anarchic, but transnational class-based hierarchy supported by distribution of wealth.
Important Actors	Nation-states, with other actors deriving their limited power and influence from states.	Nation-states, but also non-state actors with influence and legitimacy independent of states.	Nation-states and non-state actors, but deriving their power from transnational economic classes.
Nature of Interaction	Competitive, often conflictual, cooperative when it serves short-term interests.	Competitive, sometimes conflictual but often cooperative on economic and other issues.	Competitive and exploitative in North–South relations, cooperative within transnational classes.
Other Labels	Realpolitik, power politics	Liberal internationalism, liberal institutionalism, transnationalism.	Marxism, socialism, socialist internationalism.

RATIONALISTS, CONSTRUCTIVISTS, AND REFLECTIVISTS

In the last chapter, we used the restaurant menu as an analogy for the notion that actors in world politics adopt policies and take action based on their preferences, but that the courses of action available to them are enabled and constrained by the decision environment. This way of conceptualizing actors and action in the international system is compatible with all three of the perspectives we have just discussed—realism, liberalism, and radicalism—and it has been the point of departure for a majority of social scientists who conduct research in the field. The approach is often referred to as **rationalism**. The individuals or "agents" being studied—whether states, flesh-and-blood decision makers, or collective entities such as insurgencies or multinational corporations—are treated as rational actors with interests and capabilities. Actors interact within a social context or "structure," domestic and international, and although this structure places limits on what actors can and cannot do, what they do (or don't do) also affects this social structure, which in turn enables or constrains their future interactions. It is as if the restaurant menu gradually adjusts to the preferences and choices of diners, providing them with new options and perhaps new prices as they continue to patronize the establishment. The main difference is that a rationalist approach to the study of world politics sees this process occurring somewhat autonomously, without intervention from an entity like a head chef who is ultimately in charge of revising the menu.

As an example, think about how we might go about studying interstate relations during the cold war. If trying to explain, say, the U.S.–Soviet nuclear arms race, we would want to begin with the interests and military capabilities of the two superpowers and then explore the various factors that seemed to lead to an action–reaction process whereby nuclear weapons development and deployment by one side was matched by the nuclear deployments of the other side, resulting in an escalating spiral of resource expenditure by both. Our study could focus on the competitive dynamics of this process and the degree to which the superpowers' nuclear postures deterred a hot war between them, as a realist might approach the subject. Or, more in line with a liberal perspective, we could examine the role of international legal frameworks, such as the series of arms control treaties signed by the two countries, in helping to manage and eventually diffuse the superpower competition. Or we could pursue the type of questions posed by radicals and study the influence of the military–industrial complex, in both the United States and the Soviet Union, as a driving force behind the arms race. Each of these research questions would lead us to consider not only the preferences and choices of the actors but also the opportunities and constraints they faced because of the social structure associated with the cold war. In adopting a rationalist approach, however, we presume that this social structure is simply the aggregate by-product of actors pursuing their interests in cooperation or conflict with other actors.[6]

Although this approach does not preclude the possibility that actors' interests may change as a consequence of their interaction within a social setting, rationalists have been criticized for neglecting the processes by which actors in world politics formulate their interests and, in particular, for not giving due attention to the impact of ideas and norms. An alternative approach, known as **constructivism**, seeks to correct this bias by drawing attention to the tendency of some rationalists to objectify certain practices by states and other actors in the international system. Realists can be especially guilty of this—for example, believing that an anarchic system, which lacks central authority, naturally leads to suspicion and competitive policies whereby states strive to balance the power of potential opponents by enhancing their own capabilities. Although constructivists do not necessarily dispute this pattern of behavior highlighted by realists, they do dispute the notion that such behavior is dictated by the "realities" or logic of anarchy. Rather, constructivists suggest that we need to recognize that the interests of states and other actors, as well as threats to them, are socially constructed. This is not to deny that interests or threats are real. It simply means that actors' perceptions of them are the result of ongoing social processes, and thus are not predetermined by geography, military capabilities, or other material factors that rationalist analyses tend to emphasize.[7]

Returning to the menu analogy, imagine visiting a sushi bar for the first time, despite the fact that you do not find the prospect of eating raw fish particularly

---

[6] The connection between individual preferences and behavior and aggregate outcomes, in various social contexts, is nicely illustrated by Thomas C. Schelling in *Micromotives and Macrobehavior* (New York: W. W. Norton, 1978). See also Robert Axelrod, *The Complexity of Cooperation: Agent-Based Models of Competition and Collaboration* (Princeton, N.J.: Princeton University Press, 1998), chap. 3.

[7] See, for example, Alexander Wendt, "Anarchy Is What States Make of It: The Social Construction of Power Politics," *International Organization* 46 (Spring 1992), pp. 391–425; Jutta Weldes, *Constructing National Interests: The United States and the Cuban Missile Crisis* (Minneapolis: University of Minnesota Press, 1999).

appealing. However, after multiple visits and the allure of the restaurant's social scene, you may actually acquire a taste for several offerings on the menu. The menu, and the social context in which it is presented, does more than delimit your choices in this case; it has constructed your preferences. You may even become obsessed with sushi, making it reasonable to say that the menu has constructed your identity as a sushi lover. Again, the fish is real, and some of it is really raw, but the social structure represented by the sushi bar and its menu are an integral part of the "flavor" you now find so appealing.

The power of ideas is, not surprisingly, central to the constructivist approach to world politics. For example, in trying to understand the Asian financial crisis we might ask why, beginning in the late 1980s, so many Asian countries embarked on fairly drastic programs of financial liberalization, programs that would soon leave them vulnerable to massive capital flight and currency collapse. Part of the answer is that the "American model" of free-market capitalism was increasingly accepted as legitimate by Asian political and economic elites (many of whom trained at American universities). Asian leaders had witnessed the demise of the socialist model with the collapse of the Soviet Union and watched the American economy outperform the Japanese economy, which had once been the model for Asian economic development, throughout the 1990s. The risks of financial liberalization became only too apparent in 1997 and 1998. The point is not that Asian leaders made the wrong decisions to liberalize or were somehow irrational in adopting the American model, or that they were right to do so. The point is that the set of ideas associated with the American model emerged as legitimate through a complex process of social interaction and several Asian states came to identify their political-economic interests in these terms.

Constructivism, like rationalism, is not a substantive theory of world politics; it is an analytical approach that can be applied to questions and theoretical propositions derived from the realist, liberal, or radical schools of thought. Some theorists have argued that many of the differences between rationalism and constructivism boil down to analytical convenience; some questions are best approached from the "bottom-up" approach to social structure associated with rationalism, whereas others may call for contructivism's "top-down" perspective on interest and identity formation.[8]

Other constructivists, however, see little common ground and maintain that the two analytical perspectives cannot be reconciled. This position, which is also shared by scholars who do not consider themselves constructivists, has been called **reflectivism**. In attempting to model the social scientific study of world politics on modes of analysis employed in the natural sciences, rationalists aim to provide explanations that are objective and supported by factual observations. This has long been the predominant approach in the social sciences, but rationalists are distinguished by their commitment to the notion, discussed above, that international events and institutions are best understood as the outcomes of interacting agents,

---

[8] See James Fearon and Alexander Wendt, "Rationalism v. Constructivism: A Skeptical View," in Walter Carlsnaes, Thomas Risse, and Beth Simmons, eds., *Handbook of International Relations* (London: Sage, 2002).

whether they be individuals, states, or other collective entities. Reflectivists, on the other hand, do not believe that a social scientific approach to world politics can be modeled on the natural sciences and are suspect of rationalist agent-based theoretical explanations. Theory and research, in world politics and in other social scientific disciplines, are distinctive in that we are part of the social world we study. Reflectivists therefore conclude that scientific objectivity is unachievable and, more to the point, the knowledge we generate about the world as social scientists affects the world we study. This concept of "reflexivity" underpins the skepticism with which reflectivists view the mainstream theoretical schools of thought and the rationalist orientation that has been so influential in each of them.[9]

SOCIAL SCIENTIFIC STUDY OF WORLD POLITICS

Just as there have always been different views about the current or desired nature of world politics, there have also been different views about how world politics should be studied. In a book like this, we cannot hope to do justice to the philosophical issues that divide rationalists, constructivists, and reflectivists; this is a subject that is best left for more advanced courses on international relations theory. However, given the predominance of rationalism in the discipline, it is useful to examine in greater depth the social scientific approach to world politics associated with this view.

COMPARISON AND GENERALIZATION

In the debates over the causes of World Wars I and II, realists emphasized the study of diplomatic history—accounts of the international actions and policies of national governments. This seemed to follow from the overwhelming importance they placed on nation-states as actors. Idealists tended to focus on the study of international law and organization, which reflected their hope that warfare might become a thing of the past if states would abandon the practice of power politics in favor of different mechanisms for resolving conflicts. Both approaches were highly descriptive, providing detailed records of how states *actually* behave. They were also often prescriptive, setting forth ways in which states *should* behave, sometimes with legalistic or moral arguments.

Historical and legal approaches often entailed the description of particular international events, legal rules, and institutions and sought to understand them. In light of the crucial world problems that appeared after 1945, many analysts felt that a more systematic approach to the study of world politics was required if solutions were to be found. The danger of war took on new meaning with the advent of nuclear weapons. The interdependence and complexity of interstate relations increased as the Western colonial empires broke up, scores of new states were

---

[9] In addition to some constructivists, a reflectivist position is adopted by various other approaches to world politics: critical theory, poststructuralism, and some versions of feminism. The term *reflectivism* was first applied to these otherwise diverse perspectives by Robert O. Keohane in "International Institutions: Two Approaches," *International Studies Quarterly* 32 (December 1988), pp. 379–396.

created, and political and economic hierarchies around the world were reordered. The traditional methods of explanation seemed inadequate to deal with these new uncertainties.

One post–World War II intellectual reaction to the earlier approaches was to study international relations in a scientific manner, using procedures and methods borrowed from the natural sciences. Other disciplines of study, such as economics and psychology, had borrowed from the natural sciences, and the tactic seemed to be paying off in the accumulation of knowledge. The idea was to stress comparability rather than uniqueness—to look for recurring patterns and to understand particular events as emerging from these larger patterns or processes. The new "social scientific" approach, then, assumed that knowledge could be acquired by investigating patterns of *social behavior*—which is why the social sciences are sometimes called the *behavioral* sciences—and that includes international behavior. These patterns may be investigated cross-nationally (that is, by comparisons of several states at a particular time) or longitudinally (by comparisons of conditions in one or more states at several points in time). This approach to world politics assumes that over the long run, many historic parallels will transcend the specific times, places, and people involved.[10]

Thus, the social scientific approach to the study of international relations can be distinguished from the study of international history and international law. Some critics, including some historians, believe that humanity is the least promising area for scientific study because social behavior and events—especially international events—are too complex and singular. If every historical event is truly unique, and thus incomparable, the gulf between the social scientist and the critic is indeed unbridgeable. Although some scholars maintain this position, we do not believe it (and perhaps neither do they). Everyone has compared two events at some time. By comparing things, we admit the possibility of certain similarities across events. Using a single event to illustrate some more general phenomenon also accords with the principle of comparison and the possibility of patterns. The most basic rationale for the study of social relations—that the past can be used as some sort of guide to the future—must rest on the comparability of events and the existence of regularities.

Although scientists believe that things are comparable and that we should search for explanations that cover many cases, it is not true that science (even the physical, or "hard," sciences) promises general laws that will explain everything and predict exactly what will happen. All science is based on models, propositions, or laws that are *contingent*, that will hold only under certain conditions. As the world approximates such conditions, the probabilities that the events proposed by a model or theory will occur increases if the model or theory is valid. That the study of international relations does not now and may never look like physics, with some apparent "universal laws," does not mean that international relations

---

[10] On comparative analysis, see David Collier, "The Comparative Method," in Ada W. Finifter, ed., *Political Science: The State of the Discipline*, 2nd ed. (Washington, D.C.: American Political Science Association, 1993). For an overview of the scientific approach to the study of world politics, see Michael Nicholson, *Causes and Consequences in International Relations: A Conceptual Study* (London: Pinter, 1996).

cannot be scientific. As James Rosenau warns us, "To think theoretically one must be tolerant of ambiguity, concerned with probabilities, and distrustful of absolutes." The use of *probabilistic explanation* is what Jacob Bronowski called the "revolution" of thought in modern science: "replacing the concept of the inevitable effect with that of the probable trend. . . . History is neither determined nor random. At any moment it moves forward into an area whose general shape is known, but whose boundaries are uncertain in a calculable way."[11] To understand world politics we need to have a high tolerance for uncertainty and the imperfect state of human knowledge.

THEORY AND EVIDENCE

A key element in science is the development of **theory**. Theory is an intellectual tool that provides us with a way to organize the complexity of the world and helps us see how phenomena are interrelated. Theory simplifies reality, thus allowing analysts to separate the important from the trivial by pointing out what we really wish to look at and what we may safely ignore for our current purposes.

Theories are sometimes called *models,* and they serve much the same purpose as the model airplanes used by aeronautical engineers in wind tunnels. To study the effects of different wing designs on the maneuverability of aircraft under conditions of air turbulence, engineers need not replicate every detail of real aircraft in their models; they can, for example, ignore the interior layout of the plane and the electrical and communication systems. Because they concentrate on one aspect of air travel—the maneuverability and structural integrity of an aircraft in flight—their theories and models simplify all aspects of air travel that are not relevant to this concern. No aeronautical engineer would suggest that these other aspects of air travel are unimportant, only that they are not relevant when studying wing designs. This is why theory is so central—it affects not only which answers we come up with, but also what questions we ask in the first place. What questions would a realist, liberal, or radical ask about the end of the cold war? We will suggest some possibilities in the following discussion.

If they are to be evaluated scientifically, theories must be stated in a clear and precise way. A good theory is one that can be supported or rejected using information, or data, about the world. Obviously, we prefer that our theories are supported by the data, but a theory that cannot be tested at all—one that cannot be disproved in any conceivable way—will not get us very far. Think, for example, of the proposition, "People always act to advance their own self-interest, no matter how much they delude themselves or others into thinking they are acting in someone else's interest." Because the proponent of such an argument can always support the argument ("The people in question are deluding themselves about their motives") and the statement cannot be checked against evidence (we cannot look

---

[11] James N. Rosenau, "Thinking Theory Thoroughly," in James N. Rosenau, ed., *The Scientific Study of Foreign Policy,* rev. ed. (London: Pinter, 1980), p. 28; Jacob Bronowski, *The Common Sense of Science* (London: Heinemann, 1951), pp. 86–87. See also Benjamin A. Most and Harvey Starr, *Inquiry, Logic and International Politics* (Columbia: University of South Carolina Press, 1989), chaps. 1, 5.

inside a person's mind), the self-interest proposition cannot be disproved, or "falsified." It is not a scientific statement because any evidence can be interpreted as agreeing with it. We do not want our theories to be disproved, but a theory is of little use if it is so vague or self-evident that we cannot even imagine how it might be disproved.

Where do theories come from? Some of the most sophisticated and elaborate theories are the result of painstaking study and deep familiarity with the subject matter. However, even these theories often start out as hunches about the way the world works. Theories come from all aspects of human experience, and many of the most successful scientists, such as Louis Pasteur or Thomas Edison, had a creative knack by which they could look at things differently and draw analogies where others could not.

Theories tell us what to look at and how the things we look at relate to each other. Because we can come up with opposite yet plausible reasons for almost every aspect of human interaction—"absence makes the heart grow fonder" or "out of sight, out of mind"—we need systematic evidence to test a theory. Science assumes that at least some of the patterns described by a theory can be observed and measured in some way. We can therefore collect information with the intention of evaluating the validity of our theory; this is our **evidence**. Of course, evidence should be collected in such a way as to be relevant to the question at hand and should not bias the results of our evaluation. The procedures by which the evidence has been collected ought to be *transparent*. Otherwise, it will be difficult to judge whether the evidence has been slanted in some way, which may call into question the credibility of the entire analysis. Science, therefore, is a systematic way of obtaining information and making and supporting generalizations.

As some experienced social scientists point out, much of what we know about social phenomena is "ordinary knowledge" that is not derived from systematic scientific endeavors. Ordinary knowledge, or "common sense" as we often call it, reflects the general understanding of people at a particular time and place. It might include the statement that there is a war going on somewhere at virtually all times, that countries tend to trade more with neighboring states, and that children represent the majority of the world's poor. However, we must also know when to doubt what passes as ordinary knowledge, when to question it, and how to supplant or supplement it by scientific knowledge when needed. Common sense can be untrue, as were the formerly held beliefs that the Earth is flat and that human intelligence is related to brain size. Common sense may be the result of changing intellectual fashions, as in the relationship between Isaac Newton's physics and previous knowledge, or the relationship between Einstein's physics and earlier, Newtonian beliefs. Most important, common sense is often contradictory. Social science should be directed at key points of inquiry where ordinary knowledge is suspect.

HYPOTHESES AND ASSUMPTIONS

Theoretical statements that relate to possible observations are called **hypotheses**. The testing of hypotheses—checking their predictions against observed data—is a central activity of science. Hypotheses that are confirmed in virtually all classes of phenomena to which they are applied are often known as *laws*. In the social sciences, interesting laws are quite rare. The phenomena of social science are so complex, with so many different influences or causes, and our knowledge of these complex phenomena is so imperfect that few laws have been established. Even with much more theory and research, we are likely to have only **probabilistic explanations** that state, given some antecedent conditions, that most phenomena of a given class will behave in a certain way most of the time. This is why social scientists find it hard to predict how particular events will develop; for example, which Soviet leader, at what specific point in time, would be willing to let the East European states go their independent ways. At best, the social scientist can indicate a probability that a particular action (a threat, a promise, a concession) will be followed by a specific result (armed conflict, capitulation, compromise).[12]

When we say that we hope to make general statements about phenomena in world politics, we do not necessarily mean generalizations that apply to all actors or events at all times. Such generalizations may be approximated in some areas of physics, but they are hard to come by in the social sciences. Even when states are widely observed to react to certain stimuli, such as an increase in their rivals' military power, they may do so in any number of ways—by building their own military power, by joining an alliance, or by launching a preemptive strike, for example. In other words, one reaction may "substitute" for another, depending on the state's opportunities (whether military resources or powerful allies are available) and its willingness to act on those opportunities. The same cause may have different effects in different contexts. In May 1998, after India tested five nuclear bombs, there was virtual certainty that India's arch rival, Pakistan, would react in some way, but it was not a foregone conclusion that it would react by detonating its own nuclear devices. Many countries sought, unsuccessfully, to convince Pakistan to pursue an alternative course of action. One opportunity available to Pakistan in the aftermath of India's nuclear tests might have been to enhance its military strength by acquiring advanced conventional weapons from the United States.[13]

If statements have been supported by evidence, then it is also important that they identify the *process* or *causal relationship* underlying the observed patterns. For example, the statement, "Young drivers have more traffic accidents than do older drivers" may be a correct statement of fact—an observed correlation—but it tells us little of interest about causality, about *why* young drivers tend to crash their cars more frequently. Often it is very difficult to uncover the process of causation that accounts for an observed correlation. In this example, is it because younger drivers are more reckless or less experienced? Or might it be because they drive older cars, with fewer safety features? (See Box 2.1 for further discussion of causality in relation to the concepts of opportunity and willingness.)

---

[12] See John Lewis Gaddis, "International Relations Theory and the End of the Cold War," *International Security* 17 (Winter 1992/1993), pp. 5–58; and James Lee Ray and Bruce Russett, "The Future as Arbiter of Theoretical Controversies: The Scientific Study of Politics and Predictions," *British Journal of Political Science* 26 (October 1996), pp. 441–470.

[13] Theoretical statements that specify the set of contingencies that usually lead to one type of foreign policy response versus another have been called "nice laws." See Most and Starr, *Inquiry, Logic and International Politics*, especially chap. 5.

IN GREATER DEPTH

| BOX 2.1 | OPPORTUNITY, WILLINGNESS, AND CAUSALITY |

Causality is one of the most elusive concepts in the social sciences. A simple definition of a *cause* is a condition or set of conditions that must exist if the behavior or event in question is to occur. In the context of a policy maker choosing a course of action, we have referred to such antecedent conditions as contributing to either opportunity or willingness. This can be illustrated using a diagram:

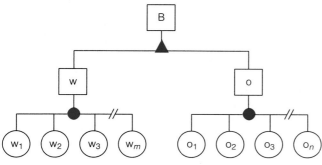

The behavior that interests us is represented as B. As an example, suppose we want to understand why a state leader would use military force to seize a piece of territory currently possessed by another state. Factors contributing to the leader's willingness to seize the territory might include its mineral wealth or its being home to ethnic kin. We can designate these as w_1 and w_2 and further recognize that there may be many (as many as w_m) factors

contributing to willingness. Probably not all m factors need to be present, but one or more of them must be, perhaps in different combinations, and we can represent this "or" requirement with a circle (●). The opportunity to seize the disputed territory might include some newly acquired military capability or the other state's preoccupation with a domestic ethnic conflict elsewhere. We can use o_1 and o_2 for these opportunities and again recognize that among all of the n factors there are different combinations that may provide the leader with the opportunity to make the grab. But neither willingness nor opportunity alone is sufficient. It is their *conjunction* that causes behavior B, and we can represent this "and" requirement with a triangle (▲).

When dealing with the sorts of complex processes that we encounter (or suspect) in world politics, it is often helpful to "formalize" the causal logic of our theories and hypotheses in this or some other way.

Note: For a more detailed discussion of these and related ideas, see Claudio Cioffi-Revilla and Harvey Starr, "Opportunity, Willingness, and Political Uncertainty: Theoretical Foundations of Politics," in Gary Goertz and Harvey Starr, eds., *Necessary Conditions: Theory, Methodology, and Applications* (Lanham, Md.: Rowman & Littlefield, 2003), pp. 225–248.

All theories include **assumptions**. In contrast to hypotheses, we do not systematically test assumptions against actual data. This is either because our assumptions are fairly straightforward statements about the world, with which most people agree, or because examining the accuracy of these statements must be deferred until later, at which time they can be treated as hypotheses to be tested. Assumptions simplify the task of theory building, and we sometimes make assumptions that we know are not correct or not fully correct. For example, we can assume that the speed of a falling body is not slowed by friction with the air. Sometimes this assumption is close enough to reality that it does not affect our conclusions about the acceleration of objects of different weights. The resistance encountered by iron and lead balls may be minimal when they are dropped from the Leaning Tower of Pisa. But if the assumptions were wildly incorrect for a particular set of problems, then the results would be irrelevant at best, and possibly disastrous. What if we assumed that air resistance would make no difference in the speeds of a feather and a lead ball dropped from the tower? By following the precepts of scientific inquiry, a careful analyst will always be alert to the nature of their assumptions, to ways in which they may differ from reality, and to the conditions under which the difference may affect one's conclusions. A careful analyst will want to be clear about what has been simplified and will have some sense of how that simplification may compromise predictions.

We suggested earlier that realists treat nation-states as rational, unitary actors—that is, they *assume,* for purposes of building a realist theory of world politics, that states are rational and unitary entities. Of course, realists know that states consist of many societal groups, which may have an impact on the process of foreign policy making, and that the parties directly involved in policy making sometimes make miscalculations and adopt what appear to be irrational strategies. However, for realists, these details are unimportant when explaining the dimensions of state behavior with which they are most concerned. That is, when all is said and done, states behave *as if* they were rational, unitary actors. Because most realists agree with this assessment, it is a common assumption in realist theories of world politics. Liberals and radicals are often not willing to make such an assumption, so their explanations and predictions can look quite different.

SPECIFYING AND TESTING HYPOTHESES

Social scientists often proceed in the following way: First, identify some behavior that needs to be explained. Second, offer some tentative hypotheses, perhaps derived from some theory purporting to explain that behavior. Third, evaluate the hypotheses in light of available evidence. Fourth, if the evidence supports the hypotheses, then consider the implications—the additional statements (or predictions) that can be deduced from these confirmed hypotheses. Finally, treat these new statements as hypotheses and evaluate them in light of available evidence.[14] In the social sciences, analysis along these lines often takes the form of a "quasi-experiment." In a clinical or laboratory experiment, the researcher randomly varies actual conditions and records the effects that the changes have. Sometimes we can conduct experiments with students or citizens. We might tell a group of them that the president in a political crisis made a demand against another country, which rejected the demand. We could tell one-half of the group that the president then took military action, and tell the other half that he did not. Then

---

[14] This basic procedure comes from R. E. Lipsey, *Introduction to Positive Economics* (New York: Harper & Row, 1963), as described by Martin Hollis and Steve Smith, *Explaining and Understanding International Relations* (Oxford: Clarendon, 1990), pp. 50–52.

we could compare the president's approval ratings in each group.[15] But with organizations and nations, we cannot conduct true experiments, mainly because we do not have the same control over the conditions of our research. Although we might wish to conduct an experiment to see if there is evidence to support the hypothesis that trading states have more peaceful political relations, we cannot manipulate the "dose" of commercial transactions between two particular states and then record the effect on their diplomatic or military interactions. We can, however, observe different pairs of states and see if those with more commercial ties are also those experiencing fewer political and military tensions.

When a hypothesis has been formulated, but conducting an experiment or quasi-experiment is not practical, perhaps because not all the necessary evidence has been collected, it may still be useful to proceed with a very tentative analysis. This might resemble a "thought experiment" in which one considers the implications of a hypothesis being true and then tentatively evaluates the hypothesis in light of logic or anecdotal evidence. For example, we can examine Gorbachev's decision not to use Soviet troops to suppress East German dissidents in 1989 in an effort to save its Communist government. This was one of the most dramatic and important decisions that permitted an end to the cold war. As an exercise, we propose several hypotheses derived from the realist, liberal, and radical perspectives and offer tentative evaluations of their plausibility.

Hypothesis 1   Gorbachev did not use force to support the East German government because he feared a NATO military response, which might culminate in World War III. A realist might say that the NATO allies could not have resisted the opportunity to gain a critical power advantage; in this case, to bring all East Germany under their control. A radical might say much the same thing but give as the reason the West's continuing wish to expand the realm of free-market capitalism and to bring down the competing system of economic and political organization.

Evaluation   One problem with either version of this hypothesis is that the NATO countries had passed up similar opportunities in the past. When the Soviet Union crushed the Hungarian revolution in 1956 and the liberalization of Czechoslovakia, known as the Prague Spring, in 1968, the West did virtually nothing. NATO countries implicitly acknowledged that the Soviet Union had the right to do as it wished within Eastern Europe, which was its sphere of influence, and that the risks involved in any NATO military response were much too great. There is little reason to think that in 1989 they would have judged the situation in East Germany differently.

Hypothesis 2   Gorbachev did not use force because he secretly held goals very different from those of other Soviet leaders. Perhaps he really was a "closet democrat" who wanted noncommunist governments in East Germany and the rest of Eastern Europe (a liberal explanation), or perhaps he really was an agent of the U.S. Central Intelligence Agency (CIA) whose aim was to betray communism (a radical explanation).

---

[15] An experiment like this appears in Michael Tomz, "Domestic Audience Costs in International Relations: An Experimental Approach," *International Organization* 61 (Fall 2007), pp. 821–840.

Evaluation   There are virtually no facts to support either version of this hypothesis. Gorbachev acted much more like a reformer of communism, with no fully formed goal in mind, than like someone who wanted to do away with the communist system entirely. He came out of much the same set of party and government experiences as did other Soviet leaders and gave no hint of a desire to make a complete break with the past. As for deliberately betraying the system as a Western agent, that belief requires enormous faith in the effectiveness of the CIA. We find both versions of this hypothesis implausible.

Hypothesis 3   Gorbachev feared that repression would not be effective in East Germany and the effort to impose this solution would only hasten the spread of revolution across Eastern Europe (a liberal hypothesis).

Evaluation   This hypothesis draws its strength from the increasing growth of transnational communications links that carried new information and ideas into and out of Eastern Europe. It implies that people would rise up in support of those ideas and in support of one another, even in the face of terrible costs. Perhaps the Soviet people and Soviet troops would also have rebelled rather than permit wholesale repression. It is true that transnational linkages had grown substantially, yet during the Prague Spring in 1968 there were also many linkages within Eastern Europe, and they had little effect. Therefore, while one cannot completely dismiss this hypothesis, it is weak as a primary explanation.

Hypothesis 4   Gorbachev knew that the use of force would alienate the Western countries, on which he was relying for technological and military assistance to rebuild the Soviet economy. No Soviet leader with such a goal could afford to do something that would cut off the possibility of trade with the West (another liberal hypothesis).

Evaluation   This hypothesis also has some plausibility, but it does not fit some of the facts very well. Western responses to previous Soviet crackdowns on dissent had not been strong. When, in December 1981, the Communist government of Poland violently repressed the Solidarity movement with Soviet approval and encouragement (but no Soviet troops), there was only a partial and ineffective Western trade embargo; the same was true in response to the Soviet military intervention in Afghanistan. Gorbachev might have thought that once again the West would accept the Soviet sphere of influence and not enforce severe economic sanctions.

Hypothesis 5   Gorbachev did not intervene because Eastern Europe had become a serious drain on Soviet resources rather than an asset. He thought that the national interest of the Soviet Union would be better served economically and politically by letting the satellites go (a realist hypothesis).

Evaluation   There is a lot of evidence that Eastern Europe had long been an economic drain, receiving many overt and hidden subsidies, such as cheap Soviet oil.

On the one hand, such considerations had earlier had little effect; on the other hand, we now know that the Soviet economy was in far worse shape than suspected by most analysts. One problem with this hypothesis is that it rests on the sometimes vague concept of national interest, and such explanations risk being nonfalsifiable.

Hypothesis 6   Gorbachev did not intervene because the Soviet Union no longer needed the political and military buffer that Eastern Europe had provided. Gorbachev no longer, if he ever had, feared a NATO attack (another realist hypothesis).

Evaluation   Gorbachev might finally have decided that the West did not wish to attack his country. But it is not clear why Western intentions should have so recently—in the years of tough rhetoric from the Reagan administration about the Soviet "evil empire"—come to seem more benign, or why Gorbachev in particular should have reached that conclusion. Evidence for the realist view may be found in the growing Soviet and American realization that in a world of nuclear parity, nuclear weapons could not be used credibly for anything but the defense of one's homeland, and certainly not to coerce another superpower. Thus, as long as it retained a rough nuclear parity with the United States, the Soviet Union could protect itself without allies or the kind of in-depth defense that a shield of reluctant East European satellites might provide. After 1986, Gorbachev abandoned most of his previous rhetoric advocating the total elimination of nuclear weapons from the world, and he may have come to see them as even more necessary than the satellites.

We did not totally reject any of the hypotheses, although the first two seem the least compelling. Even the last two, which are probably the strongest, are expressed in ambiguous terms; neither can be confidently accepted or rejected. The important part of the exercise, however, is not to make a definitive choice among them but to confront various hypotheses and consider the kind of logic and evidence that would make one more plausible than another. Each hypothesis stresses different variables, and even different levels of analysis. For example, the individuality of Gorbachev is emphasized in hypothesis 2. This is a microlevel explanation based on understanding how a particular individual views the world. Hypothesis 5 emphasizes economic conditions within formerly communist-ruled areas, and hypothesis 6 focuses on military relations between two superpowers possessing most of the nuclear capability in the international system. Both are macrolevel explanations highlighting factors from the global political environment. Making the hypotheses more precise, with sharper definitions of economic burdens or the nuclear balance, would make it clearer how—and whether—they could be tested by confronting systematic evidence from the real world.

THE STUDY AND PRACTICE OF WORLD POLITICS

We can analyze a decision or event from different theoretical approaches to world politics and at various levels of analysis. In later chapters we focus on characteristics of the global system (Chapter 4) and the relations between nation-states (Chapter 5). We emphasize the large-scale, highly aggregated units of analysis, identifying theories that hold that the most important, persistent influences on world politics and the global economy are found at the highest levels. This kind of analysis is part of the grand sociological tradition shared, in different ways and with different theoretical details, by writers such as Émile Durkheim and Karl Marx. The case for this perspective is well argued by Nazli Choucri and Robert North in their analysis of the conditions that brought about World War I:

> The dynamics of national growth and expansion, the conflict of national interests, patterns of growth in military expenditures, alliance-formation, and violence-behavior ... were not the immediate cause of WWI. The processes set the stage, armed the players, and deployed the forces, but they did not join the antagonists in combat. They created the conditions of an armed camp within which the assassination of the Austrian archduke was sufficient to trigger an international crisis and a major war.[16]

Even if the crisis following the murder of Francis Ferdinand had been resolved by wiser and more effective decision makers, from this perspective the underlying international dynamics of national expansion were certain to create further crises, and one or another of them was very likely to escalate out of control. Thus, it is important to understand the great forces that regularly produce situations fraught with the threat of war rather than to study the behavior of decision makers alone. Although individuals may be able to extricate themselves from one crisis, they cannot be expected to do so repeatedly in an environment where basic systemic forces continually produce such situations.

THE QUESTION OF POLICY RELEVANCE

Social scientists often work at levels of analysis different from those that policy makers find most relevant when facing situations requiring immediate decisions. This difference can be illustrated by comparing the work of a medical researcher and a practicing physician both concerned with coronary illness. Research scientists have established that a number of personal characteristics and environmental conditions contribute to heart disease. They now know that an individual's probability of suffering a heart attack is greater if that person is male and middle-aged or older and if one or both parents suffered heart attacks. Factors that increase the likelihood of heart disease include being overweight, smoking, a diet high in cholesterol-rich fats, and lack of exercise. High blood pressure also contributes to this likelihood, as do stress and anxiety at work or at home. Finally, some people with aggressive, hard-driving personalities appear especially prone to heart disease. For the scientist, all these influences may seem interesting and provide information that may, at some point, prove important.

For the physician who must treat patients, however, different influences are not of equal interest. Some are beyond the control of the individual patient or doctor: The patient cannot stop aging or change sex—at least in a way that would affect coronary health—and cannot change biological parents. A patient, to some degree,

---

[16] Nazli Choucri and Robert North, *Nations in Conflict: National Growth and International Violence* (San Francisco: Freeman, 1975), p. 9. In contemporary international relations theory, this macro perspective is most often associated with the work of Kenneth N. Waltz. See his *Theory of International Politics* (Boston: Addison-Wesley, 1979).

may be able to change lifestyle or even quit a stressful job, but most people cannot do much about their basic personality. A doctor may actually increase the danger of a heart attack by frightening an already worried or anxious patient.

Other influences, however, can be more readily controlled. High blood pressure or high cholesterol, for instance, can be reduced by medication. A patient can be told to lose weight, stop smoking, change diet, or get more exercise. Controlling just one of these conditions may be enough, especially if two contributing influences, such as smoking and obesity, interact. In a particular patient, heart disease may be "overdetermined"; that is, any one of the several contributing conditions is sufficient to produce a high risk of disease, and therefore all must be eliminated. Here, very careful theory, as well as detailed understanding of a particular case, is essential for responsible treatment. Patients who refuse to take any steps to reduce their risks can at least be advised to keep their life insurance premiums paid up— prediction is of some value, even without control over the medical events! Finally, some ethical considerations may also apply. Suppose a patient also suffers from a painful and terminal cancer. Should that patient be saved from a heart attack only to be faced with a difficult death from cancer shortly thereafter? Neither the doctor nor the patient can be indifferent to such a question, whatever their answers.

In our concern with world politics, we must take into account many considerations similar to those facing the physician.[17] At times the student of world politics proceeds chiefly with the kind of concern typical of scientists—at other times, with that typical of policy makers, policy advisers, or citizen activists. A scientist wants to understand the causes of a particular outcome. Because both the causes and the outcome vary (they are "variables"), we hope to find those causes (or "independent variables") that make the greatest difference in bringing about that outcome (the "dependent variable"). In other words, certain causes may account for most of the variation in the outcome. These causes, therefore, should figure most prominently in our theory. The social scientist may not be immediately concerned with whether those causes identified as most important are readily manipulable by policy makers. If pure knowledge is what interests us, then, in principle, there should be no reason for preferring an explanation that highlights one set of independent variables over another. Of course, because most scientific endeavors are driven partly by practical concerns, the social scientist will care about finding ways to make a difference (say, in promoting peace or justice). But the social scientist is not necessarily looking to put acquired knowledge to immediate use.

The policy maker, by contrast, *is* centrally concerned with putting information to use, especially with an eye toward changing outcomes from what they might otherwise be. To change outcomes, the policy maker must identify variables that are not just important but also manipulable. Explanations that identify causes that are controllable are more useful to policy makers than those that identify broad historical forces on which policy makers can have little impact. They are likely to

---

[17] The analogy between medical science and the study of world politics is also found in Bruce Russett, "Violence and Disease: Trade as Suppressor of Conflict When Suppressors Matter," in Edward Mansfield and Brian Pollins, eds., *Economic Interdependence and International Conflict: New Perspectives on an Enduring Debate* (Ann Arbor: University of Michigan Press, 2003).

be much more interested in explanations about how a crisis can be resolved short of war than in knowing about the sociological developments that brought about the crisis. Although "knowledge for knowledge's sake" often drives social scientific research, the fruits of that research are not always immediately useful to foreign policy makers.

Suppose we can show that states with systemwide interests are more likely to be involved in world-endangering military crises. Would a policy maker for such a government want to fundamentally alter the state's alliances and other international relationships, even if the necessary steps could be identified? An explanation of how decision makers perceive and act under crisis conditions may seem more pressing. Suppose we are fairly certain that the growth and liberalization of global financial markets increase the likelihood of future currency crises. Does that mean policy makers will want to find a way to return to the days when states could better manage currency exchange rates? It's probably not possible, so it is more useful to know how to calm volatile markets when a crisis seems to be brewing. Or suppose we conclude that Islamic terrorism has its roots in political repression and the lack of economic opportunities available to young males in some Middle Eastern societies. Policy makers in countries targeted by terrorist organizations would like to see these social problems addressed, but their immediate concerns are more likely to be securing their homelands. In short, policy makers may have little control over the external environment but may believe that it is possible to exert substantial influence over the decision processes that operate in times of crisis, whether in governments or markets, in order to improve crisis management.

THE QUESTION OF VALUES

Werner Heisenberg, the German theoretical physicist and Nobel laureate, was best known for his uncertainty principle, which states that one cannot simultaneously determine both the precise position of a particle and its velocity. The reason for this is that when a scientist measures a particle's velocity, he or she essentially bumps into its environment and therefore cannot know with certainty the particle's exact position—and vice versa. The implications for the classical view of science, and social science, are quite important. Heisenberg put it this way:

> We can no longer speak of the behavior of the particle independently of the process of observation. . . . Science no longer confronts nature as an objective observer, but sees itself as an actor in this interplay between man and nature. The scientific method of analyzing, explaining and classifying has become conscious of its limitations, which arise out of the fact that by its intervention science alters and refashions the object of investigation.[18]

Although science can help us understand the world, we know that in the process of acquiring knowledge we impact what we study. As we have seen, reflectivists attach great importance to this point. Every day political decision makers take

---

[18] Werner Heisenberg, *The Physicist's Conception of Nature*, trans. by Arnold J. Pomerans (New York: Harcourt, Brace, 1958), pp. 15, 29.

actions that affect the lives and happiness of millions of people; some of these actions are informed by social science research. While recognizing that action is necessary, we must retain a sense of humility about the limits and uncertainty of our knowledge.

Similar self-consciousness is needed for statements of value. We make such statements all the time: One painting is more beautiful than another; one act is morally right, and another wrong. We all make these judgments, with varying degrees of confidence, and we often disagree about them. The systems of thought by which we deduce statements about goodness and beauty may start from very different premises. A Buddhist, a Sunni Muslim, an evangelical Christian, and an atheist may well agree that certain elements of life, such as decent living conditions and essential liberties, constitute, in some sense, "basic human rights." However, they will differ in how they arrive at that common conclusion, about the specific forms those rights should take, and about the relative importance of each.

In adopting a scientific approach to the study of world politics, one decides to concentrate on **empirical theory**—constructing models of what international actors do, how they do it, and why, with the expectation that these models can be evaluated through observation. The rightness or wrongness of what they do, the justice or injustice of the outcomes, are the concerns of **normative theory**. Of course, matters of right and wrong do affect the choices that leaders make and even the menu of alternatives from which they choose. In that sense, values are an important element of many empirical theories in international relations. However, when, as students of world politics, we attempt to judge right and wrong in world politics, we have entered the realm of normative theory. Religion, ethical systems, and other elements of culture, as well as economic conditions, influence people's values and moral judgments. The methods of social science can establish the impact of different sets of values on actual behavior, but they cannot determine the moral superiority of one set of values over another.

Most, but not all, research in contemporary international relations has been guided by empirical theory, but this has not always been the case. Normative theory has a long and distinguished pedigree in political philosophy, and some of the issues we discuss in this book—the ethics of war, human rights, global poverty— are, first and foremost, matters of international justice.[19] Furthermore, as we pointed out in the beginning of the chapter, world politics as a contemporary field of study emerged with a normative concern to address the military, political, and economic maladies that many believed were responsible for World War I. It was this normative preoccupation—misguided, according to the realists—that earned liberal internationalists the labels of "idealists" and "utopians." We should hasten to add, however, that realism itself is not as value free as many proponents would like to believe. George Kennan, for instance, a realist architect of post–World War II American diplomacy, seemed to argue in his writings that there were strong

---

[19] For an introduction to contemporary normative theory in international relations, including its philosophical foundations, see Chris Brown, *International Relations Theory: New Normative Approaches* (New York: Columbia University Press, 1992). See also Molly Cochran, *Normative Theory in International Relations: A Pragmatic Approach* (Cambridge: Cambridge University Press, 1999).

normative reasons that moralizing should be kept out of foreign policy, that the world could be a better place if the United States would refrain from promoting American ideals.[20]

The line between empirical and normative theory can be very fine. Many individuals who are most committed to an objective, scientific approach to world politics have strong ethical views about the subject they study. In conducting research, we may be relatively successful in not allowing our ethics to cloud the collection of data and the evaluation of our hypotheses. But our values are reflected in the very questions we ask about world politics. There is nothing inherently wrong with this; indeed, it is what attracts many people to the study of world politics in the first place. It is wrong, however, to pretend that a social scientific approach is completely value free. Reflectivists start with this realization about the study of world politics and go on to explore the implications of asking some questions and not others, of gathering some types of evidence and not others, and of evaluating that evidence in some ways and not others. In examining such previously unexamined issues, they hope to shed new light on the incompleteness—or worse, the bias—of our current understanding of world politics and the analytical approaches we employ.

Most people involved in the study and practice of world politics want to understand and to effect change. In the long run, even what appears as a given in world politics is subject to change. Great powers rise and fall; entrenched systems decay. Sometimes all it takes is a nudge by citizens who care enough. Occasionally, change is spontaneous and far-reaching, as happened when democratic revolution spread throughout Eastern Europe and helped bring about the collapse of the cold war system. More often, perhaps, change is slow and arduous, if sometimes jarring, like the processes that ultimately led to the abolition of slavery, the dismantling of colonial empires, or the willingness to intervene to stop humanitarian disaster. Whether sudden or gradual, violent or tranquil, the wheels that set such transformations in motion can often be found in changes in the ethical systems held by individuals, groups, and societies at large.[21]

In this book we try to offer some understanding of world political phenomena without necessarily providing readily manipulable levers to solve problems. We shall address basic questions about war, peace, development, governance, and justice, which will be around for many decades and will require concerted, long-term effort. We look at explanations of why wars occur, how crises can be managed to peaceful conclusions, and why crises arise at all. We look at problems of economic and political interdependence among the industrialized countries of the world; at how economic conditions can constrain national governments; and at the implications of the spread of democracy. We look at relations between rich and poor

---

[20] See especially George Kennan's *American Diplomacy 1900–1950* (Chicago: University of Chicago Press, 1951) and *Realities of American Foreign Policy* (Princeton, N.J.: Princeton University Press, 1954); also Hans J. Morgenthau, *The Purpose of American Politics* (New York: Knopf, 1960).

[21] See, for example, Neta C. Crawford, *Argument and Change in World Politics: Ethics, Decolonization, and Humanitarian Intervention* (Cambridge: Cambridge University Press, 2002); Martha Finnemore, *The Purpose of Intervention: Changing Beliefs about the Use of Force* (Ithaca, N.Y.: Cornell University Press, 2003).

countries: questions of national wealth and development, and questions of dependence, national autonomy, and the internal distribution of economic and political rewards. We also look at problems of global resource availability and distribution, population growth and migration, and pollution, as well as at other issues that transcend national borders such as international human rights and transnational crime.

Some of these problems would have been discussed in a textbook written forty or fifty years ago; others are quite new. There have been some very important changes in the world around us. Environmental damage, for example, certainly is perceived as far more threatening now than it was a few decades ago. Yet pollution has been carried across international borders for centuries—for example, the industrial discharge swept down the Rhine River—without being considered a major political issue. Small countries have always been dependent on big ones, but concerns about the causes and consequences of that dependence have been given voice only with the great increase in the number of politically sovereign states during recent decades. Terrorism, as a tactic of violent intimidation, burst onto the international scene in the late nineteenth and early twentieth centuries with a wave of high-profile assassinations, but the threat of terrorism today derives from the creation of transnational networks and their potential access to weapons of mass destruction.

Facts change, values change, problems change, and theories change. This book, therefore, will help you determine *how to think* about world politics. This will not only aid your understanding of particular contemporary problems but also give you a set of analytical tools to apply to new problems many years from now. Then you will have to search for your own manipulable levers—levers appropriate to your circumstances, your political resources, your understanding, and your values.

INTERNATIONAL ACTORS: STATES AND OTHER PLAYERS ON THE WORLD STAGE

CHAPTER 3

HUMANS IN GROUPS: NATIONALISM AND THE NATION

Now that we have provided some basic conceptions of world politics and how the subject is studied, one further preliminary issue must be discussed: Exactly what sorts of groups of people are we concerned with—whose behavior interests us? We start our discussion of the actors on the world stage at the most basic level. World politics begins with the idea of *relations,* which are the outgrowth of inter-actions between collective social entities. Thus, we begin with the notion of humans forming *groups.*

Perhaps one of the things that makes us human is our need to affiliate into groups. Aristotle observed that people are social animals, a view supported by such social scientific disciplines as anthropology and sociology. Because our evolu-tionary heritage provides us with genetic material open to forces and influences from the physical environment, we also require a *social environment* for brain development and for the acquisition of skills such as speech and written communi-cation. As physical and social creatures, human beings throughout their existence as a species have formed into groups.

The comfort, security, and other advantages that a group provides for its mem-bers are central to the study of sociology and psychology. Given the limitations of the human animal, people must form groups to meet physiological and psychologi-cal wants and needs. So, along with the idea of the group goes the idea of identifi-cation. Individuals will identify with groups, give their loyalty to them, and act to maintain their character, security, and survival. Group identity gives individuals a basic sense of belonging and self-esteem. We can say that a group of individuals has developed a group identification and a group loyalty when a certain amount of "we-feeling" exists—when members feel more like "we" than like some other "they."

The group is defined and held together by complex nets of *social communica-tions* among people. Barriers to social communication—due to distance, language, or different belief systems about how the world works based on such things as religion, ideology, or historical experiences—help create differentiated groups of people. The more easily social communication flows, the greater the probability that such we-feelings and identity will develop. These notions of social communication and the development of loyalties underlie group identification from the smallest tribal organization to the nation-state.[1] When people identify with groups, they become differentiated from people not in those groups. Much of what occurs in world politics boils down to this separation of "we" and "they." They are different; they are not normal, are inferior in some way, are dangerous. They always want something that we have. Can they be trusted? What do they really want?

In discussing the nation-state, we start with the idea of a **nation**, a people who feel themselves part of some large identity group. Ernest Renan, the nineteenth-century French philosopher, captured the essence of a nation when he wrote:

> A nation is a soul, a spiritual principle. Two things, which in truth are but one, constitute this soul or spiritual principle. One lies in the past, one in the present. One is the possession in common of a rich legacy of memories; the other is present-day consent, the desire to live together, the will to perpetuate the value of the heritage that one has received in an undivided form.... A nation is therefore a large-scale solidarity, constituted by the feeling of the sacrifices that one has made in the past and of those that one is prepared to make in the future.[2]

Nationalism refers to the complex set of psychological, cultural, and social forces that drive the formation of a nation. The development of the concept and reality of the state is similarly complex. Historically, as we shall see, state building occurred in Europe over a period of several hundred years before 1648, when the Treaty of Westphalia was signed to end the Thirty Years' War. Kings and princes extended their central authority over territories that had formerly been a disconnected hodgepodge of feudal fiefdoms. Centralization and consolidation continued throughout Europe until World War I. Each group that identified itself as a people sought representation through the **state**—a legal entity consisting of a government that manages the affairs of a population in a given territory; that is, peoples who identified themselves as nations sought their own states, resulting in what we now call **nation-states**. Although *nation, state,* and *nation-state* do have specific meanings, the three terms are often used interchangeably.

IMAGINED COMMUNITY

State building can take the form of unification. Neither Italy nor Germany was finally united into a nation-state until the latter half of the nineteenth century,

---

[1] These ideas were developed in Karl Deutsch's classic work, *Nationalism and Social Communication* (Cambridge, Mass.: MIT Press, 1953). On the psychological role that group identity plays for humans, see Henri Tajfel, *Human Groups and Social Categories: Studies in the Social Psychology* (Cambridge: Cambridge University Press, 1981).

[2] Ernest Renan, "What Is a Nation?," trans. by Martin Thom, in Homi K. Bhabha, ed., *Nation and Narration* (London: Routledge, 1990), p. 19. For an overview of concepts and theories related to nationalism, see Anthony D. Smith, *Nationalism: Theory, Ideology, History* (Cambridge: Polity, 2001).

when war and diplomatic maneuvering were used to forge single political units out of many smaller principalities or city-states. Other European nationalities sought to establish their own states by separating from the larger empires that dominated much of Europe until World War I. These imperial entities included the Turkish Ottoman Empire, which had begun its spread westward into Eastern and Central Europe in the early 1300s and then retreated only slowly after its defeat before the gates of Vienna in 1683. The Austro-Hungarian Empire was the descendant of the Austrian Empire, and before that, the Holy Roman Empire of the Hapsburgs. Under Charles V, Holy Roman Emperor from 1519 to 1558, the Hapsburg territories dominated the Continent. When his Hapsburg inheritances were combined with the areas under nominal control of the empire, Charles's dominions included what is now Spain (and its New World possessions at that time), the Netherlands, Belgium, most of Italy, Austria, and many of the states of Central Europe. A third multiethnic and multinational grouping was the Russian Empire. Turkish rule in Europe was ended with the two Balkan wars of 1912–1913. The process by which nations separated from larger entities to form their own states culminated, in the aftermath of World War I, with the dissolution of all three of these empires.

The desire of national groups to separate from larger empires and form their own states was the predominant manifestation of nationalism until the end of World War II. Nationalistic separatism reemerged as an important social force in world politics in the 1990s as modern-day "empires" (Soviet Union) and multiethnic states (Yugoslavia) similarly disintegrated. The ongoing struggles of other groups to achieve statehood (for example, the Kurds and the Palestinians) have had serious implications for regional stability and continue to command the attention of the international community.

It is crucial to note that this process may work in reverse. As we have seen in the post–World War II period of decolonization, it is possible for states to govern populations that do not possess single national identities—these are states without nations. This condition is found in areas outside Europe, and especially in Africa, where territorial boundaries were artificially drawn by Western colonial authorities. Thus, in states such as Nigeria or India, the process then becomes one of creating a nation—a we-feeling—to coincide with the already existing state.

So far, nationalism has been discussed primarily in terms of we-feeling—a condition of the mind, a feeling of identification or loyalty to some group of people. This is probably the key factor—that people *feel* themselves to be American or German or Algerian or Bulgarian or Cuban. What produces the we-feeling? A number of factors have been identified. One is simply sharing a *common territory*. People living and interacting in the same area, and facing similar problems and challenges, often develop a common feeling and identity. Closely related is the effect of participating in a common economic system, of engaging in related types of commercial activities, relying on the same resource base, and dealing with the similar conditions of scarcity. All these provide people with a common view of the world and a sense of shared interests.

Obviously, when we speak of groups as large as nations, direct face-to-face interaction occurs only among small subgroups of individuals. Common experiences in the absence of direct interaction often do not extend much further. What can account for the development of these larger national identities, or what Benedict Anderson has called "imagined communities"?[3] This brings us to a second set of factors related to *cultural similarity*. A common language is an extremely important aspect of nationalism. Indeed, in attempting to increase national cohesion, political leaders have reinstituted languages that were dead or had been used only infrequently. The resurrection of the Welsh language by nationalists in Wales is at best a partially successful attempt to use language to reinforce or create nationalistic feelings, whereas the use of Hebrew in Israel has been quite successful in drawing together a diverse people. Other common cultural factors that have proven particularly powerful in today's world are a common ethnic background and a common religion. And maybe most important of all is the existence of a set of past experiences perceived as a common history. What Ernest Renan observed more than a century ago about the importance of "a rich legacy of memories" is still highlighted by contemporary scholars of nationalism.

Nationalism involves loyalty to a larger group—an imagined community—and contemporary world politics is also witnessing a growth of loyalties to nonstate groups based on communal ties of various kinds. It is increasingly clear that "maps which show the world neatly divided into countries, each with its own boundaries and territory, convey a misleading image of people's political identities."[4] The rise of religious fundamentalism is one example of the forces of fragmentation confronting the nation-state today. For example, an individual may identify first as a member of the Shammar tribe, then as a Sunni Muslim, and then as an Iraqi in a loyalty chain that finds the state last on the list. Fragmentation has been a major force in world politics, increasing the number of independent actors and shrinking the size of many existing states. Having expanded from a small area around Kiev in the ninth century, "Russia" first became the Russian Empire and then expanded further into the USSR; it is now Russia again, but with only about half the population and three-quarters of the land area of the Soviet Union. What was a single federated state of Yugoslavia in 1991 is now six independent states—with a seventh, Kosovo, recognized as independent by many, but not all, members of the international community.

THE STATE AS INTERNATIONAL ACTOR

Despite a number of trends to the contrary, the state (or the nation-state) has been, and remains, the primary actor in the global system. The number of states in the system has risen steadily since the end of World War II, a trend that averages out to an increase of about two states per year. In the 1960s alone, the number of states in the international system grew by more than one-third. Another indicator is the growth in the membership of the United Nations: In 1945, there were 51 charter members of the UN; now there are 192 members. Of the thirty-seven

[3] Benedict Anderson, *Imagined Communities: Reflections on the Origin and Spread of Nationalism*, new ed. (London: Verso, 2006).

[4] Ted Robert Gurr and Barbara Harff, *Ethnic Conflict in World Politics* (Boulder, Colo.: Westview, 1994), p. 1.

states joining since 1990, two-thirds were the result of the drive for separatism, especially the fragmentation of formerly communist systems. Eleven other new members were microstates, including Andorra, which has long been part of the international system. The near quadrupling of membership since the establishment of the United Nations illustrates the continuing desire of groups to achieve statehood—and to be recognized by the international community as states—no matter their size or previous status.

MODERN STATE SYSTEM

There have been large-scale political organizations for 7,000 years, starting with the city-states and empires of the Tigris and Euphrates and the Nile. However, the state, or nation-state, in its present form is relatively new. Although many scholars date the modern nation-state from 1648 and the Treaty of Westphalia, the state as it existed in the seventeenth century was the result of a convergence of processes that had been occurring for more than 500 years before Westphalia. The 200 years from about 1450 to 1650 mark the transition from one historical epoch to another when the combination and interaction of political, economic, technological, and religious factors were decisive in bringing about the shift to the **modern state system.**

For hundreds of years before this transition period, Europe consisted of a complex system of feudal entities. With the disintegration of the Roman Empire during the fifth century, the Germanic tribes that overran Roman settlements in western Europe remained organized on only the most local level, cutting their political or economic ties to the Mediterranean region. The Frankish empire of Charlemagne, established in 800, began to create the outlines of what we now know as Europe, but it too was overrun by barbarians from the East. Even after the fall of Rome, the Roman Catholic Church maintained a presence and spiritual authority across Europe, and both waves of invaders were assimilated into Christianity. By the eleventh century, a system composed of large numbers of local political entities was in place, based on the feudal relationships between lord and vassal and involving little interaction with other parts of the world. At the geographic and political center of the European system was the successor to Charlemagne's empire, the Holy Roman Empire.

The leaders of these various feudal entities, and their subjects, were enmeshed in a web of multiple loyalties. The various levels and ranks of nobility were both lords and vassals, receiving fealty (loyalty or obedience) from those below them and giving fealty to those above. In theory, such loyalty culminated in two figures: the Holy Roman Emperor in the secular realm, and the pope in the spiritual realm. Thus, in stark contrast to the state system that was to develop, the principle of authority was *hierarchical.* At the same time, actual authority was diffuse. The ability of those at the top of the hierarchy to truly exercise their authority over large territories was, in fact, limited.

European politics during this time was more about the interaction of nobles and princes than it was about dynastic relations among European monarchs, or about relations between the monarchs and the Holy Roman Emperor or the pope. But what characterizes the fifteenth and sixteenth centuries is the gradual growth of monarchical power and influence. Scholars studying the rise of the nation-state in western Europe focus on two central elements: capital and coercion. As monarchs struggled against the feudal nobility in their efforts to expand, centralize, and consolidate their control over large swaths of territory, they needed economic and especially military resources. Certain factors provided the opportunities that enabled kings to engage in this process and ultimately succeed against the lesser nobility.

One key factor was economic. Manufacturing, trade, and communication had become increasingly concentrated, resulting in the growth of cities and towns. Eventually, a money economy developed to replace the system of barter that characterized feudal exchange, and a merchant class began to emerge. Each town or city came to represent a larger regional economy, encompassing the surrounding areas of agricultural production. The merchant class, whose newfound wealth derived from its commercial activities, desired continued growth and expansion of these regional economies, including greater trade with agricultural areas and with other towns and cities. This expansion required security and order—an authority to provide for roads and communication and otherwise reduce barriers to economic expansion.

Here is where the interests of the merchant class and the monarchy coincided. If the kings were to effectively challenge the military power of the nobility and thereby establish their authority across their realms, they needed to raise their own mass armies. To do so, they needed to extract resources from the prosperous urban areas, drawing especially on the wealth of the commercial classes. Merchants, bankers, and others benefiting from economic expansion could, for their part, enjoy the order and stability that came with the establishment of a single political authority in their territory.

To raise and support armies, monarchs needed administrators. Elaborate bureaucracies evolved in order to extract resources, in the form of taxes, and to administer military camps and hospitals. Raising mass armies was a substantial undertaking; only monarchs had at their disposal the necessary resources and, increasingly, the ability to extract them. The nobility continued to rely on much smaller, mainly mercenary, forces led by warriors drawn from the aristocratic classes. Technological factors were also crucial. Advances in military technology, especially gunpowder and the cannon, made it possible for individuals with enough resources to overcome the castle strongholds of knights and other nobility. As military victory brought more territory under monarchical control, that territory in turn needed to be administered by larger and larger bureaucracies. We can see in this expansion of bureaucracy the origins of the formal administrative institutions that have come to characterize the modern state. The process was summarized well by Charles Tilly: "The state makes war, and war makes the state."[5]

The interrelationships among the commercial class, monarchs, and the bureaucracy in Europe promoted the rapid development and use of the military technology that also made possible European expansion into other parts of the globe. In

---

[5] Charles Tilly, *Coercion, Capital, and European States*, A.D. *990–1990* (Oxford: Blackwell, 1990); see also Perry Anderson, *Lineages of the Absolutist State* (London: Verso, 1979). The contemporary manifestation of this process in the developing world is examined in Brian D. Taylor and Roxana Botea, "Tilly Tally: War-Making and State-Making in the Contemporary Third World," *International Studies Review* 10 (March 2008), pp. 27–56.

fact, Paul Kennedy attributes the "European miracle," or the rise of Europe rather than areas seemingly more advanced, to the interaction of all these factors. The continual wars and rivalries between kings and nobles, and then among kings, pushed each to find some advantage in arms or wealth and led to rapid technological and scientific innovations (in areas such as weaponry, transportation, navigation, and cartography), as well as innovations in commerce, finance, and administration. The upward spiral occurred not only in arms, wealth, and power but also, and perhaps more important, in scientific knowledge. All these factors promoted a European expansion that, in turn, provided another source of wealth for the European states.[6]

SOVEREIGNTY AND THE NATURE OF THE STATE

A final element that created the opportunity for the rise of the state system was religion, which connected all these interrelated elements. In 1517, Martin Luther challenged the spiritual authority of the pope and the Church of Rome, and his challenge was taken up by a number of German princes. Lutheranism spread across much of north-central Europe, resulting in a series of increasingly destructive religious conflicts that dominated the history of the sixteenth and early seventeenth centuries and culminated in the Thirty Years' War. The war began in 1618 when Ferdinand II, a member of the Catholic Hapsburg dynasty of Austria and the sitting Holy Roman Emperor, sent imperial forces into Bohemia to quash a challenge to his authority by Protestant princes. With help from Philip IV of Spain, also a Hapsburg, the first phase of the war saw the reimposition of Catholicism in central Germany but not before the other monarchs in Europe became concerned about Ferdinand's larger designs. Denmark entered the conflict against the Hapsburgs, followed by Sweden and then France. After three decades of destructive warfare, the attempt to assert transcontinental authority on behalf of the Hapsburg dynasty had been defeated, but all parties were exhausted. The war ended with the **Peace of Westphalia** in 1648, and it is with this event that we usually date the birth of the modern state system. Indeed, we often refer to ours as the *Westphalian state system.* (Map 3.1 shows the political geography of Europe at this time.)

The central principle of the Peace of Westphalia was simple: *Cuius regio, eius religio* ("He who rules a region determines its religion"). This principle had been articulated as early as the Peace of Augsburg in 1555, which had sought to end the religious strife of the Reformation. Despite its simplicity, this principle had enormous consequences. The major issue of the day—religion—was to be determined by the local ruler, not by an external authority, whether the Holy Roman Emperor or the pope. No longer was there even the pretense of religious or political unity in Europe. Authority was dispersed to the various kings and princes. In each territory there were no longer multiple loyalties and authorities, only one singular loyalty to the authority of the king or prince. The territory and

---

[6] Paul Kennedy, *The Rise and Fall of the Great Powers: Economic Change and Military Conflict from 1500 to 2000* (New York: Random House, 1987), chap. 1.

MAP 3.1 | EUROPE IN 1648

Authority was overlapping and hierarchical in pre-Westphalian European politics. The Thirty Years' War represented a challenge to transcendent authority as asserted by the pope and the Holy Roman Emperor, and the Peace of Westphalia in 1648 marked the emergence of an anarchical system populated by territorial states. However, the areas labeled as German states and Italian states were not yet politically unified and consisted of many small independent units.

the people in that territory belonged to the ruler, who did not have to answer to an external authority. Thus, the Westphalian state system distinguished itself not only from the earlier feudal principle in Europe but also from similar principles of suzerainty that existed elsewhere at that time—in India, China, the Arab Islamic world, and the Mongol-Tatar region.

The key elements of the modern nation-state were now all in place: a people, a territory in which they lived, and a bureaucracy administering the affairs of the monarch, whose authority over the people of his territory was established by international law (the treaties signed at Augsburg and Westphalia). The king, with his administrative bureaucracy, was recognized as the agent of the state—a *legal* entity having the special status of **sovereignty**. The very term *state*, which arose in the sixteenth century, derived from the Latin *status*, meaning "position" or "standing"—in this case, the position or standing of a sovereign, or ruler.

We can now begin to answer the question of why the state was, and is, the main international actor. The notion of separate secular and spiritual entities disappeared, and the authority that had been vested in both was assumed exclusively by the state. Consequently, the international norms and laws that developed provided the state with a status enjoyed by no other actor. Perhaps the operative word here is *law*. The state is a legal entity; it has been invested with a legal status that is denied to other actors on the global stage. Like a corporation, the state technically has no concrete existence. It is a legal abstraction. Its agent is a government, and representatives of that government undertake legal commitments on behalf of the state. Government officials sign treaties, join international organizations, and take other acts that create rights and responsibilities for the state.

Sovereignty should be seen as indicating a special, theoretical relationship between each state and all other states. Hedley Bull noted that sovereignty includes both "internal sovereignty," meaning supremacy over all other entities within one's territory, and "external sovereignty," meaning independence from authorities outside that territory.[7] During the period preceding the Peace of Westphalia, the monarchies of western Europe had pretty much established their internal sovereignty vis-à-vis the nobility within their own territories (though it was a continuing process). It was really external sovereignty that was consecrated at Westphalia. No other national or international entity can legitimately dictate a state's activities; *there is no authority above the state*. This **anarchy** is the essence of the modern international system we have today.

In principle, this means that within state boundaries a single entity has a monopoly over the legitimate use of force. No other authority has a right to exercise force or maintain order within the territory of the state. Similarly, through international law, the state has been given a legal monopoly on the use of force in the global arena. Piracy and nonstate terrorism are considered illegal, in part, because they entail the use of violent force by actors other than states. When

---

[7] Hedley Bull, *The Anarchical Society: A Study of Order in World Politics* (London: Macmillan, 1977), p. 8. The exact meaning of sovereignty and the state, and the implications of differing definitions, are complex and subject to debate among scholars. For a review of that debate, see Joseph A. Camilleri and Jim Falk, *The End of Sovereignty* (London: Elgar, 1992).

implemented by a state, force can be pinpointed, responsibility can be assigned, and other rules of conduct can be invoked. For example, until the creation of the League of Nations after World War I, international law was concerned with how states behaved during a special legal condition called war. This condition could exist only between two equal units—equal in the legal sense of being sovereign states. Once this condition existed, belligerents were designated by declarations of war, and neutrals by declarations of neutrality. Participants and nonparticipants had rights and responsibilities according to the status they had declared. The various structures of international law were rarely seen to apply to peoples who were outside the system of states, such as aboriginal populations and peoples in non-European areas, which could be "legitimately" conquered, colonized, and dominated by the European nation-states.

In addition to its special legal status, the state has another important characteristic that is basic to its dominance of the international system: territory. The government of the state represents a group of people who inhabit a piece of territory. Commentators who argue that the state is no longer dominant in the world system must confront the fact that every person lives in territory controlled (at least nominally) by a state. John Herz reminds us that "[t]hroughout history that unit which affords protection and security to human beings has tended to become the basic political unit."[8] This proposition can be applied to the feudal knight and the protection that his castle provided to the villagers. This changed with the advent of gunpowder and the larger military forces developed by kings. The basis of the state was its ability to protect people through its size—its physical territory, which created a "hard shell" around the population in an era of gunpowder and the professional armies of monarchs. Although weapons of mass destruction (nuclear, biological, and chemical) and modern delivery systems make the hard shell of the state increasingly penetrable, in general the *territoriality* of the state still protects its citizens from most conflicts with other states.

Sovereignty and territoriality provide the state with major advantages over nonstate actors in the global arena. The European version of the state expanded throughout the world because it had first won out in the European competition. To survive in Europe, a country needed large amounts of capital, a large population, and significant military forces, all of which came with control of land. European states occupied about 7 percent of the world's territory in 1500; by 1914 they controlled 84 percent. As Charles Tilly summarizes it:

> Because of their advantages in translating national resources into success in international war, large national states superseded tribute-taking empires, federations, city-states, and all their other competitors as the predominant European entities, and as the models for state formation.... Those states finally defined the character of the European state system and spearheaded its extension to the entire world.[9]

---

[8] John Herz, "Rise and Demise of the Territorial State," *World Politics* 9 (1957), pp. 473–493.

[9] Tilly, *Coercion, Capital, and European States*, pp. 160, 183; see also Hendrik Spruyt, *The Sovereign State and Its Competitors: An Analysis of Systems Change* (Princeton, N.J.: Princeton University Press, 1994).

THE STATE SYSTEM SINCE WESTPHALIA

The anarchic system of states recognized by the Peace of Westphalia has undergone various transformations. Its initial principle of internal sovereignty incorporated the institution of dynastic succession, the inheritance of royal authority from one generation to another. The dynastic ruler embodied that sovereignty. However, the French Revolution of 1789 challenged all that. The notion of popular sovereignty—boldly asserted half a world away in the American Declaration of Independence—was gaining favor over the divine right of kings. The ultimate source of governmental authority was said to reside in the people—the public—and not the monarch. This "republican" principle proved a powerful organizing and empowering force. It fueled the enthusiasm for enlistment of a huge army of citizens, which proved to be far larger and displayed more ideological fervor than that shown by previous professional armies serving royal authority. The *levée en masse* enabled revolutionary France to turn back the forces of its neighbors, which had tried to reinstate the old regime, and then to expand French power by appealing directly to its neighbors' own populations.

When Napoléon Bonaparte seized power, France retained the republican spirit of governance even as Napoléon consolidated his own authority by proclaiming himself emperor. However, while enhancing his internal sovereignty, Napoléon challenged the principle of external sovereignty: He sought hegemony. Not content with maintaining French security by balancing power with other European monarchs, in his military campaigns he tried to make France the dominant power in Europe. Napoléon absorbed some of his neighbors into France and attempted to reduce the rest to vassals. The Napoleonic Wars were to determine whether the Westphalian system would survive.

The system did survive with the victory by a coalition of all the other great powers—Britain, Russia, Prussia, and Austria. Yet the victors recognized their close call. They learned from the failure of the old system and tried to revise it even as they reinstituted it. Like the parties that signed the treaties at Westphalia, those participating in the Congress of Vienna in 1815 sought to provide for an era of peace following a catastrophic period of continent-wide warfare. They tried to restore dynastic authority but in a form tempered to the republican spirit, which could not be erased from the European consciousness. The great powers allowed France to recover and reenter the system, essentially within its pre-1792 borders, and to participate as an equal partner in great power politics. This partnership, the so-called Concert of Europe, was an arrangement among the great powers to meet periodically so that they might resolve emerging conflicts between them before they erupted into open warfare. It rested on certain normative principles of proper behavior: States had a right to security and independence, and they had an obligation to respect one another's legitimacy, observe international law, and negotiate to settle their differences.

Military power was to back up these hopes. No state was to aspire to dominance nor be permitted to make the effort. An expansionist state was to be "balanced" (actually, overpowered) by the combined effort of the others. In this constellation, Britain and Russia, as the most powerful states, played key roles. Britain was the world's leading naval and industrial power; Russia was Europe's leading land power with the largest population and army. Insofar as the two powers pursued expansionist aims, those aims were concentrated outside Europe. They did not directly threaten other major European powers and, because of their geographic separation, they could not substantially threaten each other. As long as Britain and Russia were basically in agreement, no other state could hope to dominate Europe.[10]

This restored, but modified, Westphalian system worked reasonably well for a full century. A wave of popular and nationalist revolution swept much of central Europe in 1848, but most of the revolutionary movements were put down by force or tempered in practice. There were only two major wars during the century, neither of which approached the scope or ferocity of the Napoleonic Wars. Britain and France fought Russia in the Crimean War of 1854, but in a limited locale and for limited goals. More far-reaching in its effects was the Franco-Prussian War of 1870, which capped the unification of Germany as the most powerful state on the European continent. Furthermore, by its territorial settlement, which transferred the provinces of Alsace and Lorraine from French to German control, the war left a legacy of bitterness and demand for revenge in France. Even so, there was no further war between any of the major powers in Europe until 1914, when everything seemed to collapse. Tensions increased, and alliances rigidified. New military technology appeared to favor offense over defense and fed regional arms races. Long-term demographic and industrial trends threatened to enhance German or Russian power, to the endangerment of their neighbors. A continent-wide war, expanding to world war, was the result. It reached a level of killing that surpassed even the Napoleonic Wars.

Again the victorious powers recognized that the system had failed in its most important purpose—preserving peace and the sovereignty of its core states. U.S. President Woodrow Wilson championed the rights of national groups to self-determination; internal sovereignty now seemed to mean the right of an ethnically homogeneous people to govern itself. Some new states in central Europe had their boundaries drawn to reflect those principles. However, the ethnic map of Europe did not fit easily into any kind of political map. Peoples were mixed together in ways that often defied the creation of any neat or territorially defensible borders. Some peoples' aspirations were deliberately submerged to those of more powerful groups. In legitimating an outburst of demands for national self-determination that could not be satisfied, Wilson helped promote a force that would be as disruptive as it was pacifying.[11]

The victorious powers were also looking for a principle of international relations by which to restore order and security. Wilson's vision was of a system of collective security, embedded in a League of Nations, by which all members would agree to oppose jointly a threat to the security of any one of them from any

---

[10] See Paul Schroeder, *The Transformation of European Politics 1763–1848* (New York: Oxford University Press, 1994). Henry Kissinger was greatly impressed by European diplomacy during this period, which he had studied before becoming U.S. secretary of state; see his *A World Restored: Metternich, Castlereagh, and the Problems of Peace, 1812–1822* (London: Weidenfeld & Nicolson, 1957).

[11] See Daniel Patrick Moynihan, *Pandaemonium: Ethnicity in International Politics* (Oxford: Oxford University Press, 1993), especially chap. 2.

quarter. But this vision fit badly with the view that the threat to peace stemmed primarily from a few particular states, especially Germany. This latter view, which was expressed most vigorously by France, required cutting territory away from Germany and imposing economically debilitating war reparations in order to weaken that state (and also excluding it, at least initially, from the new League of Nations). In the negotiations leading to the signing of the Treaty of Versailles in 1919, the French position predominated. Furthermore, the U.S. Senate—by then representing the world's strongest power and the one potentially best able to restrain any possible hegemonic aggressor—refused to ratify the treaty, thus precluding American membership in the League.

The attempt to institute a new set of rules for the system failed at the outset. Germany recovered its strength and nurtured its sense of injustice at the Versailles settlement. Eventually Adolf Hitler came to power at the head of a fascist and totalitarian government that was determined to impose a new order on Europe and perhaps the world. Britain, France, and the Soviet Union could not agree on how to resist him; the Americans stood aside while Italy and Japan allied with him. In 1939, he began the most dangerous bid for dominance since Napoléon, driven by an odious ideology of German racial superiority. World War II ended with somewhere between 40 million and 55 million people dead, more than half of them civilians.

Yet again, in 1945, the victors met to pick up and rearrange the pieces. The United Nations was to replace the League. This time the United States would join. Again the world organization was founded primarily on the principle of collective security, including the intention of making available to the United Nations military forces earmarked for its use in maintaining international peace and security. By the charter of the new organization, the U.N. Security Council was empowered to authorize and carry out collective military action against anyone it declared to be a threat to the peace. The principal victors—Britain, the Soviet Union, and the United States (with China and France added as something of a courtesy)—were designated as permanent members of the Security Council. As such, each was given the power to veto any military or other action against a state. The reasons for giving them this veto power were straightforward. First, the major victors insisted on it. Second, the founders of the United Nations were practical; they understood that, for the foreseeable future, the permanent members would have to provide most of the military muscle. Moreover, if a great power felt that a particular proposal for U.N. action violated its vital interests, it would surely oppose such an action whether or not it had a veto. A United Nations that tried to go ahead with such an action would risk world war anyway. Thus, the veto merely recognized the realities of power at the time. Smaller powers were given no veto. Many of them did not like this two-tiered distinction—it smacked of great-power privilege, like the earlier Concert of Europe—but they could not effectively resist it.

In creating the Security Council, the founders were not being naive but pragmatic. As it happened, the hope for great-power cooperation did not last long. The cold war was thoroughly under way by 1948, and the Soviet Union had already exercised its veto many times. In effect, the Security Council could act only in those disputes in which the permanent members had no vital interests at stake. No U.N. military force could be created. The Council did, however, prove able to authorize action in cases where the great powers' vital interests did not conflict or where their interests would be endangered if the conflict were not contained (as in the Middle East).

The end of the cold war (often dated from the symbolically striking fall of the Berlin Wall in 1989) provided yet another opportunity to revise and strengthen these principles of international organization. The Soviet Union (and its successor state, Russia) cooperated with the Western powers and almost entirely stopped using its veto. China could be persuaded, by a variety of positive and negative inducements, not to use its veto. Thus, it became possible for the Security Council to agree that important events or actions constituted a threat to international peace and security and to authorize collective action to deal with them. The most spectacular such action was the 1991 war against Iraq to restore the independence of Kuwait by an international coalition as authorized by the Security Council. But unity in the Security Council was short-lived. When the council debated a second war against Iraq in 2003, the United States and Britain were strongly opposed by the other permanent members.

Sovereignty, the principle of interstate relations enshrined by the Peace of Westphalia, is the foundation on which the state system has evolved since the seventeenth century. The great struggles between states, and the agreements that concluded them, have often demonstrated both the dangers of an anarchic international system and the fragility of efforts to move beyond anarchy. Whether, at the dawn of a new century, the members of the international community have the will or the capability to forge a new set of principles to bring more order to this enduring anarchic system is a question as yet unanswered.

ALL STATES ARE EQUAL
(BUT SOME STATES ARE MORE EQUAL THAN OTHERS)

In *Animal Farm,* George Orwell's allegorical indictment of the Russian Revolution, the last and most important of the seven principles of "Animalism" is that "all animals are equal." The pigs, however, are able to capitalize on their advantages over other animals and before long come to dominate the farm. The seven principles are now reduced to one: "All animals are equal, but some animals are more equal than others."

By the principles of sovereignty and in the eyes of international law, all states are equal. But one of the truisms in world politics is that on the face of the globe nothing is distributed equally—not people or their talents, not resources, not climate or geographic features, not technology, not air quality. In fact, many things are distributed in a highly unequal manner. The differences between nation-states in terms of resources and capabilities—the opportunities provided by their available menus—can be staggering. In Chapter 5 we discuss in detail the concepts of power and influence, the whole range of state capabilities, and the ways in which states attempt to exert their power and influence on others. Here, however, we may simply point out that states range widely in size—from the Russian Federation, with 6.6 million square miles (almost twice the size of the United States), to Nauru, with 8 square miles (about one-tenth the size of Washington, D.C.). The smallest member of the United Nations is Monaco, with less than 1 square mile of territory (only 480 acres). Similarly, the People's Republic of China had a population of nearly 1.3 *billion* in 2008, whereas in that same year, the microstate of Tuvalu had a population of around 12 *thousand*. (These and other important characteristics of states can be found in Appendix B.)

State sovereignty carries with it only the *principle* of independence from outside authority. It does not ensure equality in capabilities or freedom from the outside interference, which has led one scholar to refer to the notion of sovereignty as "organized hypocrisy." Sovereignty has also come to imply that the government of a state has the capacity and ability to carry out the internal responsibilities of a sovereign state. This has led some to differentiate between *juridical statehood,* the rights and responsibilities accorded to sovereign states by international law, and *empirical statehood,* the state's capacity to enforce its external independence and provide for internal stability and well-being. No official authority controls states in the contemporary world system, but many are subject to powerful unofficial forces, pressures, and influences that penetrate the supposed hard shell of the state. Moreover, many of these same states can scarcely provide the internal security that we have come to expect of sovereign states. Indeed, they have been called "quasi-states."[12]

The question of the relationship between small and large states is a perennial one. Although there are any number of ways to divide states in order to categorize and classify them, one division has always existed and been used in interstate interactions: the hierarchy of size and power. We may always find large and small units, the strong and the weak, the influential and the ineffectual. Like the debates at the Constitutional Convention in Philadelphia over the representation of states in the U.S. Congress, the major conflicts in setting up the United Nations were over size. Although there were plenty of arguments between the Soviet Union and the Western allies, the biggest disagreements were between the major powers and the smaller states. Small countries were particularly vocal in their opposition to any departure from the principle of one state, one vote.

Several scholars have proposed that there has been a growing observance of international norms that outlaw war, especially war waged by the strong against the weak, which in earlier eras would have led to the disappearance of the weakest states as sovereign entities.[13] The defense of Kuwait in the Gulf War can be seen as an affirmation of the principle of sovereignty and a rejection of the use of violence to conquer and annex another state. This was the key normative principle on which virtually all governments of weak states could unite (and that the United Nations, as an organization of states rather than peoples, itself embodies). Small states in the post–World War II period were unusually free from blatant military coercion by larger states. Thus protected, they have proliferated because

---

[12] Robert H. Jackson, *Quasi-States: Sovereignty, International Relations and the Third World* (Cambridge: Cambridge University Press, 1990). "Organized hypocrisy" is Stephen Krasner's term; see his *Sovereignty: Organized Hypocrisy* (Princeton, N.J.: Princeton University Press, 1999).

[13] See Jackson, *Quasi-States*; also John Mueller, *Retreat from Doomsday: The Obsolescence of Major War* (New York: Basic Books, 1989); and James L. Ray, "The Abolition of Slavery and the End of International War," *International Organization* 43 (Summer 1989), pp. 405–439.

TABLE 3.1 | WORLD BANK'S CLASSIFICATION OF STATES, 2006

Classification	Total Population (Millions)	Average GNP/capita (Dollars)	Life Expectancy (Years)	Adult Literacy (Percent)
Low income	2,420	1,860	60	61
Middle income	3,088	6,451	71	90
High income	1,031	34,933	79	99

Source: World Bank, *World Development Indicators 2008 CD-ROM* (Washington, D.C.: World Bank, 2008). GNP per capita figures are adjusted for purchasing power parity. Literacy rates are for 2005.

the potential ruling elites seek the status and prestige of statehood and the chance to have a country of their own to govern.

Analysts have divided countries into many other categories as well. For years we simply had the first world (the industrialized Western democracies), the second world (the communist bloc of Eastern Europe), and the third world (all the rest). Today these terms are of little use to us, although "third world" is still a commonly used label. Currently, the World Bank uses three basic categories of country groups based on per capita national income: low-income economies, middle-income economies, and high-income economies. Roughly 30 percent of all states, with 40 percent of the world's population, fall into the low-income category. Contrast this to the high-income category consisting of 25 percent of all states but a mere 15 percent of the world's population. High-income countries come predominantly from the Organization for Economic Cooperation and Development (OECD), sometimes called "the rich man's club." Some of the characteristics of the income-based groups are presented in Table 3.1. There are substantial differences among states in regard to some basic indicators of quality of life: gross national product per capita (wealth), life expectancy (health), and literacy (education).

NONSTATE ACTORS IN THE CONTEMPORARY SYSTEM

A variety of other, nonstate actors are increasingly involved in the crucial issues of world politics. These actors form an important part of the global environment, affecting the possibilities and probabilities of state actions. As we view world politics, the global system can be seen as a chessboard and the actors as the pieces that move around it. Alternately, as did Shakespeare, we can consider the world a stage; those groups, organizations, and individuals who interact on it are the actors. This is a useful metaphor for several reasons. First, the word *actor* conveys a broad spectrum of interacting entities; it is large enough to encompass all the entities we wish to study. Second, our emphasis is on behavior, and the word helps convey the idea of an entity that behaves or performs an action. In relation to nonstate actors, the term also helps to convey the idea that different actors have different roles—that some are stars and occupy center stage while others are bit players in the chorus. Yet they all interact in creating the finished production.

However, the state is still the dominant international actor on most important issues in world politics. Thus, one way to identify a significant nonstate actor is to ask whether it is taken into account in the calculations and strategies of the leaders of states and whether its continuing functions have an impact on the world stage. Any organized unit that commands the identification, interests, and loyalty of individuals and affects interstate relations becomes a major competitor among nation-states. As we survey the types of nonstate actors, think of consequential interactions between state and nonstate actors over the past several years—between the United States and al Qaeda since 9/11, between Iraq and U.N. weapons inspectors before the Iraq War, or between Myanmar and international relief organizations after the 2008 cyclone. In each case, conflict arose when the nonstate actor or actors challenged the sovereignty of a nation-state, either in terms of its security or its control over internal military, political, or economic matters. The dramatic acts of international terrorism by nonstate groups offer only the most striking example of this competition. Here, groups other than states employ substantial violence in the global system, directly challenging the monopoly of force that international law has traditionally granted to nation-states.

INTERGOVERNMENTAL ORGANIZATIONS

Nonstate actors in the contemporary global system include *international organizations* (IOs), and one type of IO is the **intergovernmental organization (IGO)**. IGOs are composed of states, and the individuals who are sent as delegates to such organizations represent the interests and policies of their home governments. Although IGO membership is limited to states, quite often these organizations have headquarters staffed by individuals whose primary commitment is to the organization itself, not to their home governments. Thus, the permanent administrative staff of the United Nations, the Secretariat, is an international civil service of individuals who put the interests of the organization ahead of their states. This structure may create an atmosphere of competition between the IGO and the state for the loyalty of individuals. The total number of IGOs increased almost fourfold from 1945 to 1995, when they hit a post–World War II high of 348; their number has declined slightly since then (IGO growth is shown graphically in Figure 3.1).

IGOs may be usefully classified according to the scope of their membership and the scope of their purpose (see Table 3.2). In one category, we have *universal* political organizations such as the old League of Nations and the UN, which aim to include as wide an international membership as possible. Such organizations are also *general-purpose* organizations in that they perform political, economic, military, sociocultural, and other functions for member states. Other general purpose organizations have more *restricted memberships;* the Organization of American States (OAS) and the Organization of African Unity (OAU) are examples. Usually, limited membership IGOs are regionally based, but not always. The Commonwealth of Nations is not regional; its membership is spread across the globe but is limited to countries with former colonial ties to the British Empire. The Group of Eight (G8) consists of the world's most advanced industrialized states from North America, Europe, and Asia. Nevertheless, regional organizations account for more than 70 percent of all IGOs today.

A significantly greater number of IGOs serve *limited purposes* and are sometimes called "functional IGOs" because they perform specific functions on behalf

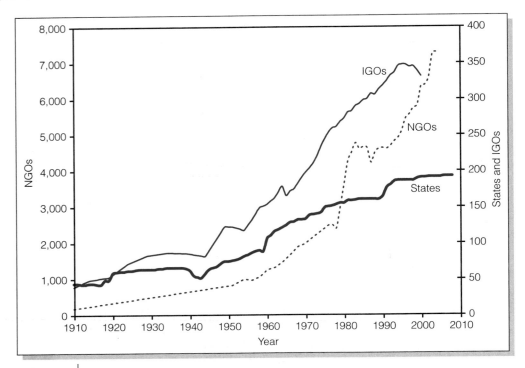

FIGURE 3.1 | GROWTH OF STATES, IGOS, AND NGOS, 1910–2008

The number of states in the international system increased steadily throughout the twentieth century, with the most rapid growth occurring with decolonization after World War II. This was accompanied by a very rapid increase in the number of both intergovernmental organizations (IGOs) and nongovernmental organizations (NGOs) during the postwar period.

Sources: Data on states come from the Correlates of War Project, "State System Membership List, v2002.1," April 21, 2003; available at <http://www.correlatesofwar.org>, updated by the authors. IGOs (1910–1964) and NGOs are compiled from Union of International Associations, *Yearbook of International Organizations* (Munich: UIA, various years). IGO data for 1965–2000 are from Jon C. Pevehouse, Timothy Nordstrom, and Kevin Warnke, "Intergovernmental Organizations, 1815–2000: A New Correlates of War Data Set," December 23, 2003; available at <http://www.correlatesofwar.org>. Some data for IGOs and NGOs are interpolations.

of member states. Many of these organizations are affiliated with the United Nations or are related to the European Union (EU). Those organizations connected to the United Nations often have, or aim for, universal membership. Some provide various social services—for example, the World Health Organization (WHO) and the International Labor Organization (ILO)—and others, such as the IMF and the World Bank, are involved in monetary matters and economic development. Many more have restricted membership. Some, like NATO and the former Warsaw Pact, serve primarily military functions. Others are concerned mainly with economic matters; examples are the various organs of the EU and organizations such as the Association of Southeast Asian Nations (ASEAN) and South America's Common Market of the South (Mercosur). The list becomes almost endless if we include groups with even more specific functional activities such as the International Statistical Institute,

TABLE 3.2 | CLASSIFICATION OF IGOs BY MEMBERSHIP AND PURPOSE

	Universal Membership	Restricted Membership
General purpose	League of Nations UN	OAS OAU British Commonwealth G8
Limited purpose	IMF World Bank WHO ILO	EU ↑ NATO MERCOSUR ASEAN

the International Bureau of Weights and Measures, the International Wool Study Group, or the Desert Locust Control Organization for East Africa.

Both the membership and purpose of IGOs evolve over time, making them difficult to classify. The Arab League, for instance, was formed in 1945 with the central purpose of opposing, both politically and militarily, the formation of the Jewish state in Palestine. More recently, however, it has become more concerned with Arab economic relations and development. Similarly, NATO, the cold war military alliance of Western powers, has become active in promoting democracy and economic reform among new and aspiring members in Eastern Europe. Indeed, a more general-purpose IGO, the Euro-Atlantic Partnership Council (EAPC), has been formed, consisting of the twenty-six member states of NATO plus another twenty-three aspirants. The EU is probably the best example of a limited-purpose IGO that has expanded its purview—from matters of economic integration to include the partial, if halting, coordination of European foreign and defense policies.

Without going into great detail on the workings of the individual IGOs—we discuss the United Nations, EU, and other organizations in subsequent chapters—let us review them as international actors.[14] First, they have a significant and continuing impact on interstate relations. The international role of many IGOs is clearly institutionalized in that states and citizens expect them to act in certain areas. They expect the United Nations to help calm areas of conflict, as it did in East Timor to keep the peace and prepare for the transition toward independence beginning in 1999. Both the EU and the Organization on Security and Cooperation in Europe (OSCE) attempted to resolve the violence in Yugoslavia starting in 1991, although without much success. When states find themselves in serious economic trouble, they almost automatically look to the World Bank or the IMF for various kinds of aid, as they did during the Asian financial crisis in 1997 and 1998 or the Argentine economic crisis of December 2001. In addition, IGOs are international actors to the extent

---

[14] On the role of IGOs in world politics, see Michael Barnett and Martha Finnemore, *Rules for the World: International Organizations in Global Politics* (Ithaca, N.Y.: Cornell University Press, 2004); Kenneth W. Abbott and Duncan Snidal, "Why States Act through Formal International Organizations," *Journal of Conflict Resolution* 42 (February 1998), pp. 3–32.

that states join the organization and value the continuation of membership. Merely sending representatives to an organization, employing resources to maintain IGO membership, and interacting with others through such organizations has an impact on the state and its foreign policy. Perhaps most important, IGOs may be considered important actors because state leaders believe they are. When state leaders deliberate over major foreign policy actions, they almost always find themselves considering repercussions that may involve one or more IGOs.

IGOs have this effect in several ways. Most clearly seen in the workings of the United Nations, but common to many other IGOs, is the function of acting as a forum in which the member states can meet, communicate, and negotiate. The IGO may act passively, serving only as a line of communication or a meeting place, or actively, as a mediator. IGOs perform a number of regulative functions across such areas as economics, health, communication, and transportation; examples range from the African Postal Union to the International Atomic Energy Agency. Here IGOs, with the consent of member states, set standards so that states can interact smoothly, efficiently, and with mutual benefit in a functional area of concern. This management or coordination role is essential to the orderly functioning of day-to-day global relations.

A very small number of IGOs can be considered **supranational authorities**. Member states have granted them the authority to act independently and to make decisions that are binding on members even if some members disagree with those decisions. These IGOs indeed appear to take a degree of sovereignty away from their member states. No IGO in existence today is completely supranational, but in the evolution of the EU, various organs of that organization, especially the European Commission, have developed extensive independent authority. The mix of intergovernmentalism and supranationalism in the EU has been aptly described as "pooled sovereignty," a topic we will examine more closely in Chapter 14.

NONGOVERNMENTAL ORGANIZATIONS

IGOs are not the only international organizations that have an impact on world politics, helping to shape the menu for state leaders and the range of state behavior. Whereas IGOs are organizations composed of states, **nongovernmental organizations (NGOs)** are private international actors. The important distinction regards membership: NGOs are organizations that cut across national boundaries—they are *transnational*—and are made up of individuals or national groups, not official representatives of national governments. They exist "below" the level of the state.[15] Like IGOs, they deal with a great variety of matters. There are religious bodies, professional organizations, sports organizations, trade union groups, and political parties. Their membership may be composed either directly of individuals (the International Studies Association) or of various national societies that themselves

---

[15] See, for example, Thomas Risse, "Transnational Actors and World Politics," in Walter Carlsnaes, Thomas Risse, and Beth Simmons, eds., *Handbook of International Relations* (London: Sage, 2002), pp. 255–274; John Boli and George M. Thomas, eds., *Constructing World Culture: International Nongovernmental Organizations since 1875* (Stanford, Cal.: Stanford University Press, 1999). These organizations are often referred to as INGOs (*international* nongovernmental organizations).

are composed of individuals (like the International Red Cross, composed of the various national Red Cross organizations). International NGOs are now quite numerous, having increased from fewer than 200 in 1909 to 700 in 1945 to more than 7,000 today (see Figure 3.1).

Most often these organizations perform rather low-level, specifically functional tasks, promoting contact across state boundaries on matters of common interest and providing nongovernmental means of communication among individuals of many nations. NGOs help knit the global society together in much the same way that private groups do within a country, although the portion of the global population with membership in NGOs is very small when compared to the portion of the national population associated with one or more domestic interest groups in a developed democracy. Sometimes an NGO can function as a pressure group affecting national governments or international organizations. An example is the role of the International Red Cross in mobilizing world concern and aid for African populations facing starvation, or Greenpeace on matters ranging from whaling to nuclear testing. A great many NGOs are formally consulted by IGOs concerned with the same problems (for example, health and medical organizations are consulted by WHO). Some NGOs, such as Amnesty International and the Roman Catholic Church, can exert significant influence on the policies of various states.

Although individuals are important to the operation and impact of NGOs and contribute in other ways to the transnational linkages between and among states (in tourism, student exchange, business and commercial links, and so on), individuals are most often powerless in international politics except when they can, through an official or unofficial role, affect the policy of a government. One analyst, however, claims that this situation is changing and that private individuals are having an ever greater impact on world affairs. Through the growing interdependence of the world system and the growing awareness of individuals of their place in the world, individual acts produce significant impacts. For example, Mathias Rust, a West German teenager acting "on behalf of world peace" landed his light plane in Red Square in 1987, exposing the vulnerabilities of Soviet air defenses and leading to the dismissal of the defense minister. Bono, the lead singer of U2, has capitalized on his celebrity to raise public awareness of the AIDS epidemic in Africa, as has the American actress Angelina Jolie in regard to the plight of refugees.[16]

TRANSNATIONAL CORPORATIONS

Some of the most powerful transnational actors are **multinational corporations (MNCs)**. The number and importance of MNCs have grown enormously in recent years. In 2005, more than 75,000 firms were conducting business in foreign countries—more than a sixfold increase since the early 1990s—with more than 650,000 affiliates, most of them located in the developing world. The top 100 MNCs (industrial, not financial) controlled $8.7 trillion in assets, had $6.6 trillion in

---

[16] James N. Rosenau, *People Count! Networked Individuals in Global Politics* (Boulder, Colo.: Paradigm, 2008). See also Andrew F. Cooper, *Celebrity Diplomacy* (Boulder, Colo.: Paradigm, 2008).

sales, and employed more than 15 million people worldwide. On average, half of their assets, sales, and employment was foreign. Of all transnational business activity worldwide, almost 90 percent is conducted by MNCs based in the United States, Japan, and EU countries. The United States was home to about one-fourth of the top 100 MNCs in 2005, the EU to one-half (most of these British, French, or German), with most of the rest based in Japan.[17]

Clearly, giant corporations like these cannot help but affect the policies of many governments and the welfare of many people. Oil companies, for instance, would still have tremendous impact with their pricing and marketing policies even if they did not try to influence the policies or personnel of national governments. Some believe that the MNC has emerged as one of the major competitors to the nation-state. Whereas nonstate liberation movements and separatist groups have challenged the military and political authority of specific nation-states, the MNC is a much more broadly based and subtle competitor. This is partly because MNCs may become deeply involved in the domestic political processes of host countries—by outright bribery, by support of specific political parties or candidates, or by financing coups. Examples are the actions of the United Fruit Company in the overthrow of the Arbenz government in Guatemala in 1954, the actions of British Petroleum in the removal of the Mossadegh government in Iran in 1953, and the role played by ITT in the coup against the Socialist regime of Salvador Allende of Chile in 1973.

Many multinationals predate the states that have been created since the end of World War II. MNCs also have their own spheres of influence through the division of world markets. They often engage in diplomacy and espionage, traditional tools of state interaction. Most important, MNCs have very large economic resources at their disposal, which gives them an advantage over not only many of the newer and smaller states but also some of the established ones. For example, in 2005, the U.S. firm ExxonMobil had gross sales in excess of the GNPs of all but twenty-four nations. Even top-100 firms that figure near the bottom of the sales ranking have total sales exceeding the GNPs of one-third of the world's nation-states. Of course, GNP and gross sales are not directly comparable accounting terms; the most accurate comparison would be between GNP and "value added" by the corporation. Nevertheless, the comparison suggests how very large some modern MNCs are compared with the often small, developing states with which they deal.

NATION-STATE VERSUS NONSTATE LOYALTY

Although there are competitors to the nation-state, some very formidable in certain ways, the state continues to enjoy great advantages over other international actors. In addition to the legal status of formal sovereignty, the state generally also possesses demographic, economic, military, and geographic capabilities unmatched by other actors. IGOs or MNCs may have the loyalty of some individuals, but the

---

[17] United Nations Conference on Trade and Development, *World Investment Report 2007: Transnational Corporations, Extractive Industries and Development* (New York: United Nations, 2007), pp. 229–231. Multinational corporations are also often called *transnational corporations* (TNCs).

nation-state commands the loyalty of very large numbers of people. One clear ramification of the combination of the nation with the state (which is what actors such as the Palestinian Authority want to achieve) is that the state comes to embody the nation and is strengthened through the continuing process of nationalism; that is, the government of the state is seen by the people as representing and protecting cultural values as well as history and tradition. Combined with the idea of sovereignty, this relationship is a powerful force indeed—one rarely matched by nonstate actors. Before the outbreak of World War I, the Socialist parties of Europe, meeting together under the aegis of the Second International, called for unity among the proletariat and for workers anywhere in Europe to refuse to take up arms against other workers if called upon to do so by their governments. Here was a direct clash between an NGO and the states of Europe: competition for the loyalty of the workers within the various European countries, especially Germany, France, and Britain. When the war came and choices had to be made, for a variety of reasons the workers rallied to the nationalist stands of their respective states, not to the flag of international Socialism.

Two concluding, if somewhat contradictory, comments are in order. The first is that states possess, in general, a far wider range of capabilities than do nonstate actors and thus have a much larger and more varied menu for choice. Although there has been a tremendous growth in both IGOs and NGOs and the transnational interactions among them (and between them and states), nonstate interactions clearly reflect the structure and distribution of the power of the states in the global system. The growth of nonstate activity has both mirrored and derived from the expansion of the state system itself in the postwar period. The second point, however, is simply that IGOs and NGOs do exist as important actors. And in a world system characterized by high and growing levels of interdependence (which we discuss in subsequent chapters), such actors inevitably and consistently affect the menu of constraints and possibilities facing states. As players on the world stage, they must be taken seriously by states and by one another.

THE WORLD SYSTEM: INTERNATIONAL STRUCTURE AND POLARITY

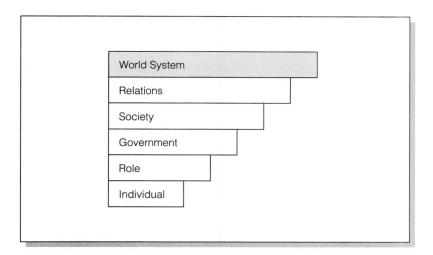

| World System |
| Relations |
| Society |
| Government |
| Role |
| Individual |

THE INTERNATIONAL ENVIRONMENT

Starting our analysis at the level of the world system, we have the most general picture of world politics. Nation-states and their foreign policy makers are embedded in an international environment, as are nonstate actors. This environment provides important components to the menu from which decision makers make their choices. How exactly does the international environment affect the menu? How does it affect what is possible and probable in state behavior? To answer these questions, we might begin by considering the geopolitical and technological dimensions of this environment.

GEOPOLITICAL SETTING

An important aspect of international relations is **geopolitics**. This includes the crucial dimension of "spatiality"—the location of entities in relationship to other entities, as well as how capabilities are distributed among these entities. Every nation-state operates within a context shaped by many other states and nonstate actors. Some of these entities are large and some are small; some possess great military and economic capacity and others do not; some control important natural resources and others are resource poor. The arrangement of states includes their political-geographic arrangement as well. This means that physical location of states is an important consideration, for both students and practitioners of world politics. For example, China and Russia still share more than 2,000 miles of common land border, whereas the United States has a common land border with neither. Britain and Japan are islands, whereas France and Germany border several other states. Some states are distant from the centers of international activity. Australia, for instance, possesses substantial military and economic capabilities but is located at the geopolitical periphery of the international system. Others states such as Egypt, Israel, and Iraq are located along historical trade routes or paths of invasion.

The political-geographic arrangement of the international system includes not only location but also topographical features. States keep an eye on their neighbors—how many there are, how close or how far, how big or how small—and they are also concerned with the features of land and sea. The menu of a particular nation-state is different if it is an island or a continental power; lies at the end of a peninsula or at the center of a continental landmass; has long shorelines and good ports or is landlocked; has mountains, deserts, rivers, swamps, or other natural barriers along its borders or open, flat plains. The arrangement of these physical features will limit or enable the movement of both economic goods and military capabilities.

The physical arrangement of the international environment also includes less obvious features. Useful natural resources—drinkable water and arable land, as well as forests, animal life, and mineral resources—are unevenly distributed. And the definition of *useful* changes over time. States that possessed uranium before the advent of nuclear power did not gain in either wealth or influence. A major shift to the use of renewable resources (solar and wind energy, biofuels, and so on) will diminish the strategic importance of the oil-rich Middle East. Climate also varies across the globe in ways that may be relevant for the agricultural and other capabilities of states. All these factors affect opportunities for certain types of state interaction. Just as the layout of a chessboard (or any other game board) and the distribution of pieces and their capabilities at a particular moment in time constrains or enables the subsequent movement of the pieces, the geopolitical setting affects the behavior of states in the international system.

Research shows that geographic location strongly affects state interaction. States tend to get into wars more often with neighbors than with others because they interact more with countries close by than with those far away. Contiguity is one factor that helps to identify "dangerous dyads"—pairs of states such as India and Pakistan or Iran and Iraq that are most inclined to engage in military conflict.[1] One view of the relationship between the closeness of states and their opportunities for interaction was put forth by Kenneth E. Boulding. According to Boulding, any state's power is greatest at home but then declines along a "loss of strength gradient" as the distance from home is increased. This occurs because of the time and cost associated with transporting one's military resources. Because of this, Boulding proposes an axiom: "[T]he further the weaker."[2] As a consequence, a state should be most concerned with its immediate neighbors and less concerned with those far away.

Interaction is most intense in what some researchers call a state's *politically relevant international environment* (PRIE), an area that a state's decision makers see as important in their calculations of both opportunity and willingness. For most states, this includes their contiguous neighbors and perhaps the neighbors of those neighbors. Thus, states are usually concerned most with their geographically proximate regions, or "neighborhoods." These may be "good neighborhoods" or "bad neighborhoods." An example of the former is the diffusion of democracy, whereby democratic governance in one state encourages the adoption of democratic governance in neighboring states. Examples of the latter include the spread of civil war or clusters of "failed" or "failing" states. The exceptions to these geographic arguments, of course, are the great powers, which may be part of the PRIE of many states not spatially close to them. Great powers are those states with enough resources to overcome the disadvantage of distance. Indeed, a major component of U.S. military superiority today is its capacity, far exceeding that of other states, to transport large numbers of military forces over long distances in relatively short amounts of time.

TECHNOLOGICAL SETTING

Decision makers are faced with a number of factors that are generally unchanging: geography, the constellation of neighboring states, and more distant states. Another factor that is more amenable to change, but sometimes only gradually over time, is the prevailing level of technology in the international system. As we noted when discussing opportunity in Chapter 2, technology plays a major part in determining what is physically possible. In the fourth century B.C.E., Alexander the Great could not communicate instantaneously with King Darius of Persia, but Richard Nixon could do so with Leonid Brezhnev during the superpower crisis triggered by the 1973 Yom Kippur War in the Middle East.

Technology is the application of scientific understanding to accomplish human purposes. Human creativity has continually led people to develop new technologies to overcome the limits of space and time, to generate power for economic and

---

[1] For evidence of this effect, see Stuart Bremer, "Dangerous Dyads: Conditions Affecting the Likelihood of Interstate War, 1816–1965," *Journal of Conflict Resolution* 36 (June 1992), pp. 309–341. On the use of the geographic information system (GIS) in international relations research, see Harvey Starr, "Opportunity, Willingness, and Geographic Information Systems: Reconceptualizing Borders in International Relations," *Political Geography* 21 (February 2002), pp. 243–261.

[2] Kenneth E. Boulding, *Conflict and Defense: A General Theory* (New York: Harper & Row, 1962), chap. 4. See also Kieran Webb, "The Continued Importance of Geographic Distance and Boulding's Loss of Strength Gradient," *Comparative Strategy* 26 (July 2007), pp. 295–310.

military purposes, to communicate and transport ideas and objects. Obstacles presented by mountains, deserts, or distance are overcome by inventions—the railroad, the automobile, the airplane, rocketry. Obstacles to the spread of ideas and ideologies have been overcome by the development of radio, television, communications satellites, and the Internet. These technologies bring news from all over the world into our homes even as events are happening. Technology also permits us to overcome obstacles posed by disease and age. Advances in medical knowledge and skills have played a large part in the explosive growth of population since World War II by lowering the rate of infant mortality and the death rate in general. New technologies also permit the extraction of resources that had been literally out of reach. The development of synthetic chemical and other materials can expand a menu otherwise limited by the Earth's resource endowment.

In short, the technology that exists in the international system at any time is an important factor for understanding what is possible or probable in world politics. But technology is not static. Research and development by governments, industry, universities, and individual inventors are continually changing prevailing technology and thus the international environment. Such change has become ever more rapid, and it has been taking less and less time for new discoveries to become operational in our world. The gap between Marconi's first radio set and commercial broadcasting was thirty-five years; but the atomic bomb went from discovery to use in six years, and the transistor made the journey in five years. The first cloned mammal (a sheep named Dolly) occurred in July 1996. Medical and commercial applications of this technology are around the corner, although sharp ethical debate has accompanied advances in mammalian cloning and may slow the process somewhat.[3] Technological development alters the menu, and state leaders are well aware of this fact. Forward-looking governments and other organizations, when faced with a set of opportunities that they find overly constraining, will direct the efforts of their research-and-development establishments with the intention of expanding their menus.

THE GLOBAL SYSTEM

A **system** is a set of elements, or units, interacting with each other. It is more than a collection of entities; in a system, the elements are interconnected such that changes in the properties of some elements, or changes in their interactions with other elements, produce changes elsewhere in the system. A set of billiard balls moving about on a pool table constitutes such a system, for the balls collide with one another and these collisions produce changes elsewhere on the table. The international system, which is infinitely more complex, is a set of states and other actors interacting (and often "colliding") with each other. Sometimes it is useful to treat the international system as consisting only of states interacting like billiard balls, all with similar internal compositions and affected only by the behavior of each other. Thus, we would concentrate on how the unit France interacts with other

---

[3] See, for example, the United Nations Declaration on Human Cloning, passed by the UN General Assembly in 2005, which encourages restraint in this area of research; available at <http://www.un.org/Depts/dhl/resguide/r59.htm>.

units such as Italy and China. However, we have indicated that the international system is infinitely more complex than a set of billiard balls. Why is this so?

Not only are other actors, both within nation-states and outside them, important elements in the system, but also the kinds of interaction, and the number of factors affecting those interactions, are much more numerous. The billiard balls act on one another only through the expenditure of energy, which can be measured on a single scale. If you know the initial location of the balls on the table, the energy-absorbing capacity of the balls and banks, the friction created by the felt, the amount of energy exerted through the cue, and the initial angles of interaction, then it is possible to make a good prediction of where the balls will end up. The prediction requires quite a lot of information, some of which (such as the angles) is very hard to measure if you are not an accomplished player, but the number of different variables at issue is relatively small. Furthermore, these are the only variables that matter. If you had all the information for them, the effects both of chance (an earthquake) and of ignored variables (atmospheric pressure) would be quite low. The typical billiard player doesn't make formal computations but does recognize certain variables as important and takes them into account based on experience and intuition. The player who "knows" the table (specific characteristics of the banks and pockets) will also have a good idea of how much force to use on the cue and the angle to try in order to get the desired distribution of the balls. Achieving the right shot may not always be possible, but the player knows how to attempt it.

The analysis of international systems requires, or at least seems to require, information about a great many more variables. We say "seems to require" because we are often not sure which variables exert a great deal of influence and which, like the atmospheric pressure in the billiards room, can be safely ignored without misleading our analyses. Any system is defined by the characteristics of its component units and by the nature, pattern, and number of interactions among those units. Therefore, when applying these ideas to the international system, there are several important factors to consider. As we shall discuss shortly, the *number and relative size of state actors* is the primary structural feature of the international system.

The numbers and types of *nonstate actors* are also important. In addition to the intergovernmental and nongovernmental organizations mentioned in the previous chapter, we should also include geographic or political groups of states as actors. Because of their common interests and linkages, such groupings have been called *blocs*. This is the sense in which many observers commonly used the term *Soviet bloc* during most of the post–World War II period. They assumed that the linkages among these countries were so numerous and strong that the states would often act as a coherent unit, delegating decision-making power to an IGO (Warsaw Pact) or to the dominant member (the Soviet Union). When such regional groupings, blocs, or alliances act together on a range of issues, they contribute to a serious modification of the overall arrangement of the international system. No longer does the system consist entirely of independent states relating to one another like billiard balls; now the system includes one or more clusters of linked billiard balls.

There is more to understanding the international system than grasping its arrangement or structure. The nature of the linkages or *interactions* among state and nonstate actors is also key. These include official government-to-government interactions as well as transactions across societies. The latter may take the form of trade, investment, movements of citizens (by tourism, migration, and student exchanges), communications between private citizens (via mail, telephone, fax, or the Internet), or mass media (radio, television, print). From the viewpoint of the political analyst, any single event—a particular purchase, a single e-mail message, one student exchange—is rarely of interest. Rather, it is the aggregate number or pattern of such acts that is of concern—in other words, whether the total volume of trade or communications is high or low. Alternately, there may be a certain class of events, or acts, of special interest. Official acts such as signing a treaty, issuing a threat, or mobilizing troops convey messages to other governments and are frequently studied forms of state interaction.

Finally, we need to consider the degree of **interdependence** existing between interacting state and nonstate actors. Interdependence is a relationship in which changes or events in any single part of a system will produce some reaction or have some significant consequence in other parts of the system. As we stated at the outset, this is what distinguishes systems from other collectivities in which inter-action is minimal and inconsequential. For example, in the human body (a biologi-cal system) an infection will affect the blood and trigger its white cell defenses; it can cause a fever and speed up the heartbeat. Similarly, by increasing the air in the carburetor of a car engine, we affect the ignition within the cylinders and the speed and smoothness of the ride. The Asian financial crisis described in Chapter 1 is a good example from world politics: The economies and financial markets in Southeast Asia had become so interdependent that developments in Thailand set off an immediate chain of events throughout the region, which ultimately had implications well beyond the region. A high degree of interdependence means that "the entire system exhibits properties and behaviors that are different from those of the parts." Failure to recognize the irreducibility of the system's "emergent prop-erties" is to commit the so-called fallacy of composition.[4] It is why we can learn some things about world politics by approaching our topic from the system level of analysis that we cannot learn from other levels.

EMERGENCE OF THE CONTEMPORARY SYSTEM

Interaction and interdependence make a system out of otherwise separate units. Many social, technological, economic, and political factors affect the rate and kind of inter-action. Where interaction is much greater among a certain set of actors than between those actors and others outside the set, the interacting units constitute a subsystem. If the rate of interaction between members of the set and outsiders is extremely low or nonexistent, we may simply refer to it as a system rather than a subsystem. Regional systems existed as far back as recorded history—for example, the Zhou Dynasty in China from 1122 to 221 B.C.E. or the Greek city-states from 800 to 322 B.C.E.—but they were relatively isolated and not part of a larger global system.[5]

---

[4] Robert Jervis, *System Effects: Complexity in Political and Social Life* (Princeton, N.J.: Princeton University Press, 1997), pp. 6, 12–17.

[5] For an analysis of international systems and subsystems in historical context, see Barry Buzan and Richard Little, *International Systems in World History: Remaking the Study of International Relations* (Oxford: Oxford University Press, 2000).

As we discussed in the last chapter, until the fifteenth century C.E., European states did not interact at all with the Western Hemisphere, and they interacted in no significant way with Africa south of the Sahara or with East and Southeast Asia. Communication and transportation technologies were too primitive to permit interaction across long distances. With improvements in navigation and sailing technology, Spain, Portugal, Holland, England, and France were able to build huge colonial empires around the globe, affecting an expansion of the European system. For the first time, a worldwide capitalist economic system emerged. Many peoples and areas were linked to this system only weakly, but many others—slaves producing sugar in the Caribbean, indigenous peoples put to work in the silver mines of South America, farmers on spice plantations in Southeast Asia, consumers in Europe—found their fortunes linked to, and interdependent with, economic conditions halfway around the world. The world political system still remained fairly fragmented, however. No single state dominated the world, and for a long time it was still possible for many non-European actors to ignore Europe for most purposes. Large parts of Africa and Asia retained substantial independence until the final wave of European colonial acquisition in the second half of the nineteenth century. The United States, with its strength and relative physical isolation, was able to ignore most European political quarrels until World War I.

One indicator of the rapid integration of the global system since the height of the colonial period is the movement of people over large distances. Figure 4.1

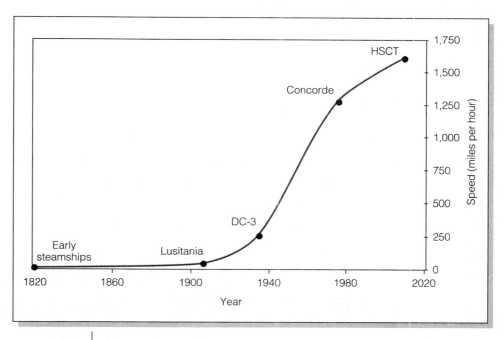

FIGURE 4.1 | MAXIMUM SPEED ATTAINABLE FOR INTERCONTINENTAL PASSENGER TRAVEL

Awareness of the world around us expands as we come into contact with more people and places. Remarkable advances in the speed of passenger travel were made during the twentieth century and will continue into the twenty-first, although there is an upper limit to the speed of human transportation.

tracks changes in transportation technology since the early nineteenth century. Beginning with sailing vessels and the earliest steamships (which moved at about five miles per hour), the curve gives the approximate maximum speed of civilian transportation over intercontinental distances. The graph rises to the speeds attained by oceangoing passenger liners at the turn of the century and then begins to advance rapidly with the development of civil aviation in the 1930s. The era of supersonic transport was inaugurated in the 1970s, and although there is certainly an upper limit for physical transportation, development projects under way in high-speed civilian transport (HSCT) are currently targeting speeds of mach 2.4 (about 1,600 mph) by the year 2015. With these and other changes, including the explosion of Internet-based communication and commerce, the whole world has become irrevocably bound into a closely knit system.

Coupled with the enormous growth in wealth of the industrial powers over the past century, new technology provides the means for great powers to make their influence felt virtually everywhere and for the entire collection of international actors to operate as an interacting system. The major powers are particularly involved in interactions with one another and with middle and minor powers. During the cold war era, each superpower had parts of the globe (or regional subsystems) that it dominated and within which it sharply limited the influence of other major powers. The United States was long dominant in Latin America, and the Soviet Union came to occupy such a position in Eastern Europe within a few years following the end of World War II. China has exercised influence in parts of East Asia, competing first with the USSR and now with Japan and Russia, and its expanding global position increasingly brings it into competition with the United States. Britain and France once had large spheres of influence in Africa and elsewhere but no longer dominate these regions. At the same time, although some major powers have clearly predominated over others in particular regions during certain time periods (for example, Latin America and Eastern Europe), most of the smaller powers within such areas usually maintain significant ties—economic, political, cultural, or military—with one another and with other outside powers as well.

STATUS AND HIERARCHY IN THE INTERNATIONAL SYSTEM

A system perspective focuses our attention on component units, their interactions, and the emergent whole. Both the characteristics of these units and their interactions will indicate how the units or, in our case, state and nonstate actors stand in relationship to one another. In the last chapter, we emphasized that the modern state system is, formally, an anarchy—no *legal* authority exists above the nation-state—but that states vary immensely in their resources and capabilities. Therefore, in discussing international systems it is useful to examine the degree of hierarchy that does, in fact, exist informally in the international system.[6] By **hierarchy**, we simply mean an arrangement in which it is evident who has the most of something

---

[6] See David A. Lake, *Hierarchy in International Relations: Authority, Sovereignty, and the New Structure of World Politics* (Ithaca, N.Y.: Cornell University Press, 2009); Ian Clark, *The Hierarchy of States: Reform and Resistance in the International Order* (Cambridge: Cambridge University Press, 1989).

(wealth, military might, prestige), who has the least, and who is positioned in the middle. Hierarchy can also indicate how states are linked together in their interactions, either essentially as equals or only through the intermediary of one or more great powers. Several writers see a feudal aspect to much of historical and contemporary international politics. They posit a world of several influence spheres, each dominated by a big power that interposes itself between small powers within its sphere and limits as far as possible the penetration of other major powers into those spheres. For instance, telephone calls between Senegal and Gabon in West Africa once had to go through Paris, and air travel in many parts of the Third World was possible only through London, Paris, or other major cities in the developed world.

When examining international politics from the perspective of the world system, we need to take into account the unequal distribution of power and influence among states as well as the principle of sovereign equality that governs their relations in the eyes of international law. The arrangement of state and nonstate actors in the international system consists of both—the principle of authority and the distribution of power—and together they constitute the *structure of the international system*. Some realist scholars argue that this structure can tell us a great deal about the relations between states, and in particular whether the system will witness more or fewer destructive wars between the major powers.[7] We return to this question at the end of the chapter.

SPHERES OF INFLUENCE

A system perspective often directs our attention to *competition* among great powers as they move to limit each other's influence in their respective spheres of influence. But we can also examine *dominance* of the weak by the strong and the limited autonomy or independence exercised by those at the bottom of the hierarchy. The menu of policy options for smaller states may be highly constrained when a major power identifies national interests of its own in the vicinity of those states, and even more so if they sit within the major power's sphere of influence. However, if two major powers are competing in an area, as the superpowers did in the Middle East during the cold war, each is limited by the presence of the other; each restrains its behavior in anticipation (or fear) of the other's response. The competition of two or more major powers can actually expand the menu of smaller states, allowing the tails to wag the dogs. These are just some of the possible constraints imposed on states, weak and strong, by the structure of the international system.[8]

One simple hierarchical structure is illustrated in Figure 4.2, with the lines indicating the degree of interaction that states have with one another. Thus A and B, two major powers, interact extensively with each other and with minor powers in

[7] See, for example, Kenneth N. Waltz, *Theory of International Politics* (Reading, Mass.: Addison-Wesley, 1979); John J. Mearsheimer, *The Tragedy of Great Power Politics* (New York: Norton, 2001).

[8] Groups of interacting smaller states located in the same region can be conceptualized as subsystems and have been referred to as "security complexes." See Barry Buzan and Ole Wæver, *Regions and Powers: The Structure of International Security* (Cambridge: Cambridge University Press, 2003); David A. Lake and Patrick M. Morgan, eds., *Regional Orders: Building Security in a New World* (University Park: Pennsylvania State University Press, 1997).

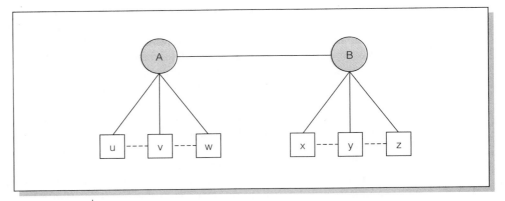

FIGURE 4.2 | A HIERARCHICAL SYSTEM

In a system of sovereign states, there is no legal authority above the nation-state; the system is anarchic. However, the distribution of power may introduce elements of hierarchy into the system, whereby great powers interact on a more equal basis, while minor states within each great power's sphere of influence have limited interaction with each other and no interaction with states outside the sphere.

their own spheres of influence (as indicated by the solid lines). The minor powers—*u*, *v*, *w*, *x*, *y*, and *z*—interact very little with each other (the broken lines), even though they might be in the same geographical region and have many common interests. Theories about spheres of influence tend to be concerned chiefly with relations among the great powers, or the "view from above." What goes on among the small powers at the periphery of the world system is generally regarded as inconsequential, except that additions or losses to spheres of influence may change the distribution of power among the system's major actors and perhaps the likelihood of war. This is the perspective of realism, which was typical of U.S. and Soviet theorizing during the cold war era. During that period, theorists in Europe and especially in the third world saw the situation very differently. Their "views from below" were much more concerned with how to avoid becoming arenas for superpower rivalry and obtain some freedom of action for their countries. From below, great-power competition looks like great-power dominance.

The end of several enduring conflicts in the late 1980s—in areas such as Angola and Namibia, Central America, Cambodia, and between Iran and Iraq—owed much to the end of the superpower rivalry and the evolution of a policy of mutual restraint between the United States and the Soviet Union. No longer would the two powers automatically support opposing factions in local disputes. But superpower competition also provided benefits to some smaller countries by fostering the interest of one superpower in areas that might be of importance to the other. Smaller countries found that they could play the superpowers against each other in a competition over the provision of economic and military aid. This process halted dramatically in the post–cold war era when Soviet inability to compete in many areas also promoted American neglect. A similar phenomenon occurred during earlier periods of U.S.–Soviet détente. The volume of U.S. economic assistance to other countries declined from 0.8 percent of GNP to about 0.3 percent from 1962 to 1983, during a period when U.S.–Soviet relations were improving (it has since dropped to less than 0.1 percent). Likewise, after the Soviet Union completed its military withdrawal from Afghanistan in 1989, the United States, having supported the anti-Soviet muja-hedeen, also left the country to its own devices. The instability and lawlessness that gripped Afghanistan came under some semblance of control only in 1996 with the rise of the Taliban and its harsh Islamic system of governance.

Just as theories of great-power politics look mainly at horizontal relations among approximate equals in power, theories that start from the standpoint of small powers stress vertical relationships of dominance and exploitation. As noted, some theories characterize international politics as essentially feudal; a related theo-retical perspective focuses on the dependence of small, developing states on large, industrialized ones. The central issues addressed in such theories are usually different from those emphasized by theories of great-power politics; they are less concerned with war and international political alignments and more concerned with patterns of economic and political development in the Global South. In particular, they exam-ine the effects of big powers' economic, political, and cultural penetrations of small powers. We discuss some of these perspectives at length in Chapter 15.

ALLIANCES

Alliances tell us much about the political and military structure of the international system: about the geopolitical relationships among states, about the distribution of friendship and enmity, and about the distribution of military capability. Like tech-nology, alliances can be used to overcome distance and geographic obstacles, creat-ing new opportunities as well as risks for the states involved. Alliances, through their impact on the distribution of power, can be central to system structure and thus to the menu of policy options presented by the international system.[9]

Alliances combine elements of cooperation and conflict. They involve interstate cooperation (between allied states) while addressing an existing or potential conflict with one or more other states. Generally speaking, cooperative behavior can be both formal and informal. Informally, two states are *aligned* if they act in a similar way toward some third international actor. Their common policies toward other actors may be a coincidence, but alignment often means that they act cooperatively because they have shared interests and choose to coordinate their behavior toward other actors but without signing a formal agreement. Essentially, they behave as a *coalition*.[10] The United States and Israel are aligned; the two countries have been part of the same coalition in many international forums, especially at deliberations of the United Nations. Military **alliances** involve more than this. Here the coalitions are *formalized* in written treaties, and these involve agreements to cooperate

---

[9] For a review of alliance theory, see Glenn H. Snyder, *Alliance Politics* (Ithaca, N.Y.: Cornell University Press, 1997); see also Stephen M. Walt, *The Origins of Alliances* (Ithaca, N.Y.: Cornell University Press, 1987).

[10] Theories of alliances often draw on models of coalition formation in political science; a classic work is William H. Riker, *The Theory of Political Coalitions* (New Haven, Conn.: Yale University Press, 1962). See also Mancur Olson, Jr., *The Logic of Collective Action: Public Goals and the Theory of Groups* (Cambridge, Mass.: Harvard University Press, 1966).

specifically on matters of military security. The agreements specify the rights and obligations of the alliance membership, generally for stipulated periods of time.

Military alliances take different forms. A *defense pact* involves the greatest commitment on the part of the signatories: Each promises to come to the defense of any member in the event of an attack. NATO is a defense pact, as was the Warsaw Pact (officially, the Warsaw Treaty Organization). When states sign a neutrality agreement, or *nonaggression pact*, they promise not to attack each other or to give assistance to an attacker. An infamous example is the Molotov–Ribbentrop Pact, a nonaggression pact signed by the foreign ministers of the Soviet Union and Germany in 1939, which stunned the world for having been signed by two countries at opposite sides of the ideological spectrum. Although they shared few common interests, Hitler was convinced that without Soviet help France and Britain would do nothing serious to oppose Germany's invasion of Poland, which was imminent. For his part, Stalin hoped to buy some time to build up the Soviet Union's military strength and to secure a defensive position in Eastern Europe. Stalin assumed Hitler's nonaggression promise would not last, and it didn't. Hitler launched Operation Barbarossa two years later.

A third type of alliance is an *entente*. As implied by this French word for understanding, an entente does not entail the same degree of formal military commitment as does a defense pact, often because relations between the parties are not especially friendly. Before World War I, relations between France and Britain were competitive, particularly in regard to the scramble for colonial territory in Africa and the Far East. This rivalry prevented the two countries from concluding a formal defense treaty, but, as German power began to look more and more threatening, they did sign an entente in 1904 whereby they tried to resolve at least some of their differences. Russia, having earlier concluded a defense pact with France, concluded its own entente with Britain in 1907—the two countries had clashed over control of the Turkish Straits and in Persia—giving rise to a three-way alliance, the Triple Entente. Thus, different types of military alliance reflect different degrees of military commitment and often reflect the degree of closeness between allies and the extent to which they share common interests. In fact, researchers have found that systematically comparing "alliance portfolios" is a good way to measure shared interests in the foreign policy realm.[11]

Alliances are sometimes used by large nations to control and dominate smaller alliance partners and by smaller allies to manipulate larger alliance partners. An alliance leader may use alliances to create an orderly international environment in which that state is safe, secure, and in a position to promote its interests. Order requires organizing relations among the leader's allies, which may include restraining their behavior toward other states within and outside the alliance. In the post–World War II period, both the United States and the Soviet Union used their alliances in this way, particularly in Europe. NATO was officially founded in 1949 as

---

[11] The pioneering work was done by Bruce Bueno de Mesquita; see, for example, *The War Trap* (New Haven, Conn.: Yale University Press, 1981). A refined approach is presented in Curtis S. Signorino and Jeffrey M. Ritter, "Tau-b or Not Tau-b: Measuring the Similarity of Foreign Policy Positions," *International Studies Quarterly* 43 (March 1999), pp. 115–144.

a means to protect Western Europe from Soviet invasion. The Warsaw Pact was established in 1955 as a response to West Germany's entry into NATO; German militarism was still a recent memory among the Soviets and East Europeans. Their respective alliances served the security interests of the United States and the Soviet Union. However, both alliances also served to keep the lesser allies—especially the two German states—in line. Lord Ismay, the first secretary-general of NATO, once said that the purpose of that alliance was "to keep the Russians out, the Americans in, and the Germans down."

Smaller allies have often engaged their larger partners in war by painting them into a corner whereby the larger partners have little choice but to fight if they expect to be taken seriously (by friends or enemies) in subsequent confrontations. Austria-Hungary's aggressive behavior toward Serbia and Russia before World War I illustrates this relationship. Germany became a belligerent supporter of Austria-Hungary because backing down before Russia would surely mark the end of the Austro-German alliance. Nor are such relationships limited to formal alliances. According to the late President Richard Nixon and former Secretary of State Henry Kissinger, one of the most dangerous moments in U.S.–Soviet relations occurred in 1973, when the Soviet Union threatened to intervene in the October war to prevent Egypt from being defeated. This would have forced the United States to intervene on behalf of Israel.

Alliances provide both opportunities and constraints. They permit the combining of capabilities, thus adding elements of flexibility to state policy and making more complicated the calculation of relative power among states. Supplementing military capabilities with those of allies can afford states a better defense against external threats, and at less cost, than having to devote additional resources of their own. For parties to a dispute, alliances provide opportunities to pursue bolder courses of action than might otherwise be the case if they were acting in isolation. For their allies, however, policy options become constrained to those consistent with the terms of the alliance, which often means participating in armed hostilities initiated or provoked by alliance partners. The process has been called "chain ganging"—alliance partners are basically shackled by a defense pact and march toward war in lockstep behind their aggrieved partner. Alliances have indeed been found to be important factors in the spread, or *diffusion*, of war.[12]

NONALIGNMENT

States may also try to go it alone, avoiding alliances by adopting a policy of neutrality or by attempting to isolate themselves from the system of states as much as possible. Of course, a state's geopolitical position and the structure of the international system are important considerations for leaders in selecting a strategy for security and survival. In the past, a strategy of isolation was more useful for large countries that were self-sufficient and could retreat from international society without harm to their national

---

[12] Thomas J. Christensen and Jack Snyder, "Chain Gangs and Passed Bucks: Predicting Alliance Patterns in Multipolarity," *International Organization* 44 (Spring 1990), pp. 138–168. See also Randolph M. Siverson and Harvey Starr, *The Diffusion of War: A Study of Opportunity and Willingness* (Ann Arbor: University of Michigan Press, 1991).

development. Japan was able to do this until the nineteenth century, as was the Soviet Union, to some degree, during the 1920s. However, in the contemporary system, large countries with many economic and political ties and a network of economic, monetary, and resource interdependencies find it difficult to withdraw from the international system. It has chiefly been smaller countries on the geographic peripheries of international activity that attempt this strategy. Two good examples are Albania and Myanmar (formerly Burma); another is Cambodia after the communist victory in 1975.

Because of their economic and political needs, many small states in the contemporary system have opted for a nonaligned foreign policy. The expression "third world" was originally coined to characterize all the less-developed countries that avoided alliance with the first world of the industrialized West and the second world of the communist East. Choices of alliance or **nonalignment** have been strongly affected by the structure of the post–World War II international system. Many states chose, or were forced, to ally either with the Western bloc in some form or with the Soviet Union. The traditional reasons for allying with great powers have been security, stability, and status. However, during the cold war, allying with one of the great powers often brought just the opposite: a perceived threat from the other superpower, internal instability resulting from the clash of Western- and Eastern-oriented political factions, and a decline in autonomy for states that became dependents of one or the other superpower. Allying with other small powers may have been tempting, but no military combination could have challenged either superpower or its military alliance. The Arab League was formed in 1945 and is the only example of a small-power (non-European) military alliance since the end of World War II.

Thus, although alliance was a possibility, the international situation that developed after World War II made a nonaligned strategy attractive to smaller powers for several reasons. For states that had recently achieved independence from a colonial status, it permitted at least the appearance of an independent foreign policy stance. Nonalignment in the form developed by India and Yugoslavia starting in the 1950s—not simply the refusal to join the Eastern or Western coalitions, but an active and assertive policy directed toward independence, world peace, and justice—also gave smaller states a purposeful policy and a positive diplomatic identity. The Non-Aligned Movement (NAM), a coalition in its own right, has since grown to include nearly 120 otherwise diverse states. During the cold war, it often acted as a third force in world affairs, but since then its role has diminished significantly.

POLARITY IN THE INTERNATIONAL SYSTEM

In any social system, however small or simple, the number and size of the participants makes a difference. The number and size of actors in the international system affects the way states can and must behave, the likelihood of war among them, and even their very survival as independent actors. Realist analysis, in particular, attempts to understand the structure of the international system by focusing on the number of state actors, their relative capabilities, and the existence of state coalitions in the form of military alliances.

Perhaps the most important feature distinguishing the international system at different points in history is the *number of major actors*, whether states or coalitions of states. These are the "poles" in the system, and each is assumed to act with a significant degree of independence relative to the other major actors. A pole often consists of a single nation-state—a major power or superpower—but poles also comprise cohesive alliances led by major powers, coalitions that frequently bring together smaller states as well. States may behave quite differently in a system composed of two alliances, each including several major powers, than in a system with two major powers unallied with other states. Because states in an alliance usually retain substantial independence, at least potentially, negotiating and bargaining may be required for members of an alliance to act together to confront shared security challenges. The possibility that an alliance will not behave like a unified actor introduces instabilities and uncertainties in the calculations of individual states as they consider courses of action that may require the assistance of allied powers.

At one extreme is a system in which a single state dominates all other states, whether individually or in coalition with each other. Never in previous centuries was there a true **unipolar** global system, though a world empire would probably take such a form. The period immediately after World War II, when the European powers, including the Soviet Union, lay exhausted and the United States had a monopoly on nuclear weapons may be a partial, if short-lived, exception. Dominated systems of less than global extent were known in the past; the region of China and East Asia several centuries ago is a good example. To the extent that a major power may be called a "pole" if it possesses a combination of significant military, economic, and political power, some observers now characterize the current period as unipolar. The United States is seen as the "unchallenged" dominant actor, the "only country with the military, diplomatic, political and economic assets to be a decisive player in any conflict in whatever part of the world it chooses to involve itself."[13] Certainly the global menu changed considerably with the end of the cold war and the demise of the Soviet Union as an opposing superpower, and American foreign policy entered a period of uncertainty deriving in part from the difficulties of adjusting to the drastically different set of opportunities and constraints that accompanied this structural change in the international system.

Systems with multiple power centers, **multipolar** systems, have been very common in the past. During most of modern history, a precarious multipolar system of many great powers existed in Europe. Occasionally, it broke down through the dynamic and aggressive growth of one member (for example, Napoléon's France) or because of rigidities introduced by very close alliances or longstanding, and often ideologically based, antagonisms. When two or more alliances form among a larger number of major powers, we say that the system has become *polarized*, much as metal filings cluster around the two poles of a magnet. In almost all the international systems we can identify, polarization is the phenomenon whereby a multipolar system is transformed by alliance formation into one with perhaps only

---

[13] See Charles Krauthammer, "The Unipolar Moment," *Foreign Affairs* 70 (Winter 1990–91), pp. 23–33, who argues that the United States can (and should) aim to preserve its unipolar status and freedom of action. See also Stephen G. Brooks and William C. Wohlforth, *World Out of Balance: International Relations and the Challenge of American Primacy* (Princeton, N.J.: Princeton University Press, 2008).

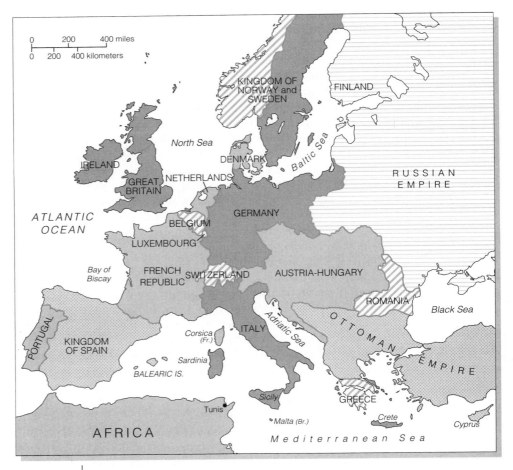

MAP 4.1 | A MULTIPOLAR SYSTEM: EUROPE IN 1900

After the unification of Germany, there were five great powers in Europe: Great Britain, France, Russia, Austria-Hungary, and Germany. On the eve of World War I, this multipolar distribution of power became polarized into two rival groupings: the Triple Alliance (Germany, Austria-Hungary, Italy) and the Triple Entente (Britain, France, Russia).

two opposing power groupings. The more closely they cluster, the more polarized, or "tight," the system has become.

The distinction between major powers as relatively independent actors on the one hand, and alliances as collective actors on the other, is often important. Around 1900, there were several states of similar size and resources: Britain, France, Russia, Germany, Italy, and Austria-Hungary. With so many great powers, Europe at that time was a multipolar system, and many of the alliances that existed among those powers were neither very close nor permanent (see Map 4.1). But just before World War I, in 1914, the great powers became so committed to rival alliance groupings—the Triple Alliance (Germany, Austria-Hungary, and Italy) and the Triple Entente (Britain, France, and Russia)—that the European states became highly polarized and prepared for major war. The possibility that two rival alliances will form, with more than one major power on one or both sides, is common in world politics and seems to be a serious source of instability in multipolar systems.

After World War I, the victorious states—Britain, France, Italy, and the United States, along with their allies—dominated the system. Austria-Hungary was fragmented into several small countries (Austria, Hungary, Czechoslovakia, and parts of Poland, Yugoslavia, and Romania), Germany was defeated and disarmed, and Russia was shattered by defeat and civil war. Nevertheless, the winning alliance quickly broke up. The United States and Japan emerged as major powers, and by the 1930s both Germany and Russia had substantially recovered. This reconstructed multipolar system was composed of several states of similar power potential. However, by the outbreak of World War II in 1939, it too had become much more polarized, as in 1914. Germany, Italy, and Japan (the Axis powers) allied themselves against France and Britain. Both the United States and Russia remained somewhat aloof from the others until they were drawn into the war on the side of Britain and France (the Allied powers).

POLARIZATION AND THE COLD WAR

Tight **bipolar** systems with only two really big powers are not too common in world history. A well-studied one, in ancient Greece during the Peloponnesian Wars of the fifth century B.C.E., consisted of Athens and Sparta as opposing great powers, each with its respective allies (see Map 4.2). Another was the United States and the Soviet Union, each with its allies, during the period immediately after World War II. At that time, the basis for a multipolar system had been destroyed. Germany, Italy, and Japan were totally defeated. Though France was officially a victor, it too was greatly weakened by its initial defeat and the German occupation in 1940. Britain was clearly a victor politically but was drained economically and was soon to lose its major colonies. China was poor and in the midst of civil war between the nationalists and the communists; its status as a great power was only nominal. The United States and the Soviet Union were clearly the most powerful states in the world (though the United States was certainly the stronger of the two). Their superiority was reinforced and dramatized by the fact that for most of the period they were the only two powers with large numbers of hydrogen bombs and the sophisticated missile systems necessary to deliver these weapons against a technologically advanced defender. Even today, the United States and Russia still have great nuclear advantages over any other state.

The two superpowers quickly formed opposing alliances. Many states in Western Europe and elsewhere sought protection against the possibility of Soviet expansion by allying with the United States. The United States then brought other countries—notably the Federal Republic of Germany (West Germany, the largest part of divided Germany)—into NATO or into its other alliances such as the Rio Pact among Latin American states and the Southeast Asia Treaty Organization (SEATO). After installing communist governments in most Eastern European countries, the Soviet Union then incorporated those states into its new alliance, the Warsaw Pact, and formed a separate alliance with the new communist government of

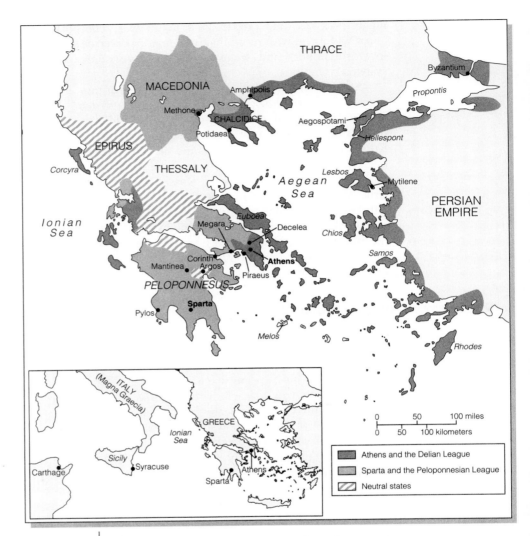

MAP 4.2 | A BIPOLAR SYSTEM: GREECE IN THE FIFTH CENTURY B.C.E.

At the start of the Peloponnesian War, the city-states of ancient Greece were aligned around two major powers: Athens, a commercially oriented democracy, led the Delian League, while Sparta, an agrarian oligarchy, headed the Peloponnesian League.

China. Thus, the bipolar system became increasingly polarized. Not only were the two superpowers much stronger than anyone else, but also each now was strengthened by important allies.

The polarization was never complete, however, because quite a number of Asian and African nations, as well as a few European ones, stayed nonaligned, remaining apart from the rival alliance groupings. Polarization is limited to the extent that states with significant bases of power stay apart from the two contending blocs or else flexibly switch alignment from one bloc to the other. A combination of processes during the 1970s and 1980s loosened this tight bipolar structure. Alliance ties weakened as a result of disagreements over security policy; the Sino–Soviet split was the most significant. The distribution of economic strength became more diffuse with the recovery and growth of China, Germany, and Japan and the development and growth of the European Union. The direct U.S.–Soviet confrontation also softened, partly as the result of increased familiarity (and fatigue) after decades of intense competitive interaction.

Then, at the end of the 1980s, changes came in a flood (as we detailed in Chapter 1). Popular revolutions in all of the Warsaw Pact nations replaced their sitting communist governments, mostly with anticommunist leaders. The new leaders demanded that Soviet troops leave their territories, and the Warsaw Pact collapsed. In 1990, East Germany rejoined West Germany, and the newly unified country inherited West Germany's membership in NATO and the European Union. Hungary, Poland, Czechoslovakia, and longtime neutrals like Austria and Sweden sought admission to the EU. Barriers to trade, travel, and other exchanges tumbled. Many Russian citizens, especially Jews, emigrated. The economically distraught countries of Eastern Europe repudiated central planning, moving toward a capitalist market economy. They, and Russia, and the rest of the states of the former Soviet Union sought massive inflows of private investment capital and loans from Western governments and international agencies. The Eastern pole dissolved, losing much of its discreteness along with its formal structure. The defining economic and institutional bonds disintegrated beyond reconstruction, and the bipolar confrontation came to an end.

Of course, in reality international systems never fit abstract models perfectly. The U.S.–Soviet bipolar system was never one of two equally matched rivals. The United States and its partners were substantially more powerful economically than the Soviet bloc. For example, in 1960 the American economy, when measured by GDP, was three times as large as that of the USSR, and the Western alliance (NATO plus Japan) had four or five times the wealth of all the communist states. By the time the cold war ended, the Soviet Union approached equality with the United States on only one dimension—military capabilities—and even here many questioned the notion of superpower parity in light of American technological superiority. That superiority was never so great, however, that the American leadership saw fit to use it against the Soviets. Though the United States between 1945 and the late 1960s could almost surely have inflicted more damage than it received in a general war, the likely damage to itself posed prohibitive risks. Except for the most serious threats to national survival, which fortunately never materialized, the United States would not resort to direct military conflict with the USSR. Also, at virtually all times during the cold war the Soviets had the ability to destroy America's Western European allies, a fact that doubtless helped restrain U.S. leaders.

POST–COLD WAR POLARITY

Difficult analytical problems may arise when we try to move from the idealized abstractions of theory to an examination of real world conditions. How much of a departure from the theoretical notion of equal capability can be tolerated without departing from the essential characteristics of a bipolar or multipolar system? How much power preponderance is required for unipolarity? And what are the relevant dimensions of equality or preponderance—population, wealth, military forces, or nuclear and thermonuclear weapons only? In regard to weapons capable of mass destruction, during the cold war only the United States and the Soviet Union could credibly threaten the other or threaten to obliterate any middle-range power. However, as it became clear that the nuclear weapons of a superpower were unusable in a quarrel between that state and a smaller one—either from moral restraint or out of fear that such use would invite a response from the other superpower in support of the opposing side—superpower leaders had to carefully consider whether they could subdue distant, small states with conventional weapons only. Distances from the great powers' bases, plus the logistical difficulties of fighting far from home, nullified many of the superpowers' advantages vis-à-vis lesser powers during the height of East–West confrontation. In addition, there were many circumstances in which military might was not easily used or threatened—was not "fungible"—for example, in UN deliberations, in trade negotiations, in disputes over access to raw materials. Such political processes often looked as if they were taking place in the context of a diffuse multipolar system.

What are the prospects for the reemergence of a bipolar system, or a multipolar one? Russia remains a major nuclear power, but with the Warsaw Pact disbanded, Russia no longer leads a major bloc or coalition. It has reduced its own conventional military capabilities and would have a difficult time supporting substantial military activities beyond its borders. Even though China has some nuclear weapons and its population (more than 1.3 billion people) is more than four times that of the United States, its GDP of $7 trillion is half that of the United States and the Chinese economy lacks the defense-industrial base even to challenge Russia militarily. China could defend its own territory against virtually any assault, but its army is ill equipped for major offensive action. A pole composed of the twenty-seven members of the EU, with a combined population of 490 million and a total GDP of $15 trillion, might be considered a potential counterweight to the United States. But a fully integrated political unit in Europe, with a common defense policy, does not yet exist and is not likely in the near future. Finally, Japan has avoided building nuclear weapons or a capacity for military action far from its shores, despite its powerful economy and growing defense expenditures. Thus, neither bipolarity nor multipolarity is a very good description of the international system now and will not be for at least the next several years.

It is possible, and perhaps probable, that the United States will not maintain its current position in the global hierarchy and that the system will return to a bipolar or multipolar distribution of power. It is also theoretically possible that there may someday be a large number of states, none of which is especially more powerful than any of the others, and that no widespread or long-term alliances will form. In the realm of commercial transactions, economists describe this sort of market structure as one of perfect or near-perfect competition; no single buyer or seller is big enough to affect the market price of other buyers or sellers. (Box 4.1 connects the concept of international structure to market structure.) However, such a condition has not existed in any of the international political systems or subsystems of recent history and is therefore little more than speculation.

IN GREATER DEPTH

BOX 4.1 | **STATES AND SYSTEMS, FIRMS AND MARKETS**

Kenneth Waltz is best known for his theory relating the behavior of states to their international environment—that is, to the structure of the international system at a given moment—and because his theory falls within the realist school of thought, it commonly identified as an example of *structural realism*. For Waltz, there are three features of an international political structure, and he illustrates his conceptualization by way of an analogy from economics. The first feature is the international system's *ordering principle*, by which he means the formal principle of authority. As we saw from Chapter 3, since the Peace of Westphalia in 1648, the system's ordering principle has been anarchic; there is no recognized authority above the nation-state. The contemporary state system is therefore like an unregulated free market in which self-interested producers and consumers interact and through this interaction attempt to improve their lot.

The second structural feature of an international system concerns the character of the units the system comprises. When we examine world politics from the system level of analysis, the primary units are nation-states. Likewise, in microeconomics, the basic units are firms. In Waltz's theory, nation-states are similar units. In addition to sovereignty, all states have essentially the same functions—to promote and protect the security and well-being of their citizens—even though their capacities to carry

out these functions vary considerably. Again, states are like firms in this regard. The basic function of all firms is to generate salaries and profits for employees and stockholders through the sale of goods and services in the marketplace, and, as with nation-states, firms vary in their capability to carry out this function.

The last essential feature of an international system's structure is the distribution of capabilities among the units of the system. In this chapter, we have discussed unipolar, bipolar, and multipolar distributions of power. The corresponding ideas from microeconomics are monopolistic, duopolistic, and oligopolistic markets—that is, markets dominated by one firm, two firms, or a few firms. In Waltz's system-level theory, it is this third element, the distribution of power, that distinguishes more conflictual periods from less conflictual ones. His reasoning is that because the other two features of the system's structure—the anarchic ordering principle and the basic functions of nation-states—remained essentially unchanged during the modern era, the only structural variable that truly varies, along with periods of stability and instability, is the distribution of capabilities among nation-states.

Note: See Kenneth N. Waltz, *Theory of International Politics* (Reading, Mass.: Addison-Wesley, 1979), chap. 5.

POLARITY AND INTERNATIONAL STABILITY

Because different systems provide different menus for states, both large and small, we might suspect (although little has been proved) that different systems are characterized by different patterns of state behavior. Aside from the consideration that most people would rather live in a powerful and secure country rather than a weak and vulnerable one, are there any reasons to prefer one distribution of power to another? Is there anything about one type of system that makes it prefer-able—for large states, for small states, or for most of the world's population, regardless of where they live? These questions have become increasingly significant as the world has moved away from the bipolarity of the cold war period.

One widely preferred characteristic of an international system is **stability**. In one sense, stability means *not being prone to war*. This, however, is a very ambigu-ous criterion; it might mean simply that wars are infrequent. But if the wars that do occur drag on for many years, the advantages of infrequency might pale. Thus, the duration of wars is also clearly important. So is severity. One can easily imagine systems where wars are rare but, when they do occur, are savage, include most members of the system, and are fought to the point of unconditional surrender. If "frequency" is the number of wars fought by a given number of states in a particu-lar period and "duration" is the number of months or years each war lasts, then an index of "severity" might be based on the number of people who are killed.

These are not merely sterile academic distinctions among variables that are closely related in the real world. On the contrary, a survey of all wars between major powers over the past five centuries shows an inverse relationship between the number of wars begun within various twenty-five-year periods and the number of casualties; in other words, periods with more wars tended to have fewer casual-ties.[14] Wars may be frequent or severe, depending on other characteristics of the international system. Bipolar systems, for instance, are marked by the continuing confrontation of two major powers. Many bloody wars would drain the two antagonists of their wealth and resources, either reducing them both to a level so near the second-rank powers that the system would become multipolar, or destroy-ing the weaker one and leaving the way open for unipolar domination. If a system is to persist, its wars—at least among the major powers—must be either infrequent or not very severe.

The bipolar system that developed after World War II produced many crises and confrontations. Confrontations, however, do not necessarily produce violent conflicts and military fatalities; on the contrary, in the postwar period there were no acknowl-edged, direct, violent conflicts between the two superpowers. (Actually, a fair num-ber of American fliers and Soviet antiaircraft crews killed each other during the Korean and Vietnam Wars, but neither state acknowledged this publicly.) Both sides feared that, should any such direct conflict begin, it would be very hard to contain at a low level of intensity, and escalation would carry the risk of enormous damage to both sides. Nor were there violent conflicts between any of the major powers, save for a border skirmish between China and the Soviet Union in 1969.

The battlegrounds for almost all the violent conflicts that occurred from the end of World War II until the end of the cold war were in the less developed coun-tries, although there was a surge in European-based conflict—in the Balkans—in the 1990s.[15] Many of the quarrels involved a superpower and a small state. At

---

[14] Jack S. Levy and T. Clifton Morgan, "The Frequency and Seriousness of War: An Inverse Relation-ship?" *Journal of Conflict Resolution* 28 (December 1984), pp. 731–749.

[15] On the location and frequency of post–cold war conflicts, see Lotta Harbom and Peter Wallensteen, "Armed Conflict, 1989–2006," *Journal of Peace Research* 44 (September 2007), pp. 623–634.

least thirteen of these conflicts arose between 1945 and 1991, with ten involving the United States (North Korea and China from 1950 to 1953, Lebanon in 1958 and 1983, Cuba in 1962, Indochina from 1961 to 1973, the Dominican Republic in 1965, Grenada in 1983, Libya in 1986, Panama in 1989, and Iraq in 1991) and three involving the Soviet Union (Hungary in 1956, Czechoslovakia in 1968, and Afghanistan beginning in 1979). Most of these episodes were quite limited and did not result in heavy casualties. The Korean, Indochinese, Afghanistan, and Iraqi cases are exceptions: The first three were of long duration, and all four were intense actions involving tens or hundreds of thousands of casualties. The superpowers, however, proved very successful in restraining conflicts among their own allies. With only a few exceptions—one or two in Central America, between Turkey and Greece over Cyprus, and between Britain and Argentina over the Falkland Islands (known to the Argentines as the Islas Malvinas)—wars between the allies of one superpower were avoided.

Another definition of stability is *continuity in the fundamental pattern of interactions* in the international system. Changes in the number or identity of major actors affect stability only insofar as they affect that pattern. A unipolar system would be marked by interactions involving dominance and submission to the will of the dominant state. A bipolar system is characterized by sustained competition and conflict between two actors. A system with three major actors witnesses shifting patterns of conflict and cooperation. If an alliance between two of the actors becomes tight and permanent, then it is no longer a three-actor system but a bipolar one, with substantial cooperation between the two formerly autonomous actors, both of which are in conflict with the third. It may be that in politics, as in love, three-actor systems are almost always unstable, falling too easily into two-against-one confrontations that end in the destruction of one of the original parties. Both the Soviet Union and the United States often feared that an alliance between the other and China might be cemented. The addition of a fourth actor to that three-actor system might have made for a more reliable pattern of shifting conflict and cooperation. However, there is always the possibility that the growth of many formal and informal linkages will create a bloc among two or more actors that formerly moved independently. What was once a multipolar system could become polarized; there would still be several major powers, but they would be combined into two opposing alliances.[16]

A system that always had four or more major actors within it might be stable even if the identity of the powers changed frequently because of wars, growth, or internal dissension in some states. When the number or identity of major actors (whether national actors or alliance blocs) changes, we say that the system has been transformed into a new system only if the changes seem to produce fundamentally different patterns of interaction. In cases where there are more than four major actors, it is hard to know whether the addition of yet another actor would

---

[16] For an analysis of tripolar systems, with an emphasis on Hitler's preoccupation with Soviet and U.S. power, see Randall L. Schweller, *Deadly Imbalances: Tripolarity and Hitler's Strategy of World Conquest* (New York: Columbia University Press, 1998). The tripolar relationship among the United States, the Soviet Union, and China is analyzed in Joshua S. Goldstein and John R. Freeman, *Three-Way Street: Strategic Reciprocity in World Politics* (Chicago: University of Chicago Press, 1990).

fundamentally change interactions. The difference between a multipolar system with four actors and one with five might be substantial. Beyond that point, as conditions approached those of perfect competition, the pattern of interactions might again be different.

BALANCES AND IMBALANCES OF POWER

Both aspects of stability, low levels of conflict and predictable interaction, have been examined by political scientists and historians wanting to assess the advantages and disadvantages of different distributions of power. How prone international systems are toward war is a topic we address in some detail in Chapter 8, but here we want to mention two common views, both associated with the realist approach to world politics.

Many theorists and practitioners believe that international stability is most likely when there is a **balance of power**. A balance exists when no single state or coalition of states dominates the international system; it operates in multipolar or bipolar systems but not in unipolar systems. According to balance-of-power theory, the development of imbalances among a system's major power centers is especially dangerous and threatens to engulf the system in destructive warfare.[17] The nineteenth century Concert of Europe worked well because the Continent's major powers were roughly equal in military strength. As Sir Eyre Crowe of the British Foreign Office put it in 1907: "The only check on the abuse of political predominance has always consisted in the opposition of an equally formidable rival, or a combination of several countries forming a league of defense. The equilibrium established by such grouping of forces is technically known as the balance of power." Indeed, British diplomats saw a special role for their country in the balance of power. Britain had long performed the role of balancer, or "holder of the balance"—a role that Winston Churchill considered both noble and essential to the defeat of tyranny on the European continent:

> For four hundred years the foreign policy of England has been to oppose the strongest, most aggressive, most dominating Power on the Continent. . . . [I]t would have been easy and must have been very tempting to join with the stronger and share the fruits of his conquest. However, we always took the harder course, joined with the less strong Powers, made a combination among them, and thus defeated the Continental military tyrant whoever he was, whatever nation he led.[18]

Stability in Europe was thus reinforced by Great Britain's tendency to throw its weight behind the lesser state or coalition when the balance was threatened by the rise of a would-be tyrant—for example, during the repeated contests between

---

[17] See, for example, Dale C. Copeland, *The Origins of Major War* (Ithaca, N.Y.: Cornell University Press, 2000). Different realist views of the balance of power are discussed in Richard Little, *The Balance of Power in International Relations: Metaphors, Myths and Models* (Cambridge: Cambridge University Press, 2007).

[18] Winston S. Churchill, *The Second World War*, vol. I, *The Gathering Storm* (Boston: Houghton Mifflin, 1948), p. 207. Crowe is quoted in James Joll, *The Origins of the First World War* (New York: Longman, 1984), p. 36.

France and the Hapsburg dynasty and during the Napoleonic Wars. However, these dynamics have become so closely associated with the diplomacy and relative stability of nineteenth-century Europe that we sometimes speak of this multipolar period as *the* balance-of-power system.

BALANCING AND BANDWAGONING

As a general concept, then, **balancing** refers to a policy of joining with the less strong. Many realists argue that this is exactly the type of state behavior we observe when looking back through history, and that there are good reasons for it: reasons of self-interest and survival as opposed to nobility in the defeat of tyranny. Logically, states should avoid the temptations of **bandwagoning**—"to join with the stronger and share the fruits of his conquest"—because there is nothing to prevent the stronger from subsequently turning on its allies whenever that suits its purposes. On the other hand, by joining the weaker coalition, a state becomes an important partner, and therefore not hostage to the whims of its allies once the dangers that occasioned the alliance have passed. Although the logic may seem compelling, there is some debate about whether balancing power against power is as prevalent in diplomatic history as some realists maintain. Small and medium powers often bandwagon, as did the German states of Bavaria, Baden, Hesse-Darmstadt, and Württemberg when they joined Napoléon's Confederation of the Rhine in 1806 at the height of French power. And although Hitler and Mussolini shared certain fascist designs for their societies, Italy's alliance with Germany was very much at odds with balance-of-power reasoning.[19]

Realists believe that states pay attention to the distribution of power in the international system; if they don't, and they fail to stem disadvantageous shifts in the power balance, their national survival is at risk. There are differences within the realist school of thought concerning what drives states to accumulate power in response to the policies of their potential rivals. *Defensive realists* maintain that a rational foreign policy is designed to preserve the state's relative position in the distribution of power. If potential opponents do not seek to augment their power, then there is no reason to augment one's own. History does, of course, record instances of policies that had the effect of destabilizing the balance of power, but these are explained as departures from good judgment or some other perversion of the policy-making process. For example, the dangerous military buildups preceding World War I, as well as the provocative force-mobilization plans that seemed to make major war inevitable once a crisis began, resulted from a widely held but misguided faith in the advantages of offensive military postures and strategies—a "cult of the offensive." Likewise, major powers have overextended themselves, according to defensive realists, not because they were sensibly balancing power against power, but because their leaders were driven by "imperial myths" promising that national security could be achieved

---

[19] See, for example, Paul Schroeder, "Historical Reality vs. Neo-realist Theory," *International Security* 19 (Summer 1994), pp. 108–148; Randall L. Schweller, "Bandwagoning for Profit: Bringing the Revisionist State Back In," *International Security* 19 (Summer 1994), pp. 72–107.

only through expansion.[20] When contemplating U.S. grand strategy today, these realists worry that an overly assertive foreign policy will not only hasten the emergence of counterbalancing coalitions but may entangle the United States in unnecessary wars and occupations far from home.

Offensive realists argue that states have an incentive to maximize, and not just preserve, their relative power—though few can aspire even to regional dominance, let alone global dominance. Those in a position to push their advantages will do so, at least until confronted by sufficient opposing force. Thus, in contrast to defensive realists, offensive realists see nothing inherently irrational or perverse in aggressive or expansive foreign policies, especially when there are power vacuums to be filled. Although realists of all stripes have little patience for the niceties of international law or the United Nations, offensive realists are more inclined than most to sanction **unilateralism**—an approach to statecraft that places a premium on freedom of action and regards international cooperation as worthwhile only when it clearly serves the national interest narrowly defined. According to this view, the United States today should seize the opportunity its disproportionate power affords to keep in check China, Russia, the EU, or any other state or coalition that seeks regional military dominance and is not otherwise opposed by neighboring major powers—a policy known as "offshore balancing."[21]

AMERICAN PRIMACY AND WORLD ORDER

A view seemingly opposed to balance-of-power theory is that a preponderance of power held by a single state is most conducive to international stability. The theory of **hegemonic stability** emphasizes that this state's preponderance, which rests on its disproportionate share of military and economic capability, allows it to establish and enforce the international "rules of the game" and thus a stable global environment conducive to its own interests. Hegemonic stability theory does not propose that the system leader truly dominates all others, including the other major powers, so *hegemony* is probably too strong a term for its power and influence. Nevertheless, the nineteenth century has been called a period of British hegemony. Britain's preponderance of economic power and naval supremacy gave it both the willingness and the opportunity to promote and maintain the rules of international free trade. Likewise, American hegemony is said to have characterized the post–World War II period. During this time, the United States had similar incentives and capabilities to take the lead in building institutions that would support international order and promote prosperity. Neither period was unipolar, however. Rather, each so-called hegemon more closely approximated a "first among equals," and its preponderance allowed the system leader to break down, whether through coercion or beneficence, the barriers to free trade that were often the source of conflict between

---

[20] Stephen Van Evera, *Causes of War: Power and the Roots of Conflict* (Ithaca, N.Y.: Cornell University Press, 1999); Jack Snyder, *Myths of Empire: Domestic Politics and International Ambition* (Ithaca, N.Y.: Cornell University Press, 1991). See also Waltz, *Theory of International Politics*.

[21] See, for example, Mearsheimer, *The Tragedy of Great Power Politics*; Christopher Layne, *The Peace of Illusions: American Grand Strategy from 1940 to the Present* (Ithaca, N.Y.: Cornell University Press, 2006).

the major powers. These periods are thus referred to as *Pax Britannica* and *Pax Americana*—the British Peace and the American Peace.[22]

Although it may be an overstatement to call these previous periods of British and American predominance "hegemonies," most analysts really do regard the current period of American power as unique in the history of the Westphalian state system. The international system today is, if not unipolar, then at the very least a system characterized by U.S. **primacy**. Indeed, critics as well as supporters of the exercise of American power are even inclined to use the term *empire* to describe the global profile of the United States in the early twenty-first century and thus to distinguish it from the U.S. position after World War II. This is hyperbole to be sure, but it does draw our attention to the unprecedented concentration of global power and the potential for fundamentally new patterns of state interaction.

Realists debate the best American strategy for an era of U.S. primacy. Defensive realists caution that the United States should exercise its power judiciously and with restraint lest it provoke potential rivals such as China or Russia, or even France and Germany, into a counterbalancing coalition that will erode U.S. freedom of action. Although there are no real military challengers on the horizon, when other states conclude that the sole remaining superpower is overstepping, there are ways to impose restraints that do not require the formation of military counterweight to U.S. power, an approach that some call "soft balancing."[23] For example, the United States has tried to get its allies to share the costs of its military conflicts. Germany, Japan, Saudi Arabia, and Kuwait paid virtually all the financial costs of the first war against Iraq. But because few countries supported the U.S. assessment of the Iraqi threat in 2003, it had to foot almost the entire bill of the second war, the postwar occupation, and its continuing military presence. Offensive realists acknowledge that the United States may as well resign itself to the rise of new challengers like China; that is inevitable in a system governed by a balance-of-power logic. Nevertheless, this view holds that the United States should begin putting into place the sort of policy that worked so well against the Soviet Union during the previous period of bipolarity: containment. Such a policy of confronting and containing potential rivals will provide the best environment for the maintenance and expansion of American power.

The liberal view of American primacy is closer to the defensive realist view. Both question the notion that states do, or should, seek always to maximize their power relative to other states, but liberals highlight the importance of **multilateralism** for the maintenance of world order. A multilateral foreign policy is one that treats international norms as binding on all states at all times, and not simply applicable when it suits a state's interests. In the current period of unchallenged American

---

[22] G. John Ikenberry, *After Victory: Institutions, Strategic Restraint, and the Building of Order after Major Wars* (Princeton, N.J.: Princeton University Press, 2001). On the hoped-for pacifying effects of American hegemony in the twenty-first century, see Niall Ferguson, *Colossus: The Price of America's Empire* (London: Penguin, 2004).

[23] Robert A. Pape, "Soft Balancing Against the United States," *International Security* 30 (Summer 2005), pp. 7–45; Stephen M. Walt, *Taming American Power: The Global Response to U.S. Primacy* (New York: W. W. Norton, 2005).

power, liberals tend to advocate multilateral policies reminiscent of those pursued by Roosevelt, Truman, and to some extent Eisenhower during the early years of the cold war when, despite the country's unchallenged power, its leaders promoted international cooperation by helping to create and underwrite international institutions like the UN, the IMF, and the World Bank. For liberals, unilateral actions—such as the George W. Bush administration's early decisions to reject international agreements to curb global warming, stem the proliferation of biological weapons, and join an international criminal court—are likely to be interpreted as an arrogance of power, and may even provoke long-standing allies. The "coalition of the willing" assembled by the Bush administration to prosecute the war against Iraq in 2003 was dismissed as pseudo-multilateralism, aptly described by one commentator as occurring when "a dominant great power acts essentially alone, but, embarrassed at the idea and still worshiping at the shrine of collective security, recruits a ship here, a brigade there, and blessings all around to give its unilateral actions a multilateral sheen."[24]

Another perspective on post–cold war American primacy has achieved some currency in recent years but is viewed with skepticism by many liberals and realists alike. Its proponents share with offensive realists the position that U.S. power can and ought to be deployed unilaterally and without embarrassment. However, they depart from realists in advocating forceful policies designed to promote the spread of American ideals—namely, individual liberties within a framework of democratic government and free-market capitalism. George W. Bush highlighted this departure from realism in his speech to the UN in September 2004: "Our security is not merely found in spheres of influence, or some balance of power. The security of our world is found in the advancing rights of mankind." Although this view is premised on the belief that the promotion of political and economic freedoms worldwide is consistent with U.S. national interests, realists have long been wary of foreign policies infused with such messianic zeal; when advocated by liberals after World War I, such policies were lambasted as hopelessly idealistic. Indeed, although there is as yet no widely recognized label for this point of view, the term "offensive idealism" seems fitting. The 2003 Iraq War was justified by offensive idealists as providing an opportunity to remake Iraq in the American image. A liberated Iraq would, in turn, serve as a beacon of hope for others yearning to be free, particularly in the Middle East, which has long been characterized by a "democratic deficit." Liberal critics of that war opposed the unilateral means; realist critics, the utopian ends.[25]

---

[24] Krauthammer, "The Unipolar Moment," p. 25. For the liberal view, see John M. Owen, IV, "Transnational Liberalism and U.S. Primacy," *International Security* 26 (Winter 2001/02), pp. 117–152; G. John Ikenberry, "Is American Multilateralism in Decline?" *Perspectives on Politics* 1 (September 2003), pp. 533–550.

[25] The offensive idealist view is defended by Lawrence F. Kaplan and William Kristol in *The War over Iraq: Saddam's Tyranny and America's Mission* (San Francisco: Encounter Books, 2003). For a realist critique, see John J. Mearsheimer and Stephen M. Walt, "An Unnecessary War," *Foreign Policy* 134 (January/February 2003), pp. 50–59. For a liberal critique, see Bruce Russett, "Bushwhacking the Democratic Peace," *International Studies Perspectives* 6 (November 2005), pp. 395–408.

The debate between the different schools of thought on the nature of U.S. primacy and the implications for contemporary world order is no closer to resolution today than it was when the bipolar system came to an end in 1991. Views often differ because definitions differ—definitions of order and stability, but also the meaning of power and influence—so it is time we examine the concept of power more closely.

RELATIONS BETWEEN STATES: POWER AND INFLUENCE

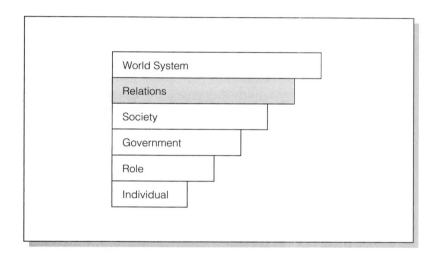

```
World System
Relations
Society
Government
Role
Individual
```

TWO ASPECTS OF POWER

The menu of policy choices available to a state is affected by its own capabilities as well as those of the other entities with which it interacts. Relationships between states can be seen in two ways, both of which will be described in our discussion of power. First, we can look at how two states compare on a set of national attributes or characteristics deemed important for achieving their respective goals. Second, we can look at the actual set of interactions between pairs of states.

We will be concerned with power both as a set of national attributes or *capabilities* and as a process of exercising *influence*. Capability and influence become meaningful only when compared with the capabilities of others and their own attempts to influence outcomes. In looking at the U.S. decision to drop the atomic bomb, the key elements were the actual existence of the weapon (a military

105

capability, derived from the skill, knowledge, and resources that created the bomb) and the arguments about how the bomb should be used to influence the behavior of Japan. Remember also that comparison implies measurement. What do policy makers look at when attempting to assess the capabilities of other states? What do social scientists look at? While contemplating power both as a set of capabilities and as influence, we highlight the problems of creating indicators to measure power.

POWER AND INFLUENCE

In an era of growing interdependence, power may simply mean the ability to have an impact on the behavior of other actors—to affect the opportunities available to others and their willingness to choose particular courses of action. Some see power as the ability to reduce uncertainty in the environment, and for some it is a means to an end. For others, power has come to mean causality, because knowing who has power explains why things happen. Power, some say, is like money in the sense that it can be saved and spent. Another view is that power is primarily a psychological phenomenon: You have it if others think you do. The list could go on and on.

As we noted in Chapter 2, the realist view of international politics begins with the observation that actors seek power and aim to dominate others. Hans Morgenthau, the most widely read exponent of this approach, stated the matter succinctly in his classic textbook, *Politics Among Nations*. The section titled "International Politics as a Struggle for Power" opens with these words: "International politics, like all politics, is a struggle for power. Whatever the ultimate aims of international politics, power is always the immediate aim."[1] This view of power concentrates on struggles among sovereign states within an anarchic international system, usually characterized by the use and manipulation of military resources.

Other observers, however, object to the realists' emphasis on constant struggle and the highly conflictual, coercive, and militaristic interpretation of the concept of power. Critics argue that although power is central to international politics, it takes many forms. Stressing the military aspects of conflict and struggle may distort how states actually behave as they attempt to reach their objectives in international politics; power is not exercised only in situations of armed conflict or potential armed conflict. What does power mean, and how is it to be measured among highly interdependent actors who share a common view of the world, have similar economies, and have excluded military options from their interactions? The realist emphasis on military power does not appear applicable to just such a group of European, North American, and other industrialized countries (including Japan, Australia, and New Zealand).

So, in our discussion, what will we mean by "power"? Let us start with a very broad definition and then break the concept down into more manageable components. **Power** is *the ability to overcome obstacles and influence outcomes*. This is a

---

[1] Hans J. Morgenthau, *Politics Among Nations: The Struggle for Power and Peace*, 6th ed. (New York: Knopf, 1985), p. 31.

useful formulation because it indicates that power is the ability to get what you want, to achieve a desired outcome through control of your social and physical environment.

In most areas of social interaction, including international interaction, to influence outcomes does not mean prevailing in conflict involving violence or the threat of violence. States, like people, have disputes with others every day on a wide variety of issues; they continually find themselves in situations where there is some form of incompatibility or *conflict of interest*. In dealing with China over trade imbalances, with Mexico on illegal immigration, and with Saudi Arabia on oil production, to name just a few examples, the interests and objectives of the United States have been incompatible in some way with the interests and objectives of these other states. As long as there are any incompatibilities between these sets of interests and objectives, conflicts will arise. However, the manner in which these conflicts are resolved and the ways in which the United States attempts to prevail may bear little resemblance to the struggle for power so often highlighted by realists, and it is not likely to involve military coercion. It will, however, involve some form of *influence*.

Exercising influence is a method by which people and states get their way. If one state has gotten its way, then the implication is that another state has not. This relational aspect of power is captured in Robert Dahl's classic definition: *A*'s ability to get *B* to do something that *B* would not otherwise do.[2] Influence takes many forms. One involves actually changing the existing policy of another actor: switching voting positions in the United Nations, leaving one alliance and joining another, dropping restrictions on the importation of foreign automobiles. Because influence has been used to change the behavior of another state, this is sometimes called *behavioral power*. It means influencing another country to halt a course of action it is already pursuing or to commence with a course of action it is not pursuing—an exercise of power known as **compellence** or, in the context of world politics, *coercive diplomacy*. During the Yom Kippur War in October 1973, the Organization of Oil Exporting Countries (OPEC) imposed an oil embargo in an effort to compel the United States to stop its airlift of military supplies to Israel, and generally to take a more balanced stance on the enduring conflict in the Middle East. OPEC was unsuccessful in stopping the airlift, but the United States did announce its willingness to adopt a more evenhanded policy, and the embargo was lifted in early 1974.

In contrast to compellence, **deterrence** aims to influence another actor *not* to do something it would otherwise do. During the cold war, the U.S. policy of nuclear deterrence (which we discuss in Chapter 9) was intended to deter the Soviet Union from attacking the United States or its allies. Soviet nuclear policy, similarly, was designed to deter U.S. attack. There are many theories and speculations about deterrence, and in practice it is hard to measure the concept satisfactorily. It is easier to recognize the actions that a state has been compelled to perform than those actions it has been persuaded not to perform. For example, did NATO's military strength and doctrine truly deter a Soviet attack on Western Europe, or did the

---

[2] Robert A. Dahl, "The Concept of Power," *Behavioral Science* 2 (1957), pp. 201–205.

USSR never intend to attack in the first place? An action that apparently was deterred might not have happened anyway, in which case a policy of deterrence is really not responsible for the outcome. Analyzing actions that did not occur, whether as causes or effects of other actions, is a difficult task for the social scientist because it involves *counterfactual* reasoning.[3]

Also hard to measure, but still very important for understanding world politics, is *potential influence*. Influence is a partly psychological phenomenon, based on the perceptions of the capabilities and intentions of other states. Potential influence rests on other policy makers' perceptions of the capabilities one may bring to bear in specific situations. If a state has potential influence, other states will not even attempt certain activities because they know those activities will fail or be very costly. As with deterrence, it is very difficult to measure state *A*'s successful influence in a case where state *B* never seriously considers a policy option because the costs involved are so high as to make an action inconceivable. How many times during the 1920s and 1930s might Panama have wanted to demand that the United States leave the Canal Zone? We have no idea because we cannot measure how many times the desire occurred and then was suppressed out of fear of American reaction.

SOFT POWER

When we look for the exercise of power in world politics, we cannot limit our attention to cases in which one state has directly influenced the behavior—action or inaction—of another state. In some situations, states may never have had the opportunity to behave in a certain way, to pursue policies that might have been in their interest to pursue. Powerful states can influence more than the choices of other states; they also influence other states' menus by removing some options altogether. This has been called *structural power* because it involves the ability of state *A* to influence the context or environment surrounding state *B*'s decisions—that is, the structure of the situation in which *B* finds itself.[4] Once the purview of radical scholars of world politics, this notion of power has become widely accepted and applied by realists and liberals as well.

One important way in which states exercise structural power is by influencing the agenda of issues under consideration. Often this takes the form of keeping certain things *off* the international agenda. During the periods of British and

---

[3] Compellence and deterrence are discussed in Paul Gordon Lauren, Gordon A. Craig, and Alexander L. George, *Force and Statecraft: Diplomatic Challenges of Our Time*, 4th ed. (New York: Oxford University Press, 2007), chaps. 9 and 10. On counterfactual reasoning, see Jack Levy and Gary Goertz, eds., *Explaining War and Peace: Case Studies and Necessary Condition Counterfactuals* (London: Routledge, 2007); Geoffrey Parker and Philip E. Tetlock, "Counterfactual History: Its Advocates, Its Critics, and Its Uses," in Philip E. Tetlock, Richard Ned Lebow, and Geoffrey Parker, eds., *Unmaking the West: "What-If?" Scenarios That Rewrite World History* (Ann Arbor: University of Michigan Press, 2006).

[4] Susan Strange, "What About International Relations?" in Susan Strange, ed., *Paths to International Political Economy* (London: Allen Unwin, 1984), pp. 183–197. Some theorists have referred to this as *metapower*; see, for example, Stephen D. Krasner, *Structural Conflict: The Third World Against Global Liberalism* (Berkeley: University of California Press, 1985).

American hegemony, for example, the idea that anything other than the free market should govern the flow of goods and capital across state boundaries was not debated much. International deliberations largely concentrated on how best to achieve this liberal economic order. It was not until the influence of British and American hegemony waned that alternatives to the free market got a place on the international agenda. Thus, the increased influence of OPEC in the 1970s stimulated discussions in the UN about how nonmarket mechanisms might be used to stabilize commodity prices and curtail some of the more exploitative practices of multinational corporations.

Foreign policy makers know well the importance of controlling the agenda. Human rights violations and other nondemocratic practices, for example, are usually declared internal affairs (matters of national sovereignty) by states subjected to international criticism. That the issue of human rights is, in fact, increasingly discussed by states gives some indication of the structural power exercised by the United States and other Western democracies in world politics. By concentrating exclusively on whether and to what extent states such as China or Iran or Cuba actually change their behavior in response to U.S. policy, we might miss this more subtle exercise of power.

Another, even more subtle, form of structural power is influence over the values held by other states, and therefore what they take to be *their own* interests, goals, and desired outcomes. Joseph Nye has called this **soft power**—exercising influence through attraction, as opposed to coercion (that is, hard power). Compared to influencing the behavior of others by getting them to do things they would not otherwise do, more can be achieved, and at less cost, if you can get others to want what you want. A state, like the United States, with soft power, is in a position where its influence over outcomes does not always require changing the behavior of other states or seizing control of the agenda at the United Nations. When the state's culture, ideology, and institutions enjoy widespread appeal—for instance, American-style democracy and free-market capitalism—other explicit and more transparent exercises of power are unnecessary. "Indeed, is it not the supreme exercise of power to get another or others to have the desires you want them to have . . . to secure their compliance by controlling their thoughts and desires?" In world politics, the concept of soft power is normally applied to U.S. influence, but observers of China's rise to power have noted that country's own "charm offensive."[5]

Of course, soft power can appear quite insidious depending on one's perspective, which is why it is interpreted by many radicals as "cultural imperialism." In the aftermath of the 9/11 attacks, many Americans were stupefied by what they perceived to be widespread resentment of the United States in the Arab world. "Why do they hate us?" has been a common refrain in the post–9/11 public discourse in the United States, and the question reflects a failure to appreciate the hostility that soft power can generate from those it does *not* sway. Although Osama bin Laden, in justifying the attacks, pointed to what the United States was doing—stationing

---

[5] See Joseph Nye, Jr., *Soft Power: The Means to Success in World Politics* (New York: PublicAffairs, 2004); Joshua Kurlantzick, *Charm Offensive: How China's Soft Power Is Transforming the World* (New Haven, Conn.: Yale University Press, 2007). The quote is from Steven Lukes, *Power: A Radical View* (London: Macmillan, 1974), p. 23, a classic exploration of this dimension of power.

military troops in Saudi Arabia, supplying the Israeli military—it was clear that the rage in the "Arab street" was also directed at what the United States *stood for.* Like those realists who predict that the predominance of U.S. military power will be met by the rise of new challengers, restoring the equilibrium of a balance of power, some believe that there are limits to soft power as well, and that Americans need to brace themselves for a "clash of civilizations"—an argument we scrutinize more closely in the final chapter of this book.

POWER AND CAPABILITY

National attributes or capabilities greatly influence the menu of activity available to states. What is possible or probable relates to the means at one's disposal. This is especially important in gauging the actions and reactions of specific states in specific situations. Capabilities include any physical object, talent, or quality that can be used to affect the behavior (or desires) of others. Capabilities are important because they affect others' perceptions, including what one has the opportunity to do and what one is willing to do.

Threats and promises are common instruments of influence, but they have to be *credible.* Capabilities are crucial to two different aspects of a state's credibility. First, for a threat or promise to be credible, the targeted party has to believe that the other party is able to carry it out. One debate over using the atomic bomb against Japan concerned demonstrating the capability—the destructiveness deliverable by the bomb—to the Japanese so that they would believe that more destruction could be rained down on the country if they did not surrender. Credibility, of course, also implies a perceived willingness to carry out a threat. In 1979, during the Camp David negotiations, the U.S. promise to deliver economic aid to Egypt and oil to Israel if they would negotiate a peace treaty was credible not only because the United States had both the wealth and the oil to deliver on its promises but also because President Jimmy Carter displayed a willingness and resolve to see the accord brought to fruition.

If threats and promises do not work, then punishments—political, economic, or military—are often carried out. States require capabilities in order to impose the costs or the pain necessary to coerce others to behave as they wish. By doing so, and by doing so effectively, a state also enhances its credibility by showing that it is willing to carry out threats in a way that gets results. If this occurs, then at some point in the future threats may not have to be carried out; the mere hint of punishment will bring about the desired action. Thus, reputation can be central to successful compellence or deterrence. However, the actual use of military force in foreign affairs, while a major element of power, may also be seen as a *failure of influence.* The use of military force means that a state has failed to persuade another state to do something and has had to resort to armed coercion.[6]

---

[6] Jonathan Mercer, *Reputation and International Politics* (Ithaca, N.Y.: Cornell University Press, 1996); Paul Huth, "Reputations and Deterrence: A Theoretical and Empirical Assessment," *Security Studies* 7 (Autumn 1997), pp. 72–99.

The ability to get others to do one's bidding will differ with the object of one's influence. Capability is relative. What Iraq could do to Kuwait, it could not do to the United States; what the United States could do to Iraq, it cannot do to China. Knowing a state's capabilities and nothing else is of no use to our analysis of world politics; they must be examined in the context of an attempt to exert influence. Capabilities of states take on meaning only when they are viewed in relation to the objectives of the state and to the capabilities and objectives of others. For example, in 1998 when India was criticized by the international community for testing nuclear weapons even while it maintained conventional military superiority vis-à-vis Pakistan, India responded that its nuclear program was directed not toward Pakistan, but toward China. According to Indian leaders, the country's capabilities were adequate in one context but not the other. Therefore, now we must ask: What capabilities are important in which situations?

NATIONAL CAPABILITIES: TANGIBLE ELEMENTS

National capabilities are resources that a state can draw upon in order to achieve a desired outcome. Some of these resources are more tangible than others. Those who study international power and influence usually develop a set of attributes on which a state's power is based, consisting of some sort of power inventory or power potential. It is often not important which specific set of attributes is used. What is important is that the analyst of international politics has some such system for representing the variety of possible power bases; without a systematic and explicit checklist, the analyst is likely to pay far too much attention to certain power attributes and completely forget about others. For example, there is a tendency to pay a great deal of attention to the military and economic bases of power but often overlook the moral stature of international actors. This is, in part, a legacy of the realist view of international politics, which tends to focus on material capabilities. When informed that the pope was critical of his policies, Josef Stalin was reported to have asked, rhetorically, "How many divisions does the pope have?" Stalin would have been surprised at the impact of Pope John Paul II's visits to Poland in 1979 and Cuba in 1998. State leaders such as Mohandas Gandhi of India and Nelson Mandela of South Africa have also been able to exercise influence on behalf of their nations because of their moral authority. We will not neglect such intangible sources of power in this chapter, but first we turn to the more tangible ones.

GEOGRAPHY AND DEMOGRAPHY

States are constantly assessed in terms of size: We speak of superpowers, major and minor powers, small states, microstates. The national attributes of land mass and population are central elements of a state's base of power and potential power. They are also among the more tangible and readily measurable set of capabilities we associate with powerful states. Although sheer land area and population by themselves are not sufficient to make a state a great power, a large area often comes with a generous natural resource endowment and, along with a large population, can support a sizable agricultural and industrial base.

A large land mass makes a state difficult to conquer, as both Napoléon and Hitler learned when they marched their armies toward Moscow. Small countries are much more vulnerable to being overwhelmed by a sudden military attack. The Benelux countries (Belgium, the Netherlands, and Luxembourg) could do little to prevent invasion by German armies on their way to France during both world wars; Kuwait was helpless in the face of the Iraqi onslaught in 1990. However, a large landmass is also difficult to defend. During periods of hostility, the Soviet Union and China expended large amounts of resources policing their shared 2,000-mile-long border. Topography—the physical features of the land, especially along a state's borders—is another geographic factor that leaders must consider when planning for national defense. Mountainous terrain, like Switzerland's, provides a natural barrier to military conquest; plains and deserts are much easier to traverse. The Golan Heights is dear to Israel because it is one of very few spots in an otherwise flat terrain that is readily defensible. Physical location (like America's straddling two oceans), political location (like Poland's between sometimes hostile great powers), and climate (like Russia's extremely cold winters) are other physical elements that may contribute to, or detract from, a state's ability to defend itself militarily.

Like large physical size, a large population may be either an asset or a liability, although it seems difficult to be a major power or superpower without one. As well as numbers, we also must look at the age, sex, and spatial distribution of a population and the quality of human resources—the degree to which a people's capabilities have been developed by education or good health care so that they can contribute to the state's economic, military, and cultural bases of power. For example, to understand Israel's military success in the Middle East, we must note the advantages a state gains over its neighbors by having an educated, skilled, and healthy population of men *and* women.

An important dimension of a state's human resource endowment is what Harold Lasswell and Abraham Kaplan called "enlightenment": the extent of higher education among the populace and access to specialized knowledge in science, engineering, and the professions. Obviously, a state's military strength depends in large part on mastery of scientific knowledge. Building modern weapons requires a body of scientific and technical expertise that is unavailable to small, poor countries and is not uniformly available to big, rich ones. More broadly, a state needs physicians, chemists, engineers, architects, social scientists, educators, administrators, and many others with advanced training and ability. Many possible measures of this capability can be found, among them the number of students receiving higher education, the number of trained scientists and engineers, and the number of articles published in scientific and technical journals.

Many aspects of enlightenment are related to wealth and material development; it is expensive to train and equip scientists. This can also be true for the more basic level of knowledge that Lasswell and Kaplan labeled "skill." Skill is what it takes to get along in modern life, even at a rather low level of sophistication—literacy, primary or secondary education, familiarity with machinery or computers. Literacy is especially important because it is required for learning many other skills and for taking advantage of other kinds of enlightenment. But universal education, even only to produce literacy, is costly and difficult for a poor state to provide. Even a country such as Pakistan, which is technologically advanced enough to produce nuclear weapons, has seen the proliferation of *madrassas,* or religious schools, many established by Islamic charities in poor regions of the country where public schooling is sparse or nonexistent.

Another aspect of a state's human resources is the health and well-being of the population. What access do people have to good medical care? How long do they typically live? How free is the country from various contagious diseases that are now, in principle, preventable? Does the state possess first-class centers of medical treatment where the latest knowledge is available? How evenly distributed is good health throughout the population? Are there substantial minorities whose health facilities are markedly poorer than the average? The health of a state's population is an important base of influence. Because both industrial and military power depend in part on having a healthy population of young people, access to basic medical facilities must be available to the entire population, regardless of income.

In short, although a large population is an important factor in providing a country with the potential for great-power status, the quality of its people—their level of *human development*—can be the difference between population as a national resource and population as a burden. A useful indicator has been constructed by the UN Development Programme (UNDP), which examines countries' achievements in three basic dimensions of human development: longevity, knowledge, and a decent standard of living. The UNDP's *human development index* (HDI) is a composite measure consisting of life expectancy, educational attainment (literacy rate, school enrollment), and per capita income.[7] We will see later which countries score highest on this index of national capability.

ECONOMIC AND MILITARY RESOURCES

A state's economy is vital to its ability to wield influence in world politics. We often measure economic size by calculating gross domestic product (GDP), and economic performance by computing the percentage change in GDP from one period to the next. The wealth and economic growth of a state are also related to the availability of natural resources. Energy sources (such as petroleum, coal, and natural gas) and resources critical to industrial capacity (such as uranium for power and cobalt and chromium for making steel) are particularly important. Abundant natural resources not only give a state the ability to develop and gain wealth from others through trade but also may provide a state with a greater degree of *autarky*, or economic self-sufficiency. The more self-sufficient a state, the less vulnerable it is to economic coercion by other international actors. For example, for much of the post-1945 period, the Soviet Union, China, and the United States were more self-sufficient than most countries, but each steadily became less so (especially Russia since the mid-1990s).

---

[7] UN Development Programme, *Human Development Report 2007/2008: Fighting Climate Change— Human Solidarity in a Divided World* (New York: Palgrave Macmillan, 2007); Mahbub ul Haq, *Reflections on Human Development* (Oxford: Oxford University Press, 1995).

Economic production relative to population—GDP per capita—is a good indicator of economic development, which shows how well a state has mobilized and used its natural and human resources. Economic production, both per capita and in the aggregate, provides a clue to the state's ability to turn its resources into military capabilities, and its ability to expand its menu of foreign policy choices. At one extreme we find the United States, with a 2007 GDP of almost $14 trillion. By itself, the United States accounts for more than one-fifth of all goods and services produced worldwide. Current analyses indicate that the size of the Soviet economy had been overestimated for many years, and substantial *declines* in GDP—partly resulting from the breakaway of economically productive territories such as the Baltic states—meant an end to number two ranking held by the USSR during most of the cold war. In 2007, Russia's GDP was only $2.1 trillion, which placed it between those of Britain and France.

Military capability, of course, is a crucial element of state power and, to most analysts of international security, the most important indicator. China, Russia, and the United States have millions of their populations under arms, whereas Iceland, Costa Rica, and Mauritius have no armies at all. One might also wish to count specific items in the arsenals of states such as nuclear delivery systems, bombers, supersonic fighters, and tanks. The sophistication of weapons technology has become increasingly important. The performance of America's "smart weapons," first demonstrated during the 1991 Gulf War, caused many states to reevaluate their entire military establishments—from strategy, to research and development (R&D), to procurement. After the war, there were major debates within the Russian and Chinese defense establishments on the technological and organizational bases of U.S. military power and how best to replicate, or at least neutralize, U.S. advantages.

A useful summary measure that takes into account many of these elements of military capability is military expenditure. Again, during the cold war, the Soviet Union and the United States far outdistanced the rest of the world; by 1989, each was spending about $320 billion on its military establishment. Their closest competitors (France, Germany, and China) spent only about 15 percent of that. When comparing defense expenditures in different national currencies, it is sometimes difficult to obtain reasonably accurate data, and determining whether expenditures encompass similar military activities may require a bit of guesswork. Russian defense spending has always been difficult to calculate—because of government secrecy in the Soviet era and because of instability in the value of the ruble in the post-Soviet era. In general, however, if employed carefully, this rough measure is useful for evaluating most countries' military efforts.

Since 1945, a key element of the military capabilities of a select few states has been the size and composition of their nuclear arsenals. How many warheads (bombs) does a state have? What types of delivery systems does it have, and in what numbers? How much megatonnage can a state deliver against an opponent? How vulnerable or invulnerable is a state to a first strike? Here, too, the superpower status of the United States and Russia is still evident. In September 1990, before the Strategic Arms Reduction Treaty (START) was signed, the United States had more than 12,500 deliverable strategic warheads; the Soviet Union had more than 10,000. START I reduced the U.S. arsenal to 8,500 and the Russian arsenal to 6,500. The Strategic Offensive Reductions Treaty (SORT) commits the two sides to a ceiling of 1,700 to 2,200 deployed warheads, although in 2008 their stockpiles remained considerably above that level: about 3,600 for the United States and 3,100 for Russia.[8] The other major-power members of the nuclear club—Britain, France, and China—had fewer than 1,000 weapons *combined,* and the arsenals of India, Pakistan, and Israel would add around 200 to that total.

Of course, there is more to military capability than just the numbers of weapons and soldiers in uniform. The morale and training of officers and troops, the quality of deployed weapons, and the distance these forces must travel to engage the opponent are among the many other factors that decision makers must consider when assessing the state's ability to exercise military influence. Moreover, even with nuclear weapons there are questions of accuracy, dependability, the state of computer technology, and the effectiveness of the command-and-control system.

COMPARING CAPABILITIES: INDEXES OF POWER

Power and influence are multifaceted and depend on a combination of capabilities. Attempts have been made to devise indexes based on two or more indicators of national capabilities.[9] We need to look at how the various capabilities may be related to one another and at the possible results of using different combinations of indicators. Table 5.1 is illustrative, showing how states rank on different indicators of capability. (Further comparisons can be made by consulting Appendix B at the end of the book.) The table lists the top ten states based on each of several criteria—two measures each from the categories of geography/demography, economic/military strength, and human resources. Area and population, measures of a nation's physical size, give some sense of the basic endowments with which a state begins. Russia still figures at the top of the area ranking, despite having lost much territory with the breakup of the Soviet Union (including Kazakhstan, itself in the top ten). In terms of population, some developing countries make the list; in the case of Bangladesh, however, its population is at present more a burden than a strength, given its limited resources in so many other areas.

The United States and China rank at the top in economic and military strength, although the raw numbers show that the United States is way ahead on GDP and military expenditures. China spends more on its military than any other country except the United States, largely because it has more people in uniform than any other country (3.6 million, compared to 1.5 million for the United States and 1.4 million for Russia).[10] Russia is a formidable military power, but maintaining this position has been difficult during periods of economic restructuring and poor

---

[8] See Robert S. Norris and Hans M. Kristensen, "U.S. Nuclear Forces, 2008," *Bulletin of the Atomic Scientists* 64 (March/April 2008), pp. 50–53, 58; Norris and Kristensen, "Russian Nuclear Forces, 2008," *Bulletin of the Atomic Scientists* 64 (May/June 2008), pp. 54–57, 62.

[9] For a review of various approaches, see Ashley J. Tellis, Janice Bially, Christopher Layne, and Melissa McPherson, *Measuring National Power in the Postindustrial Age* (Santa Monica, Calif.: RAND, 2000).

[10] World Bank, *World Development Indicators 2008 CD-ROM* (Washington, D.C.: World Bank, 2008).

TABLE 5.1 | STATE CAPABILITIES: TOP TEN LISTS

Rank	Geography and Demography		Economic and Military Strength		Human Resources	
	Area	Population	GDP	Military Expenditures	Scientific Articles	Human Development
1	Russia	China	United States	United States	United States	Iceland
2	Canada	India	China	China	Japan	Norway
3	United States	United States	Japan	United Kingdom	United Kingdom	Australia
4	China	Indonesia	India	France	Germany	Canada
5	Brazil	Brazil	Germany	Russia	China	Ireland
6	Australia	Pakistan	United Kingdom	Germany	France	Sweden
7	India	Bangladesh	Russia	Japan	Canada	Switzerland
8	Argentina	Russia	France	Saudi Arabia	Italy	Japan
9	Kazakhstan	Nigeria	Brazil	Italy	Spain	Netherlands
10	Sudan	Japan	Italy	Brazil	South Korea	France

economic performance. Japan is not often considered a military power, but its economy is so large that even the relatively small percentage of GDP devoted to the military (1 percent) puts it among the top military spenders.

Other indicators of capability reflect the quality of the human resources states can draw upon. Those countries that rank highest in terms of economic and military strength tend also to be home to the largest number of scientific and technical journal publications, reinforcing the notion that a nation's natural resources cannot be synthesized into usable capabilities without an advanced knowledge base. The other measure of human resources shown in Table 5.1 is the index of human development discussed earlier, which combines national performance in the areas of longevity, education, and wealth. Of all the indicators of national capability, the HDI may produce the most surprises. Six of the top ten nations—Iceland, Norway, Ireland, Sweden, Switzerland, and Netherlands—appear in none of the other rankings. Of the states exhibiting the greatest economic and military capabilities, only the populations of France and Japan are among the ten most developed by this measure (although the United States, Britain, and Italy are among the top twenty).

Analysts have also tried to produce composite indexes of national power that combine various elements. Because the individual components of any such index may be only moderately correlated with one another, index rankings will differ with the use of different components, and there is no perfect all-purpose indicator. One study compared eight different indexes of power, which include anywhere from two to twenty variables combined in very different ways. Roughly, the various indexes include some measurement of demographic capabilities, industrial capabilities, and military capabilities; many include some indicator of area or territory. The study compared the rank orderings of states produced by these various indexes and found "no appreciable change in outcome."[11] The lesson is twofold: (1) Accurate measurement requires a clear conceptual understanding of the phenomenon one is trying to measure (in this case, state capability), and (2) when using such a conceptual underpinning, composite indicators of power capability will give us a generally similar picture.

An index that is commonly used in international relations research is the one assembled by the Correlates of War (COW) Project. The measure combines demographic capabilities (urban and total population), industrial capabilities (energy consumption, iron and steel production), and military capabilities (military expenditures and number of armed forces). Thus, the COW composite index is a measure of states' *material* capabilities; it does not include such components as the quality of human resources. Of course, measures of human development, those we have discussed as well as others, often require data that are not available for many countries and for long periods of time. One nice feature of the COW index is that researchers have gathered the required data for a large number of countries, in many cases dating back to the end of the Napoleonic Wars in 1815, which enables historical comparisons. As an illustration, Figure 5.1 plots this capability index for the United States, Russia, and China from 1900 through the end of the twentieth century. At one level, the pattern is

---

[11] Richard L. Merritt and Dina A. Zinnes, "Alternative Indexes of National Power," in Richard J. Stoll and Michael D. Ward, eds., *Power in World Politics* (Boulder, Colo.: Rienner, 1989), p. 26.

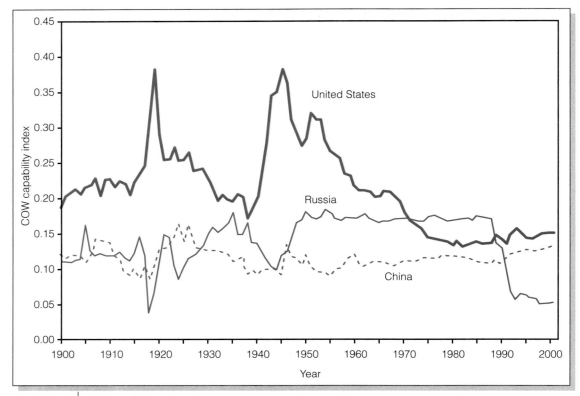

FIGURE 5.1 | NATIONAL CAPABILITIES: UNITED STATES, RUSSIA, AND CHINA, 1900–2001

The Correlates of War Project uses an index of national capabilities consisting of six separate measures in three broad categories: demography, industry, and military. The spikes in U.S. capabilities are clearly associated with wartime, which boosts the military component of the index. The index also shows Russia's capabilities dropping off substantially after the end of the cold war and the breakup the Soviet Union. However, it seems to underrepresent the power gap between the U. S. and China during this same period.

Source: Correlates of War Project, "National Material Capabilities (v3.02)," June 6, 2005; available at <http://www. correlatesofwar.org/>.

what we would expect to see, especially the spikes in U.S. capabilities as American society was mobilized to fight World Wars I and II and the sudden decline of Russian power with the breakup of the Soviet Union at the end of the cold war. However, given our discussion of American primacy in the last chapter, we might expect that the index would show a greater gap between U.S. and Chinese capabilities in the period after the cold war, despite China's status as a rising power. China's power index is probably exaggerated by its huge but poorly equipped army and its vast but still fairly poor population. The COW measure does not seem to capture the extent to which technology and the quality of human resources serve to multiply the potency of a state's material capabilities. On the other hand, many experts believe that China is bound to narrow the gap in technology and human development. If so—and barring a successful effort to keep China down—the index suggests that those who wish for American primacy in perpetuity are in for a rude awakening.

NATIONAL CAPABILITIES: INTANGIBLE ELEMENTS

Any state requires more than the mere existence of the resources that make up national capabilities. It must also maintain the political, social, and economic structures that will permit it to *mobilize* for governmental use the resources that exist within its borders and to *convert* those resources into instruments of foreign policy influence. When looking at the political system of any state, we must ask whether that system efficiently administers the nation-state's resources. What is the quality of political leadership at all levels, especially the highest? Can the leaders motivate the people to support the government's policies and to sacrifice so that the state's resources can be devoted to military capabilities or heavy industry rather than to consumer goods? Can the leadership achieve and maintain the support of the people and their continued loyalty to the state? In other words, can the resources be converted into capabilities, and capabilities into influence?

Such intangibles can be crucial. In sports, a weak team will sometimes beat one much higher up in the rankings. The weaker side does not always lose a war, and the stronger does not always win—as the French learned in Indochina and later in Algeria, and as the Americans learned in Vietnam. Despite the stunning military conquest of Iraq in 2003, it became increasingly unclear whether the United States would, in fact, emerge victorious, especially given its goal of bringing stability and democracy to that country. Intangibles such as leadership, belief in a cause, and especially the cohesion resulting from a threat to survival are important assets for smaller states and groups embroiled in unequal, or asymmetric, conflicts. The weaker party, being willing to fight for survival against a larger adversary, increases its war power through its willingness to persevere and to suffer not only the enemy's direct threat but also the sacrifices required by higher levels of resource extraction. The larger state, although possessing greater tangible capabilities, often is far from the conflict, is not threatened by the smaller opponent, and is less willing to suffer the costs of war.

As a dimension of power, the willingness to suffer can be a stumbling block for advanced democratic societies. The notion that the people in democracies do not wish to bear the costs of war was advanced long ago by the philosopher Immanuel Kant and was evident during the post-colonial struggles that followed World War II. Contemporary figures such as Vo Nguyen Giap (North Vietnamese strategist and defense minister), Saddam Hussein, and Osama bin Laden have echoed this sentiment. Because the citizenry ultimately bears the costs of war, and because it also ultimately determines its leaders, democratic states are wary of becoming embroiled in long, drawn-out struggles over anything that is not of the utmost importance to national security. Thus, Saddam Hussein doubted that the American people would have the "stomach" for a prolonged military engagement far from home. He probably was not wrong about that; the Iraqi military simply lacked the capability to prolong the conflict. The question then became whether Iraqi insurgents possessed that capability.

We must also look at the skill and efficiency of the state's administrative organs. The size, organization, and effectiveness of the bureaucracy will determine how well the state can penetrate society for purposes of extracting resources and directing effort in pursuit of national goals. As we discussed in Chapter 3, the precursors of modern state bureaucracies emerged as a means of collecting revenue on behalf of the monarchy, especially for purposes of maintaining the king's armies. The ability to raise tax revenues and to put them to good use is no less important today. Theda Skocpol has suggested that "a state's means of raising and deploying financial resources tell us more than could any other single factor about its existing (and immediately potential) capacities."[12] Of course, the bureaucracy may also be very skillful at penetrating society as a means of repression, but that can backfire, undermining the state's legitimacy and its ability to mobilize the citizenry.

Finally, we return to the notion of credibility. The effect of attempts at influence based on promises or threats depends to a large extent not only on a government's ability to carry out the action but also on perceptions of its willingness to do so. One major intangible, then, is the reputation that a government acquires in its international dealings. Our general conclusion about political intangibles is a simple one. If a government—that is, its leadership, its bureaucracy, and the political system within which both work—is so inadequate or inefficient that it cannot bring the state's capabilities to bear in a particular international situation, then those capabilities will remain latent. Capabilities that are not mobilized cannot be used to exercise influence in the international arena.

Similar questions can be asked about the economic and social systems of a state. Does the economic system reduce waste and loss? Is it efficient in the use of the state's resources? Does the social system (including the prevailing values and cultural practices in society) promote a unified national effort, or are there major groups that feel alienated? Is the social system oriented more toward principles of fairness and respect for human rights or toward a system of privilege? The answers to all these questions will affect how thoroughly, rapidly, and efficiently a society will be able to mobilize resources and how unified a society is in supporting its government's foreign policies. Here we might speak of national morale, a somewhat elusive notion concerning the "state of mind" of a nation.

Shifts in national morale occurred in both France and the United States during their armed conflicts in Indochina. In both countries, as their respective wars wore on, support for military involvement decreased and governmental policy was increasingly challenged. Vo Nguyen Giap stated bluntly that the Western powers would lose, that he could make the war go on long enough for their people to tire of the war and its costs. Neither France nor the United States was able to drive the North Vietnamese to a breaking point, not so much because of French or U.S. military failures but to an unimaginable willingness of the North Vietnamese to accept losses much higher than those of previous wars (for instance, battle deaths as a share of prewar population were twice as high as those the Japanese suffered in

---

[12] Theda Skocpol, "Bringing the State Back In: Strategies of Analysis in Current Research," in Peter B. Evans, Dietrich Rueschemeyer, and Theda Skocpol, eds., *Bringing the State Back In* (Cambridge: Cambridge University Press, 1985), p. 17. See also Jacek Kugler and Marina Arbetman, "Relative Political Capacity: Political Capacity and Political Reach," in Marina Arbetman and Jacek Kugler, eds., *Political Capacity and Economic Behavior* (Boulder, Colo.: Westview, 1997), pp. 11–46.

World War II).[13] In the end Giap was right, and the reluctance of the American public to bear the costs of long military engagements is still referred to as the "Vietnam syndrome."

INTELLIGENCE

A very different aspect of a state's intangible capabilities of power and influence is its ability to collect and analyze information—that is, the quality of its **intelligence**. In *The Nerves of Government*, Karl Deutsch observed that "it might be profitable to look upon government somewhat less as a problem of power and somewhat more as a problem of steering."[14] That is, in the uncertainty of the anarchic international system, any government that knows how to get to where it wants to go has an advantage. Any government that can reduce the uncertainty of the international environment through knowledge has an advantage. Any government that can reduce the number of times it is surprised—that can provide itself with the time for planning, preparation, and preemption of the actions of other states—has an advantage.

Power may indeed be the ability to steer. To know how to act, how to respond, and whether to continue one's policies or to correct them, a government needs information. To know how to influence states or other international actors, a government needs information about them. The information that governments seek falls into three broad categories. Earlier in this chapter we noted that in order to exercise influence, decision makers have to take into account their own goals and capabilities and the goals and capabilities of others. The first type of information, then, deals with the goals, plans, and intentions of other international actors. States can steer more carefully through the international environment with fore-knowledge of the impending behavior of other states. The many books about the Allies' acquisition of secret intelligence during World War II indicate that advance warnings of German military moves had great payoffs. And it is the *failure* of intelligence-gathering organizations to provide warnings that really shows the importance of such warnings. Consider just a few examples: The Americans were surprised when the Japanese attacked Pearl Harbor in 1941. The Japanese were surprised when the Nixon administration devalued the U.S. dollar in 1971. Israeli intelligence failed to anticipate the Arab attack that commenced the 1973 Yom Kippur War. Saddam Hussein's invasion of Kuwait in 1990 was unexpected by most observers, as were India's nuclear weapons tests in 1998.

The most spectacular recent failure—and most vivid for having been instantaneously and repeatedly broadcast around the world—was the inability of the U.S. intelligence services to "connect the dots" leading to the 9/11 attacks, an event that has led to a renewed appreciation of the importance of intelligence gathering and the need for transnational cooperation between the intelligence services

---

[13] John Mueller, "The Search for the 'Breaking Point' in Vietnam: The Statistics of a Deadly Quarrel," *International Studies Quarterly* 24 (December 1980), pp. 497–519.

[14] Karl W. Deutsch, *The Nerves of Government: Models of Political Communication and Control* (New York: Free Press, 1963), p. xxvii.

of states pursuing common goals and facing common threats. This failure, combined with the "false positive" assessment of Iraq's weapons of mass destruction, which the Bush administration acted on when it went to war in 2003, prompted the U.S. government to consider the most significant reorganization of its intelligence community since the CIA was created in 1947.[15]

We cannot know how best to use our tools of influence if we do not know the plans or intentions of others or if we must continually react to surprising situations. The same is true if we do not know the capabilities—and vulnerabilities—of others. Thus, the second kind of information is knowledge of others' military and economic strength, internal political situation, domestic unrest, and, in the case of transnational actors, the scope of their organization and bases of operation. Much intelligence work involves the collection of a great deal of information about other states, using readily available sources of information and standard research techniques. Other work is clandestine and sometimes raises difficult ethical questions. The third type of information is feedback. Governments seek information about the effects of their own decisions on the actions of others and steer accordingly. Feedback helps a government determine whether to continue its policies or to alter them in some way. American policy in Indochina during the 1960s can be seen as a classic case of the failure of information-gathering and -processing activities, as well as the failure of analysts and political leaders to assess feedback information correctly.

Intelligence involves the collection, analysis, interpretation, and storage of information, as well as the transmission of information to top-level foreign policy decision makers. One reason why we consider intelligence capabilities as an intangible component of national power relates to the unreliability of the intelligence process. As we shall see in Chapter 7, information may be lost or distorted within the government, misunderstood or disbelieved by policy makers, or never collected at all. Nonetheless, governments keep up their efforts. During the cold war, the United States and the Soviet Union spent vast sums on intelligence activities. Most countries with immediate and pressing security problems devote substantial energy to intelligence gathering, and it has been identified as perhaps the most important tool in the fight against international terrorism.

Before states can attempt to influence others, then, they must obtain certain information about the world. How well a state collects and handles information will affect the utility of all its other capabilities. How well a state collects and handles information will also affect its goals and objectives and how it seeks to achieve them. Once a set of objectives or goals exists, foreign policy decision makers must try to translate their capabilities into the influence required to achieve their objectives; they must implement their foreign policy decisions. They have a wide range of tools, techniques, and methods with which to deal with other states. Now we shall look further at some of the methods through which states exercise influence.

---

[15] On intelligence failures surrounding 9/11, see *The 9/11 Commission Report: Final Report of the National Commission on Terrorist Attacks upon the United States* (New York: Norton, 2004). For a more general survey and analysis, see Richard K. Betts, *Enemies of Intelligence: Knowledge and Power in American National Security* (New York: Columbia University Press, 2007).

DIPLOMATIC INFLUENCE

A British diplomat once said, "Foreign policy is what you do; diplomacy is how you do it."[16] Although this distinction is a good place to start, it is also incomplete—there are a wide variety of techniques for the implementation of foreign policy, not all of them diplomatic. **Diplomacy** usually involves direct, government-to-government contact whereby officials interact in order to communicate desires and accomplish goals on behalf of states. Diplomacy is normally regarded as a peaceful (if often contentious) means of state interaction; although the limited use or threat of force is sometimes characterized as "coercive diplomacy," most people would agree that such acts are more coercive than diplomatic.

Diplomacy is the central technique of foreign policy implementation and the only truly direct technique. Other techniques are often combined with diplomatic instruments in order to more effectively influence other states. For example, after a major military victory, it is usually through diplomatic interaction that the defeated party indicates whether it will surrender or modify previously held peace conditions. The military instrument has had an effect on another state, but that effect can be exploited and enhanced only through diplomacy. Indeed, Zhou Enlai, the Chinese head of state from 1949 to 1976, stated that "diplomacy is the continuation of war by other means" (a twist on Clausewitz's famous dictum). The same may be said in regard to diplomacy and economic coercion such as embargoes and other sanctions that deprive a state of needed commodities.

The central features of diplomacy are representation and communication. Modern diplomatic practice can be traced back to the fifth century when permanent diplomatic missions were established by various Italian city-states so that monarchs would have representatives in other courts to facilitate reliable and continuous communication with their counterparts. Diplomatic missions and most of the other legal trappings of diplomacy were established to maintain clear channels of communication and to reduce misunderstanding and distortion in interstate dialogue. French, widely spoken by aristocrats in most European states during the Renaissance period, became the *lingua franca* of diplomatic exchange. The rules of *protocol* were established to reduce conflicts over rank and status among diplomats; *diplomatic immunity* prevents host governments from interfering with the diplomatic representatives of other states; norms of *noninterference* prohibit diplomats from becoming involved in the domestic political processes of their hosts. These practices permit representatives to get on with the business of diplomacy, and they constitute an important pillar of international law.

Diplomacy has several functions in addition to the general aims of representation and communication between states: negotiation and conflict management; protection of citizens and other interests abroad; promotion of economic, scientific, and cultural exchanges between states; and management of the foreign policy decisions of one country in regard to others.[17] Each of these diplomatic activities

---

[16] Paul Henry Gore-Booth, *With Great Truth and Respect* (London: Constable, 1974), p. 15.

[17] See, for example, Sir Ernest M. Satow's classic guide for diplomats, originally published in 1917: Paul Henry Gore-Booth, ed., *Satow's Guide to Diplomatic Practice*, 5th ed. (London: Longman, 1979). For a review of the contemporary literature on diplomacy, see Christer Jönsson, "Diplomacy, Bargaining and Negotiation," in Walter Carlsnaes, Thomas Risse, and Beth Simmons, eds., *Handbook of International Relations* (London: Sage, 2002).

involves communicating the views of one's government and receiving the views of other governments. Each may be part of a continuous diplomatic process involving a variety of related activities. For example, after negotiating the end of military hostilities, additional diplomacy is often required to clarify how the agreement will be fully implemented, talks that may stretch on for months or even years. After the Arab–Israeli ceasefire was achieved in 1973, some very hard bargaining was required to separate Egyptian and Israeli forces on the Sinai Peninsula. The resulting Israeli–Egyptian talks on the "Kilometer 101" disengagements, as well as the implementation of the less-than-precise peace treaty of 1979, are good illustrations of the importance of postagreement diplomacy.

So far we have discussed diplomacy as a means by which one state directly influences another state. But diplomacy serves another major function, one aimed not primarily at the other party in the interaction, but at third parties observing the diplomatic activities at hand. In this case, the importance of diplomacy is less to reach an agreement with the opposing party than to influence other parties through propaganda, undermining the position of the opponent, revealing the opponent's bargaining positions and other confidential information, or taking stances calculated to impress, frighten, or reassure third-party observers. Many of the U.S.–Soviet negotiations over the years were aimed at their various allies, at third world states, and perhaps especially at China.

Disagreement over how much diplomatic communication should be open and how much should remain secret became a major issue in the twentieth century. After World War I, there was a reaction against the old diplomacy of the great European powers. In addition to a general feeling that diplomacy was a devious and dishonest business, many observers felt that the secret treaties that characterized the pre–World War I period were responsible for the outbreak of the war. Idealists like President Woodrow Wilson attacked the immorality of secret treaties that offered territory if states would help others in military offensives. Wilson called for "open covenants . . . openly arrived at" (the first of his Fourteen Points). The League of Nations promoted the idea of open treaties by publishing their texts after they were negotiated. Article 102 of the UN Charter provides for the compulsory registration of treaties with the UN. If a treaty has not been so registered, it cannot be invoked within the UN system.[18]

Openness has undermined some of the previous utility of diplomacy because public statements are often infused with propaganda. Various speeches made in the UN General Assembly and Security Council exemplify how the propaganda function of diplomacy, as opposed to problem-solving or conflict-resolution functions, can prevail. After World War II, a hybrid form of diplomacy became prevalent. It combined private negotiations between diplomats with public declarations of what had been achieved—in press conferences, in joint statements, or by the publication of agreements (usually by the UN). Former Secretary of State Henry Kissinger was a master of the private conversation and the public spectacle. His techniques were a return to traditional diplomacy: hard bargaining in private,

---

[18] Treaties registered with the UN, in accordance with Article 102, are available online; see "United Nations Treaty Collection" at <http://untreaty.un.org/english/treaty.asp>.

secret trips and agreements (revealed to the public only after their completion), and a style that combined the use of force with the use of words to bring about an agreement acceptable to every side but one that required every side to make concessions and compromises. Informal, unofficial negotiations between states, conducted out of the public eye by trusted confidants of top policy makers (in or out of government), have been called "track-two diplomacy." The 1993 Oslo Accords, which provided for the creation of the Palestinian Authority to administer portions of the West Bank and Gaza Strip vacated by withdrawing Israeli forces, is a good example of what can be accomplished when negotiations over highly sensitive issues are taken out of the limelight.

In the past, the bulk of routine diplomatic communication, as well as the most important talks and conferences, took place between the regular diplomatic representatives of the foreign ministries of states. Both day-to-day activity and major talks were handled by the diplomatic personnel of the embassies located in each state's capital. Today much of this activity, especially for smaller and less developed countries, occurs in multilateral forums such as the UN. This *parliamentary diplomacy* includes both the regular meetings of the international body to which permanent representatives are assigned and informal discussions that occur in a single location, where a state's diplomats can meet with representatives of many other states. The larger powers, taking advantage of instantaneous communication facilities between governmental leaders, faster transportation, and the desire to bring together officials from the highest level of government, have tended to skip over embassy personnel and ambassadors and conduct more and more of their business through the interaction foreign ministers, finance ministers, and the like. These activities range from the bilateral cold war "summits" of U.S. and Soviet leaders to multilateral conferences such as the regular meetings of the Group of Eight—the heads of government of the seven major Western industrial countries (United States, Japan, Germany, France, Italy, Britain, and Canada) plus Russia.

The modern U.S. secretary of state has regularly engaged in "shuttle diplomacy" of some sort, flying between the capitals of states in conflict to facilitate communication between opposing parties who usually will not sit down together. Kissinger popularized this activity in his work in the Middle East in 1973. Reagan's secretary of state, Alexander Haig, pursued it in trying to settle the Falklands dispute between Britain and Argentina in 1982. James Baker, the elder Bush's secretary of state, engaged in similar travels in 1991 as he attempted to revive a Middle East peace process following the Gulf War, and George W. Bush's secretary of state, Condoleezza Rice, did the same following a period in which the administration had largely disengaged from the process to focus on the war on terrorism. Lower-level representatives, or *envoys,* have also been active in American diplomatic efforts in recent years. During the Clinton administration, special envoys achieved considerable success in resolving issues between conflicting parties in Bosnia and Northern Ireland.

BARGAINING AND NEGOTIATION

Bargaining and negotiation are, or can be, important elements in the practice of diplomacy. The two terms are often used interchangeably, but **bargaining** is actually a broader concept: the process by which two or more parties attempt to settle on the terms of an exchange. A bargaining process will often include **negotiation**—verbal communication aimed at resolving the parties' incompatible goals—but it need not be limited to negotiation. Bargaining can be tacit, whereby intentions and commitment are demonstrated through behavior rather than by direct communication. The use of military force, which we discuss below and examine in more detail in Chapter 8, may therefore be understood as an extremely coercive form of bargaining. As one analyst puts it, "if fighting is expected to lead to an agreement then fighting must be considered as part of the bargaining process and not an alternative to it."[19]

In some respects, bargaining resembles a *debate* in which "opponents direct their arguments at each other" and "the objective is to convince your opponent, to make him see things as you see them." It also resembles a game in which each party must take into account "the potentialities and evaluations of alternative outcomes" and the object is to outwit the opponent.[20] Thus, persuasion as well as threats and promises are employed in bargaining as each side presents its conditions and demands and attempts to convince or coerce the other side to accept as many of these as possible. Threats and promises must be credible. Each side must try to figure out how far to push demands and how far to push the opponent—when to make concessions and when to dig in and say, "I have nothing more to give." A state's bargaining credibility is a function of its reputation for bluffing, standing fast, telling the truth, and honoring commitments (or not).

Bargaining in all its forms involves the complex interactions of mutual influence and expectations, with each party both anticipating and reacting to the other. A feeling for the complexity of the bargaining process is given by Thomas Schelling, one of the pioneers in the study of international strategy and bargaining:

> Each party's strategy is guided mainly by what he expects the other to accept or insist on; yet each knows that the other is guided by reciprocal thoughts. The final outcome must be a point from which neither expects the other to retreat; yet the main ingredient of this expectation is what one thinks the other expects the first to expect, and so on. Somehow, out of this fluid and indeterminate situation that seemingly provides no logical reason for anybody to expect anything except what he expects to be expected to expect, a decision is reached. These infinitely reflexive expectations must somehow converge on a single point, at which each expects the other not to expect to be expected to retreat.[21]

Bargaining, therefore, is a strategic interaction in which each side attempts to communicate to the other—directly through negotiation or indirectly through other forms of behavior—what it wants the other to believe about its preferences,

---

[19] R. Harrison Wagner, "Bargaining and War," *American Journal of Political Science* 44 (July 2000), pp. 469–484. See also James D. Fearon, "Rationalist Explanations for War," *International Organization* 49 (Summer 1995), pp. 379–414.

[20] Anatol Rapoport, *Fights, Games, and Debates* (Ann Arbor: University of Michigan Press, 1960), pp. 10, 11.

[21] Thomas Schelling, *The Strategy of Conflict* (New York: Oxford University Press, 1963), p. 70.

capabilities, and commitments. Sometimes what is communicated is an accurate representation of the party's true position; sometimes it is a misrepresentation.

Negotiation, a particular form of bargaining, usually unfolds in stages.[22] The first stage is making a commitment to deal in *good faith*. This means that both parties are negotiating for the purpose of reaching an agreement. Each party must calculate that the benefits of reaching agreement outweigh the sacrifices that may be necessary. Often this stage requires one party to convince the other that an agreement of some sort would be in the interest of both sides. States do not always negotiate in good faith. A state may negotiate to gather information about the capabilities, aims, and problems of the other side, or to give the opponent misleading information about its own intentions and capabilities. States sometimes choose to negotiate simply to maintain contact with the other side, even if chances of an agreement are slim, in hopes that as long as both sides are talking neither will resort to armed conflict. This may have been an objective of the U.S.–Japanese talks that were in progress before Pearl Harbor.

Once the intention to deal in good faith has been communicated, the parties move on to discuss preliminary issues, which often seem as important to both sides as the agreement itself. The *location* of the negotiations must be fixed. States prefer a neutral site when bargaining with an adversary; Paris was the site of the U.S.–North Vietnamese peace talks; Vienna, Helsinki, and Geneva were used for the U.S.–Soviet Strategic Arms Limitation Talks (SALT). Naming the *parties* to be represented can present a problem because participation defines who has a legitimate standing in the issue. In this era of nonstate actors trying to obtain territory, and ultimately sovereignty, simply recognizing their existence is a major substantive concession. Thus, by agreeing to their participation in negotiations, a state has made more than a procedural concession. This was a sticky point for the United States in Paris regarding the Viet Cong and was continually a central issue in the protracted conflicts in Northern Ireland and between Israel and the Arabs. Until the dramatic breakthrough with Egypt in 1977, no Arab state recognized Israel's existence. Israel, in turn, refused to recognize the Palestine Liberation Organization (PLO). The 1993 peace agreements negotiated in Oslo and signed in Washington— for which Yitzak Rabin, Shimon Peres, and Yasser Arafat received the Nobel Peace Prize—could come about only after an array of such nonrecognition barriers fell.

The second stage of negotiation is the bargaining over the actual *terms of the agreement*—that is, defining solutions and working out accords. Although each side has different and conflicting objectives, the range of outcomes acceptable to both sides provides the negotiators with something over which to bargain. The objective for each side is to identify this range of feasible agreements and then persuade the opposing side to settle on a particular solution as close as possible to one's own ideal point. (In Box 5.1, we present a simple model of a bargaining situation involving India and Pakistan.)

---

[22] See, for example, Christophe Dupont and Guy-Olivier Faure, "The Negotiation Process," in Victor A. Kremenyuk, ed., *International Negotiation: Analysis, Approaches, Issues*, 2nd ed. (New York: Jossey-Bass, 2002). The literature on negotiation is reviewed in I. William Zartmann, "Conflict Resolution and Negotiation," in Jacob Bercovitch, Victor Kremenyuk, and I. William Zartmann, eds., *The Sage Handbook of Conflict Resolution* (London: Sage, 2008).

IN GREATER DEPTH

BOX 5.1	**BARGAINING AND COMMON GROUND**

Theories of bargaining and negotiation are often formalized—that is, presented in mathematical or geometric terms. Consider a simple example in which India and Pakistan are negotiating over disputed territory in the Kashmir region. In coming to the negotiating table, the two sides have concluded that they have more to gain from a bargain than from the status quo, which is a continual source of tension and overt military conflict. Think of a two-dimensional space representing all possible bargains, where the gains to be made by India increase as we move eastward along the horizontal dimension and the gains to be made by Pakistan increase as we move northward along the vertical. That is, any bargain in this space will provide **utility**—an improvement over the status quo—to both India and Pakistan. To simplify, suppose that for either state the more territory recognized as its own, the better. At the intersection of the horizontal and vertical axes in the bottom-left corner is the "conflict point"—a situation in which no bargain is struck, thereby bringing no additional utility to either party.

This bargaining space is bounded by a **frontier**, shown as a curve, which represents the limit of all possible bargains that could be made by the two states. A particular bargain, B, to formally recognize a certain division of Kashmir will be an improvement for India, equal to U_I, and an improvement for Pakistan, U_P. A bargain anywhere inside the large zone of agreement but not on the frontier can be improved upon; the utility for both sides increases by moving to any point on the frontier northeast of that point. The frontier is often called the *Pareto optimal* frontier, after Italian economist Vilfredo Pareto, whose concepts of economic efficiency are employed widely in the social sciences today. A Pareto optimal outcome is one in which neither side can do better without making the other side worse off. You can see that any point on the frontier meets that condition; these outcomes are thus **socially optimal.**

The challenge for negotiators is first to define the bargaining space and identify the zone of agreement and then to strike a bargain at or near the Pareto frontier. That is not easy. Imagine that India and Pakistan, in the process of negotiations, are zeroing in on a bargain at point B but that India is having second thoughts and wants to increase the portion of Kashmir to be recognized as sovereign Indian territory. Although any point on the frontier southeast of B is still Pareto optimal, Pakistan could be expected to reject that move. The two sides,

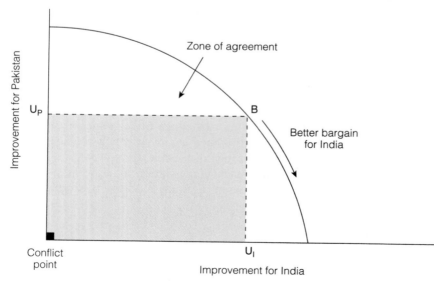

| BOX 5.1 | **BARGAINING AND COMMON GROUND** |

perhaps with the help of third-party mediators, need to try to find a bargain that is both socially optimal and perceived as "fair." One solution is to find a bargain that maximizes the product of the two sides' utilities (that is, a point on the frontier tangent to the largest rectangle that could be drawn inside the zone of agreement, which in this case is, in fact, point B). This is the *Nash bargaining solution*, named after John Nash, whose mathematical work on bargaining and noncooperative game theory (which we introduce later) earned him a Nobel Prize in economics in 1994. As bargains move closer to one axis or the other—as they disproportionately favor one side or the other—this conception of fairness will not be met.

Note: For an overview of the use of bargaining theory in the analysis of conflict, see Robert Powell, "Bargaining Theory and International Conflict," *Annual Review of Political Science* 5 (June 2002), pp. 1–30. Nash's solution is presented in John F. Nash, "The Bargaining Problem," *Econometrica* 18 (1950): 155–162.

CONFLICT RESOLUTION

Conflicts of interest, including those that are or could become violent, can be resolved in many ways. The use or threat of force—through conquest, forcible submission, compellence, or deterrence—is one means. But conflicts are also resolved through diplomacy: negotiated compromise, third-party mediation or arbitration, or adjudication of some other sort (by international courts, multilateral conferences, or international organizations).

For successful conflict resolution, the parties involved must be willing to confront the issues in dispute in a rational atmosphere of some mutual respect and open communication. Each side must try to identify the genuine differences between them and avoid taking positions merely to establish favorable conditions for the bargaining process. John Burton, a former Australian diplomat, even argues that the haggling associated with most bargaining situations should be avoided. His position is that conflicts are based on misunderstandings and that the important thing is to get people to sit down face to face. The largest issues may be set out in the presence of a mediator, who will help the parties see where misunderstandings exist. Once favorable conditions exist for analyzing the misunderstanding that underlies the conflict, the process of conflict resolution is well on its way.[23] This view that most conflicts are based merely on misunderstandings is extreme, but, as we have noted, the early stages of negotiation can be very important.

Most conflicts are more than misunderstandings. Incompatibilities do exist in the global arena: the desire to occupy the same territory, to control the same governmental machinery, or to fish the same waters. Disagreements often exist over the manner in which certain groups of people—say, coreligionists or people of the same ethnic or linguistic background living within the borders of other states—should be treated. We can recognize the objective basis of most conflicts of interest and at the same time understand that the process of conflict resolution is highly subjective because of the complex nature of bargaining.

[23] John W. Burton, *Conflict: Resolution and Prevention* (New York: St. Martin's, 1990).

Roger Fisher and his associates have distinguished between positional and principled negotiation as a means of conflict resolution, or "getting to yes." *Positional negotiation* is competitive; each side has an opening position and bargaining proceeds to a point of settlement somewhere between these two positions, perhaps closer to one side's opening position than to the other's. Fisher argues that this form of negotiation is inefficient and may not lead to optimal agreements. The parties can do better through *principled negotiation,* whereby the bargaining process begins by identifying both sides' interests, rather than their positions. "Your position is something you have decided upon. Your interests are what caused you to so decide."[24] Bargaining positions are almost always mutually exclusive, whereas interests often overlap. Getting the parties to focus on their interests instead of their positions will help to locate larger regions of common ground and more potential points of settlement.

When bargaining to resolve conflicts, the least coercive forms of influence are often the most useful, at least initially. Promises of rewards, persuasion, reliance on the legitimacy of claims, and sensitivity to the opponent's position seem to be better methods of influence than are threats of force. Emphasizing the legitimacy of one's own position so as to appeal to values held by the opponent is especially helpful. Many argue that states should be concerned with precedent and reciprocity in order to make their demands legitimate in the eyes of the opponents—to appear to act in a way consistent with their principles.

A way to do this is to appeal to international law and international organizations. During the cold war, no organization was very successful at managing conflicts between members of the different blocs. The UN was reasonably effective in non–cold war disputes, however, doing best in the area of resource conflicts (see Chapter 10). Regional organizations do well in managing conflicts not involving force, whereas the UN had some modest success with high-intensity conflicts. When the cold war wound down at the end of the 1980s, the UN was able to do things that previously would have been impossible. With the United States and Russia cooperating, the Security Council and the secretary-general helped to end a number of civil and international wars (including ones in Namibia and Cambodia). The UN also played a key role in bringing the international community together against Iraq after its invasion of Kuwait. And in 1998, when the United States was preparing a military response to the Iraqi government's refusal to grant free access to UN weapons inspectors, it was Secretary-General Kofi Annan who brought about a peaceful settlement. At the outset of a dispute, the legitimacy of an international organization like the UN may be the only thing on which states can agree.

MILITARY AND ECONOMIC INFLUENCE

We have noted several times that influence may be achieved through the application of force. Throughout history, rulers have used war and violence to overcome obstacles. There is no doubt that the use of military capabilities is generally a

---

[24] Roger Fisher, William Ury, and George Patton, *Getting to Yes: Negotiating Agreement Without Giving In,* 2nd ed. (New York: Penguin, 1991), p. 46.

coercive means of influence. It is also possible, however, to use these capabilities for *rewarding* others. The most obvious rewarding activity is the use of military aid. States, particularly larger states, may thereby attempt to influence commitment to an alliance, UN voting, or general political orientation. Powers such as the United States, Russia, Britain, and France have the technology, expertise, and capability to produce the kind of advanced weaponry that most of the world's countries cannot. Other countries such as China, Brazil, Israel, and India have also become important suppliers of arms to developing countries, but the variety and sophistication of their exports tend to be more limited; plus, they are more inclined to be seeking economic benefits than political influence.

Influence gained through providing weapons may be only temporary. Egypt illustrated how a recipient state can turn on its arms supplier when Anwar Sadat ejected Soviet military advisers and other personnel from the country in 1971. Even if it is sometimes effective, the exchange of aid for influence is far from predictable. U.S. influence on Israeli policies has been quite variable—from none to some. None of Iraq's arms suppliers, including the Soviet Union, was able to influence Iraqi policy in the six months before the Iran–Iraq War broke out. Indeed, in the aftermath of the war, major arms suppliers were forced to recognize the limited influence that arms supplies provided, along with the harm that such weapons could inflict within various regions.

USE OF FORCE

Most instances involving the military tool of foreign policy are based on exploiting the use of force or the threat thereof. Force is coercive; it is the ability to destroy or kill or take away, to occupy and control through violence. Force directly affects the distribution of security, political control, territory, and wealth in the international system. Force is used because decision makers expect to benefit from the new distributions that are anticipated after it has been used. States are influenced by the threat of force because they fear what they will lose if it is actually used. The objective of using force is the same as that of using any other technique in a bargaining situation: to influence outcomes.

This view of force was most powerfully argued and popularized by the Prussian officer and military historian Carl von Clausewitz, who wrote his classic *On War* following his military service against Napoléon. Clausewitz clearly saw the military instrument as a way to influence the opponent: "War therefore is an act of violence intended to compel our opponent to fulfill our will." Clausewitz also argued that war is a means to an end, that it cannot be separated from the political goals of states and indeed must be subordinated to those goals. His famous dictum reads: "War is a mere continuation of policy by other means . . . , not merely a political act, but also a real political instrument, a continuation of political commerce, a carrying out of the same by other means."[25]

---

[25] Carl von Clausewitz, *On War*, edited and with an introduction by Anatol Rapoport (New York: Penguin, 1968), pp. 101, 119.

The use of force can be a means to completely destroy an opponent. Brute force overcomes an obstacle by annihilating it, as the Romans overcame Carthage in the Third Punic War (149–146 B.C.E.). Rome did not employ force to influence Carthage to engage in desired behavior: There was nothing Rome wanted Carthage to do. Rome simply wanted to wipe its enemy from the face of the Earth. When the use of force is aimed at the destruction of an opponent, influence is not the object. In most situations where force is used, however, influence is the aim. The use of force is usually meant to hurt the opponent until the latter's will to resist further is broken.

Alternatively, one can merely *threaten* to use force, exploiting an opponent's knowledge of one's ability to hurt and inflict costs. Military capabilities are exploited explicitly through diplomatic channels, especially when the aim is deterrence; the deterrer must make clear to the opponent just what actions are forbidden and what will happen to the opponent if those actions are taken. Beyond the threat of force, other techniques exist for the use of military capabilities without actually resorting to violence. The aim is to convey to others the military capabilities one possesses in order to influence their view of the situation and to limit their menu of options. States often want to be perceived as being militarily powerful, willing to use their capabilities and thus not to be challenged or thwarted. Such a demonstration may be implicit, or it may be made explicit through the display of military capabilities—to impress others with one's military strength and to achieve status and prestige as a powerful state. In today's system, nuclear weapons are the most obvious element of military capabilities used for prestige or status. India's nuclear explosions in 1974 and again in 1998 were motivated in part by its quest to rival the status and prestige of China, both in Asia and in the eyes of third world countries around the globe.[26]

Stationing one's forces abroad may serve to influence others in any or all of the ways we have discussed: to reward allies or to threaten opponents, to support deterrence, or to project power and status. Although the end of the cold war brought about a substantial reduction in foreign-based troops, at its height almost 2 million military personnel from twenty-eight different countries were stationed in ninety-one foreign countries on almost 3,000 military bases or installations. More symbolically, states may display their military capabilities to outside observers through a variety of activities: nuclear tests, war games, military parades and air shows, and a demonstrated willingness to send aircraft carrier groups around the world. Mobilizing forces or putting them on high-readiness alerts, as Nixon did during the 1973 Yom Kippur War, can also be used to communicate to an opponent the seriousness of a situation. Here a state is less interested in demonstrating its capabilities than its willingness to use them in a critical situation.

---

[26] Scott Sagan, "Why Do States Build Nuclear Weapons? Three Models in Search of a Bomb," *International Security* 21 (Winter 1996/1997), pp. 54–86. The importance of this motivation in the Indian case is questioned in Šumit Ganguly, "India's Pathway to Pokhran II: The Prospects and Sources of New Delhi's Nuclear Weapons Program," *International Security* (Winter 1998/1999), pp. 148–177.

ECONOMIC PERSUASION

States rely on each other for resources and commodities that enable them to develop and sustain their economies and the well-being of their peoples. Economic resources can be manipulated by those who possess them to influence those who do not. As we stressed in the last chapter, nothing in the international system is equally distributed. This applies to economic resources as well as to the economic requirements of various states. States that possess a surplus (or a monopoly) of resources may achieve greater economic influence; states that lack the resources and commodities they require are more vulnerable to economic influence. The economic resources of states can be used across the whole range of influence mechanisms.[27] In comparison to diplomacy, however, economic means of influence may be considered indirect. Rather than direct interaction with governmental leaders, the objective is to affect some aspect of the state's society—its wealth, productivity, or material well-being—so that leaders are persuaded to alter their policies.

As with other types of influence, economic influence may be achieved through the use of rewards (the "carrot") or punishments (the "stick"). For either to work, the target state must be economically *vulnerable*. In one way or another, all states have economic needs that they cannot satisfy. They are therefore vulnerable to the influence of states who have leverage of some kind—who have what they need. In the past, states such as Bangladesh, the Soviet Union, and many African countries have required more food, especially grain, than they could produce. Most states require petroleum, which is extracted on a large scale in only a handful of countries; in this regard, Japan and the states of Western Europe are particularly vulnerable, and the United States has become increasingly so over the past two decades. In the 1970s, Henry Kissinger tried to use a policy of détente as a way of enmeshing the Soviet Union within a web of world trade. If the USSR became more dependent on the goods and markets of other states, the Soviets not only would become more vulnerable to the exercise of leverage by Western states but also would develop an interest in the smooth functioning of the global capitalist economy. He hoped that the Soviets would thus become "more responsible" world citizens.

There are many possible ways to threaten or apply economic coercion. A developed country may withhold foreign aid from a poor one; a less-developed state may nationalize the corporate investments of industrialized states or increase the price of its natural resources; trade relations may be reduced or cut off entirely. In many cases, the punishment or threat of punishment consists of withdrawing an economic resource that previously had been available. Interference with normal channels of economic interaction with another country means that both sides are deprived of possible future instruments of influence over each other's policies. Throughout the 1990s, there was a debate in the United States about how best to respond to the Chinese government's violation of human rights. Although many people argued that the United States had no business doing business with the

---

[27] For an overview of economic foreign policy tools, see David A. Baldwin, *Economic Statecraft* (Princeton, N.J.: Princeton University Press, 1985); on economic sanction in particular, see Daniel W. Drezner, *The Sanctions Paradox: Economic Statecraft and International Relations* (Cambridge: Cambridge University Press, 1999).

communist government of China—one that had massacred hundreds of pro-democracy students in Tiananmen Square in June 1989—others responded that cutting economic ties to China would eliminate one of the few instruments of U.S. influence over Chinese policy.

In contrast to the various methods of applying the economic stick, foreign aid can be a major carrot. It involves the transfer of economic goods or services from the donor to the recipient. These might include any resource or commodity, money, services, or technical advice. In economically developing countries, the need for development capital (money and goods) and for the technical and technological skills to build a modern economy are particularly high. Aid is therefore very useful in dealing with most of the states in the international system today. Giving or withholding aid, attempting to create dependencies through its use, and attempting to substitute aid from one state for aid from another are all common strategies for influence (or escape from influence).

Aid may be used for economic development or relief. The aid may come as outright grants, loans, sales, or technical assistance. In the 1950s and 1960s, grants were the preferred form of aid. More recently, technical assistance and loans have assumed a greater role. Bilateral aid, which is provided by one state directly to another, is particularly susceptible to manipulation. Dependence relationships can be created, and aid may go to states where the donor country wants to strengthen its trading interests or to establish new investments. Donor countries often provide bilateral aid with strings; the recipient may be required to buy or trade for goods it does not want or need if it is to receive the aid it desires. Much of bilateral economic aid goes to countries where the donor expects to gain some clear benefit for its foreign and national security policy. About half of all U.S. bilateral economic assistance, for example, goes to just two countries, Egypt and Israel. Israel has long been an important U.S. strategic ally, while American aid to Egypt displaced Soviet influence and compensated for the loss of Arab economic aid as a result of Egypt's decision to enter into a separate peace agreement with Israel in 1979.

In this chapter, we have reviewed some of the basic techniques states use to interact and exert influence over one another. We have taken only a brief look at the major diplomatic, military, and economic methods for exercising influence; we will return to these at various points in Parts II and III. Other topics, such as psychological means of influence, have been touched on only in passing. The ideological overlay of the cold war prompted heavy use of this indirect technique, whereby states attempt to influence the values, attitudes, and behavior of the people (or specific groups of people) in other countries. Radio and television (such as Voice of America and Radio Free Europe), films, and websites are aimed at the populations of opponents, allies, and neutrals alike. Propaganda is an important tool in attempting to increase other people's respect or improve their images of your rectitude.

A state's menu depends in large part on the array of techniques it possesses to influence other international actors and their attempts to influence it. The tools available for influence very much depend on the state's capabilities and how those capabilities stand in relation to the capabilities of others. In the next chapter, we shall move within the domestic system of a state and look at the characteristics of the society and government. We have already provided a very general idea of how these domestic factors might influence the foreign policy menu of decision makers; now we will examine these topics in depth.

DOMESTIC SOURCES OF FOREIGN POLICY: SOCIETY AND POLITY

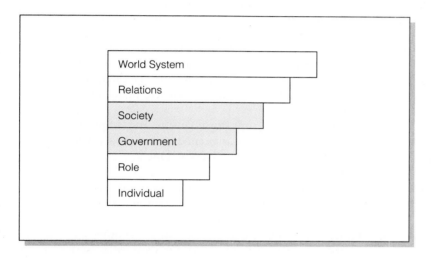

CHAPTER 6

FOREIGN POLICY

Statesmen generally feel constrained by two sets of influences: politics, power, and the actions of other states; and domestic constraints ranging from public opinion to the culture of the governmental bureaucracy. The effective statesman must be able to take both into account and master them. Henry Kissinger, who would later become U.S. Secretary of State, observed that statesmen throughout history have often failed to deal with one or the other of these sets of constraints. A foreign policy maker must understand these constraints and then be able to transcend them, bending them to his or her own will.[1]

---

[1] Kissinger expressed these sentiments in "Domestic Structure and Foreign Policy," *Daedalus 95* (1966), pp. 503–529.

We can begin our analysis of foreign policy by breaking it down into its component parts. A *policy* is a program that serves as a guide to behavior intended to realize the goals that an organization has set for itself. The notion of sovereignty helps us distinguish domestic from *foreign*. Sovereignty means control over territory delimited by internationally recognized boundaries. Anything beyond those legal boundaries, in areas where the state has no legal authority, is foreign. **Foreign policy** is thus a guide to actions taken beyond the boundaries of the state to further the goals of the state. We must also recognize, as Kissinger did, that what goes on within the state's borders may have important implications for the government's outwardly directed behavior, and so foreign policy analysis cannot be limited to an examination of the international environment.

The intention of foreign policy is to affect the behavior of other actors, even if only in general terms. Because nothing is distributed equally in the global system, every state requires resources, economic goods, military capabilities, political and strategic support, and the cooperation of other actors. Foreign policy thus concerns behavior toward some other actor for some reason. Whether the actual behavior of a state matches its intentions is another matter. Much of foreign policy analysis is directed at the links between the intentions of behavior and its consequences. Realist and radical views of foreign policy, which stress the centrality of power and dominance in world politics, claim that foreign policy revolves around the idea of continually trying to influence or control other actors, to get them to behave in ways beneficial to one's own interests. There are, however, many kinds of goals and many kinds of influence.

We need to study foreign policy—both formulation and implementation—comparatively, looking for patterns of behavior associated with different types of states under different conditions and within different contexts. One key question is: *What* to compare? What behavior or outcomes are we trying to explain (what is the dependent variable)? What contributed to that behavior or those outcomes (what are the independent variables)? That is, in trying to understand foreign policy—the policy-making process, the content of the policies, or their consequences—what factors, influences, and characteristics should be investigated? Another question is: *How* to compare foreign policies? Should one try to compare many states at one point in time, one state over many time periods, or a large number of states over different time periods? Do we compare foreign policies by evaluating their success or failure or by making normative judgments about whether the foreign policy produces "good" or "bad" outcomes? The answers depend to a great extent on just what research problem we are confronting.

Most current efforts in the comparative analysis of foreign policy focus on describing or modeling the foreign policy process: identifying the important decision-making units, looking at how individuals and groups perceive foreign policy problems and solutions, and describing the dynamics of interaction between groups of decision makers (either within the same government or across state boundaries). Which parts of the environment, or the menu, will be most closely considered by the decision makers of a particular state, under what conditions, and at what stage of the foreign policy-making process? This process begins with the formulation of foreign policy goals and continues as policy makers attempt to adapt these goals to both the domestic and international environments.

GOALS AND OBJECTIVES OF FOREIGN POLICY

A state leader pursues foreign policy objectives on behalf of the nation. As objectives evolve there is usually debate over how best they ought to be pursued. Rarely is there national consensus on either the goals of foreign policy or the means for achieving them. Some goals remain fairly consistent, while others are more sensitive to changes in the domestic and international environments. But even long-standing foreign policy objectives, like the U.S. effort to contain Soviet influence during the cold war, can change abruptly when a country finds itself occupying a new position in the global power structure.

We may think of a foreign policy objective as a vision of a future state of affairs that policy makers aspire to bring about by influencing the behavior of other state and nonstate actors. Objectives may be very concrete: Iraq sought territory in Iran that would give it control over the Shatt al-Arab waterway (and so started the Iran–Iraq War). Objectives may be much less concrete: creating images or promoting a specific set of values such as "making the world safe for democracy." Some objectives, often geopolitical ones, remain constant over long periods of time such as the Russian desire for warm-water ports or the British desire for command of the seas. Others are transitory, perhaps changing from month to month, such as the foreign economic policy objective of what currency exchange rate to target. Some objectives have consequences that affect the whole state, like the deterrence of nuclear attack. Still others involve the interests of only a small portion of society, perhaps the wealthiest or the most politically influential citizens.

Governments often pursue objectives that are incompatible with other foreign or domestic policy objectives. Such was the case when the United States sold huge quantities of wheat to the Soviet Union in 1971 and 1972. The deal was designed to improve relations with the Soviet Union and ultimately help the Nixon administration disengage from the American involvement in Vietnam. On the other hand, the administration wanted to control inflation by keeping food prices down, an objective that then became much harder to achieve. Israel's policy of encouraging Jewish immigration to Palestine (Zionism) often conflicted with another Israeli foreign policy objective: the Arab states' recognition of Israel's right to exist in peace with its neighbors.

In sum, leaders of states seek a wide range of public, and sometimes private, objectives—some concrete, some quite abstract, and some very often in conflict. One factor distinguishing the realist, liberal, and radical perspectives is the central objectives that each associates with the foreign policies of states. Realists stress the immediate military and security objectives of states and downplay economic ones. For liberals, key foreign policy objectives involve the longer-term economic and social welfare of society. Radicals also highlight the economic objectives of states but argue that foreign policy is often designed to promote the interests of particular classes in society, not society as a whole.

NATIONAL INTERESTS AND PRIORITIES

Hans Morgenthau emphasized that, more than anything else, interest "defined in terms of power" determines the behavior of states. All governments, whether democratic or authoritarian, pursue such interests in the anarchy of world politics, a realm that realists liken to the state of nature described by the seventeenth-century English political philosopher Thomas Hobbes—a condition "as is of every man, against every man." They tend to look at states as *unitary actors*, entities guided by a single overriding set of values, preferences, and objectives, that essentially speak with one voice (consistent with *the* national interest). Foreign policy objectives are designed to maximize the state's power, or at least to maintain it so as to secure the state's position in the global power hierarchy. One difficulty with such conceptions is that they can easily become mere tautologies, statements that are true by definition and hence impossible to refute. That is, one can readily construct arguments to show that nearly any action—whether initiating a war or keeping the peace, whether in accordance with international law or in blatant disregard of it—is intended to enhance or preserve the power, and thus the interest, of the nation-state.

Even when this kind of argument is avoided, the fact that different countries have different histories, cultures, and socioeconomic and political structures means that foreign policy preferences, objectives, and ultimately strategies derive in large part from domestic society and not simply from the state's place in the international system—its position on the billiard table. Nor can we ignore the fact that within any given nation-state, different individuals, groups, and classes have different interests. Workers share some interests with factory owners (for instance, in seeing that their products can be sold), but they differ sharply on others (such as who should gain more from the production of those goods or whether it is better to manufacture goods with high-priced domestic labor or inexpensive foreign labor). Some manufacturers are interested in selling consumer goods in a peaceful world; others want to sell armaments that have a market only in a world where states are at war or threatened by war. It then becomes essential to ask: Whose particular interests are reflected in any particular governmental policy or act? Which individuals, groups, or classes are most influential in determining government policy? Does this change from time to time or under different international or domestic conditions? Are there some issues on which one group or class has a dominant influence and others on which another group is dominant?

In a large, complex bureaucracy such as the United States government, a major foreign policy decision is rarely made for a single purpose; rather, different individuals and groups will have different purposes and goals that they may seek to accomplish through the same basic policy. The invasion of Iraq in 2003 was supported in different parts of the government for different reasons. Some believed that Iraq was a national security threat, a state in possession of weapons of mass destruction and committed to acquire more. Some, concerned about the humanitarian suffering caused by Iraq's tyrannical regime and the sanctions imposed by the international community, felt that the Iraqi people had to be liberated. Others had grandiose visions of democracy for the Middle East and believed Iraq provided the opportunity to show that representative government could take root there. Still others saw an opportunity to establish American bases in Iraq to more effectively secure oil supplies and project American military power. Not all of these motives were given equal weight in the decision, and not all of them appeared in public statements by officials. But all of these proponents could come together on the same decision—to overthrow Saddam Hussein.[2]

Although the assumption that states are unitary actors with a single purpose may be convenient for some types of analysis, oftentimes that assumption will obscure what is really important. Unless we know how different interests are reconciled into a single decision, we cannot know what particular policy will result. By examining who gets involved in the foreign policy-making process, who is in charge, how compromises are reached, and how these procedures differ under different circumstances, we begin to understand *whose* interests become the national interests and how. That is why it is vital to know about the state's *structure of government* and the *societal influences* on it. Whose particular interests will the government serve at any particular time? Does the structure of the economy give particular groups particular clout on a particular issue? Do cultural practices or shared experiences incline certain societies, or groups within them, to adopt particular outlooks on world affairs? Reference to *the* national interest may indicate certain core values or goals that most citizens share to some degree (for example, peace, prosperity, and security), but until we break away from the notion of a unitary state—that is, until we know how different groups' interests are aggregated—we really know very little about national *priorities* or how they will be pursued in international politics. (In Box 6.1, we discuss a well-known paradox associated with aggregating group interests and objectives into a single "social choice.")

SOCIETAL INFLUENCES ON FOREIGN POLICY

Decision makers act on behalf of their states. As we have seen, countries differ in size, income level, and other characteristics that affect their capabilities and foreign policy goals. They also differ in their histories as nations, in the ways their societies and economies are organized, and the structures of their governments. Contemporary analysts increasingly stress the linkages between domestic and international politics. In conducting foreign policy, government leaders also confront domestic pressures and must create domestic political coalitions. In effect, they must play a "two-level game," adjusting their preferences and strategies in response to simultaneous developments at the international and domestic levels.[3] President Bill Clinton's visit to China in summer 1998, for example, was like a walk on a tightrope. He had to neutralize domestic opposition to his visit by publicly criticizing China's human rights record while at the same time not offending his Chinese hosts to the point of scuttling U.S.–Chinese trade and investment opportunities. The Chinese government's willingness to engage Clinton in a discussion of human rights and

---

[2] For a journalist's account of how these various positions were expressed and came together, see Bob Woodward, *Plan of Attack* (New York: Simon & Schuster, 2004). For an insider's account, see Douglas J. Feith, *War and Decision: Inside the Pentagon at the Dawn of the War on Terrorism* (New York: HarperCollins, 2008).

[3] See Robert D. Putnam, "Diplomacy and Domestic Politics: The Logic of Two-Level Games," *International Organization* 42 (Summer 1988), pp. 427–462. Formal models can be found in Bruce Bueno de Mesquita, Alastair Smith, Randolph M. Siverson, and James D. Morrow, *The Logic of Political Survival* (Cambridge, Mass.: MIT Press, 2003).

IN GREATER DEPTH

| BOX 6.1 | THE VOTING PARADOX AND THE PROBLEM OF SOCIAL CHOICE |

A simple example can illustrate the importance of taking into account the foreign policy preferences of different groups in society and their relative influence in the political process. After Iraq invaded Kuwait in 1990, there was a debate in the United States about the appropriate response. Suppose there were only three possible courses of action: go to war, impose economic sanctions, or do nothing. Suppose also that there were only three groups in American society with strongly held preferences, each of roughly equal size—call them the militarists, the pacifists, and the humanitarians—and that they had the following **preference orderings** (where ">" is read "preferred to"):

Militarists:	war > sanctions > nothing
Pacifists:	sanctions > nothing > war
Humanitarians:	nothing > war > sanctions

In other words, the militarists supported a coercive policy, and the more coercive, the better. The pacifists thought that war should be avoided at all costs, but they approved of nonmilitary coercion to compel Iraq to end its military occupation of Kuwait. The humanitarians mostly wanted to do nothing, but actually preferred war to sanctions because the costs of sanctions would be borne primarily by the civilian population. Of course, this is an extreme simplification, but it serves as a useful heuristic.

How could these individual preferences be aggregated into a **social choice**? If society was asked to vote between war and sanctions, society would prefer war (both militarists and humanitarians prefer war to sanctions). If the choice was between sanctions and doing nothing, the social choice would be sanctions (militarists and pacifists agree that sanctions are better than doing nothing). Finally, if the choice was between war and doing nothing, the choice would be to do nothing (the preference of pacifists and humanitarians). Aggregating these pairwise contests presents a paradox: *Society*: war > sanctions > nothing > war …

How could society prefer war to sanctions and sanctions to doing nothing, but at the same time prefer doing nothing to going to war? There is an inconsistency (a "cycling") in society's preference ordering; we say that its preferences are *intransitive*. This voting paradox was first noted by the Marquis de Condorcet in the eighteenth century. Kenneth Arrow, a 1972 Nobel Prize winner, further demonstrated that it is impossible to devise a method for aggregating individual preferences to produce a social preference ordering that always satisfies an additional set of criteria we would normally associate with "fairness." This more generalized version of Condorcet's voting paradox is known as "Arrow's impossibility theorem" or, more commonly, *Arrow's paradox*.

The implications of Arrow's paradox for making foreign policy choices in a democracy are profound. What was *the* national interest that prompted the United States to go to war with Iraq in 1991? It is possible that a majority of those Americans who had an opinion did in fact prefer war when compared to any single alternative course of action; not all social choices are confounded by Arrow's paradox. However, the important point is that we should not assume that war was preferred by society just because that was the *chosen* course of action. If group preferences resembled those in our illustration, then the U.S. response to the Kuwait invasion may have been an artifact of the way U.S. options were presented to the American public. If doing nothing was not considered a serious option (which is how the militarists might pose the problem), then indeed war may have been preferred by most people. It is important to know which groups were vocal in making their preferences known, but we also need to know which groups were able to seize the agenda of political debate.

Note: These sorts of dynamics are discussed in Kurt Taylor Gaubatz, "Intervention and Intransitivity: Public Opinion, Social Choice, and the Use of Military Force Abroad," *World Politics* 47 (July 1995), pp. 534–554; see also Kenneth J. Arrow, *Social Choice and Individual Values*, 2nd ed. (New York: Wiley, 1963).

other matters previously considered off-limits—which, to the surprise of many, included a live television broadcast of his condemnation of the 1989 suppression of pro-democracy activists in Tiananmen Square—seemed to suggest that the Chinese were aware of their visitor's domestic political predicament.

The ability of a government to control society and the ability of society's interest groups to communicate their needs and demands to government are both related to the openness of government. **Political openness** is the extent to which a government is subject to influences from society. This means that a government is accountable; it must satisfy the demands of its citizenry or it can be removed from office by regular political procedures that are regarded as fair by most in society. Being open means that opposition groups in society can contest groups in government for the right to control the government, typically through some sort of electoral procedure. Being open also means that such opposition groups can present their positions to the public through a free press and other media, and no group is systematically prevented from opposing the government as long as it does not threaten public order. In the contemporary era, "democracy" denotes a country in which nearly everyone can vote, elections are freely contested, the chief executive is chosen by popular vote or by an elected parliament, and civil rights and civil liberties are substantially guaranteed.

People in government have their own personal interests: to keep or increase their political power, their wealth, and their status within society, or to promote their values and beliefs. These and other interests lead political leaders to seek societal support in order to gain control of government, remain in office, and then implement their policies. To do this, public officials must recognize and respond to the needs of society. Compelled to meet societal demands—fixing high tariffs for the protection of certain industries, sending in the Marines to protect foreign investments, or establishing hard-line policies toward dictators to protect freedom and encourage the spread of democratic government—governmental leaders are just as constrained as they are by the state's material capabilities.

Societal support can also enhance leaders' willingness to act. As we noted in Chapter 5, neither human resources nor economic and military capabilities count for much if a government cannot mobilize them. Governments do not just passively respond to societal demands; they also try to shape and control them. If a government cannot persuade people to get behind its policies and use those capabilities to support its policies, then the capabilities are useless. If the people are not willing to act militarily—for example, because they fear a hopeless, drawn-out involvement—the government itself may be reluctant. Officials in the Reagan administration tried to evade a congressional prohibition on aid to Nicaraguan rebels in the 1980s, which led to the so-called Iran–Contra scandal. President George H. W. Bush, on the other hand, very carefully built up popular, congressional, and international support before going to war with Iraq in 1991. Congress may reflect general public unwillingness to get involved and may refuse to support military intervention, as during the war in Bosnia. The governments of Germany and Japan, when asked to contribute military forces to the Gulf War, responded that they could not do so because of popular opposition to military instruments of foreign policy.

POLITICAL AND STRATEGIC CULTURE

The common experiences of citizens—and the selective memories they have of the experiences of their forebears—help provide the basic structure of belief and ideology through which these citizens view their place in the world, and hence the appropriate roles and actions of their governments. It is therefore important to understand culture, cultural differences, and the impact of culture in the formation and implementation of foreign policy. Analysts have examined states' geopolitical environments, their historical experiences, and political cultures in an effort to account for "national styles" in the conduct of foreign policy. This is sometimes referred to as *strategic culture*.[4] It is instructive to compare, for example, the United States and Russia.

The United States is a country founded largely by immigrants who came to develop a vast and sparsely populated land and to construct a society in a wilderness. Except for the slaves, most people came to the New World to realize hopes that were constrained in their home countries—hopes for political or religious expression or for economic well-being. Their experience in America often offered opportunity and rewarded individual initiative. Especially important for foreign policy, the United States was largely safe from external enemies. Once independence had been won from Britain, the limited transportation technology of the time insulated America from Europe's national wars and provided a security that prevailed for a century and a half.

Russia, by contrast, is inhabited by people who have traditionally lived in insecurity, typified by the wooden stockade fortresses that once dotted the harsh Eurasian plains. Russia was periodically invaded or conquered by Mongols, Poles, Swedes, and Germans, among others. It was ruled by autocratic leaders whose chief virtue was their ability to provide a measure of national unity and strength to ward off attackers. In time, the Russian state expanded, ruling its neighbors instead of being threatened by them. As a multinational empire, czarist Russia, and later the Soviet Union, governed or repressed many subordinate nations, whose total population approached that of Russia itself. Economically, czarist Russia was a relatively primitive society, following well behind Europe in the development of industry and the accumulation of capital. When the Communists took power in 1917, their ideology seemed a threat to the entire capitalist world as they proclaimed the virtues of world revolution. From 1918 to 1920, European, American, and Japanese forces intervened indecisively on the side of the czarist counter-revolutionaries. The communists ultimately consolidated their power, but only by confirming and deepening the Russian autocratic tradition. They built a modern, centralized, industrial state, one finally capable of providing security from invasion. At the same time, they became a constant threat to their neighbors.

Thus, Americans live with a tradition of security that allows them periodic forays into world politics but protects them from basic threats to national survival. Russians, by contrast, live with a tradition of insecurity and mutually threatening

---

[4] For a review of the literature on strategic culture, see Colin S. Gray, "Strategic Culture as Context: The First Generation of Theory Strikes Back," *Review of International Studies* 25 (January 1999), pp. 49–69.

relations with others. Americans live with an economy developed by individual enterprise that provides an unusual measure of opportunity for many (economic development is thought to proceed best when it is least fettered by state interference). Today's Russians live in an economy in which capitalist development began late and was cut short and in which, under the communists, development was controlled and directed by the state bureaucracy. Americans live in a society where the government provided the religious and political liberty so many of its immigrants sought, and where economic freedom was regarded as indispensable for industrial capitalist development. Russians live in a society where people often welcome state control; without control, there can be no unity, no security, and little prosperity.

Individuals, groups, and classes dominant within societies use their power to perpetuate a belief system that will reinforce their power. Americans are taught an ideology that praises freedom and extols capitalism as the engine of prosperity. Russians were taught an ideology that praised the state as the provider of individual and collective security. Though something of a caricature, we might say that in the United States the form of the economy shaped the kind of state that emerged: relatively decentralized, plural centers of economic power whose interests were best served by limiting state control. By contrast, in Russia, the strength of the state determined the kind of economy that emerged; state ownership of the means of industrial production, collectivization of agriculture, and centralized planning during the Soviet era were consistent with Russian political culture. In many respects, the conditions under which both nation-states developed no longer apply. The United States is no longer isolated or completely secure within its borders, the continent is no longer undeveloped, and its economy is well integrated into the global economy. The Soviet Union achieved an unprecedented degree of military security, but the state bureaucracy became a burden on individual and national development, leading to the predicaments facing post-communist Russia today.

How much difference do these contrasting histories make for foreign policy? In an analysis that would become the cornerstone of the U.S. cold war strategy of containment, George Kennan wrote of caution and flexibility in Soviet foreign policy:

> Again, these precepts are fortified by the lessons of Russian history: of centuries of obscure battles between nomadic forces over the stretches of a vast unfortified plain. Here caution, circumspection, flexibility and deception are the valuable qualities.... Its political action is a fluid stream which moves constantly, wherever it is permitted to move, toward a given goal. Its main concern is to make sure that it has filled every nook and cranny available to it in the basin of world power.

Kennan and many others characterized Soviet foreign policy as essentially opportunistic: not bent on world domination but never shying away from opportunities to enhance Soviet power and influence. By contrast, many saw (and continue to see) a crusading spirit in U.S. foreign policy. Inverting Woodrow Wilson's wartime goal "to make the world safe for democracy," they wonder instead how to make American democracy safe for the world. Kennan himself pointed to this dangerous tendency in U.S. foreign policy, which he believed derived from American pride in its history and institutions: "It behooves us Americans, in this connection, to repress, and if possible to extinguish once and for all, our inveterate tendency to judge others by the extent to which they contrive to be like ourselves."[5] Critics once again voiced these concerns when the United States decided to invade (and "liberate") Iraq in 2003.

POWER ELITE OR PLURALISM?

Questions about national style or strategic culture raise further questions about how exactly the foreign policy-making process is influenced by the attitudes and opinions held by members of society. We ought to consider the content of public opinion and ask how public opinion is expressed or shaped within different governmental forms. In what way does it make sense to say that the foreign policy decisions of a democracy represent the wishes of the public? How can public opinion place constraints on the leadership, and what opportunities do the leaders have to frame public debate? We shall look especially at ideas and information about the United States, both because a wealth of information is available and because, in such a well-established democracy, we would expect public attitudes to have a relatively significant effect.

A radical perspective starts with the proposition that interests among the leadership groups in American society converge. In this view, a "power elite" drawn from the highest echelons of society (government, business, the military) determines the nation's goals. Attitudes among most of the public are thus not even relevant. In the words of C. Wright Mills, the most famous proponent of this view:

> The conception of the power elite and of its unity rests upon the corresponding development and the coincidence of interests among economic, political, and military organizations. It also rests upon the similarity of origins and outlook and the social and personal intermingling of top circles from each of these dominant hierarchies.[6]

This perspective holds that those who occupy the leading positions of power in American society basically agree on the fundamental principles by which the society is organized and governed. Although they may disagree about details or the implementation of particular policies, their commitment to the principles of a market economy, regulated yet also protected by the ruling political structures, provides a basic common denominator. These like-minded individuals are held together by common upper-class origins, educational experience, and social and professional mingling.

The contrasting "pluralist" view of American society is held by most liberals and is typified in this comment:

> A substantial part of the government in the United States has come under the influence and control of narrowly based and largely autonomous elites. But these elites do not act cohesively with each other on many issues. They do not "rule" in the sense of

---

[5] George F. Kennan, *American Diplomacy 1900–1950* (Chicago: University of Chicago Press, 1951), p. 127. The long quote is from Kennan [X, pseud.], "The Sources of Soviet Conduct," *Foreign Affairs* 25 (1947), p. 575. See also Joan Hoff, *A Faustian Foreign Policy from Woodrow Wilson to George W. Bush: Dreams of Perfectibility* (Cambridge: Cambridge University Press, 2007).

[6] C. Wright Mills, *The Power Elite* (New York: Oxford University Press, 1956), p. 292. See also G. William Domhoff, *Who Rules America? Power and Politics*, 5th ed. (New York: McGraw Hill, 2005).

commanding the entire nation. Quite the contrary, they tend to pursue a policy of non-involvement in the large issues, save where such issues touch their own particular concerns.[7]

Proponents of this view argue that there is no single power elite, but rather a plurality of elite groupings. Different elites tend to wield influence over different issues (in defense, education, health, and so on); they fight and win different political battles. Although there may be some overlap in the membership of these elite groups, power in American society is not nearly as concentrated as radicals would have us believe. Pluralists emphasize the diversity of opinion and the unpredictability of particular political outcomes rather than any fundamental consensus on the form of political and economic order.

In a sense, the conflict between these two perspectives is irreconcilable. One stresses that diversity, unpredictability, and the clash of opinion surely are real. (Will the defense budget be increased? Will military bases be closed? Will the North American Free Trade Agreement be renegotiated?) The other dismisses this diversity as trivial and stresses the fact that certain values—liberal democracy, free enterprise, and the support of free enterprise by the government—are common denominators for most people in elite positions in the United States (or, for that matter, in Japan or Western Europe). Advocacy of alternative forms of economic or political order (socialism or fascism) is clearly outside the mainstream, being undertaken only by a small minority and without the "sound" perspectives essential for those considered fit for high positions of public trust.

Both views actually are correct. There are important differences within and between elite groups. At the same time, by long-term historic or global standards, the spectrum of respectable opinion on major public-policy issues in America is not especially wide. That spectrum, however, had undergone periodic shifts. Until the Japanese attack on Pearl Harbor, isolationism had many adherents from both the right and the left. By the 1950s, the number of proponents of this view had shrunk to a small minority, which was held in ill repute by the elite. There was instead a substantial consensus on a policy of military alliances, a strong defense, some foreign aid (at least to pro-American and pro-capitalist states), and a generally active involvement by the United States in world affairs. This policy consensus began to break down during the Vietnam War years, as opposition to American military involvement in foreign countries grew. After the Vietnam War was over and the United States seemed to suffer a series of policy reversals with respect to the Soviet Union and its allies in the third world, opposition to an active American foreign policy again became less common and less respectable. The cycle came around once again with the end of the cold war, as there were renewed calls from some circles for American retrenchment from the world scene, and especially strong arguments that the United States should avoid becoming the world's police force. This trend was abruptly halted in 2001 with the George W. Bush administration's

---

[7] Grant McConnell, *Private Power and American Democracy* (New York: Knopf, 1966), p. 339. The best known proponent of the pluralist view is Robert A. Dahl; see especially his *Who Governs? Democracy and Power in an American City* (New Haven, Conn.: Yale University Press, 1961).

"war on terrorism," and sustaining this policy seems to require something very much like an American-led global police force. Public support for this policy began to wane as costs mounted during the U.S. presence in Iraq.

ELITE OPINION AND FOREIGN POLICY

When considering public opinion in general and the opinions of leaders in particular, we should distinguish among various segments of the population. About 20 percent of the American public, for instance, has little or no interest in or information about foreign affairs, or even about politics in general. This group is typically unaware of most international events. For example, in February 2006 more that 60 percent of Americans surveyed could not name the President of Russia (Vladimir Putin) and more than 40 percent could not name the U.S. Secretary of State (Condoleezza Rice).[8] Above the nonpolitical 20 percent is a "middle mass" of 50 to 60 percent of the populace, whose attention moves in and out of politics, depending on the issue and on events. The attentiveness and knowledge of this group usually are not deep.

About one-quarter of American adults—the "attentive public"—are somewhat knowledgeable about foreign affairs; they follow news about other countries and have attitudes that are fairly stable over time. Some of these people talk about foreign affairs with others and discuss their own positions. But only about 5 percent of the population can be considered politically active. Because of their interests and, to a lesser degree, their social roles (for example, teachers, clergy, and active participants in civic affairs), some are considered to be opinion leaders. Within this group is a small segment of the population that gives money or time to political activities and communicates opinions beyond personal acquaintances. These people typically write, speak in public, or otherwise reach an extended audience. Constituting no more than 1 or 2 percent of the populace, this group includes party politicians, business and labor union executives, senior civil servants, professional political commentators ("pundits"), public intellectuals, activists, and leaders of other interest groups involved in political activities.[9]

CONTENT OF ELITE OPINION

Membership in the segment of opinion leaders is closely correlated with education, income, and professional status. People who have a lot of information and are politically active tend to have reasonably consistent attitudes and relate various facts and principles to produce a coherent set of beliefs about the world.

Americans of higher social and economic status have been more inclined to support official policy even more strongly than the average American, whatever that

---

[8] See Gallup, "Gallup Quizzes Americans on Knowledge of World Leaders," February 20, 2006; available at <http://www.gallup.com/poll/21541/Gallup-Quizzes-Americans-Knowledge-World-Leaders.aspx>.

[9] W. Russell Neuman, *The Paradox of Mass Politics: Knowledge and Opinion in the American Electorate* (Cambridge, Mass.: Harvard University Press, 1986); Lawrence R. Jacobs and Benjamin I. Page, "Who Influences U.S. Foreign Policy?" *American Political Science Review* 99 (February 2005), pp. 107–123.

policy has happens to be. In the 1950s and early 1960s, when an activist foreign policy and a strong defense were popular, highly educated, professional, upper-income Americans were even more supportive of U.S. assistance to South Vietnam than were people of lower status. When a withdrawal from some overseas commitments and a smaller defense establishment became popular later in the Vietnam War period, higher-status Americans held those views even more than did the total population. When, in June 1979, SALT II was still fairly popular nationwide and it looked as though it would be ratified by the Senate, higher-status people especially favored it. In the 1980s and 1990s, American elites tended to favor foreign aid programs, both economic and military, and were generally more inclined than the average American to favor sending troops or military assistance to U.S. allies if they should be attacked. In Western Europe, too, the college-educated were much more likely to favor their country's continued membership in NATO than were their less educated fellow citizens, who often endorsed a policy of neutrality toward the two superpowers.

The general tendency of elite opinion to be more supportive of official policy does not mean that American elites are of one mind on such matters. One study has shown that the foreign policy opinions of elites correspond closely to their domestic ideological orientations, which differ greatly. Those who adopt conservative views on such domestic issues as school prayer, environmental regulation, homosexuality, and welfare also tended to adopt a hard-line attitude toward the Soviet Union and were more inclined to advocate militant foreign policies generally (the quest for military superiority, destabilization of hostile regimes, and so on). This link between domestic and foreign policy orientation seems to make foreign policy attitudes resistant to change. This resistance was apparent even after the collapse of the Soviet Union and the end of the cold war, a major transformative event. Domestic conservatives continued to be more wary of the "new world order," and although they revised their assessment of the post-Soviet Russian threat, they seemed to retain a measure of suspicion regarding Russian intentions.[10] Table 6.1 shows some of the striking differences between conservative and liberal elites on various post–cold war foreign policy issues and how earlier views on domestic policy (in 1988) continued to be reflected in foreign policy attitudes four years later—despite the end of the cold war.

Many scholars believe that the general support for official American foreign policy among American opinion leaders has unraveled. One major project has periodically surveyed top-level American leaders since 1974. The first of these surveys found a fragmentation of opinion among those leaders, which the investigators attributed primarily to the impact of the Vietnam War. A small segment of the elite reported that it wanted to seek a complete military victory both at the beginning and at the end of U.S. involvement in Vietnam. Another segment tended to favor a complete withdrawal from Vietnam, not only at the end, but also when the war first became a political issue. Among the two-thirds of the leaders who fell in between these two extremes or who changed their positions in the course of the war, very different conclusions have been drawn about the war and very different preferences for policy are held today. Although these elites in some sense make up

---

[10] See Shoon Kathleen Murray, *Anchors against Change: American Opinion Leaders' Beliefs after the Cold War* (Ann Arbor: University of Michigan Press, 1996), chaps. 4, 5.

TABLE 6.1 | FOREIGN POLICY ATTITUDES OF AMERICAN ELITES AFTER THE COLD WAR

Opinion in 1992	Domestic Political Orientation in 1988 (Percent Approving or Agreeing)		
The United States ...	Conservatives	Liberals	Difference
needs to keep ahead of Russia in strategic nuclear weapons.	79	40	39
needs to develop strategic missile defenses to protect against attack.	81	19	62
must use military force to stop aggression; economic sanctions are not enough.	78	37	41
cannot let down its guard; there are other powerful and aggressive nations.	94	57	37
may support dictators because they are friendly toward us.	59	22	37

Source: Select data from Shoon Kathleen Murray, *Anchors Against Change: American Opinion Leaders' Beliefs After the Cold War* (Ann Arbor: University of Michigan Press, 1996), Table 5.24.

the center of opinion, they show little unity. They have been divided on arms control and security issues, on whether the United States should intervene militarily abroad, and on policy toward human rights and economic development in less developed countries.[11]

These data suggest that there is little elite consensus on the means by which foreign policy should be pursued or even on which ends are most important. It should hardly be surprising that similar divisions exist among the general public and that shifts in policy are often undertaken when a new group of political leaders takes charge of the government after an election or when a transformative world event seems to demand a change in course. This may lead to the emergence of a broad consensus in public opinion, as coalesced around the Bush administration's war on terrorism following 9/11, but such unities of purpose invariably loosen as new policies run into difficulties and as momentous events fade in the public memory.

THE IMPACT OF MASS PUBLIC OPINION

Mass public opinion is no more fixed than elite opinion. Fluctuation in Americans' attitudes regarding foreign threats is illustrated by a public-opinion survey question that has been asked repeatedly for more than sixty years. Although the wording of the question has varied slightly, its basic form has been quite stable: "Do you think we are spending too much, too little, or about the right amount for national

---

[11] Ole R. Holsti and James N. Rosenau, *American Leadership in World Affairs: Vietnam and the Breakdown of Consensus* (Boston: Allen & Unwin, 1984); Ole R. Holsti, *Public Opinion and American Foreign Policy,* rev. ed. (Ann Arbor: University of Michigan Press, 2004).

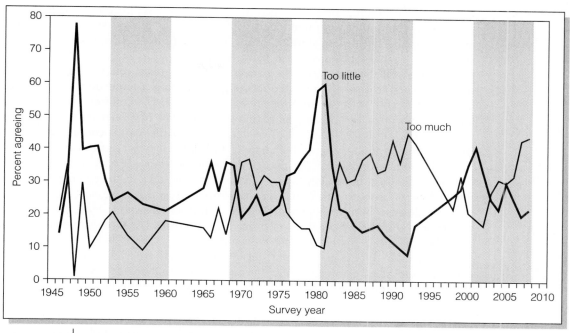

FIGURE 6.1 | AMERICAN PUBLIC OPINION ON DEFENSE SPENDING, 1946–2008

Public opinion on national defense issues often fluctuates over time in response to both domestic and international development. This graph shows the movement in American attitudes toward defense spending levels, based on similar survey questions asked at irregular intervals since the end of World War II. One pattern, especially since the mid-1970s, is that fewer people come to believe that defense spending is too low during Republican administrations (shaded), while more begin to hold that view during Democratic administrations (not shaded).

Sources: Percentages are annual averages from various surveys. 1946–1964 data computed from Bruce Russett, "The Revolt of the Masses: Public Opinion on Military Expenditures," in Bruce Russett, ed., *Peace, War, and Numbers* (Beverly Hills, Calif.: Sage, 1972), pp. 301–306; 1965–1990 data from Thomas Hartley and Bruce Russett, "Public Opinion and the Common Defense: Who Governs Military Spending in the United States?" *American Political Science Review* 86 (December 1992), pp. 905–915; 1991–2008 data from The Gallup Organization, "Military and National Defense," 2008; available at <http://www.gallup.com/poll/1666/Military-National-Defense.aspx>.

defense and military purposes?" Figure 6.1 shows the pattern over time. The graph shows substantial fluctuation in the early years of the cold war, before a popular and elite consensus was established. After the Korean War, a period of stability ensued, during which more people preferred increasing rather than reducing defense spending, but the majority of the population was content with the existing level. This consensus was shattered by the antipathy toward the military generated by the Vietnam War. Since then, opinions on this matter have proved very fluid. The antimilitary mood of the early 1970s faded and was then abruptly reversed by worsening relations with the Soviets, the Iranian seizure of American diplomats as hostages in 1979, and then the Soviet invasion of Afghanistan. But by the mid-1980s that mood, too, had passed, leaving almost half the population feeling that the Reagan defense buildup had gone far enough. The Gulf War was popular and marked the beginning of a new period of increasing support for higher defense budgets, a trend that continued until defense spending rose sharply after 9/11. Since the mid-1970s, these shifting trends in public opinion have been closely associated with changes in the political party holding the presidency.

Throughout the cold war, U.S. national security policy, and the public attitudes that supported it, seemed anchored in the great ideological and power rivalry with the Soviet Union. A basic component of that policy, U.S. military spending, was largely predictable by looking at changes in the level of Soviet military spending and at public support for increases or decreases in American spending. The end of the cold war brought remarkable changes in both policy and attitudes. Rationales for U.S. military spending, for the use of military force abroad, and for international cooperation have likewise changed. As people revised their beliefs about the Soviet Union between 1987 and 1988, attitudes toward some specific policies—such as defense budgets—also moved in a dovish direction. Since then, as the uncertainties of the post–cold war order and the threat of terrorism have become manifest, the move has been in a hawkish direction.

The public, of course, does not speak with a single voice, and many of the divisions we see in elite foreign policy attitudes also hold for the populace at large. Those with conservative opinions on domestic issues tend to be hawkish on issues pertaining to foreign affairs; domestic liberals tend to be dovish. Moreover, what separates American opinion leaders from the masses helps to account for differences within mass public opinion. Generally speaking, those with higher incomes and higher levels of education have been somewhat more likely to support arms control—according to Gallup polls, the gap can vary from 5 to 10 percent—reductions in defense spending, lower tariffs, and fewer restrictions on immigration. But higher education and income does not always translate into dovish foreign policy attitudes. These groups were more likely to support U.S. air strikes against the Serbs during the Bosnia and Kosovo conflicts, as well as the dispatch of U.S. troops to keep the peace. In 1995, when surveys were conducted on attitudes toward the U.S. atomic bombing of Japan fifty years after the event, these groups were also more likely to approve of that decision.

THE GENDER GAP

Women at all education and income levels are generally more dovish on foreign policy than men—the so-called **gender gap**. Public opinion polls in 1991 indicated that fewer women than men approved of the decision to use U.S. military force to liberate Kuwait. Women were also less likely to approve of NATO air strikes on Bosnian Serb positions in 1995, although they did not differ significantly from men when it came to sending U.S. peacekeepers to Bosnia. Women's retrospection on the atomic bombings of Hiroshima and Nagasaki has tended to be much more critical than men's as well.

In 2001, in the aftermath of the September 11 attacks in New York and Washington, the level of public support for a U.S. military retaliation against al Qaeda was around 90 percent—for *both* men and women—leading many to point to the disappearance of the gender gap. However, when we begin to scratch below the surface, we see that a gender gap actually remains, as is clear from

TABLE 6.2	GENDER GAP IN THE UNITED STATES: SUPPORT FOR MILITARY RETALIATION FOR 9/11 TERRORIST ATTACKS		

	Percent Supporting Retaliation		
Conditional on	Men	Women	Gap
U.S. ground troops used in an invasion	85	76	9
Military draft reinstituted	84	72	12
U.S. military action lasting several years	74	58	16
1,000 U.S. troops killed	76	55	21
Further terrorist attacks occurring in United States	85	72	13
Less money to spend on social programs	83	72	11
Overall support	90	88	2

Source: The Gallup Organization, "Men, Women Equally Likely to Support Military Retaliation for Terrorist Attacks," 5 October 2001, available at <http://www.gallup.com/poll/4963/Men-Women-Equally-Likely-Support-Military-Retaliation-Terrorist-Attacks.aspx>.

Table 6.2. Women's support for retaliation is more conditional. As women were asked to consider the potential costs—on the battlefield or on the home front—a majority still support retaliation, but their level of approval diminishes sharply relative to men. The largest gap emerges over the question of U.S. battle deaths, where 21 percent fewer women than men would support military action if these costs were high. Before the second war against Iraq in 2003, women were more opposed to U.S. military action than men by nine percentage points.

The precise explanation for the gender gap is a subject of debate among feminist scholars. One view, sometimes called *standpoint* or *cultural* feminism, suggests that aggression and violence are masculine characteristics and that women are more forgiving and peace-loving. Although an extreme version of this sort of explanation would trace these differences to the very biological essences of man and woman (an "essentialist" view), most of these scholars emphasize the differences between masculine and feminine roles as they have emerged from social practice.[12] Above all, women in American society, and in most others, fulfill a nurturing role. The standpoint feminist view holds that because women's identities have become so closely tied to childbearing and child rearing, women are inclined to oppose foreign policy actions that present a threat to human life. Thus, society's gender roles explain women's support for foreign policies that bring about peace and, more generally, improve the quality of life. This perspective offers not only an explanation of the gender gap, but also a normative argument that solutions to some enduring

---

[12] An argument sympathetic to the essentialist view is Francis Fukuyama, "Women and the Evolution of World Politics," *Foreign Affairs* 77 (September/October 1998), pp. 24–40; see also the reactions in "Fukuyama's Follies: So What If Women Ruled the World," *Foreign Affairs* 78 (January/February 1999), pp. 118–129.

problems in world politics are better approached by drawing upon women's unique experiences.

A different view, derived from "liberal" feminism, disputes any natural inclination of women to differ from men in their attitudes about world politics, whether based on biological essence or socially constructed gender roles. This view suggests that at least some of the observed differences between men and women really boil down to differences in education and income. If women enjoyed the same socio-economic opportunities as men, the so-called gender gap would vanish. Liberal feminists frequently point to women leaders who have broken through society's "glass ceiling"—Margaret Thatcher (Britain), Indira Gandhi (India), and Golda Meir (Israel), for example—as evidence that women behave no differently from men in the conduct of foreign policy. Nor have women holding high positions in the U.S. foreign policy establishment—Jeanne Kirkpatrick, Madeleine Albright, and Condoleezza Rice—necessarily championed more dovish postures than their male counterparts.[13]

The underrepresentation of women in the highest echelons of government, and especially in the corridors of the foreign policy making, seems especially pronounced in the United States, but the gender gap is not an exclusively American phenomenon. As Table 6.3 suggests, women in Europe were less inclined than men to have their nation support the U.S. war on terrorism launched in 2001, whether by making available their national intelligence services, military bases, or soldiers. European women are also less supportive of arming groups who fight

TABLE 6.3 | GENDER GAP IN EUROPE: SUPPORT FOR RESPONDING FOR 9/11

Response	Percent Supporting Response		
	Men	Women	Gap
National intelligence service available to U.S.–led coalition	73	68	5
Military bases available to U.S.–led coalition	65	51	14
Contribute troops to U.S.–led coalition	54	43	11
Supply weapons to groups opposing states harboring terrorists	37	30	7
Humanitarian aid to civilian victims of the conflict	90	90	0

Source: EOS Gallup Europe, "Flash Eurobarometer 114: International Crisis," December 2001, available at <http://europa.eu.int/comm/public_opinion/flash/fl114_en.pdf>. Surveys were conducted in each of the European Union member states, and figures are EU-wide percentages.

---

[13] Other feminist views more closely align with the constructivist and reflectivist approaches discussed in Chapter 3. See, for example, Cynthia Enloe, *Globalization and Militarism: Feminists Make the Link* (Lanham, Md.: Rowman & Littlefield, 2007); Charlotte Hooper, *Manly States: Masculinities, International Relations, and Gender Politics* (New York: Columbia University Press, 2000).

against governments that sponsor terrorists (although men are not much in favor of that either). Although research continues on its generality and ultimate causes, the gender gap in foreign policy attitudes is an empirical fact in many countries and on many issues. State leaders in democracies can ill afford to ignore it.

PUBLIC APPROVAL OF STATE LEADERS

Although King Louis XIV's claim "l'État c'est moi" no longer applies (if it ever did), the head of state is often said to embody the national interest. He or she is at the top of the political pyramid and is responsible for bringing together all the separate individual and group interests. Personality, character, experience, and leadership style surely matter in determining what choices a leader makes. Also relevant is the relationship he or she has with advisers and subordinates, the people who provide information, help make decisions, and are responsible for implementation. We look at individual characteristics and decision-making roles in the next chapter. Here we want to ask another kind of question: How constrained is the top leader by mass and elite opinion in the society? Does public opinion matter to the chief? If so, when and how?

According to one view, mass opinions set limits on the range of actions that a political leader may safely take. For example, the anticommunist ideology—and, at times, hysteria—among the American public imposed some constraints on the U.S. government's freedom of action in international affairs. Policy makers in the 1960s feared a backlash from the general populace in reaction to major foreign policy reverses in the government's effort to contain international communism. They remembered the domestic political costs incurred by the Truman administration resulting from the trauma of "losing China" and the witch-hunting of the 1950s. Referring to Senator Joseph McCarthy, who led the campaign against alleged communist subversives, former Senator Sam Ervin once said to an interviewer, "You can't believe the terror that man spread among politicians." Politicians came to fear electoral defeat as a punishment for perceived foreign policy setbacks, even though they themselves were too sophisticated to accept the premises behind those public attitudes.

Consequently, believing that the American people would not tolerate the "loss" of Vietnam, senior officials in Washington resolved that Vietnam would not be lost—at least, not during their term in office. They would hang on and escalate when necessary to avoid defeat, even though they knew that the long-term prospects for holding the country were poor. They could hope to postpone the day of reckoning until a time when they themselves would not be held responsible, perhaps even hoping against all available evidence that events would break favorably so that the ultimate outcome would not be disastrous.

A very different point of view, however, maintains that the leader has a deep reservoir of potential support among the populace for virtually any kind of foreign policy initiative. A leader can take either hawkish or dovish initiatives and, with the authority and respect he or she commands, still be backed by a substantial portion of the population. The ability of a nation's leader to gather popular support for foreign policy initiatives, especially during an international crisis (and provided the leader is perceived as doing something about it), has been termed the **rally-'round-the-flag** effect. The phenomenon can be seen in the experience of almost all

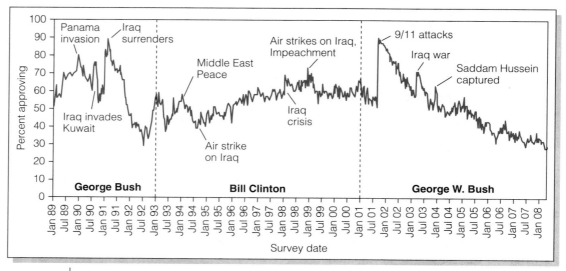

FIGURE 6.2 | PRESIDENTIAL JOB APPROVAL, 1989–2008

American public approval of presidential job performance, like other attitudes, responds to both domestic and international developments. A foreign policy crisis can have an especially strong impact, producing a rally-'round-the-flag effect in the form of a spike in approval ratings. These are often short-lived, however, as quick military campaigns end and public attention turns elsewhere or as conflicts wear on and the public increasingly disapproves of the costs. *Source: The Gallup Poll Monthly* (Princeton, N.J.: The Gallup Poll), various editions. The most recent data are from The Gallup Organization, "Presidential Job Approval in Depth," 2008; available at <http://www.gallup.com/poll/1723/Presidential-Job-Approval-Depth.aspx#2>.

recent U.S. presidents. Figure 6.2 illustrates the pattern of responses to a standard Gallup survey question asked two or three times every month: "Do you approve or disapprove of the way [name] is handling his job as president?" Fluctuations in job approval are the result of many influences, including domestic events and the state of the economy as well as foreign policy and international events. Presidents generally begin with a "honeymoon" bump in popularity immediately after taking office, and nearly all presidents experience some decline in their popularity over their terms in office as they carry out policies that displease various groups in the population. The elder George Bush had that experience, and in his case the long-term decline was magnified by his sharp, but temporary, bursts of popularity associated with major initiatives in the field of national security. Bill Clinton seems to have defied this tendency, at least through the middle of his second term, perhaps because his initial popularity was rather modest compared to that of many other U.S. presidents.

When, in December 1989, President George H. W. Bush ordered U.S. troops to invade Panama to depose the government of Manuel Noriega, his popularity rating rose by nine percentage points. It then fell fairly sharply until Iraq's invasion of Kuwait in August 1990, which triggered Bush's quick decision to impose an economic embargo and send American troops to defend Saudi Arabia against a possible Iraqi attack. That rally, however, was very short-lived, as people began to fear war with Iraq and the country was deeply divided about the wisdom of war. In the beginning of 1991, by which time Bush had carefully cultivated national and international support, negotiations with Iraq failed. Bush's support rose by an extraordinary amount—about 19 percentage points—with the beginning of the air war, then went down for a while, and rose again by nine points with the short and successful land campaign of Operation Desert Storm. However, we see from Figure 6.2 that all these rallies were extremely brief. They usually waned within two or three months, and they did not prevent a long-term decline in Bush's popularity, which, by mid-1992, brought his ratings nearly as low as Jimmy Carter's lowest ratings.

With the end of the cold war and the absence of anything that could be depicted as an immediate threat to vital American interests, President Clinton gained very little benefit from rally effects. As Figure 6.2 shows, he got a short blip of popularity (7 points) in June 1993 by ordering an air strike against Iraq in retaliation for a plot to assassinate former President Bush. A somewhat larger increase (10 points) followed in September when Yitzak Rabin and Yasser Arafat traveled to Washington for the historic Declaration of Principles by Israel and the Palestinian Liberation Organization—and a historic handshake. But that gain was short-lived because many blamed Clinton for the October 1993 deaths of American peacekeepers in Somalia. Most popularity changes associated with any Clinton foreign policy action were very small and may have been nothing more than chance variations. International economic achievements have not generated substantial praise from the American public; there were no jumps accompanying the passage of the North American Free Trade Agreement (NAFTA) in November 1993 or the General Agreement on Tariffs and Trade (GATT) world trade agreement in December 1994, none accompanying U.S. efforts in February 1995 to stem the fall of the Mexican peso, and none in January 1998 to contain the East Asian financial crisis.

The rally-'round-the-flag effect is not just a preoccupation of survey researchers and presidential advisers. Indeed, it caught the imagination of Hollywood with the release of the 1997 film *Wag the Dog*, a fictional account of presidential advisers who, when the chief executive is accused of molesting a Girl Scout, concoct an international crisis requiring U.S. military action in the hope that the president's approval rating will recover in time for his reelection. In an uncanny case of life imitating art, the film was playing in theaters when President Clinton's alleged involvement with a White House intern was made public in January 1998, right in the midst of a mounting confrontation with Iraq over UN weapons inspections. As the U.S. military prepared for an armed response to Iraqi intransigence, Clinton was accused by many, including the Iraqis themselves, of using the confrontation to deflect public criticism of the alleged affair (his approval rating went up 10 points during the last week of January). The rally-'round-the-flag effect had by then become such common knowledge that the Clinton administration went to great pains in an effort to reassure critics that the president was not trying to take advantage of it. Future American presidents may have to do the same.

Leaders of other countries may also try to take advantage of a rally-'round-the-flag effect. In spring 1982, British Prime Minister Margaret Thatcher gained great personal popularity by her tough response to the Argentine seizure of what Britain calls the Falkland Islands, and she won the next election handily.[14] The Argentine

---

[14] David Sanders, Hugh Ward, and David March, "Government Popularity and the Falklands War: A Reassessment," *British Journal of Political Science* 17 (March 1987), pp. 281–314.

military government also hoped to benefit from a rally. It chose a time when it was politically unpopular and the Argentine economy was stagnating to rekindle the long-standing dispute with Britain and invade the islands. However, the effort to make itself popular backfired when it lost the war, and the military government was then overthrown.

The head of state cannot do whatever he or she wants and expect general public support. There is some evidence that threatening or using force against foreign adversaries is initially more popular than are conciliatory or cooperative acts. The former seem to produce a rise of four or five percentage points in the president's popularity; the latter, only a one- or two-point change, often downward. But public's reaction depends partly on its images of the president. Presidents perceived by the public as doves, as Carter was, tend to be most approved when they talk or act tough, as Carter did to the Soviet Union when it invaded Afghanistan. President Reagan, who was generally seen as a hawk, gained especially from more dovish acts. While the public approved his military action in Grenada in 1983, it also approved when he withdrew the Marines from Lebanon. In 1987, to the consternation of some of his military and hard-line political advisers, Reagan signed an agreement with the Soviets on nuclear arms control in Europe. One motivation may have been to restore some of his flagging popularity. Major steps forward in Israel's acceptance of eventual Palestinian statehood have been taken by prime ministers such as Yitzhak Rabin and Ariel Sharon, whose hard-line credentials had been amply demonstrated during Israel's past wars.

The ability of a leader to shape public opinion and thus to generate support in a crisis usually holds for the short term only, and even in the short term may be negligible unless the government devotes some effort to framing the event for public consumption.[15] The life of a burst of popular support is four or five months at the most, and more often it is only about two. By the end of that time, support usually returns to its previous, lower level. The reason for this is related to the reason for the rally in the first place. In the first week or two after a sudden military action or major diplomatic event, criticism of the president, even by opposition political leaders, is usually muted. The president has the most information about foreign policy and security affairs, especially in fast-breaking crises. Opposition leaders who criticize the president risk being exposed as poorly informed. The absence of criticism looks like bipartisan support to much of the public, so ordinary people are also reluctant to criticize. In time, however, as either the government's policy begins to falter or less favorable information about the circumstances becomes available, opposition political leaders become bolder, and their renewed criticism is picked up by the media and then by the general public. The rally effect then decays.

These tendencies were all visible during the presidency of George W. Bush. The astounding bounce in public support after the September 11 attacks illustrates particularly well the social-psychological dimension of the rally-'round-the-flag effect.

---

[15] Shoon Kathleen Murray, "Tough Talk, Public Predispositions, and Military Action: Reassessing the Rally-'Round-the-Flag Phenomenon," in Harvey Starr, ed., *Approaches, Levels, and Methods of Analysis in International Politics: Crossing Boundaries* (New York: Palgrave, 2006).

Within two weeks of the attacks, Bush's job approval rating was 90 percent: 39 percentage points higher than on September 10 (the highest gain and highest over-all approval rating in the history of the Gallup poll). Although partisans on both sides debated the administration's immediate reaction to the attacks, most would agree that there was nothing the Bush administration was actually *doing* in the days following 9/11—sealing the country's borders, reassuring the public, rounding up suspected terrorists and material witnesses, and so on—that could fully account for the near-universal approval of his job performance. Even before the ultimatum to the Taliban regime in Afghanistan to turn over Osama bin Laden, the president's rating stood at 86 percent. The country simply felt victimized, and it reacted by ral-lying around its leader. The remainder of the president's first term witnessed a steady decline in public approval to pre-9/11 levels—punctuated by significant pos-itive spikes during Operation Iraqi Freedom in 2003 and at the time of Saddam Hussein's capture in mid-December. As his second term was coming to an end in 2008, his approval stood at near-record lows for any departing U.S. president. Par-allel to that was a fall in the confidence of the people in other countries; surveys in twenty countries found that the percentage of the public expressing approval of the U.S. war on terrorism had dropped an average of twenty-one points between 2002 and 2007.[16]

DO WARS WIN ELECTIONS?

The shorter the decision time available to a leader—and it may be quite short dur-ing an international crisis—the less constrained by public opinion he or she is likely to be. The short-term rally effect helps powerfully. This effect is especially strong in national security affairs because people tend to feel that the commander-in-chief has special competence and access to the best (often secret) information. However, if a crisis drags on, dissenting voices become more widely heard and constraints built into the democratic system of governance become more effective. The elder Bush was careful to make clear to American critics of his policy that the United States had many allies and UN approval for his action against Iraq. Even so, Amer-ican strategy was geared to a short war with few American deaths so as to end the conflict before domestic opposition could build. The younger Bush has continu-ously reminded the American public that the war on terrorism will be a long one and that they should expect casualties, in effect trying to lower the public's expec-tations of a "quick and clean" campaign. Nevertheless, the image of his May 2003 appearance on the deck of the USS *Abraham Lincoln,* framed by a banner reading "Mission Accomplished," would repeatedly come back to haunt the administration as the U.S. presence in Iraq dragged on.

An American president who wishes to respond militarily to a foreign adversary can mount an action with existing military forces and without prior approval from

---

[16] This and much similar information on international perceptions can be found in Ole Holsti, *To See Ourselves as Others See Us: How Publics Abroad View the United States after 9/11* (Ann Arbor: Uni-versity of Michigan Press, 2008).

Congress. A majority of the public will probably support the action and, if successful, it may be widely applauded. The year-in, year-out maintenance of military action abroad, however, requires ongoing congressional approval and appropriation of funds; trade-offs with domestic welfare and civil liberties become much more apparent and politically salient. For example, the willingness of the American public to accept restrictions on civil liberties in exchange for enhanced national security—as provided in the Patriot Act, passed by both houses of Congress with wide margins—was quite high in the immediate aftermath of 9/11, but had declined significantly by the end of 2004.[17] Domestic constraints may therefore limit the president's menu of choices in a crisis by favoring those forms of military action (aerial bombardment, massive ground assault, possibly even the use of nuclear weapons) that bring quick results, rather than protracted warfare with heavy American casualties.

In the long run, wars almost always diminish the political capital of those who conduct them. After a brief spurt of national unity, wars typically produce a loss of social cohesion and low popular morale, manifested in higher rates of strikes, crime, and violent political protest. Least healthy for a leader is, of course, to lose a major war; every great-power government that lost a major war in the past century was overthrown from within, if not by its external enemies. But even leaders, and their parties, who conduct and win costly wars are likely to be punished by the voters. Winston Churchill, the popular British World War II leader, lost the 1945 election to the Labour party by a landslide. Governments lose popularity directly in proportion to the length and cost (in blood and money) of the war. All of America's wars of the past century showed this pattern, with the president who was in office when the war began (or his party) faring poorly in subsequent elections.[18] The invasion and subsequent occupation of Iraq became the single most important issue in the 2008 presidential campaign, despite the fact that U.S. combat fatalities were low by historical standards.

Political leaders, especially in a democracy, live a precarious life in which the demands made on them always exceed the leaders' capacities to satisfy. They are expected to solve many (and often contradictory) social problems, to provide employment and prosperity without inflation, and, of course, to maintain peace while confronting dangers. They know that they will be rewarded or punished at the polls in proportion to the healthiness of the economy, but modern economies are complicated systems, often beyond ready political control. Government taxation and spending will help some people and hurt others; leaders may be unable to buy electoral popularity by filling their constituents' pocketbooks. If leaders cannot control the economy, they may then turn to international armed conflict in order to increase their domestic support, a tactic known as **diversionary war**.

---

[17] See Darren W. Davis, *Negative Liberty: Public Opinion and the Terrorist Attacks on America* (New York: Russell Sage Foundation, 2007).

[18] Sometimes they won the elections, but by a smaller margin than would be predicted from the prosperous state of the economy. See Timothy Cotton, "War and American Democracy: Voting Trends in the Last Five American Wars," *Journal of Conflict Resolution* 30 (December 1986), pp. 616–635.

According to one study, a U.S. president is more likely to use or escalate military force if he is seeking reelection during a developing or ongoing war—the proverbial "October surprise"—because he knows that voters will be more concerned than usual about foreign affairs and therefore more likely to hold it against him if the war goes badly. He is also more likely to win congressional approval on even unrelated international issues in the month following a use of force. Another study showed that over the past century, U.S. presidents have been more likely to use, or threaten to use, military force internationally in years when the economy was doing badly or when there was a national election. As an authority on the U.S. presidency says: "The desperate search is no longer for the good life but for the effective presentation of appearances. This is a pathology because it escalates the rhetoric at home, ratcheting expectations upward notch by notch, and fuels adventurism abroad."[19]

Leaders of other democratic governments show similar behavior. A study of Israeli decisions to use force found that the Israeli government was more likely to respond militarily before a national election or when the economy was doing poorly. An example was the raid on the Iraqi nuclear reactor on June 7, 1981. That was just three weeks before Menachem Begin, the incumbent prime minister, was to face voters in a general election. However justified the military strike may have been, it could have been postponed for a few months with little harm to Israeli security. As it was, Begin's party benefited greatly from an outpouring of public approval despite severe economic difficulties from inflation. In states without obvious military enemies, the rally effect can be dramatic, even in the event of a policy conflict with their allies. For example, support for a ban on nuclear weapons entering New Zealand almost doubled (from 40 percent to 76 percent) after the government adopted such a ban and the United States responded with a confrontational policy.[20] If countries are more likely to engage in international military disputes when periods of domestic political turmoil coincide with opportunities abroad, this does not mean that leaders deliberately involve their countries in war solely to boost their own electoral chances. Sometimes they may actually be taking dramatic steps for peace or arms control or, more often, they may be tempted to talk tough, make threats, or indulge in small-scale displays of military force to impress the voters or divert their attention from economic troubles. The risk is that sometimes these acts can get tragically out of hand.

The evidence that leaders often do try to divert attention from domestic problems with foreign adventures is nevertheless mixed. Some studies have not found any such pattern. Perhaps most democratic leaders are less cynical than we might imagine. Alternatively, the leaders of foreign countries may anticipate their reactions. Expecting democratic leaders to be tempted to undertake foreign diversions

---

[19] Theodore Lowi, *The Personal President: Power Invested, Promised Unfulfilled* (Ithaca, N.Y.: Cornell University Press, 1985), p. 20. The two studies are Richard J. Stoll, *U.S. National Security Policy and the Soviet Union* (Columbia: University of South Carolina Press, 1990), chap. 3; Charles W. Ostrom and Brian L. Job, "The President and the Political Use of Force," *American Political Science Review* 80, 2 (June 1986), pp. 541–566.

[20] James W. LeMare, "International Conflict: ANZUS and New Zealand," *Journal of Conflict Resolution* 31 (September 1987), pp. 420–437.

near election time, when the economy is doing badly, or just when the government's popularity is down in the polls, potential antagonists may be especially careful not to act in a provocative manner. By behaving cautiously, they would be behaving strategically, thinking ahead in the continuing "what will they do if I do this?" game of international politics.[21]

WHO GOVERNS? PUBLIC OPINION MATTERS

Presidents and prime ministers do worry about their popularity with the public. It affects not only their own or their party's prospects for reelection but also their ability to get support for their legislative programs. Franklin Roosevelt was the first president to use scientific opinion polling extensively; he closely watched public opinion before Pearl Harbor to determine his strategy for moving the United States into World War II. He first chose greater military spending and lend-lease—not the draft or direct intervention—because those instruments offered the greatest potential for domestic approval. President Reagan developed an extensive organization to monitor public opinion and used that information in making decisions. President Clinton was even accused of "governing by public opinion poll." Leaders thus, in some sense, both respond to and manipulate public opinion. They respond to it by doing what will be popular in the short run when domestic economic and political conditions encourage them to maximize votes. They also may manipulate it by trying to increase their popularity without correcting the underlying causes of mass discontent that endangered their popularity in the first place.

The U.S. Congress is said to be especially sensitive to the needs and demands of particular, narrow interests. More precisely, members of Congress are likely to be especially sensitive to the needs of major interests in their constituencies or other interests that provide them with support at election time. Defense industry executives can expect a favorable hearing from U.S. representatives in whose districts they employ many workers. Representatives from Iowa will care about foreign grain sales. The representative who chairs the House Merchant Marine Committee is likely to be solicitous of shipowners, shipbuilders, and merchant sailors, wherever their interests are located. They can provide (or withhold) financial and other support at election time.[22]

Yet international and security issues are remote for most people, even those of the upper socioeconomic classes. Only a small proportion of the population directly benefits from military spending. In any given year, relatively few citizens travel very far abroad and even fewer obtain much information relevant for evaluating complex foreign policy issues. Foreign policy is thus a prime candidate for what has been termed "symbolic politics," situated as it is well beyond most

---

[21] Brett Ashley Leeds and David R. Davis, "Domestic Political Vulnerability and International Disputes," *Journal of Conflict Resolution* 41 (December 1997), pp. 814–834; Alastair Smith, "Diversionary Foreign Policy in Democratic Systems," *International Studies Quarterly* 40 (March 1996), pp. 133–153.

[22] For a comprehensive examination, see James M. Lindsay, *Congress and the Politics of Foreign Policy* (Baltimore: Johns Hopkins University Press, 1994).

people's day-to-day lives and not affecting their immediate welfare.[23] People do have opinions about foreign policy, sometimes strong ones, but not necessarily because the implementation of foreign policy imposes costs or benefits on their material existence (like their wallets).

Elites seem more likely than others to support official policy. They are no more or less likely than others to be personally affected by foreign policy, nor do they have distinct beliefs or psychological needs. But they are more likely to live in a social environment in which international affairs are considered important. When cues in their environment change, they are more likely to change their opinions for two reasons. First, new information indicating that a given foreign policy is inconsistent with personal beliefs and interests is more likely to reach elites, who are better informed than the mass public, thus prompting them to reassess their beliefs. Second, because such a reassessment is more common among higher-status groups, support from their social environment for the old beliefs will diminish and support for new beliefs and corresponding foreign policy will be reaffirmed.

One example is security policy in Western Europe during the cold war. Support for official NATO defense policy was always strongest among the elites there. The mass public was often less committed to NATO and to specific policies concerning nuclear weapons. During the Reagan administration, nuclear strategy underwent a change (which we discuss in Chapter 9), and the revised strategy entailed the deployment of new intermediate-range missiles in Europe during 1983. Despite near-solid support among European governments (and elites), the general public was very skeptical. Official NATO policy was always that NATO would never start a war but that it reserved the right of enacting a "flexible response" to a Soviet attack, including the option of using nuclear weapons. The new deployment of nuclear missiles in Europe seemed to increase that likelihood in the minds of most ordinary Europeans, who were extremely worried about the consequences of using nuclear weapons in that densely populated region of the world. Fewer than 20 percent in the major countries (Britain, France, Italy, and West Germany) said that they approved of a first-use policy. This long-standing tension between elite and mass attitudes in Europe posed problems for Western security policy and the unity of NATO. It required the pursuit of double-track negotiations: deploying new nuclear forces while simultaneously trying to negotiate a mutual disarmament pact with the Soviet Union.

Sometimes leaders are able to implement defense or foreign policy measures even when public opinion opposes them, as suggested by NATO's deployment of missiles in the face of widespread public protest in Europe. Similarly, in 1978, President Carter urged senators to do the "statesmanlike" thing and support the Panama Canal treaties, despite the sentiment against the treaties, which was evident in most opinion polls. Two-thirds of the Senate did support the treaties, which were ratified. The next year, however, Carter met with failure. SALT II was favored by

[23] David O. Sears, "Symbolic Politics: A Socio-Psychological Theory," in Shanto Iyengar and William J. McGuire, eds., *Explorations in Political Psychology* (Durham, N.C.: Duke University Press, 1993); Murray Edelman, *The Symbolic Uses of Politics*, 2nd ed. (Champaign: University of Illinois Press, 1985).

more people than opposed it, but many either had no opinion or had never heard of the treaty. With such lukewarm approval in the mass public and a worsening international atmosphere, a majority of the Senate remained unconvinced. SALT II was dropped by the Reagan administration when it took office.

A review of public opinion and government policy changes between 1935 and 1979 found that in two-thirds of all cases (including foreign policy issues) where there was a shift in public opinion and a subsequent change in public policy, the policy change was in the same direction as the public opinion change.[24] This evidence seems to indicate that the American democratic form of government is fairly responsive to the will of the general public. We must nonetheless be cautious with this interpretation because we do not know why public opinion changes. It may well be that public opinion changes because opinion leaders and elites—including government officials—first express a preference and then persuade both the attentive public and the mass public to voice that preference. Then Congress, including some of the very people who helped change public opinion, can "respond" to that public change. Certainly this possibility often seems more plausible than the simple notion of Congress merely being obedient to the "will of the people."

Overall, our view of the importance of public opinion and the interaction between opinion change and policy change is complex. The impact of public opinion depends very much on the kind of issue, the circumstances, the level of government at which the decision is made, and other specific features of the political context. Certainly there is no immediate, automatic connection, even in a democracy, between public opinion and foreign policy. Political decision makers are skilled leaders of opinion, with ready access to television, newspapers, and other media; they shape opinion as well as respond to it. Always we are bedeviled by the problems of making inferences about power and of differentiating between the activity of people or pressure groups and their influence. It is clear, however, that public opinion does matter. What Robert Dahl said about New Haven, Connecticut, applies to the United States as a whole and to many other countries, even on matters of foreign policy: "If we ask 'Who Governs?' the answer is not the mass nor its leaders but both together."[25]

---

[24] Benjamin I. Page and Robert Y. Shapiro, *The Rational Public: Fifty Years of Trends in Americans' Policy Preferences* (Chicago: University of Chicago Press, 1992). A more recent and less approving view is Benjamin I. Page and Marshall Bouton, *The Foreign Policy Disconnect: What Americans Want from Our Leaders but Don't Get* (Chicago: University of Chicago Press, 2006).

[25] Dahl, *Who Governs?*, p. 7.

Individuals and World Politics: Roles, Perceptions, and Decision Making

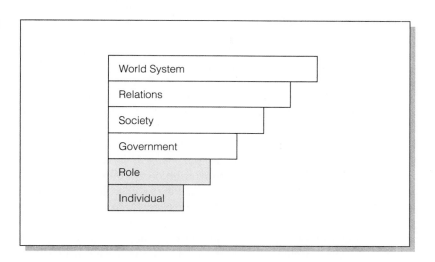

| World System |
| Relations |
| Society |
| Government |
| Role |
| Individual |

RATIONAL DECISION MAKING

Foreign policy decisions are made by people, either as individuals or as part of a group. The individual foreign policy decision maker is embedded in a decision-making environment that constrains and limits in many ways what the decision maker is able or is likely to do. Each layer of this environment blends into others. There are connections between international and societal factors, between societal and governmental factors, and between governmental and role factors. In this chapter, we examine the individual in world politics as affected by role and by personal idiosyncrasies. These factors impinge directly on the individual decision maker who plays a part in the development and execution of foreign policy.

The foreign policies of states are constantly in motion. At the center of a state's foreign policy are individuals engaged in **decision making**—the process of evaluating and choosing among alternative courses of action. When we study foreign policy decision making, we look not only at the chosen courses of action (the *content* of foreign policy) but also at the factors that influence how and why decisions are made (the foreign policy *process*). Many of the factors that affect the foreign policy menu of states derive from the perceptions and images of individuals in government. If a restaurant menu is illegible; if the diner misinterprets the menu, thinking, for example, that wine is served free of charge (when it is not); or if an individual feels pressured, say, to order an appetizer just because others in the party are doing so, then the diner's choice has been affected. Our concern in this chapter is with those things that affect how individuals perceive world politics and how they make foreign policy decisions—that is, how they act upon their willingness when presented with opportunities.

Foreign policy analysis often involves making judgments regarding good and bad decisions. Many discussions stress the idea that the best decision is the most "rational" one. However, **rationality** is a complex and contested concept, one that carries different connotations for different analysts.[1] In the simplest formulation, rational behavior is purposive behavior, so "instrumental rationality" is an ability to relate means to ends. Exactly how closely means and ends are related, with what certainty they are related, and how closely the actual consequences of behavior match the consequences that are desired all depend on an understanding of the decision-making process. We can identify two basic views on these questions. One view of rationality assumes that decision makers possess all relevant information, which is used to determine the course of action that maximizes benefits relative to costs. The other view points to the difficulties encountered by humans (and organizations) when they try to digest large amounts of information, especially in an effort to calculate the costs and benefits associated with all possible courses of action. This view agrees that rationality involves purposive behavior, but it also recognizes the limits imposed by human and organizational capability.

The first view is an idealized picture of decision making, a checklist of "perfect" conditions that would permit "perfect" decisions. No one claims that these conditions can be achieved by foreign policy makers; in fact, a great deal of research has demonstrated why these conditions cannot be achieved. However, policy makers do attempt to approximate this ideal, with varying degrees of success. Graham Allison identified the essential elements of this **rational actor model**. Faced with a given problem or opportunity, the rational decision maker first clarifies the foreign policy *goals* of the nation and determines which should take priority over others. National values and priorities provide guidance in the search for the best policy response, a search that adheres to certain "decision rules." The rational actor model assumes that the decision maker identifies all *options* available for achieving the nation's goals and then evaluates the *consequences* of these alternative courses of action. Because alternative courses of action and their consequences involve both benefits and costs, they must be ordered

---

[1] See Jonathan Mercer, "Rationality and Psychology in International Politics," *International Organization* 59 (Winter 2005), pp. 77–106; Bruce Bueno de Mesquita and Rose McDermott, "Crossing No Man's Land: Cooperation From the Trenches," *Political Psychology* 25 (April 2004), pp. 271–287.

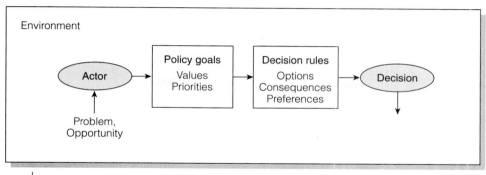

FIGURE 7.1 | RATIONAL ACTOR MODEL OF DECISION MAKING

The rational actor model provides an idealized view of how actors make foreign policy decisions. Once a stimulus is received from the environment, actors clarify their goals, evaluate their options and determine their preferences, and then make a decision. "Rationality" refers to this instrumental process of decision making, not to the goals or preferences that actors adopt or to their estimates of success.

from most to least preferred on that basis. Finally, the decision maker *chooses* the course of action that ranks highest in this preference ordering.[2] This idealized decision-making process is depicted in Figure 7.1.

A good analogy for the rational actor model is an individual playing a game such as chess. In chess, the goal is to trap the opponent's king. There may be other intermediate objectives, such as capturing the opponent's queen and protecting one's own, but the ultimate goal is checkmate. At each turn, the player considers his or her alternatives and the consequences of possible moves. What are the costs and benefits of each move? Will it position the pieces for checkmate? Will it result in the loss of a pawn, a bishop, the queen? Based on this assessment, the player chooses a move. Whether the decision turns out to be a good one or a bad one depends largely on how thoroughly and accurately the player considered the alternative moves and assessed the risks of each.

One approach to analyzing world politics is to conceptualize an international interaction as a game being played by two or more players. Alternative courses of action available to each player are seen as possible *moves,* and the combination of moves made by all players leads to an *outcome.* Each outcome has a *payoff* or *utility* for each player equal to the sum of all benefits derived from that outcome minus the costs. By using available information about outcomes and their utilities, a player will make the move that **maximizes** utility. Because outcomes are not always certain—they depend on one's own moves and on the moves of other players, with perhaps an element of chance as well—players also need to estimate the probability of achieving a given outcome. When they take into account both the utilities associated with different outcomes and the probabilities of achieving them, they maximize their *expected utility.*

---

[2] See Graham Allison and Philip Zelikow, *Essence of Decision: Explaining the Cuban Missile Crisis,* 2nd ed. (New York: Longman, 1999), chap. 1. Allison's pioneering study was first published in 1971.

Models of foreign policy that represent the decision-making process in this way are called *formal models,* and, because they rest on the assumption of instrumental rationality, they are also called *rational choice models.* If a strategic situation involving two or more actors is set up in this way—with players, moves, outcomes, and utilities (or at least preference orderings) specified—then *game theory* can be used to predict players' moves and the most likely outcome of their interaction.[3] (In Box 7.1 we illustrate how a border conflict might be examined using simple game theory, and in subsequent boxes we will give more developed examples involving such things as an arms race, nuclear deterrence, and trade negotiations.)

The notion of perfectly rational decision making was questioned many years ago by Nobel Prize–winning economist Herbert Simon. He pointed out in a famous formulation that the decision maker does not maximize utility but rather **satisfices**. This means that the rational decision maker searches for an *acceptable* choice, one that satisfies a minimal set of requirements. Instead of reviewing *all* possible alternatives, the "satisficer" will usually pick the *first* alternative that meets this minimal set of requirements. Simon argued that people do attempt to achieve the best outcomes for themselves, but their actions are guided by a "bounded rationality." That is, rational choice is limited by the capacity to process information and the tendency to adopt a necessarily simplified conception of the world. During the Vietnam War, for example, there was a tendency within the U.S. military to focus on the number of enemy deaths as an indicator of the successful prosecution of the war, when a more exhaustive evaluation of available information would have told them otherwise and might have led to less disastrous choices.[4]

RISK TAKING

Other refinements of the rational actor model focus on the concept of utility. Utility is defined very generally in game theory as the total worth that a player attaches to a particular outcome. In world politics, this worth may be composed of material benefits and costs (in terms of wealth, territory, military capability, and so on) as well as intangibles like status and prestige. The rational actor model assumes that the decision maker estimates utility by engaging in a cost–benefit analysis of each possible outcome, but that begs the question of what goes into such a calculation. Nor does the model address the possibility that individuals sometimes approach costs and benefits differently. Decision makers clearly wish to maximize their gains and minimize their losses; but considering a range of different possibilities, they may be inclined to embark on a course of action that maximizes their minimum

[3] For an overview of the rational choice approach, see Duncan Snidal, "Rational Choice and International Relations," in Walter Carlsnaes, Thomas Risse, and Beth Simmons, eds., *Handbook of International Relations* (London: Sage, 2002). For a critique of this approach to security studies, see Stephen M. Walt, "Rigor or Rigor Mortis? Rational Choice and Security Studies," *International Security* 23 (Spring 1999), pp. 5–48; see also the rejoinders in *International Security* 24 (Fall 1999).

[4] See Herbert Simon, *Models of Bounded Rationality* (Cambridge, Mass.: MIT Press, 1982). For an application to wartime decision making, see Scott Sigmund Gartner, *Strategic Assessment in War* (New Haven, Conn.: Yale University Press, 1997).

IN GREATER DEPTH

BOX 7.1 | **WORLD POLITICS, GAMES, AND GAME THEORY**

When the rational actor model is a reasonable approximation of the foreign policy-making process, analysts often treat actors (typically states) as players engaged in a **game** consisting of moves and countermoves. As an example, consider the border dispute between Peru and Ecuador. The two countries have long disputed ownership of portions of territory along their common border. In December 1994, Peruvian intelligence notified the leadership that Ecuadorian base camps had been established in one such region in the Cenepa Valley. A crisis commenced early in 1995 when Peru launched air and ground attacks, which was followed by a six-week border war. Of course, this was a serious incident in which many lives were lost and was not a "game" like chess and bridge are games. But the initiation of an international crisis involving Peru and Ecuador can be represented as a series of moves and examined using **game theory**— a mathematical approach to analyzing strategic interactions between two or more players.

In our example, the two *players* are Peru (P) and Ecuador (E), and one way to represent their interaction is with a game tree. In the following diagram, Ecuador has a choice to make: to challenge Peru (by establishing base camps) or to not challenge Peru. Thus, the first *choice node* (●) on the tree is labeled E, and two branches extend from that node indicating Ecuador's two possible *moves*. If Ecuador does not mount a challenge, then the *outcome* (■) is the status quo. If Ecuador does challenge, then the play of the game moves to the second node, labeled P. Peru now must choose whether to defend its claim to the territory (in which case the outcome is a crisis) or to not defend its claim (in which case Peru capitulates). When an interaction is represented in this way as a series of sequential moves (here, just two moves), the game is said to be in "extensive form."

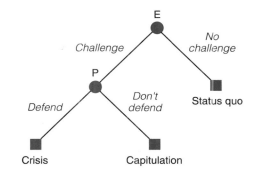

Now imagine that the interaction was structured somewhat differently. Suppose, in the context of escalating verbal threats, the Peruvian leadership felt that there would be no time to deliberate over what to do in response to an Ecuadorian move into the disputed region. The military would need to be given instructions on whether to respond to a challenge *before* knowing if Ecuador planned to mount a challenge. That is, the moves we are considering are not sequential but simultaneous because Peru lacks information about Ecuador's opening move. Instead of a game tree with choice nodes, this interaction can be represented as a two-by-two matrix in which both sides choose their moves without knowing the choice of the other side. In our particular example, although there are four possible combinations of moves by Ecuador and Peru—the four cells in the matrix—there are really only three possible outcomes, as before. If an Ecuadorian challenge does not come, the outcome (the status quo) is the same whether the Peruvian military was instructed to defend or not defend its claims. In contrast to the extensive form, here the game is represented in "strategic form."

continued

BOX 7.1 | WORLD POLITICS, GAMES, AND GAME THEORY *continued*

	P Don't defend	Defend
No challenge	Status quo	Status quo
E		
Challenge	Capitulation	Crisis

example, not so simplified as to leave out key aspects) and if we have a good idea of the utility that each outcome has for each player, then the solution to the game should correspond to what actually happened—or to what will happen. (We take up game solutions in subsequent boxes.) Accurate predictions (and even "post-dictions") are not easy to achieve in the social sciences, but game theorists have made significant strides in this regard, especially in the field of economics. Game theory is now widely used to study politics, including world politics, although many doubt it will meet with the same degree of success as in economics.

Game theory not only provides a way to represent strategic interactions between players but also a way to analyze their interactions in order to predict an outcome. This is called "solving" the game. If the interaction is appropriately represented (for

Note: A good introduction to the game theory, with many examples from international relations, is James D. Morrow, *Game Theory for Political Scientists* (Princeton, N.J.: Princeton University Press, 1994). See also Scott Gates and Brian D. Humes, *Games, Information, and Politics: Applying Game Theoretic Models to Political Science* (Ann Arbor: University of Michigan Press, 1997).

gains (a *maximin* strategy) or, alternatively, that minimizes their maximum losses (a *minimax* strategy). This is largely a question of one's attitude toward risk.

Such matters have been a central concern of psychologists, and one body of work known as **prospect theory** has found that individuals do indeed have a tendency to treat gains and losses differently. Decision makers seem to fear losses more than they covet gains, which translates into a willingness to take greater risks to protect what they have and fewer risks to acquire what they want. The status quo—for example, a state's current territorial possessions—often becomes a *reference point,* which helps to predict "risk-averse" or "risk-seeking" behavior. But the status quo is not always the reference point, and knowing a decision maker's actual reference point is important. Generally, we would expect states to take fewer risks to acquire territory than to prevent the loss of territory. This may be part of the reason why in 1990 the United States and other countries dismissed early signals that Iraq would invade Kuwait. The fact that Saddam Hussein considered Kuwait to be Iraq's rightful territorial possession—part of the Basra province of ancient Mesopotamia, which was his reference point—should have indicated to observers that they should take seriously the possibility that he would engage in risky behavior (military invasion) to repossess Kuwaiti territory.[5]

---

[5] For a review of prospect theory and the implications for foreign policy decision making, see Jack S. Levy, "Prospect Theory, Rational Choice, and International Relations," *International Studies Quarterly* 41 (March 1997), pp. 87–112. See also Rose McDermott, *Risk-Taking in International Politics: Prospect Theory in American Foreign Policy* (Ann Arbor: University of Michigan Press, 1998).

None of these challenges to the rational actor model imply that decision makers are irrational, only that actual decision making departs from the ideal model in various and significant ways. Nor do they suggest that rational choice approaches to the study of world politics are doomed to failure because of these imperfections. Game theory and its applications to international relations are constantly undergoing innovation to take into account decision makers' attitudes toward risk, the availability of only limited information, and other insights into the decision-making process. Like any approach, game theory's usefulness rests on its ability to explain behavior in the real world.

GOVERNMENTAL DECISION MAKING

Governments differ in many ways. They differ in the types and numbers of their component organizations and institutions, the distribution of influence among them, the numbers and types of personnel in the organizations and institutions, and the societal interests they represent. Some governments are large, made up of many organizations and staffed by hundreds of thousands of people; some are small, with far fewer organizations and people to staff them. Some governments centralize power in one institution or group; others distribute governmental power among a number of institutions. Some have strong executives who make most foreign policy; some have weak executives or executives restricted by other governmental bodies. Governments also have different forms of executives. In the United States, a president shares foreign policy powers with Congress; Britain's system is a parliamentary system run by a cabinet and a prime minister. In France, there is both a president and a prime minister, who are sometimes from different parties. Other systems are ruled by single parties or single individuals, as in communist governments or military dictatorships.

Some analysts argue that closed, centralized governments can act more quickly and efficiently with less public input into the process. Others maintain that more open systems can get the most out of their societies and that, although democratic governments work more slowly and with less unity of purpose, they produce better foreign policy because they get more diverse and accurate information from society, giving them a better grasp of the constraints they face in both the domestic and foreign environments. Open and closed systems also differ in the quality of their information processing. Analyzing how well information is collected and employed may be the most useful way we have for comparing governmental structures as producers of effective foreign policies, including how well they "learn" and adapt to the world.[6] In this section and the next, we also look at information processing in units smaller than whole governments—at how information is handled by individuals and variously sized groups when making decisions.

How any individual affects a foreign policy decision and its implementation depends on the individual's role within the government as well as personal factors.

---

[6] Jack S. Levy, "Learning and Foreign Policy: Sweeping a Conceptual Minefield," *International Organization* 48 (Spring 1994), pp. 279–312; and Dan Reiter, *Crucible of Beliefs: Learning, Alliances, and World Wars* (Ithaca, N.Y.: Cornell University Press, 1996).

We must take into account where each person stands in the government (within which organization, how close to the central decision maker). The nature of decision unit is particularly important. One group of scholars has defined the "ultimate decision unit" as a group of actors who have both the ability to commit resources and the power and authority to do so. They also identify three broad types of decision units: a predominant leader, a single group, and multiple autonomous groups.[7] There are many examples of predominant leaders (especially in authoritarian systems), among them Joseph Stalin and Saddam Hussein. Single groups would include the Soviet and Chinese politburos and the British cabinet. In the conduct of American foreign policy, a single group constitutes the ultimate decision unit under certain circumstances; on matters of war and peace, this is usually the National Security Council. During the Cuban missile crisis in 1962, when the Kennedy administration discovered that the Soviet Union had secretly placed medium-range missiles in Cuba despite assurances that it would not do so, it was President Kennedy's Executive Committee (the ExComm) that dealt with the situation.

The decision unit changes depending on the type of decision being made. A standard typology distinguishes among crisis decisions, general foreign policy decisions, and administrative decisions. *Crisis decisions* generally involve a few, very high-level decision makers. A crisis consists of a perceived threat to the decision makers and their state and a finite time period within which to make a decision (usually very short). Some analysts also add the element of surprise to the characteristics of crisis. *General foreign policy decisions* set out future foreign policy, looking at the present and into the near future (and often beyond). The positions of the European Union states on potential membership for former Eastern bloc countries, China's efforts to develop relationships with states in a position to supply its future energy needs, and the Bush administration's turn to military action as a primary means of combating international terrorism are all examples of general foreign policy decisions. *Administrative decisions* are concerned with very specific situations; they are usually handled by a specific part of the foreign policy bureaucracy. They involve routine situations calling for the application of the expertise and standard operating procedures of foreign policy organizations.

Crises are defined by their position along three dimensions—level of threat (high), decision time (short), and awareness (surprise)—and these dimensions can be used to construct a "decision cube" like the one depicted in Figure 7.2. Crisis decisions are located toward the front, lower-left corner of the cube. Especially intense crises, such as the Cuban missile crisis and the 9/11 attacks by al Qaeda, are located closest to that crisis corner. For example, when the top leadership in the Bush administration received word that hijacked passenger jets had crashed into the World Trade Center towers and the Pentagon, a decision had to be made in a matter of minutes to scramble fighters and instruct pilots to shoot down any additional passenger planes that might be approaching the White House or the Capitol. Here a surprise event required decision makers to choose a course of

---

[7] Margaret Hermann and Charles Hermann, "Who Makes Foreign Policy Decisions and How: An Empirical Inquiry," *International Studies Quarterly* 33 (December 1989), pp. 361–387.

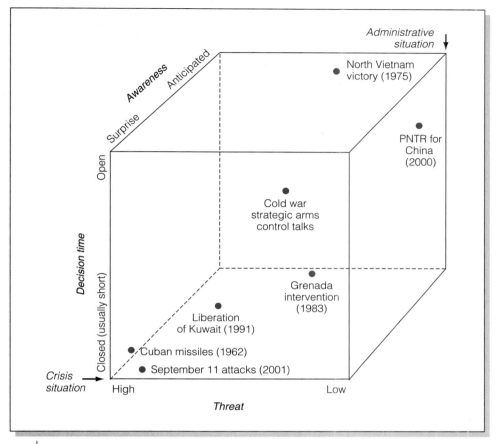

FIGURE 7.2 | A DECISION CUBE (AMERICAN PERSPECTIVE)

Foreign policy decisions can be located according to the degree of threat faced by the nation (horizontal axis), the time allowed for deliberation (vertical axis), and prior awareness that a decision is required (receding axis). Crises are unanticipated, involve high levels of threat, and require quick decisions; the Cuban missile crisis and the 9/11 attacks are good examples. Other decisions, such as the granting of permanent normal trade relations to China, are anticipated well ahead of time, involve nonthreatening situations, and allow much more time for deliberation.
Source: Modified from Charles F. Hermann, "International Crisis as a Situational Variable," in James N. Rosenau, ed., *International Politics and Foreign Policy* (New York: Free Press, 1969), Figure 1.

action in an extremely short time in order to avert an extremely high threat to the country's top leadership.

In contrast to crises, administrative decisions involve little threat and can usually be anticipated well in advance of the time when a decision must be made; they are located toward the back, upper-right corner of the cube. The American response to the fall of Saigon in 1975 was not an administrative matter, but the event was clearly anticipated and, with most U.S. combat personnel out of South Vietnam by then, the military threat to the United States was modest. (On the other hand, how to evacuate the American embassy as the North Vietnamese army approached did take on crisis proportions for local U.S. officials.) General foreign policy decisions typically fall somewhere between the two extremes of crisis and administrative decisions, with their exact positions determined by the particular characteristics of the policy situation. During the cold war, it was U.S. policy to engage the Soviets in strategic arms-control negotiations. Although the Soviet nuclear arsenal was threatening to American security, the threat was not imminent, especially when the two sides were talking. That provided negotiators with an open-ended time line for arriving at a decision, and, indeed, the Strategic Arms Limitation Talks lasted years.

The participants in a crisis decision are of the highest level and relatively few in number. General foreign policy decisions usually involve a large number of medium-level officials interacting with one or two of the high-level foreign policy players. Administrative decisions usually involve low-level officials. This is why different observers come up with different descriptions of how people make decisions. A variety of decision processes can be identified, generally involving different groups of decision makers (or different decision units) as well as different types of foreign policy situations. The problem becomes even more complicated if we look at the distinct stages of any particular decision. Decisions may be broken down into a predecisional stage, a formulation stage, and an implementation stage. The *predecisional* stage involves the collection of information and views and the scanning of the foreign policy horizon for possible problems and issues. The *formulation* stage involves the actual selection of an alternative after evaluating the possibilities. In the *implementation* stage, the decision has been translated into some form of action or foreign policy behavior.

INFORMATION: SCREENING AND PROCESSING

We can think of organizations, individuals, or any self-regulating system as having to react to the environment—to *steer* through it by learning. Steering requires *feedback*: the receipt of information from the environment about the consequences of existing policies. Positive feedback usually amplifies or reinforces our behavior, encouraging us to continue our current policy. Negative feedback indicates that we are moving away from our goal or missing it by ever greater distances and that our policy must be changed to bring it back toward the target. How information gets back to us and how it is processed along the way (by governmental organizations or by individuals) affects our image of the world and how to behave in it. In the early 1960s, when the United States was becoming involved in Vietnam, in what direction should the nation have steered? Should it have continued involvement, or should it have changed course and disengaged? Similar questions concerning steering—of taking a series of steps that ultimately lead away from one's goals—were raised about the U.S. invasion of Iraq and the continued deployment of large numbers of American troops there, troops that could have been more effectively deployed in Afghanistan against resurgent al Qaeda and Taliban forces.

The rational actor model of decision making tends to assume "perfect information"—the notion that all of the information pertinent to a decision is available and processed by the decision maker. But individuals, especially those occupying high-level positions in government, cannot acquire and comprehend all the relevant data, even when it is available. Some of it is screened out. Some information is simply ignored; some is reinterpreted so as not to upset existing views or beliefs; some is looked at quickly and then discarded. Both individual mental processes and collective organizational processes perform this **screening** function. The decision maker's ideology or worldview makes some things look more important and others less so. Different people in different parts of government, or different people occupying the same position in government (the same role) but at different times, may not all see similar situations in similar ways. Various factors combine to affect the way a person sees a problem, and because these factors vary across individuals, not all people see the same problems when they survey the foreign policy landscape.

Information overload forces us to choose which information to consider and which to ignore. In World War II, the Allies' strategy for locating the D-day landings consciously took advantage of information overload by deluging the Germans with information, much of it false. Under this onslaught of intelligence, it was hoped that the Germans would miscalculate the invasion site—and that was exactly what happened. Today, citizens and emergency personnel in the United States and other countries are often warned that there has been an increase in "chatter"—intercepted communications from suspected terrorist cells, the content of which is not well understood. Some of this chatter certainly pertains to ongoing or planned operations, but it is also possible that it is sometimes used deliberately to provoke a reaction by governing authorities.

In a government broken up into various organizations, each organization will often deliberately pass along only information that is beneficial to itself and not all the information that might be relevant to the situation. In the Bay of Pigs fiasco in 1961, the CIA gave President Kennedy only select information, that which suggested a high probability of success in overthrowing Castro's government. Because of individual psychological screens or organizational screens, decision makers may ignore or fail to grasp the significance of important information that they do have. All the information necessary to anticipate a Japanese attack on Pearl Harbor was in the possession of the American government before December 7, 1941, but because there was so much "noise"—unimportant or irrelevant pieces of data—the true signals were missed. Those signals that did get through to decision makers, especially those stationed at Pearl Harbor, were dismissed through the working of psychological screens.

The rational decision-making model confronts a paradox. As a decision maker is bombarded by more and more information, more and more screens, both organizational and psychological, are used to deal with information overload. Decision makers must reduce the amount of information received so that they can function. Nearly 200 nation-states, hundreds of IGOs, thousands of NGOs, and many other nonstate actors send out information through words and deeds, while hundreds of diplomats as well as intelligence-gathering agencies are charged with reporting on this activity. Decision makers in the contemporary system can be overwhelmed with information. Overload forces decision makers to decide what to decide. Paying attention to one issue, situation, or crisis forces them to ignore others. The paradox: In order to function, decision makers must distort their view of the real world, a deviation from the rational decision-making model. The issue then becomes what degree of distortion is acceptable and how we can recognize and deal with it when it is not.

ORGANIZATIONS AND BUREAUCRACIES

Governments, including those portions involved in the foreign policy process, are made up of many parts—individuals and organizations. Therefore, decisions are the products of the interaction, adjustment, and politics of people and organizations. Decision making often proceeds according to a *quasi-mechanical process* by reference to past decisions, precedents, or routines—the "standard operating procedures" of organizations. Organizations within governments all have a catalog of past behavior on which to draw. Bureaucrats tend to be conservative and reluctant to try new approaches; they are happy with incremental changes based on past decisions and behavior. One way to reduce the complexity of the world and thus reduce uncertainty is to act as one has acted before. Organizations tend to have rule books, guides, and manuals that indicate how things should be done. Anyone who has requested special treatment at the department of motor vehicles or the university registrar knows how difficult it can be to get a clerk to deviate from standard operating procedures.

Graham Allison discusses a second model of decision making that contrasts sharply with the rational actor model. This **organizational process model** suggests that what occurs today (at time t) is the best predictor of what will happen tomorrow (at time $t + 1$). The model may be summarized by three main points. First, the government is not a monolith but a constellation of interlocking organizations steered by political leaders at the top. Second, most activity within these organizations is programmed; specific situations are dealt with according to already established routines. Third, organizational activities that follow these standard operating procedures tend to be inflexible and adapt to unpredictable circumstances with great difficulty. Foreign policy is thus an "outcome" of this rather mechanical organizational process, which affects both the decision that is made and its implementation.[8]

The organizational process model highlights the importance of role factors in decision making. Role is important because it affects the way an individual *thinks* he or she should act. It has been defined as those aspects of an actor's outlook and behavior derived from his or her policy-making responsibilities, aspects that are expected to characterize *any* person filling the same position. In most cases, an individual in a governmental position is in a situation where precedents exist—behavioral patterns established by individuals who previously held the office. A strong personality, unafraid to innovate, shock, or take political risks, may overcome the constraints of precedent. Others may find it comfortable to tread a well-worn path.

---

[8] Allison and Zelikow, *Essence of Decision*, pp. 166–178. On the impact of organizational processes on war, see Jack S. Levy, "Organizational Routines and the Causes of War," *International Studies Quarterly* 30 (June 1986), pp. 193–222.

The individual who performs a specific role is often expected to follow the needs and requirements of the organizational setting rather than personal convictions. Before World War I, Winston Churchill deplored the naval arms race between Germany and Britain, recognizing that both states were spending large sums of money and raising international tensions in a competition to build more and better battleships. He also recognized that when the process was over, both sides would be in approximately the same relationship as before, and all the effort would have been futile. However, as First Lord of the Admiralty, he went before Parliament and requested more funds for naval construction. Colin Powell, who served as chairman of the Joint Chiefs of Staff during the first Bush and Clinton administrations, was often at odds with officials in the Pentagon when he served as secretary of state under George W. Bush. His insistence that the United States attempt to work through the United Nations before resorting to military force against Iraq was due in part to his personal inclinations, but it also reflected the interests and diplomatic mission of the organization he headed.

In addition to the quasi-mechanical dimension to decision making in large organizations, there is a social element. In a *social process,* decision makers interact and the result of that social interaction and maneuvering is a decision. Foreign policy making involves politics; it emerges from a normal process of political competition and compromise, a process that includes elements of bargaining, adjustment, arm twisting, favor trading, and the like. This is the heart of Allison's third model of decision making, the **governmental politics model**. This image of foreign policy decision making starts with the organizational process model but goes further to integrate the social element. Foreign policy decisions are not merely the outcomes of organizations following standard operating procedures. They are "resultants" of various bargaining games among bureaucratic players within the government. Each player—president, prime minister, first secretary, adviser, senator, foreign minister, general, cabinet member—sets goals, assesses alternatives, and makes choices, as we would expect of any rational actor. But given the limitations on information processing and other imperfections in the decision-making process, each individual player falls short of the ideal posited by the rational actor model. Still, most of what should be considered will be considered because others are involved in the process, each with his or her own goals and information about alternative courses of action and their consequences.

Members of different organizations see different sides of a situation, depending on how that situation affects (and perhaps threatens) their organization. As Allison summarizes the situation, "where you stand depends on where you sit." An individual's priorities and self-interests are seen to derive in large measure from the organization's self-interests. In contrast to the notion that there exists some single *national* interest, there is an array of organizations and therefore *bureaucratic* interests. Of course, each organization (or bureau) argues that its interests are similar to, or necessary ingredients of, the national interest. But in reality there are many separate interests, and those interests must be reconciled in the social process of foreign policy making.

Organizational process and governmental politics can be seen as two sides of the same coin. The parochial nature of organizations is a core concept of Allison's organizational process model. Each organization within a government has a narrow range of interests and priorities. The mission of an organization requires capabilities—people and money—which is where bureaucratic "pulling and hauling" comes in. To acquire the necessary resources, an organization needs influence within the government, especially on budgetary matters and decisions that distribute new programs and responsibilities to government organizations. Members are deeply concerned with "organizational health," the protection (and often the expansion) of the organization's mission, especially as measured by budgetary and staffing allocations. A navy, for example, sees its mission as combat and combat support on the high seas. The only problem is that submariners think this mission is best achieved by subs, proponents of air power support the use of aircraft carriers, and advocates of sea power stress the importance of surface ships.

Organizational health can also be protected by demonstrating how successful the organization is or by highlighting mistakes made by competing organizations. One reason why organizations follow standard operating procedures is to cut down on uncertainty and risk. Organizations behave incrementally for the same reason. However, the protection of the organization also entails providing information to top-level decision makers that shows the organization in the best light. This involves withholding information that would embarrass the organization and implementing top-level decisions in a way that meets its best interests, even if not necessarily in the spirit intended by top-level decision makers.

PRINCIPALS AND AGENTS

Organizations provide individuals with roles and the expectations attached to them. The longer a specific role exists, the more precedents are set and the more widely held are the expectations of other government members for people assuming that role. As an institution becomes older and more complex, it is more difficult for an individual to shape the role to his or her own suiting. New positions in government, on the other hand, provide more leeway for an individual to shape the role rather than be constrained by it. Tom Ridge, the first secretary of the U.S. Department of Homeland Security, had more maneuverability within his bureaucracy than his counterparts in the Departments of State or Defense. In addition, the higher the position is in the governmental hierarchy, the fewer constraints that role will impose on the individual who fills it; one has fewer superiors and is more likely to be confronted with new or unexpected situations that call for innovative responses.

The impact of a role also depends on the individual's personal characteristics and especially his or her political skills. The governmental politics model considers the power and skill of individual players to be important. Much of the power derives from an individual's position in government, but this power can be expanded or reduced, depending on the personality and skill of the players involved. Although William Rogers was secretary of state for most of the Nixon years, Henry Kissinger was the unquestioned primary adviser to the president on foreign policy and national security matters. In Kennedy's administration, the secretary of defense, Robert McNamara, played a more central part in foreign affairs than did Secretary of State Dean Rusk. And during the George W. Bush administration, Dick Cheney wielded a degree of influence unprecedented for a vice president.

Individual capacities to overcome role constraints does not necessarily translate into the ability to control policy implementation. Even presidents have thrown their hands up in despair at their inability to get various sections of the bureaucracy to do what they want in the way they want. Franklin Roosevelt likened the navy to a feather pillow—no matter how hard or how long one punched it, it always came out the same. During the Cuban missile crisis, Kennedy ordered the Strategic Air Command (SAC) to go to Defense Condition 2. This was the first time that the U.S. military had been taken to this level of alert; it involved placing the nuclear missile force and airborne strategic bombers on an exceptionally high degree of launch readiness. Normally, the military communications accompanying the alert process are encoded. The signal that Kennedy intended for Khrushchev was to be sent and received as Soviet intelligence observed the U.S. military activities associated with the alert. But in this case, Soviet intelligence was able to intercept unencoded U.S. military communications between SAC's senior commanders—a flaunting of U.S. nuclear superiority that must have alarmed Soviet leaders.

> Equally extraordinary, and not known in Moscow, was that this remarkable display of American power was unauthorized by and unknown to the president, the secretary of defense, the chairman of the Joint Chiefs, and the ExComm as they so carefully calibrated and controlled action. . . . The decision for bold action was taken by General Thomas Power, commander-in-chief of SAC, on his own initiative. He had been ordered to go on full alert, and he did so. No one had told him how to do it, and he decided to "rub it in."[9]

This is a good illustration of the **principal–agent problem**. A principal is an individual (or group) with ultimate authority, but who must delegate tasks to an agent, usually because the principal does not possess the resources (like time or expertise) necessary to accomplish those tasks. The problem arises because the interests of the principal and the interests of the agent can and often do diverge. In this example, the objective of the principal—both Kennedy and McNamara—was crisis management and the aversion of a U.S.–Soviet war. The agent, General Power of SAC, presumably was not interested in provoking a nuclear conflagration but seems to have had his own ideas about how best to deal with the crisis. Agents often have better access to information and other resources than do principals, and this allows them to pursue their own or their organization's interests at the expense of the interests of their principals. Economists and political scientists who study principal–agent relations within large organizations tend therefore to focus on ways in which the behavior of agents can be brought into line with the objectives of principals—and how both of these can be brought into line with the public interest.[10]

---

[9] Raymond Garthoff, *Reflections on the Cuban Missile Crisis*, rev. ed. (Washington, D.C.: Brookings Institution, 1989), p. 62.

[10] See, for example, Peter D. Feaver, *Armed Servants: Agency, Oversight, and Civil-Military Relations* (Cambridge: Harvard University Press, 2003); Deborah D. Avant, "Are the Reluctant Warriors Out of Control? Why the U.S. Military Is Averse to Responding to Post–Cold War Low-Level Threats," *Security Studies* 6 (Winter 1996/1997), pp. 51–90.

SMALL GROUP INTERACTION

Sociologists and psychologists who study organizational and group behavior have found that being a member of a small group can strongly affect both the perceptions and the behavior of the individual. One advantage of social decision processes noted earlier was that, although each individual has limited information and a narrow set of perceived alternatives, when that individual interacts with others, a wider range of information and alternatives becomes available. But countervailing forces also operate. Pressures to conform to the view of the group often alter the individual's perceptions of both the situation and role he or she should play in the decision-making process. In a series of laboratory experiments, groups of six to eight people were asked to compare visual images—the length of two lines or the size of two cubes, for example. However, only one member of the group was actually being observed each time this experiment was performed; the others (unbeknownst to the single subject) had been instructed to give false answers. Subjects, after repeatedly hearing the other members of the group say that the shorter line was longer or that the smaller cube was larger, reacted with puzzlement and dismay. But as the experiment continued, they began to conform and described the objects as the others did.[11]

GROUPTHINK

The pressure on an individual to conform to the views seemingly held by others in small-group settings has been examined closely by Irving Janis. The psychological dynamics he observed gave rise to a phenomenon he called **groupthink**. In one study, Janis looked at a number of American foreign policy decisions—such as the Bay of Pigs invasion in 1961, the Cuban missile crisis of 1962, and the escalation of the war in Vietnam—and summed up his general findings as follows: "The more amiability and esprit de corps among the members of a policy-making in-group, the greater is the danger that independent critical thinking will be replaced with groupthink, which is likely to result in irrational and dehumanizing actions directed against out-groups."[12]

Janis identifies eight interrelated symptoms of groupthink, two of which involve the group's self-image. A close and friendly group will produce an *illusion of invulnerability*. This feeling is associated with excessive optimism that the courses of action considered by the group will succeed in achieving their foreign policy goals, and thereby encourages risk taking. Similarly, the group tends to have an *unquestioned belief in its own morality,* that this assemblage of decent people is unlikely to settle upon any course of that is not right and proper under the circumstances. This symptom fosters group screening by encouraging the group members to ignore the ethical or moral consequences of their

---

[11] These now legendary experiments are reported in S. E. Asch, "Effects of Group Pressure upon Modification and Distortion of Judgment," in Darwin Cartwright and Alvin Zander, eds., *Group Dynamics: Research and Theory* (Evanston, Ill.: Row, Peterson, 1953), pp. 189–200.

[12] Irving L. Janis, *Groupthink*, 2nd ed. (Boston: Houghton Mifflin, 1982), p. 13; the symptoms of groupthink, presented below, are summarized on pp. 174–175. See also, *Groupthink in Government: A Study of Small Groups and Policy Failure* (Baltimore: Johns Hopkins University Press, 1994); Paul A. Kowert, *Groupthink or Deadlock: When Do Leaders Learn from Their Advisors?* (Albany: State University of New York Press, 2002).

decisions. Another symptom is a *stereotyped view of the opponent's leadership* as too evil to engage in good-faith negotiation or too inept to counter the policies being considered by the group. In other words, our counterparts are a mirror image of ourselves.

The groupthink process leads to a *shared illusion of unanimity* that often overcomes members' personal inclinations and influences deriving from their organizational roles. This sense of unanimity is an artifact of the small-group setting because members exert *direct pressure* on any individual who argues against the stereotypes the group produces or because an individual whose viewpoints deviate from the perceived group consensus engage in *self-censorship*. Groupthink also occurs when efforts are made to *rationalize the group's decisions,* to justify them no matter what they might be, screening out warnings or contrary information that might lead the group to reconsider its decisions. Finally, the group cohesiveness that is most conducive to groupthink is fostered when the group is isolated from outsiders and outside views, and especially when one or more members behave as *mindguards* by filtering out information that might challenge the predominant images held by the group.

The appearance of a group leader who promotes a preferred solution is another major influence on the creation of groupthink. For this effect to take place, it is not necessary that the others in the group be toadies. A person becomes a leader because of any number of personal and role characteristics. Others in the group may fall into line because the leader controls promotion decisions, because they share the leader's values, or due to the sheer force of the leader's personality. The U.S. decision in 1950 to send military aid to South Korea as soon as the administration was informed of the North Korean attack illustrates the impact a leader may have on the deliberative process of a small group. After President Truman walked into the meeting of his advisers and expressed his initial approval of the plan presented by Secretary of State Dean Acheson, the rest of the discussion was based on Acheson's view rather than on any other. In contrast, during the Cuban missile crisis, President Kennedy consciously removed himself from a number of the ExComm sessions so that his presence would not inhibit the broadest possible review of options. Groupthink appears to have been minimized because each participant was encouraged to be skeptical and think "outside the box" in an atmosphere lacking a formal agenda or rules of protocol.

A variety of possible remedies for groupthink have been suggested by researchers, including "devil's advocacy"—assigning someone the role of challenging the group's seeming consensus—but the symptoms of groupthink probably cannot be eliminated altogether because of natural human psychological processes. For example, the U.S. Senate's Select Committee on Intelligence came to this conclusion about the information and analysis that led to the decision to invade Iraq in 2003:

> The Intelligence Community (IC) suffered from a collective presumption that Iraq had an active and growing weapons of mass destruction (WMD) program. This "group think" dynamic led Intelligence Community analysts, collectors and managers to both interpret ambiguous evidence as conclusively indicative of a WMD program as well as ignore or minimize evidence that Iraq did not have active and expanding weapons of mass destruction programs. This presumption was so strong that formalized IC mechanisms established to challenge assumptions and group think were not utilized.

There can be little doubt that, as information becomes available on the decision-making process leading to the Bush administration's decision to go to war against Iraq, as well as subsequent decisions concerning the continued U.S. presence there, it will be examined closely by psychologists and political scientists for symptoms of groupthink.[13]

INDIVIDUAL PERCEPTIONS AND BELIEFS

Foreign policy is made and implemented by people; states are not monolithic, impersonal creatures that somehow behave on their own. The particular individuals who occupy governmental and nongovernmental roles—presidents, prime ministers, foreign ministers, revolutionary leaders, peace activists—can strongly influence the foreign policy processes of their own states and other states. Therefore, the way these people see the world is important. The unique characteristics that influence an individual's decision making and behavior include a number of things that are relatively easy to study and some others that are quite difficult: values, personality, political style, intellect, past experience, and so on. But anyone who endeavors to grasp their impact on foreign policy starts with the assumption that individuals matter.

As our previous discussion suggests, people hold images of the world around them, and these images are not always accurate representations of the "real" world. Understanding the images held by foreign policy makers involves learning about their belief systems and how their perceptions of other peoples, states, leaders, and situations affect their decisions. New information, modifying information, even contradictory information may be incorporated as a decision maker adjusts his or her image to fit the newly perceived reality. Or, for various psychological reasons, images may be highly resistant to change; contradictory information is ignored or interpreted selectively so that only the bits and pieces that reinforce one's preconceptions are retained. Decision makers' images are therefore constructed and reconstructed by cognitive screens that filter incoming information.

Even if we could obtain perfect information about policy alternatives and their consequences, problems of perception call into question the notion of an ideal, or perfectly rational, choice among those alternatives. The meaning attached to the information before them partly depends on decision makers' beliefs and preconceptions. **Misperception** occurs when information received about the behavior of another actor diverges from what has actually taken place, or when the interpretation of the behavior diverges from meaning intended by the other actor.[14]

There are a number of psychological mechanisms by which decision makers process information on the basis of held images. One is the conscious or subconscious pursuit of **cognitive consistency**—a state of mind in which various cognitive images do not clash with or contradict each other. Sometimes new information is

---

[13] The reconstructions provided by journalist Bob Woodward are suggestive; see his *Plan of Attack* (New York: Simon & Schuster, 2004) and *State of Denial: Bush at War, Part III* (New York: Simon & Schuster, 2007). Excerpt from the Select Committee on Intelligence, U.S. Senate, "U.S. Intelligence Community's Prewar Intelligence Assessments on Iraq," Report 108301 (July 9, 2004), p. 18; available at <http://intelligence.senate.gov/108301.pdf>.

[14] See Robert Jervis's pioneering study, *Perception and Misperception in International Politics* (Princeton, N.J.: Princeton University Press, 1976). See also Jerel A. Rosati, "The Power of Human Cognition in the Study of World Politics," *International Studies Review* 2 (Fall 2000), pp. 45–75; also Yaacov Y. Vertzberger, *The World in Their Minds: Information Processing, Cognition, and Perception in Foreign Policy Decisionmaking* (Stanford, Calif.: Stanford University Press, 1990).

so at odds with the decision maker's held images that it creates a state of *cognitive dissonance*. Rather than embark on a reappraisal of this challenged set of beliefs, an individual may simply ignore or reshape the incompatible information. Wishful thinking reflects just such a psychological process. For example, national leaders who strongly hoped to avoid war with Germany were reassured in 1938 when British Prime Minister Neville Chamberlain returned from Munich exulting that he had achieved "peace in our time." Never mind that appeasing Hitler came at the cost of Czechoslovakia's dismemberment and there was little in Germany's other actions to suggest that Hitler would remain content with the acquisition.

Perceptions are also distorted by the use of imperfect or superficial *historical analogies* whereby decision makers notice those details of a present episode that looks like some past event while ignoring crucial differences. Indeed, Chamberlain's appeasement of Hitler has become one of policy makers' most often used historical analogies, and the frequency with which this case is invoked, accurately or inaccurately, is commonly called the *Munich syndrome*. For the British, the Suez crisis of 1956 was generated in part by the selective perceptions of Prime Minister Anthony Eden, who saw Egypt's Nasser as another Hitler, and thus as someone who could not be appeased. Saddam Hussein was viewed in the same light after Iraq invaded Kuwait in 1990. And in a speech to the Israeli Knesset in 2008, George W. Bush recalled the German invasion of Poland in 1939, deriding those who advocate dialogue with rogue leaders as seeking "the false comfort of appeasement, which has been repeatedly discredited by history."[15]

IMAGE OF THE ENEMY

Some common misconceptions recur in foreign policy. Foreign policy decision makers often do not realize that their words and deeds may not convey what they intend to communicate. There is also a tendency to see other states, particularly adversaries, as more threatening than they are—in regard to their intentions, their capabilities, or both. In his 2002 State of the Union address, President Bush referred to Iraq, Iran, and North Korea as an "axis of evil." The reaction to this statement both at home and abroad was swift and rather critical, not so much because there was a great deal of sympathy for these countries, but because of the implication that they were somehow in cahoots. Most commentary was quick to point out that Iran and Iraq were not on friendly terms and that the North Korean regime was isolated and not inclined toward collaboration. One wonders whether Bush's statement was deliberately provocative, but either way it was an illustration (perhaps exaggerated) of how state leaders often perceive their opponents.

When confronting a hostile environment, individuals tend to construct a particular *image of the enemy*. Decision makers interpret the behavior and intentions of other states not only as especially hostile but also as deliberate and coordinated. There is an inclination to ignore or underestimate the role of chance, missteps, and the influence of

---

[15] On the misuse of this analogy, see Robert J. Beck, "Munich's Lessons Reconsidered," *International Security* 14 (Fall 1989), pp. 161–191; Jeffrey Record, *Making War, Thinking History: Munich, Vietnam, and Presidential Uses of Force from Korea to Kosovo* (Annapolis, Md.: U.S. Naval Institute Press, 2002).

bureaucratic politics on the foreign policy behavior of other states and instead assume that the rational actor model captures what is going on within the enemy camp. Decision makers view the other government as monolithic, acting in a calculating way and with a unity of purpose; every event and utterance is intended and has transpired for a reason. Thus, when others act in the way we want, the tendency is to overestimate the influence we have had on the opponent's behavior; but when the adversary does something undesired, the tendency is to find internal forces in the opposing state to explain that behavior. Seeing others as opponents or enemies has a powerful influence on the perceptions and behavior of the leaders of states.

The image of the enemy derives partly from psychological **defense mechanisms**. These act to protect the individual from things that would otherwise make him or her uncomfortable and anxious. One defense mechanism is *projection* onto others of feelings, characteristics, and desires that we cannot admit exist in ourselves. One common result is the creation of a scapegoat. An enemy serves as a scapegoat when it is accused of bringing about an outcome that was actually perpetrated by another, perhaps even oneself. The accusation is used to justify one's own behavior, which is similar to that foisted on the opponent. In foreign relations, an enemy is usually seen as aggressive, seeking dominance and conquest, and capable of evil and brutality. Being able to crusade against such an opponent brings great psychological satisfaction. One can ignore one's own behavior and preserve one's self-image because no matter how badly one is behaving, the object of that behavior is an enemy that is even more evil. Much of this sort of behavior was observed in the United States during the Vietnam War, when some Americans failed to question various U.S. tactics such as napalm bombing, the torture of prisoners, or the killing of civilians. The post–9/11 war on terror exhibited a similar willingness to adopt degraded standards of behavior to combat an implacable foe.

Having an enemy allows decision makers the satisfaction of recognizing their own moral superiority and the rightness of the nation's cause. Having an enemy permits us to see the world in clear-cut distinctions of good and evil—a nasty "they" helps to define a righteous "we." During World War II, the Japanese and Americans each held strong images of their own superiority and the other's barbarism; these images then excused the commission of terrible atrocities by both sides. On the American side, there were pronounced differences in the way the German and Japanese enemies were portrayed in wartime propaganda, which historian John Dower attributes to racism. Whereas Germany (usually Hitler and his military leadership) was portrayed as evil and bent on world domination, the Japanese (usually *all* Japanese) were very often depicted as subhuman—monkeys, rodents, insects (Figure 7.3 is an example). Such subhuman caricatures of the enemy encouraged a view of war fighting as extermination. As Dower writes, "it was in this atmosphere that precision bombing of Japanese military targets was abandoned by the United States and the 'madmen' and 'yellow vermin' of the homeland became primary targets."[16]

---

[16] John W. Dower, *War Without Mercy: Race and Power in the Pacific War* (New York: Pantheon, 1986), p. 300. See also Peter Gottschalk and Gabriel Greenberg, *Islamophobia: Making Muslims the Enemy* (Lanham, Md.: Rowman & Littlefield, 2007).

FIGURE 7.3 | IMAGE OF THE ENEMY: AMERICA'S ADVERSARIES IN WORLD WAR II

Our enemies are often portrayed as subhuman, especially during wartime. Although this is true of American portrayals of both Germany and Japan in World War II, studies have revealed recurring differences in the images of these two enemies. These differences suggest a degree of racial prejudice in America's enemy images and may account for the willingness to abandon restraints on the conduct of the war against the Japanese, including the use of atomic weapons against Japanese cities.

Source: Washington Post. Copyright © 1942, The Washington Post. Reprinted with permission.

BELIEF SYSTEMS

A **belief system** is a reasonably coherent set of images, conceptions, and values that give meaning to an individual's perceptions of the physical, social, and perhaps spiritual world. They are built upon past and present experiences and give rise to expectations for the future, especially for "what ought to be." One's belief system performs some very important functions. It helps orient the individual to the environment, integrates often competing perceptions (and thus aids in achieving cognitive consistency), and provides as a guide to behavior. Belief systems that are composed of a rather narrow range of conceptions and understandings, yet provide the basis for a fairly comprehensive guide to action, especially political action, are often referred to as *ideologies*. Not all belief systems are entirely coherent; some foreign policy decision makers do not begin with a clear or highly integrated set of preconceptions about the world. Although belief systems influence political behavior, behavior in office also helps to shape policy makers' belief systems.[17]

Belief systems generate policy preferences in both the domestic and international arenas. For example, the never-ending argument concerning the redistribution of wealth and whether to help the needy runs through both domestic and foreign policy debate. In international affairs, these beliefs appear in attitudes about combating world hunger or giving aid to less developed countries; domestically, they appear in attitudes about the merits of progressive taxation and the welfare system. Competing beliefs about the utility and desirability of violence and its use as a deterrent also span these two realms. In foreign policy, belief systems provide guidance on matters relating to military intervention, covert operations, and civil–military relations; domestically, we see distinct belief systems at work in debates over crime fighting and the death penalty. The joining of liberal (domestic) views to dovish (international) views, and conservative to hawkish views, has been found repeatedly in research on both mass and elite opinions in the United States.[18]

An **operational code** is that part of an individual's (or group's) belief system that guides thinking about the repertoire of appropriate responses to various situations and therefore serves as a guide to political action. In a classic study, Nathan Leites reviewed Russian literature and the writings of the Bolsheviks in order to reconstruct the operational code of the Soviet Politburo. Ole Holsti used a similar approach to analyze the views of John Foster Dulles, Eisenhower's secretary of state from 1953 to 1959. He found that two of Dulles's operative beliefs about the conduct of foreign policy were: when one's opponent is strong, one should avoid conflict; and when one's opponent is weak, one should be willing to run risks. Dulles also seems to have projected his own beliefs onto Soviet leaders, for he held an "inherent bad faith" image of the Soviet Union, believing that it could not be trusted and would only act in a friendly way when weak or afraid.[19]

PERSONAL CHARACTER AND HUMAN PHYSIOLOGY

Certain leaders stand out as historical figures because we think they were instrumental in bringing about important world events; the course of history would have been different had someone else occupied that role at that time. Chancellor Otto von Bismarck seemed to defy both international and domestic forces in

---

[17] Deborah Welch Larson, "The Role of Belief Systems and Schemas in Foreign Policy Decision-Making," *Political Psychology* 15 (March 1994), pp. 17–33; Mark Laffey and Jutta Weldes, "Beyond Belief: Ideas and Symbolic Technologies in the Study of International Relations," *European Journal of International Relations* 3 (June 1997), pp. 193–237.

[18] See, for example, Shoon Kathleen Murray and Jonathan A. Cowden, "The Role of 'Enemy Images' and Ideology in Elite Belief Systems," *International Studies Quarterly* 43 (September 1999), pp. 455–481.

[19] Nathan Leites, *The Operational Code of the Politburo* (New York: McGraw-Hill, 1951); Ole Holsti, "The 'Operational Code' Approach to the Study of Political Leaders: John Foster Dulles' Philosophical and Instrumental Beliefs," *Canadian Journal of Political Science* 3 (March 1970), pp. 123–157. See also Stephen J. Walker, Mark Schafer, and Michael D. Young, "Presidential Operational Codes and Foreign Policy Conflicts in the Post–Cold War World," *Journal of Conflict Resolution* 43 (October 1999), pp. 609–625. Related psychological concepts include *cognitive maps, schemas,* and *scripts.* in

securing Germany's position on the continent as a status quo power. Having recently defeated Denmark, Austria, and France in the Wars of German Unification and continuing its military and industrial expansion, Germany should have been subject to a counterbalancing coalition of European powers—a situation Bismarck managed to short-circuit through masterful diplomatic maneuvering. He also managed to restrain prowar impulses emanating from within the German government bureaucracy, including the military, and the German populace. Kaiser Wilhelm II, on the other hand, after removing Bismarck in 1890, "brought Bismarck's architecture crashing down through sheer force of idiocy." The Kaiser flaunted Germany's strength and insisted on its rightful "place in the sun." In permitting Bismarck's successors to take a series of diplomatic missteps, he brought about an encirclement of Germany that Bismarck had so deftly avoided—setting the stage for the First World War.[20]

Unlike many of the organizational and psychological factors that affect the foreign policy decision-making process, the personal characteristics that contribute to exceptional leadership, or to especially inept leadership, are often idiosyncratic and unpredictable features of the decision-making context. Quality of leadership is also hard to predict because so much depends on the opportunities presented by the international environment. Only then will we be able to connect personal character to a leader's ability to seize the day, whether to good effect (as in the case of Mohandas Gandhi) or bad (Hitler). However, there are conditions that are more likely to allow individual leaders to escape some of the constraints that might otherwise stifle the sort of bold, innovative, or judicious action we often associate with episodes of great leadership throughout history. When the political structure of the state concentrates authority in the hands of the executive, or when it has been permitted or manipulated to do so, the personal character of the state's leader may loom large and exert a strong impact on foreign policy. Individual leaders can overcome constraints when political authority is diffuse as well, especially if bureaucratic actors or interest groups in society are at odds and essentially cancel out the influence of each other. The fluidity and unpredictability of international events may also give individuals an upper hand relative to bureaucratic or societal interests, which can be slower to react to rapidly changing circumstances.

These condition are often present at wartime, so it is no surprise that a many of those we consider pivotal leaders of the past either rose to power or rose to the occasion when their countries were at war: Woodrow Wilson, Winston Churchill, Franklin Roosevelt, Joseph Stalin, Mao Zedong, Ho Chi Minh, Mustafa Kemal Atatürk, David Ben Gurion, Ayatollah Khomeini—to name several from just the twentieth century. Others such as Hitler and Saddam Hussein started their own wars and continued their already established dominance over the foreign policy process. During wartime, executives are freed from some of the domestic constraints they experience during peacetime (if they face any) because they are

---

[20] Daniel L. Byman and Kenneth M. Pollack, "Let Us Now Praise Great Men: Bringing the Statesman Back In," *International Security* 25 (Spring 2001), pp. 107–146; quote from p. 121. Henry Kissinger, long before entering government, also argued that individuals can make a big difference in world politics; see *A World Restored: Metternich, Castlereagh and the Problems of Peace, 1812–1822* (Boston: Houghton Mifflin, 1957).

granted emergency powers by the other institutions of government or simply because governmental and societal actors choose to defer to national leaders under extraordinary conditions. But wars may also mobilize groups with sharply divergent interests to check the influence of their domestic opponents with similar consequences: a freer hand for national leaders and a greater likelihood that personal character will prove instrumental in the policy process.

PERSONALITY TRAITS

There have been many personality studies of individual foreign policy decision makers, as well as comparative analyses of leaders' psychological profiles and personality traits. In one of the classic studies of this genre, Alexander and Juliette George concluded that Woodrow Wilson's approach to a number of issues involving power and control over others, including his unwillingness to compromise with political opponents, was rooted in his childhood. This was later manifest in his handling of the Treaty of Versailles, which the U.S. Senate refused to ratify, thereby killing Wilson's dream of American participation in the League of Nations. Wilson's need to dominate others apparently stemmed from his competition with and aggression toward his father: "Political power was for him a compensatory value, a means of restoring the self-esteem damaged in childhood." Kaiser Wilhelm is reported to have had an analogous insecurity complex of massive proportions.[21]

Extreme personality disturbances are relatively rare among leaders of large bureaucratized organizations like nation-states, especially under normal conditions where a potential leader has to work his or her way up through the organization over a long time. People who think or act in very peculiar ways will be weeded out of positions of leadership or will fail to be promoted. A person with a severe personality disorder is likely to spend so much energy coping with psychological problems that he or she will be unable to perform at the level required for high achievement in a large organization. During times of great social and political upheaval, however, a person with very unusual personality characteristics may achieve power in situations where normal people are unable to cope with social problems. Hitler, for instance, came to power in a period of terrible inflation and unemployment in Germany; Stalin during the upheaval following a revolution and civil war. Moreover, the behavior of such a leader—especially one entrenched for many years in an authoritarian system—may become much more abnormal over time. Both Hitler and Stalin became even more aberrant after their first decade in power.

When accession to political power is more routine, the range of personality types found in office will be substantially narrower. Even so, there is enough variation to warrant the use of psychoanalytic techniques to study foreign policy decision makers, sometimes through the use of a classification scheme. The most

---

[21] Alexander George and Juliet George, *Woodrow Wilson and Colonel House: A Personality Study* (New York: Dover, 1964), quote from p. 320; see also their *Presidential Personality and Performance* (Boulder, Colo.: Westview, 1998). On Kaiser Wilhelm (and Hitler), see Robert G. L. Waite, "Leadership Pathologies: The Kaiser and the Führer and the Decisions for War in 1914 and 1939," in Betty Glad, ed., *Psychological Dimensions of War* (Newbury Park, Calif.: Sage, 1990).

famous of these is James David Barber's typology for understanding American "presidential character." The character and style of any president, he argues, are rooted firmly in his political experiences very early in his career. These experiences help to explain whether the individual is "active" or "passive" (energy devoted to the job) and whether the individual is "positive" or "negative" (actually enjoys the job). An engaged and confident president who enjoys the job—an active-positive character—would be one like Franklin Roosevelt or John Kennedy or Bill Clinton. The opposite, a president with little liking for the office and low activity and self-confidence, is a passive-negative—Calvin Coolidge, for example. Some recent U.S. presidents have been active-negative: almost compulsively active in office but not deriving much pleasure from the job because of low self-esteem and confidence; examples are Lyndon Johnson and Richard Nixon. Ronald Reagan was considered to be passive-positive—receptive and compliant, with superficial optimism and a strong need for consultation, even affection. The same classification may apply to George W. Bush.[22]

Psychobiographical studies of Henry Kissinger have attempted to link his past experience to his personality and style, which in turn affected his behavior in the foreign policy arena. Kissinger's boyhood experience in tumult of Nazi Germany is said to have been the source of "inner chaos" that ultimately motivated his search for order in the external world. The picture that emerges is of an active-negative, a man of incredible energy and drive who never quite succeeded in dispelling unease over the chaos that might recur at any time. Perhaps it is not unusual that two active-negatives such as Nixon and Kissinger were able to work well as a foreign policy team. Studies of Ronald Reagan indicate that from childhood he found success through an "energetic attack on obstacles in his path and the avoidance of emotional and intellectual ambiguities." His turn to the political right in the late 1940s "was an adaptation to a personal and political crisis. Anti-communism served certain ego defensive and social adjustment needs for him at a time when his personal and private life had bottomed out."[23]

STRESS AND STRAIN OF FOREIGN POLICY MAKING

Knowing that foreign policy is the product of human behavior, we ought not overlook the fact that decision makers are physical beings, constrained by their physiology and possibly by their genetic heritage. Whether information is received and the extent to which it can be processed and interpreted depend partly on the physical capabilities individuals, as we pointed out in our discussion of bounded rationality. Thus, the physical as well as the mental health of decision makers can affect the decision-making process. The strain of high public office is great; look at before-and-after photographs of almost any U.S. president since World War II and notice

---

[22] James David Barber, *The Presidential Character: Predicting Performance in The White House*, 4th ed. (Englewood Cliffs, N.J.: Prentice-Hall, 1992). See also Fred I. Greenstein, *The Presidential Difference: Leadership Style from FDR to George W. Bush*, 2nd ed. (Princeton, N.J.: Princeton University Press, 2004).

[23] Harvey Starr, *Henry Kissinger: Perceptions of International Politics* (Lexington: University Press of Kentucky, 1984); Betty Glad, "Ronald Reagan's Mid-life Crisis and the Turn to the Political Right," *Political Psychology* 10 (December 1989), pp. 593–624.

the effect of not just the passage of four or eight years but also the job itself. It does not help that many political leaders, particularly the heads of governments and senior ministers, are older individuals and therefore even more susceptible to the strains of office. Some remain in office to an advanced age such as Robert Mugabe (age eighty-five in 2009), Mao Zedong (eighty-four), Fidel Castro (eighty-three), Charles de Gaulle (seventy-nine), Ronald Reagan (seventy-seven), and Leonid Brezhnev (seventy-five). The former communist countries seemed particularly susceptible to groups of aged leaders. The average age of the Eastern European leaders in 1989, when communism fell, was seventy-six. None of the Chinese communist leaders who were responsible for the Tiananmen Square attack, also in 1989, were under age seventy-five.

People today are basically the same physical creatures that evolved as plains hunters tens of thousands of years ago. Human physiology operates so that in a situation provoking fear, anger, or anxiety, the body gears up for "fight or flight." Physiological reactions—increased heartbeat, the release of adrenaline, the movement of blood to the muscles—prepare the body for physical combat or for running away as fast as possible. The stress that builds up in the body is released by one or the other of these physical actions. The body chemistry of today's foreign policy decision maker still works that way, but "fight or flight" is only a metaphor. The modern official does not run screaming down the White House lawn or across Red Square but sits in conference or talks on the telephone or broods alone in an office. The internalized stress is not released as intended, potentially impairing the health of the decision maker—and the handling of information and clarity of thought during a crisis.

Medical histories of twentieth-century political and military leaders indicate an extremely high rate of medical disabilities. These ailments and the drugs and other treatments taken for them have a number of physiological effects on individuals that can affect their perceptions of the world and decision-making procedures.[24] A good example of these effects is the behavior of British Prime Minister Anthony Eden during the Suez crisis of 1956. Eden was ill, suffering from hypertension and nervous disorders. Reports at the time indicated that he was also taking benzedrine, which imparts a feeling of control and confidence. We know that Eden's decision-making behavior during the crisis differed markedly from the behavior he had displayed in other situations; he was much more secretive and consulted only a very small group of colleagues. The prime minister suffered a physical breakdown right after the crisis.

Many American presidents and other high-level decision makers have suffered from major physiological problems. Critics of Franklin Roosevelt claim that he was too ill from high blood pressure during the 1945 Yalta Conference to negotiate effectively with Stalin and that he delayed decisions and gave in on issues to speed the conclusion of grueling bargaining sessions so that he could

---

[24] Roy Lubit and Bruce Russett, "The Effects of Drugs on Decision Making," *Journal of Conflict Resolution* 28 (March 1984), pp. 85–102.

rest.[25] Woodrow Wilson had a stroke during his stressful and unsuccessful campaign to promote the League of Nations. Some analysts blame the stroke, rather than lifelong psychological problems, for his stubborn, uncompromising, and counterproductive behavior thereafter. Eisenhower's heart attacks weakened his control over policy; his turning over the government to Vice President Nixon partly prompted the adoption in 1967 of the Twenty-fifth Amendment to the Constitution on presidential disability and succession. Many have suggested that Ronald Reagan's failing memory allowed the activities that culminated in the Iran–Contra scandal to go unchecked (he was diagnosed with Alzheimer's disease after he left office). The death of top decision makers or their inability to function can bring the decision-making processes of government to a halt or cause great confusion. The ill health of Brezhnev, Andropov, and Chernenko in the early to mid-1980s brought instability and uncertainty to the conduct—and analysis—of Soviet foreign policy.

CONCLUSION TO PART I

In Part I we have looked at a series of environments and contexts within which states and nonstate entities interact, as well as sources of influence and constraint on the foreign policy-making process itself. We began with the world system and concluded with a look at the individual and his or her psychological environment. Processes operate at various levels to exert an impact on the opportunities facing decision makers and their willingness to act—their menus and their choices. One way to review these processes, at various levels of analysis, is to consider the extent to which they change over time, as summarized in Table 7.1.

Notice the general pattern regarding change. Factors that operate at more aggregated levels of analysis (world system, international relations) tend to change rather slowly compared to those operating at lower levels (role, individual). Anarchy, the principle of authority underlying sovereignty in the international system since the seventeenth century, has obviously been quite resistant to change. States' natural endowments change very little unless their borders change; historical legacies and political cultures also endure. Most of the factors we have discussed fall within an intermediate category of change. In some instances, when change does occur it is a momentous event—as with the end of the cold war and the resulting change in system polarity and spheres of influence, as well as governmental structure and openness in the case of Russia. Other factors affecting foreign policy undergo moderate change because shifts tend to be gradual; states' military and economic capabilities are examples, as are changes in social structure and public mood. Changes in the organizational and bureaucratic processes described earlier in this chapter are also noteworthy for their incremental nature.

---

[25] Robert H. Ferrell, *The Dying President: Franklin D. Roosevelt, 1944–1945* (Columbia: University of Missouri Press, 1998), says he was "in no condition to govern the Republic" p.4.

TABLE 7.1 | FACTORS AFFECTING FOREIGN POLICY AND THEIR SUSCEPTIBILITY TO CHANGE

Level of Analysis	Factor Affecting Foreign Policy		
	Slow Change	Moderate Change	Rapid Change
World system	Anarchy	Polarity Spheres of influence Technology	
Relations	Geography Demography	Military capability Economic capability Diplomatic practice	
Society	History Political culture	Social structure Public opinion National interests	
Government		Government structure Openness	
Role		Decision unit Organizational process	Information flow
Individual	Human physiology		Misperceptions Beliefs Personalities

Source: Adapted from James N. Rosenau, "The Study of Foreign Policy," in James N. Rosenau, Kenneth Thompson, and Gavin Boyd, eds., *World Politics* (New York: Free Press, 1976), p. 18.

Aside from the physiological elements above, which apply generally to the human race, the processes operating on individual decision makers tend to provide for relatively rapid changes in foreign policy. It is not that the perceptions and belief systems of individual policy makers change so readily—indeed, we have repeatedly emphasized their resistance to change in the face of new information—and most do not possess multiple personalities. Rather, these factors tend to reside in the minds of individuals; they accompany foreign policy makers when they ascend and descend from positions of influence. The constant circulation of individuals through the corridors of power, along with their peculiar images of the world and personal idiosyncrasies, is the predominant source of unpredictability in world politics.

Yet in all times, kings and persons of sovereign authority, because of their independency, are in continual jealousies, and in the state and posture of gladiators.
—**Thomas Hobbes**

Against uncertain fears, protection must be sought in divine providence and innocent precaution, and not in the exercise of our strength.
—**Hugo Grotius**

INTERNATIONAL CONFLICT AND COOPERATION

PART **2**

MILITARY CONFLICT: WHY STATES AND OTHER ACTORS RESORT TO FORCE

CHAPTER 8

VIOLENT CHANGE IN WORLD POLITICS

When the nuclear age dawned, many observers hoped that the use of military power would become obsolete. Launching nuclear weapons against another nuclear-armed state seems to provide no political utility at all. Either the state that used them would then be destroyed by a retaliatory attack, or the devastation would be so great that no territory, wealth, or population could be gained after their use. The costs of a nuclear war would be unprecedented. Given the complex interdependencies of modern society, because of the importance of cities and their vulnerability to disruption, nuclear attack is likely to bring society to a standstill within a few hours. Distance and time, elements that once protected states in war, are cut short in an age of intercontinental ballistic missiles. Moreover, nuclear weapons are of no use in preventing guerrilla operations or terrorism. The main value of nuclear weapons seems to rest in their nonuse—in their *posture* as a deterrent to attack by a nuclear opponent.

Some took (and still take) the position that any use of force presents extreme danger because of the risk of escalation; even a small war could spread and engulf the nuclear powers. They proclaimed that *all* war had become obsolete. However, the use of large-scale military force—by Iraq to take Kuwait, by the American-led coalition to repel Iraq, by NATO against Serbia, and by the United States in Afghanistan and (with Britain) in Iraq again—provides ample evidence that this is not the case. The actual use or threatened use of conventional military force against nonnuclear powers (particularly those not located in Europe) retains value for decision makers under certain circumstances, as does the use of force by nonstate actors for separatist or revolutionary purposes. War has been ubiquitous throughout history, and the use of war as a tool to advance state or group interests continues to the present day.

The legitimacy of force or the threat of force is maintained in several ways. The UN Charter permits states, either individually or collectively in alliances, to use force for self-defense. The collective security function of the UN rests upon the

Security Council's authority to employ the collective force of its membership in response to an actual or threatened breach of international peace and security. This authority was exercised against the North Koreans in 1950 and Iraq in 1991. Staunch neutrals such as Switzerland and Sweden have based their neutrality on strong military establishments, which they believe deters would-be aggressors. Other states have used force when it was convenient or necessary. Even India, whose first leaders were so outspoken in opposition to violence, has turned to military force on several occasions since independence—in 1961 against Portugal in a dispute over Goa; in 1962 in a border war with China; and in the 1947, 1965, and 1971 wars with Pakistan—and its army now stands poised to engage Pakistani forces all along their disputed border region.

John Mueller argues that norms against the use of force were on the rise even before World War I but were spurred on by that conflict and by World War II. There are, in fact, indications that this is still happening. As will be discussed later in this chapter and again in Chapter 11, democracies rarely fight each other. In addition, there are broader patterns. According to data from the Correlates of War Project, about 15 percent of all "militarized disputes" escalated to war in the period from the Napoleonic Wars to World War II, while only about 3 percent have done so since then.[1] During the cold war, each superpower deterred the other from using nuclear weapons against itself or against its allies (assuming there was any intention to attack). The superpowers and their allies in Europe also refrained from the direct use of conventional force on the continent, although they often employed military force elsewhere. A look at which states are engaging in conflict and in which parts of the world suggests that any argument about the obsolescence of the military tool has applied mainly to the East–West standoff during the cold war and to relations among advanced industrial democracies.

A central object of violent struggle has been the control of the state. Since World War II, almost 150 governments have been created. Because of the multi-ethnic or multitribal populations of many of these states and the persistence of ideological and religious clashes, governments have been under constant siege. Force has been used as a principal tool by nonstate actors to challenge established governments for control of a state or a region that hopes to become a state in its own right. The use of force by nonstate actors is one of a number of challenges to the nation-state in the contemporary system. As we have discussed in earlier chapters, sovereignty is the legal status that gives the state a monopoly on the use of force. This monopoly has been and continues to be severely contested.

HUMAN AGGRESSION

Of all forms of international interaction, war is the most studied. In a pioneering examination of the causes of war, Kenneth Waltz located various theoretical

---

[1] John Mueller, *Retreat from Doomsday: The Obsolescence of Major War* (New York: Basic Books, 1989); see also Michael Mandelbaum, "Is Major War Obsolete?" *Survival* 40 (Winter 1998–99), pp. 20–38. Findings from the Correlates of War Project are discussed in Daniel S. Geller and J. David Singer, *Nations at War: A Scientific Study of International Conflict* (Cambridge: Cambridge University Press, 1998).

explanations at three different levels of analysis—what he called *images*. The *first image* focuses on human nature and the psychological needs and deficiencies we all supposedly possess by virtue of our genetic makeup. First image explanations are therefore a subset of the individual level explanations we discussed in the last chapter. "The locus of the causes of war is found in the nature and behavior of man. Wars result from selfishness, from misdirected aggressive impulses, from stupidity."[2]

Many have speculated about human nature, wondering if there is a built-in human instinct for violence, aggression, and domination. The debate over "nature versus nurture" is an old one. What accounts for human actions: innate genetic characteristics or the cultural environment? A form of the debate continues between those in the fields of ethology (the study of animal behavior) and anthropology. The most extreme view informed by ethology maintains that biological influences on violent behavior by humans are very powerful. A more moderate *sociobiological perspective* places less emphasis on instinctual elements and more on the evolutionary forces of natural selection in which certain forms of behavior are passed from one generation to the next because they are conducive to survival. Political scientists who have applied some of these ideas to the study of contemporary warfare disagree on the implications for rational choice. Some believe that an evolutionary explanation reinforces the notion of human egoism central to classical versions of realist theory. Natural selection preserved the genetic predisposition toward selfish behavior as a means of survival in a competitive environment; no wonder foreign policy makers behave similarly in the anarchic environment of international politics. Others believe that the evolutionary perspective highlights the importance of emotions like fear and honor, which tend to get downplayed in rational choice explanations of crisis decision making.[3]

Critics of sociobiological and related evolutionary explanations argue that violence, aggression, and warfare are not hardwired into the human genome or reinforced through human evolution. The famous anthropologist Margaret Mead maintained that war was simply "an invention like any other of the inventions in terms of which we order our lives." John Mueller suggests that war, like slavery and dueling, can be "unlearned."[4] Although ethology and sociobiology provide us with some interesting analogies and explanations for human violence, they cannot explain decisions either to go to war or to act cooperatively in international relations. We are all human, and thus we share the same human nature—yet some

---

[2] Kenneth Waltz, *Man, the State, and War: A Theoretical Analysis* (New York: Columbia University Press, 1959), p. 16.

[3] See, respectively, Bradley A. Thayer, *Darwin and International Relations: On the Evolutionary Origins of War and Ethnic Conflict* (Lexington: University Press of Kentucky, 2004); Stephen Peter Rosen, *War and Human Nature* (Princeton, N.J.: Princeton University Press, 2005). Classic statements of earlier, more extreme views include Konrad Lorenz, *On Aggression* (New York: Harcourt, Brace, 1966), and Desmond Morris, *The Naked Ape* (New York: Dell, 1967). The pioneer in the field of sociobiology is Edward O. Wilson; see his *On Human Nature* (Cambridge, Mass.: Harvard University Press, 1978), chap. 5.

[4] Margaret Mead, "War Is Only an Invention—Not a Biological Necessity," in Leon Bramson and George W. Goethals, eds., *War: Studies from Psychology, Sociology, Anthropology* (New York: Basic Books, 1964), p. 270; Mueller, *Retreat from Doomsday*.

societies are much more peaceful than others. Though something of a stereotype, the people of modern Scandinavia are widely regarded as opposed to war; Sweden, for instance, has not fought a war since its conflict with Russia ended in 1809. Their ancestors, however, were the fierce Vikings who pillaged and looted all around Europe during the Middle Ages. The contrast between Hagar the Horrible and Dag Hammarskjöld is striking.

Under the auspices of the Spanish National Commission of the United Nations Educational, Scientific, and Cultural Organization (UNESCO), a group of leading biologists and social scientists from twelve countries (and five continents) formulated the Seville Statement on Violence in 1986. The statement, adopted by numerous academic and professional organizations in many disciplines and countries, specifically rejects the proposition that armament and war are inevitable because of the inherent influences of human nature. It regards as "scientifically incorrect" claims that we humans have inherited a proclivity to make war from our animal ancestors and that violent behavior is instinctual or programmed into our genes. Instead, we would do much better to look at how certain types of situations affect an individual's perceptions and feelings and, ultimately, individual and group decision making.[5]

AGGRESSION AND DEPRIVATION

Perceptions of status and deprivation are subjects of common study in psychology, sociology, and political science. One important theory asserts that aggressive behavior stems from frustration arising out of a feeling of **relative deprivation**. People may act violently or aggressively, not because they are poor or deprived in some absolute sense but because they *feel* deprived—relative to others, or relative to their expectations of what they should have.[6] Perhaps the best example is pre–World War I Germany's demand for its "place in the sun." Important elements within German government and society felt that the country was not receiving its due recognition as a great power (especially in comparison to Britain), a feeling of resentment exacerbated by Kaiser Wilhelm's own personal insecurities and jealousies. Similarly, before the Seven Weeks' War in 1866 between Prussia and Austria, Prussia's grievances with Austria had been related to "pride of place," a demand for equal status with Austria in the German Diet.

Feelings of relative deprivation can arise when contemplating past, present, and expected future conditions. Assessment of this condition is strongly affected by where one's country sits within the hierarchy of various global or regional systems based on status, prestige, military power, wealth, and so on. Feelings of relative deprivation are likely to arise when a formerly prosperous society experiences a severe economic setback. Such feelings are widespread during recessions and

---

[5] UNESCO, "Seville Statement on Violence, Spain, 1986 (Subsequently Adopted by UNESCO at the Twenty-Fifth Session of the General Conference on 16 November 1989)," available at <http://www.unesco.org/cpp/uk/declarations/seville.pdf>.

[6] This concept was first applied by Ted Robert Gurr to the study of internal war; see his *Why Men Rebel* (Princeton, N.J.: Princeton University Press, 1970).

depressions and often result in severe political unrest. Karl Marx thought that revolutions would occur as the result of the increasing impoverishment of the working class. Prolonged, severe depression in Germany in the 1930s played a key part in creating an environment conducive to Hitler's rise to power (not the sort of revolution Marx had in mind, of course), and Indonesia's economic collapse during the Asian financial crisis of 1997 to 1998 resulted social upheaval sufficient to upend the seemingly entrenched Suharto regime.

On the other hand, in some cases it is an improvement in people's material conditions that releases unrest. This is how Alexis de Tocqueville described the situation before the French Revolution: "It was precisely in those parts of Europe where there had been most improvement that popular discontent was highest. . . . Patiently endured so long as it seemed beyond redress, a grievance comes to appear intolerable once the possibility of removing it crosses men's minds."[7] A different hypothesis combines these two views and asserts that the most dangerous time for social unrest, or for challenges to the status quo in any sort of system, is when a sustained period of improving conditions is followed by a sudden, sharp setback. The period of improvement leads people to expect continuing improvement; when the setback occurs, it causes more distress than if it had followed a period of unchanged conditions.

Another perspective emphasizes the importance of people's comparisons with one another. One group may be satisfied, even with a bad lot, providing that others are doing no better. But to the degree that the group finds its situation relatively poor compared to others, it is likely to be dissatisfied. Here it is necessary to specify what group is relevant for comparison. People in the slums and barrios of the developing countries, for instance, may be better off economically than they had been, but satellite television and the Internet (if they can gain access) have made them more aware of how well people in other countries are doing, or how well elites in their own country are doing. Generally, such feelings seem more severe for comparisons among people in close contact than for widely separated social groups or strata. For the landless peasant in a traditional society, the condition of the rich landlord may be beyond the peasant's dreams, but the modest prosperity of the middle peasant (the kulak in Russia after the 1917 revolution, for example) may arouse acute feelings of relative deprivation. Poor whites may feel angrier and more threatened by the gains of blacks than they do about the privileges of rich whites, even though poor whites as well as blacks may be better off than their parents were. Importantly, the revolution in communications technology has fostered this phenomenon across continents, cultures, and economic classes. This is the problem of "rising expectations"—improved conditions.

These two perspectives, emphasizing comparisons across time and across groups, can be usefully combined. The first suggests when serious discontent may arise; the second suggests where in the social system it will be most manifest. Theories of relative deprivation have received a good deal of attention. Part of the

---

[7] Alexis de Tocqueville, *The Old Regime and the French Revolution* (Garden City, N.Y.: Doubleday, 1955), pp. 176–177.

reason is that the present day seems to be a period of substantial change in people's status or in their awareness of differences in status.

CONFLICT BETWEEN STATES

Military conflict between states has varied widely both in terms of severity (the extent of death and destruction involved) and scope (the number of participants involved). The most severe form of interstate conflict is, of course, called *war*; those that have involved numerous participants, including multiple great powers, are called *global wars* or *systemic wars*. Table 8.1 lists these global wars beginning with the Thirty Years' War, which inaugurated the contemporary state system. The Thirty Years' War was the longest global war and was especially destructive by the standards of the time (more than 2 million battle-related fatalities), giving urgency to the clarification of sovereign rights at Westphalia in 1648. It was not until the wars of the French Revolution and Napoléon's bid for European supremacy that war would result in a greater loss of life. The two world wars of the twentieth century saw the advances of the industrial revolution put to use on the battlefield; the toll was an exponential increase in destructiveness, especially considering the relatively short duration of these conflicts compared to previous global wars.

TABLE 8.1 | GLOBAL WAR IN THE CONTEMPORARY STATE SYSTEM

War	Dates	Great Power Involvement	Battle Deaths
Thirty Years' War	1618–1648	Britain, France, Hapsburgs/Austria, Netherlands, Spain, Sweden	2,071,000
Dutch War of Louis XIV	1672–1678	Britain, France, Hapsburgs/Austria, Netherlands, Spain, Sweden	342,000
War of the League of Augsburg	1688–1697	Britain, France, Hapsburgs/Austria, Netherlands, Spain	680,000
War of the Spanish Succession	1701–1713	Britain, France, Hapsburgs/Austria, Netherlands, Spain	1,251,000
War of the Austrian Succession	1739–1748	Britain, France, Hapsburgs/Austria, Prussia, Russia, Spain	359,000
Seven Years' War	1755–1763	Britain, France, Hapsburgs/Austria, Prussia, Russia, Spain	992,000
French Revolutionary/ Napoleonic Wars	1792–1815	Britain, France, Hapsburgs/Austria, Prussia, Russia, Spain	2,532,000
World War I	1914–1918	Austria-Hungary, Britain, France, Germany, Italy, Japan, Russia, United States	7,734,300
World War II	1939–1945	Britain, France, Germany, Italy, Japan, Russia, United States	12,948,300

Source: Jack S. Levy, *War in the Modern Great Power System, 1495–1975* (Lexington: University of Kentucky Press, 1983) and Levy, "Theories of General War," *World Politics* 37 (1985), 344–374.

WHY STATES FIGHT

States have fought over many things. In a study of the range of issues that have led states into conflict, Kalevi Holsti identified 177 wars and major armed interventions as having occurred between 1648 and 1989. Several interstate conflicts occurring since 1989 can be added to that list.[8] Some have been wars of the more traditional type such as the Iraqi conquest of Kuwait (1990), the U.S.–led wars against Iraq (in 1991 and 2003), and border conflicts between Ecuador and Peru (1995), India and Pakistan (1999), and Ethiopia and Eritrea (from 1998 to 2000). Others have been internationalized civil wars such as the conflict between Azerbaijan and Armenia over Nagorno-Karabakh (in 1992 and 1993), the wars between Yugoslavia and the breakaway republics of Croatia and Bosnia-Herzegovina (from 1992 to 1995), the NATO intervention against Yugoslavia over Kosovo (1999), and the Second Congo War (1998–2003)—the deadliest conflict since World War II, involving regular military forces from the Democratic Republic of Congo, Rwanda, Angola, Uganda, Chad, Sudan, Zimbabwe, and Namibia.

Holsti found that territorial disputes are the single most common issues contributing to war; territory has been at issue in almost half of all interstate wars fought since the Peace of Westphalia in 1648.[9] International disputes related to the creation of new states—resulting from national liberation and unification movements as well as secession—are also common. The importance of this issue became apparent during the nineteenth century with the rise of national independence movements accompanying the wave of European colonization beginning in the 1870s. The wave of *decolonization* following World War II—the ultimate success of these movements—accounts for the centrality of this issue as a source of international conflict in the second half of the twentieth century. Most of these conflicts were not really interstate wars but rather wars waged by European states in their own colonial territories. Such colonial conflicts were fought by the Netherlands in Indonesia (1945–1949); by France in Vietnam (1946–1954), Tunisia (1952–1956), Morocco (1953–1956), and Algeria (1954–1962); by Britain in Palestine (1946–1948), the Malay Archipelago (1948–1960), and Cyprus (1955–1960); and by Portugal in Guinea (1962–1974), Mozambique (1965–1975), and Angola (1968–1974). Decolonization was not a peaceful transition.

Economic issues—those involving commercial navigation, access to resources, colonial competition, and protection of commercial interests—were much more likely to figure prominently in wars during the seventeenth and eighteenth centuries than during later periods. The first round of European colonization that began in the fifteenth century had as its primary motive the acquisition of foreign territory and control of trade routes designed to enhance states' wealth and power. Frequent

---

[8] Kalevi J. Holsti, *Peace and War: Armed Conflicts and International Order, 1648–1989* (Cambridge: Cambridge University Press, 1991). Conflicts since 1989 are discussed in Lotta Harbom and Peter Wallensteen, "Armed Conflict, 1989–2006," *Journal of Peace Research* 44 (September 2007), pp. 623–634.

[9] See also Paul K. Huth, *Standing Your Ground: Territorial Disputes and International Conflict* (Ann Arbor: University of Michigan Press, 1998); Miles Kahler and Barbara F. Walter, eds., *Territoriality and Conflict in an Era of Globalization* (Cambridge: Cambridge University Press, 2006).

wars were fought as the European powers confronted one another in their imperial quests. The First Anglo–Dutch War (1652–1654), for example, grew out of an attempt by Britain to challenge Holland's predominance in commercial shipping in the Baltic Sea. The Second Anglo–Dutch War (1665–1667) had similar roots; this time it was Britain's interference in the Dutch slave trade out of western Africa and Britain's seizure of New Amsterdam (New York). Czar Peter the Great, in seeking to open up Russian trade routes to western Europe, presented a challenge to Swedish hegemony, thereby precipitating the Great Northern War (1700–1721). These sorts of wars became rare by the nineteenth century, but economic issues have nonetheless been a factor in one-fifth of the wars fought since 1945. Access to disputed oil reserves was a major issue in Iraq's invasion of Kuwait in 1990, and some of the more cynical observers of the liberation of Kuwait and the 2003 invasion of Iraq believe that oil was the primary motive for U.S. military action.

The role of ideology in generating international conflict has increased over time and became the most prominent issue after World War II. There was a shift away from disputes over concrete issues, like territory and commerce, toward conflicts over ideas about proper forms of political, economic, and social interaction. The cold war, in which the forces of capitalism were pitted against the forces of communism, provided a conducive atmosphere for this type of conflict. Related to conflicts over ideology are conflicts over religion and ethnicity; states have often gone to war in order to protect their religious or ethnic brethren or to support them in their "irredentist" efforts to unite with their own kind in adjacent states. The most recent example of this sort of conflict was the one between the former Soviet republics of Armenia and Azerbaijan over the treatment of Armenians in Azerbaijan's Nagorno-Karabakh region. Accompanying these and other issues is often predation—the desire to completely eliminate another state as a sovereign entity—in which case the target state is fighting for its very survival. Predation has been ever present in the contemporary international system but was at its height in the period between the two world wars, the best example being the 1939 conquest of Poland by Nazi Germany from the west and Soviet Russia from the east. In the post–World War II period, Israel's right to exist was an issue in the Arab–Israeli wars of 1948, 1967, and 1973.

It is clear that policy makers still perceive utility in the use of force. Historians and political scientists have examined in great detail the sequence of events, and the decisions preceding them, that erupted in specific wars like World War I, as well as those that stopped short of war like the Cuban missile crisis. The wealth of historical detail available to students of war and peace makes constructing general models of prewar decision sequences a very difficult exercise, but, as we mentioned in Chapter 7, many have turned to game theory in an effort to explore the deadly logic that leads states down the path to violent conflict—what Bruce Bueno de Mesquita has called "the war trap."[10] In Box 8.1 we illustrate how game theory can help us model crisis decision making and understand and even predict the outcomes that follow.

---

[10] Bruce Bueno de Mesquita, *The War Trap* (New Haven, Conn.: Yale University Press, 1981). See also Bueno de Mesquita, "Game Theory, Political Economy, and the Evolving Study of War and Peace," *American Political Science Review* 100 (November 2006), pp. 637–642; James D. Morrow, "The Ongoing Game-Theoretic Revolution," in Manus I. Midlarsky, ed., *Handbook of War Studies II* (Ann Arbor: University of Michigan Press, 2000).

IN GREATER DEPTH

| BOX 8.1 | THE GAME OF INTERNATIONAL CONFLICT: IS THERE A "SOLUTION"? |

In Box 7.1 we introduced game theory as a tool for analyzing strategic interaction in world politics, and nowhere is the use of game theory more prevalent than in the study of interstate conflict. For example, the conflict between the United States and Iraq over UN weapons inspections can be examined using an extensive-form game. In January and February 1998, and again in November of that year, the United States was on the verge of mounting a military action against Iraq for its refusal to give UN weapons inspectors unfettered access to suspected weapons sites in accordance with the terms of surrender that concluded the Gulf War in 1991. On both occasions when Iraq refused to grant access to the inspectors, the United States (U) had a choice to make: either demand compliance with the UN inspection regime or content itself with the status quo of no access. In response to a U.S. demand, Iraq (I) could capitulate and allow UN inspections, or it could make its own demand, like an easing of economic sanctions. The United States, in turn, could treat the Iraqi response as a reasonable one and opt for a negotiated settlement to the dispute, or it could reject the demand and use military force to destroy suspected weapons sites.

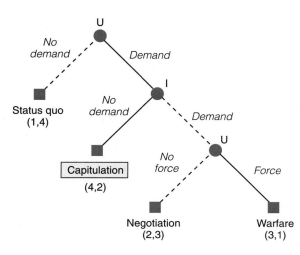

To predict the outcome of this interaction, we must have information about the utility of each possible outcome to the United States and Iraq. The Iraqis most preferred the status quo of suspended inspections and least preferred an American use of force. If they did have to permit inspections, they preferred that this be accompanied by an easing of economic sanctions. We can therefore order these four outcomes for Iraq, assigning 4 to the most preferred and 1 to the least preferred. (In the diagram, these values are listed second in the parentheses below the four outcomes.) The United States most wanted to see an unconditional resumption to UN weapons inspections. The status quo was the worst alternative for the United States. A negotiated settlement was only slightly more acceptable, worse even than having to resort to military force. Iraq had repeatedly flouted the UN inspections and the United States was determined to see them continue unimpeded. (U.S. values are listed first under each outcome.)

In a game-theoretic model of a crisis like this, we might assume that each side tries to anticipate future sequences of events and then eliminates current courses of action that may result in the least favorable outcomes. American leaders, looking ahead to their second choice node and faced with an Iraqi counterdemand for an end to the sanctions, know that their chosen course of action would be military force (so the no-force branch is dashed). The Iraqis, anticipating the U.S. choice at this stage and realizing that the outcome will be their least preferred, therefore do not want the crisis to get to that stage (this branch too is dashed); they choose to capitulate to the U.S. demand. At the beginning of the crisis, then, when it must choose between the status quo and a confrontation, the United States demands Iraqi compliance because it expects Iraq to capitulate, an outcome the U.S. clearly prefers to the status quo. Thus, Iraqi capitulation is the predicted outcome in this game. It is a

| BOX 8.1 | THE GAME OF INTERNATIONAL CONFLICT: IS THERE A "SOLUTION"? |

Nash **equilibrium** outcome, one that results when both sides make their best moves in response to each other, and we are able to identify this equilibrium outcome—to "solve" the game—using *backward induction*. All branches in the game tree leading to capitulation are solid lines, indicating that this series of moves is *on the equilibrium path*.

In both February and November 1998, inspections were in fact allowed to resume and military action was averted. The actual story, of course, is more complicated than this game-theoretic rendition, though here we probably have the essence of the strategic interaction between the United States and Iraq during these two crises. But U.S. military action was not averted during a subsequent crisis in December 1998. What happened? One possibility is that Iraq misjudged U.S. preferences. If Iraq believed that the United States preferred a negotiated settlement to the use of military force, then Iraq may have expected that its refusal to capitulate would result in a negotiated settlement (confirm this by using backward induction with a different U.S. preference order). Such a miscalculation could

account for the war outcome. Another possibility is that Iraq actually preferred to endure military strikes to capitulation. Several observers suggested that Iraq really had nothing left to lose by provoking U.S. strikes, and possibly something to gain if those attacks served to split the permanent members of the UN Security Council, whose unanimity seemed central to a continuation of both the inspection regime and the economic embargo.

Solving games using backward induction requires accurate information about each side's preferences and the assumption that both sides possess this information. When this assumption of *complete information* is not reasonable, a different solution is required. Game theorists use different solution concepts depending on the amount of information they believe was (or is) available to each side in a particular strategic interaction.

Source: The game tree used in this example is a portion of the "international interaction game" presented in Bruce Bueno de Mesquita and David Lalman, War and Reason: Domestic and International Imperatives (New Haven, Conn.: Yale University Press, 1992), p. 30.

CAPITALISM AND IMPERIALISM

Returning to Waltz's classification, according to *second image* explanations, "the internal organization of states is the key to understanding war and peace."[11] One dimension of a state's internal organization is its form of governance. We have mentioned that many researchers and policy makers contend that democratically governed countries are less warlike, at least toward other democracies, than authoritarian countries; this "democratic peace" is explored at greater length in Chapter 11. Another dimension of internal organization is the state's economic structure, and the relationship between economic organization and war has also been studied extensively.

Realist theories of world politics assume that it does not matter much how differently countries' economic systems are organized. Equally rich and powerful countries will have about the same goals, whether they have capitalist or socialist

---

[11] Waltz, *Man, the State, and War*, p. 81.

economies. Liberal theories, however, say that it does make a difference. Some liberal theorists have argued that capitalists' interests in free trade and prosperous foreign markets promote world peace; as poor countries develop along capitalist lines, they too contribute to building a more peaceful world order. But other theorists, especially Marxists and other radicals, have long claimed that capitalist countries are likely to have particularly aggressive foreign policies. This aggression is not limited to acts of war. Capitalism is sometimes considered the cause of a variety of imperialist acts, loosely defined as efforts to exert political or economic control over smaller or weaker states. Political and military interventions in less-developed countries are of special interest.

Theories differ substantially as to which particular aspects of capitalism cause imperialism or war. Some radicals cite the alleged needs of the entire capitalist economy, claiming that the capitalist system as a whole (or at least the capitalist economy of any major power) is dependent on military spending or on continued access to foreign markets for goods or investment opportunities. Others point to the interests and powers of particular groups or classes. Foreign investors, the military–industrial complex, or other economically defined groups may have an interest in an aggressive or expansionist foreign policy that can potentially yield great gains for them, even though many other members of the system—capitalists as well as workers—suffer net losses from such a policy. A minority of economic interests, therefore, may successfully maintain a policy that benefits them even though it may be detrimental to the capitalist economy as a whole. Finally, some theories go beyond readily definable material interests and focus on the value structure—that is, the ideology supporting capitalist systems. According to these theories, this value structure, concerned as much with the desire to preserve the capitalist system as to extend it, produces behavior that is excessively responsive to economic growth and the incentive of material rewards. The resulting foreign policy is thus expansionist and hostile to socialist states with different value structures.

Most of the classical economic interpretations attribute imperialism to demands arising from the organization of production in capitalist economies. Writing at the turn of the twentieth century, English economist J. A. Hobson argued that the very unequal distribution of income and wealth in capitalist countries, especially England, left the poor unable to consume much. "Underconsumption" in the domestic market in turn forced capitalists to invest their capital abroad and to compete with others to control foreign markets. The capitalist system of the time was to blame, but according to his theory imperialism was not inherent in capitalism. Aware that the foreign policy of the state had been hijacked to promote the private interests of a select few, the majority could (and should) reassert their popular sovereignty and redirect foreign policy to the pursuit of truly national interests.[12]

Marxists writing at about the same time developed their own theories of imperialism, some of which would become hugely influential. Most famous is the work

---

[12] J. A. Hobson, *Imperialism: A Study*, introduction by Philip Siegelman (Ann Arbor: University of Michigan Press, 1971); see also David Long, *Toward a New Liberal Internationalism: The International Theory of J. A. Hobson* (Cambridge: Cambridge University Press, 1996).

of V. I. Lenin. Like Hobson, Lenin observed that underconsumption led to the accumulation of surplus capital, a process that became especially pronounced with the emergence of monopoly production. Because industrial and banking interests combine to gain effective control of the state, the drive to export surplus capital became a competition among countries rather than simply a competition among corporations, ultimately leading to war among the capitalist powers. Imperialism was therefore the "highest stage" of capitalism. Imperialist wars—Lenin considered the ongoing (First) World War just such a war—were the predictable outcomes of this stage of capitalist development and would be recurring until the system was overthrown.[13] Later Marxist writers drew similar conclusions from capitalist countries' need for market outlets for their products as well as their capital, and their continual need for new sources of raw materials.

All these theories came from an effort to explain European colonialism, which divided up the world into competing empires in the decades preceding World War I. The arguments put forth have been the subject of intensive criticism, however, with a number of studies supplying empirical evidence that refutes their central claims. For example, most British foreign investment did not go to the African and Asian colonies or other less-developed countries; instead, more than three-fourths went to the United States, to the predominantly white-settled countries of the British Empire, and to other advanced capitalist countries, which should have been plagued by the same surplus capital conditions supposedly existing in Britain.

Realist theorists have offered primarily political or strategic explanations for imperialism, taking account of economic factors but arguing that the typical situation was one of investments in the service of diplomacy, not vice versa. In an early challenge to predominantly economic explanations of imperial expansion, Eugene Stanley argued:

> Private investments have usually, in actual practice, been subordinated by governments to factors of general political or military strategy which have a more direct bearing on power. Thus, it is that private investors have received strong, even outrageously exaggerated governmental backing where they have been tools and agents of power and prestige politics, while other investors whose projects seemed to run counter to the government's line of political endeavor have experienced official indifference or even active opposition.[14]

Other writers, carefully examining British actions in Africa, also declared that British objectives were political and strategic, not economic. On the other hand, such strategic interests arose for Britain because of its existing imperial holdings in India—the jewel in Britain's imperial crown—which leaves open the possibility that the basic motivation for British imperialism in Africa was to protect its economic interests on the Asian subcontinent. Nevertheless, Karl Polanyi pointed out that

---

[13] V. I. Lenin, *Imperialism: The Highest Stage of Capitalism* (London: Pluto Press, 1996). For a review of early liberal and radical perspectives on imperialism, see Bernard Semmel, *The Liberal Ideal and the Demons of Empire: Theories of Imperialism from Adam Smith to Lenin* (Baltimore: Johns Hopkins University Press, 1993).

[14] Eugene Stanley, *War and the Private Investor: A Study in the Relations of International Politics and International Private Investment* (Garden City, N.Y.: Doubleday, 1935), pp. 361–362.

"business and finance were responsible for many colonial wars, but also for the fact that a general conflagration was avoided. . . . For every one interest that was furthered by war, there were a dozen that could be adversely affected. . . . Every war, almost, was organized by the financiers; but peace also was organized by them."[15]

Joseph Schumpeter is the best-known theorist to stress the noneconomic forces driving imperialism. Although he acknowledged that some monopolists had an interest in the conquest of lands producing raw materials and foodstuffs, he regarded it as a "basic fallacy to describe imperialism as a necessary phase of capitalism, or even to speak of the development of capitalism into imperialism." Some capitalists may gain but only a small minority. The gains from war for capitalists as a class are more than offset by their losses and burdens. Imperialism is primarily an affair of politicians and military personnel. Basically, imperialism stemmed from attitudes and behavior patterns among militarists, a group that evolved historically, in the precapitalist era, to defend the state and establish its security, but whose policies of foreign conquest had become "objectless" in an era of free trade.[16]

WAR AND THE DISTRIBUTION OF POWER

In addition to first and second image explanations of war, there is a *third image*. "The requirements of state action are, in this view, imposed by the circumstances in which all states exist."[17] War, in other words, can be explained by the characteristics of the international system, especially the distribution of power. As we discussed in Chapter 4, some believe that bipolar systems are most successful in avoiding major war, despite the fears and hostilities likely to be built up between the two principal antagonists. In a bipolar system, the two major powers are rather evenly matched and neither has a good chance of easy victory. War would be long and costly, and the risks of losing, even for the side that may initially seem stronger, would be substantial.

At the end of the cold war, people began to ask more insistently why there had been such a long peace—forty-five years without war between major powers, an almost unprecedented situation. Bipolarity is indeed one possible explanation. Realists, who think that the structure of the international system very much affects the likelihood of great-power war, began to predict that with the end of the bipolar cold war system we would be entering a period of great uncertainty and risk. On the other hand, nuclear weapons may have been an equally important influence, given the particular caution that the mutual vulnerability of the United States and the Soviet Union fostered. Nuclear weapons made any major-power war seem

---

[15] Karl Polanyi, *The Great Transformation: The Political and Economic Origins of Our Time*, 2nd ed. (Boston: Beacon, 2001), p. 16. On British actions in Africa, see Ronald Robinson and John Gallagher, *Africa and the Victorians: The Climax of Imperialism* (Garden City, N.Y.: Doubleday, 1968).

[16] Joseph Schumpeter, *Imperialism and Social Classes* (New York: Meridian, 1955), quote from p. 89.

[17] Waltz, *Man, the State, and War*, p. 160.

impossibly costly.[18] Yet World War II, which was fought with only conventional, nonnuclear weapons until the very end, was also hideously costly in both lives and economic destruction, demonstrating to many people that sustained war between developed industrialized states would always be a losing proposition. By this argument, all the chief antagonists of World War II learned that lesson and would have avoided war with each other again, even if nuclear weapons had not been a factor and regardless of whether the postwar distribution of power was bipolar or multipolar.

War between states also arises from change in the international system. Scholars concerned with the rise and decline of system leaders and their challengers have focused on the differential growth rates among the great powers. Especially rapid economic growth can increase a state's capabilities even without a conscious decision by its leaders to increase the state's influence in the international system. Technological innovation may occur faster in one state than in another—affecting production, creating new means of exploiting resources, or producing a potent new generation of weaponry. Slowdowns in the growth of state power can come from *imperial overstretch*, to use Paul Kennedy's term, or from a variety of domestic political and economic conditions. High levels of civil conflict, or even revolution, can seriously weaken a state, as can economic stagnation. Thus, economic and military capabilities may shift significantly, sometimes in relatively short periods of time. A variety of economic, technological, or sociocultural changes may lead to the breakdown of one system and the emergence of another.[19]

The threat to international stability stems directly from both the differential growth of power and the frequent trials of strength that test new power relationships. Such conflicts are an integral part of the balance-of-power system. If wars do occur, sometimes a major power may be eliminated or fatally weakened because of a miscalculation, bitter hatreds among citizens of the victor toward the vanquished, or the lack of internal cohesiveness of the loser. For instance, at the beginning of World War I, none of the major enemies of Austria-Hungary expected that empire to break up and utterly disappear from the ranks of major powers. When a major power is eliminated, it may be very hard to find another state capable of filling the void. Some big states will continue to grow bigger despite the efforts of others to restrain them. Thus, there are certain processes in any system that tend to eliminate some major powers and to strengthen others, making precarious the maintenance of the sensitive balance required in the long run.

The importance of changes in systems as a cause of war is clear from a careful look at Europe before the outbreak of World War I. Between 1900 and 1914,

---

[18] For the debate over bipolar stability, see John J. Mearsheimer, "Back to the Future: Instability in Europe after the Cold War," *International Security* 15 (Summer 1990), pp. 5–56; Dale C. Copeland, "The Myth of Bipolar Stability: Toward a New Dynamic Realist Theory of Major War," *Security Studies* 5 (Spring 1996), pp. 38–47. On the role of nuclear weapons, see Scott D. Sagan and Kenneth N. Waltz, *The Spread of Nuclear Weapons: A Debate Renewed*, 2nd ed. (New York: Norton, 2003).

[19] Paul Kennedy, *The Rise and Fall of the Great Powers: Economic Change and Military Conflict from 1500 to 2000* (New York: Random House, 1987). See also Dale C. Copeland, *The Origins of Major War* (Ithaca, N.Y.: Cornell University Press, 2001).

Europe was increasingly polarized, most notably by the addition of previously unallied England to the entente of France and Russia, by increases in the tightness of the opposing alliance, and by a growing shift in military capabilities in favor of the new Triple Entente. States that are the furthest apart on measures of power are the least likely to fight each other. Both sides can easily calculate who would win in a military showdown, and the weaker is likely to give in to all but the most extreme demands. Of course, the weaker side does not always give in, as was apparent in the confrontations between the United States and Iraq. Nor does the stronger state always win a war. The United States easily vanquished Iraq in 1991 and had no trouble toppling Saddam Hussein in 2003; the occupation of Iraq, however, was much more difficult and many observers feared a replay of the U.S. defeat in Vietnam.

Why is change so threatening to international peace and stability? A. F. K. Organski argued that "nations are reluctant to fight unless they believe they have a good chance of winning, but this is true for both sides only when the two are fairly evenly matched, or at least when they believe they are." Organski focused on the period of *power transition* when a rising challenger approximates the power of the dominant state: "If great change occurs within a single lifetime, both challenger and dominant nation may find it difficult to estimate their relative power correctly, and may stumble into a war that would never have been fought if both sides had foreseen where the victory would lie." It is this condition of change and uncertainty that affects calculations of relative power. The challenger may start a war because it thinks that now, for the first time, it has a good chance to win, or the dominant power may foresee its own strength declining and thus calculate that it is better to fight now, while it still has some advantages, than to risk waiting until its position may be significantly worse. Change makes calculations of power and war outcomes difficult because the evidence is ambiguous (even though the decision makers may not see the ambiguity). Decision makers may miscalculate; miscalculations may then lead to the escalation of small wars, creating a period when major wars are especially likely.[20]

Other analysts associate system change with international instability but go further to suggest that these transformations, and the global wars that go with them, occur at fairly regular intervals. George Modelski, for example, has identified "long cycles" in global politics, each lasting approximately a hundred years. Modelski says that global wars, fought by major powers, result in the establishment of a dominant world power and a high concentration of political, military, and economic capabilities. This concentration cannot last forever. Dominant states lose their economic dynamism; they overextend themselves militarily and may lose their will to dominate. As dominance wanes over a century-long period and new challengers rise, the conditions for the next global war are created. More recent

[20] A. F. K. Organski, *World Politics*, 2nd ed. (New York: Knopf, 1968), pp. 294, 480. Studies of the link between power transition and war include Douglas Lemke, *Regions of War and Peace* (Cambridge: Cambridge University Press, 2002), and Kelly M. Kadera, *The Power-Conflict Story: A Dynamic Model of Interstate Rivalry* (Ann Arbor: University of Michigan Press, 2001).

work finds global cycles of shorter duration, with periods of economic expansion making it possible for the major powers to sustain big wars.[21]

What might third image explanations tell us about the current international system and the prospects for stability and peace? The essentially bipolar structure of the cold war is gone. The changes in the relative strength of the poles came first from differing internal rates of economic growth (the failure of Soviet-style command economies compared with market economies) and then from the Soviet Union's loss of allies. The end of the cold war involved no power transition; no power transition was even approached. Systemic change occurred, but without general war. In this case, the challenger simply faded back. If we were to take seriously the arguments about why bipolar systems are more stable than multipolar ones, we might fear that the new configuration would become more prone to war—especially if we considered the new system closer to a multipolar one than to a unipolar one. A rapid change in the relative power of the leading states could be grounds for concern. What if the Russian economy experiences a serious downturn, or if a rapidly growing China and a new, anti-Western government in Russia were to ally with each other? Alternatively, the problem of a new power transition, with China surpassing the United States, may present itself.

Most third image theories in international relations do not allow us to predict war and peace in the future unless we can also predict, independently, the conditions that make war or peace more likely. Whether the international system will be peaceful in, say, 2050 depends on whether the distribution of power is bipolar, multipolar, or in transition—and currently we have no way of knowing which of those conditions, or any others, will exist. But here theories of long cycles stand out as an exception. These theories differ on the exact duration of the long cycle, but they agree that global war is associated with decline of hegemonic power and that the current hegemon is the United States. Predictions for the next phase of hegemonic decline, the most dangerous phase of the long cycle, vary from circa 2020 to 2050, depending on the analyst. Such scenarios for the outbreak of global war are not pleasant to contemplate, and we can hope only that other developments in world politics will invalidate long-cycle theory for the twenty-first century and beyond.

CONFLICT WITHIN STATES

Conflict within states is of concern for two reasons. First, and perhaps most obviously, internal conflict can be enormously destructive and long-lasting, taking a large toll on society in terms of the loss of life, the breakdown of civilian infrastructure, and enduring conditions of poverty and underdevelopment. Conflict between states often imposes the same costs, of course, but incompatibilities and misunderstandings that seem to drive conflict within states are especially hard to resolve,

---

[21] George Modelski, *Long Cycles in World Politics* (Seattle: University of Washington Press, 1987). On the relationship between economic cycles and war cycles, see George Modelski and William R. Thompson, *Leading Sectors and World Powers: The Coevolution of Global Economics and Politics* (Columbia: University of South Carolina Press, 1995); Joshua S. Goldstein in *Long Cycles in War and Economic Growth* (New Haven, Conn.: Yale University Press, 1988).

making the history of internal war a tragic one. Internal wars can be both the cause and consequence of **failed states**—states that are internationally recognized but whose governments (if they exist) cannot provide their citizens with even the minimum level of security and well-being expected of sovereign states.

Conflict within states is also a concern because it may provoke conflict between states. For example, revolutions—disruptive, often sudden, and usually violent changes of political systems—also alter the international environment and thus change the menu of other states. In the post–World War II period, revolutionary political change in Vietnam, Ethiopia, Mozambique, Iraq, and Nicaragua also brought military conflict with a neighboring state (and, in the case of Vietnam and Nicaragua, with the United States). The classic example, however, is the French Revolution. The overthrow and execution of the French king shocked the other monarchs in Europe. Their disapproval of the events unfolding in France, and their veiled threats, caused resentment within the new Legislative Assembly, which declared war on Austria in 1792, the first in the series of French Revolutionary Wars lasting ten years. The internal upheaval had subsided with the rise of Napoléon in 1799, but French militarism had not; Napoléon's personal ambitions simply came to replace revolutionary zeal as the driving force behind the continuing warfare that did not end until 1815. Stephen Walt has summarized the connection between internal revolution and external war this way:

> In short, revolutions exert far-reaching effects on states' estimates of the threats they face, and they encourage both the revolutionary state and the onlookers to view the use of force as an effective way to deal with the problem. Each side will see the other as a threat, but neither can estimate the real danger accurately. For all these reasons, revolutions exacerbate the security competition between states and increase the likelihood of war.[22]

The Uppsala Conflict Data Project reports that during 2006 there were thirty-two separate armed conflicts in progress in twenty-three states (see Table 8.2). None of these was a traditional interstate conflict, although the wars in Iraq and Afghanistan involve forces from other states, and Israel's conflict with Hezbollah has been fought mainly in southern Lebanon. The rest were almost entirely internal: conflicts over the composition of government or the type of political system ("government") or conflicts over secession or territorial autonomy ("territory"). Most conflicts involved fewer than 1,000 battle-related deaths in 2006 (labeled "minor" conflicts), but more than that number of deaths occurred in Iraq, Afghanistan, Sri Lanka, Chad, and Sudan; those conflicts are designated as "wars."

Asia and Africa have long been the most conflict-ridden regions of the globe, and still are, experiencing three-fourths of the conflicts in 2006. That is no coincidence, considering the conditions that promote civil wars. One of these conditions is *poverty*. In reasonably rich countries, the government has resources with which to satisfy demands from the most discontented groups in the society; governments

---

[22] Stephen M. Walt, *Revolution and War* (Ithaca, N.Y.: Cornell University Press, 1996), p. 6. See also Patrick J. Conge, *From Revolution to War: State Relations in a World of Change* (Ann Arbor: University of Michigan Press, 1996); Harvey Starr, "Revolution and War: Rethinking the Linkage Between Internal and External Conflict," *Political Research Quarterly* 47 (June 1994), pp. 481–507.

TABLE 8.2 | ARMED CONFLICTS IN 2006

Location	Issue	Intensity
Europe (1)		
Russia	Territory (Chechnya)	Minor
Middle East (5)		
Iran	Government	Minor
Iraq	Government	War
Israel	Territory (Palestine)	Minor
Israel	Territory (Southern Lebanon)	Minor
Turkey	Territory (Kurdistan)	Minor
Asia (15)		
Afghanistan	Government	War
Burma/Myanmar		Minor
Karen	Territory	Minor
Shan	Territory	
India		
Assam	Territory	Minor
Kashmir	Territory	Minor
Manipur	Territory	Minor
Nagaland	Territory	Minor
Tripura	Territory	Minor
Other opposition	Government	Minor
Nepal	Government	Minor
Pakistan	Territory (Baluchistan)	Minor
Philippines		
Mindanao	Territory	Minor
Other opposition	Government	Minor
Sri Lanka	Territory (Eelam)	War
Thailand	Territory (Patini)	Minor
Africa (9)		
Algeria	Government	Minor
Burundi	Government	Minor
Central African Republic	Government	Minor
Chad	Government	War
Ethiopia		
Ogaden	Territory	Minor
Oromiya	Territory	Minor

Location	Issue	Intensity
Somalia	Government	Minor
Sudan	Government	War
Uganda	Government	Minor
Americas (1)		
Colombia	Government	Minor

Source: Data compiled by the Uppsala Conflict Data Program and published in Lotta Harbom and Peter Wallensteen, "Armed Conflict, 1989–2006," *Journal of Peace Research* 44 (September 2007), pp. 623–634. A minor conflict is one involving between 25 and 1,000 battle-related deaths in 2006; a war involves more than 1,000 battle-related deaths in 2006.

in poor countries do not. In a rich country, most individuals have peaceful and productive kinds of employment available to them. But in a poor country, a pool of unemployed and uneducated young men provides a source of recruitment for violent groups promoting ideological or religious goals or simply offering a means to steal the property of others. Africa and much of Asia are the locations of some of the poorest regions of the world. By contrast, in Western and Central Europe only the Balkans—indeed, the poorest part of Europe—have experienced major civil war in the last half century.

The *lack of democracy* is another condition that may promote civil war. Especially for wars that stem from ethnic or religious conflicts, a group's lack of democratic rights can threaten the core of its ethnic identity and reduce the possibility of redressing its grievances. But it's not a simple matter of greater democracy equaling a lower risk of civil war. Really tough dictatorships, like the old Soviet Union, can repress and suppress rebellion by overwhelming force. They are willing to do so, and have the capability. Truly democratic governments, on the other hand, are ready and often able to recognize group and individual rights and so lower the grievance level. Consequently, there are very few civil wars in the democratic countries of Europe and North America. (It also helps that those governments are also rich enough to distribute resources to discontented groups.) The greatest risk of civil war comes in countries where the government is neither tough enough to repress effectively nor democratic enough to satisfy grievances. Yugoslavia, after the cold war, went through a limited process of liberalization from the old dictatorship but fell well short of full democracy—and fell apart with the expression of old and new ethnic hatreds.[23]

Various forms of internal conflict—political unrest and instability, as well as civil war—are key predictors of state failure, along with poverty, lack of

[23] Håvard Hegre, Tanja Ellingsen, Scott Gates, and Nils Petter Gleditsch, "Toward a Democratic Civil Peace? Democracy, Political Change, and Civil War, 1816–1992," *American Political Science Review* 95 (March 2001), pp. 33–48. A review of the literature on democracy and conflict within states can be found in David Kinsella and David L. Rousseau, "Democracy and Conflict Resolution," in Jacob Bercovitch, Victor Kremenyuk, and I. William Zartman, eds., *The Sage Handbook of Conflict Resolution* (London: Sage, 2008).

democracy, and external war. These factors have clustered in certain geographical regions, most notably sub-Saharan Africa, creating a "bad neighborhood" of failed states or states at risk of failure. The effects of poverty, bad government, and internal conflict also have been found to spread to neighboring states and nearby regions.[24]

ETHNIC CONFLICT

Many conflicts in contemporary international politics arise from threats (or perceived threats) to group identification and loyalty. One problem is that states and nations may not coincide on the same territory. The separate nationalisms of different ethnic groups may threaten to tear a state apart, as they did former Yugoslavia. Different national identities within a state may tempt another state to intervene on behalf of a minority. Sometimes a feeling of nationality may spill over many states, calling into question the legitimacy of separate states (as in the case of pan-Arab nationalism). Although we commonly refer to entities in the international system as nation-states, there are in fact many multinational states and multistate nations. The mismatch of state and nation has been the cause of much conflict in world politics. Although no one factor appears to be sufficient to account for group loyalty, it may be that a cleavage along racial, tribal, linguistic, or religious lines is sufficient to bring about **ethnopolitical conflict**, also called *communal conflict*. The pressures toward separatism or fragmentation in the world system are powerful and widespread. Most modern states are mosaics of distinct peoples, and their security and aspirations often are not respected by those in control of the central government.

After decolonization, states with no geographical logic beyond the arbitrary boundary lines drawn on maps by former colonial powers were split by diverse groups and have struggled to forge group loyalty from this diversity. But postcolonial states are not the only ones, as we can see from Map 8.1. One-fifth of Russia's population is non-Russian; half of its territory consists of ethnic republics and autonomous regions. The northern Caucasus region, which includes the now-independent states of Georgia, Armenia, and Azerbaijan, is home to a very large number of ethnically based linguistic groups (see inset). Nationalism has been reinforced by religious fervor (radical Islam) in Chechnya, and the fighting that resumed in 1999 provoked a particularly brutal Russian occupation. To the west, ethnic and religious tensions between Ingushetians (Muslims) and North Ossetians (Christians) repeatedly threatened to erupt into widespread violence, while the government of Georgia tried to suppress South Ossetian demands for territorial attachment to North Ossetia, triggering a Russian invasion in August 2008. To the east in Dagestan, ethnic tension has been infused with hostilities between different Islamic sects; further south, the Lezgins in Azerbaijan, like the Ossetians in Georgia, want to unite their territory with that inhabited by Dagestanian Lezgins in Russia.

---

[24] Zaryab Iqbal and Harvey Starr, "Bad Neighbors: Failed States and Their Consequences," *Conflict Management and Peace Science* 25 (Winter 2008), pp. 315–31.

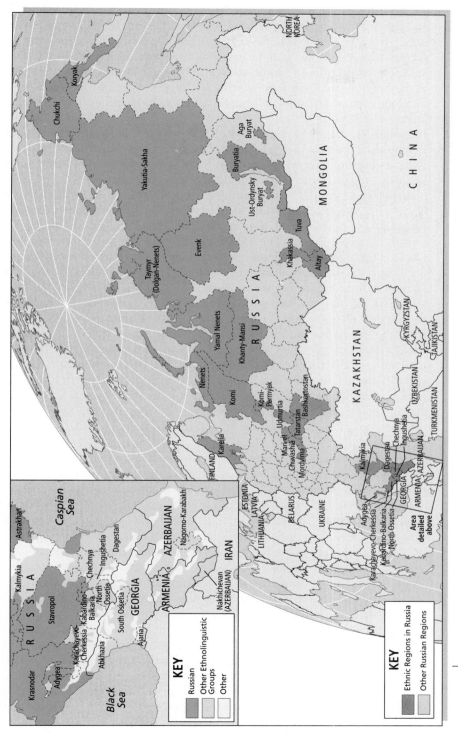

MAP 8.1 | ETHNIC REGIONS IN RUSSIA AND NORTHERN CAUCASUS

Ethnic tensions in Russia have come to the surface since the disintegration of the Soviet Union. The northern Caucasus region is especially volatile, where ethnic and linguistic differences are often combined with opposing nationalist sentiments and religious identities. These forces raise not only the specter of ethnopolitical warfare in Russia but also of interstate conflicts between Russia and states that were formerly part of the Soviet Union.

States have fought intense civil wars over unity or separation. The Ibo rebellion and the attempt to establish Biafra were defeated by the Nigerian government in a three-year war that ended in 1970. In contrast, the Bengali secession from Pakistan was successful, though not without external assistance. The Bengali population of East Pakistan rose in riots and instituted a general strike in March 1971 after being denied victory at the polls. Though sharing a common religion, East and West Pakistan differed in ethnicity, language, and economic factors and were separated by approximately 1,000 miles of Indian territory. West Pakistani armed attacks on the East Pakistanis led to the December 1971 war between India and Pakistan. The Indian victory permitted the Bengalis to declare their own independent state, Bangladesh. India, a large and diverse country, has itself been wracked by conflict among different linguistic, regional, racial, and religious groups. Violence involving the Sikh religious minority in the Punjab was responsible for the assassination of Prime Minister Indira Gandhi in 1984. Her son, Prime Minister Rajiv Gandhi, was assassinated in 1991 by a Tamil group that blamed him for India's abandonment of the Tamil separatist movement in Sri Lanka. The 1990s also saw the intensification of a Muslim drive for an independent Kashmir and insurgent separatism in the northeast state of Assam. Such communal conflict was intensified by a revival of Hindu nationalism and the rise to power of the Bharatiya Janata Party.

Fears of nationalistic meltdowns, however, are not confined to the less-developed states or only to those states formed since World War II. Loyalty is based on group interaction. If some part of a group feels it is being exploited or that mutual benefits from association with the larger group no longer exist, then the loyalty and we-feeling will disintegrate. The *process* of national integration is a continuous one, and the nation may be susceptible to disintegration if that process is neglected. The most graphic instance of disintegration is seen in the violence accompanying the breakup of Yugoslavia. We can also see its effects in the rapid dissolution of the Soviet Union and the ethnic troubles that continue to plague Russia.

Even the older and intact states of Europe must continually work to make ethnic minorities feel a nationalist connection to the nation-state as a whole. There are more-or-less well-organized nationalist movements among the Basques in Spain, the Welsh and Scots in Britain, and the Bretons and Corsicans, who are governed by France. In Canada, French speakers in the province of Quebec have a long tradition of separatist politics. Canada's handling of this problem is a good example of how an established and developed state risks being broken apart and of the dilemmas that a democracy faces in such a situation. Attempts at nation building included the institutionalization of bilingualism, special constitutional arrangements, and the creation of specifically Canadian images for the national flag and national anthem (the previous flag had incorporated the British Union Jack, and the anthem had been "God Save the Queen"). That political crises continue to occur in Canada over the proper constitutional arrangements required to deal with the separatist movement in Quebec and yet satisfy the western provinces indicates the difficulties of building and maintaining a state.

According to the Minorities at Risk Project, more than 280 substantial ethnic groups are politically active in more than 100 countries. In about half of these states, ethnic groups constituted more than one-quarter of the total population. In

2003, nearly 60 of these groups were engaged in active *rebellion* against the central government: banditry, campaigns of terrorism, insurgency, or civil war. Many groups are also engaged in *intercommunal* conflict. In 2000, about 70 groups participated in sporadic violent attacks against other groups or antigroup demonstrations, and one-fourth of them took part in more severe communal rioting or warfare. The human costs of ethnopolitical conflict are immense. More than 60 million people have been killed in ethnic violence since the end of World War II. Roughly 35 million are displaced each year; more than half of them typically cross interstate borders, straining the resources of neighboring countries and increasing the risks that civil conflicts will become international ones.[25]

The Rwandan genocide was a tragic illustration of the extreme brutality of unchecked ethnic conflict and the inability (or unwillingness) of the international community to fashion an effective response when the killing is contained within a state's borders. The genocide was triggered when the Hutu president's plane was downed on its approach to Kigali airfield in April 1994. The majority Hutu, marginalized by foreign administrators before Rwandan independence, were hostile toward the minority Tutsi, who had long enjoyed an advantageous political and economic position in society. Ethnic violence was ongoing, even before the genocide; the mainly Tutsi Rwandan Patriotic Front (RPF) had been fighting the government since 1990, prompting armed intervention by French troops in 1993 and the stationing of UN observers to monitor the ceasefire. The resurgence of ethnic warfare in 1994 was spurred on by expanding executions by a paramilitary group, the Interahamwe, which originally functioned as the Hutu palace guard. The violence toward Tutsi and moderate Hutu quickly spiraled out of control, and in a matter of months between 500,000 and 800,000 had been slaughtered at the hands of Hutu extremists. Despite feeble efforts by the international community to stem the violence, it was not until the RPF seized the capital that the genocide was stopped—but not before Tutsi revenge attacks killed another 25,000 to 45,000 Hutu in Rwanda, while RPF forces pursued as many as 200,000 to their deaths in Zaire (now the Democratic Republic of the Congo). By August, about one-quarter of Rwanda's population had died or fled the country.[26]

Once the full extent of the Rwandan genocide came to light, as well as the primitive means by which it was conducted (knives, machetes, and small arms), many observers concluded that this sort of ethnic violence could have been—and ought to have been—prevented by decisive armed intervention by the international community. One decade later, the latest chapter in the long-running civil war in Sudan seemed to contain many of the same elements as the Rwanda crisis: a central government, dominated by one ethnic group (Arabs), fighting an insurgency drawn

---

[25] Figures for deaths and displacements come from Wilma A. Dunaway, "Ethnic Conflict in the Modern World-System: The Dialectics of Counter-Hegemonic Resistance in an Age of Transition," *Journal of World-Systems Research* 9 (Winter 2003), p. 26. Other figures are compiled from data released by the Minorities at Risk Project (2005); available at <http://www.cidcm.umd.edu/mar/>.

[26] On the UN role, see Michael Barnett, *Eyewitness to a Genocide: The United Nations and Rwanda* (Ithaca, N.Y.: Cornell University Press, 2002); and Roméo Dallaire, *Shake Hands with the Devil: The Failure of Humanity in Rwanda* (New York: Carroll & Graf, 2004). Dallaire was UN force commander in Rwanda during the genocide.

from a different ethnic population (blacks); a pro-government militia (the Janja-
weed) terrorizing civilians, causing widespread death and upheaval (200,000 dead
and 2 million displaced since 2003). Yet the international community was again
slow to respond—and was especially reluctant to use the term *genocide* to describe
what was going on there, preferring instead such phrases as "massive violations of
human rights" or some other characterization that did not invoke the same obligation to act. It was not until 2007 that the Security Council authorized a combined
UN and African Union peacekeeping force for the region.

GREED AND PREDATION

Deprivation—poverty and the lack of political and civil rights—can cause populations to rebel against the central government, and when economic and political
rewards are distributed unequally among ethnic groups within society, conditions
are ripe for eruption of ethnopolitical conflict. Other conditions allow civil war to
persist. One is *external assistance*. Arms and money supplied by the United States
and Pakistan to the rebels in Afghanistan was crucial to their persistent fight
against the Soviet-supported government during the 1980s and, ultimately, to the
rise of the Taliban. Indeed, the pattern of Soviet support for one side in a civil war
and American support for the other was common during the cold war. Wars in
Angola, Ethiopia, Mozambique, Nicaragua, and El Salvador are some of the examples, calling to mind the African proverb, "When elephants fight, it is the grass that
suffers." Many of those vicious wars ended when the cold war did. Russia could
no longer support its side, and with its strategic competitor gone the United States
lost interest.

Another factor in ongoing civil wars is the *presence of lootable resources*, like
gold, diamonds, drugs, or other high-value commodities, especially in otherwise
poor countries. Dissident groups have a problem in launching and sustaining rebellion—what one scholar has called "the rebel's dilemma."[27] Combat is dangerous;
most individuals are not highly motivated to fight and possibly die and would
rather let someone else do it. But lootable resources provide the incentive and a
means for leaders to reward their fighters and keep their loyalty. We see the consequences in many places. The rebellion in Colombia is sustained by the drug traffic,
and in places such as Sierra Leone and Angola rebellion was propped up by diamond smuggling. Virtually all civil wars are fed in part by bribery, corruption,
and black market dealings. And rebels are not the only beneficiaries of lootable
resources. During the Angolan civil war, for example, the government maintained
its forces with the aid of large and steady receipts from coastal oil wells operated
by Gulf Oil in areas secured by government forces.

Some people question the importance of perceived deprivation as an explanation for the emergence of civil conflict because such grievances are so widespread
in the world; not everyone who feels cheated by the government or the dominant
group in society takes up arms in revolt. Dissident leaders motivated primarily by
greed are often able to stir up supporters by playing upon their grievances while at

---

[27] Mark Irving Lichbach, *The Rebel's Dilemma* (Ann Arbor: University of Michigan Press, 1995).

the same time promising that the rebels can enrich themselves by looting whatever resources they can bring under their control. Grievances are not irrelevant, but they are seen as secondary—used merely as a more politically acceptable justification for an armed rebellion otherwise motivated by greed and sustained by predation.[28]

To the extent that greed is the central motivation behind certain rebel movements today, the prospects for lasting peace settlements are disturbing. Insurgencies, whatever their motivation, thrive where the government is absent and order has broken down. Rebels gain the support of the population in these areas when they are able to provide a new social order, and that new order may be legitimate in the eyes of locals even if it is not lawful. Thus, there are many willing participants in the narco-economy in Colombia; in rural areas devoted to coca cultivation, rebel groups function as "shadow states," providing the order and protection that citizens otherwise expect from the central government in Bogotá.[29] As shadow states become established and achieve a degree of local legitimacy, loot seeking and predation might be better understood as rent seeking and taxation, but the purpose is the same: to sustain a rebel movement posing as an alternative to the central government. However, if the shadow economy is serving the interests of both the local population and the rebels, the incentive to "win" the war with the government is much diminished. Assuming control of the government carries with it a responsibility to enforce the law of the land, and that means abandoning a local political and economic arrangement beneficial to the rebels. Rebels may prefer the status quo—a central government with truncated control over the state's territory, with rebel political and economic fiefdoms in the periphery—and may choose to prolong the civil war indefinitely, or at least as long as the government attempts to extend its reach. Afghanistan, with its regional warlords, exhibits this pattern as well, which is why President Hamid Karzai has been dubbed the "Mayor of Kabul."

Internal conflict weakens governments, but it is also a symptom of state failure. As we discuss in Chapter 14, globalization is a process that erodes the capacity of many governments to manage cross-border flows of goods, people, and ideas. Although the free flow of capital and labor may be conducive to economic efficiency and industrial development, the free flow of refugees, guns, and disease puts the local population at risk. At the root of what Mary Kaldor calls "new wars" is identity politics: the mobilization of opposition movements around ethnic, racial, or religious identity in reaction to the inability of ruling groups to provide for security and well-being of the rest of the population. The failure of states to blunt the economic shocks of globalization is also a factor in the emergence of shadow economies. The result is that "a new retrograde set of social arrangements

---

[28] Paul Collier, "Rebellion as a Quasi-Criminal Activity," *Journal of Conflict Resolution* 44 (December 2000), pp. 839–853; James D. Fearon and David D. Laitin, "Ethnicity, Insurgency, and Civil War," *American Political Science Review* 97 (February 2003), pp. 75–90. See also, in regard to the war in Sierra Leone, Macartan Humphreys and Jeremy M. Weinstein, "Who Fights? The Determinants of Participation in Civil War," *American Journal of Political Science* 52 (April 2008), pp. 436–455.

[29] William Reno, "Shadow States and the Political Economy of Civil Wars," in Mats Berdal and David M. Malone, eds., *Greed and Grievance: Economic Agendas in Civil Wars* (Boulder, Colo.: Rienner, 2000).

is being established in which economics and violence are deeply intertwined within the shared framework of identity politics."[30]

UNCONVENTIONAL CONFLICT

The labels *unconventional* and *irregular* are often used to describe conflicts that do not take the form of mass armies engaging one another on the battlefield, or the traditional air- and sea-based military operations that support them. Guerrilla warfare—operations conducted by paramilitary forces in enemy-held territory—has been labeled as such, but guerrilla tactics have become so widespread since World War II, especially since the wars of decolonization, that it hardly seems correct to call them unconventional.[31] In any event, the kind of conflicts we have in mind are those in which combatants on one or more sides in a dispute avoid pitched military battles with the enemy. In the case of guerrilla warfare, combatants stage raids, ambushes, and sabotage from remote and inaccessible bases in mountains, forests, jungles, or the territory of neighboring states. Virtually all conflicts within states have at one time or another involved guerrilla warfare, and most have also witnessed the use of terrorist tactics.

Although governments and other actors usually intend to morally condemn unconventional tactics when they refer to "guerrillas" or "terrorists"—as opposed to "freedom fighters"—these groups usually resort to such tactics out of necessity. They typically command few resources and must pursue cost-effective methods of military combat and political disruption. In the modern era in which there are great disparities in the capacity of different groups to muster political, economic, and military power, it is perhaps not surprising that more and more of those at a disadvantage have turned to unconventional means. These tactics do have a long history, however. In the first century C.E., the Jewish Zealots employed them in their attempt to dislodge Roman forces occupying what is now Israel, culminating in the storied siege of Masada by the Roman Tenth Legion. In the period leading up to the American Revolution, the minutemen of New England (who assembled to fight the British at a minute's notice) are best described as guerrilla fighters. And many in the late-nineteenth-century anarchist movement in Western Europe and Russia advocated the use of terrorist methods, especially political assassination. In the span of less than a decade, French President Marie François Sadi Carnot, Spanish Prime Minister Antonio Cánovas, Italian King Humbert I, and U.S. President William McKinley were all victims of anarchist assassination.

---

[30] Mary Kaldor, *New and Old Wars: Organized Violence in a Global Era* (Stanford, Calif.: Stanford University Press, 1999), p. 107. For a skeptical view of primarily economic explanations of internal war, see I. William Zartman, "Need, Creed, and Greed in Intrastate Conflict," in Cynthia J. Arnson and I. William Zartman, eds., *Rethinking the Economics of War: The Intersection of Need, Creed, and Greed* (Baltimore: Johns Hopkins University Press, 2005).

[31] See, for example, Terry Terrif, Aaron Karp, and Regina Karp, eds., *Global Insurgency and the Future of Armed Conflict: Debating Fourth-Generation Warfare* (London: Routledge, 2007).

INTERNATIONAL TERRORISM

The principal purpose of **terrorism** is not the actual destruction produced but its dramatic and psychological effects on populations and governments. The objectives of terrorism are to frighten target audiences through the use of dramatic and shocking acts, which include bombings, assassinations, kidnappings, the taking of hostages, and hijackings. Although guerrilla groups sometimes employ such tactics, terrorism is not the same as guerrilla warfare. Terrorist acts are not typically directed toward enemy combatants; their targets are civilians, government workers, or noncombatant military personnel. Terrorism involves the systematic use of violence—often suicidal violence—for political ends, acts intended to produce fear that will change attitudes and behavior toward governments and their policies.[32]

Nonstate actors at various points in time have sought to undermine governments by making them appear weak, ineffectual, and unable to protect the population. Terrorists wish to gain publicity and attention and to convince the government and population that they are a potent political force. Terrorism also weakens governmental support when the government responds indiscriminately to terrorist acts, "retaliating" on sectors of the population not connected with the terrorists. Because governments find it so hard to find and punish those responsible for terrorist acts, terrorism can be a frustratingly effective political weapon. Some of the most prominent terrorist groups in recent years include Aum Shinrikyo in Japan, the Basques (ETA) in Spain, Hamas in Palestine, Hezbollah in Lebanon, the Irish Republican Army (IRA), the Tamil Tigers (LTTE) in Sri Lanka, the Kurdistan Workers' Party (PKK) in Turkey, and the Shining Path (Sendero Luminoso) in Peru.

The twin bombings of the American embassies in Kenya and Tanzania in 1998, attributed to Osama bin Laden and his al Qaeda organization, sparked talk of a new kind of international terrorist—one without commitment to any particular territory (and without well-defined territorial aspirations), and skilled in the use of transnational communications and financial networks as a means of coordinating and supporting the activities of dispersed operatives. The September 11 attacks on the World Trade Center and the Pentagon in 2001 made combating al Qaeda's brand of terrorism the top priority of the United States, and the Bush administration's war on terror received considerable support from nations throughout the world. However, although the Taliban (al Qaeda's hosts in Afghanistan) had been routed within months of 9/11, bin Laden and several of his top lieutenants remained at large and a surprisingly large number of people in the United States and elsewhere had resigned themselves to the likelihood that al Qaeda or an affiliated group would strike again, and in a big way. In time, as questions emerged about the Bush administration's anti-terror strategy overseas (especially the diversion in Iraq) and its willingness to curtail civil liberties at home, support for the U.S.–led war on terror began to dissolve.

---

[32] See, for example, Bruce Hoffman, *Inside Terrorism* (New York: Columbia University Press, 1998); Andrew H. Kydd and Barbara F. Walter, "The Strategies of Terrorism," *International Security* 31 (Summer 2006), pp. 49–80. On the use of suicidal violence, see Robert E. Pape, *Dying to Win: The Strategic Logic of Suicide Terrorism* (New York: Random House, 2005).

Many analysts of contemporary terrorism have focused on the flexibility and resilience of their organizations, which often take the form of networks (see Figure 8.1). A network is a nonhierarchical, or partially hierarchical, form of organization consisting of nodes (physical sites, people, or organizations) linked in various ways for various purposes. Network forms of organization have been extremely important to modern societies because they incorporate "redundancy" and thereby facilitate the flow of people, goods, and information, even when parts of the network experience disruption or overload. Traffic can become maddeningly slow, whether on city streets, in air corridors, or over the Internet, but it rarely comes to a complete standstill. The information revolution has enhanced the smooth functioning of *physical networks* such as transportation, communications, and power grids, but it has also enabled the creation and maintenance of geographically far-flung *social networks* (users of websites like Facebook and MySpace can attest to this). International terrorist groups, including al Qaeda, are similarly organized. As with physical networks, an

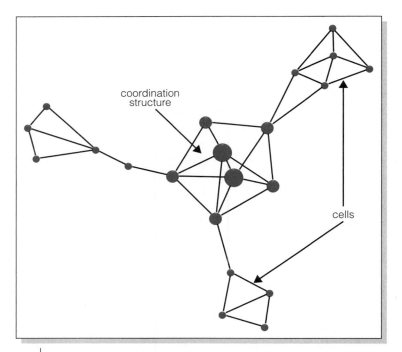

FIGURE 8.1 | STRUCTURE OF A HYPOTHETICAL TERRORIST NETWORK

Terrorist networks often combine centralized and decentralized forms of organization. Centralization allows for the coordination of objectives and strategic planning, while decentralization allows for relatively autonomous tactical planning and execution. Attempts to disrupt the network by attacking the centralized coordination structure may leave the decentralized cells intact and functioning.

attack on one part of a terrorist or criminal network, even its command and coordination structure, may leave other parts of the network free to adapt and carry on with the organization's central mission. On the other hand, networks are far from invulnerable; counterterrorism experts continuously worry about weak nodes in the social infrastructure and the danger of cascading network failures like the one that caused the electric power failure in the northeastern quadrant of the United States in 2003. Combating modern transnational terrorism therefore requires an understanding of networked forms of organization, their resiliencies, and their vulnerabilities.[33]

It is important to distinguish dissident terrorism from establishment terrorism, or **state terrorism**. Governments also use terror tactics against their own populations to gain or increase political control through the manipulation of fear. These tactics include torture, murder, expulsion or exile, the toleration of vigilante groups (as in Rwanda and Sudan), and widespread arrests and kidnappings (like the "disappearances" in Argentina and Chile). This form of terrorism also has a long and sordid history. The Reign of Terror in France in the 1790s and Stalin's "purges" in the Soviet Union during the 1930s are two of countless examples. One scholar has chronicled "democide"—genocide and mass murder—during the twentieth century. From 1900 through the end of the cold war, almost 170 million people were killed by their own governments, far more people than killed in wars. The major "megamurderers" during this period were the most authoritarian states—the Soviet Union, the People's Republic of China, Germany (from 1933 to 1945), and Nationalist China (from 1928 to 1949); the least murderous countries were democracies. The author's conclusion: "Power kills, absolute power kills absolutely."[34]

Another form of terrorism is **state-sponsored terrorism**—international terrorist activity conducted by state officials or, more often, the support of terrorist groups through the provision of arms, training, safe haven, or financial backing. In sponsoring terrorism against another government, a state pursues the same objective mentioned previously: weakening the control of that government by hurting and embarrassing it. In this sense, states are using the actions of terrorist groups in surrogate warfare. After regime change in Iraq in 2003, the U.S. state department's list of state sponsors of terrorism was reduced to six, and after Libya renounced terrorism and forswore the development of weapons of mass destruction in 2006, it was reduced to five. Iran and Syria are accused of supporting the Hezbollah in Lebanon, the Palestine Islamic Jihad, Hamas, and other groups. Cuba, North Korea, and Sudan are regarded as less active state sponsors but remain on the list and are therefore subject to strict economic and financial sanctions.

Figure 8.2 shows the trend in international terrorism since 1970. During this time, the number of international terrorist incidents rose steadily to its peak of

---

[33] Marc Sageman, *Leaderless Jihad: Terror Networks in the Twenty-First Century* (Philadelphia: University of Pennsylvania Press, 2008); Steve Ressler, "Social Network Analysis as an Approach to Combat Terrorism: Past, Present, and Future Research," *Homeland Security Affairs* 2 (July 2006).

[34] Rudolph J. Rummel, *Death by Government: Genocide and Mass Murder since 1900* (New Brunswick, N.J.: Transaction, 1994).

665 incidents in 1987; since then, the number of terrorist acts has shown a general downward trend, though with considerable variability from year to year. Terrorism-related casualties have shown no clear trend over the last three decades. The sarin gas attack on the Tokyo subway system by Aum Shinrikyo killed only 12 but injured 5,700. The 1998 U.S. embassy bombings in Kenya and Tanzania killed 300 and injured 5,000, mostly Kenyans. Of course, the 3,000 deaths resulting from the 9/11 attacks were unprecedented; no other terrorist attack in history killed more. If tallies of terrorist attacks and resulting deaths are expanded to include incidents of domestic as well as international terrorism, the numbers increase by two orders of magnitude in recent years, not least because such tactics are frequently employed by insurgents in Afghanistan and Iraq. Not surprisingly, this is the U.S. state department's current method of tracking global terrorism, and its recent counts are shown on the far right of Figure 8.2.

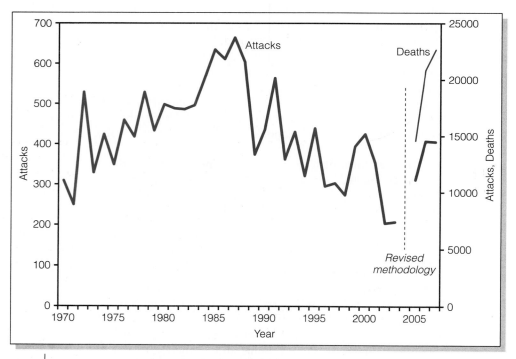

FIGURE 8.2 | TERRORIST INCIDENTS WORLDWIDE, 1970–2007

From the late 1960s until the mid-1980s, the U.S. Department of State reported a gradual increase in the incidents of international terrorism worldwide; thereafter the trend reversed until 2003. Beginning in 2005, the state department began using a revised methodology for counting terrorist incidents, which resulted in significantly higher counts of both attacks and resulting casualties (vertical axis on right). About half of the attacks reported since 2004 have occurred in Iraq and Afghanistan.

Source: Compiled from various editions of the U.S. Department of State's *Patterns of Global Terrorism* (for 1970–2003) and *Country Reports on Terrorism* (for 2005–2007). Recent versions of both titles are available at <http://www.state.gov/s/ct/rls/>.

INFORMATION WARFARE

Access to information has long been an important element in warfighting. In the fourth century B.C.E., the philosopher-general Sun Tzu wrote, "Though the enemy be stronger in numbers, we may prevent him from fighting. Scheme so as to discover his plans and the likelihood of their success. Rouse him, and learn the principle of his activity and inactivity." In making one's own plans, he continued, "the highest pitch you can attain is to conceal them; conceal your dispositions." The success of the Golden Horde against numerically superior forces in Russia and eastern Europe during the thirteenth century rested on continuously updated information about the enemy's whereabouts and formation. Scouts and messengers (the "arrow riders") were able to apprise Batu Khan of developments within four or five days, which during this period was the closest thing to "real-time" intelligence. At the same time, Mongol advantages in mobility and deception enabled them to keep their own location secret. Armed with superior information, the Horde could strike at the enemy's communications causing disarray and undermining any numerical advantage. When the Mongols advanced into Syria and Egypt, however, they met their match in the Mamelukes who, among other displays of military prowess, made use of carrier pigeons.[35]

Information warfare involves the manipulation, corruption, or denial of information. It can include many things, from disruption of an opponent's ability to command and control its military forces to psychological tactics, like the broadcasts of Tokyo Rose during World War II or the rock-and-roll music blasted by U.S. Marines during the 1983 Panama invasion in an effort to drive dictator Manuel Noriega out of the Vatican embassy. Other forms still inhabit the realm of speculation, especially those tactics that are often referred to as *cyberterrorism* or *hacker war* or some other term meant to capture the enlistment of computing technology for purposes of disruption and violence. Although we have not yet witnessed widespread and sustained use of this sort of information warfare, there have been numerous cases of political activism undertaken by hacking into or inundating target computer systems—"hacktivism." For example, in September 1998 the Electronic Disturbance Theater (EDT) registered its support for the Zapatista movement in Mexico by overloading Mexican government websites (along with those of the Pentagon and Frankfurt Stock Exchange) with hundreds of thousands of browser hits per minute during a period of several hours. A more serious series of cyberattacks came to light in 2001 when U.S. officials lodged a formal complaint with the Russian government. In an operation investigators would name "Moonlight Maze," hackers penetrated Pentagon computers regularly over the course of three years from Russian Internet addresses, although it was not certain that the intruders were operating from Russian territory. Imagining the forms that more damaging attacks might take and protecting against them has become a

---

[35] Sun Tzu, *The Art of War*, edited by James Clavell (New York: Delacorte, 1983), p. 28. The contemporary relevance of the Mongol way of warfare is discussed in John Arquilla and David Ronfeldt, "Cyberwar is Coming!" *Comparative Strategy* 12 (Spring 1993), pp. 141–165.

preoccupation of the defense establishments of the United States and many other industrialized countries.[36]

Technological advances in communication and computation have been integrated into the modern military as part of the so-called revolution in military affairs. Many aspects of information warfare, therefore, represent advances in the conduct of conventional conflicts between states or between state and nonstate actors. The precision-guided munitions ("smart bombs") first launched by American forces against Iraq's communications network during the Gulf War represented the application of new technology to an otherwise old objective in warfare. The psychological operations conducted by the U.S. Army before the 1994 invasion of Haiti, in which pro-Aristide leaflets were tailored to specific segments of the population based on market-research techniques, was simply a sophisticated use of wartime propaganda.

Other techniques of information warfare, as yet untried (or as yet unsuccessful), may become tools for waging unconventional conflict. Cyberterrorism might take the form of inserting a computer virus into telephone-switching software thereby disrupting the phone system, or planting a "logic bomb" set to go off at a specified time to wreak havoc on the electronic routers controlling a commuter rail line. Air and ground transportation, financial and stock markets, telecommunications systems, electric power grids, and many other aspects of modern civil society rely on computer programs and networks for their smooth functioning and, hypothetically at least, could be subject to hacker attacks. Because terrorists cannot muster the resources necessary to engage the enemy militarily, a laptop and wireless network card would seem ideally suited to their needs.

There may also be a tendency to overstate the importance of information warfare for future conflict between and within states. As we have said, targeting an opponent's command and communications facilities and engaging in psychological operations have long been elements in military conflict. The information revolution has enhanced such capacities in the case of modern militaries, but it did not invent them. Information warfare targeted at the civilian population—sometimes called *netwar* because it aims at the networks connecting society—would constitute more of a break with the past. Still, it is somewhat ironic that the very developments that seem to usher in the possibility of information warfare also suggest limits to its effectiveness. For every accomplished hacker, there is an equally accomplished computer security specialist. Moreover, networks, including computer and communications networks, are webs with multiple pathways between any two points. Although that may provide the cyberterrorist many more points of entry for hacking into crucial systems, for every way in there is a way around. Well-designed backup systems take advantage of network redundancy, allowing the stream of information to seek out alternative channels in the event of disruption.

---

[36] The EDT action is discussed in Dorothy E. Denning, "Activism, Hacktivism, and Cyberterrorism: The Internet as a Tool for Influencing Foreign Policy," in John Arquilla and David Ronfeldt, *Networks and Netwars: The Future of Terror, Crime, and Militancy* (Santa Monica, Calif.: RAND, 2001). On Moonlight Maze, see James Adams, "Virtual Defense," *Foreign Affairs* 80 (May/June 2001), pp. 98–112.

It is perhaps a sad commentary on human evolution that advances in technology are almost immediately integrated into our methods of disruption and destruction. Indeed, as we will see in Chapter 12, the quest for improved military capability has often been the driving force behind technological progress. The Internet itself was a by-product of an effort by the U.S. defense establishment to create a robust communications infrastructure that would not collapse during a nuclear war. The relationship between technology, weaponry, and conflict is a complex one, which we continue to explore in the next chapter.

THE SECURITY DILEMMA: ARMAMENT AND DISARMAMENT

CHAPTER 9

ARMED FORCES

Armed forces play an important role in politics between and within states. The need to support and supply mass armies was a central driving force in the evolution of the institutional apparatus of the modern state in fifteenth- and sixteenth-century Europe. Even today, the armed forces are at the forefront of state building and modernization in many countries, often in relatively young states that were formerly part of colonial empires. The conduct of foreign relations throughout history has been so infused with the acquisition, display, and use of military power that the study of international relations is sometimes, though erroneously, equated with the study of military affairs—or simply "bombs and rockets." Although no student of world politics (having gotten this far in the book) would make such a mistake, this chapter is in fact about bombs and rockets and about the politics and policies that surround their deployment, management, and, in the case of arms control, their decommissioning.

The military as an institution can trace its roots at least as far back as ancient Mesopotamia's standing armies equipped with bows and spears. Since then, armies and their means of conducting warfare have gone through many transformations, the most significant ones being linked to the evolution of technology, which greatly expands the opportunities available to decision makers. The horse-drawn chariot gave birth to the cavalry, gunpowder made possible explosive munitions, and the Industrial Revolution led to the development of mechanized fighting forces. Armies took to the air with the advent of air travel, while the exploration of space permitted the intercontinental delivery of bombs by self-propelled ballistic missiles. Of course, the most profound and threatening of these many military-technological advances was the development of the atomic bomb. The deployment and proliferation of nuclear weapons prompted not only fundamental shifts in military strategy but also a widespread desire for progress in the area of arms control and disarmament.

In Chapter 12 we will explore the political economy of defense and disarmament, which includes topics relating to military technology and the role of the state in promoting technological advancement in the pursuit of national security. In this chapter we focus more generally on arms acquisition by states, the dynamics of arms races, and the mixed historical record of arms control.

ARMS ACQUISITION

Why do countries arm? One straightforward explanation is that states acquire arms in response to the arms acquisitions of their adversaries. Lewis F. Richardson, a pioneer in the study of states' arms acquisition processes, pointed to the "very strong motive of fear, which moves each group to increase its armaments because of the existence of those of the opposing group."[1] When both sides are ensnared in this action–reaction process, we have the makings of an **arms race**. In the early cold war years, it seemed to many Americans that the action–reaction phenomenon was all one way: The United States was reacting to Soviet militarization (and other forms of aggressive behavior). However, when the period of isolation under Stalin drew to a close and Soviet and U.S. scientists began to make contact with each other, it became apparent that Soviet citizens typically held the mirror image of the American perspective: They saw the Soviet Union as simply reacting to American threats. From this exchange, people developed a more general understanding that in some real sense each side was reacting to the other and that it was extraordinarily difficult to sort out particular causes, especially once the action–reaction process was under way.

Figure 9.1 shows that Soviet and American military expenditures were fairly steady from the end of the Korean War until the early 1960s when they begin to move upward. An arms race need not imply an ever-escalating spiral. A race does imply competition, but if two long-distance runners maintain a steady pace, the race is progressing just as much as if their speeds were continually increasing. It is this element of competition, or *interaction*, that characterizes an arms race. Such interaction seemed to be present in Soviet and U.S. behavior throughout the cold war. It was not always a mechanical process of action and reaction but moved in fits and starts in response to particular decisions that seemed especially provocative and was conditioned by other developments in the superpowers' foreign and domestic environments. The analogy to a race surely does not explain every element of superpower relations. It may tell us about interaction in arms spending at a general level but not about the presence or absence of competition in the acquisition of specific weapons systems. Moreover, the idea of interaction does not explain what happened in the 1970s. The action–reaction hypothesis suggests that the Soviet Union would have moderated its military spending once the Americans slowed down theirs after Vietnam. No such moderation took place, as we can see from Figure 9.1. Something other than a straightforward action–reaction process was driving Soviet military spending during these years.[2]

Other explanations for arms acquisitions focus on domestic influences, including bureaucratic pressures or "inertia" within the government. As we discussed in Chapter 7, the leaders of large organizations are typically concerned with the well-being of their organizations, especially in maintaining or increasing their budgets.

---

[1] Lewis F. Richardson, *Arms and Insecurity: A Mathematical Study of the Causes and Origins of War* (Pittsburgh: Boxwood Press, 1960), p. 13. For an overview of different conceptions of the arms acquisition process, see Barry Buzan and Eric Herring, *The Arms Dynamic in World Politics* (Boulder, Colo.: Rienner, 1998).

[2] David Kinsella and Sam-man Chung, "The Long and the Short of an Arms Race," in Murray Wolfson, ed., *The Political Economy of War and Peace* (Boston: Kluwer, 1998), pp. 223–246; Michael D. McGinnis and John T. Williams, *Compound Dilemmas: Democracy, Collective Action, and Superpower Rivalry* (Ann Arbor: University of Michigan Press, 2001).

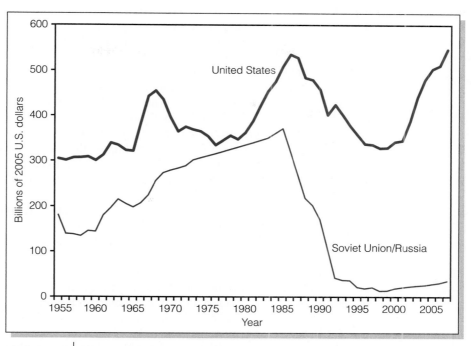

FIGURE 9.1 | AMERICAN AND RUSSIAN MILITARY EXPENDITURES, 1955–2007

Throughout much of the cold war and post–cold war period, U.S. and Russian military expenditure levels moved together, a general upward movement characteristic of the superpower arms race. The downward movement after the late 1980s shows the end of the race and opened up a large gap between the spending levels of the former rivals. This gap has opened even further with increases in U.S. military spending associated with the war on terrorism.

Source: Stockholm International Peace Research Institute, *SIPRI Yearbook: World Armaments and Disarmament* (Oxford: Oxford University Press, various years).

Moreover, a leader's own power in the government and in society at large depends heavily on the size of the organization. Just about the best predictor of the size of any organization's current budget is the size of its last budget, and military organizations are no exception. Usually, when a major weapons system becomes outmoded or obsolete, the military presses to either modernize the weapons or replace them with something else that will do a similar job and keep the same people and resources employed. For example, as the B-52 bomber neared obsolescence, Air Force generals looked around for a new bomber, and the B-1 was developed to replace it. And because of the Air Force's organizational interests, the generals' evaluations of the merits of a proposed new strategic bomber were unlikely to be entirely objective.[3]

---

[3] For a review of theory and research on military organizations, see Theo Farrell, "Figuring Out Fighting Organizations: The New Organizational Analysis in Strategic Studies," *Journal of Strategic Studies* 19 (March 1996), pp. 128–142. Organization dynamics in the Soviet military are examined in Kimberly Marten Zisk, *Engaging the Enemy: Organization Theory and Soviet Military Innovation, 1955–1991* (Princeton, N.J.: Princeton University Press, 1993).

This argument does not imply that military leaders are corrupt or that their advice to maintain or acquire a weapons system is necessarily mistaken. Their evaluation of the national interest and that of most objective observers might well coincide. But it does imply that decisions to reallocate resources within a government will be strongly resisted by organizations, including the military, that are faced with budget reductions or the elimination of programs. Indeed, there are many elements of society—labor unions, defense contractors, politicians, as well as government bureaucrats—have a stake in maintaining a high level of military spending and continuing current procurement programs. Together they constitute a "military–industrial complex" and, according to the radical perspective, their influence is especially strong in capitalist states. A more balanced view recognizes the undue influence of an analogous military–industrial complex in communist societies as well. (We return to this topic in Chapter 12.)

Arms acquisitions are also caused, or at least facilitated by, an expanding economy. In a growing economy, more resources can be devoted to military purposes without reducing anyone's share of the expanding pie. By the same token, a stagnating economy may force leaders either to squeeze civilian needs or to cut back their military expansion. Part of Gorbachev's interest in arms control and bringing an end to the cold war stemmed from the relative decline of the Soviet economy due to the accumulated strain of decades of military buildup. Indeed, economic troubles may well have been the most important force working to end the arms race for both superpowers.

Taken together, domestic influences seem so strong that some analysts have maintained that military–industrial complexes are essentially autistic actors that insulate themselves from outside social stimuli and respond only to their own domestic and organizational imperatives. By this characterization, the arms race is not really a race at all, if by *race* we mean that the competitors really care about each other's positions. The governmental and societal leaders in an autistic system maintain a level of military capability almost solely as a result of demands and pressures from within their own countries, not as a result of international incidents or military gains by potential enemies. At most, the international environment is described as hostile so that societal elites have an excuse to demand sacrifices and allocate resources for military programs. The enemy's actions thus become useful, domestic propaganda to support policies that leaders desire on other grounds. Such an explanation certainly does not rule out some collusion between the leadership groups of two ostensibly competing countries, each acting aggressively to permit the other to justify its own buildup.

Many difficulties arise in analyzing arms races. Establishing an action–reaction process requires that we study the behavior of competing states over a period of time, and even the lengthy cold war rivalry between the United States and Soviet Union provides only sketchy information. The data available on arms acquisitions tend to be highly aggregated; usually we must deal with total military spending rather than, say, spending for strategic arms, which might be the most relevant information to examine for evidence of an arms race. The quality of the data on military spending by some states is very poor and subject to rather wide differences in interpretation. Time lags in the budgetary process—weapons systems are funded over the course of several years—add further complications. As a result, any analysis is bound to include a substantial degree of uncertainty. Moreover, both the organizational process and action–reaction explanations lead us to expect very similar behavior—namely, steady or gradually increasing expenditures by both sides. Given these and other difficulties, it can be very hard to separate different causes and to document those differences in a convincing way. Often we can say only that both domestic and international influences have an effect on arms races and that these influences, from different levels of analysis, often reinforce each other.[4]

GLOBAL MILITARY PRESENCE

In 1985, the eve of the end of the cold war, all nations together spent about $1.2 trillion on their militaries (in constant 2005 dollars). In 2000, they spent about $800 billion—a decline of one-third. In 1985, military expenditures represented 6.2 percent of the value of world production; in 2000, the military accounted for only 2.3 percent. Global military spending had returned to and surpassed its 1985 level by 2007, amounting to more than $1.3 trillion. The reversal of the post–cold war downward trend resulted in large part from increased military spending by the United States, which accounts for 45 percent of the world total. U.S. spending represents about 4 percent of the country's GDP, but worldwide military spending is still only 2.5 percent of world production.[5]

Recent trends notwithstanding, the military downsizing following the end of the cold war was rather impressive and serves to highlight the profound impact that the cold war had on the perceived requirements of national security. Developing states, including those recently freed from colonial rule, looked to the major powers in the international system for cues when building their own defense establishments. Often they did not need to look far. In 1991, the United States had more than 425,000 troops stationed in twenty-three foreign territories or at sea; the Soviet Union deployed nearly 400,000 troops abroad in more than twenty countries. France and Britain also stationed substantial numbers of armed forces abroad. As Table 9.1 indicates, the U.S. military presence was still quite substantial in 2007, although about half of its overseas deployments (not at sea) had been mobilized to fight the war in Iraq. The global military presence of the other major powers was much diminished because of the collapse of Soviet military power and the demise of the East–West rivalry.

Maintaining a large military is expensive, especially when large numbers of forces are stationed overseas. Since the end of the cold war, the number of American active-duty personnel has been decreased by more than 25 percent, and before the Iraq War the number deployed overseas was less than half of what it was in 1991. The United States still seeks to maintain the capacity to prevail in two "nearly simultaneous" regional conflicts, down from two and a half during the cold war. But the very real difficulties the U.S. military has encountered in Afghanistan and Iraq suggests that this capability may be beyond its grasp when prevailing requires occupation, pacification, and nation

---

[4] The academic literature on arms racing was most extensive during the cold war; for a review, see Craig Etcheson, *Arms Race Theory: Strategy and Structure of Behavior* (New York: Greenwood, 1989). On contemporary approaches to studying arms races, see J. Paul Dunne and Ron P. Smith, "The Econometrics of Military Arms Races," in Todd Sandler and Keith Hartley, eds., *Handbook of Defense Economics, Volume II: Defense in a Globalized World* (Amsterdam: North-Holland, 2007).

[5] Stockholm International Peace Research Institute, SIPRI *Yearbook 2008: Armaments, Disarmament and International Security* (Stockholm: SIPRI, 2008).

TABLE 9.1 | GLOBAL MILITARY PRESENCE, 2007

	Defense Budget ($ Billion)	Armed Forces	Ready Reserves	Foreign Deployment
United States	622.4	1,498,200	1,082,700	Afghanistan, Australia, Bahrain, Belgium, Canada, Colombia, Diego Garcia (United Kingdom), Djibouti, Egypt, Germany, Greece, Greenland, Guantánamo (Cuba), Honduras, Iraq, Italy, Japan, Kuwait, Netherlands, Norway, Oman, Portugal, Qatar, Saudi Arabia, Singapore, South Korea, Spain, Thailand, Turkey, United Arab Emirates, United Kingdom Total: 334,800
Russia	33.0	1,027,000	2,000,000	Armenia, Georgia, Kyrgyzstan, Moldova, Syria, Tajikistan, Ukraine Total: 24,600
France	51.7	254,900	135,300	Afghanistan, Central African Republic, Chad, Djibouti, Gabon, Germany, Ivory Coast, Lebanon, Senegal, Tajikistan Total: 19,600
United Kingdom	61.1	180,500	199,300	Afghanistan, Belgium, Belize, Brunei, Canada, Cyprus, Germany, Iraq, Italy, Kuwait, Netherlands, Oman, Saudi Arabia, Sierra Leone, United States Total: 40,500
Germany	43.2	245,700	161,800	Afghanistan, Djibouti, France, Poland, United States, Uzbekistan Total: 4,700
China	46.7	2,105,000	800,000	None
Japan	43.7	240,000	41,800	Kuwait Total: 210

Source: Compiled from International Institute for Strategic Studies, *The Military Balance 2008* (London: Routledge, 2008). Foreign deployment does not include off-shore deployments, deployments in dependency territories, peacekeeping missions, relief missions, or small (less than 50) detachments.

building, and not merely invasion and defeat of an opponent's regular military forces. Nevertheless, the United States is really the only country with truly global military reach. The dissolution of the Soviet Union and the subsequent downsizing of the Russian military have left it with less than one-third the number of troops marshaled by the Soviet military in 1991, while Russian forces abroad in 2007 were less than 10 percent of Soviet forces abroad in 1991. China has a very large military—considerably more personnel than even the United States and Russia—but a limited capacity to project power much beyond the East Asian theater. China's power will continue to grow, and if relations with the United States go sour, a Chinese–American arms race might emerge.

WEAPONS OF MASS DESTRUCTION

The destructive potential of modern weapons needs little emphasis. The largest conventional bombs detonated during World War II (the so-called blockbusters) could seriously damage buildings within one-tenth of a mile. The atomic bomb dropped on Hiroshima at the end of that war had a yield of approximately 15,000 tons of TNT and destroyed most buildings within a mile and a half of the blast. Later scientific developments raised this figure substantially, to about 18 miles for big 25-megaton hydrogen bombs (the destructive equivalent of 25 *million* tons of TNT). In contrast to conventional weapons, **nuclear weapons** use the massive amounts of energy released by atomic nuclei when they split (fission) or combine (fusion).

Before World War II, military aircraft had a combat radius of only a few hundred miles and could carry only a ton or so of high-explosive bombs. Today, bombers and missiles are able to reach halfway around the globe, carrying payloads with explosive power nearly 100 million times that of a pre–World War II bomber. Indeed, one Trident submarine can carry weapons equal in firepower to three times that used in all of World War II. Studies of possible full-scale nuclear exchanges between the United States and the Soviet Union during the cold war (using thousands of warheads on urban and industrial targets) indicated the devastating results to both societies. For example, estimates of American deaths within thirty days of such an exchange ranged from one-third to two-thirds of the total American population. Such studies also demonstrated the vulnerability of modern, urban, and technologically based societies. Far more than half the American population (as well as more than 70 percent of its doctors) lives in its seventy largest urban areas. Gas pipelines, oil pipelines, and electricity grids would be fragmented. Without fuel, the entire transportation system would be crippled. Railroad lines would be chopped up. Water supply and sewage facilities would break down everywhere, creating epidemics and further straining the already impossibly overburdened medical facilities. If food were still available (and not contaminated) in agricultural areas, it could not be processed and shipped because those facilities are generally in metropolitan areas. No possible level of preparation or civil defense could significantly ease this disaster.

We have not even mentioned long-term ecological results such as depletion of the ozone layer, selective destruction of some plants and animals and survival of the hardier forms, cancer from radioactive fallout, and so on. Worse yet, scientific studies have raised the possibility of a "nuclear winter" and global climatic catastrophe. Dust and especially soot from fires following nuclear explosions might bring on a period of darkness—making it much too dark to see, even at midday, for a week—and a substantial temperature drop in the Northern Hemisphere. The temperature, even in summer, would remain below freezing for months and an entire growing season for crops might be lost.[6]

---

[6] These studies first appeared during the latter part of the cold war. A recent study is Alan Robock, Luke Oman, and Georgiy L. Stenchikov, "Nuclear Winter Revisited with a Modern Climate Model and Current Nuclear Arsenals: Stil Catastrophic Consequences," *Journal of Geophysical Research* 112 (July 2007).

Nuclear weapons, along with chemical and biological weapons (to be discussed later), are referred to as **weapons of mass destruction (WMD)** because they are, of course, immensely destructive. But they also are designed to distribute their effects over large areas, at least in most cases, and therefore are not likely to discriminate between military and nonmilitary targets. Nuclear weapons have been used on only two occasions—the American bombings of Hiroshima and Nagasaki, discussed in Chapter 1—but the human suffering that followed left an indelible mark on the conscience of the international community and gave rise to what many have called a "nuclear taboo."[7] That is why the vast majority of the effort devoted to arms control and disarmament has concentrated on nuclear weapons, despite our relative inexperience with their effects.

A BRIEF HISTORY OF THE NUCLEAR COMPETITION

Let us now examine the evolution of the nuclear arms race between the United States and the Soviet Union during the cold war and its undoing over the course of the last twenty years. The deployment of offensive nuclear weapons by the two superpowers during this period is plotted in Figure 9.2. How did the world enter, endure, and survive the era of superpower nuclear confrontation, and what might happen in the event of another confrontation involving either established or emerging nuclear powers?[8]

Period of U.S. Nuclear Monopoly: 1945–1950   After World War II, the United States and, to a lesser degree, the Soviet Union both disarmed from the high levels achieved during the war. The atomic bomb was the central element in America's policy of deterrence. Although the Soviet Union retained large land forces (which could have threatened Western Europe), for all practical purposes, the Soviets had no atomic weapons. They exploded their first bomb in 1949, but they lacked intercontinental bombers capable of reaching the United States, and it was several years before they built up a stockpile adequate for fighting a war. The Americans could have bombed the Soviet Union, inflicting substantial damage, though the number of American bombs was not large (probably only about 300, even at the end of this period). They were also *fission* (atomic) weapons rather than the much more devastating *fusion* (thermonuclear, or hydrogen) weapons that were deployed later.

Period of U.S. Nuclear Dominance: 1951–1957   The Korean War, which began in June 1950, was the culmination of a series of threatening incidents in the emerging cold war—the communist takeover of Czechoslovakia and the Berlin blockade in 1948, a communist victory in China, and the Soviet atomic bomb explosion in

---

[7] Nina Tannenwald, *The Nuclear Taboo: The United States and the Non-Use of Nuclear Weapons Since 1945* (Cambridge: Cambridge University Press, 2008); George H. Quester, *Nuclear First Strike: Consequences of a Broken Taboo* (Baltimore: Johns Hopkins University Press, 2005).

[8] A comprehensive history of nuclear strategy is Lawrence Freedman, *The Evolution of Nuclear Strategy*, 3rd ed. (New York: Palgrave, 2003); see also Joseph Cirincione, *Bomb Scare: The History and Future of Nuclear Weapons* (New York: Columbia University Press, 2007).

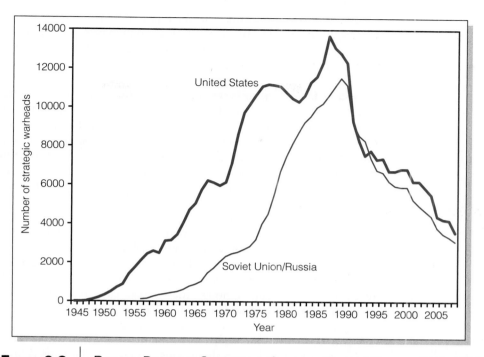

FIGURE 9.2 | RISE AND DECLINE IN SUPERPOWER OFFENSIVE NUCLEAR FORCES, 1945–2008

Since the end of World War II, U.S. and Russian nuclear-stockpile levels have shadowed each other even more closely than their military-expenditure levels. Unlike general military spending, which is undertaken to address a wide range of national security needs, the two nuclear powers' offensive strategic arsenals were directed almost exclusively at each other. Strategic nuclear armament—and now disarmament—decisions have been tightly coupled.

Source: For 1945–2002, National Resource Defense Council, "Archive of Nuclear Data," available at <http://www.nrdc.org/nuclear/nudb/datainx.asp>; for 2004–2008, Robert S. Norris and Hans M. Kristensen, "U.S. Nuclear Forces" and "Russian Nuclear Forces," *Bulletin of the Atomic Scientists* (various issues). Totals include warheads carried by bombers, intercontinental missiles, and submarines; they exclude warheads deployed as theater forces (even when capable of striking U.S. or Russian territory).

1949—and it initiated a great American program of rearmament, during which annual U.S. defense expenditures nearly tripled. U.S. Secretary of State John Foster Dulles declared that the United States would respond to any further communist attack on "free world" nations "in a manner and at a place of our own choosing." In other words, in the face of any such "proxy war" the United States would feel free to strike not at the small communist ally but directly at the Soviet Union, in "massive retaliation" with nuclear weapons. Such a threat was credible because the United States had by then built up a very large stockpile of nuclear weapons, including the hydrogen bomb (first tested by the United States in 1952 and by the Soviets in 1953), and an intercontinental bomber force to deliver them. The ability to inflict damage was so greatly imbalanced in favor of the United States (which also maintained bases in Europe and Asia quite near the USSR) that we can speak of this era as the period of American strategic dominance. In response, the Soviet leaders pursued a very cautious and generally unprovocative foreign policy—and a major rearmament effort.

Period of U.S. Preponderance: 1958–1966   American dominance over the Soviet Union faded from 1958 to 1966; it is more accurate to describe American superiority at this time as nuclear *preponderance*. The United States could still consider the option of attacking the Soviet Union with nuclear weapons in response to a military move against an American ally. U.S. nuclear forces retained some **first-strike capability** in that they could hit the Soviet Union first and limit the Soviet ability to retaliate to "acceptable levels." Any American temptation to relax was eliminated by the shock of *Sputnik.* In 1957, the USSR became the first country to put a satellite into orbit around the Earth, indicating that the USSR had perfected very large rockets that could also be used as intercontinental ballistic missiles (ICBMs)—the delivery vehicles for nuclear and thermonuclear bombs. Behind in this technology, the United States feared that the Soviets now might achieve a first-strike capability—that they would build enough ICBMs to attack and destroy the bombers on which the United States relied for its deterrent. Although the "missile gap" many feared would never actually materialize, the United States embarked on a crash program to develop and deploy a new generation of land- and sea-based ICBMs.

American preponderance was maintained even while the Soviet Union was increasing its capability to do serious damage to the United States in retaliation, if not in a first strike. Partly to remedy this imbalance, in 1962 the Soviets put a variety of nuclear-armed missiles and bombers into Cuba, precipitating the Cuban missile crisis of October 1962. During the thirteen-day crisis, President Kennedy made it clear that the United States was prepared to launch a nuclear first strike against the forces in Cuba and perhaps against the Soviet Union if those missiles were not removed. Because the United States had an overall nuclear superiority (as well as local nonnuclear superiority in the Caribbean, an area of vital importance to the United States), the Soviet leaders believed the American threat and withdrew their missiles and aircraft. However, in reaction to this very public demonstration of their weakness, the Soviet leaders began a new program of strategic armament, revealed in steadily expanding stockpiles of nuclear warheads and rising levels of military expenditure after 1965 (see Figures 9.1 and 9.2).

Period of Essential Equivalence: 1967 to the End of the Cold War   From 1966 until 1975, the United States was deeply involved in another long, painful, and costly land war in Asia, this time in Vietnam, during which American military expenditures climbed to new heights. By 1973, in reaction to the war, American military expenditures dropped below the pre-Vietnam level and remained there until 1977 and then resumed a slow climb. Meanwhile, the Soviet Union maintained its military buildup in conventional as well as nuclear arms. By the 1970s, it was spending nearly the same as the United States on its military, was keeping up with the United States in the expansion of strategic nuclear warheads (though it remained behind in absolute numbers), and now possessed more nuclear launchers. Most observers characterize this period as one of essential equivalence when all elements of strategic weapons are taken into account. Through the mid-1960s, the United States maintained a clear quantitative (and qualitative) superiority in all classes of strategic delivery vehicles: ICBMs (land-based missiles like the Minuteman), SLBMs (submarine-launched ballistic missiles like the Trident), and long-range bombers like the B-52. By the 1970s, however, the Soviet Union had developed very large rockets and warheads and surpassed the United States in numbers of ICBMs.

The result was a situation in which neither side could attack the other without suffering enormous damage from the opponent's retaliation. This gave the United States and the Soviet Union a capability of **mutual assured destruction,** sometimes abbreviated MAD. In other words, each side possessed a **second-strike capability:** the capacity to absorb an enemy attack and have enough weapons remaining to retaliate and inflict unacceptable damage on the opponent. Thus, no matter how the size of nuclear arsenals was measured, for all intents and purposes, neither side could win a nuclear war. The logic of the strategic relationship was quite simple. A country with first-strike capability might be tempted to attack by the *belief* that the opponent could not retaliate (and therefore had no effective deterrent threat). In a situation where *both* sides had achieved second-strike capabilities and both were able to retaliate, the deterrent threats of each were believable, and neither was tempted to strike. The situation was thus "stable"—neither country had an incentive to launch an attack and start a war.

Period of Strategic Debate: End of the Cold War to the Present   With the end of the cold war and the dissolution of the USSR, the strategic rivalry basically collapsed. As the result of arms-control agreements (discussed later), the United States and Russia are very near strategic nuclear parity, both in terms of warheads and delivery vehicles, and at levels much below their peaks in the mid- to late 1980s. Table 9.2 summarizes this strategic nuclear balance as of 2004. Further cuts in nuclear forces may occur, which provides a context for an ongoing debate over nuclear strategy and force postures in a world where the United States and Russia still possess the lion's share of nuclear weaponry, but where the primary nuclear threat facing each state may not be its former cold war rival.

In contrast to MAD, if the U.S. and Russian nuclear arsenals may eventually be brought down to very low levels—1,000 to 2,000 total warheads for each side have been discussed—then both states would be moving toward strategies of

TABLE 9.2 | AMERICAN AND RUSSIAN STRATEGIC NUCLEAR FORCES, 2008

	Bombers	ICBMs	SLBMs	Total
United States				
delivery vehicles	72	488	288	891
warheads	1,083	764	1,728	3,575
Russia				
delivery vehicles	79	430	176	685
warheads	884	1,605	624	3,113

Source: Robert S. Norris and Hans M. Kristensen, "U.S. Nuclear Forces, 2008," *Bulletin of the Atomic Scientists* 64 (March/April 2008), pp. 50–53, 58; Norris and Kristensen, "Russian Nuclear Forces, 2008," *Bulletin of the Atomic Scientists* 64 (May/June 2008), pp. 54–57, 62. Figures include operational warheads; they do not include reserves, spares, or those awaiting dismantlement.

minimum deterrence similar to those of other nuclear powers. Like MAD, a minimum deterrent requires only a second-strike capability, but when no other state possesses a large nuclear force this can be achieved with a relatively small stockpile. China effectively pursued a strategy of minimum deterrence throughout the cold war with an arsenal of a few hundred warheads. This became the most realistic model for nuclear stability in the India–Pakistan relationship once their nuclear weapons tests in 1998 obviated the previous situation of "existential deterrence"— deterrence of major war resulted from the existence of nuclear arms production *capacity*, but not the weapons themselves.

Both Russia and the United States, however, continue to modernize their weapons, and the United States continues to pursue a capacity for **national missile defense (NMD)**, which has prompted widespread rethinking about the force levels necessary for minimum deterrence. Most proponents of NMD imagine a system that would protect the U.S. homeland from a ballistic missile strike from a "rogue state" like North Korea or Iran, but not so elaborate as to be able to shield an attack from Russia, thereby upsetting the stability of the U.S.–Russian balance. While Russia may be placated by American assurances that its NMD will not undermine Russia's second-strike capability, the Chinese remain wary of the latest developments in American nuclear policy and the implications for their posture of minimum deterrence in the event of a war over Taiwan. Thus, by pushing forward with NMD, the Bush administration altered the menus of not only potentially nuclear rogue states but also long-standing nuclear powers who must now contemplate the impact on their once-stable nuclear relationships with the United States.[9]

PROLIFERATION

Weapons **proliferation** refers to the increase in the number of states (and potentially nonstate actors) that possess a certain class of weaponry. The proliferation of nuclear weapons, ushering in what some have called a "second nuclear age," involves a number of dangers. New nuclear powers, which would likely include authoritarian and potentially aggressive states, lack the experience and maybe the resources necessary to develop the elaborate command and control capabilities essential for managing a nuclear crisis. This is especially true of the less-developed countries. Many of these governments may be involved in serious local conflicts, which now have the potential to cross the nuclear threshold. For example, because both India and Pakistan conducted a series of nuclear weapons tests in 1998, many observers fear that their long-running conflict over Kashmir might become the spark that ignites the world's first nuclear war.[10]

---

[9] For a review of the military and political issues surrounding national missile defense, see Charles L. Glaser and Steve Fetter, "National Missile Defense and the Future of U.S. Nuclear Weapons Policy," *International Security* 26 (Summer 2001), pp. 40–92. On Chinese and Russian reactions, see Alastair Iain Johnston, "China's New 'Old Thinking': The Concept of Limited Deterrence," *International Security* 20 (Winter 1995/1996), pp. 5–42; Celeste A. Wallander, "Russia's New Security Policy and the Ballistic Missile Defense Debate," *Current History* 99 (October 2000), pp. 339–341.

[10] Paul Bracken, "The Structure of the Second Nuclear Age," *Orbis* 47 (Summer 2003), pp. 399–413; Stephen Peter Rosen, "After Proliferation: What to Do If More States Go Nuclear," *Foreign Affairs* (September/October 2006), pp. 9–14.

Despite some arguments that a system in which *everyone* possessed nuclear weapons would be quite stable—due to a megabalance of terror of all against all—a world of many nuclear powers would be a perilous one indeed. The belief that the "long peace" during the cold war was in some measure the result of mutual U.S.–Soviet deterrence is a dubious basis for arguing that the widespread proliferation of nuclear weapons in the current system is a recipe for stability. A second danger is the opportunity proliferation provides for terrorists to gain control of nuclear materials (which may have been acquired by governments for peaceful purposes) or finished nuclear weapons. Perpetrators of "nuclear terrorism" could be based within the countries they wish to harm, or far away, simply taking advantage of opportunities to acquire nuclear materials from governments that are unable to take sufficient security precautions. Such possibilities emerged with the end of the cold war and will be multiplied with the proliferation of nuclear states.[11]

To meet the threat of proliferation, several different kinds of incentives for the acquisition of nuclear weapons must be recognized. For some countries, the problem of security against present nuclear powers may be paramount. Pakistan's nuclear program is directed toward perceived security threats from India, which first demonstrated its nuclear potential in 1974. India's program is directed, at least in part, toward China. South Korea is concerned about North Korea. Often security is sought against local powers that are not yet nuclear. Israel has been motivated by security threats from the Arab countries and Iran. For still other states, military security may not be a primary concern; rather, they may wish to secure big-power prestige or the technological advances that can be obtained from the development of nuclear capabilities (as was possibly the case in past Argentine efforts). For still others—India, for example—all three kinds of incentives may be involved.[12]

Nuclear arms are not the only weapons of mass destruction. Stemming the proliferation of **chemical weapons** also presents a major challenge because some can be assembled with widely available chemical agents and commercial equipment. Easily produced and potentially very destructive, they have been called the "poor man's atomic bomb." Chemical agents, like tear gas, are commonly used in riot control, but those used in chemical warfare are more nefarious, attacking the body's nervous system, blood, skin, or lungs. Chlorine and mustard gas were first used in the trench warfare of World War I. Napalm was used in flamethrowers during World War II and was made infamous by American forces in Vietnam who used it (along with the herbicide known as Agent Orange) as a jungle defoliant. Iraq used mustard gas and nerve agents to defend against Iran's "human wave" attacks during the Iran–Iraq war as well as against Iraqi Kurds at the end of that war. In

---

[11] Kenneth Waltz has advanced the argument in support of proliferation, which is rebutted by Scott Sagan. See Sagan and Waltz, *The Spread of Nuclear Weapons: A Debate Renewed*, 2nd ed. (New York: Norton, 2002). On nuclear terrorism, see Graham Allison, *Nuclear Terrorism: The Ultimate Preventable Catastrophe* (New York: Times Books, 2004); Michael Levi, *On Nuclear Terrorism* (Cambridge, Mass.: Harvard University Press, 2007).

[12] Etel Solingen, *Nuclear Logics: Contrasting Paths in East Asia and the Middle East* (Princeton, N.J.: Princeton University Press, 2007); Jacques E. C. Hymans, *The Psychology of Nuclear Proliferation: Identity, Emotions, and Foreign Policy* (Cambridge: Cambridge University Press, 2006).

1995, the Japanese group Aum Shinrikyo released sarin gas in the Tokyo subway system, killing 12 people and injuring more than 5,000, thus highlighting the danger of chemical proliferation to nonstate actors engaging in terrorism.

Even more than chemical weapons, **biological weapons** have acquired a sinister reputation for their capacity to produce potentially frightening effects on the cheap. Biological agents consist of living organisms (bacteria, fungi) and viruses, as well as the toxins derived from them, that cause disease and death to humans, livestock, or agricultural crops. The use of biological weapons during warfare has been less frequent, or at least less blatant, than the use of chemical weapons, although the early history of human warfare includes accounts of biological agents introduced into drinking water and food supplies. When the plague struck Tatar forces laying siege to Kaffa (in the Crimea) during the fourteenth century, corpses were hurled over the city walls spreading disease among the city's inhabitants, eventually forcing their surrender. Japan's notorious Unit 731 conducted biological warfare experiments on Chinese prisoners of war during the Japanese occupation of Manchuria in the 1930s, culminating in the actual use of bacteriological (bubonic plague) bombs against Chinese cities beginning in 1940.

It is nearly impossible to stem the proliferation of chemical and biological weapons by restricting access to the substances and technologies necessary for their production. Punitive measures—like the 1998 American bombing of a Sudanese chemical plant suspected of producing elements of the chemical agent VX—may be only marginally more effective. Perhaps limiting chemical and biological proliferation must rest on moral persuasion or simply the fear conjured up by images of the uncontrolled stockpiling of these weapons of mass destruction—and their increasingly probable use.[13] A new problem arises from the revolution in molecular biology. Common and relatively benign infectious organisms (like the flu virus) could be genetically modified to carry an existing deadly disease or even a brand new pathogen. The frontiers of medical research for life-giving ends could inadvertently lead to the development of brand-new plagues that are then employed for terrorist purposes.

THE SECURITY DILEMMA

Sovereignty, the fundamental principle of authority underlying contemporary interstate relations, helps to explain the forces driving arms acquisitions and arms races, as well as the difficulties associated with arms control. Sovereignty means that states exist in a formally anarchic environment. No legitimate or legal authority is empowered to control, direct, or watch over the behavior of sovereign states (as, for example, the federal government of the United States does over the fifty states of the union). One consequence of such a system of sovereign states is that each state must take responsibility for its own security and survival.

If there is no legitimate authority to enforce order and punish rule breakers, then there is no legal or formal recourse if allies or friends fail to assist a state—they cannot

---

[13] On the moral stigma attached to the use of chemical weapons, see Richard Price, *The Chemical Weapons Taboo* (Ithaca, N.Y.: Cornell University Press, 1997).

be sued to fulfill their alliance commitments! Thus, self-help in the international system means that each state must take measures to provide for its own defense. A tragic flaw of the formally anarchic state system is that this self-help imperative often leads to what John Herz long ago called the **security dilemma**:

> Wherever such anarchic society has existed—and it has existed in most periods of known history on some level—there has arisen what may be called the "security dilemma" of men, or groups, or their leaders. Groups or individuals living in such a constellation must be, and usually are, concerned about their security from being attacked, subjected, dominated or annihilated by other groups and individuals. Striving to attain security from such attack, they are driven to acquire more and more power in order to escape the power of others. This, in turn, renders the others more insecure and compels them to prepare for the worst. Since none can ever feel entirely secure in such a world of competing units, power competition ensues, and the vicious circle of security and power accumulation is on.[14]

States may never feel safe because they never know how much is "enough" for their security. But they become trapped by this logic; uncertainty becomes fear when their efforts to enhance security spur on the efforts of others, erasing any sense of safety that had been achieved and throwing them into "the vicious circle of security and power accumulation."

The formally anarchic system of sovereign states seems to promote a realist vision of struggle in world politics in which the security dilemma demands that state leaders be preoccupied with threat, military power, and self-help. The need for military power, and for constant alertness as to its accumulation and use by others, stems directly from the structure of a system of sovereign states and—if we subscribe to classical realist assumptions—the power-seeking dimensions of human nature. The security dilemma is central to many aspects of interstate relations besides arms races, and analogous forms of competitive state behavior appear in international political economy as well, as we shall see in later chapters. How states cope with these conditions creates some degree of order out of anarchy.

THE PRISONER'S DILEMMA

The continuing and parallel increases in superpower military spending and the deployment of nuclear forces are two manifestations of an arms race. Game theory, introduced earlier as a method for analyzing international conflict (see Boxes 7.1 and 8.1), attempts to capture the interdependence of each side's choices and the combination of competition and cooperation found in many social situations. As an approach to the study of world politics, game theory comprises many different "games" that have been constructed by analysts for purposes of examining situations commonly encountered in relations between states (as well as nonstate actors). One well-known game, called the **prisoner's**

---

[14] John Herz, "Idealist Internationalism and the Security Dilemma," *World Politics* 2 (January 1950), p. 157.

dilemma, illustrates how people—including the leaders of states—can become trapped by self-defeating acts.[15]

The basic story of the prisoner's dilemma is simple. Two individuals are held incommunicado in a police station after having been arrested for an armed robbery. Each prisoner is presented with a pair of unattractive options, and each is questioned separately and given a choice by the district attorney: "I'm pretty sure that you two were responsible for the robbery, but I don't have quite enough evidence to prove it. If you will confess and testify against your partner, I will see to it that you are set free without any penalty, and your accomplice will be sentenced to ten years in prison. You should be aware that I am making the same proposal to your buddy, and if he accepts my offer, you will be the one locked up for ten years; he will go free. If you both confess, then my prosecution need not hinge on your testimony alone, or his alone. We will have a little mercy, but you'll both go away for seven years. If you both keep quiet, we won't have the evidence to convict you of armed robbery, but we can convict you on a concealed weapon charge, which carries a sentence of one year in prison. If you want to take a chance that your partner in crime will keep quiet, go ahead. But if he doesn't—and you know the sort of guy he is—you will do very badly. Think it over."

What will the prisoners do in this situation? What would you do? If your partner has confessed, unbeknownst to you, then your decision to confess is best: You get seven years instead of ten. If your partner has kept quiet, then your best choice is still to confess: You go free rather than spend a year in jail on the weapon charge. So, either way, you ought to confess. Unfortunately, the same logic holds for your partner, which means the likely outcome is that you both confess and therefore receive seven-year sentences. This is the dilemma, for had you both kept quiet you both would have done better with just one year in prison. (Box 9.1 illustrates this same logic using a game matrix.)

Consider the U.S. and Soviet arms acquisitions during the cold war. Now we move from a situation of easily specified choices (confess, keep quiet) and easily measured outcomes (years in prison) to one with choices and outcomes that are much harder to measure. We must simplify the situation while at the same time capturing the essence of strategic situation. Assume that each superpower had but two options, to arm or to restrain from arming—that is, to defect or to cooperate. Given these options, it seems that each side's preference ordering among the four possible outcomes was analogous to that of each prisoner in the prisoner's dilemma. Unilateral armament was preferred to mutual restraint because the superior power could use its military advantage as leverage (like one prisoner confessing while the other has kept quiet, thereby going free). Mutual restraint was preferred to mutual armament because a military balance could be struck without diverting resources from domestic needs (both prisoners keep quiet and serve just one year). Mutual armament was preferred to unilateral disarmament because preventing

---

[15] The game was originally developed by researchers at the RAND Corporation, a think tank established after World War II to advise the U.S. Air Force on military (including nuclear) strategy and tactics. See William Poundstone, *Prisoner's Dilemma: John von Neumann, Game Theory, and the Puzzle of the Bomb* (New York: Doubleday, 1992).

IN GREATER DEPTH

BOX 9.1   ### THE PRISONER'S DILEMMA GAME

To help predict the outcome of a prisoner's dilemma, we could construct a decision tree similar to the one presented in the last chapter (see Box 8.1). However, because each prisoner must make a decision without knowledge of the decision made by the other, the strategic form, a 2 × 2 matrix, works well. The two prisoners, labeled Blue and Red, each have to decide between two options: confess or keep quiet. The uncertainty for each prisoner is whether there exists "honor among thieves," so we use the label *cooperate* for keeping quiet (upholding honor among thieves) and the label *defect* for confessing to the district attorney (squealing among thieves). With two players, each with two options, there are four possible outcomes. If Red confesses (defects) and Blue keeps quiet (cooperates), then Red goes free and Blue gets ten years. That is the best of the four possible outcomes for Red (we assign it a value of 4) but the least attractive outcome for Blue (a value of 1), and it is represented by the northeast cell in the matrix. The exact opposite outcome results if Blue confesses and Red keeps quiet, as shown in the southwest cell. If both confess, then they both get seven years, which is bad, but not the worst, for both (a value of 2), as shown in the southeast cell. The northwest cell is the outcome when both keep quiet—not the best for both, but still a relatively short time in prison (a value of 3).

If Blue is rational, then that prisoner would reason as follows: "Let me first assume that Red cooperates. In that case I should defect, because going free [4 in the southwest cell] is better than a year in jail [3, northwest]. Next let me assume that Red defects. Again I should defect; seven years in prison is not good [2, southeast], but it's better than ten years [1, northeast]. Looks like either way, I should confess." In other words, Blue has a **dominant strategy**: to make the same choice (defect) no matter what Red does. Unfortunately for Blue, Red has the same dominant strategy, to defect. The outcome is therefore predictable: Each prisoner, rationally looking out for his own self-interest, squeals on the other and both end up spending seven years in prison. Had they been able to cooperate in upholding honor among thieves, they both would have been better off—hence the dilemma.

Recall from Box 8.1 that a Nash equilibrium outcome is one that results when both sides make their best moves in response to each other. The defect–defect outcome is the equilibrium in a prisoner's dilemma because neither Blue nor Red has an incentive to switch unilaterally from defect to cooperate. Doing so would increase the sentence to ten years for the one cooperating, which is not the prisoner's best response. Recall from Box 5.1 that a Pareto optimal outcome is one in which neither side can do better without making the other side worse off. In the prisoner's dilemma, cooperate–cooperate is Pareto optimal because both players together cannot do any better; the other cells represent outcomes in which one or both prisoners do worse than one year in prison. The dilemma in a prisoner's dilemma is that the equilibrium outcome is not socially optimal. Sadly, many situations in international relations have this feature.

	Red	
	Cooperate	*Defect*
Cooperate	3,3	1,4
Defect	4,1	2,2

Blue

manipulation by a militarily superior opponent was worth the diversion of resources (both prisoners confess; seven years is bad but not as bad as ten for being a sucker). Because the strategic interaction between the United States and the Soviet Union had the same structure as the prisoner's dilemma, the outcome was similarly predictable: mutual armament. Unfortunately for the superpowers, both would have been better off had they maintained a military balance without becoming embroiled in an arms race.

Given each side's preferences in a prisoner's dilemma, are two countries in an arms race condemned to the risk and waste of a never-ending, costly arms competition? In 1950, that seemed to be the case. President Truman's scientific advisers told him that they could build a powerful new thermonuclear weapon—the hydrogen bomb—hundreds of times more powerful than the atomic bomb. Some Americans would have liked best to be sole owner of the new bomb (unilateral armament), but would have settled for a situation in which no country had it (mutual restraint). However, the Soviets had pretty much the same scientific knowledge that the Americans had, and neither power would consider allowing the other to have such a fearsome weapon unless it also had one. It seemed better to go ahead and build the hydrogen bomb if the Soviets were going to build it also (mutual armament). Even though building a hydrogen bomb would leave both countries exposed to its dangers, it seemed better than being at the mercy of the Soviets without a counterweapon (unilateral restraint). Lacking any prospect of an enforceable agreement that neither side would build hydrogen bombs, each felt forced to build a weapon that it wished did not exist.[16] This is the essence of the security dilemma. One may lose greatly by failing to trust the other, but one risks losing even more if the trust proves misplaced.

OVERCOMING THE DILEMMA

Obviously the superpower arms race did end, contrary to what the prisoner's dilemma leads us to expect. Does that mean such models are unhelpful for understanding major changes in interstate relations like the end of the cold war? No, it just means that the prisoner's dilemma no longer captured the essence of American and Soviet preferences toward the end of the cold war period. How might we account for this transition?

As applied to the arms race, the prisoner's dilemma assumes that the best outcome for oneself is military superiority or unilateral defection. But instead, what if the United States decided that the alleged advantages of superiority, especially strategic nuclear superiority, were overrated? When both sides have large and secure nuclear retaliatory forces (MAD), the side with more nuclear weapons may not be able to derive much military or political advantage from its numerical edge. Although the United States might have preferred to have more weapons than the Soviet Union, at some point it grew tired of the arms race and came to prefer bilateral arms control, perhaps even limited disarmament, to a one-sided outcome in its

---

[16] See Richard Rhodes, *Dark Sun: The Making of the Hydrogen Bomb* (New York: Simon & Schuster, 1995).

favor that absorbed large amounts of resources without having much use. At the same time, the United States wanted to avoid disarming while the Soviet Union continued to arm. In short, what was once the most preferred outcome for the United States became the second-most preferred outcome; American policy makers would prefer mutual cooperation above all. (In the matrix shown in Box 9.1, reverse Blue's payoff values in the northwest and southwest cells.)

Unlike the prisoner's dilemma, where defecting was a dominant strategy for the United States, now its best choice depends on what the Soviets do. If the United States thinks the Soviets will cooperate, then it should cooperate and achieve its most preferred outcome of mutual restraint; if the Soviets will defect, then so should the United States. Although it may now appear that there is a way out of the arms race, there is not. The American side will discern that the Soviets still have an incentive to defect—Soviet preferences are assumed to remain unchanged—in which case the Americans must do the same. This calculus was, in fact, quite common in American cold war rhetoric. It was easy to believe that the Soviets had more malign intentions than our own: We wanted to avoid an arms race but nevertheless found ourselves in one, and it was convenient to assume that the Soviets were to blame. Because it was hard to see what the Soviets were actually doing, and we had little chance to judge their intentions firsthand, we readily attributed hostile intentions to them (recall the discussion of groupthink and the image of the enemy from Chapter 7). If we had reasons to doubt the Soviets' intentions or were suspicious merely because of inadequate contact, then the safest line of action was to continue defecting. An opportunity for mutual disarmament may have been lost, but the risk of being in a militarily inferior position was avoided. Even in a one-sided prisoner's dilemma, the likely outcome is mutual defection and thus an arms race.

It is disheartening to note that defection on the American side may have been driven not by Soviet preferences, but by *perceived* Soviet preferences. If the Soviets too preferred mutual restraint to their own strategic superiority, there was no escaping the security dilemma unless and until the Americans understood that— and vice versa. Because the one-sided prisoner's dilemma captures well the importance of what each side *thinks* about the other's preferences, it has been called the "perceptual dilemma." Indeed, there is survey evidence suggesting that *both* U.S. and Soviet leaders judged their own most preferred outcome to be mutual restraint while believing that their counterparts still sought superiority.[17] How much earlier might the cold war have ended had their perceptions of each been different?

The de-escalation and termination of the arms race accompanying the end of the cold war suggests that the superpowers' preferences did indeed change. They may have changed because it became impossible to achieve meaningful superiority because each power decided that military superiority could not bring any political utility or because the high levels of armament accumulated by both sides in their pursuit of superiority became too risky. In the real world, people do change how much they trust each other, and their preferences about what they want, what

---

[17] S. Plous, "The Nuclear Arms Race: Prisoner's Dilemma or Perceptual Dilemma?" *Journal of Peace Research* 30 (May 1993), pp. 163–179.

they may be capable of achieving, and what they want to achieve.[18] Both super-powers revised their preference orderings; having coming to better understand each other's preferences, they became engaged in a strategic interaction that was no longer a prisoner's dilemma. (In Box 9.1, in addition to Blue's revised payoff values, now reverse Red's in the northwest and northeast cells.)

When both sides do best by cooperating, it would seem odd that such an outcome was nevertheless so hard to achieve. But it is not so odd if we keep in mind that both sides did not do worse by defecting. The arms race was costly, but letting one's guard down was judged to be potentially more costly, possibly a great deal more costly. Successive leaderships in both the United States and the Soviet Union had inherited competitive foreign policies from their respective predecessors, so it seemed sensible to carry these policies forward—to change course midstream would leave the nation at the mercy of its rival. It would take a forward-looking leadership, and one willing to take some risks, to escape this trap. One nation would have to lower its guard long enough to demonstrate its good intentions, even at the risk of being taken advantage of, but in the hopes that the other side would then see its way clear to the mutually cooperative outcome most preferred by both sides.

Gorbachev seems to have been guided by precisely this calculus when embarking on the Soviet foreign policy known as "new thinking." As Jack Snyder wrote in 1987, "Gorbachev and his circle see America as innately hostile, but they believe that America's aggressiveness can be defused through Soviet self-restraint and concessions." Among many other concessions, Gorbachev accepted the Reagan administration's "zero option" for intermediate, nuclear force reductions, which required a greater Soviet sacrifice, and agreed to disproportionately deep cuts in Soviet (and Warsaw Pact) conventional forces in Europe, which also assumed a very defensive force posture. Fortunately, after much hesitation in some parts of its foreign policy establishment, the United States reciprocated, setting the arms race (and the cold war generally) on a downward spiral.[19]

REPEATED ENCOUNTERS

Confrontations between the same parties occur repeatedly in international politics. In these circumstances, a country's actions at a particular time have consequences not only for that interaction but also in subsequent confrontations if those actions reveal information about its interests or strategy. It is a logical next step, then, to consider what happens when players interact in what they think will be a repeating series of games (sometimes called *iterated games*). Experimental psychologists and other researchers have asked subjects to play games with payoffs like those in a prisoner's dilemma in order to observe their behavior over time. There is a typical sequence that many players adopt. At the beginning, participants often play

---

[18] Andrew H. Kydd, *Trust and Mistrust in International Relations* (Princeton, N.J.: Princeton University Press, 2005) contains a good combination of history and game theory on the cold war.

[19] Jack Snyder, "The Gorbachev Revolution: A Waning of Soviet Expansionism?" *International Security* 12 (Winter 1987/88), p. 118.

cooperatively, yielding rewards to each side. After a short while, however, one player can no longer resist the temptation to defect. The other player will usually retaliate after being betrayed once or twice, settling into a pattern of mutual defection in which both receive lower payoffs. At this point, each may try to reestablish cooperation, but because the game does not allow them to communicate openly that is difficult to do. Without any assurance that a player's cooperation will be reciprocated, would-be cooperators avoid their least preferred outcome by continuing to defect (a maximin strategy).

In international politics, too, it may be very hard to break with established patterns and shift to cooperative behavior. The first initiatives may not be seen as cooperation at all, or if perceived as such they may be interpreted as a sign of weakness that should be exploited. For example, many Americans were wary of Gorbachev's new thinking. Soviet reforms, they suspected, were merely designed to give the Soviet military some breathing space. Once the economy was streamlined, there would be a new infusion of resources into the military and the Soviet Union would resume its offensive military posture. And all this just as the United States had been lulled into complacency. Others thought that Soviet concessions were a sign of vulnerability, an opportunity to be exploited in order to force a complete collapse of the Soviet economy and substantial military retrenchment.

In psychological experiments, after a good deal of trial and error, many players do eventually succeed in returning to a consistent pattern of cooperation. In the interim, repeated plays of the game often serve as a means of communicating, through one's actions, a desire to achieve a jointly optimal outcome in later plays. In this way, the game resembles the ongoing politics among states, where cooperation breeds expectations of future cooperation and defection breeds expectations of defection. Ultimately, over many plays, it becomes possible to develop trust as the players become increasingly confident that each knows how the other will behave if suitable conditions can be established.

Repeated plays convey information not only between the players currently engaged in the interaction but also to those third parties observing the interaction. That is, a player can establish a reputation, which will inform the choices of others when they find themselves engaged in a similar interaction with this player. A player with a reputation for defecting will have an especially difficult time soliciting cooperation from other players, even when behaving cooperatively; others are likely to view this behavior with suspicion and will be disinclined to reciprocate. Likewise, a player who develops a reputation for cooperating will have an easier time getting others to reciprocate cooperative behavior, and are more likely to be forgiven for an occasional defection.

Robert Axelrod conducted an interesting experiment with implications for how rational people learn to cooperate in conflictual situations in which there is little or no communication between them. He designed a computer tournament involving thirteen social scientists who were each asked to submit a programmed strategy for playing a repeated prisoner's dilemma game. Because the measure of success was the total number of points accumulated in all matchups, it turned out that players who defected too often fared poorly overall even though they often bested their opponents. Defecting brought short-term gains, but it also brought reciprocal defections and bad outcomes for both players. Of all the strategies played, Axelrod found that **tit for tat** (cooperating after the opponent cooperated, defecting after a defection) was most successful, especially when coupled with *optimism* (opening with a cooperative move) and being somewhat *forgiving* (punishing once, and then trying again to cooperate). Interestingly, in any paired matchup, the tit-for-tat player can at best tie an opponent; tit for tat never wins an individual match. However, because the strategy elicits cooperative behavior from others, resulting in socially optimal outcomes in those rounds, the overall performance of tit for tat was better than other strategies that are less adept at bringing out the best in their opponents. What allows for this evolution of cooperation is the expectation that players will encounter one another again—a sufficiently long "shadow of the future."[20]

In experiments with human players, it makes a difference how the investigator describes the purpose of the game to the players before they begin. The object may be: (1) that each player does his or her best, regardless of what happens to the other player; (2) that each player does better than the other; or (3) that both players do well. Not surprisingly, people cooperate least often when the experimenter emphasizes doing better than the other. Players' preconceptions about international politics may also affect the way they play the game in an experimental setting. Some are inclined to be concerned about others and are therefore more likely to seek joint rewards, while others think in stark realist terms and are less ready to cooperate. When we believe that the overriding goal is to maximize our own interests over all others, non–zero-sum situations may be interpreted as zero sum, and the outcome of our interactions becomes mutual misery.

Thinking back to the prisoners in the police station, imagine how different their situation would have been if each firmly subscribed to the principle of honor among thieves and possessed a prickly conscience that made it painful to betray the other. The utility of each outcome would not coincide merely with jail terms. In these circumstances, where the pangs of conscience associated with squealing now make unilateral defection a distasteful outcome, the prisoners would actually get what would be for them the best possible outcome: Both would refuse to defect and thus would receive the very short jail sentence. In international politics, it is often easy to dismiss the effect of moral conscience, but such considerations should not be ignored.

Even though the détente of the early 1970s did not last, many of its elements (scientific and cultural exchanges, the Helsinki Accords, certain arms-control agreements) survived and provided the basis for the dramatic East–West thaw that began in the 1980s. In their repeated encounters, both sides learned from past mistakes of extreme suspicion as well as misguided trust. We must always remember that world politics requires both conflict and cooperation. This is a fundamental argument against excessive pessimism and suspicion when thinking about international problems and their solutions. The idealism of one side alone cannot make all conflicts go away, but if we insist on seeing the world as a constant struggle, we are condemned to a world of our making.

---

[20] Robert Axelrod, *The Evolution of Cooperation*, rev. ed. (New York: Basic Books, 2006). Axelrod's results were originally published in 1980. See also Robert Hoffmann, "Twenty Years On: *The Evolution of Cooperation* Revisited," *Journal of Artificial Societies and Social Simulation* 3 (March 2000).

DETERRENCE

With the dissolution of both the Warsaw Pact and the Soviet Union in 1991, and with Russia entering the Partnership for Peace with NATO in 1994, the cold war ended without escalating into a hot war, nuclear or conventional. How was this achieved? If one of the costs of arms races is the steady increase in destructive potential, how is this process reversed before that destructive potential is put to use?

Both the United States and the Soviet Union spent many billions of dollars on the research, development, and procurement of advanced weapons, and pursued a range of strategies to protect their second-strike capabilities. They *produced large numbers* of delivery vehicles and *distributed them widely,* multiplying the number of targets an attacker would have to hit and making it impossible for one attacking warhead to wipe out more than a few delivery vehicles. Bombers were dispersed among many air-fields, and ICBM silos were separated. They *hardened launching sites.* For example, U.S. missile silos were built to be enclosed in enough steel and concrete to withstand the blast of a near miss. They *concealed* some of their delivery vehicles and made others *mobile* because such targets are difficult to track and hit. Because nuclear-armed submarines operating hundreds of feet below the surface of the ocean are both concealed and mobile, SLBMs are regarded as the most dependable and secure elements of a second-strike force. Lastly, the superpowers adopted a policy of *launch under attack.* This meant that land-based ICBMs that were vulnerable to a first strike would be launched before they could be struck by incoming missiles. This would have been a desirable policy only if we could have been totally confident of avoiding false alarms (and maybe not desirable even then).

Neither side depended solely on one type of weapons system in its strategic forces. Each possessed large numbers of bombers capable of attacking the other's home territory, land-based ICBMs, and SLBMs on submarines. Together they formed a **nuclear triad,** with each leg having different capabilities and each protected in different ways. This formed the core of the strategic planning of both sides. Even though one or even two parts of the triad might become vulnerable through technological change, the other element(s) would still be secure. Neither side could have had a secure first-strike capability, and deterrence remained stable.

CRISIS INSTABILITY

In the cold war confrontation between the United States and Soviet Union, stability depended on the fact that neither side possessed a first-strike capability. With a first-strike capability, one side can attack and destroy enough of the other side's capability to launch an unacceptably costly retaliatory strike, and it may become very tempting to launch such an attack when any military crisis between the two begins to escalate. Stable deterrence, by contrast, requires that each side possess a second-strike capability—the capacity to absorb a first strike and still retaliate causing unacceptable damage. Because each side is assured that the other can inflict enormous destruction on an attacker, neither is tempted to attack.[21]

---

[21] For contemporary analyses of deterrence theory and practice, see Frank C. Zagare and D. Marc Kilgour, *Perfect Deterrence* (Cambridge: Cambridge University Press, 2000); Patrick M. Morgan, *Deterrence Now* (Cambridge: Cambridge University Press, 2003).

The normal, noncrisis mode of nuclear deterrence is a "balance of terror." The best choice for both sides is restraint, and under normal conditions the balance of terror produces this outcome. A policy of restraint is acceptable only so long as neither side has a first-strike capability and so long as each is confident that the other is not bent on acquiring that capability. This stability can be undermined by a great technological breakthrough for one side. For example, the development of extremely accurate MIRVs (multiple independently targeted reentry vehicles) raises the probability of a first strike being effective, and an extremely effective missile defense would reduce the damage expected from whatever was left of the opponent's retaliatory force. Even the perception—correct or mistaken—that the adversary is about to achieve such a technological breakthrough might suddenly change a country's calculations. If an adversary appears to be on the verge of gaining the ability to attack, then a preemptive nuclear strike might seem like the rational thing to do.

The technological changes that transpired during the cold war did not shake the foundation of stable deterrence because both superpowers maintained their nuclear triads along with extensive nuclear research and development programs. What was more likely to upset the stability of nuclear deterrence was an escalating military crisis like the Cuban missile crisis of 1962. According to Henry Kissinger:

> If crisis management requires cold and even brutal measures to show determination, it also imposes the need to show opponents a way out. Grandstanding is good for the ego but bad for foreign policy. Many wars have started because no line of retreat was left open. Superpowers have a special obligation not to humiliate each other.[22]

As it happened, in 1962 President Kennedy was careful to give Khrushchev an opportunity to withdraw the Soviet missiles with some dignity. But suppose that Kennedy had dramatized the outcome of the missile crisis as an American victory and a great loss of prestige for the Soviets. Suppose also that Kennedy had followed up with efforts to overthrow the Castro government. Under these circumstances, the value of mutual restraint to the Soviets—and especially to the humiliated Khrushchev, who would have faced immediate ouster—might have taken second place to nuclear attack as long as there was a possibility that the damage imposed by the American retaliation would fall short of annihilation. At the same time, Khrushchev might have interpreted Kennedy's actions as indicating that the Americans had great confidence in their first-strike capability, raising substantially Soviet estimates of the damage the United States could inflict if the Soviet Union did not strike first. Although some on both sides were thinking along these lines, we are fortunate that cooler heads prevailed.

BRINKMANSHIP

Many international crises do not resemble the prisoner's dilemma so much as they do the adolescent game of **chicken**, which was popularized during the 1950s. Two youths would line up their cars facing each other on a deserted stretch of road.

---

[22] Henry Kissinger, *Years of Upheaval* (Boston: Little, Brown, 1982), p. 595.

Each car would have its left wheels on the center line, and they would drive toward each other at high speed. Friends might be riding in the cars; others would stand on the sidelines, cheering on the contestants. If neither car swerved, they would collide, and the occupants would be badly injured or killed. That, of course, was the worst outcome. But the next worst was to be the driver who swerved first, the "chicken." An acceptable, if not especially satisfying, outcome was to swerve at exactly the same moment as the adversary. The best outcome was for the other driver to swerve. At minimum, this produced immense satisfaction at having made a chicken out of the other driver, but sometimes the payoffs were much higher, as when the chicken had to forfeit title to his automobile. The usual result was that one driver would swerve; less often, both players would pull away simultaneously. No one really intended to kill or be killed, but occasionally there was the sobering result (and a little sobering often was in order) when both players miscalculated and neither swerved in time.

International crises often resemble games of **brinkmanship** like chicken, contests of nerve to see who will be first to give in. The Cuban missile crisis was such an instance; the goal was to make the adversary change course. Only if absolutely necessary, if it appeared that the adversary was going to resort to the use of nuclear weapons—or if the risk of accidental use by either side was becoming too great—would one's own course be changed. It was Khrushchev who swerved during the missile crisis, and the chicken game suggests that this was the rational thing to do. However, Soviet leaders swore they would build up their forces so that the United States could never threaten them that way again. Chicken is a dangerous game. In nuclear diplomacy, it assumes that both sides will be able to control their forces well enough that war will not occur accidentally and that at least one party will be fearful (and sensible) enough to swerve in time. But a player who was once humiliated may be unwilling to swerve in a subsequent crisis.

Deterring a nuclear "bolt from the blue" was not the central problem for American and Soviet strategists during the cold war because that sort of surprise attack did not present a credible threat in an era of MAD. The problem, especially for U.S. policy makers, was how to credibly threaten a nuclear response to lesser forms of aggression, like a Soviet invasion of Western Europe, when nuclear retaliation would surely follow. Jonathan Schell summed it up nicely when he said that each superpower's nuclear arsenal was "like a gun with two barrels, of which one points ahead and the other points back at the gun's holder. If a burglar should enter your house, it might make sense to threaten him with this gun, but it could never make sense to fire it."[23] (Box 9.2 shows this logic in game-theoretic terms.)

One solution adopted by the United States was not unlike the tactic used by a bold driver in the game of chicken who would take his hands off the steering wheel as the cars approached each other. An important feature of nuclear command and control is that the authority to launch nuclear weapons devolves during times of crisis. If sole authority remained with the high-level military commanders (including the president, as commander in chief), then U.S. retaliatory capacity might be neutralized by a "decapitating" Soviet first strike. In reality, as a crisis escalates,

---

[23] Jonathan Schell, *The Abolition* (New York: Knopf, 1984), p. 54.

IN GREATER DEPTH

BOX 9.2 | NUCLEAR CRISIS AND THE GAME OF CHICKEN

The game of chicken as played by two youths can be depicted as a 2 × 2 game in strategic form. The worst outcome for both is when neither swerves (southeast cell), while the best for either driver is for the other to swerve (northeast and southwest cells). When they both swerve, they avert a crash but neither has prevailed in making a chicken of the other (northwest cell). There are two Nash equilibria in this game—one stands firm, and the other gives in—but neither is the Pareto optimal outcome of mutual cooperation. Thus, like the prisoner's dilemma, chicken also presents its players with a dilemma.

	Red *Give in*	Red *Stand firm*
Blue *Give in*	3,3	2,4
Blue *Stand firm*	4,2	1,1

One common tactic employed in chicken was for the driver to take his hands off the steering wheel, thereby communicating to the other driver that he no longer controlled his vehicle and their mutual fate was no longer in his hands. The other driver, being rational, would have no choice but to swerve. As contestants became wise to such tactics, more desperate measures were called for in order to demonstrate lack of control, like jumping into the passenger seat. In precommitting himself to stand firm, one driver was in effect transforming a simultaneous-move game into a sequential-move game in which that driver made the first move. It is easy to see why this strategy worked when we examine the extensive form of the chicken game. Using backward induction (recall Box 8.1), there is one Nash equilibrium in the sequential chicken game. The one who moves first (pre-commits) drives straight on while the other swerves.

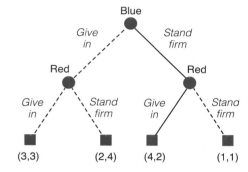

The difficulty with nuclear deterrence is not so much preventing a bolt-from-the-blue first strike by the adversary, but figuring out how to make a retaliatory threat credible once a nuclear crisis is under way and your side has lost the initiative in a game of chicken. To continue with Jonathan Schell's metaphor: On most days your deterrent keeps the burglar out of your house, but what if somehow he manages to get in? Your threat to pull the trigger of that suicidal gun is just not credible. You need to find a way to convince your opponent that you will indeed go down the retaliatory path (stand firm) knowing full well that doing so will bring destruction to both of you. Only then can you be sure he won't ever be tempted to enter your house.

more and more authority passes to local military commanders to use the nuclear weapons in their possession. If the Soviets attacked Western Europe with all their conventional military might, there was not much that U.S. forces in Europe could have done to repel the invasion. But the Soviets had to consider the prospect that local U.S. commanders, their forces overrun (and their families in danger), had nuclear weapons at their disposal. From the perspective of American nuclear strategists, this was like taking your hands off the steering wheel: "Look, we are no longer in full control of our nuclear response, so it's up to you to swerve." It is what Thomas Schelling called "the threat that leaves something to chance."[24]

Strategists may have devised a way to enhance the credibility of nuclear retaliation, but this solution was rather frightening to the rest of us. (Who wants to ride with a driver willing to let go of the steering wheel?) Scenarios for nuclear attack may seem improbable, but in fact they were not. At the time of the Cuban missile crisis, Kennedy said that he thought the chances of nuclear war were about one in three. Perhaps he was mistaken, but even if the odds were lower, such a belief can become a self-fulfilling prophecy. Making plans—deploying weapons, proclaiming doctrines, picking targets, instructing commanders—with every intention of not putting them in motion provides no assurance that they will not be put in motion. In the 1914 crisis, the great powers' competitive mobilization plans worked in lockstep, making World War I almost unavoidable once mobilization was under way. Plans we adopt in the name of nuclear deterrence could be activated when a crisis occurs; then it is too late for second thoughts. The problem with brinkmanship is that human leaders are fallible. They can easily misunderstand each other's intentions, especially under the enormous pressures of a nuclear crisis.

We might be inclined to rest a little easier because the United States and Russia no longer stand at the edge of the nuclear chasm. Conflicts over spheres of influence have largely abated, and military crises are much less likely. Good political relations have defused much of the danger posed by both sides' strategic nuclear technologies. But there is huge destructive capacity harnessed in the nuclear weapons that the United States and Russia still deploy, not to mention those deployed by the other nuclear states. With India and Pakistan—the two most recent members of the nuclear club—eyeing each other across contested Kashmir, it is clear that the dangers of crisis instability and nuclear escalation remain very real. Nuclear proliferation also poses the risk that a future nuclear crisis will be multilateral; we can imagine that China may well become involved in an Indo–Pakistani conflict. Such crises—and the brinkmanship they might encourage—could be much harder to control than the bilateral crises of the past.

ARMS CONTROL AND DISARMAMENT

The nuclear balance of terror and the fear of accidental or uncontrolled nuclear launches highlighted for world leaders and the general public the need to restrain the U.S.–Soviet arms race and the proliferation of weapons of mass destruction.[25] When reviewing the history of arms control, especially the bilateral agreements

---

[24] Thomas Schelling, *The Strategy of Conflict* (Cambridge, Mass.: Harvard University Press, 1960), chap. 8.

[25] On the possibility of nuclear accidents, see Scott D. Sagan, *The Limits of Safety: Organizations, Accidents, and Nuclear Weapons* (Princeton, N.J.: Princeton University Press, 1993); Bruce G. Blair, *The Logic of Accidental Nuclear War* (Washington, D.C.: Brookings Institution, 1993).

signed by the United States and the Soviet Union, it is important to remember that arms control is not necessarily disarmament. **Arms control** is a process that produces agreements on the production, deployment, management, or use of weapons. Arms-control agreements aim to create or enhance stability by limiting the availability of weapons for intentional or accidental use, and that does not necessarily involve reducing their numbers. The aim of **disarmament** is indeed to reduce the numbers of weapons. Thus, arms control may sometimes be seen as a distraction from the quest for disarmament, while some kinds of disarmament could work against the stability sought through arms control (for instance, by undermining a state's second-strike capability).

Generally, multilateral treaties attempt to prevent the spread of weapons of mass destruction to areas and countries where they have not already been deployed. Treaties regarding Antarctica, outer space, the seabed, and environmental modification all provide that signatories will continue to refrain from doing something they have not yet done. Other agreements call on states to destroy what they do not need. Biological and chemical weapons agreements have called for destroying stocks of weapons, but most analysts of modern warfare agree that both biological and chemical weapons are generally inferior to nuclear ones as weapons of mass destruction. But the most important targets of biological and chemical weapons agreements are the nonnuclear states, which might seek to acquire these weapons as substitutes for nuclear weapons (perhaps while they conduct nuclear weapons research).[26]

NUCLEAR ARMS CONTROL

In January 1994, Presidents Clinton and Yeltsin said that the United States and Russia would stop targeting each other's territory with strategic nuclear missiles. Although perhaps considered unremarkable in the post–cold war atmosphere, such an event was the result of a long process of arms control, both between the two superpowers and in multilateral agreements covering various forms of weapons of mass destruction. The major multilateral arms-control agreements since World War II are listed in Table 9.3; the final column indicates the number of countries that either signed the original agreement (whether or not they have formally ratified it) or acceded to the agreement since it entered into force.

The limitations on weapon types, characteristics, and deployment can be broken down into several basic categories. Some arms-control agreements *create nuclear free zones* in an effort to exclude arms races from certain areas by forbidding the deployment of nuclear weapons there. Some of these have been created in frontier areas, such as Antarctica, outer space, and the seabed. Other treaties declare the intention of signatories not to see weapons introduced into their own regions; states are forbidden from either acquiring nuclear weapons themselves or allowing external powers to station nuclear forces on their territories. Such agreements, like those signed by countries in Latin America, the South Pacific, Southeast

---

[26] For a comprehensive guide to arms control, see Jozef Goldblat, *Arms Control: The New Guide to Negotiations and Agreements*, 2nd ed. (London: Sage, 2002)

TABLE 9.3 | MULTILATERAL ARMS-CONTROL AGREEMENTS SINCE 1959

Signed	Agreement	Provisions	Signatories
1959	Antarctic Treaty	Prohibits all military activity in the Antarctic area.	45
1963	Partial Test Ban Treaty	Prohibits nuclear explosions in the atmosphere, outer space, and underwater.	134
1967	Outer Space Treaty	Prohibits all military activity in outer space, including the moon and other celestial bodies.	131
1967	Latin America Nuclear Weapon Free Zone Treaty	Prohibits Latin American countries from acquiring, manufacture, testing, using, or stationing nuclear weapons.	33
1968	Non-Proliferation Treaty	Prohibits acquisition of nuclear weapons by nonnuclear nations.	191
1971	Seabed Arms Control Treaty	Prohibits emplacement of nuclear weapons and other weapons of mass destruction on the ocean floor or its subsoil.	118
1972	Biological Weapons Convention	Prohibits development, production, and stockpiling of biological agents and toxins intended for hostile use and requires destruction of existing stocks.	185
1977	Environmental Modification Convention	Prohibits manipulation of the dynamics, composition, or structure of the earth, including its atmosphere, and of outer space for military or other hostile purposes.	89
1979	Celestial Bodies Agreement	Prohibits military deployments on or around the moon and other celestial bodies.	20
1980	Protection of Nuclear Material Convention	Establishes guidelines for international transport of nuclear material and the protection, recovery, and return of stolen nuclear material.	115
1981	Certain Conventional Weapons Convention	Prohibits and restricts use of excessively injurious and indiscriminate conventional weapons	111
1985	South Pacific Nuclear Free Zone Treaty	Prohibits countries and territories of the South Pacific from acquiring, manufacture, testing, using, or stationing nuclear weapons.	13
1987	Missile Technology Control Regime	Seeks to restrict the export of ballistic missiles, space launch vehicles, unmanned air vehicles, and related technologies.	34
1990	Conventional Armed Forces in Europe Treaty	Reduces NATO and Warsaw Pact forces in the Atlantic-to-Urals region. Former Soviet states agree to USSR obligations in 1992 Tashkent Agreement.	30
1992	Open Skies Treaty	Parties allow a quota of overflights of their territory for purposes of observing military activities.	32
1993	Chemical Weapons Convention	Prohibits development, production, and stockpiling of toxic chemicals intended for hostile use, and requires destruction of existing stocks by 2007.	188
1995	Southeast Asian Nuclear Weapon Free Zone	Prohibits Southeast Asian countries from acquiring, manufacture, testing, using, or stationing nuclear weapons.	10

(Continued)

TABLE 9.3 | *(Continued)*

Signed	Agreement	Provisions	Signatories
1996	Wassenaar Arrangement on Export Controls	Seeks to restrict the export of conventional weapons, dual-use equipment, and their production technologies.	40
1996	Comprehensive Test Ban Treaty	Prohibits all nuclear explosions, including those intended for peaceful purposes.	176
1996	African Nuclear Weapon Free Zone Treaty	Prohibits African countries from acquiring, manufacture, testing, using, or stationing nuclear weapons.	53
1997	Anti-personnel Mine Convention	Prohibits production, stockpiling and use of anti-personnel mines, and requires destruction of existing stocks.	158
1999	Inter-American Convention on Illicit Arms	Western Hemispheric countries commit to prevent the production and transshipment of illicit weapons and other dangerous materials	20
2006	Central Asian Nuclear Weapon Free Zone Treaty	Prohibits Central Asian countries from acquiring, manufacture, testing, using, or stationing nuclear weapons.	5

Source: UN Department for Disarmament Affairs, "Multilateral Arms Regulation and Disarmament Agreements"; available at <http://disarmament.un.org/TreatyStatus.nsf>. Signatories are the number of states that have signed, ratified, or acceded to the agreement.

Asia, and Africa, also include promises by the nuclear powers to respect these prohibitions. The latest multilateral arms-control agreement, signed in 2006, creates a nuclear free zone in Central Asia.

Arms control may be aimed at *minimizing risks of accidental nuclear attacks*, especially those that might result from miscommunication. In the first bilateral agreement signed by the United States and Soviet Union, which followed the Cuban missile crisis, the superpowers agreed to install a "hotline" providing for emergency communication between their heads of state. Communication between their foreign policy and defense officials has been facilitated more recently by the creation of a "nuclear risk reduction center" in each country. These agreements have sought to make it easier to control crises that could escalate beyond the nuclear threshold.

Arms control has long sought to *set limits on the characteristics of weapons*, both nuclear and nonnuclear, including their capacity for inflicting human suffering. In the twelfth century, the second Lateran Council under Pope Innocent II disallowed the use of crossbows against Christians (though not against non-Christians). The Hague Agreements of 1899 and 1907 outlawed the use of exploding and expanding ("dumdum") bullets because they caused unnecessary human suffering. Following on the Hague Agreements, which also banned the use of projectiles armed with poison gases, the Geneva Protocol of 1925 recognized that "the use in war of asphyxiating, poisonous or other gases, and of all analogous liquids, materials or devices, has been justly condemned by the general opinion of the civilized world" and sought to extend the ban to include bacteriological methods of warfare. These agreements provided the basis for the 1972 Biological Weapons Convention and the 1993 Chemical Weapons Convention, both of which prohibit not only the use of these weapons but also their development, production, and stockpiling.

Some weapons characteristics are considered especially destabilizing. As a result of the Strategic Arms Limitation Talks, the two superpowers agreed in 1972 to limit their deployment of antiballistic missile (ABM) systems because they undermined the second-strike capabilities that provided the foundation for mutual deterrence. Subsequently, the Reagan administration's Strategic Defense Initiative (SDI)—a plan to develop and deploy a surface- and space-based system to intercept incoming ballistic missiles—was criticized for being destabilizing and for violating the ABM Treaty. Committed to moving forward with national missile defense and unwilling to do so within the confines of the ABM agreement, the George W. Bush administration withdrew the United States from the treaty in 2001 and has since tested various components of a system for national missile defense.

Other bilateral arms-control agreements between the United States and the Soviet Union, and later Russia, *set limits on the number of nuclear weapons* that can be deployed. The Strategic Arms Limitations Talks were the first forum for their efforts and the resulting treaties (SALT I and SALT II) succeeded in slowing the growth of the superpowers' nuclear arsenals. The 1987 Treaty on Intermediate Nuclear Forces (INF) represented a milestone in arms control for two reasons. Although the treaty covered only about 4 percent of the superpowers' nuclear forces, it was the first arms-control agreement that actually reduced the number of nuclear weapons. The SALT agreements had only established ceilings that could not be exceeded by future deployments. INF provided for on-site inspections and other verification procedures that had been insurmountable hurdles in previous talks. Verifying the elimination of an entire class of nuclear weapons would prove far easier and less intrusive than verifying whether some numerical or qualitative limit had been exceeded.

The INF agreement and its successful implementation, even though almost insignificant from a military point of view, proved to have a substantial impact on political relations between the superpowers, which is the second reason it became a milestone in the history of arms control. Arms-control treaties, in almost any form, *build confidence and trust* among the parties to the agreement. The INF treaty had that effect, setting into motion a process that has culminated in the very deep cuts required by the two Strategic Arms Reduction Treaties (START I and START II), cuts that are graphically displayed in Figure 9.2. Even SALT II, which was never ratified by the U.S. Senate as a result of the Soviet invasion of Afghanistan six months after its signing, built confidence and trust between the superpowers for as long as they continued to adhere voluntarily to the limits set by the treaty. The latest U.S.–Russian agreement, the Strategic Offensive Reductions Treaty (SORT), signed by George W. Bush and Vladimir Putin in Moscow in 2002, commits the former nuclear rivals to reduce their offensive arsenals to levels unimaginable during the height of the cold war.

Most observers agree that *stemming the proliferation of weapons of mass destruction* will continue to be the central issue of arms control in the years ahead. In signing the Non-Proliferation Treaty (NPT) of 1968, states that did not already have nuclear weapons promised not to acquire them, and states that did have nuclear weapons promised not to transfer them to nonnuclear states. The bargain between the nuclear powers and nonnuclear states in the NPT was that this "horizontal" proliferation of nuclear capability would be restricted in return for real reductions in the nuclear powers' existing arsenals—that is, an end to "vertical" proliferation. As an effort to dampen the upwardly spiraling arms race, SALT was welcome; but it was only with the START agreements that the United States and Russia began to live up to promises long overdue. Meeting in New York in May 1995, parties to the NPT agreed to extend the original treaty permanently into the future. There are now 191 parties to the agreement, making it the most widely adhered to treaty in the history of arms control. Only Israel, India, and Pakistan have refused to sign, and North Korea withdrew from the NPT in 2003, the only country to have done so. All four are nuclear states (Israel unofficially), and becoming a party to the treaty now would require them to disarm; the treaty recognizes as nuclear states only those that tested a nuclear device before 1967.

Despite widespread adherence to the NPT, the spread of nuclear materials and technology remains an issue. By the 1980s, Israel, India, and South Africa (which was not a signatory to the NPT at the time) had crossed the threshold to actual possession of a nuclear capability. Until 1998, there was some uncertainty about Pakistan's nuclear capability, but that was put to rest when it engaged in dueling nuclear tests with India in May of that year. Other non-NPT states, such as Argentina and Brazil, were moving in the same direction during the 1980s and early 1990s, as were NPT states like South Korea and Taiwan. But beginning in 1992, with the U.S.–Russian arms reduction agreements and the accession of France and China to the NPT, these subthreshold states began dismantling their nuclear weapons programs. South Africa destroyed all seven of the bombs it had built and signed the NPT in 1991; three states (Belarus, Ukraine, and Kazakhstan) that inherited nuclear weapons from the old Soviet Union gave them up. Argentina signed in 1995, while Brazil signed in 1998. A worrisome development was the emergence of a new group of "rogue states": parties to the NPT who try to acquire nuclear weapons. The states attracting the most attention have been North Korea (now a nonparty) and Iran, with their ever-changing policies regarding on-site inspection of nuclear facilities. The U.S. invasion of Iraq in 2003, though ostensibly undertaken to rid the country of weapons of mass destruction, confirmed the International Atomic Energy Agency's judgment that Baghdad had, in fact, dismantled its nuclear weapons program. Libya was also in violation of its NPT commitments but began dismantling its program in 2004 under international supervision.

Although they also help to control proliferation, some arms-control efforts to curb nuclear testing have had as a central purpose *limiting environmental damage*. One of the first arms-control agreements of the cold war was the Partial Test Ban Treaty, signed in 1963, which banned nuclear test explosions everywhere but underground—explosions that might cause "radioactive debris to be present outside the territorial limits of the state under whose jurisdiction or control such explosion is conducted." The 1996 Comprehensive Test Ban Treaty (CTBT) closes off two avenues left open for nuclear testing by the Partial Test Ban: Underground testing and testing for "peaceful purposes" are now included in the prohibition. The CTBT has been signed by 176 nations and places serious constraints on nuclear weapons development and qualitative improvement. Within months of their May 1998 nuclear tests, both India and Pakistan expressed their intention to accede to the treaty but still have not done so.

CONTROLLING CONVENTIONAL WEAPONS AND TECHNOLOGY

Most arms-control agreements target weapons of mass destruction, but there have been some noteworthy efforts to address the proliferation of conventional weapons, as well as advanced weapons technology. Following on fifteen years of Mutual and Balanced Force Reduction (MBFR) talks, NATO and Warsaw Pact countries began negotiations on Conventional Armed Forces in Europe (CFE) and in 1990 concluded a treaty requiring substantial cuts in the number of tanks, armored vehicles, artillery, combat helicopters, and aircraft deployed in the European theater. The most celebrated recent accomplishment in conventional arms control is the Anti-Personnel Mine Convention outlawing the production and use of landmines, which entered into force in 1999. The movement to ban landmines was a truly grassroots effort spearheaded by the International Campaign to Ban Landmines, for which the NGO and its coordinator, Jody Williams, received the 1997 Nobel Peace Prize. The United Nations, spurred on by a number of NGOs, has also held a series of conferences on regulating the trade and small arms and light weapons.[27]

The U.S.–led war against Iraq in 1991 and its aftermath heightened interest in the acquisition of advanced-technology weaponry throughout the world, including missile-delivery systems. Such interest in turn raised concern among the five permanent members of the UN Security Council: the United States, Russia, China, Britain, and France—the countries responsible for about 80 percent of the global trade in conventional weapons. Earlier, in 1987, the Missile Technology Control Regime (MTCR) had been established as a voluntary association of countries committed to establishing guidelines for the export of missiles (and missile-production know-how) that might be used to deliver weapons of mass destruction. A more concerted effort seemed to be required, so meetings were held beginning in 1991. These efforts were only partially successful, but ended in late 1992 when China walked out in protest over U.S. sales of jet fighters to Taiwan. The effort to replace the cold war–era Coordinating Committee for Multilateral Export Control (CoCom)—mainly NATO members cooperating to restrict the transfer of military technology to the Warsaw Pact—was more successful. In 1996, the Wassenaar Arrangement was announced, whereby member states (this time including former Warsaw Pact countries) agreed to new restrictions on the export of conventional weapons and advanced weapons technology.

Many people—government leaders, citizen activists, and scholars—have devoted their energies to reducing the prospects of war and reducing the number and destructiveness of weapons with which wars might be fought. Our review of arms-control and disarmament efforts since World War II leaves us with a mixed picture. There has been progress. The world has not blown up; no nuclear weapon

---

[27] On the role of NGOs in the campaigns against landmines and small arms, see Frank Faulkner, *Moral Entrepreneurs and the Campaign to Ban Landmines* (Amsterdam: Rodopi, 2007); Denise Garcia, *Small Arms and Security: New Emerging International Norms* (New York: Routledge, 2006).

has been exploded in war since 1945. By historical standards, that is a very long time without a really big war. Despite the common fears voiced in each decade, there has not been a steady proliferation of nuclear weapons. Beyond the United States, Russia, Britain, France, and China, only India and Pakistan have exploded nuclear devices—although North Korea claims to have done so and Israel could and might. As we have seen, there have been international agreements to ban nuclear weapons from several places and to prohibit nuclear testing and proliferation. Chemical and biological weapons of mass destruction are being controlled, while international public opinion has turned sharply against states willing to deploy inhumane weapons like landmines. Such progress should not give way to complacency, however. There are still a lot of nuclear weapons in the world, and there are nagging uncertainties about the ability of some states to control them during times of interstate crisis and keep them out of the hands of aspiring nuclear terrorists. Not all states have signed the most comprehensive arms-control treaties, and not all those who have can be depended on to abide by their terms. It may not be a realist dog-eat-dog world out there, but neither is it an idealist utopia.

INTERNATIONAL LAW AND ORGANIZATION

ETHICS, LAW, AND WAR

The last two chapters concentrated on the historical record of military conflict and arms acquisition and some analytical perspectives that aid in our understanding of their causes and consequences. There are also ethical questions to be asked and answered. We have alluded to moral and ethical considerations as possible restraints on both conflict and armament, but that has been the extent of our discussion of ethics. We have not considered such issues as what kinds of actions are moral or what ethical principles *should* guide our behavior and the behavior of our leaders in times of war and peace. Nor have we considered the principles and laws that *do* guide behavior in world politics or the ways states have organized themselves in order to encourage proper behavior. These are the kinds of issues we will now take up.

Moral or ethical propositions concern how people ought to behave, not necessarily how they do behave. This is the stuff of normative theory. Ethical reasoning is essentially *deductive* reasoning. One starts with a few basic principles—such as "all humans are created equal"—and deduces from them a set of propositions that provide further guidance for identifying behavior consistent with those principles. Many social scientists are reluctant to engage in ethical discussions because of the great difficulty we have, in modern industrial societies, of establishing a common frame of reference. Few people live in cultures where a single value system is dominant. Although modern values are heavily influenced by Greek and Judeo-Christian traditions, there is no commonly accepted authority, and only a few propositions are shared across most contemporary religions and other ethical systems. Humanists, Marxists, agnostics, and atheists share some common ground with religious believers, but that ground is not very extensive. Even within many of the major traditions, authority is repudiated and a wide variety of opinions are tolerated.

Despite the difficulties, we cannot neglect such issues in our discussion of deterrence and war. When is war justified? Are there circumstances in which nuclear weapons should never be used or even deployed? Are there targets that should never be attacked, whether by nuclear or conventional weapons? In a system in which states are the primary actors, can anyone be held personally responsible when moral limits are crossed? Our purpose here is not to insist on answers but to offer a number of considerations essential to an informed discussion of the issues.

REALISM AND PACIFISM

At one end of the spectrum of ethical thought about warfare are views associated with realism. The most extreme view is that war is justifiable if undertaken to serve the national interest. Those who take this position hold a very pessimistic view of international society: regardless of the moral restraints that bind our interpersonal behavior, international politics is so anarchic—a war of all against all—that mere self-preservation requires the abandonment of moral inhibitions. A more moderate realist view is that justice in foreign affairs depends on the aims of the government rather than on particular policy tools employed to achieve them. It is possible to distinguish between legitimate and illegitimate goals in world politics, but if a state's goals are just, then they ought to be pursued by whatever methods are available. This form of reasoning is called *consequentialism*.

Although many people may express their adherence to such principles—how often are we told that the end justifies the means?—it is not clear how many really believe that consequences alone are appropriate guides to action. Most adults come to believe that the law is important; there may be occasions when one feels compelled to break the law, but these are rare and should not be taken lightly. International law is sometimes regarded as one of the least authoritative and least effective forms of law, but, as we shall see, it is given considerable respect and observance, and not solely out of self-interest. This holds not only for international law in general but also the part that attempts to regulate military conflict. Despite the frequency with which we hear the adages "War is hell" and "All's fair in [love and] war," most people act as though they believe that some legal and ethical restraints are relevant to international behavior—even its most violent form.

Pacifism is very different from a realist "all's fair" position. A completely pacifist position may result from a philosophical and moral predilection for nonviolence, a principled rejection of the use of force as an instrument of national policy, a belief in the spiritually regenerative effect of a nonviolent response to violence, or an overriding concern for the preservation of human life. Like other normative theories, pacifist arguments are often based on rigorous deduction from first principles, despite the fact that many people associate pacifism only with certain forms of social activism like "draft dodging." Nor is pacifism necessarily passivity in the face of oppression. Civil disobedience, for example, is an active response to perceived injustice; it normally involves breaking the law, nonviolently, in pursuit of some higher moral purpose.

Pacifism has deep roots in a number of secular and religious traditions. It seems to have been the dominant view in the early Christian church before the Roman emperor Constantine converted to Christianity. The Roman Empire was pagan and often persecuted Christians; no Christian could in good conscience serve in the army of such a power. Pacifism is not the dominant tradition in contemporary Christianity, but it is still a common and respected view in many Christian churches. It is a central principle of the Society of Friends (the Quakers) and was practiced by Martin Luther King, Jr., in his program of civil disobedience against racial segregation. Mohandas Gandhi blended part of this Christian pacifist tradition with Hinduism in his resistance to British rule in India, and his example has had great influence worldwide. Buddhist monks protesting the war in Vietnam brought great attention to their cause by setting themselves on fire (although such acts of self-inflicted violence may not qualify as pacifism). Plans for nonviolent resistance—a war without weapons against a would-be conqueror—are commonly discussed and sometimes practiced.[1]

JUST WARS

Between the realist and pacifist positions are a variety of intermediate views commonly known as the **just war tradition**. Just war theory has its origins in ancient Greek and Roman thought, was developed in the Middle Ages by Christian theologians (most notably Augustine and Thomas Aquinas), and is the predominant Christian view today. It provides a foundation for similar positions taken by non-Christian thinkers as well. For those who accept the use of force as a legitimate instrument of state policy in some but not all circumstances, there are two sets of ethical principles to consider when judging the morality of war. "War is always judged twice," Michael Walzer points out, "first with reference to the reasons states have for fighting, secondly with reference to the means they adopt." The first judgment applies to the justice *of* war, or *jus ad bellum*, and the second to justice *in* war, or *jus in bello*.[2]

The just war tradition—both *jus ad bellum* and *jus in bello*—has evolved over the centuries, but the first comprehensive and systematic statement of just war theory is often traced to Hugo Grotius, the seventeenth-century jurist, in his *The Law of War and Peace*. Grotius identified several conditions that must be met if the resort to war is to be considered legitimate in light of prevailing international norms. Two of them, that there be just cause and that war be a last resort, also find expression in the UN Charter. For Grotius, *just cause* mainly meant the right of **self-defense**, as it does in the UN Charter, which identifies "the inherent right of individual or collective self-defense if an armed attack occurs" (Article 51). The principle of *last resort* suggests that states should exhaust all peaceful means of resolving disputes before resorting to military force, a condition that is met when a state has been attacked and is merely engaging in self-defense. This principle is also expressed in Article 33 of the UN Charter, which calls on states to "first of all, seek a solution by negotiation, enquiry, mediation, conciliation, arbitration" and other nonviolent means.

In addition to self-defense, Grotius and others writing in the just war tradition have argued that states need not wait to be attacked; imminent aggression may

---

[1] Classic statements in the pacifist tradition are Leo Tolstoy, "Last Message to Mankind" and Betrand Russell, "War and Non-Resistance," both in David Kinsella and Craig L. Carr, eds., *The Morality of War: A Reader* (Boulder, Colo.: Rienner, 2007); M. K. Gandhi, *Non-Violent Resistance (Satyagraha)* (Mineola, N.Y.: Dover, 2002).

[2] Michael Walzer, *Just and Unjust Wars: A Moral Argument with Historical Illustrations*, 4th ed. (New York: Basic Books, 2006), p. 21. On the historical evolution of just war theory, see James Turner Johnson, *Just War Tradition and the Restraint of War: A Moral and Historical Inquiry* (Princeton, N.J.: Princeton University Press, 1981).

justify the *preemptive* use of force. Preemptive self-defense is recognized in customary international law as a just cause for war, even though the UN Charter (Article 39) reserves for the Security Council (but not individual member states) the right to determine whether "a threat to the peace" calls for military action. The common understanding of "imminent" is that an act of aggression is in the making and will occur very soon unless it is preempted. It implies intent and capability on the part of the would-be aggressor, while the urgency of a preemptive response is typically signaled by some sort of offensive military mobilization. This is sometimes referred to as the *Caroline standard* for the preemptive use of force. In reference to a British attack in 1838 on the U.S. steamship *Caroline*, which was ferrying Canadian rebels and supplies from the New York side to the Canadian side of the Niagara River, Secretary of State Daniel Webster disputed the British claim that the attack, although a first use of force against the United States, was nevertheless justified as an act of self-defense. What was missing in this case, according to Webster, was "a necessity of self-defense, instant, overwhelming, leaving no choice of means, and no moment for deliberation."[3]

Customary international law does not recognize states' rights to undertake *preventive* war—military action against a state whose growing strength will allow it to attack in the foreseeable future but is not now an immediate threat. For example, in 1981 Israeli aircraft destroyed the Osiraq nuclear reactor at Tuwaitha near Baghdad before its first uranium fuel had been loaded. The Israelis judged that Iraq had the intent to attack, and the development of its capabilities was approaching a critical phase, after which Israeli security would be imperiled. Nevertheless, Israel was widely condemned for this attack. Before the Iraq War in 2003, the Bush administration adopted a modified view of imminent threat, one that blurs the traditional distinction between preemptive and preventive war. Their argument was that a preemptive strike becomes legitimate not so much because the would-be aggressor has the military capability and is poised to attack, but because it intends to attack, and waiting any longer for its capability to develop would make the attack prohibitively dangerous to deter or, if deterrence fails, to defeat. Here imminence applies to an approaching critical stage in the development of the *capability* to launch or facilitate an attack—including by transferring weapons of mass destruction (WMD) to terrorists—not to an actual attack.[4] So far, this reinterpretation of preemptive self-defense is not widely accepted within international legal circles or by the community of states.

The just war tradition also requires that war be declared by a *legitimate authority* and that it be *declared publicly*. These principles were meant to exclude

---

[3] Webster's words, from a letter to British minister Henry Fox in 1841, are ubiquitous in the international legal literature and have been invoked often by diplomats and jurists challenging a state's claim of self-defense.

[4] The Bush administration's rethinking of preemptive war can be found in "The National Security Strategy of the United States of America," September 2002, chap. 5, available at <http://www.whitehouse.gov/nsc/nss.pdf>. For a critique of this view, see Michael W. Doyle, *Striking First: Preemption and Prevention in International Conflict* (Princeton, N.J.: Princeton University Press, 2008). A more sympathetic view is Whitley Kaufman, "What's Wrong with Preventive War? The Moral and Legal Basis for the Preventive Use of Force," *Ethics and International Affairs* 19 (Fall 2005), pp. 23–38.

private wars and vigilante actions, which were more common before sovereign states had acquired a monopoly on the legitimate use of force. Now they mean that the established legal processes of the state must be followed. In the United States, the Congress is empowered by the Constitution to declare war, but no U.S. military action since World War II has been a declared war. Instead, the president has relied on his powers as commander-in-chief to send military forces into battle—usually with Congressional approval, but not always—and such actions generally satisfy *jus ad bellum* requirements even in the absence of a formal declaration of war. Today, new rules about the use of military force may be emerging. With the end of the cold war, there was an expectation that the United States and Russia would be able to agree on important matters of international security coming before the UN Security Council (where they, China, Britain, and France have individual veto power); the collective response to Iraq's invasion of Kuwait in 1990 was a case in point. This expectation of joint response restrains any one powerful state from unilaterally deciding that it has a just cause in defending someone else. In effect, some powers of legitimate authority may be shifting from a national to an international level. The U.S.–led war against Iraq in 2003, which was not sanctioned by the Security Council, was clearly at odds with these emerging norms. Yet the Bush administration did feel compelled to seek UN approval for its military action, even though failure to receive it did not dissuade the administration from moving ahead with its planned invasion.[5]

Jus in bello concerns proper conduct on the battlefield, and those rules of conduct have been extensively codified in that body of international law known variously as the *law of war*, the *law of international armed conflict*, and *international humanitarian law*. The most important principle governing the conduct of war is **discrimination** (sometimes referred to as *distinction*), the requirement that combatants respect the immunity of noncombatants. Discrimination forbids direct, deliberate attacks on civilians and others not engaged in or preparing for combat. World War II saw some particularly grave violations of this principle: the bombing of Dresden, a German city with no military significance; the firebombing of hundreds of thousands of Japanese civilians in Tokyo; and the atomic bombing of Hiroshima and Nagasaki, cities that were chosen as civilian, not military, targets. According to this principle, the fact that these bombings may have hastened the end of the war and even may have reduced the total number of casualties from what they otherwise would have been is not sufficient justification. Discrimination is an "absolutist" principle; it does not yield to consequentialist reasoning. Political leaders, on the other hand, have often turned to consequentialism in order to justify violations of noncombatant immunity in wartime.[6]

---

[5] On the role of the Security Council in legitimizing military action, see Erik Voeten, "The Political Origins of the UN Security Council's Ability to Legitimize the Use of Force," *International Organization* 59 (Summer 2005), pp. 527–557.

[6] Americans have had great difficulty coming to terms with this judgment in regard to the atomic bombings of Japan. See Gar Alperovitz, *The Decision to Use the Atomic Bomb, and the Architecture of an American Myth* (New York: Knopf, 1995); Robert Jay Lifton and Greg Mitchell, *Hiroshima in America: A Half Century of Denial* (New York: Quill, 1996).

In the just war tradition, the moral basis for discrimination is not guilt versus innocence. When a state resorts to unjust war, its soldiers are not considered complicit in the crime of aggression, and its civilians are not assumed to be innocent. Immunity from attack derives instead from the simple fact that noncombatants cannot do physical harm to an opposing army. Those who can do harm, soldiers, may be targeted—even though some may strenuously object to the war they are fighting, as is often the case. This same principle of discrimination affords combatants a set of rights once they are taken prisoners of war (POWs). Because POWs can no longer do harm, they may not be killed while captive and must be released when the war comes to an end. The war they fought before being taken prisoner may have been a war of aggression, but they are not responsible for that crime. If they are lawful combatants, if their conduct on the battlefield conforms to the laws of war, then the principle of discrimination gives them the right to surrender—in effect, to become noncombatants immune from attack. Injured soldiers, those who can no longer do harm, acquire this same immunity.

Another just war principle applies both when states resort to war and while they fight. Under *jus ad bellum*, **proportionality** is met when the legitimate aims sought by a state resorting to war outweigh the harm that will result from the prosecution of the war. Proportionality recognizes that all wars impose costs on the societies involved. The resort to war is just if the state is acting in self-defense *and* the stakes are sufficiently high that the likely costs of the war are worth paying. For example, it is hard to imagine any actual or imminent military attack that could justify the resort to substantial use of nuclear weapons even in self-defense. Massive civilian casualties would surely occur, even in a reactive war consisting of nuclear launches directed only at military targets, and the likely retaliatory strikes would impose costs that far exceed those suffered as a result of the initial act of aggression.

As a *jus in bello* principle, proportionality is expected to guide military actions once states are already at war. Like war itself, specific military actions should not impose costs that are not justified by the legitimate aims of the operation. As we have indicated, targeting noncombatants is never allowable under just war theory, but the principle of proportionality suggests that discrimination alone is not enough to make a military action morally acceptable. The requirements of discrimination and proportionality come together in what is sometimes referred to as the principle of **double effect**. Military actions have both good and bad effects. In order for those actions to be just, the good effect must outweigh the bad. Double effect requires that noncombatant immunity be observed (that the bad effect be unintended) but also requires that this unintended bad effect be proportional to the legitimate objective of the military action. The use of toxic defoliants by the United States in Vietnam probably violated the principle of double effect. The aim was legitimate: to reveal enemy forces, allowing them to be targeted by aerial bombardment. But the use of defoliants like Agent Orange caused long-term environmental damage and contamination. These bad effects were unintended, but we should ask whether destroying the enemy's cover was worth the adverse and foreseeable consequences for the civilian population.

LAW AND THE WAR ON TERROR

Just war theory is a tradition of political and moral philosophy and is not the same as international law, but key principles of just war theory have indeed become formalized international law by virtue of agreements signed by states. As we have said, the UN Charter prohibits states from using or threatening military force against other states but recognizes the right of self-defense when a state is attacked. The Geneva Conventions signed in 1949, along with the Protocols signed in 1977, are the most authoritative statements of the law of war and include rules pertaining to both discrimination and proportionality.[7]

We have referred to the "war on terror" on several occasions. Clearly, this is not a war in the traditional sense; it is best understood as the U.S. approach to combating international terrorism in the aftermath of the 9/11 attacks. As a whole, the war on terror was conceived as an open-ended policy allowing for the use of military force against terrorists and their state sponsors in multiple theaters and for an indefinite period. At the same time, the war on terror has included military actions that do, in fact, resemble wars in the traditional sense, namely, the wars against Afghanistan and Iraq. In this section, we examine these wars against the backdrop of just war theory and the law of war. Were they just wars? We also consider the status of prisoners seized during the war on terror—in Afghanistan, Iraq, and elsewhere—and ask whether their treatment is consistent with the law of war.[8]

Invasion of Afghanistan   States have often responded to terrorist attacks with military force. The United States bombed Libya in 1986 after it learned that Libyan intelligence agents orchestrated a terrorist attack on a West German dance club that killed several off-duty U.S. soldiers. After concluding that al Qaeda was behind the attacks on the U.S. embassies in Kenya and Tanzania in 1998, the United States launched missile strikes against al Qaeda training camps in Afghanistan and a chemical plant in Sudan, whose owners were thought to have links to al Qaeda (the evidence is disputed). Although the United States has invoked the right of self-defense in such cases—as have other states in similar circumstances—these actions are better classified as armed **reprisals** than acts of self-defense. Reprisals are actions that are themselves unlawful but are taken in response to a previous unlawful act with the intent of persuading the initial law breaker to change its ways. The U.S. strike against Libya, for example, was intended to convince Libya's leader, Muammar Qaddafi, to stop supporting terrorism against the United States

---

[7] See, for example, Christine Gray, *International Law and the Use of Force*, 2nd ed. (Oxford: Oxford University Press, 2004); Yoram Dinstein, *War, Aggression, and Self-Defense*, 3rd ed. (Cambridge: Cambridge University Press, 2001); Dinstein, *The Conduct of Hostilities under the Law of International Armed Conflict* (Cambridge: Cambridge University Press, 2004).

[8] See, for example, Helen Duffy, *The "War on Terror" and the Framework of International Law* (Cambridge: Cambridge University Press, 2005); David Kinsella, "Principles Under Pressure: Just War Doctrine and American Antiterror Strategy after 9/11," in Harvey Starr, ed., *Approaches, Levels, and Methods of Analysis in International Politics: Crossing Boundaries* (New York: Palgrave Macmillan, 2006).

and its allies. Thus, reprisals are essentially a form of vigilantism in an international system that lacks a recognized law enforcement authority. And like vigilantes, states resorting to reprisals are often condemned by others in the international community for taking the law into their own hands.

The 2001 U.S. invasion of Afghanistan following the 9/11 attacks more closely resembled a war of self-defense. Indeed, it was consistent with the Bush administration's rejection of a law-enforcement approach to fighting terrorism in favor a *war* on terror. UN Security Council resolutions passed after 9/11 began by recognizing the inherent right of individual and collective self-defense, and went on to warn that states supporting or harboring the perpetrators of the 9/11 attacks would be held accountable. Article 51 of the UN Charter, in addition to acknowledging the right of self-defense, requires states acting in self-defense to inform the Security Council of their actions. Accordingly, in October 2001 the U.S. ambassador to the UN stated in a letter to the Security Council that the United States, exercising its right of self-defense, was commencing military operations against Afghanistan. In addition to al Qaeda, the Taliban government was named as the target of U.S. action because it allowed Afghan territory to be used as a base for al Qaeda's attacks on the United States.

Although there was some opposition to the U.S. invasion, it was relatively muted, and the silence suggested that the international community generally regarded this as a legitimate war of self-defense. However, there was an important departure from the traditional understanding of self-defense. The United States had suffered an armed attack by al Qaeda, but no other attacks followed. Was there (to quote Daniel Webster) a "necessity of self-defense, instant, overwhelming, leaving no choice of means, and no moment for deliberation"? The answer is probably no, considering that the U.S. response did not come until four weeks after 9/11. Nevertheless, because the invasion was not widely viewed as unlawful, it may be that new legal norms are emerging in regard to the use of military force against international terrorists and their state sponsors. The Caroline standard may not be the yardstick by which the international community measures the legitimacy of self-defense in the war on terror.

Iraq War   The U.S.–led invasion of Iraq in 2003 is a more complicated case because supporters of that war offered multiple reasons for its legitimacy, not all of them directly related to the larger war on terror. One was that Saddam Hussein's regime presented a clear and present danger to the United States and its allies, justifying a war of preemptive self-defense. Another was that Iraq had violated the terms of the Security Council resolution ending the 1991 enforcement action that liberated Kuwait from Iraqi occupation; the legal authority for the military action in 2003 was the same as that behind the Persian Gulf War.

In the previous section, we indicated that the right of preemptive self-defense is recognized in customary international law. This seems to place an extra burden on the preemptor to demonstrate to the international community, sometimes after the fact, that an act of aggression was imminent. We also suggested that the Bush administration's view of legitimate preemption pertained not to the threat of attack but to the threat that a potential aggressor is about to acquire a dangerous military capacity. Leaving aside the fact that many analysts do not accept this interpretation even in principle, the United States (and Britain, its chief military ally) needed to demonstrate that Iraq's nuclear capability was imminent. Most were not convinced. Furthermore, the allies had an additional burden the Israelis did not have when they struck the Osiraq complex in 1981. It stood to reason that if Iraq acquired a nuclear bomb in, say, the mid-1980s, there was a good chance that the Iraqi military could deliver it to Israeli territory once a decision was made to attack. Getting such a device to the United States (or Britain) is another matter, so the case for preemption also had to rest on the Ba'ath regime's ties to terrorist groups, particularly those with a demonstrated capability to strike the U.S. (or British) homeland. Iraq certainly could not do it. Yet that claim, too, was widely regarded as dubious at the time. Nor did any evidence surface after the invasion that would have vindicated the case for preemption.

If the Iraq War was not a war of self-defense, could it be justified as an enforcement of Security Council resolutions? States have granted the Council authority to take "action with respect to threats to the peace, breaches of the peace, and acts of aggression" under Chapter VII of the UN Charter. The Persian Gulf War was authorized by Security Council Resolution 678; the conditions for the cease-fire—most importantly, Iraq's disarmament—were stipulated in Resolution 687. In the years that followed, however, Saddam Hussein's regime was repeatedly accused of not living up to its disarmament obligations. The regime's recalcitrance led to a series of increasingly coercive responses by the United States and Britain, including strict enforcement of no-fly zones. Resolution 1441, passed in November 2002, warned Iraq that it would face "serious consequences" if it did not afford itself one last opportunity to comply with those obligations.

Because there was sharp disagreement among the members of the Council, Resolution 1441 was intentionally left vague, and while ambiguity may make good political sense, it did not make good law. The text at issue stated that the Council "decides to convene immediately upon receipt of a report" by UN weapons inspectors indicating that Iraq continues to obstruct their efforts, in which case it will "consider the situation and the need for full compliance." The French and Russian delegations took this to mean that military action against Iraq required, first, a determination by the Council that Iraq was in further breach of its obligations and, second, a separate decision to authorize the forcible disarmament of Iraq. The American and British view was that the Council could convene and "consider the situation" all it wanted; the authority to disarm Iraq had already been granted to member states by prior resolutions.

Another legal question concerned the nature of the military action implied by the reference to "serious consequences" in Resolution 1441. In 1990, the stronger language used in Resolution 678—that member states are authorized to "use all necessary means"—referred to the military liberation of Kuwaiti sovereignty and the restoration of "international peace and security in the area." In 2002 and 2003, it is possible that Iraq remained a threat to security in the area, but it is doubtful that the regime posed more of a threat than it did in 1990 before it invaded Kuwait. If the regime did pose that level of threat to its neighbors, then there was still the question of whether all necessary means implied a full-scale military invasion and overthrow of Saddam Hussein's regime, which in 1991 was considered neither necessary nor proportionate. Some, for instance, had called for military enforcement of the inspection regime, which might have been accomplished by declaring all of Iraqi airspace a no-fly zone and accompanying UN inspectors with armed military personnel.

In sum, it is hard to see the Iraq War as anything but a violation of international law.[9] In contrast to the invasion of Afghanistan, this was not a response to an armed attack; even if we accept a revised standard for preemptive self-defense, as proposed by the Bush administration, the threat presented by Iraq did not meet it. And justifying the war as an enforcement of UN Security Council resolutions required a particular interpretation of those resolutions accepted by very few states other than the United States and Britain.

Is there fault to be found in the conduct of the war in Iraq? In planning Operation Iraqi Freedom, policy makers and military planners had to take into account the "al-Jazeera effect," whereby graphic reports of civilian casualties would be broadcast into millions of homes across the Arab world (and beyond), igniting public outrage and increasing pressure to suspend the military campaign prematurely. That meant avoiding targets like roads, bridges, and other public works, as well as hospitals, schools, and mosques. It also meant relying heavily on precision-guided munitions; 65 to 70 percent of the ordnance used in Iraqi Freedom was precision-guided, compared to about 10 percent during Operation Desert Storm in 1991.

Despite these and other precautions, the order of magnitude of civilian deaths was in the thousands. High-end estimates, not surprisingly, included figures released by various antiwar groups, which are typically compiled from media reports of stray bombs and surveys of hospitals and burial sites. Iraq Body Count (IBC), a British research group, estimated civilian fatalities to be about 7,400 through the end of April 2003, when the major combat phase of the war concluded. The methodologies used by IBC and other groups are not beyond dispute, but the refusal of the U.S. and British governments to release their own figures led many observers to conclude that IBC's estimates are believable. Furthermore, most estimates of war deaths count only direct and immediate fatalities from violence. They do not include deaths that may occur in the months and years after the war from disease, malnutrition, the plight of refugees, and the destruction of health, water, and sanitation services. These indirect and long-term deaths are likely to be many times as numerous.[10] Whatever the actual tally, it surely provides a sharp

---

[9] For legal arguments on both sides of the debate over Iraq, see "Agora: Future Implications of the Iraq Conflict," *American Journal of International Law* 97 (April 2003), pp. 553–641. See also Mark A. Drumbl, "Self-Defense and the Use of Force: Breaking the Rules, Making the Rules, or Both?" *International Studies Perspectives* 4 (November 2003), pp. 409–431.

[10] IBC figures come from the Iraq Body Count, "Documented Civilian Deaths from Violence: Monthly Table," June 23, 2008; available at <http://www.iraqbodycount.org/database/>. A controversial study published in a British medical journal estimated the number of civilian causalities due to violence from the onset of the invasion through June 2006 at 601,000; see Gilbert Burnham et al., "Mortality after the 2003 Invasion of Iraq: A Cross-Sectional Cluster Sample Survey," *The Lancet* 368 (October 21, 2006), pp. 1421–1428. On the question of proportionality, see Thomas W. Smith, "Protecting Civilians . . . or Soldiers? Humanitarian Law and the Economy of Risk in Iraq," *International Studies Perspectives* 9 (May 2008), pp. 144–164.

contrast to the relatively low number of American and British combat deaths during the invasion, which was fewer than 200.

Prisoners of the War on Terror   The law of war pertaining to the treatment of prisoners is codified in the Third Geneva Convention of 1949 (amended in 1977 by Geneva Protocol I). Evaluating the conduct of captors, interrogators, and other prison officials is fairly straightforward in the case of a conventional armed conflict like the Iraq War. But determining the applicability of the Geneva rules to prisoners of the more nebulous war on terror has been difficult and quite contentious.

By the time of the Iraq War, the Bush administration had already been criticized for its handling of prisoners from the war in Afghanistan. The controversy surrounding the abuse of Iraqi prisoners held at the Abu Ghraib detention center reinforced suspicions among international legal experts and human-rights advocates that the administration did not feel strictly bound by Geneva law. Prisoners at Abu Ghraib were battered and beaten, sexually humiliated, terrorized by dogs, and otherwise subjected to physical and psychological duress, if not tortured outright. If the maltreatment of Iraqi prisoners wasn't bad enough, the lurid photographs that brought the abuse to public attention dealt a serious blow to America's image worldwide. Several low-ranking military police personnel were convicted in U.S. courts martial and sentenced to prison time. The commanders of the military police and intelligence brigades were demoted or reprimanded but not prosecuted for crimes, and there remained questions about the role of high-level policy makers and intelligence officials in directing the mistreatment of detainees, or at least in creating a permissive environment in which abuse could go on unchecked.[11] The handling of prisoners at Abu Ghraib was the greatest ignominy of U.S. conduct during the Iraq War. It certainly presents a stark contrast to the restraint and discipline shown by U.S. Army and Marine units during the ground invasion.

Even before the Abu Ghraib scandal, there was widespread criticism of the Bush administration's decision to relocate combatants captured in the Afghan theater of war to prison facilities at the U.S. military base in Guantánamo Bay, Cuba. It soon became clear that the administration viewed the detainees as something other than POWs with rights defined under Geneva law. Various reasons were offered for denying Taliban detainees POW status. Because the Taliban was recognized by only a few states as the legitimate government of Afghanistan, the administration regarded its members as irregular armed forces who nevertheless failed to meet the Geneva requirements for lawful combatancy—in particular, for not wearing distinctive insignia (like uniforms). Most legal experts disputed the classification. The Taliban was the de facto government of Afghanistan; its members constituted the country's regular armed forces and therefore were lawful combatants entitled to Geneva protections when in captivity. On the other hand, legal

---

[11] Seymour M. Hersh, *Chain of Command: The Road from 9/11 to Abu Ghraib* (New York: Harper-Collins, 2004); Mark Danner, *Torture and Truth: America, Abu Ghraib, and the War on Terror* (New York: New York Review Books, 2004).

experts generally agreed that al Qaeda fighters failed to meet the lawful combatancy requirements for irregular forces and need not be afforded POW protections.

In refusing to classify prisoners from Afghanistan or those captured elsewhere during the war on terror as lawful combatants, the Bush administration's aim was to avail itself of every opportunity to extract information. Unprotected by POW rights, the captives could be interrogated, and the conditions of captivity would not be subject to the strictures contained in the Geneva Conventions. Holding the detainees in facilities at Guantánamo, the administration hoped, would also place them out of reach of U.S. law, which grants even alien prisoners due process rights, including the right to petition a court for a writ of *habeas corpus* (that is, to challenge one's imprisonment). However, in a series of stunning legal defeats, the U.S. Supreme Court ruled that Guantánamo was not beyond the reach of U.S. law, that detainees could challenge their imprisonment in U.S. courts, and that the system created by the administration and the U.S. Congress to strip the court of its jurisdiction and use military commissions to deal with prisoners of the war on terror was unconstitutional. In one case, *Hamdan v. Rumsfeld*, the Court ruled in 2006 that the rules established for the military commissions violated the Third Geneva Convention—Article 3 in particular, which requires trial by "a regularly constituted court affording all the judicial guarantees which are recognized as indispensable by civilized peoples."[12]

The Guantánamo detentions and the Abu Ghraib scandal, as well as the apprehension of terrorist masterminds hiding in Pakistan and elsewhere, generated the sort of public debate on the pros and cons of torture that was taboo before 9/11. Some people have argued that torture ought to be allowed under legally controlled circumstances—for example, to extract information from a "ticking bomb terrorist" who has set in motion an attack that will kill a large number of innocent civilians and knows what it will take to avert it.[13] Many others refuse to endorse the use of torture but nevertheless assume that the U.S. and other governments do it anyway when dealing with "high value" prisoners. Despite the permissive environment created by the war on terror in regard to interrogation methods, torture remains a clear violation of international law and the domestic law of most nations, including the United States.

INTERNATIONAL LAW

So far we have focused on those areas of international law pertaining to the resort to military force by states and the rules of conduct during wartime. Now we step back and consider international law more generally. International law, once commonly referred to as the "law of nations," is a mechanism for maintaining and

---

[12] On the use of military commissions and tribunals, historically and during the war on terror, see Louis Fisher, *Military Tribunals and Presidential Power: American Revolution to the War on Terrorism* (Lawrence: University Press of Kansas, 2005).

[13] The best known proponent of this view is Alan Dershowitz; see *Why Terrorism Works: Understanding the Threat, Responding to the Challenge* (New Haven, Conn.: Yale University Press, 2002), chap. 4.

expanding regularized, smooth interactions among states and must be understood in a political context. It has evolved as the Westphalian state system itself has evolved, and the anarchic character of interstate relations means that the international legal system is quite unlike the mature domestic legal systems of most states. International law is in many ways primitive, more like what existed in the Wild West. If there was any law at all, it was best not to count on the local sheriff to enforce it; in the face of injustice, sometimes the better bet was to rely on one's own wit and resources (and perhaps some neighbors). But law and governing institutions did gradually take hold in the American West, and international law and institutions, too, have evolved considerably over the course of the past century. International legal considerations form an important part of the menu from which states select actions (or inaction) in their foreign relations.

NATURAL LAW, LEGAL POSITIVISM, AND REALISM

There are two main philosophical perspectives in international law. The **natural law** tradition has its roots in the concept of divine law—timeless principles and rules handed down by God and revealed through Church teaching and edicts. Beginning in the seventeenth century, natural law theorists like Grotius and Samuel Pufendorf grounded their views not in Church law but in the "law of nature"— principles accessible by human capacity to reason about the natural world. Contemporary natural law theorists generally believe that there exists a community of humankind, and members of this community share certain rights and responsibilities irrespective of their status as citizens of states. The subjects of international law, in other words, are not just sovereign states; international law is more than the "law of nations." Before the natural law tradition was fully loosened from is theological moorings, many rules (including some relating to the conduct of war) were not viewed as applying equally to Christians and non-Christian "barbarians." In time, however, and with the influence of such profound thinkers as eighteenth-century German philosopher Immanuel Kant, there was an insistence that international law and ethics be applied universally. Contemporary advocates of international human rights owe much to the natural law tradition, as do just war theorists.

Beginning in the nineteenth century, **legal positivism** became the predominant philosophical perspective on international law, and it remains highly influential today. Legal positivists are not inclined to ground the legal principles and rules of international relations in either divine law or the law of nature. Instead of relying on the authority of the Church or enlightened thinkers to determine what the law is, they look to states. International law consists of nothing more than the rules that states make for themselves, which are contained in the agreements they sign and the customary practices they follow (that is, "positive law"). Thus, legal positivists are skeptical of the natural law view that there are timeless and universal laws that apply to the entire human community. If certain laws appear to be universal, that is because all states—with the possible exception of a few rogue states—have actually consented to them.

Legal positivists acknowledge that the laws states make for themselves generally serve their own interests and the interests of the international community in stability and smooth relations between states. In this respect, they share common ground with realists. However, unlike realism, legal positivists emphasize the importance of consent and especially the obligations that follow once consent is given. States usually do feel bound by the agreements they make—*pacta sunt servanda*, agreements must be kept—even though that may clash with the national interest on occasion. Realists, on the other hand, do not deny that laws exist or even that states behave in accordance with them much of the time. What they do deny is that international law or a sense of obligations has any impact on the true motivations underlying state action—self-interest, plain and simple. States may find international law useful, but mainly as a fig leaf to conceal the otherwise crude exercise of power.

The legal positivist view of international law emphasizes not abstract philosophical conceptions of the law, but the manner in which states actually conduct their relations with other states. Although states often stretch and break international rules, as we saw in the case of the war on terror, more often they conform to those rules. One international legal scholar has summed it up well: "It is probably the case that almost all nations observe almost all principles of international law and almost all of their obligations almost all of the time."[14] In many ways, then, international law serves the same purpose as domestic law: It provides a set of rules that constrains behavior and brings order to society—the society of states.

But is international law really "law"? Domestic law consists of a set of rules found in the national constitution, legislated statutes, government regulations, and judicial decision, which are enforced by a centralized political authority. The system of sovereign states lacks a centralized government with supreme legislative, judicial, and enforcement authority; there is no international constitution. Nevertheless, institutions and practices do exist that make, interpret, and enforce international rules. These include IGOs, the official diplomatic procedures followed by states, and even legal authorities within states.[15] International law has many functions, including coordinating and regulatory functions similar to those of domestic law, and most do not require the sort of centralized political and legal structures that constitute national governments. Compared to most domestic legal systems, international law is decentralized and under-institutionalized. But if we recognize that law is more than formal command consistently backed up by force, then international law really can be regarded as "law."

SOURCES AND SUBJECTS OF INTERNATIONAL LAW

The statute of the International Court of Justice (ICJ) identifies the major sources of international law. International treaties and custom are the primary sources, but the statute also identifies "the general principles of law recognized by civilized nations" as

[14] Louis Henkin, *How Nations Behave: Law and Foreign Policy*, 2nd ed. (New York: Columbia University Press, 1979), p. 47.

[15] See, for example, Anne-Marie Slaughter, *A New World Order* (Princeton, N.J.: Princeton University Press, 2004); Michael Barnett and Martha Finnemore, *Rules for the World: International Organizations in Global Politics* (Ithaca, N.Y.: Cornell University Press, 2004).

another source. In addition to these three sources, which create international law, the statute refers to two subsidiary means for determining the content or rules of the law: judicial decisions by national courts and international tribunals (like the ICJ itself), and the writings of "highly qualified publicists" or legal scholars.

A convention or **treaty** (also known as a *covenant* or *pact*) is a formal agreement signed by states that specifies their rights and obligations in some area of international interaction. Agreements that also create new international institutions are typically called *charters* or *statutes*. States become bound by a treaty once they have signed and ratified it—different states have different domestic political processes for ratification—and the treaty has entered into force. Entry into force requires a certain number of ratifications, as stipulated in the treaty itself. If a state has signed but not yet ratified a treaty, it is not obligated by its specific terms, but the signatory may not actively seek to undermine the treaty's general purpose. For example, the administration of George W. Bush opposed the International Criminal Court and adopted policies intended to prevent its jurisdiction over U.S. personnel overseas. The Clinton administration signed the Rome Statute creating the court shortly before leaving office, and had the Bush administration simply proceeded to work at cross purposes to the statute it would have been in violation of the law of treaties. However, the administration informed the UN Secretary-General that the United States now opposed the treaty and would not ratify it. This effectively removed the U.S. signature from the Rome Statute and relieved the country of its obligations as a signatory. Treaties are often open for signature (and subsequent ratification) for a finite amount of time, after which becoming party to the treaty is known as *accession*.

We have already suggested that on matters related to international armed conflict, states have gone to great effort to codify in formal treaties the types of restraint that should be exercised during this most primitive and violent form of interstate interaction. The first major accomplishments in this regard were the Hague Conventions of 1899 and 1907, which clarified and extended the basic rules of warfare, including the treatment of civilians and prisoners, as well as issues relating to neutrality and military occupation. In light of violations of the Hague Conventions during World War I, the Geneva Convention of 1929 took up many of the same issues. Violations were less flagrant during World War II, but there were still enough to prompt another round of conferences in Geneva after the war, which gave rise to the four Geneva Conventions of 1949. The wave of internal warfare and foreign military intervention that accompanied decolonization prompted states to revisit the rules of warfare and adapt some of them to this new context; thus, in 1977 two protocols were attached to the 1949 conventions. Given that all states in the international system are parties to the Geneva Conventions and more than 160 are parties to Protocols I and II, there seems to be nearly universal agreement on at least the letter of the law of war.

In most communities, but especially in communities with underdeveloped legal systems, custom plays an important role in regulating the behavior of its members. This is certainly true of the community of states.[16] The ICJ statute states that an international **customary law** is "evidence of a general practice accepted as law."

---

[16] See Michael Byers, *Custom, Power and the Power of Rules: International Relations and Customary International Law* (Cambridge: Cambridge University Press, 1998).

That is, the general practice is followed not simply out of self-interest or benevolence; it is international custom because most states feel a legal obligation to conform—sense of duty referred to as *opinio juris*. In a case before the U.S. Supreme Court in 1900, the owners of the *Paquete Habana*, a Cuban fishing vessel seized by the U.S. Navy during the Spanish-American War, argued that the maritime law of prize, which allowed the seizure of enemy ships at sea as booty, included a customary exemption for coastal fishing vessels. The U.S. government's position was that this custom was a matter of courtesy, not law. The Court disagreed, however, stating that although the exemption grew out of comity between nations, over the course of the nineteenth century the practice had matured into a settled rule of international law, and was therefore binding on the U.S. Navy.

International treaties and customs are paramount in international law because this is a legal system in which sovereign states are the primary subjects, or "legal persons." To have legal personality means that states are the entities that acquire rights and obligations under the law, and they may press their claims against each other in whatever forums may exist for that purpose (like the ICJ). Other entities—IGOs, NGOs, individuals—may benefit from the law, but those protections generally derive from their association with a particular state. For instance, a diplomat benefits personally from diplomatic immunity—how nice not to have to worry about getting a ticket when you double park!—but that immunity is really the state's, which attaches to its representatives functioning in the territory of another state. When diplomatic immunities are violated, as they were when Iranian students seized the U.S. embassy in Teheran in 1979, individual diplomats have no claims to press before an international tribunal. The state is the injured party that may seek restitution, as the United States did before the ICJ in *U.S.A. v. Iran* (1980).

There are important exceptions, however, and the trend is that nonstate actors are gradually acquiring limited degrees of legal personality in international law. The very concept of *human* rights, as we shall see, rests on the principle that individuals have rights under international law regardless of their citizenship. The opportunities for individuals to sue, however, are still very limited. In some cases, states are willing to "espouse" the injury claims of their nationals and go before the ICJ, where only states have legal standing, in order to seek restitution on their nationals' behalf. An example is *Mexico v. U.S.A.* (2004). Mexico complained that the United States had violated the Vienna Convention on Consular Relations when officials in several U.S. states failed to inform Mexican nationals accused of capital crimes of their right to contact the Mexican consulate for legal assistance. Of course, the implications of this trend in international law cuts both ways; while individuals have acquired some rights, they have also acquired accountability. The Nuremberg Tribunal that tried Nazi war criminals after World War II famously said, "[C]rimes against international law are committed by men, not by abstract entities," and rejected the argument that these officials were immune from prosecution as representatives of the German state.

Other nonstate actors have acquired limited legal personality as well, notably IGOs. The Security Council is empowered by the UN Charter to sign separate agreements with states whereby states commit to provide the Council with military forces and facilities necessary to enforce its decisions. No such agreements have ever been concluded—collective enforcement has instead been undertaken by willing member states on an ad hoc basis—but the fact that states have given the Council the power to enter into such contracts is noteworthy. An ICJ advisory opinion issued in 1949 is also suggestive of the UN's legal personality. When presented with the question whether the UN had a claim to press because Jewish extremists had murdered a UN diplomat sent to Palestine to mediate the conflict between the departing British forces and those of the nascent state of Israel, the ICJ answered yes. Ironically, the ICJ could not decide the complaint itself, as only states have standing before the court (it was settled by negotiation).

COMPLIANCE WITH INTERNATIONAL LAW

International law exists in various forms, and most states obey it most of the time. But why do they obey it? Realists argue that state behavior that accords with international law is merely coincidental with the pursuit of national interest. Legal positivists have to acknowledge that self-interest has a lot to do with law-abiding behavior by states. If each state violated international law whenever it wanted, order would soon yield to chaos; the future would be unpredictable and dangerous. When states find themselves in highly conflictual situations and the stakes are high, treaties, customs, UN resolutions, and all the rest stand a good chance of being disregarded. But most of the time such conditions do not prevail. Order seems to be an outcome that states rank high in their preference orderings. Chaos—a truly anything-goes system, all the time, and on all issues—would be costly for all states.

States exercise restraint because they do not want to set a precedent for certain types of behavior. For example, the application of *intertemporal law* means that territorial ownership is legal if the means used to acquire territory were legal at the time; new laws concerning territorial acquisition may not be applied retroactively. Not all that long ago, it was not unlawful to seize and annex territory by military force. In its 1970 Friendly Relations Declaration, the UN General Assembly stated "no territorial acquisition resulting from the threat or use of force shall be recognized as legal" but further stated that this shall not be construed to invalidate territorial settlements concluded before the UN Charter was signed. Thus, Iraq had no legal claim to Kuwaiti territory in 1990 (no matter how the territory was lost), and few other states supported such a claim. The reaction to Argentina's claim to the Falklands was similar. Although many third world states had supported Argentina's anticolonial rhetoric, only a very few supported its military action to acquire the territory by force. Recognizing this as an excuse for military action had the potential of threatening the territorial integrity of many other states, especially relatively young ones, as well as international order.[17]

Although a common criticism of international law is that it cannot be enforced, we have provided examples of states having been compelled to comply with rules and of suffering consequences when they don't. It is sometimes forgotten that

---

[17] In international law, this is known as the principle of *uti possidetis* ("as you possess"). See, for example, Mark Zacher, "The Territorial Integrity Norm: International Boundaries and the Use of Force," *International Organization* 55 (Spring 2001), pp. 215–250.

national courts often enforce international law, as the U.S. Supreme Court did in the *Paquette Habana* case (law of prize) and more recently in *Hamdan v. Rumsfeld* (Geneva law). The U.S. Constitution states that duly ratified treaties become the supreme law of the land, and many other states have similar provisions in their constitutions or statutory law. We have also cited examples of the military enforcement of international law. The UN Security Council has done this when authorizing the use of "any means necessary" to force compliance with its resolutions. States do this unilaterally when they launch reprisals, as the United States and other states have done in response to state sponsorship of terrorist attacks.

There is yet another reason why states comply with international law, which can be illustrated with an analogy from domestic law. The vehicle code includes the rule that drivers must obey traffic signals. Not all do, but most drivers obey most traffic signals most of the time. Why do they obey? First, there is the concern for safety: Ignoring a traffic signal may result in collision and injury or death. This is not unlike states' fears of the dangers of a disorderly world system devoid of rules and norms of international conduct. Second, there is the possibility that disobeying a traffic signal will result in a traffic citation and fine in the event that the offending driver is spotted by a traffic cop. This exact mechanism of enforcement is not available in international law, but states may be subject to unilateral or collective enforcement actions by their peers.

Now suppose you are the driver. It is very late at night, the library has just closed, and you are driving home. The traffic light ahead has just turned red; there are no other motorists in sight, and no police cruisers. Do you stop? You probably do. And you probably wait for the light to turn green before proceeding, which can take frustratingly long considering the fact that there really is no traffic to regulate at that hour. You do not stop and wait because you are afraid of collision, nor do you fear punishment. You stop and wait because you have been trained as a good driver and socialized as a good citizen. It's the right thing to do. There may be occasions when you yield to temptation and run the light, but mostly you obey the law, as do most others—and for no other reason than it's the law.

We should not neglect similar motives for obeying international law. Most states want to be good citizens of international society and often appear willing to forego certain advantages to demonstrate their good citizenship.[18] Even if a state intends to violate international law when the national interest dictates, the very act of signing a treaty entails the costs of having to defend apparent hypocritical actions. Leaders justify their behavior in terms of international law and, where ambiguities might exist, try to make the case that their behavior does indeed conform to international law. A reputation as a state that others can depend on and trust enhances the state's influence in many ways. At minimum, there is the expectation that something like a golden rule operates in world politics: If a state behaves properly, it can expect proper behavior from others. While realists might be quick to point out this rule works only because states have found it to be in

---

[18] But for a skeptical view, see Stephen D. Krasner, *Sovereignty: Organized Hypocrisy* (Princeton, N.J.: Princeton University Press, 1999); Jack L. Goldsmith and Eric A. Posner, *The Limits of International Law* (New York: Oxford University Press, 2005).

their self-interest, the legal positivist would respond that this is the sort of self-interested behavior we can all live with.

HUMAN RIGHTS AND HUMAN WRONGS

Aside from the laws of war that define the rights and responsibilities of combatants and noncombatants, most international law regulates the behavior of states, not individuals. State sovereignty is the foundation upon which world politics has rested since the Peace of Westphalia in 1648, and the rights of states to noninterference in their internal affairs has been a pillar of international law to the present day. For day-to-day international conduct, this seems to be the most workable guiding principle for national leaders interested in maintaining order within the "anarchical society" of states. From a moral standpoint, however, there are other conceptions of rights and responsibilities in world politics, and the international community is becoming increasingly receptive to at least some of these alternative principles.

The normative bias of international law is **communitarian** (or, as some say, *statist*). This means that there is a tendency to accord significant moral status to political communities. Respect for state sovereignty, particularly states' independence and territorial integrity, reflects a general willingness of states to defer to each other when it comes to matters of social justice and welfare within their borders. Communitarian ethics derive from the belief that conceptions of justice and welfare emerge from the historical, cultural, and religious experiences that the members of a political community share. The "thickness" of these shared experiences is the moral basis upon which states refrain from interference in the domestic affairs of other states. However, noninterference is not a blanket prohibition for communitarians; interference is justified when a political community faces a serious threat—one emanating from its own government, or one that its government is unable or unwilling to counter.

A different view is held by those who subscribe to the **cosmopolitan** perspective. For cosmopolitans, states do not acquire moral standing simply because they are the legal representatives of the political communities inhabiting their territories. Rather, states' rights to autonomy and noninterference derive from their willingness and capacity to respect and defend the security and welfare of their citizens. Individuals are, first and foremost, members of the community of humankind; it is they who have an inherent moral standing, not states. Cosmopolitans do not deny the meaningfulness of the shared experiences that define political communities, but they want to draw our attention to the "thinner" moral principles that we have in common by virtue of our shared humanity. This is not to say that cosmopolitans are preoccupied with less significant or shallow rights and responsibilities. To the contrary, while such universal principles may be relatively few in number, "this morality is close to the bone," as Michael Walzer puts it.[19] Because the morality of states is contingent on

[19] Michael Walzer, *Thick and Thin: Moral Argument at Home and Abroad* (Notre Dame, Ind.: University of Notre Dame Press, 1994), p. 6. On the communitarian and cosmopolitan perspectives in normative international relations theory, see Chris Brown, *International Relations Theory: New Normative Approaches* (New York: Columbia University Press, 1992); Molly Cochran, *Normative Theory in International Relations: A Pragmatic Approach* (Cambridge: Cambridge University Press, 1999).

their relationships with their citizens, cosmopolitans are less inclined to treat sovereignty as a bar to interference in the domestic affairs of other states whose citizens are suffering acute hardship and privation.

The debate between communitarians and cosmopolitans is a long-standing one, but contemporary international law is more a reflection of the communitarian position. However, if we view these normative positions as located at opposite sides of a spectrum, we can at least detect some movement in the cosmopolitan direction. International legal and moral arguments over international human rights and criminality ("human wrongs") are very much about how far the international community is willing to move away from communitarianism toward cosmopolitanism. States (and, increasingly, citizens) are finding that their menus are changing in international law as in so many other realms of world politics.

INTERNATIONAL HUMAN RIGHTS

Recent activity on issues relating to **human rights**—rights possessed by individuals because they are human, not because they are citizens of one or another state—represents an expansion of the domain of international law and the influence of contemporary natural law perspectives. Concepts of universal human rights, embodied in international declarations and treaties, aim to deny states the prerogative to withhold those rights from their own citizens. Individuals are to be considered legal subjects separate from their state of national origin. Human-rights norms have increasingly become the basis for intrusion by IGOs and NGOs into the domestic affairs of states—striking at the traditional relationship of the state to its citizens and thus at principles of legitimacy and sovereignty long embedded in the Westphalian state system. Monitoring and publicizing human-rights violations (or "naming and shaming") by NGOs such as Amnesty International or Human Rights Watch has become a mechanism for deterring and restraining violators of human rights.

The fact that the international legal instruments for the enforcement of human rights remain undeveloped has not prevented the international community from identifying a rather long list of rights that should be protected.[20] The list in Table 10.1 is compiled from three international conventions, which together constitute what many people call the *International Bill of Rights*. The Universal Declaration of Human Rights adopted by the UN General Assembly in 1948 provides the most comprehensive list of asserted rights, but as little more than a statement of hopes and aspirations it is generally regarded as "soft law." The two human-rights covenants adopted in 1966 (and entering into force in 1976) overlap each other very little, reflecting the two broadly different approaches states have taken to the question of rights and responsibilities within their societies. Taken together, however, the covenants cover

---

[20] Henry J. Steiner, Philip Alston, and Ryan Goodman, *International Human Rights in Context: Law, Politics, Morals*, 3rd ed. (Oxford: Oxford University Press, 2007); Paul Gordon Lauren, *The Evolution of International Human Rights: Visions Seen*, 2nd ed. (Philadelphia: University of Pennsylvania Press, 2003).

TABLE 10.1 | INTERNATIONAL HUMAN RIGHTS

Right	Universal Declaration of Human Rights	Covenant on Civil and Political Rights	Covenant on Economic, Social, and Cultural Rights
Life	•	•	
Liberty and security of person	•	•	
Protection against slavery	•	•	
Protection against torture and inhumane punishment	•	•	
Recognition as a person before the law	•	•	
Equal protection of the law	•	•	
Access to legal remedies for rights violations	•	•	
Protection against arbitrary arrest or detention	•	•	
Hearing before an independent and impartial judiciary	•	•	
Presumption of innocence	•	•	
Protection against *ex post facto* laws	•	•	
Protection of privacy, family, and home	•	•	
Freedom of movement and residence	•	•	
Freedom of thought, conscience, and religion	•	•	
Freedom of opinion, expression, and the press	•	•	
Freedom of assembly and association	•	•	
Political participation	•	•	
Own property	•		
Seek asylum from persecution	•		
Nationality	•		
Protection against debtor's imprisonment		•	
Protection against arbitrary expulsion as an alien		•	
Protection against advocacy of racial or religious hatred		•	
Protection of minority culture		•	
Free trade unions	•	•	•
Marry and found a family	•	•	•

(*Continued*)

TABLE 10.1 │ (*Continued*)

Right	Universal Declaration of Human Rights	Covenant on Civil and Political Rights	Covenant on Economic, Social, and Cultural Rights
Special protections for children	•	•	•
Self-determination		•	•
Social security	•		•
Work, under favorable conditions	•		•
Rest and leisure	•		•
Food, clothing, and housing	•		•
Health care and social services	•		•
Education	•		•
Participation in cultural life	•		•

Source: Jack Donnelly, "State Sovereignty and International Intervention: The Case of Human Rights," in Gene M. Lyons and Michael Mastanduno, eds., *Beyond Westphalia? State Sovereignty and International Intervention* (Baltimore: Johns Hopkins University Press, 1995).

almost all of what was laid out by the General Assembly in 1948 and ground human rights more firmly in international law by virtue of their status as treaties.

The Covenant on Civil and Political Rights provides a list of rights that are familiar to citizens of many Western countries. Most can be considered "negative rights" in the sense that they are *freedoms from* the arbitrary exercise of government power, unequal application of the law, and limits on political participation. The right to life, liberty, property, freedom of expression, freedom of the press, and freedom of religion are the sorts of rights that lie at the core of liberal democratic practice, so it is not surprising that their universal application is embraced more strongly in the West than elsewhere. The Covenant on Economic, Social, and Cultural Rights, on the other hand, consists of "positive rights"—that is, *entitlements to* certain economic amenities and social welfare. Employment under favorable conditions, education and health care, and rest and leisure are highly valued in most societies, but in the West it is not as common to treat these as inalienable human rights. Instead, such positive rights have been championed by socialist and social democratic countries in which the state commands a larger share of societal resources with the purpose of providing for the well-being of the populace.

Some of the most familiar protections found in the International Bill of Rights concern individuals' rights to participate in the public sphere—the freedom of expression and assembly, for instance—but the private sphere, too, has increasingly come under scrutiny by human-rights advocates and NGOs. The best examples are in the area of women's rights. International campaigns against rape, prostitution, and sexual harassment have generally enjoyed widespread support. The targets of these campaigns are not primarily governments, as in most other areas of human-rights advocacy, but organizations and social practices that seem to condone or even encourage the mistreatment of women. More controversial are certain practices that Westerners find offensive but are rooted in non-Western cultural traditions or rituals. Thus, feminists and other groups engaged in efforts to stop female genital cutting, *sati* (widow burning), female infanticide, and forced veiling are sometimes accused of being insensitive to local social norms, or worse, behaving as agents of Western cultural imperialism.[21] Although such criticisms have not deterred women's rights advocates from pressing ahead with their appeals, they have forced Westerners to become more attuned to the different cultural landscapes encountered along the way.

Most human-rights agreements are hard to enforce, and rights-violating governments may sign on to them knowing that they have no enforcement teeth. But some treaties primarily devoted to fostering economic integration often have human-rights provisions built into them. Trade agreements can be effective in reducing violent repression when they incorporate enforcement mechanisms—like the ability to terminate trade agreements and impose sanctions on repressive member states—and not just standards of conduct unconnected to market access or other economic benefits. The Lomé Treaties between the European Union and states in Africa and Latin America have such provisions, and the Lomé Commission halted benefits after the 1994 Rwanda genocide, forcing the Rwanda army to prosecute war criminals.[22]

The evolution of international human-rights law reflects to a piecemeal erosion of the supreme moral and legal standing of the state in world politics. The individual person is still at a distinct disadvantage because of the communitarian bias of international law and practice. But where we see movement, it is toward a more cosmopolitan conception.

HUMANITARIAN INTERVENTION

Judging from Table 10.1, there is a long list of human rights that deserve protection, and this is not a minority view within the international community; there are about 160 state parties to the two human-rights covenants. As in other areas of international law, the real difficulty in promoting international human rights turns on the question of enforcement. At what point do human-rights violations call forth the use of armed force by the international community?

Armed intervention is the use of military force to affect the domestic affairs of an independent state without the consent of that state's government. An armed **humanitarian intervention** is one in which the main purpose is to relieve human suffering. We have indicated that just cause for the resort to military force is interpreted rather narrowly in international law. The principle of sovereignty seems to

[21] Sally Engle Merry, *Human Rights and Gender Violence: Translating International Law into Local Justice* (Chicago: University of Chicago Press, 2006); Diana G. Zoelle, *Globalizing Concern for Women's Human Rights: The Failure of the American Model* (New York: Palgrave Macmillan, 2000).
[22] Emilie Hafner-Burton, "Trading Human Rights: How Preferential Trade Agreements Influence Government Repression," *International Organization* 59 (2005), pp. 593–629.

sanction defense against aggression and little else, including intervention on behalf of the oppressed. Yet states have intervened militarily in the affairs of others and have often couched these interventions in terms of humanitarian obligation, if not international law. That may be convenient for states looking to justify what is, in fact, a crude use of force in pursuit of national interests. However, there have been times when such moral considerations do appear plausible, even if in these cases military intervention furthered political interests as well.[23] In 1971, India intervened to rescue the Bengalis in East Pakistan from massacre at the hands of the Pakistani army. India's military intervention saved a lot of innocent people (and stemmed a massive refugee exodus), but it also created an independent Bangladesh, thereby dismembering India's longtime military rival. In 1979, Vietnam invaded Cambodia (then known as Kampuchea), overthrowing Pol Pot and putting an end to a forced collectivization campaign that cost more than a million lives. Of course, the Vietnamese also installed a friendly regime in the process.

The UN Charter and some other instruments of international law provide room for maneuver on the matter of intervention. According to the Charter, an "act of aggression" is grounds for the collective use of force but so is a "threat to the peace." During the cold war, the Security Council almost never agreed on cases of aggression, let alone *threats* to peace. Just war theorists have been more forthright in arguing in favor of military intervention when governments savagely turn on their own people. International law, too, condemns such savage acts as genocide—the UN General Assembly approved the Convention on the Prevention and Punishment of the Crime of Genocide in 1948—but the emphasis has been on punishment of war criminals rather than prevention through military intervention. Nevertheless, with the end of the cold war has come a gradual erosion of the norm against intervention when the lives of civilians are threatened on a large scale. After the Gulf War, the UN Security Council established safe havens in northern Iraq for Kurds who had fled Iraqi repression; the movement of large numbers of refugees was deemed a threat to peace in the region. This was a first for the UN, even if its significance is somewhat diminished by the fact that Iraq had just been defeated in a UN-sanctioned war. At the end of 1992, the Security Council acted again, sanctioning a U.S.–led military intervention in Somalia where warring clans were impeding humanitarian relief efforts.

By the time a new round of "ethnic cleansing" was under way in the Balkans in March 1999, now by the Serbs in Kosovo, the Security Council was once again immobilized by internal disagreement. Although the Council had three years before sanctioned NATO air strikes against Bosnian Serb positions to relieve pressure on besieged Muslim enclaves, when the Kosovo crisis erupted, NATO acted without UN approval. Although Russian opposition to the NATO action can be understood in political terms—the Milosevic regime being a Russian ally, even if a dubious one—the intervention did represent a greater departure from the norm of noninterference than did other post–cold war interventions. In the case of Bosnia,

---

[23] Simon Chesterman, *Just War or Just Peace? Humanitarian Intervention and International Law* (Oxford: Oxford University Press, 2003); Martha Finnemore, *The Purpose of Intervention: Changing Beliefs about the Use of Force* (Ithaca, N.Y.: Cornell University Press, 2003).

NATO assistance was invited by an internationally recognized sovereign government, while in Somalia there was really no sovereign government. NATO member states justified the Kosovo action both on humanitarian grounds and as a means of checking a Serbian threat to regional peace and security. The Kosovo Liberation Army (KLA) welcomed the intervention, to be sure, but NATO did not claim that the KLA was the rightful government of an independent Kosovo. No pretense was made that this was anything other than an armed intervention into the domestic affairs of a sovereign state.

INTERNATIONAL CRIMINAL LAW

Enforcing international human rights involves not only efforts to stop ongoing abuses but also procedures for identifying and punishing those who have perpetrated such abuses. After emerging victorious from World War II, the Allies established international military tribunals at Nuremberg and Tokyo to render judgments about the wartime conduct of the vanquished. These were obviously one-sided affairs, but they established certain precedents regarding personal accountability for conduct during war. Neither government officials nor soldiers following orders from their superiors are relieved of responsibility for war crimes or crimes against humanity.

In 1960, Israeli agents abducted Adolf Eichmann, the notorious Nazi official who oversaw the extermination of Jews from German-occupied Europe, in Argentina and took him to Jerusalem where he was tried in an Israeli court for crimes against humanity. Eichmann was convicted and hanged. National courts, of course, have jurisdiction within their territories (territoriality principle). International law also recognizes the extraterritorial jurisdiction of national courts to try their own citizens who have committed serious crimes beyond their borders (nationality principle) and even to try noncitizens who have committed serious crimes against their citizens beyond their borders (passive nationality principle). But none of this applied in the Eichmann case. Eichmann was not an Israeli citizen, nor were the Jews he sent to death camps; the state of Israel did not exist when Eichmann perpetrated his crimes. Instead, the Israeli prosecutor's complaint against Eichmann rested on the concept of **universal jurisdiction**. Certain crimes, like genocide and other crimes against humanity, are said to offend the entire international community—they violate a peremptory norm, or *jus cogens*—and national courts have sometimes asserted their jurisdiction to prosecute individuals whether or not the crimes were committed by their nationals, against their nationals, or within their borders. Those acts are literally *international* crimes.

A different but equally important legal development is illustrated by the trial of Slobodan Milosevic before the International Criminal Tribunal for the former Yugoslavia. Milosevic was the first former head of state to face serious criminal charges before an international tribunal—for genocide in Bosnia and for crimes against humanity in both Croatia and Kosovo. The matter of jurisdiction was not at issue in the Milosevic case; the successor government in Belgrade had turned the former leader over to the international tribunal. But jurisdiction was an issue in the case of former Chilean dictator Augusto Pinochet, who was arrested in 1998 while receiving medical treatment in London and held for extradition to

Spain to face charges of murder, torture, and other crimes against Spanish and other nationals while he was head of state. The Chilean government had already decided not to press charges against Pinochet in the interest (it was said) of national reconciliation and healing; plus, he had been made senator-for-life and retained immunity from prosecution in Chile. The Spanish court was challenging Chile's sovereignty in this case by issuing a warrant for Pinochet's arrest, and this was an issue the British government had to address when considering Spain's request for extradition.

The saying "The king can do no wrong" sums up the legal principle of **sovereign immunity**. Under international law, sovereign states are immune from the jurisdiction of other states' courts. Because a state is a legal abstraction and does not really "act," sovereign immunity has traditionally covered the actions of the head of state. Until relatively recently, just about anything the head of state did was considered a "public act of state" and therefore beyond the jurisdiction of foreign courts (and domestic courts for that matter). Contemporary international law no longer recognizes such an all-encompassing notion of public acts of state. Manuel Noriega, the Panamanian leader seized by U.S. military forces during the 1989 invasion, had been indicted by a federal grand jury in Miami. The Florida court's jurisdiction rested on the claim that Noriega's alleged offenses (complicity in drug trafficking) were not public acts taken on behalf of the state but were acts taken for personal gain; they were not, therefore, off limits to scrutiny. In the Pinochet case, the acts in question were not taken for private enrichment. Arguably, they were taken in the interest of the security of the state or at least the government. But the British Law Lords, who had to determine whether Pinochet should be extradited to stand trial in Spain, concluded that Pinochet's alleged crimes were also not legitimate public acts. Pinochet was allowed to return to Chile, but only because he was in ill health, not because the conduct in question was judged immune from prosecution in Spain.[24]

While human-rights advocates applaud recent developments in international law, many others are concerned about the implications of universal jurisdiction. Some suggest that the fear of being held responsible for international crimes committed while head of state will persuade despots only to cling more tightly to the reins of power, making the task of national reconciliation and democratization that much more difficult. Henry Kissinger, himself the target of a number of foreign legal actions, has written: "It is an important principle that those who commit war crimes or systematically violate human rights should be held accountable. But the consolidation of law, domestic peace, and representative government in a nation struggling to come to terms with a brutal past has a claim as well."[25] Critics also point to the political motivations and

---

[24] See, for example, Naomi Roht-Arriaza, "The Pinochet Effect and the Spanish Contribution to Universal Jurisdiction," in Wolfgang Kaleck et al., eds., *International Prosecution of Human Rights Crimes* (Berlin: Springer-Verlag, 2007); Reed Brody and Michael Ratner, eds., *The Pinochet Papers: The Case of Augusto Pinochet in Spain and Britain* (The Hague: Kluwer Law International, 2000).

[25] Henry A. Kissinger, "The Pitfalls of Universal Jurisdiction," *Foreign Affairs* 80 (July/August 2001), p. 91. For a comprehensive discussion, including positions taken by various national courts, see Luc Reydams, *Universal Jurisdiction: International and Municipal Legal Perspectives* (Oxford: Oxford University Press, 2003).

capriciousness with which national courts may pursue some "criminals" and not others. Why Pinochet and not Jaruzelski of Poland or Pol Pot of Cambodia?

The Pinochet and Milosevic cases put other despots on notice that the international community had become less willing to tolerate blatant human-rights abuses perpetrated behind the veil of state sovereignty. But leaving the prosecution of international criminals to national courts would have been very unsettling to the social order of sovereign states. In 1998, states instead decided to vest that authority with a permanent International Criminal Court (ICC), which would try cases involving egregious war crimes, crimes against humanity, and genocide. The ICC was formally established in 2002 after sixty states had ratified the Rome Statute governing the Court's jurisdiction and procedures.

THE UNITED NATIONS SYSTEM

International organization refers to the ways states arrange themselves for purposes of promoting cooperative and collaborative practices in world politics, and the result of this process of arrangement is the creation of international organizations (IOs). States sign treaties, which add considerably to the body of international law. Many of these treaties take the form of charters that create international organizations, usually intergovernmental ones; such IGOs are a *product* of international law. However, a growing number of IGOs are also *sources* of international law in the contemporary system. Their charters, which detail organizational bylaws and procedures, constitute many of the rules of everyday international interaction, and their resolutions and declarations add further to the body of international rules. Some organizations, like the International Law Commission, have also helped to collect, interpret, and codify international law derived from custom, treaties, and the opinions of international courts. They have been useful in applying international law, in helping to coordinate states' compliance, in organizing states around their common interests, and in pointing out the benefits of cooperation. Large regional organizations, such as the European Union, have worked extensively to promote economic cooperation. Others, such as the Organization of American States and the African Union, have worked to control and manage conflict in their own regions.

The two most important contemporary international organizations are the United Nations and the European Union, each of which is, in fact, a system of smaller organizations arrayed around issue areas and the needs of member states and their citizens. The evolution of both the UN and the EU illustrate the great efforts that states have undertaken to bring order to the anarchic international system. Liberals, at least, would argue that both organizations—at the behest of their member states but also independently of them—have brought about profound changes in world politics and the menus of all international actors. In this section, we discuss the UN system; in Chapter 14, we will turn to the EU.

BIRTH OF THE UN

Besides being a major source of international law and the most extensive system of international organization in the contemporary world—in both the extent of its membership and the broad scope of its aims and activities—the UN has faithfully reflected the changing nature of world politics throughout the period of its existence.[26]

In the aftermath of World War II, the UN reflected the desire of the victorious states to maintain world peace and to attack the conditions that appeared to foster war: colonialism, poverty, inequality, and ignorance. The UN Charter, drawn up and signed by fifty-one states in San Francisco in 1945, was largely the product of American, British, and Soviet negotiations. Those negotiations began well before the end of the war and, in the early phases, concentrated on maintaining unity in the fight against the Axis powers, but as Allied victory neared, broader objectives relating to global peace and security came to dominate the discussions. Much of the bargaining over the goals and structure of the new international organization was conducted during the Dumbarton Oaks Conference, held in Washington, D.C., in 1944.

The founders of the UN learned much from the failures of its predecessor, the League of Nations, and from the realist critique of the idealism that clouded the vision of the League's founders. They recognized that the organization was to be composed of sovereign states; they did not see the UN as a device to take away or undercut the autonomy of states, although some later observers have felt that this *should* be the UN's role. Because the international system lacked a central authority, one strategy for promoting international cooperation was the creation of an IGO that all states, or almost all states, would be willing to join. Thus, their realism was tempered by enough idealist vision to seek new international institutions and procedures to promote common interests and manage conflict, even while maintaining state sovereignty. Mechanisms to coordinate behavior and promote political and economic cooperation would become even more crucial as international interdependencies multiplied and created new sources of potential conflict. Perhaps one reason for the remarkable survival of the UN has been its usefulness in an era when environmental, economic, and human-rights issues have joined peace and security as central matters of concern for the international community. With many new international actors, most with vulnerabilities associated with global interdependence, the Westphalian state system seems ready for a semipermanent fixture like the UN.

STRUCTURE AND FUNCTIONS

The Security Council, the General Assembly, the Secretariat, the International Court of Justice, the Trusteeship Council, and the Economic and Social Council constitute the six agencies identified in the Charter as the principal organs of the UN. They are depicted in Figure 10.1. Today's UN system of some thirty multilateral institutions has been built incrementally over the years to promote cooperation in response to new international problems. Its headquarters are in New York City but in an eighteen-acre international zone not considered to be territory of the United States.

This UN structure reflects the system within which it was created. The Security Council is the primary organ of action, and as such it reflects the unequal

---

[26] On the historical evolution of the United Nations, see Paul Kennedy, *The Parliament of Man: The Past, Present, and Future of the United Nations* (New York: Random House, 2006).

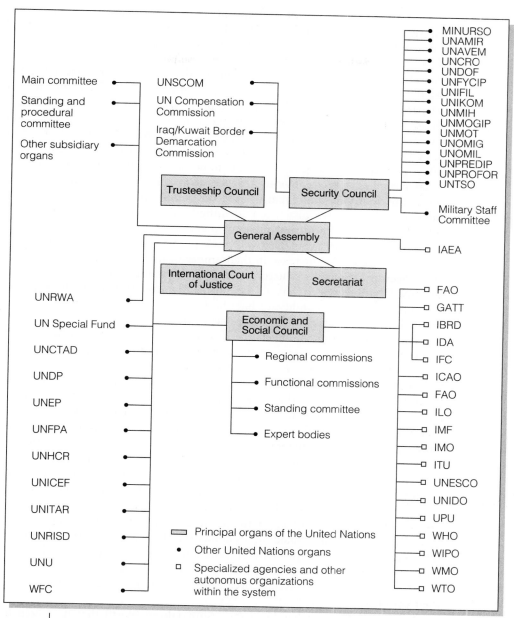

FIGURE 10.1 | THE UNITED NATIONS SYSTEM

The UN system consists of several organs and a large number of subsidiary organizations established to deal with a wide variety of issues and problems confronting member states and their citizens. Some of them, like the IMF and World Bank, have considerable political and financial autonomy as IGOs.
Source: U.S. Central Intelligence Agency, *The World Factbook 1998* (Washington, DC: U.S. Government Printing Office, 1998), Appendix B.

distribution of power in the system—at least as it existed when the UN Charter was signed at the end of World War II. The five major-power victors (the United States, Britain, France, the Soviet Union, and China) became permanent members of the Security Council (the "P5"), while ten other seats on the Council have rotated among other states. In addition to their permanent seats, each of the P5 has the right to veto actions considered by the Council. These two features give the permanent members substantial influence over matters of peace and security coming before the UN. In this way, the Charter sought to save the UN from a major weakness of the League of Nations. During the entire period of the League's existence, one or more of the great powers was not a member because it felt that its influence within the League was not commensurate with its position in the international system. The most obvious absences from the P5 given *today's* distribution of power are Germany and Japan. Based on population and total economic output, India and Brazil have also been identified as potential permanent members. In 2004, these four countries (calling themselves the Group of Four, or G4) announced that they would actively seek permanent membership on the Security Council, as well as an increase in the number of nonpermanent members. A change in the Security Council's structure and voting procedure requires an amendment to the UN Charter, which has to be ratified by two-thirds of all member states, including the P5. It is unlikely that the G4's plan or any other plan for Security Council reform will meet this requirement any time soon.

The Security Council reflects the special role that the great powers must play in the world body.[27] The veto permits each power to protect its interests by remaining in the organization. The heavy use of the Soviet veto during the early years of the UN (114 times from 1945 to 1975) was an attempt to compensate for disproportionate U.S. influence in the General Assembly, which is the UN's plenary body. Figure 10.2 shows that, in 1946, states from the Americas and Western Europe dominated the General Assembly with almost 60 percent of the membership. Although the General Assembly had been set up as a world parliament on the basis of one-state, one-vote sovereign equality (Article 2 of the Charter), it too was dominated by the great powers in the early days of the UN. When the structure of the international system was tightly bipolar but imbalanced in favor of the West, the cleavages in the General Assembly were predictable. Not only did East–West issues dominate the agenda (with about 30 percent of the membership coming from Europe), but the United States could and did exercise a great deal of influence over members' votes in the General Assembly. Even as a measure of East–West balance was introduced, for a long period many small and nonaligned countries were dissatisfied with the UN system because of its dominance by the great powers and their problems.

Since the 1970s, it has been the industrialized North that has often been dissatisfied with the UN. By welcoming all states, the UN had grown through the

---

[27] Ian Hurd, *After Anarchy: Legitimacy and Power in the United Nations Security Council* (Princeton, N.J.: Princeton University Press, 2007); Alexander Thompson, "Coercion Through IOs: The Security Council and the Logic of Information Transmission," *International Organization* 60 (Winter 2006), pp. 1–34.

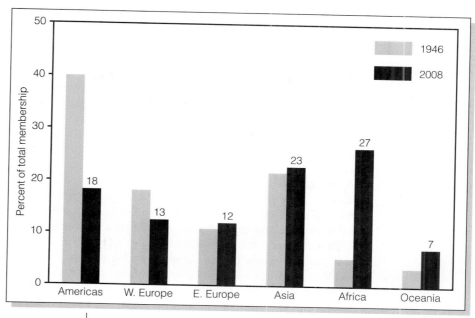

FIGURE 10.2 | UN MEMBERSHIP BY REGION, 1946 AND 2008

During the UN's early years, more than 60 percent of the organization's members were states located in the Americas and Western Europe, which gave the United States a great deal of influence in the General Assembly. Over time, the distribution of membership shifted to the point where now half of UN members come from Asia and Africa, including many of the least-developed regions of the globe, thereby effecting a change in the UN's agenda and priorities.

addition of non-Western states created by the process of decolonization. With this change, which began in earnest in 1960, came a shift in emphasis from East–West to North–South issues (which we discuss in Chapter 15). Economic issues, and particularly issues of development and equity, came to dominate many areas of UN debate. The expanded membership powerfully affected the objectives, processes, and successes of the organization, especially as the members organized into coalitions with the purpose of fostering the common interests of different groups of member states. The anticolonial stance of the newer members was often supported by the anti-Western communist states. After 1970, the United States found itself unable to command a majority in the General Assembly (as reflected in sixty vetoes the United States exercised in the Security Council between 1976 and 1990, compared to only seven by the Soviet Union). This state of affairs was strikingly evident when in 1971, despite strenuous U.S. opposition, the People's Republic of China was granted the seat occupied until then by the Republic of China (Taiwan). Because this move did not involve a change in the structure of the Security Council (only a change of credentials), it was not subject to a U.S. veto.

One of the most contentious issues in the UN has been the allocation of the organization's scarce resources. In 2008, the UN's regular budget was $2.3 billion, with another $6.8 billion going to support peacekeeping operations. Member states make contributions to the UN budget based on their relative wealth so that the eight richest states contribute more than 70 percent of both the regular and peacekeeping budgets. The U.S. assessment alone is 22 percent of the regular budget and 27 percent for peacekeeping. The budgetary process has become an issue of contention because although the secretary-general assembles UN budgets, they must be approved, and are often revised, by the General Assembly where all members have an equal voice regardless of their financial contributions (which can amount to as little as 0.001 percent for the smallest and poorest states). An informal agreement, however, ensures that the budget will be adopted by consensus, thereby giving clout to the 5 percent of UN members who contribute 70 percent of the budget total.

Some states have expressed their dissatisfaction with the budgetary politics in the UN by withholding portions of their assessed contributions. The United States is the UN's largest debtor; at the beginning of 2008 it owed the organization $2.5 billion for past and current assessments (two-thirds for peacekeeping). That was almost 40 percent of the $6.5 billion owed to the UN by all member states. To add some perspective to these figures, consider that the U.S. defense budget for 2008 was about $620 billion, including supplemental funding for the war on terror—almost seventy times what the UN spent on both its regular operations and on peacekeeping and almost 100 times what the organization was owed by all member states.

The changing nature of the UN has been influenced not only by the number of new members but also by the circumstances under which they became sovereign states. Many of these newer UN members are independent in part because of the work of the Trusteeship Council, which was established to bring an end to colonialism and to guide the former colonial areas to independent statehood as soon and as peacefully as possible. Most observers agree that the Trusteeship Council fulfilled its purpose well—so well, in fact, that with the independence of its last trust territory in 1994 (Palau), the Council suspended its regular operations. Some have proposed that the Council be used in the future to help reconstitute "failed states" where the central institutions of government have collapsed, but so far it has not been called into action for that purpose.

The Economic and Social Council is assigned the task of dealing with international economic, social, educational, and health matters. It is supposed to improve the world's living standards by attacking poverty, ignorance, and inequality as causes of war. Many health matters have been successfully dealt with; many educational and cultural dissemination programs have also had positive results. The Economic and Social Council oversees a number of programs that have received a great deal of attention, often praise, in their own right: the UN Conference on Trade and Development (UNCTAD), the Office of the High Commissioner for Refugees (UNHCR), the UN Children's Fund (UNICEF), and the UN Environment Programme (UNEP), to name a few. Other UN agencies, like the International Bank for Reconstruction and Development (IBRD, or World Bank), the International Monetary Fund (IMF), and the World Trade Organization (WTO), technically report to the Economic and Social Council but have a great deal of autonomy as IGOs.

The UN acts as a forum for diplomacy and facilitates communication among member states. Activities directly related to the settlement of disputes are listed in Article 33 of the Charter and include negotiations, inquiry, mediation, and arbitration. The UN can facilitate each of these. States make use of the UN's "good offices"—a place for formal negotiations or, as is often the case, a forum that eases communication between parties who might want to launch formal negotiations at a later date. Through its agencies and staff, the UN can also serve as a neutral investigating body that provides unbiased information relevant to a dispute and its resolution. Similarly, the UN can act as a third-party mediator, an active participant in negotiations to help states in conflict arrive at acceptable solutions. Arbitration, wherein conflicting parties agree to be bound by solutions arrived at by third parties, is another approach to conflict resolution. In 1998, Peru and Ecuador agreed to submit their border dispute to binding arbitration by the United States, Brazil, Argentina, and Chile. It is rare for states to surrender sovereignty in this way when it comes to matters of national security (Peru and Ecuador fought briefly in 1995 over this fifty-mile stretch of territory), but it may be a sign of things to come. The UN seems well suited to this role, if not now then certainly in the future as states gain more confidence in the organization's competence and fairness.

Another mechanism mentioned in Article 33 is adjudication, or judicial settlement, in which a dispute is brought before an international court. The ICJ (often called the World Court) is the judicial organ of the UN. Although its record is quite mixed, the court has proven useful in a number of cases. In addition to the influential decisions we have mentioned in this chapter, it has judged cases involving issues ranging from fisheries to frontier disputes to nuclear testing. A number of cases are submitted to the court but then withdrawn by the parties themselves. Some are settled out of court; most of the rest languish because one party refuses to accept the ICJ's jurisdiction in the dispute. Indeed, distrust of the ICJ and the reluctance to let an outside party determine a state's interests are the main reasons that many high-stakes issues are not brought before the court in the first place. States use the ICJ when they feel it would be a useful tool of their foreign policy. The United States, for instance, went to the ICJ after Iranian students seized American diplomats in 1979 but refused to accept its jurisdiction in the case brought by Nicaragua regarding the covert U.S. mining of its harbors. The ICJ issued its oft-cited judgment in *Nicaragua v. U.S.A.* (1986) anyway after determining that the court had compulsory jurisdiction in this case.

The Secretary-General of the United Nations (currently Ban Ki-moon of South Korea) heads the Secretariat, which is the organization's executive and primary administrative body. Although members of the Security Council and General Assembly are states—delegates represent the interests of their home governments and not (necessarily) those of the UN—the loyalties of the Secretary-General and the Secretariat staff are to the organization. Article 100 of the Charter states: "In the performance of their duties the Secretary-General and the staff shall not seek or receive instructions from any government or from any other authority external to the Organization. They shall refrain from any action which might reflect on their position as international officials responsible only to the Organization." The administrative tasks of the Secretariat are immense, requiring a staff of 16,000 international civil servants worldwide, and although the size of this bureaucracy is often seized upon by its critics, that is about the same number employed by the Fire Department of New York City. Perhaps the most important duty of the Secretariat has been to administer peacekeeping operations, which emerged during the cold war as practical substitutes for the collective security mechanism envisioned by the UN's founders.

COLLECTIVE SECURITY AND PEACEKEEPING

The UN Charter identifies international peace and security as the organization's first goal, and the UN's founders wanted the organization to play a central role in collective security. Recall from Chapter 4 that **collective security** means that all members agree to oppose together a threat to the security of any one of them, an arrangement that realists dismissed as idealistic after the failure of the League of Nations. Chapter VII of the UN Charter calls on all members to make available to the Security Council, by special agreements, armed forces and facilities "for the purposes of maintaining international peace and security" (Article 43). These forces were to provide the basis for UN-authorized military actions against aggressor states. Almost immediately, however, the cold war began. Soviet–American hostility made it impossible for the permanent members of the Security Council to concur on the terms for a UN military force, and no agreements with individual states were ever reached. In its first forty-five years, the UN only once designated a state as an aggressor; that was North Korea, in 1950. The designation was made while the Soviet representative was boycotting the Security Council for its refusal to recognize China's new communist government as the rightful occupant of China's seat at the UN. The subsequent war with North Korea, while authorized by the UN and conducted with troops from fifteen states, was nonetheless dominated by American military planning and personnel.

Not until 1990, after the Iraqi occupation of Kuwait, was a collective enforcement operation again authorized against a member state. Then the United States and the Soviet Union were in substantial agreement, and careful negotiations between them, and with other major powers, made possible the large-scale military action to liberate Kuwait. There was, of course, no standing UN military force for that operation either. Instead, a multinational coalition was assembled on an ad hoc basis. In this operation, too, the United States dominated the coalition and substantially controlled military and political strategy; the UN exercised only very general supervision. Many hoped that the extent of agreement among the great powers that existed at the close of the cold war would last and would allow similar collective enforcement operations in the future, or even serve to stimulate creation of some sort of permanent UN military capability that might also act as a deterrent to aggression. So far, however, there have been no repeats. Major U.S.–led military interventions—in Kosovo in 1999, Afghanistan in 2001, and Iraq in 2003—witnessed little or no direct UN involvement, and, except for Afghanistan, substantial opposition by some other members of the P5.

The other kind of operation in which the UN can employ military force is **peacekeeping**. Peacekeeping is very different from collective enforcement. Its purpose is conflict management or settlement, and it does not involve assigning guilt or identifying an aggressor. Rather, it involves recognition that a violent conflict or threat to peace is at hand. Here the role of the UN is to separate the warring parties and create conditions for them to negotiate instead of fight. Traditionally, peacekeepers (often called "the blue helmets") have been lightly armed and dispatched only after belligerents agreed to a cease-fire. Increasingly, however, UN personnel are sent into unstable situations, and rules of engagement allow them to employ military force for purposes other than self-defense. Such operations, like those employed during the disintegration of Yugoslavia, have come to be known as *peace enforcement.*[28]

During the cold war, the UN had little success with conflicts involving either superpower (or its allies) because each could veto any proposed UN action. It was often more successful, however, in dealing with medium and minor powers in situations where the superpowers were not (or not yet) strongly involved on opposite sides. The earliest deployments were observer missions only, but beginning with the Suez crisis in 1956, the UN has dispatched lightly armed peacekeeping forces of varying magnitudes to many trouble spots (earlier missions consisted of observers only). More than forty peacekeeping missions have been concluded since then—some of them not so lightly armed—and seventeen were in place in 2008 (see Table 10.2). To date, the largest peacekeeping operation was the force deployed in the former Yugoslavia from 1992 to 1995. That operation involved about 39,000 military personnel and cost $4.6 billion. The peacekeeping operation for Sudan is a joint mission with the African Union (the first of its kind) and has an authorized troop strength of 32,000 and an annual budget of $1.3 billion. Nearly 2,500 peacekeepers (including observers) have been killed in the line of duty since 1948.

Peacekeeping operations are almost always carried out only with the consent of the conflicting parties; when the UN appears to take sides in a civil war, as in Somalia, it is less successful.[29] The key feature of many operations has been the use of UN forces to separate the armies of the warring parties and to maintain a ceasefire. The importance of such activities was made painfully clear in 1967, when Secretary-General U Thant acceded to the request by Egypt's President Nasser to remove the UN forces that had been stationed on the Sinai border between Israel and Egypt (but in Egyptian territory) since the Suez War. Israel's decision to launch, preemptively, the 1967 Six Day War was strongly influenced by the absence of a UN barrier to a possible Egyptian attack, which the Israelis believed to be imminent.

---

[28] See, for example, Michael Pugh, "Peace Enforcement," in Thomas G. Weiss and Sam Daws, eds., *The Oxford Handbook on the United Nations* (Oxford: Oxford University Press, 2007); J. Michael Greig and Paul F. Diehl, "The Peacekeeping-Peacemaking Dilemma," *International Studies Quarterly* 49 (December 2005), pp. 621–645.

[29] Walter Clarke, "Failed Visions and Uncertain Mandates in Somalia," in Walter Clarke and Jeffrey Herbst, eds., *Learning from Somalia: The Lessons of Armed Humanitarian Intervention* (Boulder, Colo.: Westview, 1997). See also Kenneth Anderson, "Humanitarian Inviolability in Crisis: The Meaning of Impartiality and Neutrality for UN and NGO Agencies Following the 2003–2004 Afghanistan and Iraq Conflicts," *Harvard Human Rights Journal* 17 (2004), pp. 41–74.

TABLE 10.2 | UN PEACEKEEPING MISSIONS, 2008

Location	Mission	Start	Personnel	Deaths	Budget ($ Millions)
Africa					
Chad	MINURCAT	2007	206	0	182
Congo, Dem. Republic	MONUC	1999	22,064	125	1,116
Ethiopia/Eritrea	UNMEE	2000	888	20	113
Ivory Coast	UNOCI	2004	10,453	41	471
Liberia	UNMIL	2003	15,075	109	688
Sudan	UNMIS	2005	13,300	35	846
Sudan (with African Union)	UNMID	2007	31,569	1	1,276
Western Sahara	MINURSO	1991	500	15	48
Middle East					
Golan Heights	UNDOF	1974	1,228	43	40
Lebanon	UNIFIL	1978	13,254	272	714
Middle East	UNTSO	1948	375	49	66
Asia					
East Timor	UNMIT	2006	2,804	3	153
India/Pakistan	UNMOGIP	1949	115	11	17
Europe					
Cyprus	UNFICYP	1964	1,085	178	48
Georgia	UNOMIG	1993	432	11	35
Kosovo	UNMIK	1999	4,503	53	211
Americas					
Haiti	MINUSTAH	2004	10,877	35	535
Totals			128,728	1,001	6,559

Note: Personnel include peacekeeping troops, police, military observers, international and local civilian personnel, and UN volunteers. Deaths include all fatalities since the start of the mission. Figures for UNMID are authorized levels; as of May 2008, the total deployed was 10,506.

Source: United Nations, "Current Peacekeeping Operations," May 2008; available at <http://www.un.org/Depts/dpko/bnote.htm.>

The UN's original peacekeeping role—standing between hostile forces—has been expanded to *peace-building* activities such as maintaining security or stability within a wide area (as in southern Lebanon), providing humanitarian assistance (Cyprus), disarming insurgents (Nicaragua), and monitoring elections (Namibia, Nicaragua, and Haiti). Gradually, therefore, the UN has become important in managing conflicts within a single country rather than purely between countries and has taken on a role in helping to secure peaceful governmental transitions. The UN is increasingly helpful in aiding the establishment of democratic governments when the parties involved want such help (sometimes in collaboration with regional IGOs like the Organization of American States). Multidimensional UN peacekeeping operations—maintaining the peace militarily, rebuilding the physical and administrative structure of the country, and supporting democracy—have developed a record of substantial achievement, learning from earlier mistakes as well as successes. They typically keep the peace and establish reasonably democratic regimes for about five years, although after that unexpected shocks, like natural disasters and economic collapse, may disrupt the established order. This is superior to similar efforts mounted solely by single countries, regional organizations, or coalitions.[30]

The UN's peacekeeping and peace-building roles are continuously evolving. One recent development is the establishment of a rapid deployment force, the Standby High Readiness Brigade (SHIRBRIG), headquartered near Copenhagen. The members of this force are well trained in the complexities of conflict management and humanitarian assistance, especially in the context of intrastate conflicts, and come from countries with extensive experience in peacekeeping—for example, Austria, Canada, Denmark, and the Netherlands. SHIRBRIG is designed to be deployed for up to six months, either independently or in conjunction with other peacekeeping forces whose duties may last longer than that. In 2000, a SHIRBRIG battalion was deployed as part of the UN Mission in Ethiopia and Eritrea (UNMEE), and did in fact conclude its mission after six months even though UNMEE remained in place. Since then, however, its deployments have been much smaller and mainly to help plan for other peacekeeping missions. Nevertheless, the creation of these standby military forces takes the UN one small step closer to fulfilling its role in the realm of international peace and security as envisioned in the UN Charter.

THE THREE UNs

For all its limitations and periodic failures, the UN has become a powerful instrument for achieving **human security** in its broadest sense. It was established by founders with a broad vision of peace and security, and the UN continues to evolve within a changing global context. While it has not satisfied all their high hopes, it has accomplished far more than its detractors recognize—and more than many of its member governments have accomplished. The UN consists of organs devoted to three broadly different purposes; like organs in the human body, they complement each other and cannot be effective alone.

Of the three UNs, the most obvious is the UN of security against violence. This is the UN of the Security Council, which authorizes peacekeeping missions, applies economic and other sanctions, and carries out collective security operations against blatant aggressors and other threats to international peace. This UN also includes the Secretary-General, who has the power and capacity to promote the peaceful

---

[30] Michael W. Doyle and Nicholas Sambanis, *Making War and Building Peace: United Nations Peace Operations* (Princeton, N.J.: Princeton University Press, 2006); Virginia Page Fortna, *Peace Time: Cease-Fire Agreements and the Durability of Peace* (Princeton, N.J.: Princeton University Press, 2004).

settlement of disputes through good offices, negotiation, and mediation. Because it has been able to take only small and tentative steps into the great void of world politics—the lack of centralized enforcement authority responsible for the security of states—this UN will remain the target of criticism and disillusion for as long as its members are willing and able to use military force to resolve their differences.

The second UN, the UN of economic security and the provision of basic human needs, is less obvious. This is the UN of the specialized agencies and much of the Secretariat. It includes emergency humanitarian assistance, the Food and Agriculture Organization (FAO), the World Health Organization (WHO), and the United Nations Development Programme (UNDP). It is also the UN of the IMF and the World Bank, affiliated organizations dispensing enormous capital resources in an effort to provide international economic stability and well-being. This UN does much of its work under the radar of high politics, but it can lay claim to having improved the lives of very many people.

Often the least visible, but equally important, is the UN of human dignity and justice. This is the UN that oversaw the treatment and ultimately the transition of trusteeships like Namibia. It includes the International Court of Justice, the Electoral Assistance Unit of the Secretariat, the Commissioner of Human Rights, and the High Commissioner for Refugees. It is the UN of the Universal Declaration of Human Rights and numerous other statements on self-determination, discrimination, the rights of women and children, servitude and forced labor, and the administration of justice. Moreover, it is the UN that, in 1998, succeeded in providing for the creation of a permanent International Criminal Court to prosecute genocide and other crimes against humanity.

In all three of its aspects, the UN has achieved successes and suffered failures. Against the neglect of Rwanda and tragedy of Somalia are substantial peacekeeping and peace-building accomplishments in places such as Cambodia, El Salvador, Mozambique, and East Timor. WHO eradicated smallpox worldwide. Many underdeveloped economies have benefited from UN development assistance. The Electoral Assistance Division of the Department of Political Affairs has helped conduct democratic elections in nearly a hundred countries. UN rhetoric on human rights, while often ignored, has become embodied in international conventions and declarations that now take the form of domestic law in many states, binding governments to observe their normative principles.

The UN in its varied guises has attempted to deal with serious environmental, economic, and political problems, which may ultimately be the most crucial the world faces because of the interdependencies of the current world system. The UN has held special conferences in all these areas to bring states together to air their differences, to propose corrective policies, and to work out agreements. The three UNs have a synergy; they reinforce and build on each other. There can be little economic security if there is no security against violence, within countries as well as between them. Building peace in the wake of conflict requires reestablishing economic stability and protecting human rights for the vanquished, for minorities, and for majorities that govern democratically. These are the sort of successes that explain the relative longevity of the UN as an international organization and lead most observers to believe that it will remain a force in world politics for the foreseeable future.

CAUSES OF PEACE AND NONVIOLENT TRANSFORMATION

CHAPTER 11

THE ZONE OF PEACE

In the past five decades, the achievements in the rich industrialized countries of the world have been very impressive indeed. Despite occasional bouts of recession and inflation, these countries have seen a period of economic well-being unrivaled in history. Despite serious inequalities and remaining pockets of real poverty within many industrialized countries, at no other point in history has prosperity been as widespread. In contrast to the prosperity experienced by most of the great empires of the past, economic well-being in the industrialized world today is enjoyed by far more than just the ruling classes.

All this has happened in spite of the enormous loss of life and physical destruction caused by World War II, after which the economies of Japan, Germany, and many other states were in ruin. Moreover, all states—but especially the industrialized countries—are now tightly linked by a network of trade, investment, communications, and travel to an unprecedented degree. Most citizens of Europe and North America could probably afford an intercontinental trip, and the plane journey is a matter of hours. The prospering national economies are tightly interdependent: growth, inflation, and recession are readily transmitted from one country to another with little control. However, they have *managed* their interdependence to produce positive results for all involved.

Equally important, but not noticed as often as the achievement of prosperity, is the achievement of peace. Among the developed market economies of the Organization for Economic Cooperation and Development (OECD)—the countries of North America, Western and (now) Central Europe, Japan, South Korea, Australia, and New Zealand—there has been only one brief international war since 1945, the conflict between Greece and Turkey over Cyprus in 1974. Not only has there been virtually no violent conflict in the last sixty years, there has been no expectation of, or preparation for, war among these states. The enduring hostility between France and Germany since the nineteenth century appears well buried since the 1960s. Individual German and French citizens may not love one another, but neither do they expect the other's state to attack or wish to mount an attack themselves.

Europeans, Americans, and Japanese may still fear security threats from outside the OECD and may continue to use or threaten to use military force against small or poor states to retain their spheres of influence. But among countries within the OECD area, peace and the confident expectation of peace is the norm. When the U.S. government wanted the British and French to withdraw from Suez in 1956, it coerced them with economic sanctions, not with military force. Despite periodic—and sometimes shrill—trade disagreements between the United States and Japan during the 1980s and 1990s, there was no hint of armed violence.

The most industrialized countries of the world inhabit what many call a **zone of peace**. This is an extraordinary achievement by the standards of recent history. Until 1945, war or the expectation of war among these countries was the norm. Future OECD countries were the instigators and major combatants of both world wars, which resulted in the deaths of tens of millions of people. The preceding century saw many major wars among these same countries, beginning with the extended Napoleonic Wars involving all major states of Europe (and provoking the War of 1812 between Britain and the United States) and including several wars leading to the unification of Germany in 1870. Even in periods of peace, it was recognized that peace was precarious and depended on states being ready, willing, and able to fight; peace required the maintenance of a balance of power. Crises and war scares were common. Several conflicts threatened to provoke a general European war before one finally did in August 1914.

The vast majority of international wars since 1945, however, have been fought in less-developed countries (LDCs), and mostly among LDCs. The global incidence of violent conflict has been so lopsided that some contrast the zone of peace in the industrialized world with "zones of turmoil" in the developing world.[1] No war has been fought on the territory of an OECD country. This was partly the result of NATO's deterrence of a Soviet and East European attack on Western Europe, as well as the security guarantees extended to other OECD countries. But there is still the lack of war between OECD countries that is not so easily explained. The significance of the zone of peace is reinforced if we consider that almost all civil wars fought since World War II have taken place within LDCs (though often with outside intervention).

Peace among the OECD countries is also an extraordinary achievement by the standards of world history. The countries involved contain a total population of more than 1 billion spread over a geographic area equal to nearly half the land of the Northern Hemisphere. By both measures it is a larger zone of peace than has ever existed before. These are simple facts, but facts that cry out for explanation, particularly given the contrary expectations of realists and radicals. If we could understand why such a large set of peoples—who only recently fought bitterly and bloodily—now live at peace with one another, we would know something very important.

---

[1] Max Singer and Aaron Wildavsky, *The Real World Order: Zones of Peace/Zones of Turmoil* (Chatham, N.J.: Chatham House, 1993). See also Samuel P. Huntington, *The Clash of Civilizations and the Remaking of World Order* (New York: Simon & Schuster, 1998), who refers to "the West" and "the Rest."

Throughout this book we have addressed the possible causes of war. Applying the levels-of-analysis scheme, we have discussed power rivalries in the context of different kinds of international systems, threats and bargaining in the relations between states, economic systems as the source of societal pressures for expansion, bureaucratic politics as a source of policies unsuited to the "national interest," and fear and misperception by individual decision makers. But the question "What are the causes of peace?" is not simply the opposite side of the question "What are the causes of war?" Reversing the various social and international developments that have contributed to warfare is often not possible. It may be that other countervailing processes must operate in parallel in order to diminish the likelihood of war and bring about lasting peace. If we can explain the peace among the OECD countries, then we can have an understanding of what is happening elsewhere to expand this zone of peace to include many more countries—someday even the entire globe.

PEACE: SALAAM OR SULAH?

To some, peace is simply the absence of war, the absence of organized violent conflict. For most of us, however, that is not enough. The kind of peace we want is not a world in which every individual or group who could conceivably resort to violent conflict is simply deterred or destroyed. Ideally, we wish to achieve a stable peace—the absence of preparation for war or the serious expectation of war. Kenneth Boulding called stable peace "a situation in which the probability of war is so small that it does not really enter into the calculations of any of the people involved."[2] If we prepare for or expect violent conflict, or if we repress violent conflict by force, we have what Boulding called "unstable peace." Others have called this "negative peace." An unstable or negative peace can be enforced by deterrence (the fear of violent retribution), but we may continually fear the breakdown of peace in the event that deterrence fails.

If there is no balance—if deterrence is merely a one-way, rather than a mutual, relationship between two hostile parties—then we are speaking of repression. For some people, especially the most privileged, the absence of violent conflict even if achieved by repression and coercion may be better than the outbreak of violent conflict, but it is hardly anyone's ideal. Repression and coercion can be found in the relationships between powerful and weak states as well as between powerful and weak groups within states. People may be deprived of political liberties, made materially poor, or allowed to die from sickness or starvation without direct physical violence. Some analysts thus refer to **structural violence**—deprivations enforced, often subtly, by repressive social and political systems that are resistant to change—in contrast to the direct or physical violence of war or imprisonment.[3]

---

[2] Kenneth Boulding, *Stable Peace* (Austin: University of Texas Press, 1979), p. 13.

[3] A classic discussion of structural violence is Johan Galtung, "Violence, Peace and Peace Research," *Journal of Peace Research* 6 (August 1969), pp. 167–191. See also Paul Farmer, "On suffering and Structural Violence: A View from Below," *Daedalus* 125 (Winter 1996), pp. 261–283.

The central distinction between stable peace, under conditions that are generally acceptable to both sides, and negative peace, maintained only by threats (whether unilateral or mutual), is clear enough. But the notion of stable peace can be pushed further to describe not only the absence of any expectation of war but also the elimination of deprivation and structural violence—a condition sometimes called "positive peace." These different conceptions of peace correspond roughly to the Arabic terms *sulah*, which means only the end of hostilities or a truce, and *salaam*, which means an enduring peaceful relationship based on mutual respect and well-being.

Stable peace exists within the OECD area, and there is movement toward positive peace. Conditions of injustice, coercion, and repression have not completely disappeared, but the accomplishments of the OECD are substantial compared with most other parts of the world. The most pronounced accomplishments are evident in relations between countries. The greatest remaining hurdles to the achievement of positive peace exist in social relations within countries. The most significant cases of violent political deaths in the last decade or so have been within the United Kingdom (conflict in Northern Ireland), Spain (conflict with Basque separatists), and Turkey (conflict with Kurdish separatists). In each case, the violent acts have involved people who do not wish to be subject to their current government and seek either independence (Basque and Kurdish homelands) or inclusion in another country (the Republic of Ireland). Today, the conflict in Northern Ireland is on its way toward final resolution, but it is still true that in parts of the OECD violence directed at existing governmental institutions remains a threat.

THE DEMOCRATIC PEACE

In a controversial article published in 1989, Francis Fukuyama argued that the dismal record of Soviet-style socialism had demonstrated once and for all that there can be no serious competitor to Western liberalism—free-market capitalism plus political democracy—as an organizing principle for modern society. Fukuyama suggested that we may have arrived at "the end point of mankind's ideological evolution and the universalization of Western liberal democracy as the final form of human government."[4] He surmised that the triumph of Western liberalism—the "end of history"—would be accompanied by increasingly peaceful interstate relations, but he did not go so far as to predict the complete and total end of international conflict. Rather, when conflict does erupt, it is more likely to involve states that have not (yet) embraced Western liberalism. Conflict between nonliberal states (those "still in history") is distinctly possible, as is conflict between them and liberal states. What is unlikely is conflict between liberal states. This view is widespread, even among those who do not fully subscribe to Fukuyama's other

---

[4] Francis Fukuyama, "The End of History?" *The National Interest* 16 (Summer 1989), p. 4. See also his *The End of History and the Last Man* (New York: Free Press, 1992). His argument has been disputed by many; a recent example is Robert Kagan, *The Return of History and the End of Dreams* (New York: Knopf, 2008).

views on the triumph of the West, and the phenomenon has become known as the **democratic peace.**

Few observers of world politics dispute this empirical regularity: Stable democracies are unlikely to engage in militarized disputes with each other or let any such disputes escalate into war. Social scientific research suggests that democracy is indeed part of the explanation. Even when taking into account other factors contributing to the frequency with which countries have conflicts with one another— geographic proximity, alliance membership, economic interdependence, well-being, and so on—democratic states show a disinclination to become embroiled in violent disputes with each other. They virtually never go to war with each other and have far fewer militarized confrontations or even serious diplomatic disputes with each other than do other kinds of states. Democracies tend to reciprocate each other's cooperative behavior, accept third-party mediation or good offices in settling disputes, and generally resolve conflicts peacefully. Notice that this is a *dyadic* phenomenon. The most widely accepted empirical finding is the high probability of peace between pairs of democratic states. Although some research suggests that democratic states may be more peaceful generally, whether in their relations with other democracies or with nondemocracies—a *monadic* finding—there is less consensus behind this strong version of the democratic peace.[5]

It is the democratic form of government that seems to matter. If similarity of form of government alone were enough, then we would expect to have seen peace between the Soviet Union and China, between the Soviet Union and its Eastern European neighbors, and between China and Vietnam. Despite important differences in political values and organization among the communist countries, they were much more like one another, especially in values or ideology, than like the democracies or even like right-wing dictatorships. Yet war or the threat of war between these countries was commonplace. The relations between democracies seem to be qualitatively different. Woodrow Wilson expressed this conviction in his 1917 war message to Congress when he asserted that "a steadfast concert of peace can never be maintained except by a partnership of democratic nations."

There is, then, good reason to believe that a zone of peace exists in the industrialized world largely because it is also a zone of democracy. Since the restoration of democracy in Greece, Portugal, and Spain in the early 1970s, and Turkey in the early 1980s, all OECD countries have had democratic forms of government. Their governments are, by worldwide standards, relatively nonrepressive—certainly less repressive than many governments in the less-developed world or the former communist regimes of Eastern Europe. In this respect, the current OECD governments also differ markedly from many of their governments in the late 1930s, when

---

[5] A range of complementary and competing explanations for the democratic peace are considered and tested in Bruce Russett and John R. Oneal, *Triangulating Peace: Democracy, Interdependence, and International Organizations* (New York: Norton, 2001). On the monadic version of the democratic peace, see David L. Rousseau, *Democracy and War: Institutions, Norms, and the Evolution of International Conflict* (Stanford, Calif.: Stanford University Press, 2005). For a recent review of the social scientific literature, see David Kinsella and David L. Rousseau, "Democracy and Conflict Resolution," in Jacob Bercovitch, Victor Kremenyuk, and I. William Zartman, eds., *The Sage Handbook of Conflict Resolution* (London: Sage, 2008).

Germany, Italy, Japan, Spain, Portugal, and others were all ruled by fascist dictatorships.

Democratic Governance: Structure and Culture

Two main types of explanation have been offered for the democratic peace. One emphasizes perceptions of individual rights, expectations of limited government, shifting coalitions, and toleration of dissent by a presumably loyal opposition. By this *cultural explanation*, the perceptions and practices that permit the peaceful resolution of conflicts of interest without the threat of violence within democracies also apply across national boundaries toward other democratic countries. In short, people within a democracy perceive themselves as autonomous, self-governing people who share norms of "live and let live" and who respect the rights of others to self-determination—*if* those others are also perceived as self-governing and hence not easily led into aggressive foreign policies by a self-serving elite. The openness of society and the free flow of information that characterize democracies facilitate these perceptions. They also help prevent the development of demonic enemy images, which are often created by elites as necessary to justify war against another people. The same cultural restraints that are assumed to limit our aggression, both internally and externally, may also be expected to limit democratically governed people in other states. Even though these images may involve a significant degree of myth as well as reality, they still operate as powerful restraints on violence between democratic systems.

By contrast, such restraints do not apply when the two countries are governed according to very different norms and at least one of them is not democratic. The leaders of the nondemocratic state are seen as being in a permanent state of aggression against their own people, and thus also against foreigners. For example, the essence of U.S. cold war ideology was always that the United States had no quarrel with the Russian people, only with the communist elites who governed and repressed them. Similarly, the wars against Afghanistan in 2001 and Iraq in 2003 were cast partly as wars of self-defense (unjustifiably in the case of Iraq, as we suggested in the last chapter), but also as wars of liberation, after which peaceful relations between free and self-governing peoples would be possible. The implication, of course, is that democratic culture can and will thrive among these previously oppressed peoples if given the opportunity.

Along with cultural explanations, there are *structural explanations*. Institutional constraints—regular elections, division of powers within government, checks and balances—make it harder for democratic leaders to move their countries toward war. A leader must, to varying degrees, persuade the legislature, the government bureaucracy, and even private interest groups that the resort to military force is in the national interest. They must mobilize public opinion. In a democracy, support for war can be built by rhetoric and exhortation, but it cannot be readily compelled. The complexity of this process requires time as leaders of various institutions are convinced and formal approval is obtained; but this time also allows for negotiation and other forms of peaceful conflict resolution. In a crisis between democracies, each leadership anticipates that the other will have to engage in a difficult and lengthy process before force can be used.

Because they expect to have an opportunity to reach a peaceful settlement, they are less likely to cut short the negotiating process with preemptive military action.

An especially important structural argument starts with the observation that all national leaders are motivated by the desire to retain power for themselves or their chosen successors. To do this, they must satisfy a sufficiently large segment of those who influence the choice of leaders (democratically or undemocratically) so that they can maintain a winning coalition in the game of domestic politics. To maximize their chances of staying in power, they pursue policies that benefit society as a whole (public goods) and distribute special benefits to their supporters (private goods). All leaders generally do both, but the mix often depends on the type of regime in power. Democratic leaders have to satisfy a wide electorate, not just a small set of cronies or military officers. Rather than depending on the distribution of private goods, which may not amount to much when distributed widely, they are driven more toward providing public goods to large segments of the population. If they engage in wars that they lose or that do not benefit the general population—especially long or costly wars—they are likely to be voted out of office. Even a popular World War II leader like Britain's Winston Churchill was soundly defeated for reelection at the end of the war. So democratic leaders try to avoid getting into such wars. This gives them greater legitimacy and support from society. However, so long as its general population supports the war effort, a democracy is likely to devote a large share of its resources to the war effort, and a democratic army may be strongly motivated to fight. Democracies usually do win their wars—nearly 80 percent of the time. So another democracy is not an easy target.[6]

A dictator like Saddam Hussein of Iraq, however, cannot easily be removed from office. He took his country into three very costly wars. In the first two—against Iran in 1980, and against Kuwait and ultimately a U.S.–led coalition in 1990—the majority of the Iraqi population suffered, but there were no elections whereby voters could depose him. By buying off his clan, and to some extent the Sunni population as a whole, as well as the military and the police, he was able to stay in power; their support was all he needed. After the Gulf War, the Kurdish population in the north did fairly well under the protection of a no-fly zone enforced by U.S. and British aircraft, but the Shi'ites in the south continued to suffer. The support of neither group was necessary for Saddam Hussein to retain his unchallenged position. His third disastrous decision, to resist the U.S. invasion in 2003, did finally end his tyranny and was devastating to the Sunni minority that benefited from his rule.

Cultural and structural explanations for the democratic peace should not be understood as "contending" approaches, as though one type of explanation is

---

[6] Kenneth A.Schultz, "Do Domestic Institutions Constrain or Inform? Contrasting Two Institutional Perspectives on Democracy and War," *International Organization* 53 (Spring 1999), pp. 233–266; Bruce Bueno deMesquita, JamesMorrow, RandolphSiverson, and AlastairSmith, "An Institutional Explanation of the Democratic Peace," *American Political Science Review* 93 (December 1999), pp. 791–807. On the tendency of democracies to win when they do fight, see DanReiter and Allan C. Stam, *Democracies at War* (Princeton, N.J.: Princeton University Press, 2002).

correct and the other is not. We should instead ask if and how both could be true.[7] Various factors affect both the opportunity and the willingness of decision makers to choose among conflictual and cooperative options that exist under particular circumstances. The normative and cultural commitments shared by liberal democratic societies seem to exert their influence primarily by diminishing the willingness of democratic leaders to pursue policies at odds with those shared commitments, while the institutional and structural constraints operating under democratic forms of governance mainly serve to limit their opportunities to do so. Thus, the democratic peace results from a set of processes at work in both domestic and international politics, which has influenced not only the menu of states but also their appetites for the available selections. (Box 11.1 presents a simple game-theoretic account of the strategic choices faced by a democracy in an international crisis.)

PERPETUAL PEACE

In the last chapter, we mentioned that the writings of Immanuel Kant have greatly influenced contemporary approaches to human rights law wherein all individuals, regardless of national citizenship, are said to possess a common set of freedoms and protections. We will return to this idea again in Chapter 16 when we discuss international distributive justice. For now, Kant's ideas are relevant also for understanding the zone of peace. Writing in 1795, Kant presented three "definitive articles for perpetual peace among states":

1. The civil constitution of every state should be republican.
2. The law of nations shall be founded on a federation of free states.
3. The law of world citizenship shall be limited to conditions of universal hospitality.[8]

In his first article, by *republican* Kant meant a constitution that provides for individual freedom and equal status under the law, as well as a separation of executive and legislative powers within government. Interestingly, Kant was critical of democratic forms of government as despotic, because the will of the majority is imposed on the minority. However, what he had in mind was direct democracy in which the citizenry is directly involved in both legislation and the execution of laws, and which exists more in theory than in practice. Representative democracy, the form of democratic government we see today, does correspond to Kant's conception of republicanism. Representative government is conducive to peace, according to Kant, for the same reasons highlighted by structural explanations of the democratic peace: "If the consent of the citizens is required in order to decide that war should

---

[7] For an application of this framework to ancient Greece, see Bruce Russett, "Democracy, War, and Expansion through Historical Lenses," *European Journal of International Relations* 15 (March 2009).

[8] See Immanuel Kant, *Perpetual Peace, and Other Essays on Politics, History, and Morals*, trans. and with an introduction by Ted Humphrey (Indianapolis, Ind.: Hackett, 1992); quotes in this section from pp. 112–119. See also Burleigh T. Wilkins, "Kant on International Relations," *Journal of Ethics* 11 (June 2007), pp. 147–159.

IN GREATER DEPTH

BOX 11.1 | DEMOCRACIES AND CRISES

Some studies have attempted to integrate the cultural and structural explanations of the democratic peace by examining how both relate to the menu of options available to decision makers in democratic states, thereby conditioning their choices during periods of international crisis. Bruce Bueno de Mesquita and David Lalman argue that the dovishness of democratic states and the domestic political costs of using force mean that the calculations these leaders must make when choosing a course of action will differ from the calculations made by leaders of non-democratic states. This can be illustrated through the use of a game tree. Suppose that one side in a confrontation, after having made a demand of the other and receiving a counterdemand, must decide between using force and not using force (recall Box 8.1). That is the point in the interaction where the two states enter a crisis situation. Bueno de Mesquita and Lalman call this the *crisis subgame*:

cates the use of force, then the outcome is a war initiated by A; when B does not reciprocate, the outcome is B's capitulation. If A does not use force (the left branch), then B must decide whether to initiate the use of force. If B decides not to, the outcome is a negotiated settlement. If B does use force, A must decide whether to reciprocate the use of force. If A reciprocates, the outcome is a war initiated by B; otherwise A capitulates.

This game tree can help us predict the outcome of a crisis if we know how each side values the five possible outcomes. Leaders in a democratic state must confront the domestic political costs of war and are, therefore, inclined to rank war low in their order of preferences. If war is inevitable, they will prefer to initiate it rather than wait passively by; but if they have lost the initiative, then they may well prefer to capitulate than fight. If these leaders are also dovish—not out to forcibly impose their will—then their opponent's

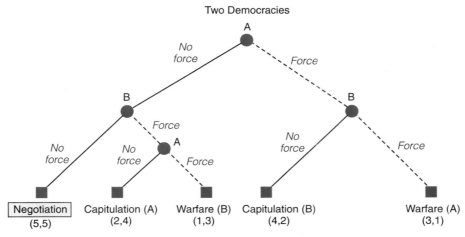

Two states—say, two democracies—find themselves in a crisis subgame because both have made demands and neither has conceded to the other. The crisis starts when state A must decide whether to use force in the face of B's recalcitrance. If A does use force (the right branch), and B recipro-

capitulation will be better than either war or their own capitulation but not as good as a negotiated settlement. Overall, then, democratic state A's preference ordering may be as follows: negotiate > capitulation by B > war initiated by A > capitulation by A > war initiated by B. If state B is also democratic,

(Continued)

BOX 11.1 | DEMOCRACIES AND CRISES (*Continued*)

it may have an analogous preference ordering. As we did for the model presented in Box 8.1, we can attach numbers to each of these five outcomes, indicating the preferences of each side. In this case, negotiation (5,5) is most preferred by both A and B, war initiated by B (1,3) is least preferred by A but ranked third from the bottom by B, and so on as indicated at the base of the game tree.

What is the predicted outcome of a crisis between two democracies? Using backward induction, let us start with B's decision once A has chosen to use force (the right branch). For B, reciprocating A's use of force leaves it worse off than capitulating, so B would capitulate under those circumstances. (B's decision to reciprocate the use of force is drawn as a dashed line to designate it as a course of action *not* chosen.) Now A reasons that if it chooses to fight, the result will be B's capitulation, the second most preferred outcome for A. In order to compare this outcome to the one that would follow if A chooses not to use force, A must look ahead to a situation in which B has been the one to initiate the use of force (down the left branch). Under those circumstances, A is better off capitulating than fighting a war initiated by B. State B can see this and therefore, if it chooses force, will expect A's capitulation. Still, although B's choice of force leaves it in a good position, that outcome is still not as good for B as a negotiated settlement.

Therefore, B will not use force. State A, having reasoned through the likely outcome of its initial decision to not use force, can now compare negotiated settlement to the likely outcome of using force: B's capitulation. Negotiation is preferable to A, so A chooses not to use force and the crisis proceeds along the (solid) path to the negotiation outcome. That is the equilibrium outcome, and that is the outcome we predict when two democracies (with these preferences) find themselves in a crisis situation.

What happens when a democracy finds itself in a crisis situation with a nondemocratic country—say, a dictatorship? First, democratic state A must consider that dictatorship C ranks the five possible outcomes differently than would another democracy. One difference is that dictatorships do not confront the same domestic political costs when they become involved in war. For a dictatorship, fighting a war initiated by an opponent may be more desirable than capitulation. Another difference is that a dictatorship may be more hawkish—preferring to bend an opponent to its will rather than negotiating. In short, dictatorship C may have the following preference ordering: capitulation by A > negotiate > war initiated by C > war initiated by A > capitulation by C. In our game tree, we need to change the second in each pair of preference orderings to reflect this different strategic situation:

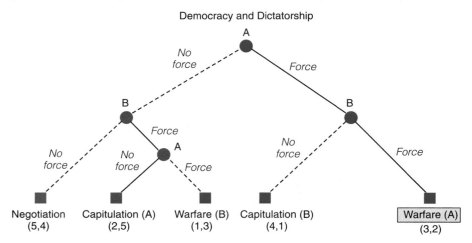

Democracy and Dictatorship

| Negotiation (5,4) | Capitulation (A) (2,5) | Warfare (B) (1,3) | Capitulation (B) (4,1) | Warfare (A) (3,2) |

| BOX 11.1 | DEMOCRACIES AND CRISES (*Continued*) |

Now when state A contemplates the use of force (the right branch), it reasons that C will reciprocate and therefore expects the outcome of this choice to be a war that it has initiated. In choosing not to use force (the left branch), again A has to imagine itself having to respond to C's use of force, and again A prefers capitulation to war. But C, predicting A's decision, will prefer that outcome to a negotiated settlement and so can be expected to resort to force even when A does not. Having thought the process through, leaders of state A must weigh their own capitulation against their initiation of war. Neither outcome is especially good for A, but war is better. Democratic state A therefore elects

to use force, and the crisis proceeds down the path to war. When a democracy becomes embroiled in a crisis with a dictatorship, we would predict that the democracy may well initiate a conflict so as to preempt the anticipated use of force by the opponent. That is the equilibrium outcome. As Bueno de Mesquita and Lalman observe, "the high domestic political constraint faced by democracies makes them vulnerable to threats of war or exploitation and liable to launch preemptive attacks against presumed aggressors."

Source: Adapted from Bruce Bueno de Mesquita and David Lalman, *War and Reason: Domestic and International Imperatives* (New Haven, Conn.: Yale University Press, 1992), quote from p. 159.

be declared, ... they would be very cautious in ... decreeing for themselves all the calamities of war."

In his second article, Kant calls for international law anchored in a federation of free states. His idea of a federation was more like a loose union or confederation, not a federal system like the American states or Swiss cantons; he certainly did not have in mind a world government. He also felt that each member had the right to demand that all other members have representative forms of government, making this a "pacific union." Kant expected that representative forms of government would spread. Because they are "inclined toward perpetual peace," the pacific union would expand as more and more states joined in order to "secure freedom under the idea of the law of nations." In contemporary international relations, the largest federation of states is, of course, the United Nations, but its membership consists of a large number of states that would not meet Kant's criteria for republicanism. Other international organizations—most notably, the European Union, but also the less formal OECD—do consist solely of representative democracies and, given their peaceful relations, they seem to fit his idea of pacific union.

In his third definitive article, Kant refers to world citizenship and universal hospitality. He was concerned that individuals be treated fairly when guests in other lands, and that as guests they should likewise treat their hosts fairly. In particular, he lamented the treatment of indigenous peoples by European "commercial states"—that is, exploitation perpetrated "under the pretense of establishing economic undertakings." But he was also critical of the inhospitality shown by the coastal inhabitants of the Barbary Coast, who interfered with European commerce in the Mediterranean and the Atlantic. Essentially, Kant was calling for the conditions that would make possible the free exchange of goods between peoples. What we refer to today as economic interdependence is more conducive to perpetual peace than the economic plundering that Kant thought so plainly violated principles of universal hospitality.

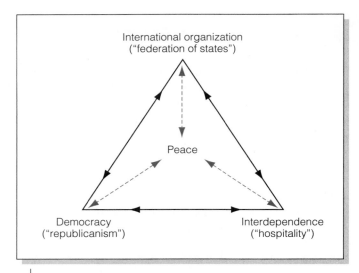

FIGURE 11.1 | KANT'S PRESCRIPTION FOR PERPETUAL PEACE

The arrows pointing toward the center of the triangle represent the effects of democracy, interdependence, and international organizations on peaceful relations between states. The arrows returning to the corners from the center represent the reciprocal effects of peace on democratic consolidation, on deepening interdependence, and on the spread and effectiveness of international organizations. Each leg of the Kantian triad is related to the other legs, thereby reinforcing the foundation for perpetual peace.
Source: Russett and Oneal, *Triangulating Peace*, p. 35.

There are, then, three legs upon which perpetual peace stands according to Kant, each corresponding to one of his three definitive articles. Figure 11.1 illustrates this idea of perpetual peace, using both Kant's terminology and the terminology of contemporary world politics. We have already discussed the democratic ("republican") leg. We now turn to the other two characteristics of the zone of peace.

ECONOMIC INTERDEPENDENCE AND GROWTH

Economic interdependence gives one state a material stake in the prosperity and stability of another's economic system. One cannot sell goods or services unless others can afford to buy them. When strong economic links work both ways, the parties have certain common interests. Trade among the OECD countries, for example, typically accounts for about 80 percent of their total international trade. The ratio of foreign trade to GDP—the importance of foreign commerce relative to the overall level of economic activity—is another useful indicator of the degree of interdependence. The total trade of OECD countries amounts to more than one-third of their collective GDP, although figures do vary for individual countries.

Trade ties give states a strong incentive for maintaining peaceful relations. To use, or even to threaten, military violence against an important trading partner is likely to disrupt commercial exchange. Military conflict endangers importers' preferred supplies of goods and services; it endangers exporters' markets. If one state's nationals have invested heavily in the economy of the other state, war could mean the destruction of the very facilities they own there. Trade and investment also serve as mediums for communication. Interests, preferences, and needs on a broad range of matters beyond immediate commercial exchange are communicated between societies in the course of regularized and stable economic relations. These communications form potentially important channels for averting militarized conflict.

Social science research largely supports the link between trade and peace. The more any two states trade with each other, the less likely they are to experience wars or militarized disputes. Moreover, this pacifying effect of trade operates in addition to the pacifying effects of democratic governance, as well as other factors making states reluctant to fight (distance, relative power, and so on). Economically interdependent states do have disputes—witness the frequent bickering between the United States and the Europeans and Japan over trade practices and access to markets—but "trade wars" are not hot wars.[9]

Economic interdependence is a dyadic phenomenon, characteristic of pairs of states with extensive trade ties. There is also an economic explanation for peace that is essentially monadic. Joseph Schumpeter, among other liberal thinkers, argued that individuals in industrialized societies are materialistic, too preoccupied with commercial production and the acquisition of wealth to be distracted by foreign conquest. Even imperial wars in pursuit of economic advantage are not worth the costs for the majority in society and really benefit only a select group. As societies become more industrialized and wealthy—and democratic, Schumpeter adds—an aversion to war will spread, and so too will the prospects for lasting peace between states.[10]

A high level of industrial activity and a high rate of economic growth are prominent features of the OECD. Virtually all OECD countries experienced rapid economic expansion after World War II. This was especially true for the defeated states, Germany and Japan, which benefited from various forms of American assistance and by 1960 had totally recovered from their wartime devastation. By contrast, the negative economic growth for most OECD countries during much of the 1920s and 1930s (the time of the Great Depression) was probably a major cause of World War II. Germany's economic difficulties, including rampant inflation followed by mass unemployment, led directly to Hitler's accession to power in 1933. Many of the industrialized countries, in an effort to maintain their own balance of payments, adopted protectionist measures to restrict imports from other industrial countries. The result was a set of "beggar-thy-neighbor" policies that reduced

[9] Theoretical and empirical issues related to this research are discussed in Edward D. Mansfield and Brian Pollins, eds., *Economic Interdependence and International Conflict: New Perspectives on an Enduring Debate* (Ann Arbor: University of Michigan Press, 2003). This thesis is challenged in Katherine Barbieri, *The Liberal Illusion: Does Trade Promote Peace?* (Ann Arbor: University of Michigan Press, 2002).

[10] See Joseph Schumpeter, *Capitalism, Socialism, and Democracy* (New York: Harper Torchbooks, 1950).

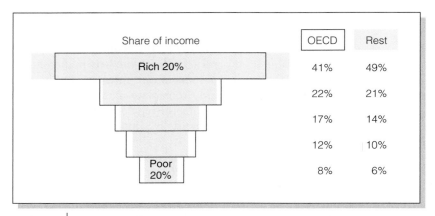

Share of income	OECD	Rest
Rich 20%	41%	49%
	22%	21%
	17%	14%
	12%	10%
Poor 20%	8%	6%

FIGURE 11.2 | INCOME DISTRIBUTION WITHIN SOCIETIES: OECD AND THE REST OF THE WORLD

The length of the bars represents the percentage of national income earned by each quintile of the population, averaged for OECD and other countries. Although the OECD includes the wealthiest and most developed countries in the world, the richest 20 percent in these countries earn a smaller share of national income than do the richest people outside the OECD. Likewise, in the OECD, each quintile below the richest earns a greater share of national income than does its counterparts elsewhere.

Source: Averages are computed from income distribution data in World Bank, *World Development Indicators 2008 CD-ROM* (Washington, DC: World Bank, 2008). Figures for some countries refer to shares of consumption rather than income. Data are available for 29 OECD and 96 other countries, and are from the 2000 to 2004 period.

---

international trade and led to a further decline in everyone's incomes. Conflicts over economic policies were a major cause of international tension and contributed to Japanese expansionist political and military actions. Here we have a good example of low or negative growth severely damaging the prospects for peace.

OECD countries are by far the world's richest, with an average GDP per capita of almost $32,000 in 2006, while the average for the rest of the world was under $7,000. Of the world's twenty-five wealthiest countries (again, in terms of GDP per capita), all but four are OECD members. Moreover, these high living standards apply more equally among the various developed industrialized countries than they do globally. Whereas worldwide GDP per capita ranged from $280 in the Democratic Republic of Congo to more than $50,000 in Norway, the range within the OECD was narrower: from Norway's $50,000 to Turkey's $8,400. That may still seem like a large gap within the OECD, but almost 100 countries in the world are poorer than Turkey.[11]

Income is also distributed more equally within these countries. Figure 11.2 shows the average distribution of household income for countries in the OECD

---

[11] These figures are purchasing power parities. See World Bank, *World Development Indicators 2008 CD-ROM* (Washington, DC: World Bank, 2008). Luxembourg is an outlier within the OECD, with a GDP per capita of $75,000.

(outlined) and those outside the OECD (shaded). The biggest contrast is for the richest in society: On average, the wealthiest 20 percent of households earn almost half of society's total income in countries outside the OECD, but among OECD countries the richest 20 percent earn only 41 percent. At the same time, the middle classes and the poorest earn a larger share of income in the OECD than they do in other countries. Certainly there are serious inequalities even within the OECD, particularly among ethnic and racial minorities or in particular geographic regions. But the fact that these societies' considerably greater wealth is distributed more equally than is lesser total wealth in other societies does represent significant social progress.

Within the OECD, however, equality is not a sufficient condition for peace. Economic inequalities, while significant, do not constitute the main grievance in Northern Ireland, where conflict has been based on religious and cultural differences. The Basques live in one of the most prosperous parts of Spain; again, the conflicts are over cultural and linguistic autonomy rather than economics. But these few exceptions are not enough to indicate that economic equality is irrelevant to peace. It still may matter in important ways, including in relations between states. Some trade relations between rich and very poor countries may not promote truly peaceful relations if they are not seen as producing rewards to both sides, or if they benefit only a select few on both sides. High levels of wealth produced by trade, and its distribution over a larger number of households, means that more citizens would have a great deal to lose in a war.

This suggests that perhaps a combination of economic interdependence, growth, and income equality may together form a powerful set of conditions for peace. This makes sense if the decision to go to war is a rational choice—made by decision makers who calculate, to the best of their ability, the probable costs and benefits of military action. It is true that decision makers value many things besides material advantage (honor, prestige, reputation, cultural autonomy, and so forth). Moreover, they often calculate poorly, on the basis of incomplete or erroneous information. What looks like a course of action that will produce more benefits than costs may in the end accomplish quite the opposite. Nevertheless, decision makers attempt to make such calculations. In a war among OECD countries, the prospective economic gains would not be high (a conquered "rich" country is not likely to be so much richer than its "poorer" conqueror). The costs of such a war, however, would be very high: economic growth would be interrupted, production facilities and capital equipment would be destroyed, and existing wealth would be severely eroded. With such high prospective costs, war with another developed market economy just does not look cost-effective at all.[12]

INTERNATIONAL ORGANIZATIONS

For Kant, a federation of free states would contribute to the maintenance of perpetual peace. Many explanations of the role of international organizations and

---

[12] See John Mueller, *Retreat from Doomsday: The Obsolescence of Major War* (New York: Basic Books, 1989). For a counterargument, see Peter Liberman, *Does Conquest Pay? The Exploitation of Occupied Industrial Societies* (Princeton, N.J.: Princeton University Press, 1996).

international law resemble both the cultural and institutional explanations for the democratic peace. Peace between democracies is based on the tendency of those states to externalize their democratic processes of conflict management and resolution. Organizations, norms, and rules are established *within* societies to reduce the costs of decision making and to enhance efficiency in the creation and implementation of policy. Democratic societies have established not only laws, but procedures for the creation, interpretation, and execution of laws. Legislatures, courts, and administrative bodies at various levels of society serve these functions. Organizations not only facilitate the use of law in conflict management, they also socialize citizens and thereby promote adherence to social norms. In general, organizations within society ease interactions between individuals and help individuals to recognize and pursue common interests.

Leaders of democracies would expect to use international organizations and international law in the same way: to reduce the costs of international interactions in the pursuit of common interests. International organizations are often regarded as weak and ineffectual, as we noted in the last chapter, particularly on matters that critically affect states' security interests. Although international organizations usually lack the same coercive power that national governments have over their constituencies, they can and do fulfill many of the same functions *among* nation-states as domestic organizations do *within* nation-states. For example, a national government coerces all of us by requiring us to pay taxes. We may grumble, but on the whole we accept this coercion as long as it is applied reasonably and fairly among people. Because we want most of the benefits that a modern government provides—social order, health care, education, national defense—we are more or less willing to be prodded into paying our taxes. Most institutions to which OECD states belong lack coercive power, but they do *facilitate* mutual attention and problem solving among the members.

IGOs may be important in promoting accurate perceptions of states' political characteristics, thus providing more correct expectations of how states will behave in crises. Democracies are more likely to use IGOs in resolving their conflicts than are other kinds of states, and regional IGOs seem to be reasonably successful in preventing violence in crises that involve democratic states. Institutions also provide legitimacy for collective decisions and so promote adherence to what has been agreed. Norms and rules developed within IGOs may facilitate arms control and delegitimize the use of force. The Agency for the Prohibition of Nuclear Weapons in Latin America and the Caribbean, for example, helped to free the region of nuclear weapons. Shared norms create common interests and enhance the prospects of cooperation. IGOs help to develop interests and preferences that are more stable than, and in some ways independent of, those held by individual member states. These can serve as a basis for influencing members in accordance with the original purposes for which the IGOs were created, and they may even create new purposes.[13]

---

[13] Some types of IGOs—for example, democratic and highly institutionalized ones—are more effective than others in serving these functions. See Jon Pevehouse and Bruce Russett, "Democratic International Governmental Organizations Promote Peace," *International Organization* 60 (Fall 2006), pp. 969–1000; Charles Boehmer, Erik Gartzke, and Timothy Nordstrom, "Do Intergovernmental Organizations Promote Peace?" *World Politics* 57 (October 2004), pp. 1–38.

This leg of Kant's perpetual peace has been the subject of less social science research than either of the other two legs. Some studies have found that dense links of IGO membership reduced the initiation of conflict in the post–World War II period; this is in addition to the effects of democracy, economic interdependence, and other factors inhibiting conflict between states. More theoretical and empirical investigation remains to be done on the connection between international organization and peace. For instance, the ways that alliances affect international relations are not the same ways that institutions with economic functions operate. In the meantime, there has been a resurgence of interest in some theoretical ideas that lay dormant for much of the cold war period: international integration and the emergence of security communities.

INTEGRATION AND PEACE

Achieving peace by integrating smaller political units into larger ones has long been a goal of political theorists and policy makers. The Roman Empire brought the *Pax Romana*—the Roman peace—to much of the world for several centuries. Although there were some revolts within the empire and continuing battles with barbarians on its borders, the Roman Empire did preside over a remarkable era of peace as well as prosperity. Of course, it was largely a peace of domination, not the kind of stable or positive peace most would prefer today. Writing in the fourteenth century, Florentine poet Dante nevertheless looked back on the Roman Empire as being far better than the situation he knew—almost constant warfare among the Italian city-states. He observed that "in a multitude of rulers there is evil" and hoped for the emergence of a unified Italy under a single crown.

Following the devastation of World War II, the second enormously destructive war in only thirty years, some adopted the principles of **world federalism**: the idea that permanent peace could be achieved only by establishing a world government. In Europe, several leaders vowed that wars among Europeans had to cease and saw some form of European unification as the means to secure that goal. There was, for example, an attempt to create a European Defense Community (EDC). Deteriorating relations with the Soviet Union were made still more threatening by the outbreak of the Korean War in 1950. Many Europeans and Americans came to the conclusion that the military security of Western Europe could not be guaranteed unless West Germany could be rearmed. After World War II, Germany had been occupied by the United States, Britain, and France in the western zone and by the Soviet Union in the eastern zone; Germany had no army and no control over its foreign policy. Because of their recent Nazi experience, the Germans were still intensely distrusted. The EDC, therefore, was conceived as a way to harness German personnel and industrial strength to the common defense. It also would have controlled German militarism by uniting all the member states' armies under a single commander. The EDC was to have a directly elected European parliament and an executive who could be dismissed by the parliament, making it virtually a "United States of Europe." But plans for the EDC were shelved in 1954 after being defeated by a vote in the French Parliament.

TRANSNATIONAL COOPERATION

An important aspect of domestic institutions is that they can forcibly keep the peace. They are the wielders of the only legitimate instruments of violence (the army and police), and as a result can impose order and compel obedience for the common good of society. They can also protect property rights and enforce private contracts. For example, a divorcing couple may make an agreement for the father to provide child support and to receive visiting rights. If the father subsequently refuses to pay or the mother refuses him access to the children, they can be compelled to do so by the courts. If there were no legal authority able to do this, perhaps the couple would be too distrustful of each other to reach any agreement at all. So they both may be better off with the possibility of a mutual commitment that both will have to keep.

The world federalists did not expect that coercive authority could be completely transferred to a world government, but their visions were very ambitious—and idealistic—in this regard. Others writing during and after World War II, like David Mitrany, were more pragmatic. Mitrany was an avid internationalist, but he felt that the proper role for international organizations was to help states solve specific problems, especially on matters that were not confined within national boundaries, like air traffic, international health and safety standards, and refugee movements. The idea was that international organizations should aim to solve problems arising in specific functional areas, and should not attempt to be all things for all states. This approach to international organization came to be called, appropriately, **functionalism.**

Mitrany and other adherents to this view believed that this was the best path to peace. Many international problems highlighted by functionalists could be handled by cooperative efforts undertaken by specialists and technicians trained in those functional areas. Politicians, for the most part, could and should stay out of the way. With the role of state leaders kept to a minimum, there would be less danger that transnational cooperation would be undermined by balance-of-power considerations or other national jealousies that seemed to preoccupy those at the top. Successful collaboration on one set of problems would encourage similar efforts in other functional areas, a process that Mitrany called *ramification*; others would later refer to this process as *spillover*. Before long, a web of international institutions would be created with overlapping membership. Solutions would be found to problems that might otherwise contribute to interstate hostility, and the costs of armed conflict would escalate because that would threaten to disrupt the transnational networks that were working to everyone's benefit.[14]

Functionalists had more success than the world federalists in seeing their vision implemented. Jean Monnet, head of the French economic planning commission and formerly an official with the League of Nations, wanted to see functionalist ideas applied in the regional context of Western Europe. One problem that needed

---

[14] David Mitrany, "The Functional Approach to World Organization," *International Affairs* 24 (1948), pp. 350–363. See also Mitrany's *A Working Peace System* (Chicago: Quadrangle Books, 1966); Per A. Hammarlund, *Liberal Internationalism and the Decline of the State: The Thought of Richard Cobden, David Mitrany, and Kenichi Ohmae* (New York: Palgrave Macmillan, 2005).

attention was the regulation of coal and steel production, an economic sector in which France and Germany were quite interdependent. Indeed, control of the mineral-rich region of Alsace-Lorraine had been a central issue of contention since France first lost it to Germany after the Franco–Prussian War of 1870–1871; possession of the territory went from Germany to France after World War I, and from France to Germany and back to France during World War II. In May 1950, Robert Schuman, foreign minister of France, announced that the French government

> proposes that Franco–German production of coal and steel as a whole be placed under a common High Authority, within the framework of an organization open to the participation of the other countries of Europe. The pooling of coal and steel production should immediately provide for the setting up of common foundations for economic development as a first step in the federation of Europe, and will change the destinies of those regions which have long been devoted to the manufacture of munitions of war, of which they have been the most constant victims. The solidarity in production thus established will make it plain that any war between France and Germany becomes not merely unthinkable, but materially impossible.[15]

From this initiative the European Coal and Steel Community (ECSC) was born a year later, including not only France and Germany but also Belgium, Luxembourg, the Netherlands, and Italy. (Monnet was the first president of the ECSC's High Authority.) This was the first major European supranational authority—that is, an institution with powers to overrule the members' national governments on certain issues.

Promoting interdependence among the heavy industrial sectors of the European economies seemed a good way to limit the independent war-making ability of individual states. Wider economic union could do so even more effectively. During the Nazi occupation of France, Monnet had declared:

> There will be no peace in Europe if States re-establish themselves on the basis of national sovereignty, with all that this implies by way of prestige policies and economic protectionism.... The countries of Europe are too small to give their peoples the prosperity that is now attainable and therefore necessary. They need wider markets.... To enjoy the prosperity and social progress that are essential, the States of Europe must form a federation or a "European entity" which will make them a single economic union.[16]

This approach to European integration led to the signing of the 1957 Treaties of Rome, which established the European Atomic Energy Community (Euratom) and the European Economic Community (EEC, also called the Common Market), by the same six countries that had formed the ECSC. These separate institutions were then merged into the European Community (EC), which expanded its membership, and its functions, and was later renamed the European Union (EU). We discuss the evolution of the EU as an integrated economic bloc of nation-states at length in Chapter 14. For now, it is important to recognize the vision of peace and

---

[15] Robert Schuman, "Declaration of 9 May 1950," available at <http://europa.eu.int/abc/symbols/9-may/decl_en.htm>.

[16] Jean Monnet, *Memoirs*, trans. by Richard Mayne (Garden City, N.Y.: Doubleday, 1978), p. 222.

prosperity that ultimately gave birth to the elaborate set of institutions that constitute today's EU.

Following Mitrany's line of argument, Monnet believed that peace could be achieved in Europe, despite the jealousies and suspicions of state leaders, by gradually expanding transnational cooperative networks below the highest levels of government. The process of European integration he imagined was almost automatic, and irreversible. For others, like Ernst Haas, integrating Europe required the active involvement of political elites. There was no "sneaking up" on the nation-state. An expanding web of European institutions would not materialize—nor would lasting peace—unless elites themselves *transferred their loyalties* to these new institutions and encouraged the process of spillover. French national interests and German national interests would have to be reconceived as European interests.[17]

It is certainly true that stable peace has been achieved among members of the EU. For countries now so highly interdependent, the EU institutions are essential in solving members' common problems and dealing with tensions that could endanger the peace. However, the zone of peace includes all the OECD countries, not just the EU. A variety of important institutions that overlap and extend beyond the member states of the EU—the Council of Europe, NATO, and the OECD itself, for example—are not in any significant way supranational organizations and therefore lack even the limited enforcement capacities possessed by some EU institutions. But there are other transnational processes that work principally through negotiation, consensus, the development of shared commitments, and perhaps even shared identity among states and societies inhabiting the zone of peace.

TRANSNATIONAL COMMUNICATION

Some scholars of international integration and peace, most notably Karl Deutsch and his associates, describe a process of integration based on a wide array of intersocietal transactions that are of benefit to the people involved.[18] These transactions facilitate mutual attention and encourage the identification of common interests and outlooks. There is a social fabric between as well as within nations that is built from such bonds as trade, travel (migration or tourism), cultural and educational exchange, and communication (telephone, television, the Internet, and so on). These ties communicate the needs and perspectives of one group of people to others; they strengthen the sense of a collective identity within the larger community. In the tradition of sociological theory, these community bonds are part of the *Gemeinschaft*, which emphasizes common loyalties and values and a feeling of belonging together, in contrast to the *Gesellschaft*, which emphasizes contractual arrangements and institutions.

---

[17] The classic works are Ernst B. Haas, *The Uniting of Europe: Political, Social, and Economic Forces, 1950–1957* (Stanford, Calif.: Stanford University Press, 1958); Haas, *Beyond the Nation-State: Functionalism and International Organization* (Stanford, Calif.: Stanford University Press, 1964). These and related revisions of functionalist thinking are labeled *neofunctionalism*.

[18] Karl W. Deutsch et al., *Political Community and the North Atlantic Area: International Organization in the Light of Historical Experience* (Princeton, N.J.: Princeton University Press, 1957).

Recall from our discussion of nationalism in Chapter 3 that social communication is important for the development of psychological attachments to a community and ultimately the formation of a nation. The community-building process is based on learning—learning that such transactions provide benefits, that such benefits outweigh the costs involved, and that there are positive payoffs in continuing and expanding such transactions. As peaceful transactions increase, peoples develop greater responsiveness to one another. They develop the we-feeling, trust, and mutual consideration that Deutsch and others adopting the "transactionist approach" thought necessary for the evolution of integrated political communities.

Though they usually seem to bind nations or social groups together, trade, tourism, and migration can also serve as irritants. The most important qualification—a serious one—is that the exchanges must be mutually beneficial, at least not harmful, and respectful of local values and norms. Ties perceived as exploitative or colonial, however strong, do not seem to bring groups together. Contacts that are involuntary for one party are not conducive to community building, nor are highly status-conscious relations. Contacts between disparate cultures may also arouse conflict rather than bring the cultures together. Tourists from rich countries to poor countries, for instance, may create animosities among their hosts and distress in their own minds. The nature of the contacts in each particular case must be examined before any firm conclusions about their effects are made. However, a very general observation can be made: ties between nations that are culturally similar and perhaps geographically close are more likely to be favorable.

SECURITY COMMUNITIES

One possible outcome of this process of transnational interaction, if it is extensive and sustained over a reasonable period of time, is the emergence of a supranational political community. Deutsch and colleagues were especially interested in the implications of the community-building process for international peace, and defined a **security community** as

> a group of people which has become "integrated." By *integration* we mean the attainment, within a territory, of a "sense of community" and of institutions and practices strong enough and widespread enough to assure, for a "long" time, dependable expectations of "peaceful change" among its population. By *sense of community* we mean a belief ... that common social problems must and can be resolved by processes of "peaceful change."[19]

In describing a security community as the result of a process of social integration, there is an emphasis on peaceful change, an ability and willingness to accommodate new demands and needs, not merely the maintenance of a status quo that may be unjust. It is a situation in which participants frequently harmonize their interests, compromise on their differences, and reap mutual rewards. There still

---

[19] Deutsch et al., *Political Community and the North Atlantic Area*, p. 5. See also Emanuel Adler and Michael Barnett, eds., *Security Communities in Comparative and Historical Perspective* (Cambridge: Cambridge University Press, 1998); Alex J. Bellamy, *Security Communities and their Neighbours: Regional Fortresses or Global Integrators?* (New York: Palgrave Macmillan, 2004).

may be some conflicts of interest, but the use or threat of force to resolve conflict is absent. This is positive peace.

Individuals' perceptions of their self-interests can be greatly broadened so that they are willing to make certain sacrifices whether those sacrifices are directly reciprocated. For example, members of a family will make sacrifices for their common welfare or for the welfare of one of them. Identification and affection may be so strong that on some matters a husband or a wife comes to prefer to do what the spouse wants rather than what he or she had originally desired. Although radicals are often critical of the subtle ways in which the internalization of common values can encourage behavior that seems to contradict self-interests, a community-building perspective emphasizes the positive aspects. In effect, there is a tacit agreement—tacit because if stated openly it becomes a very fragile affair—not to coerce others and to limit the scope of bargaining. One gives up certain bargaining options without having to admit it. Within the OECD community, for example, states have substantially given up the use of military force against each other (which flies in the face of realist beliefs). As within marriage, each partner bargains. But in a reasonably good relationship the partners recognize their common interest in keeping the bargaining limited and share a desire to avoid coercing or breaking up the union.

Integration need not involve the creation of a single political entity, or "amalgamated" security community; states may retain their sovereign independence, thereby forming a "pluralistic" security community, but one still based on a degree of shared identity.[20] The only serious violent conflict within the OECD area in recent years has been within a few countries, notably in Northern Ireland. It is not simply that an institution there—the common government—is unable to prevent violence. Rather, the common government is a *cause* of the violence. There have been many cases of civil war and secession in history; people may fight against a common government but then live in peace as separate states. Common institutions are no panacea for peace. Neither is any simple prescription for world federation, let alone world government. For early theorists of integration—functionalists like Mitrany and Haas, as well as transactionists like Deutsch—the goal was peace between and within states. Institution building often contributes to that kind of integration, but under some circumstances may diminish it.

ZONES OF TURMOIL

We have discussed various explanations of the democratic peace, Kant's prescription for perpetual peace, and notions of peace through integration. Each cluster of explanations sheds light on the zone of peace in contemporary world politics. We now can speculate on whether the experience of the OECD countries gives us any reason to hope that a stable peace based on something more than simply

---

[20] See Thomas Risse, "A European Identity? Europeanization and the Evolution of Nation-State Identities," in Maria Green Cowles, James Caporaso, and Thomas Risse, eds., *Transforming Europe: Europeanization and Domestic Change* (Ithaca, N.Y.: Cornell University Press, 2001); Richard K. Herrmann, Thomas Risse, and Marilynn B. Brewer, eds., *Transnational Identities: Becoming European in the EU* (Lanham, Md.: Rowman & Littlefield, 2004).

dominance or mutual deterrence can be achieved in other parts of the world. In doing so, we remain skeptical of realist assumptions about the inevitability of the pursuit of power and the prospect of violent conflict among all kinds of states. We are thinking like liberals—some might say idealists—in search for hints about what an alternative world might look like. Yet we are thinking "realistically" in that we are asking whether conditions that *already* exist in part of the world might be extended further.

One hopeful sign is that the global levels of political democracy, economic interdependence, and international organization can be expected to continue their upward trends. Figure 11.3 shows three important trends in world politics. One is the average "democracy score" for all countries in the world from 1965 to 2006. The index is constructed by the Polity Project to assess the degree of democratic governance in each state based on political participation, executive recruitment, and constraints of the chief executive.[21] Countries that most observers would consider democratic (like the OECD) have higher indexes, but even nondemocratic polities may have select democratic features. (Social scientists usually designate as democracies those regimes that score 7 or more on the 0 to 10 Polity scale.) The average level of democracy has been steadily increasing since the mid-1970s, and turned up rather sharply after the end of the cold war.[22] The chart also shows the trend in interdependence, as measured by the average level of economic openness (imports and exports as a share of GDP), and the trend in states' average number of memberships in IGOs (as full or associate members, or observers). Both measures also exhibit a steady rise over the period. Based on what social scientific research tells us about the contribution of each of these factors to reducing the risk of war between states, these trends do indeed encourage the hope that the peace enjoyed by the OECD can be expanded to other regions.

Many countries that had formerly been dictatorships—both communist countries and military regimes—have moved partially or almost entirely toward free democratic governments. The shift has been dramatic and almost worldwide. A key question is whether relations in all of Europe, including the former communist countries, can be those of a security community. Liberalization in the Soviet bloc began in the 1980s. By 1991, several Eastern European countries were fully democratic, and all had progressed far in that direction. That bodes well for a peaceful future in all of Europe. In some of these states, however, democracy is not secure. If perceiving another state as democratic is important to peace, one aspect of the perception must be that the other is dependably, stably democratic. That is much less certain. Few Eastern European countries have an experience of stable democratic practices and institutions (none, except for the former Czechoslovakia, had more than ten years of multiparty democracy in this century before 1990). They are beset by ethnic and nationalist rivalries. Although these rivalries led to the

---

[21] Monty G. Marshall and Keith Jaggers, "Polity IV Project: Regime Characteristics and Transitions, 1800–2004," October 24, 2007, available at <http://www.systemicpeace.org/inscr/inscr.htm>.

[22] It is also an upward trend in the *number* of democratic states in the international system. See KristianGleditsch and Michael D.Ward, "Diffusion and the International Context of Democratization," *International Organization* 60 (Fall 2006), pp. 911–933; HarveyStarr and ChristinaLindborg, "Democratic Dominoes Revisited: The Hazards of Governmental Transitions, 1974–1996," *Journal of Conflict Resolution* 47 (August 2003), pp. 490–519.

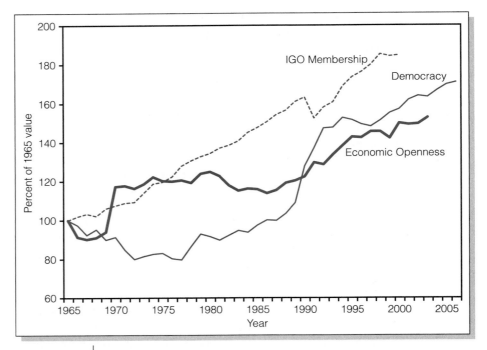

FIGURE 11.3 | TRENDS IN DEMOCRACY, ECONOMIC OPENNESS, AND IGO MEMBERSHIP, 1965–2006

The trend lines show the average level of democracy, economic openness, and IGO membership for all countries (expressed as a percent of their values in 1965). All three of Kant's ingredients for perpetual peace in the international system have generally been on the rise since the 1970s. On average, states are more democratic, trade more, and belong to more IGOs.

Source: Level of democracy is computed using the democracy index (0 to 10 scale) compiled by the Polity IV Project, "Political Regime Characteristics and Transitions, 1800–2006," October 24, 2007, available at <http://www.systemicpeace.org/inscr/inscr.htm>. Economic openness is the constant-dollar openness index (imports and exports as a share of GDP) from Alan Heston, Robert Summers, and Bettina Aten, "Penn World Table, version 6.2," September 2006, available at <http://pwt.econ.upenn.edu/>. IGO membership is the number of IGOs in which states are full or associate members, or observers; data are from Jon Pevehouse, Timothy Nordstrom, and Kevin Warnke, "Intergovernmental Organizations, 1815–2000: A New Correlates of War Data Set," December 9, 2003, available at <http://www.correlatesofwar.org/>.

peaceful separation of the Slovak and Czech Republics, they have brought violence in Russia (for instance, in Chechnya) and especially in the former Yugoslavia (Bosnia and Kosovo). The admission of many Eastern European countries to NATO and the EU is meant to solidify their commitment to democracy and free markets.

DANGEROUS DEMOCRATIC TRANSITIONS

We should probably expect that the occurrence of international conflict will decline over time if more countries adopt stable democratic forms of government. However, the process of changing from a dictatorship to a democracy may raise problems. For instance, in Chapter 6 we discussed domestic factors, like the rally-'round-the-flag effect, which may increase even a democratic state's willingness to engage in "diversionary" war. Diversionary impulses continue to interest international relations scholars, and they may be most potent in states undergoing transitions between autocratic and democratic political regimes.

It is easy to imagine reasons why democratization, or political change generally, might affect a state's foreign policy. A newly installed political system, whether democratic or autocratic, is more likely to be unstable. This could tempt neighbors to threaten or attack it while it is weak and not fully in control of the resources of government and the nation. This temptation seems to have seduced Iraqi President Saddam Hussein into attacking Iran in 1980 after the shah's monarchical autocracy was replaced by a revolutionary Islamic dictatorship headed by Ayatollah Khomeini. In addition, dramatic changes in government often occur at times of social and economic turmoil when the populace's standard of living is sharply reduced or endangered. A domestic crisis may encourage a new regime to pick a quarrel with another state in order to solidify its support at home.

The dangers of political transitions—in both the democratic and autocratic directions—are well illustrated by the French Revolution. The revolution started in 1789 with the installation of a democratic government that first sharply restricted the power of the monarchy and then violently abolished it. By April 1792, France was at war with Austria, a war that both sides apparently wanted. The war quickly widened and, by February 1792, Britain, the Netherlands, Sardinia, and Spain were added to France's adversaries. The revolutionary ideology promoted by France threatened to undermine all the monarchies of Europe. They, in turn, sought to crush the threat at its source. Meanwhile, the French republicans became increasingly radical and violent toward their domestic opponents, and France deteriorated into a reign of terror and dictatorship. In 1798, Napoléon staged a coup d'état and eventually crowned himself emperor. The Napoleonic Wars soon swept over Europe, reaching from Madrid to Moscow. Peace was restored only in 1815 with Napoléon's final defeat at Waterloo.

Revolutionary France, in both its democratic and imperial periods, waged war on many states. But are states that are undergoing democratic transitions generally more prone to become involved in international conflicts than states that have been democratic for some time? Those who say yes start with the observation that the process of democratization opens up the arena of political competition and requires elites to appeal to large constituencies if they hope to acquire or maintain political power. Nationalist themes are especially tempting because they strike a chord with a broad cross-section of society. Unfortunately, nationalism frequently goes hand in hand with belligerency, and whether this belligerency is intentionally stirred up by elites or simply a by-product of their nationalist appeals, there is a danger that hostility will be directed outward to neighboring states. In mature democracies, where political competition is more fully institutionalized, elites who embark on unwise and costly foreign adventures can expect to be held accountable by the public. Where democratic institutions are weak, as they are in the early phases of democratic transitions, elites are less likely to suffer the same consequences; demagoguery goes a long way to ensure political survival in the context of institutional underdevelopment. It is this explosive combination—electoral mobilization alongside weakly institutionalized elite accountability—that may make democratization a threat to peace.[23]

Although the experience of former Yugoslavia suggests that the emergence of open political competition may be tumultuous and sometimes quite violent, the risks of democratization may be overstated. The greatest danger lies in democratic transitions cut short. The end of autocratic rule does not always unleash forces of virulent nationalism, but when it does, the consolidation of democratic institutions is part of the solution. Virtually all instances of democratization and violence have involved states that were still incompletely democratic. These cases tell us less about the dangers posed by democratic transitions than about the risk of conflict for states that have not yet reached a high level of democracy. Once a state becomes an institutionalized democracy, the risk of external conflict falls sharply. So does the risk of serious internal conflict. Although some established democracies do exhibit severe tensions among ethnic groups, they typically manage them without major lethal violence. Democracies offer institutionalized protections to minorities, and they provide peaceful procedures and expectations for containing and resolving conflicts. Killings, when they happen, are usually the work of fringe groups representing only a minority within the minority. Full-scale civil war—not uncommon in destabilized authoritarian systems—is virtually unknown in established democracies.[24]

A brand-new democracy may be unstable and may face fierce problems of restructuring its economy and satisfying diverse interests and ethnic groups. All the East European states experienced abrupt drops in their national incomes as they lost their former assured markets and supplies in other communist countries (previously joined economically in COMECON) and, especially, as they moved painfully from socialist command economies to free-market ones. People may not indefinitely support democratic governments that cannot deliver the economic goods. We have seen a return of some aspects of authoritarian government in post-communist regimes—developments not necessarily unwelcome by a populace struggling to adapt to new economic realities. Most of the East European states have now been admitted to the European Union, under conditions requiring them to open their markets to other EU members, to remain democratic, and to settle any border disputes with their neighbors.

Russia, however, is a particular concern, partly because it is by far the biggest of the former communist countries and still a nuclear military power. Democratization and the creation of a market economy have further to go there than in most other European countries. The governing parties control much of the mass media; elections are inordinately influenced by those with money to advertise and conduct polls; many of the new capitalists who dominate the government and economy are former Soviet bureaucrats who enriched themselves with corrupt deals; and the

---

[23] Edward D. Mansfield and Jack Snyder, *Electing to Fight: Why Emerging Democracies Go to War* (Cambridge, Mass.: MIT Press, 2005); Jack Snyder, *From Voting to Violence: Democratization and Nationalist Conflict* (New York: Norton, 2000).

[24] See, for example, HåvardHegre, TanjaEllingsen, ScottGates, and Nils PetterGleditsch, "Toward a Democratic Civil Peace? Democracy, Political Change, and Civil War 1816–1992," *American Political Science Review* 95 (March 2001), pp. 33–48.

economy is a mix of freedom, central control, bribery, and chaos.[25] Vladimir Putin, having served as president for the maximum two terms under the Russian constitution, nevertheless continues to wield power as prime minister, an appointment he received from his hand-picked successor, Dmitri Medvedev. The fact that Medvedev handily won the presidential election of 2008 and Putin himself remains quite popular in Russia suggests that neither elections nor public popularity are sufficient measures of consolidated democracy. Nevertheless, despite Russia's incomplete democratic transition, it has not become embroiled in a military conflict with any other state—as the dangerous-democratizer thesis might predict.

DEMOCRATIC PEACE ... THROUGH FORCE?

The policy of "peace through strength" has long been associated with the realist view of world politics and is grounded in balance-of-power theory. A different view, one we referred to as offensive idealism in Chapter 4, goes further and subscribes to a policy of "democratic peace through force." It has long been the policy of the democratic major powers, and especially the United States, to promote democratic reform worldwide—a policy that predates the accumulation of social scientific research linking democracy to domestic and international peace. Yet the end of the cold war and the dissipation of the major ideological challenge to representative democracy and market capitalism brought with it a greater willingness to discuss the use of military force as a means of toppling authoritarian regimes, with the expectation that democratization, while good for those liberated from tyrannical rule, is also good for regional and international security.[26]

Examples commonly invoked by advocates of forceful democratization are the post–World War II experiences of the western allies in Germany and the United States in Japan. Their goal at the beginning of the war was one of avoiding defeat, not regime change per se, but as early as the Atlantic Charter in August 1941—before the United States was actually at war—Churchill and Roosevelt declared that their vision of peace in the postwar period included self-government for all peoples, a restatement of earlier Wilsonian principles. Their postwar policy was built on the belief that the former autocratic German and Japanese governments could never have been peaceful, and that it was essential to democratize their political systems. To this end they devoted enormous material and intellectual resources. Their success served to motivate those in the administration of George W. Bush who hoped to achieve a similar result in Iraq.

---

[25] Michael McFaul, *Russia's Unfinished Revolution: Political Change from Gorbachev to Putin* (Ithaca, N.Y.: Cornell University Press, 2001); Valerie Bunce, "Comparative Democratization: Lessons from Russia and the Postcommunist World," in Michael McFaul and Kathryn Stoner-Weiss, eds., *After the Collapse of Communism: Comparative Lessons of Transition* (Cambridge: Cambridge University Press, 2004).

[26] See, for example, William Kristol and Robert Kagan, *Present Dangers: Crisis and Opportunity in American Foreign and Defense Policy* (San Francisco: Encounter, 2000); Stanley Kurtz, "Democratic Imperialism: A Blueprint," *Policy Review* 118 (2003), pp. 3–21. For a critique of this policy in light of policy-relevant social scientific evidence, see Bruce Russett, "Bushwhacking the Democratic Peace," *International Studies Perspectives* 6 (November 2005), pp. 395–408.

The difficulty, as is so often the case when making policy by analogy, was that Germany and Japan were poor analogues. Not only had the allies been willing and able to carry on a long occupation and provide massive economic assistance, Germany and Japan met most of the conditions identified by political analysts as conducive to successful democratic transitions and consolidations. Iraq, on the other hand, was (and is) saddled with many of the conditions analysts identify as negative influences on democratization: low per capita income (at least over the past two decades), no previous history of democracy, and the alleged authoritarian character of Islamic and especially Arab culture. Iraq also experienced what some call the "resource curse"—an economy dependent on petroleum exports—and was long governed by an autocratic regime in which a strongman or ruling family horded wealth, doling it out as necessary to maintain social stability and acquiescence from their position of privilege. Finally, Iraq is located in a geopolitical neighborhood populated largely by dictatorships, with a history of militarization and violent international conflict. So it was a hard case from the start, even had the postinvasion occupation and reconstruction not gone so badly.[27]

Sometimes vital national or humanitarian interests may leave little choice; war might be necessary to remove a government that is a threat to international peace or is viciously oppressing its own people. The responsibility inherited by the intervening state to put the defeated country back together again with a decent government should include democratization as a centerpiece. But that is quite different from imposing democracy when truly vital national and humanitarian interests are not at stake. As a general principle, democratization by force is full of practical and moral dangers, depending on many conditions and very unpredictable contingencies. Most analysts—realists, liberals, and radicals—believe that democratization should not to be undertaken as the purpose in a war of choice. We can set aside the difficult ethical question of whether and, if so, when regime change should be engineered by force, and ask the question: Is it likely to succeed? If the odds are bad from the start, then the ethical question becomes much easier to answer.

Although there is some evidence linking U.S. military intervention to the democratization of target states, when looking at the specific cases of interventions intended (wholly or in part) to contribute to the creation or consolidation of democratic regimes, fewer than half succeeded. And democratization was almost never the by-product of U.S. interventions undertaken for purposes other than regime change. The success rate for military interventions by Britain and France is even worse. Furthermore, there is little evidence that imposing democratic reforms on a state in an otherwise nondemocratic region will serve to encourage democratization elsewhere in the region. These and other studies of intervention recognize that the promotion of democracy is rarely the sole purpose of military action by the United States or other democratic major powers. When democratic reforms prove difficult—usually they do—and threaten the intervener's other policy aims, the

---

[27] David Edelstein, "Occupational Hazards: Why Military Occupations Succeed or Fail," *International Security* 29 (Summer 2004), pp. 49–91; Larry Diamond, "What Went Wrong in Iraq," *Foreign Affairs* 83 (September/October 2004), pp. 34–56. An analysis of authoritarian government in the Muslim world is Stephen Fish, "Islam and Authoritarianism," *World Politics* 55 (October 2002), pp. 4–37.

intervening government's own electoral survival normally dictates that democratization be abandoned altogether or that it be limited to mainly symbolic reforms, even rigged elections.[28] Multilateral operations like those mounted by the United Nations, even the more forceful ones, seem to have a better track record than unilateral interventions.

International organizations, particularly IGOs composed primarily of democracies, have developed noncoercive processes to assist democratic transitions. The greater the proportion of stable democratic states in the IGO, the more credible its guarantees of assistance are, the more interested it will be in promoting reforms, and the more likely it will set constraining conditions and enforce them. IGOs can change the cost–benefit perceptions of domestic elites who may not be enthusiastic about democracy in the first place and can make continued democracy a condition for continued IGO membership.[29] NATO has such a condition. It did not eject Greece or Turkey when their governments turned autocratic in the past, but the threat is more credible now that cold war toleration of friendly dictators is over.

IGOs with serious economic assets to deploy can also provide incentives to reluctant elites. The EU began with a commitment to democracy. It was required by Article 237 of the Treaty of Rome that began the integration process in 1950. The European Parliament strengthened this commitment in 1962, by requiring that would-be members guarantee "truly democratic practices and respect for fundamental rights and freedoms." After the Greek military coup in 1967, the EU suspended its Association Treaty with Greece, and threatened to cancel the agreement entirely. Nearly half of Greece's total trade was with the EU, and even the junta's conservative supporters began to desert it. The junta fell in 1974. In newly democratic Spain in 1981, the business community helped defeat a coup so as not to jeopardize the country's entry into the EU. The democratization process in the Czech Republic, Hungary, and Poland was far advanced by the time their applications to join the EU were considered, but for later entrants the EU's democracy condition probably played a stronger role. The EU has enormous resources available for the economic development of its less-prosperous members, and its combination of carrots and sticks can deeply affect many constituencies in candidate states. It is surely the most powerful international institution in this respect. Free-trade agreements outside of Europe lack such strong incentives, but typically do require a commitment to democracy by their members.

Kant's idea was not simply that democracy, trade, and international organization separately contribute to peace. He, and subsequently the founders of the EU, also understood that each element supports the other. Causal arrows can be drawn around the outside of the Kantian triangle (recall Figure 11.1). Democracies trade more heavily with each other than dictatorships do and are more likely to

---

[28] Jeffrey Pickering and Mark Peceny, "Forging Democracy at Gunpoint," *International Studies Quarterly* 50 (September 2006), pp. 539–559; Andrew J. Enterline, "Beacons of Hope? The Impact of Imposed Democracy on Regional Peace, Democracy and Prosperity," *Journal of Politics* 67 (November 2005), pp. 1075–1098; Bruce Bueno de Mesquita and George W. Downs, "Intervention and Democracy," *International Organization* 60 (Summer 2006): pp. 627–649.

[29] See, for example, Jon C. Pevehouse, *Democracy from Above: Regional Organizations and Democratization* (Cambridge: Cambridge University Press, 2005).

join international organizations with other democracies. International organizations protect and promote trade, and trading states form IGOs among each other for just that purpose. Some IGOs—like the UN and the EU—strengthen and solidify democracy. Trade can stimulate economic growth to satisfy the material needs of people who want to govern themselves democratically. Finally, peace itself provides conditions under which democracy, commerce, and international institutions can thrive; the causal arrows can go back from the center of the triangle to its corners. The Kantian principles become a self-reinforcing system—not guaranteed to succeed but offering a basis for success by leaders and citizens who understand them.

CONCLUSION TO PART II

Part II of this book examined major themes in international conflict and cooperation. We started by discussing the basic causes of social violence and then considered several explanations for interstate conflict. Causes of war can be located at all of the levels of analysis we introduced in Part I, and the focus of researchers typically depends on the theoretical approach to world politics they find to be most persuasive. Thus, realists have examined causes at the systemic level, especially the distribution of power, while liberals and radicals often concentrate on domestic politics and economics. More recently, the rational choice approach, which models the strategic interaction of players in a "game," has provided key insights into the tragic logic that traps state leaders as they head down the road to war. We also considered the forces driving conflict within states, especially ethnonationalism, as well as various forms of unconventional conflict. Although the cold war ended two decades ago, internal conflicts and terrorism remain as disturbing features of contemporary world politics.

Hostility cannot become warfare unless states, and nonstate actors, acquire the instruments with which to fight. Clearly they have, and the capacity of modern military arsenals—particularly weapons of mass destruction—to wreak havoc on the human race, not to mention other species, is truly frightening. One wonders how the major states of the world could have arrived at such a high state of militarization considering not only the risks of mass destruction but also the substantial economic costs involved. Again, game theory illustrates well the logic that drives this security dilemma. One ray of hope has been the real progress in arms control that first accompanied, then followed the end of the cold war. Now disarmament, not just arms control, is meeting with success in certain areas.

Of course, world politics is not all about weapons and war. In most societies, violence is not the typical form of social interaction; behavior is usually guided by social norms, laws, and institutions. So, too, in the society of states. We have discussed the importance of international organization and law, including the existence and widespread (though certainly not universal) adherence to laws governing warfare, the most primitive form of state behavior. Although few mechanisms exist in world politics for the enforcement of international law—international organizations like the UN do not have the same authority in international society as national governments do in domestic society—we should not underestimate the extent to which states really do feel bound by the norms and laws that bring order to world politics. Domestic order rarely rests solely on coercion; neither does international order.

Peace, not war, is the normal state of affairs in world politics. That is no reason for complacency, however. We can learn much from the enduring peace that has emerged among the industrialized countries of the OECD and elsewhere. Explanations vary, but most emphasize pacifying effects of democratic governance as well as increased social and economic transactions between states. Can the zone of peace be expanded during the twenty-first century? We are optimistic. There is a trend toward more democratic forms of government and more open economic systems, both fostered in part by increased membership in international organizations. However, some of the biggest impediments to both domestic and international stability—and therefore to stable peace—derive from international economic uncertainties. In Part III we turn to the nexus between politics and economics in world affairs.

Commerce and manufactures gradually introduced order and good government, and with them the liberty and security of individuals.

—Adam Smith

Finance capital and the trusts are increasing instead of diminishing the differences in the rate of development of various parts of the world economy.

—V. I. Lenin

INTERNATIONAL POLITICAL ECONOMY

PART 3

POLITICAL ECONOMY OF NATIONAL SECURITY AND DEFENSE

CHAPTER 12

APPROACHES TO POLITICAL ECONOMY

Political economy, as the term implies, refers to the intersection of politics and economics. It is a concept used to describe individual and state behavior, as well as the outcomes of social interaction, that involves both political and economic considerations. **International political economy** (IPE), then, focuses on the combined political and economic behavior taking place among state and nonstate international actors. It refers equally to the politics of international economics and the economics of international politics. World politics provides few examples of purely political phenomena. Most of the issues this book has so far examined have economic dimensions; nearly all matters examined by international economists have political dimensions. However, subjects usually considered to be the focus of IPE include international trade and monetary relations between states, the activities of international institutions that facilitate economic cooperation, and global economic development. The chapters in Part III examine each of these subjects.

Other topics, like some of those discussed in this chapter, have much to do with *domestic* political economy but are relevant to world politics because they pertain to national defense and international security. Wartime industrial mobilization, the economic impact of defense spending, the dislocating effects of military base closings, and the conversion of military-related manufacturing to civilian use are examples. These issues have taken on added significance with military downsizing in the United States, Russia, and elsewhere following the end of the cold war. But before turning to such topics, let us reconsider the main theoretical approaches to world politics and their perspectives on international political economy.

REALISM, LIBERALISM, AND RADICALISM

In Chapter 2 we introduced three alternative views of international relations, and throughout the book we have highlighted the ways in which these perspectives differ on various issues in world politics, especially international conflict and cooperation. These same views—realism, liberalism, and radicalism—can be found when we shift our discussion to topics in international political economy.

The realist perspective emphasizes the role of the state in global economic affairs in much the same way that the state occupies center stage in global political affairs. The realist approach to the study of international political economy—relatively new in the long history of realist thought, which has tended to neglect the economic dimensions of world politics—is often called *neorealism*. Realists are the intellectual descendants of mercantilists. **Mercantilism** was the economic doctrine pursued by the major states of Europe before the nineteenth century. Monarchs believed that the best way to maximize wealth and to reduce the vulnerability of their states was to actively encourage exports while discouraging imports, thereby adding to their stocks of gold and silver (the currency of international trade at that time). The surplus could then be used to promote industrial development, to build the bureaucratic infrastructure of the government, and to strengthen the army and navy. In short, the nation's economic activities were to be enlisted in support of self-sufficiency and state power. Mercantilist views were not confined to Europe, however. In his famous *Report on Manufactures*, Alexander Hamilton wrote that "Every nation . . . ought to endeavor to possess within itself, all the essentials of national supply. These comprise the means of subsistence, habitation, clothing, and defense."

Realism is not the same as mercantilism, but the emphasis on the state's ability and willingness to intervene in the market in the pursuit of national interests is reminiscent of mercantilist doctrine. Indeed, the realist approach to international political economy is sometimes called *neomercantilism*. Consistent with their focus on the state as the guarantor of economic power, realists are skeptical that nonstate actors can have much of an independent impact on global political-economic relations. IGOs and NGOs, including multinational corporations (MNCs), seem to be most effective in world affairs when their activities promote the national interests of the most powerful states in the international system, not because they wield much influence by themselves.

Liberals, on the other hand, are less confident that the state occupies such an exalted position in the international political economy. To be sure, states are important actors—generally, the *most* important actors—but when it comes to the global economy, the state shares the stage with some very significant others. International organizations and MNCs may not have the resources available to major states in the international system (including, of course, national armies), but traditional forms of state power are not always effective in contemporary economic affairs. Liberals therefore tend to focus on the limits of state power and the tendency of states to redefine their national interests in the context of changing international economic conditions.

Where the realist view sees potential conflict, the liberal view sees potential harmony. If, as realists suggest, foreign economic policy is designed to maximize a state's wealth and power in world affairs, then states will be wary of policies and agreements that diminish their position in the global pecking order. In other words, states are interested in maximizing their **relative gains**, lest any emerging gaps in capabilities be turned against them in the future. But liberals argue that states pursue **absolute gains**. Arrangements that improve the welfare of society are really what motivate a state's foreign economic policy, even when those arrangements may be of greater benefit to other societies. Because it is easier to satisfy parties seeking absolute gains than those who are also jockeying for a better position relative to others, liberals are more inclined than realists to see potential for international cooperation on global economic matters. For realists, when states seem to be cooperating, it is probably because this "cooperation" has somehow been coerced (or perhaps purchased) by the most powerful states.

Liberals also tend to have abiding faith in the individual and in the market. Social harmony is possible, both domestically and internationally, and it is better achieved by deferring to the "invisible hand" of the free market than by resorting to the heavy hand of state intervention. This argument was first developed in the eighteenth century by Scottish philosopher Adam Smith—in his famous *The Wealth of Nations*—as a reaction to the mercantilist beliefs driving the foreign policies of European states during his time. Smith was not opposed to government intervention in the national economy when it was essential to national security. But, as a general matter, he believed that the wealth of the nation, and ultimately the power of the state, was better built up by free trade than by autarky: "Fleets and armies are maintained not with gold and silver, but with consumable goods. The nation which, from the annual produce of its domestic industry, . . . has the wherewithal to purchase those consumable goods in distant countries, can maintain foreign wars there."[1]

The third perspective we introduced in Chapter 2 was radicalism, or *Marxism* as it is often called. Actually, Karl Marx wrote relatively little about *international* political economy; the task of adapting Marxist thought to international relations was taken up by V. I. Lenin, among others.[2] In contrast to liberals, radicals do not expect that social harmony can be achieved among individuals of different classes. Like realists, they are suspicious of what may appear on the surface to be cooperative economic arrangements between states, especially states at different stages of economic development. Economic relations between the developed countries of the North and developing countries of the South are fundamentally unequal. But while realists believe that international cooperation is undertaken for the benefit of the most powerful *states* in the international system, radicals argue that it is the international capitalist *class* that benefits. Capitalists in the advanced industrialized countries obviously gain from international trade and from foreign investment by their MNCs, but even capitalists in less-developed countries profit from unequal economic relationships. The working classes are the losers all around, particularly in less-developed countries. According to the radical view, by treating states as if they were unitary actors pursuing wealth and power, realists

---

[1] Adam Smith, *An Inquiry into the Nature and Causes of the Wealth of Nations,* edited with an introduction by Kathryn Sutherland (Oxford: Oxford University Press, 1993), p. 285. On the strategic implications of Smith's and Hamilton's views, see Edward Mead Earle, "Adam Smith, Alexander Hamilton, and Friedrich List: The Economic Foundations of Military Power," in Peter Paret, ed., *Makers of Modern Strategy from Machiavelli to the Nuclear Age* (Princeton, N.J.: Princeton University Press, 1986).

[2] See especially V. I. Lenin, *Imperialism: The Highest Stage of Capitalism* (New York: International Publishers, 1939).

overlook important, class-based conflicts of interests in the international political economy.

The radical perspective is alive and well despite the collapse of Soviet-style socialism as a viable political-economic model for society. Contemporary radical thinkers tend to look less to Marx for insights than to Antonio Gramsci. In contrast to Marx, Gramsci was less certain about whether existing structures of political dominance would ultimately collapse at an advanced stage of capitalist development. He instead tried to explain how the position of the dominant classes becomes viewed as entirely legitimate—that is, the subject of "spontaneous consent" by the masses—through the subtle mechanisms of socialization. Many scholars have found these ideas useful for understanding globalization, particularly its widespread (though far from universal) acceptance as a natural and largely positive outgrowth of economic and technological development. Globalization does have its discontents, and the radical perspective sheds light on their grievances and often champions their acts of resistance.[3]

These three competing perspectives on the political-economic dimensions of international relations are evident in many of the issues we address in Part III. No single view dominates the study of international political economy. On some matters, realism, liberalism, and radicalism offer alternative and plausible interpretations of the same things—international trade, economic development, globalization, and so on—but they also draw our attention to different aspects of IPE, as we shall see.

ECONOMICS AND STATECRAFT

In Chapter 5 we briefly discussed the economic instruments states use to influence other states. The use of economic techniques for international influence is designed to exploit the vulnerability of another state in order to persuade its leaders to do something they would not otherwise do. Few states can completely isolate themselves economically because other states have at least some of what they need. Thus, most states are subject to attempted influence through the manipulation of these economic dependencies. Whether the manipulation of economic ties is an effective means of influence is another question and has been the subject of debate among scholars and policy makers for a long time.

ECONOMIC COERCION

Economic statecraft includes any economic means of influencing the behavior of another state and encompasses both inducements and sanctions. Negative economic sanctions are forms of **economic coercion**—actions or threats to disrupt economic exchange unless the target state modifies its behavior as demanded—and these can vary greatly in terms of severity. The use of tariffs, quotas, and other restrictions on free trade usually fall toward the less severe end of the spectrum,

---

[3] See Antonio Gramsci, *Selection from Prison Notebooks of Antonio Gramsci,* trans. by Quintin Hoare and Geoffrey Nowell-Smith (London: Lawrence and Wishart, 1971).

and we discuss these policy instruments in the next chapter. For the moment, we want to focus on more severe forms of economic coercion. The most extreme form is *economic warfare*: the use of severe economic coercion to change the behavior of an adversary, usually accompanied by political isolation and sometimes the use of military force.[4]

Like warfare in general, full-blown economic warfare is not a commonly used instrument of statecraft. Economic sanctions, especially during peacetime, more often take the form of comprehensive or partial trade embargoes, bans on investment, and the freezing of assets. Although sanctions may exact significant economic costs, one comprehensive study of economic sanctions reported that of the approximately 200 sanctions that states imposed on other states from World War I until the end of the century, 20 percent sought to bring about only modest policy changes on the part of the target. That economic sanctions need not mean economic warfare is also evident from the list of countries having experienced U.S. sanctions, which includes U.S. allies and close trading partners—like Canada and Japan (in regard to fishing)—whose specific trade or investment practices had at some point raised the ire of the U.S. Congress.[5] For example, the Helms–Burton Act, passed in 1996, sought to punish foreign companies that invest in Cuban assets formerly owned by Americans but nationalized by the Castro regime. Of course, such punishments differ markedly from the much more coercive sanctions imposed on Cuba itself.

Sanctions can have more ambitious aims, such as destabilizing an unfriendly government or impairing a target's military activities. Before the mid-1970s, such goals were about as common as attempts to bring about policy changes, but since the 1970s they have represented a much smaller share of the total; the increased use of economic sanctions has been associated with the pursuit of mostly modest goals. On the other hand, there does seem to be a greater willingness on the part of the international community to turn to sanctions as a means of punishing states seen to be in violation of fundamental international norms. During the cold war, the UN Security Council imposed sanctions only twice—against Southern Rhodesia and South Africa—in both instances for the white minority regime's systematic violation of the black majority's human rights. UN-mandated sanctions have been much more common since the end of the cold war. They were imposed on Iraq for its invasion of Kuwait, on Yugoslavia for the use of force against its former republics, on Libya and Afghanistan for their support of terrorism, as well as on Somalia, Liberia, Rwanda, Haiti, and Sierra Leone for various forms of domestic

---

[4] For a discussion of the concepts associated with economic statecraft, see David A. Baldwin, *Economic Statecraft* (Princeton, N.J.: Princeton University Press, 1985); also Jean-Marc F. Blanchard, Edward D. Mansfield, and Norrin M. Ripsman, eds., *Power and the Purse: Economic Statecraft, Interdependence, and National Security* (London: Frank Cass, 2000).

[5] Gary Clyde Hufbauer, Jeffrey J. Schott, and Kimberly Ann Elliot, and Barbara Oegg, *Economic Sanctions Reconsidered*, 3rd ed. (Washington, D.C.: Peterson Institute for International Economics, 2008). On the strategic logic of sanctions, see Daniel W. Drezner, *The Sanctions Paradox: Economic Statecraft and International Relations* (Cambridge: Cambridge University Press, 1999); David A. Baldwin, "The Sanctions Debate and the Logic of Choice," *International Security* 24, 3 (Winter 1999/2000), pp. 80–107.

repression. The UN has even targeted domestic factions *within* states. In 1993, the Security Council embargoed petroleum and petroleum products going to the National Union for Total Independence of Angola (UNITA) guerrillas fighting in Angola (in addition to arms and other forms of military assistance); in Rwanda, Sierra Leone, and the Democratic Republic of the Congo, UN arms embargoes have applied only to nongovernmental groups.

The success of economic coercion depends on how vulnerable the target is to being cut off from a particular foreign good or service (an embargo), or from a particular foreign market for its own goods and services (a boycott). The key issue here is *substitutability*. If the target state can find substitutes for the items covered by the sanction regime, and can do so at acceptable costs, then economic sanctions will fail to change the target state's behavior. At minimum, this would seem to require that prior to the imposition of sanctions the state being punished should have important economic ties with the punishing state. For example, faced with the 1973 oil embargo and price increases by Arab members of OPEC, the countries of Western Europe were strongly affected because they had based their energy policies on the assumption of a continued flow of low-priced oil from the OPEC states, which provided an overwhelming proportion of their supply.

The state being punished must also be unable to find a substitute for the sanctioned item, in terms either of goods or of markets. When the United States under President Dwight Eisenhower attempted to punish Cuba by cutting the U.S. quota of Cuban sugar, Cuba was able to substitute markets by getting the Soviet Union to purchase the newly available sugar. Similarly, when the United States and Western companies cut off Cuba's oil supplies, Castro was able to substitute Soviet oil. On the other hand, when the Arab oil suppliers decided to embargo oil to the United States, Western Europe, and Japan in 1973, there was some short-term acquiescence by European countries and Japan to Arab demands. The Arab states controlled such a large proportion of the oil supply that most of the target countries found substitution difficult. Nevertheless, one country singled out by the Arabs as "unfriendly"—the Netherlands—soon found that it could meet its oil needs by indirect routes. The Arab states produced the chief economic effects by their huge oil price increases rather than by targeting specific countries for embargo. Even then, the effects were largely shifts in target countries' rhetoric (moderated public statements, nearly meaningless votes in the UN), not more substantive shifts. Probably the most important change was simply to increase the prominence of the Arab–Israeli conflict on the agenda of world leaders (especially the United States).

There are ways to fight back against economic sanctions. For example, in response to the hardships imposed by the Arab oil embargo, Nixon announced that the American aim would be energy self-sufficiency by 1980. Until self-sufficiency could be reached, he said, people should learn to sacrifice and even learn to like it. One of the first suggestions the Nixon administration made was that thermostats be turned down in homes, adding that cooler temperatures were healthier. The speed limit on American highways was cut to 55 miles per hour, and it was argued that in addition to saving fuel, this speed was also safer. The United States also took the lead in organizing oil-consuming states into the International Energy Agency to coordinate energy policies and provide mutual aid if another embargo occurred. The Nixon strategy also included creation of a strategic petroleum reserve—a thirty-day supply of oil, which is now about 700 million barrels—increased mining of coal, expanded oil exploration, and a greater emphasis on nuclear-generated electricity. All of these measures were designed to diminish U.S. vulnerability to future oil shocks by securing substitutes for Arab oil.

The punishing state, too, must be able to substitute or be able to afford the cutbacks in supply or purchases. During the Napoleonic Wars, when Britain and France tried to prevent the other from trading with the United States by, among other things, harassing American vessels, President Thomas Jefferson placed an embargo on American exports in an attempt to coerce their recognition of American shipping rights. But the Embargo Acts of 1806 to 1808 caused great economic hardship in the United States, were wildly unpopular, and were frequently flouted by American exporters—dooming any prospects Jefferson might have entertained for a third presidential term. Critics of the increased use of economic sanctions in U.S. foreign policy have often highlighted the consequences for U.S. economic performance, especially lost jobs. For many, such costs are too high given the spotty success rate of economic sanctions as a foreign policy tool.

Changing the behavior of a target state through economic coercion can be very difficult. A major debate over the necessity of resorting to military force against Iraq in 1991 involved whether UN-mandated economic sanctions alone would have compelled Iraq to withdraw from Kuwait. It was clear that sanctions weakened the country considerably and made living conditions far more difficult. It was not clear, however, whether such effects would have moved Saddam Hussein to comply with the UN resolutions. The continued use of sanctions after the Gulf War did not oust Hussein from power, but it did prevent Iraq from rebuilding its military forces. A similar debate on the effectiveness of sanctions surrounded the moves by the South African government to dismantle the apartheid system in 1991 and the subsequent lifting of sanctions by the United States. These cases do show that the greater the number of states complying with sanctions, and the more complete that compliance (more so with Iraq than with South Africa), the greater the impact sanctions will have.

Economic sanctions are a blunt instrument for achieving desired political reform. Their effects very often fall indiscriminately upon the population of the targeted state, while governing elites—those who must persuaded to change the state's course of action—are affected last and least. One study estimated that 90,000 Iraqis died annually from disease and malnutrition caused by the sanctions put in place beginning in 1991. For sanctions to have an effect on leaders, either the leaders must care about the domestic conditions within their countries, or those deteriorating conditions must actually threaten their grip on political power. It may prove extremely difficult for those states imposing such sanctions to recognize either the extent or the gravity of the impact their actions will have on innocent populations. In the event sanctions do cause death, starvation, or disease among innocent populations, it is certainly reasonable to insist that sanctioning states change their practices and policies. But by this point, the damage has already been done. Imposing "smart sanctions"—embargoes with exemptions for the import of food, medicine, and other humanitarian essentials—may provide one escape from the moral dilemma, but then the sanction regime even less likely to have the desired effect on elites.[6]

The success of economic sanctions needs to be measured in terms of the objectives sought through sanctions. Sanctions often do not bring about compliance with major demands. They may be effective in subverting the government of another state, especially if the state is small and its government already shaky. However, they can also be used as international and domestic symbols of political support, opposition, or ideology. Not as risky or provocative as the use of military force, sanctions can still provide the public image of "doing something." This probably best accounts for their continued and even increased use in contemporary world politics, despite persistent criticism regarding their effectiveness and humanitarian impact.[7]

NATIONAL COMPETITION AND GEO-ECONOMICS

Economic warfare is often an outgrowth of a general state of war between states; rarely, if ever, have states engaged in normal economic relations while their militaries fought on the battlefield. Economic warfare has also been used by states to attempt to disrupt military campaigns against third parties. After the Japanese invasion of Manchuria in 1937, the United States began blocking the sale of oil and steel to Japan, and by 1941 the United States had imposed a full trade embargo. But economic competition can also be a cause of war. Although U.S. actions were ostensibly a response to Japan's military activities in China and Southeast Asia, some historians suggest that this should be seen as part of a larger U.S.–Japanese struggle for resources, one that precipitated the attack on Pearl Harbor and full-scale war in the Pacific. Foreign trade and investment are essential to industrial capitalism, and the attempt to secure foreign markets or commodities has often led to clashes over spheres of influence.

The 1990–1991 Gulf War (both the Iraq–Kuwait phase and the U.S.–Iraq phase) served as a reminder that states will go to war at least partly over economic resources, especially over control of such vital resources as oil. Although the George W. Bush administration preferred to stress counterterrorism and liberation as its goals, many critics of the 2003 Iraq War saw it too as a "war for oil." There were multiple reasons for that war—just or unjust, well-intentioned or misguided—but no single factor furnishes Iraq with its strategic importance to the United States and other industrialized countries more than its resource endowment.[8]

---

[6] The toll of sanctions on the Iraqi population is reported in John Mueller and Karl Mueller, "Sanctions of Mass Destruction," *Foreign Affairs* 78 (May/June 1999), pp. 43–53. See also Joy Gordon, "Peaceful, Silent, Deadly Remedy: The Ethics of Economic Sanctions," *Ethics and International Affairs* 13 (1999), pp. 123–142. Smart sanctions are discussed in David Cortright and George A. Lopez, eds., *Smart Sanctions: Targeting Economic Statecraft* (Lanham, Md.: Rowman & Littlefield, 2002).

[7] Ernest H. Preeg, *Feeling Good or Doing Good with Sanctions: Unilateral Economic Sanctions and the U.S. National Interest* (Washington, D.C.: Center for Strategic and International Studies, 1999); Nikolay Marinov, "Do Economic Sanctions Destabilize Country Leaders?" *American Journal of Political Science* 49 (July 2005), pp. 564–576.

[8] Former Chairman of the Federal Reserve, Alan Greenspan, has stated: "I am saddened that it is politically inconvenient to acknowledge what everyone knows: the Iraq war is largely about oil." See his memoir, *The Age of Turbulence: Adventures in a New World* (New York: Penguin, 2007), p. 463.

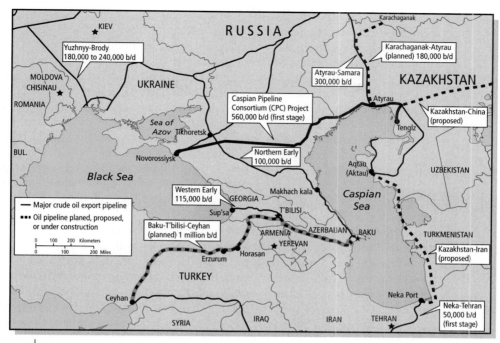

MAP 12.1 | OIL PIPELINE ROUTES IN THE CASPIAN SEA AREA

Possession of natural resources like oil gives states geopolitical and geo-economic advantages in world politics. In the case of an oil-rich country like Azerbaijan, with no direct access to global trade routes, its neighbors may also take on strategic importance (for both suppliers and consumers) to the extent that they can provide pipeline routes to the sea or around potentially hostile or volatile countries.

Oil wealth is now driving a transformation of the Caspian region into what many believe will become a new locale for great-power competition. The post-Soviet states of Azerbaijan, Kazakhstan, and Turkmenistan are well positioned to profit economically and politically from the vast oil and natural gas reserves beneath the Caspian Sea. The region is landlocked, so pipelines must be built to transport the oil to ports before it can make its way to world markets. The proposed routes have important political implications because neighboring states hosting the pipelines could manipulate the flow of oil. Possible routes from Baku, Azerbaijan, for example, might go through Russian or Georgian territory to the Black Sea, through Georgia and Turkey to the Mediterranean, or through Iran to the Persian Gulf (see Map 12.1). Given the state of U.S.–Iranian relations and volatility in the U.S.–Russian relationship, the United States government clearly preferred the route to the Mediterranean (the Baku–Tbilisi–Ceyhan pipeline) but had some difficulty persuading oil companies to take on such a costly project.[9]

---

[9] Gawdat Bahgat, "Pipeline Diplomacy: The Geopolitics of the Caspian Sea Region," *International Studies Perspectives* 3 (August 2002), pp. 310–327. See also Michael T. Klare, *Resource Wars: The New Landscape of Global Conflict* (New York: Henry Holt, 2001).

Internal pressures to expand the state's activities beyond its borders have not subsided in the contemporary world; if anything, they have increased. However, the costs of great-power war, along with changing international norms regarding the resort to force, may make violent conflict over economic resources and practices less likely, especially among the world's major powers. As Edward Luttwak puts it, there has been a shift from geopolitics to *geo-economics*: "If commercial quarrels do lead to political clashes, as they are now much more likely to do with the waning of the imperatives of geopolitics, those political clashes must be fought out with the weapons of commerce." The prefix *geo* implies more than routine economic competition among states. It suggests that the realist "logic of conflict" still motivates the global struggle for power, even though the most effective instruments for that struggle are to be found in the economic arena. Those who see international political economy in geo-economic terms seem to be putting forward a view much like neomercantilism, a view we associated with the realist perspective. However, it may be more accurate to locate proponents of the geo-economic view on some middle ground between realists and liberals, though probably closer to the realist camp.

Although geo-economists see industrial and technological development as boons for the state's military strength, along with liberals they recognize that domestic economic priorities like employment and high living standards are increasingly seen as key elements of the "national interest," especially for advanced capitalist democracies in the zone of peace. But along with realists, geo-economists see more competition than cooperation when it comes to the pursuit of these national interests—including a preoccupation with relative instead of absolute gains—and are generally suspicious of arrangements that would undermine the sovereignty and capacity of the state to secure advantages for itself. Geo-economics is thus "not more and not less than the continuation of the ancient rivalry of nations by new industrial means."[10]

POLITICAL ECONOMY OF DEFENSE

In the West and elsewhere, the end of the cold war brought renewed debate about the future of the defense-industrial base—a state's capacity to develop and manufacture the implements of national defense. Does the risk of a renewed threat from Russia, China, or emerging nuclear states require continued expenditure on expensive strategic nuclear weapons? Do ongoing regional conflicts and transnational terrorism require continued expenditure on conventional forces that can be employed for global reach? If the military and its arsenal are going to be significantly downsized, what factories and military bases, at home and abroad, should be closed? How much of the defense-industrial base should be retained in case rearmament is needed? Important economic issues are involved in such decisions, and these issues highlight the different interests, objectives, and strategies of various groups within society.

---

[10] Edward N. Luttwak, *The Endangered American Dream* (New York: Simon & Schuster, 1993), p. 34; the quote in the previous paragraph is from his "From Geopolitics to Geo-Economics: Logic of Conflict, Grammar of Commerce," *The National Interest* 20 (Summer 1990), p. 21.

MILITARY-INDUSTRIAL COMPLEX

Although realists know that societies are composed of different constituencies with different interests, they believe that on matters of national security these social cleavages tend to give way to a near unity of purpose. In the United States, for example, there emerged after World War II a domestic "cold war consensus" on the domestic priorities that would go hand-in-hand with the foreign policy of containing communist influence.[11] This is why, for realists, states can be treated as essentially unitary actors when it comes to understanding policies designed to promote the geopolitical (and geo-economic) interests of the nation. But when we take a closer look at the national security establishments within states, and the societal groups linked to them, we see that the unitary actor model misses an important part of the picture.

In his last public address as president, General Dwight Eisenhower warned about the political influence of a newly powerful **military–industrial complex**:

> We have been compelled to create a permanent armaments industry of vast proportions. Added to this, three-and-a-half million men and women are directly engaged in the defense establishment. We annually spend on military security alone more than the net income of all United States corporations. Now this conjunction of an immense military establishment and a large arms industry is new in the American experience. The total influence—economic, political, even spiritual—is felt in every city, every statehouse, every office of the federal government. . . . In councils of government we must guard against the acquisition of unwarranted influence, whether sought or unsought, by the military-industrial complex. The potential for the disastrous rise of misplaced power exists and will persist.

The term *military-industrial complex* is now a common expression. In addition to defense industries and the professional military, the military-industrial complex can be interpreted broadly to include politicians whose districts benefit directly from military spending and even labor unions whose memberships are employed disproportionately in the defense sector. The expression often carries negative connotations, as it did for Eisenhower. Whether society as a whole benefits from aggressive foreign policy and high levels of military preparedness, certain groups and sectors in the domestic political economy clearly do benefit. The harshest critics of the military-industrial complex suggest that it exerts pressure on the central government to maintain its military posture at high levels, even when foreign threats diminish, without regard to the potential economic costs imposed on other sectors of the national economy.

In Chapter 6 we discussed the radical view that states are essentially governed by a power elite composed of individuals from the highest echelons of society—politics, business, the military—whose professional paths cross regularly. One manifestation of elite interaction, according to radicals like C. Wright Mills, is overlapping membership on corporate boards, which creates a pattern of "interlocking directorates." In another pioneering study, Gordon Adams attempted to identify overall levels of personnel transfer between the U.S. Department of Defense (DoD)

---

[11] Benjamin O. Fordham, *Building the Cold War Consensus: The Political Economy of U.S. National Security Policy, 1949–1951* (Ann Arbor: University of Michigan Press, 1998).

and defense contractors in the private sector in the 1970s. This "revolving door" allows defense corporations to improve their products by making use of the scientific and technical expertise of former military officers and civilian employees of DoD. More importantly, perhaps, defense contractors can gain information about future research areas deemed important by U.S. military planners, as well as insights into the workings of the procurement process on the government side.

In general, radicals and other critics argue that the cozy relationship between politicians, the military, and defense contractors—what Adams called the "iron triangle"—corrupts the competition for military contracts. Almost any *pattern* in military procurement is suspect, because it suggests that nonmarket considerations have come into play. One analyst, for example, has identified a "follow-on imperative," whereby a contract for a new weapon system (or major component) is awarded to a company as its production of a similar older weapon is winding down. This enables the company to keep its production line open (a good thing for the contractor), but it does not necessarily mean that the contract has been awarded to the most competitive bidder. Sixteen of twenty major aerospace contracts awarded between 1960 and 1988 may be explained in part by the follow-on imperative, including the F-16 fighter as a follow-on to the F-111 (General Dynamics), the Minuteman III ballistic missile as a follow-on to Minuteman (Boeing), and the Trident I submarine-launched missile as a follow-on to Poseidon (Lockheed).[12]

Other procurement practices may be designed to benefit politicians. One study showed that U.S. defense contracts accelerated right before election time, giving a boost to the economy and allowing incumbents to take some credit for improved economic conditions. Prime contractors also tend to distribute their subcontracts among companies located in a number of congressional districts, presumably to ingratiate themselves with as many legislators as possible. Another study found that while pork-barrel politics do not account for congressional voting on major nuclear weapons projects, like the B-1 bomber or the MX missile, legislators do have their constituents in mind when they vote on matters related to military bases.[13] Such procurement decisions may improve politicians' chances for reelection, but they are not necessarily the best decisions from a strict national security point of view. Although these various findings do not lend unequivocal support to the more radical portraits of the military-industrial complex in the United States, they do point to a closer than arm's-length relationship between politicians, the military, and defense contractors, and to the fact that considerations other than cost-effectiveness and performance often enter into decisions regarding military procurement.

Whether defense procurement is seen to serve the economic interests of defense contractors or the electoral interests of politicians, or both, the implication is that it

---

[12] James R.Kurth, "The Military–Industrial Complex Revisited," in Joseph Kruzel, ed., *American Defense Annual, 1989–1990* (Lexington Mass: Lexington Books, 1989); Gordon Adams, *The Iron Triangle: The Politics of Defense Contracting* (New York: Council on Economic Priorities, 1981), especially chap. 6.

[13] See Kenneth R. Mayer, *The Political Economy of Defense Contracting* (New Haven, Conn.: Yale University Press, 1991); James M. Lindsay, *Congress and Nuclear Weapons* (Baltimore: Johns Hopkins University Press, 1991).

TABLE 12.1 | LEADING ARMS COMPANIES, 2006

Firm	Country	Arms Sales ($ Billions)	Arms in Total (Percent)
Boeing	United States	30.7	50
Lockheed Martin	United States	28.1	71
BAE Systems	Britain	24.1	95
Northrop Grumman	United States	23.7	78
Raytheon	United States	19.5	96
General Dynamics	United States	18.8	78
EADS	Western Europe	12.6	25
L-3 Communications	United States	10.0	80
Finmeccania	Italy	9.0	57
Thales	France	8.2	64

Source: Sam Perlo-Freeman and the SIPRI Arms Industry Network, "The SIPRI Top 100 Arms-producing Companies, 2006," *in SIPRI Yearbook 2008: Armaments, Disarmament and International Security* (Oxford: Oxford University Press, 2008), Table 6A.2.

does not fully and most effectively serve the interests of national security. This conclusion is disputed by those who argue that the U.S. defense establishment has been relatively insulated from domestic political and economic pressures. In direct contradiction to the radical view, they suggest that it was the high level of threat perceived during the cold war that gave the military a free hand in charting a new course for American defense policy, which included building an unprecedented peacetime defense-industrial base. It was not the cold war, but its end that has increased the vulnerability of the DoD to corporate and congressional lobbying. For example, an indication of the likely influence of private defense contractors is the volatility in company stock prices. If they enjoy a close relationship with their government customers, company shares will be seen by the market as a good and stable investment; if contractors are held at arm's length, then the fluctuation in share prices will be greater, reflecting the perceived riskiness of those investments. An analysis of defense contractors' stock prices showed a significant decrease in their volatility (relative to overall market volatility) after the end of the cold war; private investors seem to be more, not less, confident that large defense firms will be able to ensure their financial health in the post–cold war environment.[14]

As Table 12.1 indicates, the top ten arms-producing firms in world are based in the OECD, six of them in the United States. However, even though many

---

[14] Eugene Gholz and Harvey M. Sapolsky, "Restructuring the U.S. Defense Industry," *International Security* 24 (Winter 1999/2000), pp. 5–51. The relative insulation of the Pentagon from domestic political and economic pressures is also emphasized by Gregory Hooks, *Forging the Military–Industrial Complex: World War II's Battle of the Potomac* (Urbana: University of Illinois Press, 1991).

radicals link the development of a military-industrial complex to capitalism, a similar constellation of interests was evident in the Soviet Union. State industrial managers had incentives to promote the growth, power, prosperity, and technological preeminence of the arms-manufacturing plants they controlled. They, too, shared interests with their clients in the Red Army and the Strategic Rocket Forces, along with hawkish ideologues in the Communist party. A cold war—though not a hot one—helped to maintain their privileges and central roles in Soviet society.[15] On both sides of the cold war divide, therefore, entrenched economic and political interests maintained the momentum of established hard-line policies. In a perverse way, the military-industrial complex in each country helped the other. Each embodied the foreign threat that its counterpart needed to justify its own activities.

DEFENSE-INDUSTRIAL POLICY

Governments sometimes intervene in the market to correct "market failures"—when the commercial payoffs are considered so uncertain that firms are reluctant to invest resources in new areas that in the long run would benefit society. Two traditional areas for intervention are in basic research (that is, "pure science") and research and development (R&D) directly related to the central missions of governmental agencies, like public health and national defense. Governments also intervene in the market, to varying degrees, in order to enhance the economic competitiveness of certain industries or sectors within the national economy. **Industrial policy** is the set of arrangements whereby the government assists these industries—sometimes called "national champions"—deemed to be crucial to the nation's economic strength. Such arrangements include strategically targeted government purchases, capital for plants and equipment, R&D subsidies, and the promotion of exports. The United States has generally frowned on such industrial policies, adopted by some of its major trading partners in Europe and Asia, as contrary to the spirit of free trade.

One response to American criticism has been that the United States accomplishes much the same thing under the guise of national defense. Although free-market principles hold great sway in the United States and government intervention in the economy seems taboo except when the nation is at war, many point out that large peacetime defense budgets constitute a "covert industrial policy." The U.S. government has sponsored large-scale projects in the interest of military readiness that have also generated valuable "spin-offs" for civilian industry. The computer, for instance, had its origins in code breaking during World War II, and by 1950 the government was providing up to $20 million a year to support related R&D. As one analyst of the computer industry has pointed out, "government support for applied research and development would be acceptable only if aimed at a noneconomic objective, like national security."[16]

---

[15] Clifford G. Gaddy, *The Price of the Past: Russia's Struggle with the Legacy of a Militarized Economy* (Washington, D.C.: Brookings Institution, 1996); see also Steven Rosefielde, "Back to the Future? Prospects for Russia's Military Industrial Revival," *Orbis* 46 (Summer 2002), pp. 499–509.

[16] Kenneth Flamm, *Creating the Computer: Government, Industry, and High Technology* (Washington, D.C.: Brookings Institution, 1988), p. 78. See also Arthur L. Norberg and Judy E. O'Neill, *Transforming Computer Technology: Information Processing for the Pentagon, 1962–1986* (Baltimore: Johns Hopkins University Press, 1996).

The balance of military and commercial objectives in American defense-industrial policy has changed over the years. At one end of the continuum are policies in which the sole objectives of R&D programs pertain to military missions, while commercial spin-offs are unintended and unanticipated by-products of those efforts. In the late 1960s, DoD's Advanced Research Projects Agency (ARPA) began supporting research on linking computers over a wide-area network so that the defense community (including military contractors) could more easily share information and computing capacity. Development of the ARPANET pioneered technological innovations that would become the basic components of public and commercial data networks, like the transfer of data in "packets," as well as the creation of protocols for the networking of networks (thus, the Internet). Yet such commercial spin-offs were completely fortuitous; they were neither sought nor promoted by ARPA, whose objectives were strictly defense related.

At the other end of the continuum are R&D programs that concentrate on promoting technological and industrial advances in the commercial sector, which are then expected to have military applications. Such military applications are sometimes called "spin-ons" because they originate in the civilian economy. A case in point is the initiative launched in 1993 to support technological advances in flat panel display (FPD), the type of computer screens originally developed for laptops but now used in desktop workstations, televisions, personal digital assistants (PDAs), and cell phones. The military applications are ubiquitous; FPDs are the interface between the military's intelligence sources (surveillance systems, space sensors, remote probes, and so on) and the personnel who must act on this information. The FPD initiative explicitly sought to build a vibrant domestic industry out of practically nothing (the goal was 15 percent of the global market, from 3 percent in 1994). Although the military mission was the key to the Pentagon's interest in the program, military R&D was but a component of an overall national strategy to enhance U.S. competitiveness in a particular industry.[17]

Information technology is a prime example of "dual-use technology," one with both military and commercial applications. Separating government-directed activities designed to promote military industry from those that foster advances in the civilian economy has never been straightforward, and the information revolution continues to blur the distinction. The long-standing refusal of some of America's major trading partners to remove industrial policy from their menu of choice partly accounts for an increased willingness to see the balance of military and commercial objectives in U.S. defense-industrial policy tip toward the latter as a means of promoting the nation's geo-economic interests.

GUNS VERSUS BUTTER

Prosecuting a war can put enormous strains on a state's economic resources. Transforming a peacetime economy into a wartime economy requires a mobilization of

---

[17] Glenn R. Fong, "Breaking New Ground or Breaking the Rules: Strategic Reorientation in U.S. Industrial Policy," *International Security* 25 (Fall 2000), pp. 152–186, discusses the ARPANET and FPD initiatives, along with several others, in terms of the balance of military and commercial objectives.

industrial and human resources, and centralized planning is sometimes required to prioritize the war effort over other economic activities. When there is a wealth of unused resources—that is, idle industrial capacity and high levels of unemployment—wartime economic mobilization can pull a national economy out of its doldrums. For example, industrial mobilization for World War II is credited for finally ending the Great Depression in the United States. However, when there are few slack resources in a society, wartime mobilization can cause severe economic strains. Even if economic resources are not scarce when the war begins, scarcities can quickly set in as the war drags on and it may not be long before price controls and other forms of centralized economic planning become necessary to deal with shortages and bottlenecks. During World War II, the U.S. War Production Board resisted many such economic controls as "socialistic," but its restraint may well have hampered the country's war effort in the early years.

The relationship between military preparedness and economic performance during peacetime is hotly debated, and the expression **"guns versus butter"** is shorthand for the essential trade-offs identified by critics of excessive military spending. There are actually two related issues here. First, is there a connection between peacetime defense activities, especially military spending, and the overall *economic health* of the nation or regions within it? Second, does production by the military-industrial complex (guns) absorb resources that might otherwise go to *social programs* (butter) designed to improve the lot of society's poor and dispossessed?

Radical scholars and others have argued that politicians use peacetime defense spending to stimulate the national economy during periods of slow growth. In the 1930s, British economist John Maynard Keynes believed that persistent unemployment was due to a deficiency in demand for goods and services; government spending could be used to compensate for downswings in the business cycle. In Britain and the United States, this Keynesian logic motivated spending on large public works projects—fiscal policy—designed to help lift these economies out of the Depression. As a component of government spending, military spending in particular might be used in this way, as a *counter-cyclical tool*. Such a policy has been called *military Keynesianism*, and some associate this with an advanced stage of capitalism in which industrial production, including defense production, is concentrated in relatively few hands. There is a tendency in this stage of capitalism for monopolistic firms to produce more than what the market demands. Radicals say that this surplus production is absorbed through government spending in order to prevent the collapse of the capitalist system. Some social spending is acceptable, especially if necessary to pacify anticapitalist forces, but that alone cannot sustain the economy. Military spending is a preferred solution to this "underconsumption problem" because monopoly capital continues to reap profits from production. It has the added benefit of appealing to many outside the military-industrial complex who do not gain economically but who approve of high levels of defense spending for reasons of nationalism.[18]

[18] A classic study is Paul A. Baran and Paul M. Sweezy, *Monopoly Capital: An Essay on the American Economic and Social Order* (New York: Monthly Review Press, 1966); see especially chaps. 6, 7. See also Harry Magdoff and Paul M. Sweezy, *The Irreversible Crisis: Five Essays* (New York: Monthly Review Press, 1989).

It is hard to test the underconsumption thesis satisfactorily. The defense establishment does represent a large component of many national economies, in both the industrialized and developing world. In the United States, the DoD employed 670,000 civilians in 2008, with a total payroll of $60 billion, and another 3.6 million were employed in defense-related industries. Taken together, that was almost 3 percent of all employed civilians. In 2008, the U.S. government spent more than $600 billion on national defense (including defense-related energy and space expenditures and supplemental allocations for the war on terror), which amounted to 4.2 percent of all goods and services produced in the U.S. economy, and nearly half of all the world's military spending. No other country spends anything close to this much on defense. The U.S. military burden is appreciably higher than the worldwide average (2.5 percent of GDP, based on the latest available figures) and higher than that of any other NATO country. Many other countries' military expenditures, however, represent a considerably larger portion of the national economy. For example, Saudi Arabia, Oman, and Qatar each spend more than 10 percent of their GDPs on national defense, while North Korea probably spends closer to 20 percent.[19]

Does military spending have an impact on economic performance? Whether or not politicians use military spending as a fiscal stimulus, as radicals suggest, many liberals believe that the overall effect of large defense budgets is to sap the nation's *overall economic health.* Many point to the impressive postwar economic growth rates in countries like Germany and Japan (until recently), which were achieved in the context of small defense burdens. But an extensive body of social science research into the relationship between defense spending and aggregate economic performance in many countries during different time periods has turned up contradictory evidence, much of it suggesting that defense spending has no overall effect—positive or negative—on the national economy. As one scholar familiar with this vast literature concluded, "defense spending may not be the fiscal tail that wags the economic dog. Whether and how much it does so will depend in part on a country's economic structure, in part on its political institutions and culture, and in part on the incentives that motivate its officials."[20] Even in a country like the United States, with its huge defense establishment, there are a large number of factors responsible for economic ups and downs, and military-related economic activities may not stand out as especially influential.

This is not to say that peacetime military preparedness has no economic effects. Defense plants and military bases can have profound effects on a *local economy.* U.S. defense outlays for payroll (civilian and military) and for military contracts in the states of Alabama, Alaska, Arizona, Maine, Maryland, and Mississippi accounted for more than 5 percent of gross state income in 2005; in Hawaii and Virginia the figures were more than 10 percent. At the local level, the cancellation of a major weapons program, or worse, the closing of an entire plant or military

---

[19] U.S. figures are from U.S. Department of Defense, *National Defense Budget Estimates for FY 2009* (Washington, D.C.: U.S. Department of Defense, 2008); defense industry employment is for 2006, the latest available. Other figures are from U.S. Central Intelligence Agency, *The 2008 World Factbook*, February 21, 2008; available at <https://www.cia.gov/library/publications/the-world-factbook/>.

[20] Steve Chan, "Grasping the Peace Dividend: Some Propositions on the Conversion of Swords into Plowshares," *Mershon International Studies Review* 39 (August 1995), p. 68.

base, can mean laying off a large share of the local workforce, which reverberates as shopkeepers and others who serve that community see the demand for their goods and services decline or evaporate altogether. Critics of America's "permanent war economy" sympathize with the plight of local communities in such predicaments but point to the larger problem of structural dependencies in the U.S. economy that link the fate of local economies to the vagaries of weapons procurement and military planning.[21]

Critics also point to distortions that may not be apparent at the aggregate level of national economic performance (growth rates, unemployment rates, inflation, and so on). These generally have to do with *opportunity costs*—the benefits foregone by investing in the military as opposed to more economically productive or socially redeeming pursuits. Because workers in the defense industry are drawn disproportionately from the higher-skilled occupations (like the scientific and engineering community), money spent on defense could employ a lot more people if invested elsewhere. Moreover, critics say money withdrawn from weapons procurement would go further even if it remained in the high-technology sector of the economy because military contractors worry little about cost overruns when the central government is picking up the tab, which encourages "gold plating," waste, and even fraud and abuse. Customers in the civilian sector of the economy are more attentive to costs, increasing the incentives for productive efficiency. The $436 hammer and the $640 toilet seat are now legendary in annals of U.S. military procurement, and although many of these headline-catching "abuses" can be explained by innocent accounting practices—like allocating indirect costs equally among all the parts used in production—the perception is widespread that the government does not get its money's worth.

Related to this question of opportunity costs is the question of *defense–welfare trade-offs*. Many view central government expenditures as a pie of relatively fixed size; a larger military slice means a smaller slice for social programs like education, health, and welfare. It is important to keep in mind that the dynamics at issue here are essentially political, not economic. Although there may be some dispute about whether defense spending is more economically productive than social spending—which type of spending employs more people, and which adds more to the GDP—the real debate concerns social obligation and role of government in society. Research on the defense–welfare trade-off generally has not supported the hypothesis that politicians take money from social coffers to increase military spending. Trends in government spending on such things as health, education, and welfare are relatively smooth in most industrialized societies, while military spending is more volatile, responding to international crises and commitments. However, findings may differ depending on country and party in power. Figure 12.1 shows spending trends for the United States (in constant 2008 dollars). Since the 1970s, there have been three periods in which the general upward trend in social spending has slowed or stopped: during the Carter and Reagan years, the Clinton years, and

---

[21] See, for example, Seymour Melman, *The Permanent War Economy: American Capitalism in Decline*, rev. ed. (New York: Simon & Schuster, 1985). State-level figures are calculated from data in U.S. Census Bureau, *The 2008 Statistical Abstract: The National Data Book*, June 3, 2008; available at <http://www.census.gov/compendia/statab/>.

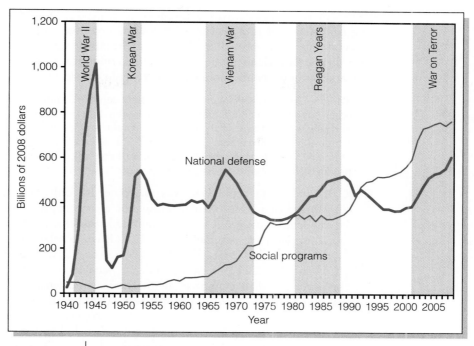

FIGURE 12.1 | MILITARY SPENDING AND SOCIAL SPENDING IN THE UNITED STATES, 1940–2008

The trend in U.S. military spending has fluctuated widely over time—mainly a reflection of the country's involvement in wars—while the trend in social spending (health, education, and welfare) has been generally upward. But during the terms of Presidents Reagan and George W. Bush, the growth in social spending stopped even as defense spending increased substantially, a pattern consistent with a defense–welfare trade-off.

Source: Social spending is the sum of three budget categories: (a) health, (b) education, training, employment, and social services, and (c) income security. Data are from U.S. Office of Management and the Budget, *Historical Tables: Budget of the United States Government, Fiscal Year 2009* (Washington, DC: U.S. Government Printing Office 2008).

George W. Bush years. During the terms of Carter and Clinton, this slowdown was accompanied by either no growth in defense spending or a decline. During the Reagan and Bush terms, by contrast, a defense–welfare trade-off is evident; the growth in social spending stopped while defense spending turned sharply upward.

MILITARY DOWNSIZING AND OUTSOURCING

Many arguments linking excessive military spending to economic ills are compelling. Yet it is often difficult to observe any clear relationship between defense expenditures and economic growth, unemployment rates, inflation, debt, or other measures of national economic performance in the short term. However, a society that continuously devotes a substantial share of its material and human resources to military production—because it is either engaged in or preparing for war—may divert valuable energies away from other more productive pursuits, achieving in the long run a level of prosperity well below its potential. After a historical survey of the economic forces propelling states to great-power status, and those that brought them down, Paul Kennedy highlighted "the conundrum which has exercised strategists and economists and political leaders from classical times onward":

> To be a Great Power—by definition, a state capable of holding its own against any other nation—demands a flourishing economic base. . . . Yet by going to war, or by devoting a large share of the nation's "manufacturing power" to expenditures upon "unproductive" armaments, one runs the risk of eroding the national economic base, especially vis-à-vis states which are concentrating a greater share of their income upon productive investment for long-term growth.[22]

Thus, the end of the cold war was welcome not only because it dissipated the looming threat of nuclear Armageddon but also because it seemed to promise a "peace dividend"—an economic windfall made possible because so many resources were freed up with the peaceful turn in U.S.–Russian relations.

By the end of the 1990s, the United States had downsized its military substantially. Compared to a decade earlier, military personnel—whether measured as active duty personnel, civilian employees of the DoD, or defense-industrial workers—had declined by one-third. Defense spending was down by almost the same amount, and the portion used for weapons procurement had dropped by 55 percent. Military infrastructure had been reduced by about 20 percent, including the closure of almost 100 major military bases and hundreds of smaller facilities. The process of dismantling sectors of the U.S. cold war economy was an instance of **defense conversion**, which entails any or all of the following: diversifying and adapting defense-industrial plants for nondefense production, transferring defense technology to nondefense firms, reorienting defense R&D toward dual-use technologies, integrating isolated defense industries into a civil and military industrial base, retraining laid-off defense workers, and helping communities adjust to the economic effects of defense cutbacks.[23]

The post–cold war adjustments and dislocations that confronted U.S. firms and communities were substantial, but the cutback in military spending paled in comparison to the one accompanying demobilization after World War II (see Figure 12.1). But despite the enormity of wartime mobilization, the post–World War II transition was remarkably smooth because, during the war itself, the Roosevelt administration had been planning for it. The cold war "mobilization," on the other hand, was more gradual and lacked the finiteness of a hot-war mobilization. Although the argument can and has been overstated, in certain respects the United States really did have a permanent war economy. Dismantling the local and regional economic dependencies that evolved over more than forty years of cold war was not an easy task. (Box 12.1 gives a brief illustration.)

---

[22] Paul Kennedy, *The Rise and Fall of the Great Powers: Economic Change and Military Conflict from 1500 to 2000* (New York: Random House, 1987), p. 539.

[23] Jacques S. Gansler, *Defense Conversion: Transforming the Arsenal of Democracy* (Cambridge, Mass.: MIT Press, 1995), pp. 40–41. See also Bonn International Center for Conversion, *Conversion Survey 2005: Global Disarmament, Demilitarization and Demobilization* (Baden-Baden: Nomos, 2005).

IN GREATER DEPTH

BOX 12.1 | GUNS, BUTTER, AND DEFENSE CONVERSION

The guns versus butter trade-off can be understood with reference to a Pareto optimal frontier (introduced in Box 5.1 to depict a dispute over territory). Here, the "dispute" is over the appropriate balance of economic effort devoted by society to military and nonmilitary endeavors. Society has a fixed amount of resources to devote to both, and if all available resources are utilized—that is, if society is producing at the Pareto frontier—then devoting more effort to guns will necessarily reduce the availability of butter, and vice versa.

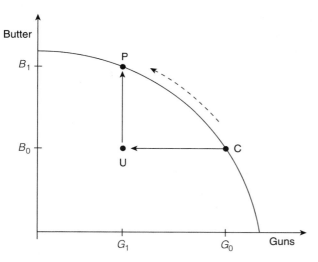

Suppose we start at point C, a particular mix of G_0 guns and B_0 butter considered socially optimal during the cold war. This is a social choice, which is not to say that all groups within society believe that C is best (recall Box 6.1) but that after the political process has worked itself out, this is the mix of military and nonmilitary effort chosen. Now suppose the cold war has ended and social preferences have changed such that the new social choice is

at point P; the world seems less dangerous, so society wants fewer guns (G_1) and more butter (B_1). A simple neoclassical economic model would suggest that moving from C to P is not problematic. As demand for guns and butter changes, prices and quantities of capital and labor will change. Markets clear, leaving no shortages or surpluses in either capital or labor. That is, moving from C to P is a smooth process and is accomplished by moving along the Pareto frontier.

The actual experience of defense conversion was considerably more disruptive. Reallocating resources from the defense sector to the civilian sector often proved difficult. Military plants and equipment were not easily converted to commercial production, and the skills of defense workers did not always translate, without substantial retraining, into the skills needed for the production of goods or the provision of services in the civilian economy. Conversion of land once occupied by military bases was also an issue, in part because there were environmental hazards—for example, deriving from the storage of both conventional and nuclear weapons materials—that had to be dealt with before the land was suitable for other uses. In short, experience has shown that moving from C to P does not take society along the Pareto frontier but through some point like U in which capital and labor are underutilized while the conversion process is taking place. High rates of unemployment were especially disruptive for some communities, creating vocal political constituencies opposed to defense conversion.

Source: Todd Sandler and Keith Hartley, *The Economics of Defense* (Cambridge: Cambridge University Press, 1995), especially chap. 11; the figure, slightly modified, is from p. 266.

Defense conversion in the Russian economy has been even more difficult. From 1992 to 1994, 1.6 million workers left defense-industrial production jobs, along with 800,000 who exited defense-related scientific institutes. This mass exodus—highlighted by most Western observers as evidence of successful market restructuring—is perhaps less interesting than the fact that roughly the same number of personnel *stayed* in these Soviet-era defense enterprises, despite dismal working conditions, low pay, and an uncertain future. And although the enterprise managers did fare better than their workers, they did not do particularly well. Yet many held tightly to their jobs even when presented with opportunities to strike out as independent entrepreneurs in the Russian free market. The endurance of the Soviet-era military-industrial complex, however shrunken, could be explained partly by "cultural notions of what it means to preserve the enterprise."[24] Such notions were powerful indeed in an industry that occupied such an exalted position in cold war Soviet society.

With post–cold war military downsizing has come military outsourcing. Private military companies perform a wide range of functions for their clients, both state and nonstate actors, only some of which involve actual combat. Nevertheless, the combat activities of Executive Outcomes (EO, a South African firm) and Sandline International (British) attracted a great deal of attention because they conjured up images—sometimes romanticized, but often sinister—of the mercenary armies and "soldiers of fortune" of previous eras. EO was hired by Sierra Leone in 1995 to help it defeat the Revolutionary United Front (RUF), which had been fighting the government from sanctuaries in Liberia since 1991. EO stopped the rebel advance on the capital of Freetown, forced the RUF to retreat deep into the jungle, and then trained local militias to help keep the rebels at bay—at a cost of $35 million over the course of two years. Shortly after EO departed, the newly elected government was overthrown in a coup and the RUF returned. Sandline, which was hired by private individuals (including the overthrown president) to engineer a counter-coup in Sierra Leone, had previously achieved some notoriety after the civilian government of Papua New Guinea enlisted the firm to train its special forces and help defeat the rebel Bougainville Revolutionary Army. That contract was strongly opposed by the Papua New Guinean army and triggered violent protests when it became public, bringing the country to the brink of civil war. Although the contract was terminated, Sandline successfully sued for full payment of the $36 million contract amount.[25] (EO and Sandline have both disbanded.)

Cases like these of weak and embattled states outsourcing their security to private companies are relatively infrequent compared to the use of military firms in consulting and support roles. Military Professional Resources Inc. (MPRI), based in Alexandria, Virginia, works closely with the U.S. government and has assisted

---

[24] Kimberly Marten Zisk, *Weapons, Culture, and Self-Interest: Soviet Defense Managers in the New Russia* (New York: Columbia University Press, 1997), p. 59; employment figures based on those reported on pp. 32–33. On defense conversion in Eastern Europe, see Yudit Kiss, *The Defence Industry in East-Central Europe: Restructuring and Conversion* (New York: Oxford University Press, 1997).

[25] These cases are described in P. W. Singer, *Corporate Warriors: The Rise of the Privatized Military Industry* (Ithaca, N.Y.: Cornell University Press, 2003). See also Deborah D. Avant, *The Market for Force: The Consequences of Privatizing Security* (New York: Cambridge University Press, 2005).

new Eastern European members of NATO in restructuring their military forces to achieve compatibility with those of other states in the alliance. Although many observers applauded MPRI's role in professionalizing and reorganizing Croatia's military prior to its successful offensive against Serb forces in 1995 (which was described as a textbook, U.S.–style campaign), the firm nevertheless sought to downplay its contribution to the combat operation itself. Kellogg Brown and Root (KBR), a subsidiary of Halliburton once headed by Vice President Dick Cheney, provides logistical support for the U.S. Army, including construction, base camp and equipment maintenance, food and laundry services, and transportation. KBR supplied its services during the wars and peacekeeping operations in Bosnia and Kosovo. It received a great deal of negative publicity as a result of its no-bid contract to assess and repair Iraq's petroleum infrastructure after the U.S. invasion and again when it was accused of overcharging on its multibillion dollar contract to feed and house U.S. troops. The industry's public image was dealt another blow when employees of Titan Corporation and CACI International, under contract for translation and interrogation services, were linked to prisoner abuse at the Abu Ghraib prison in Iraq.

The trend toward outsourcing reflects the shifting of military supply and demand since the end of the cold war. As we discussed in Chapter 8, there has been a proliferation of violent conflict, primarily internal war, in regions like sub-Saharan Africa where there are weak states and little interest on the part of extraregional powers in investing resources to resolve distant and poorly understood disputes. Furthermore, many of these are multiparty conflicts; the targets of violence and retaliation are not just the established governments and the rebel movements opposed to them, but other actors like international organizations, multinational corporations, and crime syndicates. All these actors have need of protection when operating in conflict zones and they are exhibiting a greater willingness to turn to private military firms, partly or wholly, for their security. Military downsizing since the cold war has also expanded the menus of state and nonstate actors by greatly increasing the supply of personnel in the private sector with military skills, whether in combat, organization and training, or logistical support. Even well-endowed military establishments, like those of NATO member states, are finding it cost-effective to outsource a wider range of security-related tasks, including intelligence collection and covert operations. These developments raise important political and legal questions about the accountability of both private military firms and those state and nonstate actors who employ them.

THE INTERNATIONAL ARMS MARKET

In 1934, H. C. Englebrecht and F. C. Hanighen published *Merchants of Death*, a polemical account of the *international* activities of armament makers. They pointed to the existence of small coteries of politically influential arms merchants operating in all the world's major capitals and suggested that their interests were virtually identical. Although they themselves did not consider the international arms trade to be the root cause of the "war system," they had some sympathy for those who viewed this as corrupt and dangerously irresponsible business:

They picture a group of unscrupulous villains who are using every device to profit from human suffering and death. They conjure up a picture of a well-organized, ruthless conspiracy to block world peace and to promote war. Theirs is an ethical reaction easily understood. For the business of placing all our vaunted science and engineering in the service of Mars and marketing armaments by the most unrestricted methods of modern salesmanship is indeed a thoroughly anti-social occupation.[26]

Merchants of Death became an instant best seller, fanning the flames of American isolationism that culminated in the Neutrality Acts of 1931–1939. The book's message, in essence, was that American neutrality was compromised during World War I by arms merchants with both national- and foreign-government connections, whose profit motive and strict adherence to commercial principles in peddling their wares left them little incentive to ponder either the moral dimensions of their profession or the national interest. The arms business is exactly that—a business—and business is good when nations are at war, or when they fear it.

Today the international arms trade is not strictly business. Before the passage of the Neutrality Acts and the formation of the Munitions Control Board, the export of weaponry by American merchants was effectively unregulated. By the outbreak of World War II in Europe, the U.S. government had established controls over private arms sales, and what was a means of profit for the arms merchants became for the government an instrument of foreign policy. Governmental supervision over arms exports was established during the 1930s in most European nations with significant production capabilities as well, though with typically less fanfare than in the United States. This new role for arms transfers was inaugurated in the United States with the signing of the Lend-Lease Act of 1941, which authorized the president "to sell, transfer title to, exchange, lease, lend, or otherwise dispose of . . . any defense article" to any country whose defense was deemed essential to U.S. national security. The hope was that direct American involvement in the European war could be avoided, but at minimum the United States would have to commit itself as the "great *arsenal* of democracy."

Arms transfers are an important instrument of influence in world politics, as we pointed out in Chapter 5, and for this reason state leaders must be attentive to the economic viability of the nation's arms producers. When domestic demand for armaments is insufficient to make arms production a profitable enterprise, defense firms search out export opportunities in order to maintain acceptable unit costs of production. Without arms exports, or large subsidies from the central government, production lines may become too costly to keep open. While the central government has an interest in defense-industrial efficiency, at some point corporate downsizing may threaten to shrink the country's defense-industrial base below what is considered necessary for purposes of national security. Defense industries must be able to support military mobilization in response to unforeseen international developments. They must also continually engage in military R&D if they are to supply the state with the means of engaging in military campaigns of the future. These capacities are maintained through the production and sale of armaments, whether at home or abroad.

---

[26] H. C. Englebrecht and F. C. Hanighen, *Merchants of Death: A Study of the International Armament Industry* (New York: Dodd, Mead, 1934), p. 6.

Of course, all of this begs some important and divisive questions. What are acceptable profit levels for defense firms? When profits (and salaries) depend on government purchases and subsidies, the answer to this question cannot rest solely with corporate executives and their stockholders, at least in a democracy. When arms transfers prop up oppressive regimes or threaten to destabilize precarious regional balances, as many claim, or when the potential exists that exported weaponry may be used against one's own military forces in some future confrontation—sometimes referred to as "blowback"—then profits, market share, and other economic calculations are probably not the most important ones.[27]

GLOBAL ARMS TRANSFERS

The arms trade peaked during the early 1980s. As shown in Figure 12.2, the annual trade in major conventional weapons was about $50 billion (in 2007 dollars) during that period; it dropped rather substantially after the end of the cold war to a low of $20 billion before moving up again to its current level of about $30 billion, still well below its cold war peak. The top weapons exporters and importers are shown in Table 12.2. During the cold war, the two superpowers supplied most of the world's weaponry, and in many cases competed with one another in doing so. In the years following the collapse of the Soviet Union, the United States dominated the arms market, but in recent years the former rivals have resumed positions of relative parity as global arms suppliers, though at levels below those reached during the cold war period. From the end of World War II the two superpowers were the world's *first-tier* arms suppliers. First-tier suppliers engage in innovations at the military-technological frontier—for example, today's "smart" and "brilliant" weapons—and they have the military-industrial capacity to produce (and export) the entire range of weaponry, from artillery to advanced fighter aircraft and missile systems. The United States is currently alone at the furthest reaches of the technological frontier, but the Soviet Union was an innovator throughout the cold war, and Russia retains considerable potential despite its post-cold war economic difficulties.[28]

Like first-tier producers, *second-tier* producers are able to manufacture much of the most advanced weaponry available, but their capacity for military-related scientific and technological innovation is more limited. Their most advanced arms production is often based on imported know-how, even though they may adapt it. Thus, second-tier producers like Britain, France, and Germany manufacture

---

[27] On the regional impact of arms transfers, see Gregory S. Sanjian, "Arms Transfers, Military Balances, and Interstate Relations: Modeling Power Balance versus Power Transition Linkages," *Journal of Conflict Resolution* 47 (December 2003), pp. 711–727; Cassady Craft, *Weapons for Peace, Weapons for War: The Effects of Arms Transfers on War Outbreak, Involvement, and Outcomes* (New York: Routledge, 1999). On internal repression, see Shannon Lindsey Blanton, "Policy in Transition? Human Rights, Democracy, and U.S. Arms Exports," *International Studies Quarterly* 49 (2005), pp. 647–667.

[28] For a historical overview of global arms production and supply, as well as the evolution of its three-tiered structure, see Keith Krause, *Arms and the State: Patterns of Military Production and Trade* (Cambridge: Cambridge University Press, 1992).

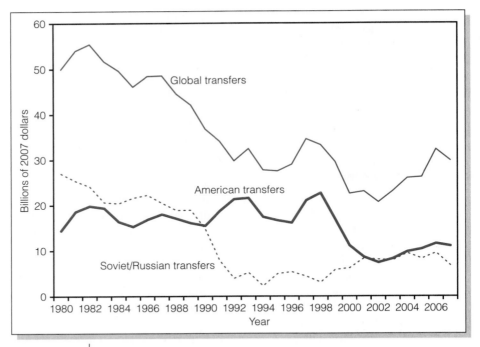

FIGURE 12.2 | GLOBAL ARMS TRANSFERS, 1980–2007

The worldwide volume of arms transfers has showed a steady decline since the late 1980s, a trend associated with the end of the cold war and, in particular, the decline in Russia's role as a major supplier of weaponry to the third world. American arms transfers remained relatively constant until the late 1990s and accounted for the largest share of the post–cold war arms trade, but there are signs that Russia is emerging once again to rival the United States as a global arms supplier. *Source:* Stockholm International Peace Research Institute, "SIPRI Arms Transfers Database," 2007, available at http://armstrade.sipri.org/. Data are estimates of the market value of major conventional weapons transfers, not what was actually paid.

indigenously designed fighter aircraft, but they do not yet produce stealth fighters; when they do, these will be based on U.S. scientific and technological innovations in the 1980s and 1990s, perhaps adapted for new and specific military purposes. Innovation at the technological frontier requires a substantial devotion of resources to military research and development. Major military R&D programs are made possible by government-subsidized initiatives—like the National Missile Defense program in the United States, successor to the Reagan administration's Strategic Defense Initiative—as well as confidence among private-industry participants that their efforts will someday be rewarded by large government purchases of newly developed weapons systems or components. Such incentives for innovation are not as strong in a second-tier country as they are in the first tier, nor is the defense-industrial base as large or diversified.

Smaller government defense budgets in second-tier countries also give an added push to arms exports as a supplement to domestic procurement. Of the total value of arms exported worldwide from 2003 through 2007, British, French, and

TABLE 12.2 | LEADING ARMS EXPORTERS AND IMPORTERS, 2003–2007

Arms Exporters			Arms Importers		
Country	Billions (2007 $)	Percent of World Total	Country	Billions (2007 $)	Percent of World Total
United States	50.8	30.9	China	19.8	12.1
Russia	41.8	25.4	India	13.4	8.2
Germany	16.0	9.8	United Arab Emirates	11.0	6.7
France	14.0	8.6	Greece	10.5	6.4
Britain	7.0	4.3	South Korea	8.1	5.0
Netherlands	6.0	3.7	Israel	6.2	3.8
Italy	3.8	2.3	Egypt	5.5	3.4
Sweden	3.2	1.9	Australia	5.0	3.1
China	3.0	1.8	Turkey	4.2	2.6
Ukraine	2.5	1.6	United States	3.8	2.3

Note: Figures are totals for the period 2003 to 2007 and are estimates of the market value of major conventional weapons transfers, not actual payments and receipts.

Source: Stockholm International Peace Research Institute, "SIPRI Arms Transfers Database," 2007, available at <http//armstrade.sipri.org/>.

German exports each accounted for more than 20 percent, up from less than 5 percent during the 1980s. In contrast to quantity, the quality of the military equipment supplied by these countries does not differ markedly from the equipment supplied by the United States or Russia. Indeed, the international arms market has become considerably more competitive than it was during the cold war. The unwillingness of first-tier producers to supply state-of-the-art equipment to anyone other than their own military forces has the effect of leveling the arms-export playing field.

Post–cold war military downsizing and a more competitive international arms market have given momentum to defense-industry consolidation in both first- and second-tier countries. For example, the Europeans have long contemplated cross-border consolidation of defense-industrial resources, because it would allow their firms to become more competitive in military R&D and in the international arms market. That has proven difficult, but there have been a number of transnational mergers and acquisitions, and the EU has actively sought to facilitate defense collaboration and ultimately the creation of a single European defense industry. In 1999, British Aerospace (BAe) merged with General Electric Company's Marconi Electronic Systems, and France's Aérospatiale, which was wholly state-owned and had already acquired a large stake in Dassault, merged with Matra. Then in 2000, Aérospatiale-Matra merged with the aerospace division of Germany's Daimler-Chrysler and Spain's Construcciones Aeronáuticas S.A., forming European Aeronautic Defence and Space (EADS), a first step toward the EU's vision. EADS had total sales of $50 billion in 2006 (arms sales were one-fourth) and employs more than 100,000. The high end of the international arms market will likely be dominated by a relatively small number of defense conglomerates.

PROLIFERATION OF MILITARY TECHNOLOGY

Some states constitute a *third tier* of arms producers, and a few of them are also fairly active in the international arms market. Third-tier arms producers rely more heavily than second-tier producers on imported technology, including weapons designs, and they are not capable of producing the same range of weaponry. When they enter the international arms market, they are typically "niche suppliers," specializing in the manufacture of specific weapons systems specially adapted for particular purposes.

The most advanced of the third-tier arms producers is China, which averaged about $2 billion worth of arms exports per year in the 1980s, but less than half that since the end of the cold war. Chinese exports represent about 2 percent of the global arms market, and it exports a wide variety of military goods. Although these facts might suggest that China is more than a third-tier supplier, China's present capacity in high-technology arms production—much based on old Soviet designs, though modified using Chinese (and Western) technology—really is not in the same league as Europe's second-tier capacity. Other important third-tier arms producers include Brazil, Israel, India, North Korea, South Africa, and South Korea. Third-tier suppliers as a group generally provide less than 10 percent of all imported weaponry.

There are several motivations for arms production in third-tier countries. Actual or potential threats to national security are exacerbated when states find themselves dependent on others for the implements of defense. States that have been subject to weapons embargoes, especially during wartime, bristle at the thought of lasting arms-import dependence, and most of today's major arms producers in the developing world experienced some sort of arms-import restrictions in the past. Another motivation is the hope that developing an indigenous arms production capacity will help promote wider economic development, a strategy commonly referred to as "military-led industrialization." Yet another motivation is symbolic. Certain national characteristics have great symbolic significance, and the possession of a nuclear weapons capability is probably the best example. The possession of advanced conventional weapons is also important, and even more important is the capacity to manufacture them. When India successfully test-fired its own intermediate-range ballistic missile in April 1999, the Indian prime minister described the Agni-II as "a symbol of resurgent India" and vowed that "yes, we will stand on our own feet."[29]

To some extent the global diffusion of advanced military technology is inevitable. In fact, many scholars anticipate an acceleration of technological diffusion in the context of the current restructuring of the international arms market. Although Europe has not yet succeeded in creating a fully integrated defense industry, there are numerous collaborative defense-industrial ventures in Europe, and many trans-Atlantic programs as well. Some involve *coproduction,* in which defense firms in two or more countries jointly produce a weapons system originally developed by one of them. Others are *codevelopment* projects, whereby companies and research institutes from different countries collaborate in the development of new weapons systems from the earliest stages of the product life cycle. Such arrangements facilitate the rapid diffusion of military technology among participating firms and countries.

These sorts of joint ventures linking first- or second-tier producers with third-tier producers are far fewer, though they are becoming increasingly common. One staple of the cold war arms trade, *licensed production,* continues to be a source of technological diffusion to the third tier. This involves a transfer of the rights and wherewithal to produce a weapons system or component originally developed and manufactured by a supplier. Licensing the production of aging weapons designs (and sometimes rather young ones) was one means of currying favor with local elites in the superpowers' cold war competition for friends and allies in the third world. Today, with increasing competition among first- and second-tier suppliers for business clients, as opposed to political clients, buyers can demand this and other forms of military-technology transfer as a condition for their purchases. Although economic motivations may have replaced political motivations on the

[29] David Kinsella and Jugdep S. Chima, "Symbols of Statehood: Military Industrialization and Public Discourse in India," *Review of International Studies* 27 (July 2001), pp. 353–373; quote from p. 353. On the relationship between arms production, trade, and development, see Jurgen Brauer and J. Paul Dunne, ed., *Arms Trade and Economic Development: Theory, Policy, and Cases in Arms Trade Offsets* (New York: Routledge, 2007).

part of arms suppliers, implications for the diffusion of military technology are the same—indeed, they may be more serious.

On the other hand, the globalization of arms production and the emergence of huge defense conglomerates in the United States and Europe may have the effect of squeezing all but a very few third-tier suppliers out of the international arms market. The resources necessary to participate in the much discussed "revolution in military affairs" for the moment seem to be available only to the United States, but Europeans and Russians can hope to be on board before too long. Countries in the developing world may come to conclude that their military preparedness in the contemporary context requires that they abandon any serious plans for military-industrial autarky in exchange for the acquisition of advanced weaponry on the international arms market.

The arms trade and other topics discussed in this chapter are examples of the close relationship between national security and both national and international economics. Economic transactions create interdependencies within and between societies. When these interdependencies derive from or have implications for national security and defense, they cease being strictly economic issues governed solely by economic logic. In the next chapter we continue our discussion of economic interdependence and its importance in world politics.

INTERDEPENDENCE AND ECONOMIC ORDER

CHAPTER 13

INTERDEPENDENCE

As new states and other international actors have come into being and as new technologies and norms have altered their menus, practices have adapted to these changes to maintain order within the international system. Although there is formal anarchy—the absence of a central authority with coercive power—within that system, we have seen that there is actually much cooperation, coordination, and collaboration in the world. Hedley Bull called the international system an "anarchical society," and such a society exists because there is *order* within the anarchy. Recurring patterns of behavior shape the expectations of the actors in the international system; behavior is often *predictable*.[1]

This is a crucial point: Order can exist without formal rules or with only a primitive system of rules. Order is difficult enough to obtain within societies that have central governmental authorities; the environment of world politics creates even more problems. The ability to create order and the frequency and virulence of conflicts depend largely on the relationships among international actors. One feature of systems and the relationships among the components of the systems is interdependence. Interdependence both contributes to the problems of creating order and creates the conditions necessary for achieving it.

This chapter looks at interdependence and its effects on order in world politics. We describe the evolution of the liberal international economic order and the practices and institutions that were designed to sustain it. We will often use the term *liberal* in this and subsequent chapters to refer to economic liberalism—principles of economic interaction and organization that emphasize the importance of private ownership, free markets, and the unhampered flow of goods, capital, and labor both within and between national economies. This does not imply that liberal theories of world politics tell us most of what we need to know about the liberal economic order. To the contrary, realist and radical perspectives also provide

---

[1] Hedley Bull, *The Anarchical Society: A Study of Order in World Politics* (New York: Columbia University Press, 1977).

compelling insights into the functioning of the contemporary political economy and the behavior of state and nonstate actors within it.

SENSITIVITY AND VULNERABILITY

In systems, things ramify; effects ripple through the system because of interdependent relationships that link actors. When there is a change in the system, there may be surprising consequences. The Yom Kippur War of 1973, for example, led to the Arab oil embargo, which led to worldwide economic problems, which led to conservation efforts that changed the way of life in advanced industrial countries. Surprise effects have a number of sources, not simply the major changes that can accompany war or revolution. Poor weather in the winter of 1971–1972 destroyed one-third of the Russian winter wheat crop. However, the government bureaucracy failed to increase the spring wheat acreage. To meet wheat demands, a massive wheat sale was arranged with the United States in July 1972, doubling the price of wheat in North America and generating public anger. In addition, North American wheat was not available for India (whose food supply had been worsened by monsoon and war) or for China and Africa (both hit by drought).

International interdependence has two different dimensions. First, international actors are sensitive to the behavior of other actors or developments in parts of the system. The degree of **sensitivity** depends on how quickly changes by one actor in one setting bring about changes in another, and how great the effects are. By "changes" we mean shifts in foreign policy or transformations of actors themselves (a new form of government, the onset of internal instability, or economic collapse, for example). States and other actors are sensitive when changes implemented or experienced by others cannot be ignored; they require some policy response. Second, actors who are sensitive to external changes may also be vulnerable to their effects. **Vulnerability** is measured by the costs imposed on a state or nonstate actor by external events, costs that the actor must absorb because it cannot pursue alternative policies that might minimize those costs.[2]

The Asian financial crisis discussed in Chapter 1 illustrates both of these concepts. The interdependence of Southeast Asian financial systems was such that when the Thai currency began its free fall in summer 1997, it sparked a similar drop in the Indonesian currency, and then in the currencies of Malaysia and the Philippines. Within a few months the currencies of South Korea, Singapore, and Taiwan had also lost much of their value. Despite great efforts by central bankers in these countries to maintain the value of their currencies, they simply did not have the resources to do so. They were vulnerable, and the economic costs imposed by the crisis were substantial. Other countries were not so vulnerable but still felt the impact of developments in the Asian financial markets. The United States, Japan, and some European countries scrambled to provide financial assistance to

---

[2] See Robert O. Keohane and Joseph S. Nye, *Power and Interdependence*, 3rd ed. (New York: Addison Wesley, 2000), chap. 1; also Robert Jervis, *System Effects: Complexity in Political and Social Life* (Princeton, N.J.: Princeton University Press, 1997). Harvey Starr, *Anarchy, Order, and Integration: How to Manage Interdependence* (Ann Arbor: University of Michigan Press, 1997), provides an overview of the issues and approaches relevant to interdependence in contemporary world politics.

help prop up the value of the Asian currencies and avert economic collapse. They were sensitive; alternatives were available to them in order to prevent the financial crisis from enveloping their own economies.

Sensitivity and vulnerability are not well-defined conceptual boxes in which states and other actors can be placed when analyzing developments in the international political economy. They are better seen as two ends of a continuum. Where an actor falls on the sensitivity–vulnerability continuum depends not only on the concrete circumstances but also on the passing of time. Japan was not as vulnerable to the financial crisis as the Southeast Asian economies, but the impact was felt much harder there than in the United States. The economies of Latin America did not feel the effects of the crisis for several months, but after about a year Brazil required an international financial bailout of its own. Thus, different systems, and different actors within those systems, may be characterized by different levels of sensitivity and vulnerability. In the current system—truly global and woven together by networks of communication, transportation, commerce, and finance— we find far more sensitivities and vulnerabilities than existed in international systems of the past.

CONFLICT AND HARMONY

Interdependence is one form of constraint on states and other actors in the international system. What is on one actor's menu depends very much on how that menu is connected to the menus of other actors. How might interdependence limit the menu? Changes by or in one actor will have some significant consequences for other actors, whether they like it or not. The images of the "global village," the "spaceship Earth," and the "shrinking planet" are all derived from this idea of interdependence and connectivity.

The liberal view of interdependence is essentially positive and optimistic; interdependence is conducive to more and more cooperation among states as they are brought together through various forms of interaction. The models of integration discussed in Chapter 11 were based on increasing the interdependent linkages between states through functional coordination and collaboration (as in the movement for European unity) or through social, economic, and political integration based on intersocietal transactions. Some theories go so far as to predict that the outcomes of these integration processes will eventually lead to world federation or a world state, although most liberals do not put a great deal of faith in such forecasts.

In contrast, the realist view points to interdependence as a constraint on states and therefore as potentially a very important source of conflict. Interdependence— especially if it is lopsided, making one party much more dependent than the other— can generate frustration and anger, as states hopelessly wish for past times when they were not inextricably linked with others and had greater freedom of action. Mutual dependence need not mean mutual reward, as is sometimes implied by liberal views of integration. When interdependence leads to vulnerability, actors acquire the capacity to injure each other. Resentment also may be fed by spreading awareness that the other side is reaping far more of the benefits of an interdependent relationship. Relative, not absolute, gains are important to states, according to realists, and therefore become potential sources of conflict.

Interdependence and the idea of sovereignty, which carries the formal and legal assumption of autonomy and equality among states, do not mix well. Consider again the Peace of Westphalia. The leaders who fashioned this settlement ending the Thirty Years' War were creating agreements that met the needs of their time. Very clear trade-offs were made between autonomy and self-control, on one hand, and the lack of order inherent in an anarchic international system, on the other. Princes who were striving for independence of action from the control of religious or imperial authority (the pope and the Holy Roman Emperor) were willing to create a system of states that had no formal source of authority to impose order. This "Westphalian trade-off," perhaps sensible at the time, has fostered a set of contemporary problems arising from growth in the levels and scope of interdependence. The Peace of Westphalia stressed independence and autonomy; interdependence generates complex problems, which require solutions involving collective, not unilateral, action. The balance has been changing, especially in the decades since World War II, and the international community increasingly has come to stress the need to reduce the formal anarchy of the system in order to solve the problems of contemporary interdependence.

INTERNATIONAL TRADE

More than $15 trillion worth of goods and services were traded between states in 2006; that was more than one-quarter of all goods and services produced worldwide. High-income countries account for most international trade (73 percent), but they are not necessarily the most open economies. The United States trades far more than any other state, but it imports the equivalent of only 16 percent of GDP. The figure for Japan is even lower (13 percent). Most countries account for tiny shares of all global trade, but trade is very important to many national economies. In some countries, like Luxembourg, Malaysia, Seychelles, and Singapore, the value of total imports exceeds 100 percent of GDP, and for another fifteen countries the figure is more than 75 percent.[3] Although there is considerable variability in the trading behavior of states, there can be little doubt that trade is a centerpiece of international interaction.

COMPARATIVE ADVANTAGE AND FREE TRADE

The basic principles behind international trade have been known for a long time. Adam Smith, writing in the eighteenth century, argued that states trade because some states can produce some goods more efficiently than others. If each state can concentrate its efforts on what it does best, it can then trade some of those goods for goods that other states produce most efficiently. As an illustration, imagine two states, A and B, each of which produces two goods, pizza and beer. Assume also that A is better at making pizza and B is better at brewing beer. Each week, a worker in state A can produce either 50 pizzas or 2 kegs of beer. A worker in state B can

---

[3] Figures from World Bank, *World Development Indicators 2008 CD-ROM* (Washington, D.C.: World Bank, 2008).

TABLE 13.1 | GAINS FROM TRADE

	Absolute Advantage			
	No Trade		Trade	
	Pizzas	Kegs of Beer	Pizzas	Kegs of Beer
State A	5,000	200	5,000	300
State B	4,000	300	5,000	300

	Comparative Advantage			
	No Trade		Trade	
	Pizzas	Kegs of Beer	Pizzas	Kegs of Beer
State A	5,000	260	5,000	281
State B	4,000	240	4,150	240

produce either 40 pizzas or 3 kegs of beer. If 200 workers in each state are split evenly between pizza making and beer brewing, then the production (and consumption) of A and B, without trade, are as shown in the top-left part of Table 13.1. What if A reallocates its 100 beer brewers to pizza making, and B sends its pizza makers to the brewery? State A could then trade those 5,000 extra pizzas for the 300 extra kegs of beer that B now has on hand. Both states benefit: A gets 100 more kegs of beer than it could produce on its own; B gets 1,000 more pizzas.

The gains from trade are easy to see in cases like this when each state has an *absolute advantage* in the production of some good. David Ricardo, a British economist writing in the early nineteenth century, extended these principles to situations in which a state possessed only a **comparative advantage**.[4] Imagine now that state A can produce both pizza *and* beer more efficiently than state B—50 pizzas and 2.6 kegs per worker per week, compared to 40 pizzas and 2.4 kegs in state B. The bottom-left part of Table 13.1 shows what A and B would produce (and consume) when they do not trade. What if they do trade? Imagine that A reallocates 75 of its brewers to produce pizzas, while the remaining 25 brewers continue to produce their 65 kegs per week. Suppose that B reallocates 90 of its pizza makers to the brewery, and the remaining 10 make their 400 pizzas. Now the 3,750 pizzas produced by A's reallocated workers can be traded for 216 kegs of beer produced by B's reallocated workers. Again, both states benefit: A gets more kegs of beer (65 + 216 = 281) than it could produce on its own; B gets more pizzas (400 + 3,750 = 4,150). Looked at in a different way, for every keg of beer A produces, it must produce about 19 fewer pizzas (50 ÷ 2.6). But for every keg that B brews, it produces only about 17 fewer pizzas (40 ÷ 2.4). Even though B is less efficient than A at

---

[4] The classic study is David Ricardo, *Principles of Political Economy and Taxation* (Amherst, N.Y.: Prometheus, 1996), originally published in 1817.

brewing beer, producing a keg of beer costs B less in terms of pizza labor; beer is B's *comparative* advantage.

Of course, specializing production in order to gain from trade is not without potential pitfalls. Our illustration assumed a straightforward barter—pizza for beer—when in reality the exchange of goods depends on their relative prices in world markets. What if worldwide demand for pizza increases, allowing state A to increase its prices? Then B gets less per keg of beer; had B continued to devote some of its resources to beer production, it could have benefited from the price increase. Economies oriented toward the production of only a few goods are more sensitive to the uncertainties of the international market, and price fluctuations can cause severe dislocations (declining wages, unemployment) for workers in affected industries. There are other considerations as well. Perhaps the nature of pizza production is such that producers in state A, hoping to tap the potential market for frozen do-it-yourself pizza, decide to experiment with automation and mass production. The technological advances in the pizza industry might be tried in other sectors, putting state A's economy on the path of advanced industrial development. In the meantime, state B's beer producers stick with tried-and-true methods of brewing handed down over the generations, which is fine for discriminating beer drinkers, but it does not contribute to technological progress. Likewise, the experiences of states specializing in the production of agricultural goods or the extraction of natural resources (referred to as *commodities*) suggests that this may not be very conducive to the technological advancement of society, which seems to be a goal of virtually all states. We shall explore these and other issues relating to the so-called international division of labor in Chapter 15.

PROTECTIONISM

Very few states in the international system can produce everything their populations need to survive and prosper. Even for those that can, pursuing an economic policy of **autarky**—minimizing trade in favor of domestic production of all goods and services required by society—is not very cost-effective, given the principles of comparative advantage. In the past, nations have sought to isolate themselves from the world economy when productive efficiency was of secondary importance to state leaders, as it was during the global depression of the 1930s. During this period the United States, Britain, France, Germany, and Japan all sought to stimulate domestic production and thereby reduce unemployment by placing restrictions on imports. Some countries, like Iraq in the 1990s, have had little choice but to pursue autarky because their economic isolation has been imposed for military reasons. For a few other countries, autarky is a choice. Economic information about Myanmar has been sketchy for several years, but in the late 1990s the country was importing only 1 or 2 percent of its GDP as a consequence of the isolationist policy pursued by the military government.

Like so many other concepts, in the real world neither free trade nor autarky are absolutes; they are instead opposite ends of the spectrum of trade practices. In between are varying degrees of **protectionism**. Protectionism is a policy of restricting, but not eliminating, imports in an effort to maintain or nurture—to protect—the economic viability of domestic industries. As we pointed out in Chapter 12, governments may elect to protect industries, like silicon chip manufacturing, because domestic production of certain goods is deemed crucial for reasons of national security. More often, domestic industries are protected for political and economic reasons. Newly industrializing countries (NICs), for example, have actively protected their "infant industries" from the effects of cheap foreign imports until they have developed and are efficient enough to compete in international markets. Developed countries sometimes engage in protectionism because foreign competition threatens the well-being of industries that wield a great deal of political influence. Automobile manufacturers in the United States and farmers in France are two groups that have had sufficient political clout to extract from their national governments some degree of protection from the competition of foreign imports.

States use various techniques to control imports of goods and services. A state can impose **tariffs** on products entering its borders. Tariffs are taxes or duties levied on imported goods in order to raise revenue or to regulate the flow of foreign goods into a country. When tariffs are imposed, a particular imported item becomes more expensive to purchase and fewer will be sold relative to similar domestically produced goods. Tariffs protect domestic industries, but they can also be manipulated in an effort to influence trading partners. When the tariffs imposed on goods imported from one state are no higher than the tariffs imposed on those same goods from any other state, the first state is said to have *most-favored-nation* (MFN) status—a term that can be somewhat misleading because a state with MFN status is actually being treated the same as most other trade partners, not better. The United States, which provides a huge export market to other countries, has often sought to exert influence by promising or withdrawing MFN status. In 1975, Senator Henry Jackson and others tried to influence Soviet policy on the emigration of Jews by holding up an agreement to extend MFN treatment to the USSR. The attempt failed. A similar situation arose with China after the brutal repression of the democracy movement in 1989; then, as now, there was considerable debate over whether the U.S. should attempt to influence China's conduct by manipulating trade relations. American leaders have generally concluded that the Chinese economy is too large for this sort of leverage to be effective. Furthermore, because the United States has need of China's cooperation to pursue nonproliferation and other U.S. foreign policy goals, the potential adverse side effects of economic coercion have usually been judged too costly, even if it did work in curbing the government's repression of internal dissent.

Protectionism includes other **nontariff barriers to trade** (NTBs). *Quotas* control imports not through prices, but through the amount of goods permitted to enter a country from a specific source for a specific time period. The United States used quotas to restrict imports of Japanese automobiles in the 1980s, although the quotas were ostensibly *voluntary export restrictions* by Japan. Other mechanisms for controlling trade include *subsidies* and *loans* to domestic industries, which effectively reduce the costs of domestic production. As we discussed in the last chapter, some forms of economic behavior have been used strictly to punish other states. These include the *boycott*, in which states cease to buy the goods, resources, or services of another state. Boycotts cut the target state off from its markets. Contrast this to an *embargo*, which stops sales of economic items to another state, thus cutting off the state's supply of resources and products from the outside.

Tariffs and NTBs constitute state intervention in the market. But not all trade barriers are the result of direct action taken by national governments. Groups within society often appeal to nationalist sentiments in an effort to sustain the viability of certain domestic industries and, especially, to protect jobs. In the United States, for example, labor unions and other industry groups often encourage consumers to purchase goods "Made in the USA." Even small businesses advertise that they are "American Owned and Operated." Similar campaigns have been undertaken in other countries as well. Japanese consumers have long been discouraged from purchasing imported rice, and some campaigns have gone so far as to suggest that the consumption of foreign rice is contrary to the essence of being Japanese. Rarely are such appeals isolated from other more explicit forms of protectionism—for instance, government subsidies to American automakers or Japanese rice farmers—but they are unique in that they constitute a form of **economic nationalism**, as opposed to economic policy.[5]

COLLECTIVE GOODS

As the world has become more tightly linked through various interdependencies, states have found themselves grouped together in international organizations and regional groupings that are economic, political, and military in nature. We may also think of each state (as well as the other international actors) as a member of a group or collective that includes the entire globe. Being a member of a group complicates what any individual member can achieve due to the sensitivities and vulnerabilities associated with interdependence. Clearly, interdependence affects how individual interests relate to group interests. Sometimes leaders of states think they are acting in their own interests when in the end they are not.

How can we, as rational actors, not act in our own best interests? Consider how individual interests relate to group interests. This relationship is clearly illustrated in *Catch-22*, Joseph Heller's satirical novel about World War II. Yossarian, a bombardier in the U.S. Army Air Force in Italy, refuses to fly any more missions. Major Major, a superior officer, in trying to persuade Yossarian to fly, asks, "Would you like to see our country lose?" Yossarian replies, "We won't lose. We've got more men, more money and more material. There are ten million men in uniform getting killed and a lot more are making money and having fun. Let somebody else get killed." Major Major then responds, "But suppose everybody on our side felt that way." Yossarian's answer is devastatingly to the point: "Then I'd certainly be a damn fool to feel any other way. Wouldn't I?"[6]

Here we have another variant of the prisoner's dilemma. If all the other fliers are willing to fly their missions—that is, to cooperate—then Yossarian would be unwise to go along. He should defect. With 10 million men in the war, his

---

[5] Dana Frank, *Buy American: The Untold Story of Economic Nationalism* (Boston: Beacon Press, 1999). On Japan, see Malcolm Trevor, *Japan—Restless Competitor: The Pursuit of Economic Nationalism* (London: Curzon Press, 2000). For an analysis of protectionism under different forms of democratic government, see Sean D. Ehrlich, "Access to Protection: Domestic Institutions and Trade Policy in Democracies," *International Organization* 61 (Summer 2007), pp. 571–605.

[6] Joseph Heller, *Catch-22* (New York: Dell, 1961), p. 107.

individual presence will not make a difference. On the other hand, if none of the others wishes to fly either—all are defecting—then his response, "I'd be a damned fool to feel any other way," is indeed sensible. His presence would again make no difference, so again he should defect. However, if all the other fliers were to take the same position, then we have a dilemma: Despite the fact that missions have to be flown, it is not rational for any single individual to participate. For the collective, the goal of winning the war can be achieved only through group action. But such group action consists of the activities of individuals, and Yossarian makes it clear that it is not in the interest of any single individual to perform the actions needed to achieve the group's goal. So how do groups of supposedly rational actors ever accomplish collective goals? Why, for example, should any single state dismantle its trade barriers when it continues to enjoy access to the open markets of other states? And why, if other states do not open their markets, should any single state do otherwise? (This dilemma is illustrated in Box 13.1.)

In our discussion of international trade we have referred to the exchange of goods—pizza, beer, automobiles, and so on. A "good" is simply the consequence or outcome of an activity. If such consequences or outcomes are tangible things that can be possessed as property or consumed by an individual, we call them *private* goods. The discipline of economics is devoted in large part to the study of private goods and the way they are allocated within or between societies. The allocation of private goods is determined by the availability of the good (supply) and how much is desired (demand). Economists study how supply and demand interact at different price levels to determine the amount of a good that will be produced and thus allocated among consumers. Under ideal conditions, the market "clears" by resolving any misallocation of goods. When something is desired but not supplied, its price rises until potential suppliers find it in their interest to make the good available to those who want it.

Suppliers of goods incur costs when producing and distributing goods to consumers, and expect to recoup those costs when the goods are sold at a particular price. But if we think of Yossarian as a potential supplier, we can immediately see certain limitations of the free market. As a bombardier, he is essentially a producer, along with his fellow soldiers, of a good: actions that lead to victory in war (hopefully). However, Yossarian elects to stop producing that good because he believes the probable cost to him (death) will never be compensated; it can't be. Furthermore, if others do supply the good—and he is sure they will—then he gets paid anyway, even though he is not a supplier. That is because the good itself, victory, is its own repayment and everyone on the winning side can partake of its benefits. Victory in war is a good, but it cannot be possessed or consumed exclusively by those who pay for it. It is a **collective good** (also called a *public good*). Although collective goods are provided through the actions of individuals, once provided they belong to the group. They are not possessed by individuals and therefore cannot be consumed or transferred or exchanged in the manner of private goods. As we shall see, free trade is a collective good that benefits the entire international community, even those states that do not fully participate in providing the good.

Collective goods possess two special characteristics. The first is *jointness of supply*. If a good is supplied to any member of a group, then it is supplied to all members of that group. In contrast to private goods, collective goods are therefore

IN GREATER DEPTH

| BOX 13.1 | TRADE, PROTECTIONISM, AND THE PRISONER'S DILEMMA |

The goal of free trade has often been elusive because there are powerful incentives to protect domestic industry, especially when external markets remain open. The situation resembles a prisoner's dilemma. Recall from Box 9.1 that in certain situations, like arms races, the rational strategy that *each side* pursues in order to maximize its own self-interest results in a *socially suboptimal* outcome—another outcome would have been better for *both sides*. Had each adopted an alternative strategy, they would have achieved the socially optimal outcome.

Now let us consider two trading states. Each state, A and B, must choose between protectionism and free trade. If state A erects trade barriers, it will be protecting its domestic industry; if state B does not erect trade barriers, its markets will remain open to A's exports. That is the best outcome for state A because it is able to screen out the "dangers" of free trade (excessive competition) while continuing to enjoy the benefits (expanded markets). All of this occurs at the expense of state B, which is why protectionist policies are sometimes called "beggar-thy-neighbor" policies. The worst outcome for A is the opposite situation: B erects barriers to A's exports while A's markets remain open. The second best outcome for both states is free trade. Their markets stay open, trade increases, and they both enjoy the benefits of comparative advantage—increased consumption and industrial efficiency due to specialization. The next-to-worst outcome is mutual protectionism. Trade declines when both sides erect barriers, the benefits of comparative advantage diminish, and the

potential for inefficiencies increase because firms have fewer opportunities to specialize their production. Such an ordering of the four possible outcomes makes this a prisoner's dilemma.

State B

	No barriers	Barriers
State A — No barriers	3,3	1,4
State A — Barriers	4,1	2,2

As in any prisoner's dilemma, both sides have an incentive to defect (erect trade barriers); no matter what the other side does, defecting will yield a better outcome for the defector. Unfortunately, the equilibrium outcome is mutual protectionism, even though both sides are better off in a free-trade relationship. But achieving free trade requires cooperation, which can be exceedingly difficult when state leaders must also contend with domestic groups seeking protection from the uncertainties of the international market.

Note: For an application of 2 × 2 games, like the prisoner's dilemma, to the study of international cooperation, see Arthur A. Stein, *Why Nations Cooperate: Circumstance and Choice in International Relations* (Ithaca, N.Y.: Cornell University Press, 1990).

indivisible. If new members are added to the group, other members who are currently benefiting from (or "consuming") the good will not receive a diminished amount. An example of a collective good is network television. When a television station broadcasts its programs over the airwaves, all households within the range of transmission can view them. And the fact that more people may tune their television sets to that station at certain times does not diminish its availability to others. Likewise, when a government provides for the common defense, that protection is jointly supplied to all residents. When Washington threatened Moscow with retaliation for an attack on the United States, it provided a good (deterrence of Soviet attack) for every individual in U.S. territory. Once one person is protected, all are protected; if California is protected, so are Montana and Delaware. An increase in population does not reduce the deterrence provided to all the rest. The addition of Alaska and Hawaii to the Union in 1959 did not diminish the protection already being provided to the other forty-eight states.

The second characteristic of a collective good is *nonexclusiveness*. A jointly supplied good may be either excludable or nonexcludable. Some jointly supplied goods, like cable television, can be withheld from members of the group. Once the cable signal is supplied to any one cable subscriber, the addition of new subscribers does not reduce the supply of the good. However, the good is excludable: Those who do not pay for the service are not hooked up to the cable and thus cannot receive the service. Jointly supplied goods can be excludable, but a collective good is jointly supplied and nonexcludable. If the United States is deterring a nuclear attack on its own territory, it cannot exclude any specific person or group of persons—foreign diplomats, illegal aliens, or citizens who do not pay taxes. All people in the territory of the United States are part of the group being protected through nuclear deterrence and none can be denied its benefits.

FREE RIDERS

The characteristics of collective goods have important implications for how individuals behave in groups. Only a small number of all regular viewers of public television make contributions during those periodic fund-raising drives. By failing to contribute, the others are not prevented from watching public TV. Victory in war has some of these same properties. If the war is won, all citizens of the victorious country will have won. Some of the benefits—say, territorial integrity and political independence—will go to all if they go to one. It is also difficult to exclude particular citizens from this collective good of victory (though there may be penalties for draft dodgers and the like). Therefore, individuals must decide whether to help achieve the good or to be "free riders" on the efforts of others. This is exactly the choice that Yossarian faces, and his reluctance to fly any more missions, if it is shared by many others, creates the dilemma identified by Major Major. If everyone wants to be a free rider—a perfectly rational position to take—the collective good may never be achieved. This **free-rider dilemma** is simply a collective version of the prisoner's dilemma, which exists between just two actors.

In a capitalist economic system, the free market allocates private goods within a society and, in the case of international trade, between societies. This mechanism does not work well for the allocation of collective goods because of their indivisibility and nonexcludability. If individuals are strictly rational in the economic sense of desiring to maximize benefits and minimize costs in the near term, a collective good may never be provided, even if all members of a group desire that good. This dilemma arises from the clash between individual interests and actions on the one hand, and group interests and outcomes on the other. The rational individual prefers to wait for someone else to shoulder the burden; indeed, only a sucker would *not* wait. Why should Yossarian rush off to fly another dangerous mission while others are making money and having fun—and when there are 10 million other men in uniform willing to do the job, or who can be ordered to do it. Economic mechanisms are insufficient to overcome the temptation to free ride, and this is why collective action is so difficult in world politics (and in other spheres of social life). The collective-goods problem, in short, is a case of "market failure."[7]

In the contemporary world system, the fact of interdependence often requires collective action if the goals of states and other actors are to be achieved. The very idea of order in the international system may be seen as a collective good. If there is some stability, predictability, and regularity in international affairs, adding new actors may not diminish it, and it is difficult (although not impossible) to exclude actors from the benefits of global order and international coordination. The "new world order" was much heralded after the end of the cold war as a condition benefiting all members of the society of states. Part of the strong reaction to the Iraqi invasion of Kuwait stemmed from the perception that just when the disintegration of the East–West conflict was opening new opportunities for global cooperation, Iraq's behavior threatened not only Kuwait but also the collective good of this new global order.

Many areas of international political economy have been studied using collective-goods concepts, including international trade, coordination of monetary policies, and the management of global resources. International environmental issues, in particular, lend themselves to this type of analysis. Cleaning up an international body of water like the Rhine or the Mediterranean requires group action. Although a state might appear to be following its own interests by electing to free ride, in the long run it may be acting against them if the good desired—a clean waterway—is never achieved. Because the condition of the waterway is jointly supplied and nonexcludable, anyone using it will benefit from its cleanliness, just as all will be harmed by its continued pollution by one or more countries. Here, free riding will stop the good of clean water from being achieved altogether, or will cause cleanup to take much longer or remain incomplete. We will return to the collective-action problem when we discuss global environmental issues in Chapter 16.

STRATEGIES FOR COLLECTIVE ACTION

In Chapter 9, we discussed the ways in which states have overcome the prisoner's dilemma and the pressures to defect, even in the context of a prolonged arms race

---

[7] A classic statement of the collective-action problem is Mancur Olson's *The Logic of Collective Action: Public Goods and the Theory of Groups* (Cambridge, Mass.: Harvard University Press, 1965); see also Luis Fernando Medina, *A Unified Theory of Collective Action and Social Change* (Ann Arbor: University of Michigan Press, 2007).

when suspicion is high on both sides. This suggests that there should also be strategies to overcome free riding and to promote collective action. Collective goods present situations in which the strictly economic forces of the marketplace cannot bring about optimal solutions and in which political action must be taken to achieve the desired outcome. We will consider several broad strategies for achieving collective goods, each of which increases the costs of defecting or the benefits of cooperating.

One way to get individuals to cooperate is through *coercion*. Yossarian, for example, was in the army because it was against the law to refuse to be drafted. While he was serving, the army could threaten imprisonment, even execution, if he refused to fight. Within states, tax systems are backed up by threats of punishment for nonpayment. When a labor union achieves a union shop, it forces all workers to join the union, eliminating free riders who would not join but would still enjoy most of the benefits of collective bargaining, like higher wages and safe working conditions.

This type of coercion is difficult in international relations. The power to tax is not readily given to IGOs because it is a threat to sovereignty. (Note, however, that the EU does have such authority in a number of areas.) Sometimes an individual state can coerce others to contribute to the collective good by threatening to end its own contribution. The United States, for example, attempted to coerce its cold war allies to take on a larger share of the burden in NATO by threatening to pull U.S. troops out of Europe. Coercion was also an important element in the Soviet Union's management of burden sharing in the Warsaw Pact. A government and its leaders may lose prestige if other governments feel that they are not pulling their weight. NATO's annual review to identify and spotlight slackers has been used in this way. Such pressure was put on states that bore low costs during the Gulf War or that dragged their feet in paying their share.[8]

In world politics, positive strategies based on *rewards* of some kind are often more useful than negative ones based on coercion. Members of a group are sometimes coaxed to participate in collective action by offers of private goods as "side payments." For example, states may join alliances and provide a share of the defense burden if they receive new and sophisticated weapons in return. This is part of the reason why former Soviet bloc countries were anxious to join NATO after the end of the cold war. Side payments can also be used to encourage certain behavior on the part of nonallies. In 1994, in an attempt to persuade North Korea to contribute to the collective good of nuclear nonproliferation, the United States promised to provide two light-water nuclear reactors, useful for purposes of generating electricity but not for the production of weapons-grade nuclear fuel. Although the administration of George W. Bush rejected this approach, after having failed to coerce North Korea into denuclearizing, the administration was finally able to secure Pyongyang's compliance in exchange for various bilateral

[8] See Todd Sandler and Keith Hartley, "Economics of Alliances: The Lessons for Collective Action," *Journal of Economic Literature* 39 (September 2001), pp. 869–896. For applications to the Gulf War, see Andrew Bennett, Joseph Lepgold, and Danny Unger, eds., *Friends in Need: Burden Sharing in the Gulf War* (New York: Palgrave, 1997).

and multilateral inducements. Not only was North Korea promised that important coercive measures would cease—it would be taken off of the list of state sponsors of terrorism, for example—but also that it would receive foreign aid and low-interest loans.

Another noncoercive strategy is *education*, which is intended to convince individual actors that their self-interests will be served by promoting the interests of the collective. For example, Malta's representative to the General Assembly, Arvid Pardo, proposed in 1967 that the General Assembly explore ways to extract the resources of the deep seabed consistent with the interests of humanity as a whole, calling these resources the "common heritage of mankind." Educational tasks have been performed by professionals acting collectively as "epistemic communities"— transnational groups "united by a belief in the truth of their model and by a commitment to translate this truth into public policy, in the conviction that human welfare will be enhanced as a result."[9] Once they understand the consequences of defection, policy makers may be more willing to confront the free-rider problem. The problem is that education can be a slow process, and a number of collective-action problems require immediate attention.

A collective good can be provided if one member of the group desires that good so much that it is willing to *pay the whole cost* (or most of it) and does not care that noncontributing group members also receive the good. In effect, one member offers to be the sucker. Besides valuing the good highly, this member is usually better endowed with resources or wealthier than other members; it can shoulder most of the burden with fewer sacrifices. Studies of some IGO budget assessments and burden sharing in alliances such as NATO and the Warsaw Pact show that the larger members will pay proportionately more to get the things they want, even if others ride free. This characterizes the U.S. willingness to provide deterrence for itself and its Western European allies right after World War II, as well as for Japan throughout the entire cold war period and beyond. Another example is the U.S. role in stabilizing international trade, as we shall see.

One other strategy for achieving collective goods is through the creation of localized or regional organizations consisting of small groups of states interested in tackling specific problems related to public goods and then to create some sort of federal structure to coordinate their various activities. This approach involves *the use of IGOs* to address collective-action problems through the creation of regimes (to be discussed in the next section). This strategy often follows the functionalist model of integration introduced in Chapter 11, which we examine more closely in Chapter 14 in regard to the EU. Using IGOs often works because collective action is easier when there are fewer members in the collective; free riders are more readily identified and may be more susceptible to pressure by other members.

General strategies for coping with and resolving collective-action problems involve both formal and informal mechanisms. These mechanisms help states coordinate their activities and collaborate in positive ways. The strategies just discussed

---

[9] Ernst B. Haas, *When Knowledge Is Power: Three Models of Change in International Organizations* (Berkeley: University of California Press, 1990), p. 41. See also Peter Haas, "Epistemic Communities and International Policy Coordination," *International Organization* 46 (Winter 1992), pp. 1–36.

only hint at a very powerful informal process that helps to facilitate the provision of collective goods. The most problematic aspect of the prisoner's dilemma is trusting the other side in a specific situation; in the free-rider dilemma, the issue of trust pertains to the rest of the group. When one or both prisoners go to jail, the question of trust is confronted once—can you trust the other guy not to squeal after having heard the DA's proposal? This is a *single-play* situation, but most relationships in social life, and certainly in international relations, are *continuous*. That is, there are multiple plays in any game, and the players can learn what will happen to them if they defect—or, in collective-action situations, if they free ride. In Chapter 9 we discussed Robert Axelrod's research showing that in experimental games players did best by following a tit-for-tat strategy: cooperating while the other player cooperates, retaliating when the other defects. If both players follow the never-defect-first principle, they end up acting cooperatively to achieve a jointly optimal outcome.[10]

It follows that it may be possible to deal with the collective-action problem if all states realize that they are involved in a continuous relationship—that is, a multilateral version of an iterated prisoner's dilemma. All plays of an iterated game take place under the "shadow of the future." In any given iteration, players know that they are likely to find themselves in a similar situation later on. In this context, the temptation to free ride diminishes so long as the final play of the game does not seem near. You might be able to hurt another player, but the other player can also hurt you; and if that player doesn't retaliate, another member of the group might. This **reciprocity** can promote something akin to the golden rule. If the circumstances are such that states can be expected to "do unto others," then cooperation becomes the best strategy, despite the temptations to defect. Mutual cooperation has thus been called the game's *nonmyopic equilibrium* because it is achieved when players take a farsighted view of their collective interests.

Reciprocity is even more important when we recall that states are engaged simultaneously with other states and international actors, and they are interacting in multiple issue areas. In other words, the games are linked, which is the essence of interdependence. A state may defect in one game (for example, environmental protection), but it may have to worry about the other player's defection in another (say, alliance burden sharing). Again, critics of a renewed American unilateralism have pointed to just this outcome. Having defected from collective action to deal with global warming (the Kyoto Protocol) and crimes against humanity (the International Criminal Court), the George W. Bush administration found that defection was reciprocated when it tried to fashion a collective-enforcement action to deal with Saddam Hussein's regime in Iraq. The idea of reciprocity is central to understanding the workings of international law and the importance of formal and informal rules and expectations. It also helps explain how we can have order and a certain amount of stability and predictability in formally anarchic situations.

---

[10] Robert Axelrod, *The Evolution of Cooperation*, rev. ed. (New York: Basic Books, 2006). For an adaptation to collective action, see Randall W. Stone, Branislav L. Slantchev, and Tamar R. London, "Choosing How to Cooperate: A Repeated Public-Goods Model of International Relations," *International Studies Quarterly* 52 (June 2008), pp. 335–362.

REGIMES AND INTERNATIONAL ORDER

If states and other international actors are to overcome the free-rider problem, how should they organize themselves? There are, as we have seen, a number of strategies for achieving collective goods. One method is for the international community to develop rules of conduct designed to prevent free riding, to which each member commits. Some of these rules may be legally binding, but the rules of conduct that affect international behavior go beyond those of international law. Scholars have developed the concept of **regime** to help us understand the full array of constraints imposed by international society. We often use the term *regime* to refer to a particular government, especially an authoritarian government, but in the context of our current discussion a regime is a set of formal or informal rules and procedures that regularizes behavior in some area of world politics. The regularization of behavior means the creation of patterns: procedures, compliance with norms and rules, and, most especially, converging expectations. As Robert Keohane points out, "What these arrangements have in common is that they are designed not to implement centralized enforcement of agreements, but to establish stable mutual expectations about others' patterns of behavior."[11]

What do these arrangements consist of and where do these common understandings come from? There are formal components and informal components; there are national components, transnational components, and international components. The set of governing arrangements consists of national rules (the domestic laws of states), international rules (international law, the charters of IGOs, and the regulations and resolutions of IGOs), and private rules (the charters of MNCs and other NGOs, as well as other regulations). These are the formal products of governments and international organizations. Regimes also include the norms and principles that are reflected in patterns of behavior not yet codified in laws or organizational charters. Norms, principles, and customs include an important psychological component in that decision makers feel they *should* act in certain ways because they are expected to (and expect others to), whether or not that behavior is required by law.

The issue areas covered by a regime may be very wide or very narrow. Their areas of concern range from monetary and trade issues to the management of natural resources, outer space, and the seabed. Regimes may also be geographically bounded, covering problems that arise within specific territories—for example, Antarctica. Some regimes have only a few participants, like the regime overseeing North Pacific fisheries, while some are very large, such as the UN conflict-management regime. Some may be enduring, like the free trade regime; others are shorter-lived, perhaps because their purposes have been achieved, like the sanctions regime applied to South Africa under apartheid.

Some of the most extensive analysis of regimes has focused on post–World War II economic relations in the West. After victory, the Western industrialized

---

[11] Robert O. Keohane, *After Hegemony: Cooperation and Discord in the World Political Economy* (Princeton, N.J.: Princeton University Press, 1984), p. 89. For a review of concepts and theories from the literature on regimes, see Andreas Hansenclever, Peter Mayer, and Volker Rittberger, *Theories of International Regimes* (Cambridge: Cambridge University Press, 1997).

countries consciously sought to create an international economic regime that would tie the states of the world together in order to promote economic growth and peace. The 1920s and 1930s were periods when economic isolationism, protectionism, and suspicion helped lead the world into war. In the immediate postwar period, the United States used its Marshall Plan aid to encourage European recovery and economic interdependence in areas like international monetary policy and trade. But interdependence involves vulnerability and sensitivity, as we have discussed. In the late 1960s and 1970s, when the spectacular economic growth of the postwar era slowed, the costs of economic interdependence were increasingly manifest alongside the benefits. The question, again, was how to manage interdependence, build new arrangements to solve newly emerging problems, and ensure that the collective goods of global economic stability and peace would continue to be provided.

HEGEMONY AND REGIMES

At the end of World War II, the Western powers seemed to agree in their basic views of the international economy. The cornerstone of their vision was a liberal economic system, one without the sorts of economic barriers that had been set up in the 1930s. This was to be a relatively unhampered economic system based on private property, the free market, and minimal barriers to trade. To make the system work, states had to cooperate. Establishing this system was seen as a major step toward creating peace and order in the world, particularly within the group of OECD states. Free trade and the movement of capital depended on stability and predictability in the world, and, most importantly, in the North Atlantic area. Thus, there was a relationship between political-military stability and economic stability. The area had to be militarily secure from outside threats as well as internally peaceful. The same state that could provide military order—the United States—was also the only state economically strong enough to provide order in the economic system. As the one dependable locale of economic growth at the time, the United States would be the engine of global economic reconstruction and development.[12]

In this international system based on U.S. military and economic predominance, the United States followed a policy of leadership—or, as some observers describe it, hegemony. In a hegemonic system, "one state is able and willing to determine and maintain the essential rules by which relations among states are governed. The hegemonial state not only can abrogate existing rules or prevent the adoption of rules it opposes but can also play the dominant role in constructing new rules." Under U.S. leadership, the major economic features of the postwar period were a rapid expansion of international trade, due to a gradual reduction in tariffs; an increase in the volume and speed of capital movements, due to the

---

[12] For discussions of this period in historical context, see G. John Ikenberry, *Liberal Order and Imperial Ambition: Essays on American Power and International Order* (Cambridge: Polity, 2006); Jeffry A. Frieden, *Global Capitalism: Its Fall and Rise in the Twentieth Century* (New York: W. W. Norton, 2006).

maintenance of a system of fixed exchange rates; and the growth and spread of huge multinational corporations.[13]

Hegemony can be a useful, if not a necessary, mechanism for helping a group to achieve collective goods. Mancur Olson pointed out that a single member of a large group can constitute a "privileged" subgroup—in this case, a group of one—in that this member is able to provide the collective good for the whole group. Similarly, Charles Kindleberger argues that a stable world economy needs a "stabilizer." This suggests that the stability of the international political economy, including the effectiveness with which states deal with collective-action problems, is affected by the presence or absence of a hegemonic power. Indeed, realists, with their emphasis on state power, have often argued that the best explanation for regime formation and transformation is the rise and decline of hegemonic states in the international system. At the end of Chapter 4, we discussed this *hegemonic stability* perspective in the context of American primacy and the current distribution of power.[14]

U.S. predominance was important in setting in motion the economic prosperity and interdependence that followed World War II and now underlies the stable peace within the OECD. In this sense there is some virtue in having one big power in the international system. If it chooses, it can not only bully others to contribute to collective goods but also can afford to make short-term sacrifices that will in the long run benefit all members of the community, not just itself. The real problem with hegemony, however, has been pointed out by Kindleberger, among many others: distinguishing between leadership and domination. The utility and desirability of having a hegemon depends on where states sit in the international economic system. As we shall see, less-developed countries (LDCs) that have found themselves in relationships of economic dependency often come to regard hegemony as domination, illegitimate, and unjust. Their views are very different from those of developed, industrialized states, who may regard it more as benign leadership, perhaps punctuated by bouts of hubris.

THE MONETARY REGIME

After World War II, a group of industrialized states led by the United States created the basis for a liberal international economic order for the developed, noncommunist states. In this section and the next we provide an overview and brief history of the contemporary monetary and trade regimes that have been central to this order.

---

[13] C. Fred Bergsten, Robert Keohane, and Joseph Nye, "International Economics and International Politics: A Framework for Analysis," *International Organization* 29 (1975), p. 14. This is a state-centered notion of hegemony along the lines discussed in Chapter 4. It is narrower than, but not necessarily inconsistent with, the class-based conception of hegemony associated with Antonio Gramsci and contemporary radical scholarship (see Chapters 5 and 12).

[14] Olson, *Logic of Collective Action*; Charles P. Kindleberger, "Dominance and Leadership in the International Economy: Exploitation, Public Goods, and Free Rides," *International Studies Quarterly* 25 (June 1981), pp. 242–254.

When individuals trade goods and services, they use currency as a medium of exchange. When trade is conducted across state borders, goods and services are valued in different national currencies. Exchange rates—the value of one currency relative to another—allow traders to compare the relative prices of these goods and services, but such price comparisons are much easier if there is a common medium of exchange (for example, gold, British pounds, or American dollars). Prices need only be converted into this common medium rather than into the national currency of each and every potential trading partner. For this kind of system to work smoothly, however, traders must be confident that the values of goods and services are relatively stable and not subject to wild fluctuation. Because changing currency values affect the values of traded goods—independent of the quality of those goods or the real costs of producing them—individuals engaged in international trade also prefer that exchange rates not be subject to wild fluctuation. Thus, international trade rests squarely on a stable international monetary system. An international **monetary regime** is designed to help states manage their exchange rates, maintain their reserve currencies (or assets like gold) used as a common medium of exchange, and regulate the movement of international capital.

In July 1944, forty-four states met at Bretton Woods, New Hampshire, intent on creating an international monetary order that would promote economic and political stability.[15] Specifically, they sought to institutionalize the strengths of the previous monetary system while avoiding the weaknesses that led to its demise during the Great Depression. Before the Great Depression, a "gold standard" was in effect; most major national currencies could be exchanged for gold on demand. This helped to stabilize currency values, for currencies were pegged to a precious metal with intrinsic worth. But there was always the temptation to devalue the national currency by raising the price of gold in the hopes that this would encourage exports, which would then be cheaper to foreign consumers. Under normal conditions, states resisted this temptation in the interest of international financial stability, but during the economic depression of the 1920s and 1930s, states succumbed and sought to stimulate exports and economic growth through currency depreciation. (The gold standard had been abandoned during World War I, but many states returned to it after the war.) There ensued a series of competitive devaluations that choked off international trade and deepened the global depression.

The monetary policies of states during the interwar period resembled a collective-action problem. Stable exchange rates were a collective good because they facilitated international trade and economic growth, yet each state was tempted to free ride by devaluing its own currency. When the temptation became widespread during the global economic crisis, the collective good of monetary stability could not be provided. Before this period, in the context of stable exchange rates, trade was made that much easier because the British pound served as a common medium of exchange. Because Great Britain had been on the gold standard since the early nineteenth century, many countries also held reserves of British

---

[15] For a history of the monetary regime, see Harold James, *International Monetary Cooperation since Bretton Woods* (Oxford: Oxford University Press, 1996).

pounds; they were "as good as gold." Most international economic transactions were conducted using pounds (much less cumbersome than using gold bullion), and this was possible as long as Britain could exchange gold for pounds on demand. But the British economy had weakened substantially by end of World War I. Although the pound was pegged to gold at its prewar price, its value was artificially high given the diminishing demand for British exports. Holders of British pounds preferred the gold; Britain's gold reserves were depleted, forcing it to end the currency's convertibility in 1931.[16]

In an effort to return to the financial stability of the gold-standard era, the agreement signed at Bretton Woods in 1944 fashioned a system of **fixed exchange rates**. The dollar would become the primary reserve asset (outside the communist economic bloc), just as gold had been used in the nineteenth century and the British pound in combination with gold at the end of the nineteenth and beginning of the twentieth centuries. It was pegged at $35 per ounce of gold, and the firm commitment of the U.S. government to convert dollars into gold meant that now the dollar was as good as gold. The value of other currencies were fixed relative to the dollar, and states would hold reserves in the form of both gold and dollars (and other foreign currencies as well, once they too became convertible).

This fixed exchange-rate system was designed to provide the financial stability necessary to promote an expansion of international trade. It disciplined states' monetary policies. During the interwar period, inflation was rampant. Germany was the most extreme example; saddled with heavy war reparations, the German government simply printed money when it ran out, totally undermining the value of the German mark. While less profligate, other countries also printed money, particularly as a means of financing post–World War I reconstruction. However, under the Bretton Woods system, expanding the money supply to the point of undermining confidence in the national currency would encourage local investors to cash in their notes for dollars because the dollar's value was more dependable. The state's dollar reserves would be depleted, making it difficult or impossible to maintain the fixed-dollar exchange rate of its national currency, as required by the Bretton Woods agreement. (To "prop up" the national currency, the state's central bank uses its foreign exchange reserves to purchase the currency so as to contract the money supply, thereby making the currency that remains in circulation more valuable.) Nor was the U.S. central bank, the Federal Reserve, free from constraints. Expanding the U.S. money supply would diminish confidence in the dollar, leading to a depletion of U.S. gold stocks as foreign central banks cashed in their weakening dollars. Stemming the outflow of gold by raising its price was not an option for the Fed under Bretton Woods; the price of gold was fixed at $35 an ounce.

The Bretton Woods agreement established the International Monetary Fund (IMF), which would help countries maintain their fixed exchange rates. The

---

[16] For a discussion of this period, see Barry Eichengreen, *Golden Fetters: The Gold Standard and the Great Depression* (New York: Oxford University Press, 1992); Beth A. Simmons, *Who Adjusts? Domestic Sources of Foreign Economic Policy During the Interwar Years* (Princeton, N.J.: Princeton University Press, 1994).

interwar experience taught observers that states would find it difficult to contract their money supplies for purposes of maintaining fixed exchange rates when doing so would have an adverse effect on economic growth and employment. The IMF, using a pool of foreign currency reserves contributed by member states, would make loans to states, allowing them to support the value of their currency during periods of economic difficulty. For states that needed a great deal of support, the IMF reserved the right to exercise some supervision over the borrower's economic policies, both monetary and fiscal—a stipulation known as **IMF conditionality**. The fixed exchange-rate regime was not overly rigid, however. Recalling Britain's experience after World War I, when the pound was overvalued relative to global demand for British products, the architects of the IMF built in provisions whereby states facing similar circumstances could devalue their currencies to ease the adjustment process and prevent the depletion of international reserves. But, again, devaluation was not an option available to the United States under Bretton Woods. Strains on the new fixed exchange-rate system would be further eased by the creation of the International Bank for Reconstruction and Development (IBRD, or World Bank), which provided loans for postwar economic recovery, as well as direct U.S. assistance by way of the Marshall Plan.

In reality, the constraints on the United States were not as limiting as those on other states under the Bretton Woods system. The United States did not need to maintain the dollar exchange rate, because all other currencies were pegged to the dollar. It had only to be willing to provide foreign central banks with gold in return for dollars. But for a time, not only was the U.S. dollar as good as gold, it was better than gold. The price of gold was fixed, while the dollar (in the form of treasury bills) paid interest. Foreign central banks willingly accumulated dollars rather than cash them in with the Fed. In fact, a "Eurodollar" market emerged wherein European banks, as well as offshore branches of American banks, began lending their dollar deposits (beyond the reach of U.S. regulators). Confidence in the dollar did not last, though.

The second half of the 1960s saw a large increase in U.S. government expenditures associated with the Johnson administration's Great Society programs to reduce poverty and America's widening involvement in the Vietnam War. The resulting price inflation fed speculation that there needed to be a devaluation of the dollar relative to European currencies. Devaluation was not a simple matter for any country under the system of fixed exchange rates, but for the United States it was especially difficult because it required a coordinated and simultaneous *revaluation* of other currencies that were pegged to the dollar. Because revaluation would raise these countries' export prices compared to U.S. goods, cooperation was not forthcoming. Faced with continued depletion of U.S. gold stocks as confidence in the value of the dollar sunk, the Nixon administration declared, in August 1971, that the United States would no longer exchange gold for dollars and would impose a 10 percent surcharge on imports—the so-called Nixon shocks. Its major trading partners agreed to revalue their currencies, but the realignment proved to be only a temporary reprieve for the fixed exchange-rate system. In February 1973, in the midst of another run on the dollar, the currency exchange market closed; when it reopened in March, most European currencies and the Japanese yen were floating against the dollar. Bretton Woods had finally collapsed.[17]

The move to **floating exchange rates** in 1973 was meant as a transition to a new system of fixed rates, one that reflected the new, less lopsided distribution of economic power within the OECD. That became complicated by developments elsewhere in the international system. As we pointed out in the last chapter, during the Yom Kippur War, several member states of OPEC showed their displeasure with American support of Israel by placing an embargo on oil exports to the United States (and the Netherlands, another supporter of Israel). There was some speculation that the embargo might be widened, causing the price of oil to be bid up as importing countries moved to secure future supplies. OPEC used its new-found leverage to increase oil prices further, and by the beginning of 1974 oil was selling for $12 a barrel, four times the market price just three months earlier. The oil shock helped to push industrialized economies, along with the economies of many nonoil LDCs, into recession. Global economic slowdown was brought on by across-the-board price increases driven by high energy costs. The combination of high prices and stagnating economic growth—until then, the two did not normally occur at the same time—led economists to coin a new term, *stagflation*.

The oil shock sealed the fate of the fixed exchange-rate system. Dealing with domestic stagflation was a difficult task in itself; the imposition of exchange-rate targets as an additional chore for economic policy was no longer realistic. Most policy makers concluded that the process of adjusting to the oil shock was smoother in the context of floating exchange rates. The degree of stagnation and inflation was different for different countries, and their fiscal and monetary policies could be more closely tailored to their own domestic economic conditions. In addition, certain government-imposed controls on the movement of international capital, necessary to maintain exchange rates, were now lifted. This benefited LDCs by making it easier to borrow in international financial markets in order to sustain domestic spending programs and economic growth.

A system of floating exchange rates has operated since 1973. This does not mean that benefits of stable exchange rates have disappeared, only that new mechanisms for stabilization have emerged since the collapse of Bretton Woods. The current system is often called a *managed float* because the monetary authorities in various states (finance ministers and central bankers) often consult and coordinate their policies so as to minimize disruptive fluctuations in exchange rates. Over time, member states of the European Union moved to fix the value of their currencies to each other until 1999, when most of them adopted a single European currency (the euro). Many developing countries peg their currencies to another currency (usually the dollar, yen, or euro), or to a basket of currencies, in order to maintain the stability of their exchange rates. Some countries have even adopted a foreign currency as their official currency—loosely known as "dollarization"

---

[17] See Peter M. Garber, "The Collapse of the Bretton Woods Fixed Exchange Rate System," in Michael D. Bordo and Barry J. Eichengreen, eds., *A Retrospective on the Bretton Woods System: Lessons for International Monetary Reform* (Chicago: Chicago University Press, 1993). On the Nixon shocks, see Joanne S. Gowa, *Closing the Window: Domestic Politics and the End of Bretton Woods* (Ithaca, N.Y.: Cornell University Press, 1983).

because in most cases the U.S. dollar has been currency of choice. Ecuador and El Salvador dollarized in 2000 and 2001, respectively; Kosovo and Montenegro use the euro.[18] Thus, despite this mix of arrangements, there is still widespread agreement that exchange-rate stability is a collective good worth pursuing.

THE TRADE REGIME

As with the monetary regime, the United States was the primary organizer and support behind the postwar system of liberalized international trade. The goal of a nondiscriminatory, multilateral, and market-based system was shared by the industrialized Western powers, in part as a reaction to the protectionism of the 1930s. Cooperation in the reduction of trade barriers, not protectionism, was to be these states' modus operandi, and the hope was that ultimately the rest of the world would follow along.

Although the United States was willing to lead in this area as well, the issues were much more complex because of the effects of trade on domestic politics. Discussions on trade policy and multilateral arrangements began in 1943, but the first element of the postwar trade regime did not take hold until the 1947 General Agreement on Tariffs and Trade (GATT). Reflecting the liberal consensus, GATT members agreed to implement the most-favored-nation principle (described in the previous chapter) and established other rules aimed at reducing trade barriers and mediating trade disputes. The agreement also included a plan to establish an International Trade Organization (ITO), which would help member states meet their GATT obligations, much like the IMF functioned with respect to the monetary arrangement negotiated at Bretton Woods. The Truman administration considered the ITO charter too restrictive on U.S. policy and never submitted the treaty for ratification. Instead, the GATT itself became institutionalized, with a secretariat, a director general, and staff to handle the work relating to trade negotiations.

The GATT was the central feature of the liberal trade regime and worked very well for the developed countries as tariffs, quotas, and other trade barriers were gradually removed and trade was encouraged.[19] Much of the postwar prosperity derived from this increase in economic interaction. Trade talks were conducted continuously under the auspices of the GATT in what became referred to as trade "rounds" (summarized in Table 13.2). A high point of trade cooperation through the GATT came with the tariff reductions achieved during the Kennedy Round of negotiations (named in honor of John F. Kennedy, assassinated the year before), which concluded in 1967. After this point, however, all the factors that caused strains in the monetary regime also brought trouble to trade relations.

---

[18] On dollarization, see Eric Helleiner, "Dollarization Diplomacy: U.S. Policy towards Latin America Coming Full Circle?" *Review of International Political Economy* 10 (August 2003), pp. 406–429; Dominick Salvatore, James W. Dean, and Thomas Willett, eds., *The Dollarization Debate* (New York: Oxford University Press, 2003).

[19] For evidence, see Judith L. Goldstein, Douglas Rivers, and Michael Tomz, "Institutions in International Relations: Understanding the Effects of the GATT and the WTO on World Trade," *International Organization* 61 (Winter 2007), pp. 37–67. For a more skeptical assessment, see Joanne Gowa and Soo Yeon Kim, "An Exclusive Country Club: The Effects of the GATT on Trade, 1950–94," *World Politics* 57 (July 2005), pp. 453–478.

TABLE 13.2 | GATT TRADE ROUNDS

Years	Primary Locations	Called	Issues	Participants
1947	Geneva		Tariffs	23
1949	Annecy, France		Tariffs	13
1950–1951	Torquay, England		Tariffs	38
1956	Geneva		Tariffs	26
1960–1961	Geneva	Dillon Round	Tariffs	26
1964–1967	Geneva	Kennedy Round	Tariffs, dumping	62
1973–1979	Geneva	Tokyo Round	Tariffs, nontariff barriers	102
1986–1993	Geneva	Uruguay Round	Tariffs, nontariff barriers, trade in services, intellectual property, textiles, agriculture, WTO	123

Source: World Trade Organization, *Understanding the WTO*, 3rd ed. (Geneva: World Trade Organization, 2007), p. 16.

Inflation and the increasing interdependence of national economies caused political discontent in certain economic sectors within countries that were being hurt by foreign competition. The problems emerging in monetary relations also became trade problems, especially as European and Japanese goods came to rival U.S. goods and helped lead to U.S. balance-of-trade deficits. In a five-year period ending in 1972, the United States went from a trade surplus of almost $4 billion to a deficit of more than $6 billion. Some European actions in particular were highly preferential or protectionist, especially provisions in the Common Agricultural Policy of the European Community (now the EU). Japanese restrictions on imports of U.S. agricultural products and U.S. restrictions on imports of Japanese textiles and electronics became continuing irritants. The United States was no longer able or willing to shoulder the burden of the free-trade regime.

From 1967 onward, pressures for trade protection and discrimination increased in the United States, Europe, and Japan. The loss of cheap oil as an energy source and, with wage increases, a loss of cheap labor contributed to the decline in competitiveness that fed these demands. The August 1971 Nixon shocks were accompanied by what would become a continuing American insistence on changes in European and Japanese trade practices. By 1973 it was clear that some new rules for the liberal trade regime had to be established. In September, representatives of about 100 states convened in Tokyo to launch a new round of trade negotiations. The Tokyo Round, lasting until 1979, took up some of the complex issues of international trade not addressed in previous rounds, including the nontariff barriers like import licensing and customs valuations. The results were mixed. There were agreements to dismantle some NTBs, but in many cases only the industrialized participants promised to adhere to the arrangements (so they were called *codes* rather than agreements).

A new round of talks was launched in Punta del Este, Uruguay, in September 1986. The agenda was very ambitious, including issues left unsettled at the conclusion of the Tokyo Round, as well as new ones like trade in services, intellectual property rights, and North–South trade. The Uruguay Round concluded in 1994 with a trade accord signed in Marrakesh, Morocco. It took three and a half years longer than intended, but its achievements were substantial. First, in the area of market access, participants were aiming for a one-third reduction in tariffs on average; the final agreement reduced them by almost 40 percent. The GATT was extended to include agreements on textiles, agriculture, dumping, export subsidies, licensing procedures, and various technical barriers to trade. Second, while the GATT had been directed mainly at the trade in goods, it was now supplemented by a General Agreement on Trade in Services (GATS) and an agreement on Trade-Related Aspects of Intellectual Property Rights (TRIPs), which covered patents, trademarks, copyright, product designs, and so on. Finally, the Uruguay Round established the World Trade Organization (WTO)—a belated, but in the end probably more effective, international organization than what was envisioned for the ITO in 1948. We return to the WTO in the next section.

For countries grouped by income level, Figure 13.1 shows trends in import duties (as a percent of all imports) from 1990 to 2006. The norm in the liberal trade regime has been to allow poorer countries a greater degree of protection for their domestic industries, and this is clear from the higher import duty levels for the low-income group. Levels declined rapidly for all income groups in the post–World War II period and over the past fifteen years, as the figure indicates, they have continued to decline. The steepest decline is for middle-income economies, although average import duties for high-income economies really cannot get much lower (certain economic sectors, like agriculture, still benefit from protection). States continue to negotiate over the protection of international property rights and barriers to trade in services, a high priority for the United States because more than 70 percent of its GDP comes from the service sector. It is a mark of continued American influence that the agenda for international trade negotiations has increasingly turned to barriers applied to products of the so-called new economy, an area in which the United States enjoys a substantial lead.

ECONOMIC DISORDER AND REALIGNMENT

The United States still plays the lead role on the world economic stage, but the supporting cast, both state and nonstate actors, have much more significant roles than before. The disorderliness of the international political economy beginning in the

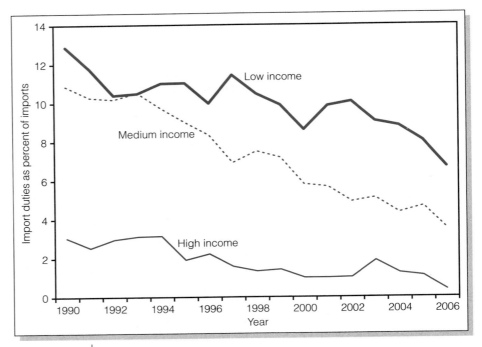

FIGURE 13.1 | IMPORT DUTIES FOR HIGH-, MEDIUM-, AND LOW-INCOME ECONOMIES, 1990–2006

Tariffs and other import duties, as a share of total imports, declined significantly as the liberal trade regime took hold in the years following World War II, and they have continued to decline in more recent years. A higher level of protectionism is tolerated for less wealthy countries in exchange for a commitment to reduce trade barriers over time. In general, countries in all income categories have been living up to these commitments.

Source: Calculated from data in World Bank, *World Development Indicators 2008 CD-ROM* (Washington, D.C.: World Bank, 2008).

mid-1970s is precisely what realist perspectives and hegemonic stability theory would have predicted for that period.[20]

HEGEMONIC DECLINE

The monetary and trade regimes established under American dominance just after World War II inevitably became complicated as the Western European and Japanese economies recovered and grew. By the late 1970s, it was clear that the U.S. economy could no longer be the sole engine of worldwide economic growth. Japan and Germany, in particular, had to share in the responsibilities,

[20] See Charles P. Kindleberger, *The World in Depression 1929–1939*, rev. ed. (Berkeley: University of California Press, 1986); Duncan Snidal, "The Limits of Hegemonic Stability Theory," *International Organization* 39 (Autumn 1985), pp. 579–614.

and the required coordination of economic policies is often a source of friction among the leading industrialized countries. One recurring pattern has been for the United States to pressure Japan and Germany to pursue expansionary policies to stimulate economic growth, while the latter resist for fear of excessive domestic inflation. Beginning in 1979, the Fed pursued a restrictive monetary policy in order to reduce U.S. inflation, which also caused a sharp appreciation of the dollar. But the rising costs of American imports, combined with rising oil prices following the second oil shock in 1979, led to price inflation abroad, thus prompting foreign central banks to pursue restrictive monetary policies as well. (The United States was said to be "exporting" its inflation.) That led to a global economic recession from 1981 to 1983, the worst since the Great Depression of the 1930s.

Poor economic performance in the 1980s, along with the mounting U.S. trade deficits that accompanied an appreciation of the dollar, translated into trade surpluses for America's major trading partners. Japan became America's largest creditor, and the trade disputes between the two countries became major issues of contention that were not easily solved. It was during the 1980s that imported Japanese cars began to account for a substantial share of the North American market. Although American consumers now tend to take the prevalence of Japanese automobiles in the marketplace for granted, the initial shift in the auto market engendered feelings of resentment among American workers, feelings frequently tinged with racism. Such attitudes resurfaced when Japanese companies began investing in American real estate and the entertainment industry. In 1989, for example, Mitsubishi acquired 80 percent of New York's Rockefeller Center; at about the same time, Sony purchased Columbia Pictures and Matsushita bought MCA/Universal—both considered icons of American popular culture. Such developments were viewed with alarm by many Americans on both ends of the political spectrum.[21]

The Japanese economic miracle was part of an economic resurgence and growth along the whole Pacific Rim, especially in the NICs of Taiwan, South Korea, Singapore, and Hong Kong (also known as the "Asian Tigers"). During the 1980s, the Pacific Rim countries replaced Western Europe as the major trading partners of the United States—and mostly with trade surpluses. The Asian NICs' currencies depreciated almost as fast as the dollar, maintaining these countries' competitiveness and allowing them to export twice as much to the United States as they imported from it. Meanwhile, rapid increases in Japanese productivity and continuing Japanese informal, as well as official, restrictions on imports of goods and services enabled Japan to export three times as much to the United States as it imported. The Pacific Rim countries of Brunei, Indonesia, Malaysia, the Philippines, Singapore, Thailand, and Vietnam are members of the Association of South East Asian Nations (ASEAN). ASEAN has facilitated economic cooperation

---

[21] For a study of American public attitudes during this period, see Gearóid Ó Tuathail, "Japan as Threat: Geo-economic Discourses on the USA–Japan Relationship in US Civil Society, 1987–91," in Colin H. Williams, ed., *The Political Geography of the New World Order* (New York: Belhaven, 1993).

among its members and represents yet another source of economic growth around the Pacific Rim.[22]

Consequently, the 1980s saw an increase in protectionist sentiments in the United States. In 1988, the U.S. Congress passed the Omnibus Trade and Competitiveness Act, which included a provision known as *Super 301* that required the president to identify states engaging in unfair trade practices and subject to possible retaliation. By 2002, when the provision expired, the U.S. trade representative had initiated more than fifty investigations into the practices of U.S. trade partners in accordance with Super 301, about one-third of them directed at Japan or members of the EU. The bill also authorized a review of foreign direct investment in the United States for potential threats to national security. The Clinton administration was especially assertive in its efforts to break down remaining trade and investment barriers, both in its bilateral economic policies and in multilateral forums like the GATT and WTO.

WORLD TRADE ORGANIZATION

The WTO, headquartered in Geneva, is the successor to the GATT's de facto organization, and its creation was the most significant single development in the liberal trade order since the GATT itself was established in 1947. The GATT is a treaty and is still binding on state parties; it was simply amended by the accords signed in Marrakesh in 1994, which included a charter for the WTO as well as revised trade rules for existing parties to the GATT. The updated agreement is often referred to as the GATT 1994. The WTO's founding members consisted of only about 60 percent of the GATT membership at the time, but the remainder had joined within two years. By 2008, after an additional 24 accessions to the GATT 1994, the WTO membership stood at 152 (with 30 more states as observers). Among IGOs, only the UN has more members.[23]

The WTO monitors compliance with the rules and procedures that emerged from the Uruguay Round. In a manner similar to the UN and other IGOs, the organization provides a forum for states to address issues relating to trade. It also provides a set of mechanisms whereby states may redress trade-related grievances against other states in an institutional setting administered by neutral parties. The WTO's Ministerial Conferences, which bring together state representatives at least once every two years, have replaced and further institutionalized the process that evolved under the GATT. The Ministerial Conference, though large and unwieldy, is nevertheless the WTO's most authoritative body and its purview includes any and all matters covered by the trade agreements. (Figure 13.2 is a diagram of the WTO's organizational structure.) The 2001 conference in Doha, Qatar, launched

---

[22] The East Asian model of economic growth is praised in James Fallows in *Looking at the Sun: The Rise of the New East Asian Economic and Political System* (New York: Pantheon, 1994). The economic crisis of 1997–1998 did much to diminish that model (see Chapter 1), but for a precrisis critique see Paul Krugman, "The Myth of Asia's Miracle," *Foreign Affairs* 73 (November/December 1994), pp. 62–78.

[23] For a skeptical view of such developments, see Judith Goldstein and Lisa L. Martin, "Legalization, Trade Liberalization, and Domestic Politics: A Cautionary Note," *International Organization* 54 (Summer 2000), pp. 603–632.

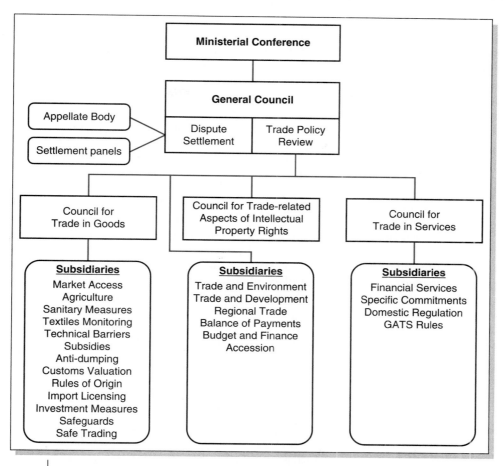

FIGURE 13.2 | STRUCTURE OF THE WORLD TRADE ORGANIZATION

The organizational structure of the WTO is designed to monitor and implement the trade rules contained in the GATT 1994—that is, provisions for reducing barriers to trade in goods and services, protections for intellectual property rights, and procedures for resolving trade disputes. All member states have representatives in the various bodies of the WTO.

what has become known as the Doha Round of trade talks. It has been a highly contentious round of negotiations focusing mainly on agricultural subsidies, especially those provided by rich states, but also labor and environmental standards, patents, and other issues. As of 2008, no agreement had been reached, and it appeared likely that the Doha Round would stretch even longer than the Uruguay Round, suggesting the sensitive nature of the topics being addressed.

The General Council of the WTO, consisting of midlevel representatives from all member states, meets regularly and is the chief decision-making body for reviewing trade policy and settling trade disputes between member states. The WTO's dispute settlement process is highly structured, with ultimate authority residing with the General Council meeting as the Dispute Settlement Body. In this capacity, the General Council typically appoints a panel of experts to investigate the dispute, identify the unfair trade practices (if any), and indicate how those practices should be changed in order to comply with the rules. Because the panel's report can only be rejected by a unanimous vote of the General Council, it is effectively binding on the parties to the dispute (although one or both can appeal). If the unfair trade practices have not been reversed within a designated amount of time, the aggrieved state can request permission to impose retaliatory trade sanctions. By June 2008, almost 400 trade disputes had been submitted to the WTO—disputes that otherwise might have been dealt with unilaterally. The United States has been the respondent in most of these (90 disputes), but it has also lodged more complaints than any other member (99). The EU, which represents its members before the Dispute Settlement Body, has also been party to a large number of disputes (78 as complainant, 62 as respondent).[24]

Reporting to the General Council are councils charged with monitoring the implementation of trade rules in each of three main areas: trade in goods, trade in services, and TRIPs. The Goods Council and the Services Council are composed of subsidiary committees and working groups with responsibilities in more specific issue areas; another set of committees dealing with cross-cutting matters reports directly to the General Council. Almost all of these bodies consist of representatives from every member state, so most of the real work of the WTO takes place in the context of smaller informal meetings, out of which larger agreements are fashioned piecemeal. Assisting in all of this is the WTO's secretariat, headed by a director-general with a staff of about 600. As with the secretariats of other IGOs, this body serves the interest of organization itself, and ultimately the trade regime.

ENDURING ORDER

U.S. leadership in world economic affairs was revitalized beginning in the latter half of the 1990s. The American "new economy" was performing well, and, after some difficult restructuring, American companies had become much more competitive in the global marketplace. At the same time, the Asian economic crisis raised doubts about the Japanese model of economic development, emulated elsewhere in East and Southeast Asia, boosting the confidence of proponents of American-style free-market capitalism. Moreover, the United States has been called upon repeatedly to help rescue countries in economic trouble. It spearheaded and contributed substantial funds to the bailouts of Mexico in 1994, as well as of South Korea, Russia, and Brazil in 1998—a sign that American leadership, if not hegemony, is alive and well in the international political economy.[25]

---

[24] See World Trade Organization, "Dispute Settlement: Disputes by Country," June 20, 2008; available at <http://www.wto.org/english/tratop_e/dispu_e/dispu_by_country_e.htm>. For an analysis of states' use of this and other multilateral forums for resolving trade disputes, see Marc L. Busch, "Overlapping Institutions, Forum Shopping, and Dispute Settlement in International Trade," *International Organization* 61 (Fall 2007), pp. 735–761.

[25] For early views that the predicted American decline was premature, see Bruce Russett, "The Mysterious Case of Vanishing Hegemony: or, Is Mark Twain Really Dead?" *International Organization* 39 (Spring 1985), pp. 207–231; Susan Strange, "The Persistent Myth of Lost Hegemony," *International Organization* 41 (Autumn 1987), pp. 551–574.

Nevertheless, the United States may need to learn new patterns of economic diplomacy. Many countries of the Pacific Rim have pursued a model of state-centered capitalism different from that of the United States. Their domestic markets, investment efforts, and export policies are characterized by a partnership between their state bureaucracies and private corporations. Lessons learned from the recent Asian economic crisis are not likely to completely undo economic practices reinforced by three decades of often stellar economic performance. The Asian countries, as well as those of continental Western Europe, traditionally have been more comfortable with protectionism than have the British and Americans. They have often pursued policies of **strategic trade**, whereby the state promotes certain export industries by providing government subsidies or other forms of assistance.[26] While the current trend seems to be in the direction of openness, it is not clear whether the structures of international free trade can be retained or whether barriers will again emerge during periods of global economic difficulty.

The rise of China as a major economic power has complicated matters further. Chinese controls on imports and foreign investment are far more restrictive than Japan's. In 2007, the U.S. trade deficit with China was more than $250 billion, or more than one-third of its total trade deficit and well in excess of its deficits with Japan, with its NAFTA partners Canada and Mexico, and with the entire EU. Although the United States has welcomed China's integration into the world economy (initiated in the late 1970s), China's domestic market is less accessible than most others on the Pacific Rim. Many Chinese firms have been accused of "pirating" computer software, audio recordings, and other high-tech goods protected by copyrights and patents in the West—not only reducing Chinese demand for U.S. imports of these goods but even allowing Chinese firms to compete sharply with the original producers in Asian export markets. China has agreed to stop these abuses, but its record of compliance is mixed. China joined the WTO in 2001, so Chinese officials are bringing their trade policies into line with the existing rules of the multilateral trade regime. WTO membership also requires some economic restructuring, and a degree of economic "transparency"—scrutiny of its trade policies and practices—that the Chinese government has not been comfortable with heretofore.

The diversity of approaches to dealing with both the benefits and costs of integration into the global economy partly reflects what John Gerard Ruggie has called the post–World War II compromise of **embedded liberalism**. Neither the laissez-faire liberalism practiced in the nineteenth century nor the economic nationalism of the interwar period seemed to offer a viable model for postwar world order. If states were to adopt liberal international economic policies, they would also need to retain the capacity to intervene in order to cushion the economic and social dislocations their citizens were likely to experience once the national economy was exposed to international market forces. Economic liberalism thus had to be

---

[26] Marc L. Busch, *Trade Warriors: States, Firms, and Strategic-Trade Policy in High-Technology Competition* (Cambridge: Cambridge University Press, 1999); Laura D'Andrea Tyson, *Who's Bashing Whom? Trade Conflict in High-Technology Industries* (Washington, D.C.: Institute for International Economics, 1992).

"embedded" within this shared understanding that had become the basis for relations between states and their civil societies. The methods that states adopt to soften the blows of global capitalism vary, but all states have endeavored to do so, and, as our discussion of American defense-industrial policy in the last chapter indicated, the United States is no exception. Therefore, American hegemony provides only part of the explanation for the order we have described in this chapter. Another part of the explanation is the willingness to enter into this compromise, and to tolerate the same on the part of other trading states. As long as the bargain holds, argues Ruggie, the prospects for enduring order in world politics are good.[27]

Whether we see order or disorder in international political-economic relations often depends on whether we are inclined to see the glass as half-full or half-empty. The initial decline of U.S. economic might relative to other countries was inevitable; the post–World War II economies of Europe and Japan could not remain in tatters indefinitely, and industrialization was bound to be successful in many developing countries, including the newly independent ones. The United States itself actively promoted economic reconstruction and development; its diminishing capacity to steer global economic affairs in many ways testifies to the success of U.S. policy, not its failure.

What most liberals find noteworthy is the extent of cooperation that has transpired in international economic relations even in the absence of a single hegemonic power. States have cooperated despite the temptations to free ride, or perhaps because free riding is no longer feasible without a hegemon willing to carry the load. If America's economic clout is not what it once was, wielding it has become less necessary as Europe and Japan have become more accustomed to sharing leadership responsibilities in helping to manage global economic stability. The annual economic summit meeting of the Group of Five (G5)—then the G7, and now the G8—beginning in 1975 epitomizes the recognition that, although the United States is often treated as first among equals, leadership in the contemporary world economy is too much for one state and must be shared. The frequent meetings of the Trade Ministers' Quadrilateral (the "Quad": the United States, Canada, Japan, and the EU) since 1982 are another indication of an increasingly institutionalized joint leadership that has emerged in the wake of American hegemony. The collaboration and economic policy coordination required to bring an element of stability to a global economic system consisting of almost 200 trading states, 65,000 multinational corporations, and about $3 trillion in currency trading per day would seem unattainable on its face. That government ministers and central bankers ever meet with success is impressive indeed.

The move toward free trade on the part of an ever increasing number of states, despite the periodic lapses into protectionism, undergirds the considerable order we find in world politics today. Trade prospers in peacetime, and the resulting web of mutual economic interest helps reinforce the peace. A commitment to order gave

---

[27] John Gerard Ruggie, "International Regimes, Transactions, and Change: Embedded Liberalism in the Postwar Economic Order," *International Organization* 36 (Spring 1982). See also Karl Polanyi's classic, *The Great Transformation: The Political and Economic Origins of Our Time*, 2nd ed. (Boston: Beacon Press, 2001). Note, however, that Russia has yet to be admitted to the WTO.

rise to the GATT after World War II and ultimately transformed the GATT's de facto organizational apparatus into the WTO, an organization with a charter under international law and nearly all states as either members or observers. Free trade thrives under conditions of monetary stability, and the Bretton Woods regime provided that for two and a half decades before the inevitable realignment of economic power forced its collapse. The commitment to monetary stability remains, as does the IMF, a core Bretton Woods institution, even though the current monetary regime allows exchange rates to float.

The degree of free trade and monetary stability is uneven worldwide. States have found that chiseling away at trade barriers and stabilizing exchange rates is easier when efforts are concentrated among fewer countries in relative geographic proximity and at roughly similar levels of economic development. Collective goods are less likely to be undermined by free riding when restricted to small groups, and this can be seen in the formation of regional trade blocs, a topic we take up in the next chapter.

REGIONAL ECONOMIC INTEGRATION AND GLOBALIZATION

CHAPTER 14

EUROPEAN UNION

Many state leaders have concluded that larger economic entities typically fare better in the modern world economy than smaller ones. Large domestic markets provide the demand necessary to support diverse industrial and service sectors. What is more, domestic demand is a great deal more dependable and predictable than foreign demand for the country's exports, which is subject to the vagaries of the international political economy, like protectionism and monetary instability. Economic self-sufficiency, or autarky, is really not an option in the contemporary international system, but large and diverse economies stand a better chance of weathering the effects of international economic crises. Large domestic markets provide no guarantees, of course; economic (and political) mismanagement can just as easily send a large economy into a tailspin as a small one. But small and specialized economies, even if well managed, can be overwhelmed by international economic forces beyond the control of state leaders or other domestic economic actors.

There may be no better single explanation for the vitality and resilience of the U.S. economy than its large domestic markets. China has become a major economic force in world affairs because of the sheer size of its economy. Its vast population has permitted industrialization even in relative isolation from the world economy, but now, with increasing openness, China presents potentially huge markets for foreign goods. The stake that industrialized countries have in seeing Russia's economy become fully integrated into the global capitalist system is similar. A prosperous Russian population would be a substantial source of demand for goods and services produced abroad. As we discussed in Chapter 5, natural endowments count for much when it comes to state power; large populations mean large markets, and large markets promote industrialization and economic strength.

The immediate goal of **economic integration** is the creation of a single market out of a number of separate markets previously circumscribed by national boundaries. Multilateral economic cooperation and policy coordination is designed to enable the free movement of goods, services, labor, and capital across state borders, which will promote economic competitiveness and prosperity in the region. The most successful effort to date has been the creation of the European Union. In this chapter we discuss the evolution of the EU as well as the emergence of other economic blocs like NAFTA. We also consider the increasingly transnational character of economic activities, such as those of multinational firms, especially the degree to which they are transforming the nature of world politics. In such developments many observers see a substantial whittling away of state sovereignty and the beginning of the end of the Westphalian state system. For some, this is a cause for celebration; for others, a cause for alarm.

FROM ROME TO MAASTRICHT

As discussed in Chapter 11, the visionaries of a united Europe thought that integration was the best way to achieve peace in a region racked by two continent-wide wars in three decades. Functionalists like David Mitrany and Jean Monnet reasoned that the interdependencies that characterized Europe's level of social and economic development gave rise to technical problems and management tasks that were best handled by specialists, not politicians. As the web of transnational problem-solving personnel and procedures grew and brought more and more benefits to European states, not only would state leaders have less to fight about, they would also think twice about trampling these transnational linkages on their way to yet another European war.[1]

The first step along the path to European unification was the formation of the European Coal and Steel Community (ECSC) in 1951 to coordinate coal and steel production by France, West Germany, Belgium, Luxembourg, the Netherlands, and Italy—the "Six" or, as the community expanded, the "Inner Six." The Six were so encouraged by the success of the ECSC that they sought to deepen their collaboration. They agreed to form the European Defense Community (EDC) in 1952. Both Europeans and Americans had come to the conclusion that the military security of Western Europe could not be guaranteed unless West Germany could be rearmed. Germany at this time was still occupied (by the United States, Britain, and France in the western zone and by the Soviet Union in the eastern zone); it had no army and no control over its foreign policy. World War II was very fresh in Europeans' memories, and most remained wary of German militarism. The EDC, therefore, was seen as a way to harness German personnel and industrial strength to the common defense. It also would have checked German militarism by uniting all member states' armies within a single organizational structure. However, the EDC Treaty, after being ratified by five of the Six, was defeated by the French Assembly in 1954. It was shelved after that, along with a draft treaty establishing a European Political Community.

---

[1] For a historical overview of the evolution of the EU, see Desmond Dinan, *Europe Recast: A History of the European Union* (Boulder, Colo.: Rienner, 2004). For a review of theory, see Mark A. Pollack, "Theorizing the European Union: International Organization, Domestic Polity, or Experiment in New Governance," *Annual Review of Political Science* 8 (June 2005), pp. 357–398.

The designs for a defense and a political community were too ambitious for Europe at that time. Not enough Europeans (especially the French) were ready to give up such sweeping powers to an international organization. In retrospect, this is not surprising; the functionalist notion of "spillover" suggested a piecemeal process of European unification. The *Treaties of Rome*, which established the European Atomic Energy Community (Euratom) and the European Economic Community (EEC) and were signed by the Six in 1957, were more consistent with this idea of gradualism. Still, Euratom was only modestly effective—atomic energy was intertwined with matters of national security and Europeans (again, especially the French) were reluctant to surrender much sovereignty in this area. The EEC was quite successful, however. The Six were to be constituted as a **customs union,** meaning that they were to first eliminate all tariffs between them and then adopt a common set of tariffs on imports from countries outside the EEC (the process was largely complete by 1968). The ECSC, Euratom, and the EEC became known collectively as the European Communi*ties,* although it was common to refer to them, and their member states, using the singular European Community (EC).

Britain viewed early moves toward European integration with considerable skepticism, and even today, as a full member of the EU, tends to remain somewhat aloof from the continental members.[2] As the Six were negotiating what would become the Treaties of Rome, Britain was pushing for the creation of a **free-trade area,** whereby tariffs within the community would be dismantled, but without common tariffs imposed on imports from outside the community as called for by a customs union. The British were partly concerned that joining the customs union would interfere in the special relationships the country had with both the United States and members of the British Commonwealth. But the Six rejected the British plan, at which point the British approached Austria, Denmark, Norway, Portugal, Sweden, and Switzerland. These seven countries formed the European Free Trade Area (EFTA) in 1960. When Britain finally did apply for EC membership, its entry was vetoed in 1963 by France. Britain reapplied in 1967, along with Ireland, Denmark, and Norway, and in 1973 the EC was expanded to nine members (Norwegian membership was defeated at the polls).

In the late 1970s, Greece, Spain, and Portugal applied for EC membership; Greece was admitted in 1981, Spain and Portugal in 1986. Actually, aside from expanding the size of the EC, the process of economic integration slowed during the 1970s and early 1980s. European economies were plagued by rising inflation, increasing unemployment, and slow growth—an economic malaise that would come to be called "Eurosclerosis" because many felt it was due to welfare-state legislation and market rigidities. Beyond achieving a customs union, the movement toward European unification, as laid out in the Rome treaties, seemed dead in the water. The treaty establishing the economic community called for a Common Agricultural Policy (CAP). Although CAP was in place by the late 1960s, it was a source of contention within the EC as well as between the EC and countries outside

---

[2] Anthony Forster, *Euroscepticism in Contemporary British Politics: Opposition to Europe in the Conservative and Labour Parties since 1945* (London: Routledge, 2002); Stephen George, *An Awkward Partner: Britain in the European Community,* 3rd ed. (New York: Oxford University Press, 1998).

the community, particularly the United States. The CAP basically entailed protecting European farmers from external competition through subsidies and price supports while fostering economic interdependence among the Six. Within the EC, tensions arose because countries like Germany, where agricultural exports were less important to economic well-being, were subsidizing agricultural production in countries where the export of farm products was more important, like France, and later Ireland, Greece, Spain, and Portugal.

After signing the Treaties of Rome, the Six were often referred to as the "Common Market." This was something of a misnomer, for although the Six did intend to form a common market—whereby barriers to the free movement of labor and capital are removed, along with remaining nontariff barriers to trade in goods—little progress had been made even by the mid-1980s. But with the signing of the Single European Act (SEA) in 1986, the creation of a common market became the EC's first priority. The Europeans were increasingly of the view that in order to compete effectively with large American and Japanese firms, European industries needed to consolidate, and this was not possible as long as there were restrictions on the flow of European capital and labor within the EC. The SEA not only specified in some detail the measures that must be undertaken in order to create a single European market but also set as its target date the end of 1992—and the project became known as *Europe 1992*. An important element of the project was a concrete plan for achieving European **monetary union**. Monetary union had long been an element in the grand plan of European unification, but the SEA now took up the question of implementation: the establishment of a central banking system and the introduction of a single European currency. We return to a discussion of monetary union later in the chapter.

The SEA breathed new life into the process of European unification; the pessimism that accompanied Eurosclerosis gave way to Euro-optimism. Member states focused their efforts on the steps required to achieve a common market in accordance with Europe 1992. They also began seriously negotiating the stages that the EC would have to pass through in order to enter into economic and monetary union. This raised the ante. Monetary policy can have a significant effect on national economic performance and therefore, in European democracies, on a sitting government's prospects at election time. Also on the agenda was political union. From 1989, with the fall of the Berlin Wall, West and East Germany were moving toward reunification. Fearful that a united Germany would wield too much influence on the continent, particularly in Eastern Europe, France and Britain eventually agreed that the EC should be strengthened through institutional reforms and movement toward a common foreign policy.

In 1992, the twelve EC foreign ministers signed the far-reaching Treaty on European Union in the city of Maastricht, the Netherlands. Because national sovereignty was at stake in the agreements on both monetary union and the common foreign and defense policy, ratification of the *Maastricht treaty* proved more difficult than state leaders expected. During the negotiations, Britain had insisted on the right not to participate in certain aspects of what was now formally dubbed the Economic and Monetary Union (EMU), as well as the Social Charter, which provided for the standardization of social policy and workers' rights essential to a single European labor market. Popular opposition elsewhere in the EC was mobilized only after the Maastricht treaty was signed. Danish voters said no to the treaty in a 1992 referendum; they approved the treaty only after it was stipulated that Denmark, too, could opt out of certain provisions. The French approved the treaty by the narrowest of margins, while domestic legal haggling prevented German ratification until the end of 1993. Finally, however, the Maastricht treaty went into effect. Somewhat confusingly, the EEC, one of the three European Communities, was itself renamed the European Community (also EC) and the wider institutional and legal arrangement officially became known as the European Union.[3]

With the addition of Austria, Finland, and Sweden to its ranks in 1995, the union grew to fifteen members (EU15), where it remained until 2004 when it undertook its largest and potentially most challenging expansion ever. As agreed in the Treaty of Nice in 2001, ten new admissions brought EU membership to twenty-five (EU25): Cyprus, the Czech Republic, Estonia, Hungary, Latvia, Lithuania, Malta, Poland, the Slovak Republic, and Slovenia. That represented a 20-percent increase in the EU population, although only a 5-percent increase in GDP. In 2007, Bulgaria and Romania joined the union (EU27).Turkey applied to join in 1987 and entered into a customs union with the EU in 1996, yet it remains a candidate country, along with Croatia (applied in 2003) and Macedonia (applied in 2004). Map 14.1 shows the geographic configuration of the EU today.

The evolution of the EU has therefore consisted of both *deepening* (tighter integration on the way to economic, monetary, and political union) and *widening* (expanded membership). These processes are not mutually reinforcing. Integration works best among a homogenous set of economies; the addition of new members, often poorer and less industrialized, has required extra provisions and more complex negotiations, thereby slowing somewhat the deepening process.[4] Widening also complicates the process of political unification. The EU's inability to present a truly united front in response to Yugoslavia's disintegration during the 1990s and the Iraq War in 2003 suggests that there will be some tough hurdles to clear if the EU is to achieve a coherent and consistent foreign policy.

INSTITUTIONS OF THE EUROPEAN UNION

The EU is more than an IGO. Like IGOs, some decisions are made by institutions composed of representatives of member states acting on behalf of their governments. This **intergovernmentalism** ensures that the core missions, policies, and structures of the EU as an organization reflect the interests of its sovereign member states. But in many important respects, decision making in the EU can be characterized as **supranationalism**. States have indeed ceded some of their sovereign

---

[3] The ECSC was abolished in 2002, so there are now just two European Communities within the EU: the EC and Euratom. For an examination of the watershed agreements that marked the rise of the EU, see especially Andrew Moravcsik, *The Choice for Europe: Social Purpose and State Power from Messina to Maastricht* (Ithaca, N.Y.: Cornell University Press, 1998).

[4] James Hughes, Gwendolyn Sasse, and Claire Gordon, *Europeanization and Regionalization in the EU's Enlargement to Central and Eastern Europe: The Myth of Conditionality* (New York: Palgrave Macmillan, 2005); Frank Schimmelffennig and Ulrich Sedelmeier, eds., *The Europeanization of Central and Eastern Europe* (Ithaca, N.Y.: Cornell University Press, 2005).

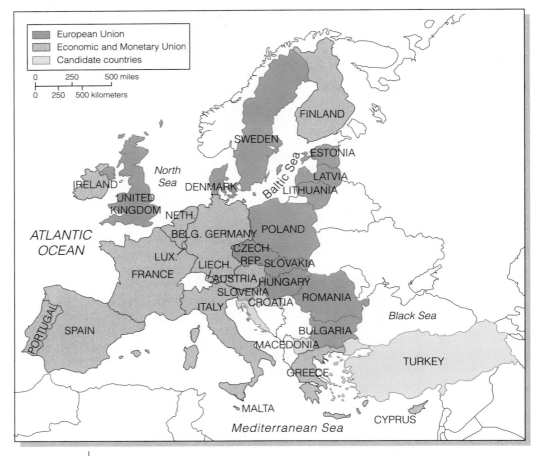

MAP 14.1 | EXPANDING EUROPEAN UNION

In 2004, the EU15 became the EU25, and with the admission of Bulgaria and Romania in 2007, it became the EU27. As a result of expansion, more economic and cultural diversity exists within the EU today, and this has sometimes been an impediment to the deepening of European integration. Of the twelve members joining after 2004, only Slovenia, Cyprus, and Malta qualified for the EMU by 2008.

authority to certain EU institutions on certain matters, and decisions made by these bodies become binding on member states even when governments feel that their particular national interests are not being well served. The balance of intergovern- mentalism and supranationalism in the EU, which is continuously evolving, is unique among international organizations.[5]

---

[5] See George Tsebelis and Geoffrey Garrett, "The Institutional Foundations of Intergovernmentalism and Supranationalism in the European Union," *International Organization* 55 (Spring 2001), pp. 357– 390; Paul Pierson, "The Path to European Integration: A Historical-Institutionalist Analysis," in Wayne Sandholtz and Alec Stone Sweet, eds., *European Integration and Supranational Governance* (Oxford: Oxford University Press, 1998).

The institutional structure of the European Union is composed of three main decision-making bodies: the European Commission, the Council of the European Union, and the European Parliament. European heads of state, often accompanied by their foreign ministers, meet as the European Council at least two times per year in Brussels (the "capital of Europe"). Although the European Council is the highest political authority in the EU, its main role is to direct the community's evolving domestic and international agendas; ordinary policy- and decision-making authority is vested with the other three bodies. The EU's primary financial institutions are the European Central Bank and the European Investment Bank, while the European Court of Justice and the European Court of Auditors serve judicial and oversight functions. The EU's institutional structure is shown in Figure 14.1.

The *Council of the European Union*—also called the *Council of Ministers* or the *Consilium*—enacts laws, often based on proposals from the European Commission, and is thus the EU's central decision-making authority. Its officials come from each member state, and which ministers constitute the Council depends on the issue under discussion. Foreign ministers come together to address foreign and security policy as well as more general matters; agricultural ministers address farm policy, economic and finance ministers take up monetary affairs, and so on. Member states have different numbers of votes (ranging from Malta's 3 votes to 29 each for France, Germany, Italy, and the United Kingdom) and most decisions in the Council require a "qualified majority" of votes (three-fourths of the 345 total). Decisions on some matters, like EU membership and taxation, require unanimity. Unanimity is also required on issues relating to foreign policy and defense, but up to one-third of the members may "constructively abstain," allowing the remainder to proceed unimpeded. Under some circumstances, known as *enhanced cooperation*, as few as eight Council members may determine a course of action that does not otherwise violate the rights of nonparticipating members. Such procedures were designed so that EU enlargement would not undermine decision-making flexibility in the Council.

The *European Commission* is the EU's main organ for proposing legislation and implementing policy. Member states have discussed the need to reduce the size of the Commission—EU enlargement has made the body unwieldy at times—but presently there are 27 commissioners, one appointed from each member state. The Commission serves a five-year term. The Commission president, who is chosen by the European Council, selects the other commissioners in consultation with the member states, subject to European Parliamentary approval of the entire group (or "college"). Unlike the Council of Ministers, the Commission's first loyalty is to the EU itself, making this body and its staff of 24,000 a favorite target of resentment and ridicule—unresponsive, faceless "Eurocrats" residing in Brussels, far removed from the concerns (and electoral reach) of ordinary citizens. Member states agree to be bound by rulings of the Commission, which gives it some measure of supranational authority, and is another source of resentment among those concerned that states are unwisely abdicating their sovereign powers and responsibilities. The Commission president, also a member of the European Council, can be very influential among European statesmen. For example, Jacques Delors, president from 1985 to 1995, played a central role in formulating the set of provisions that were ultimately encompassed in the Maastricht treaty, including the plan for monetary union.

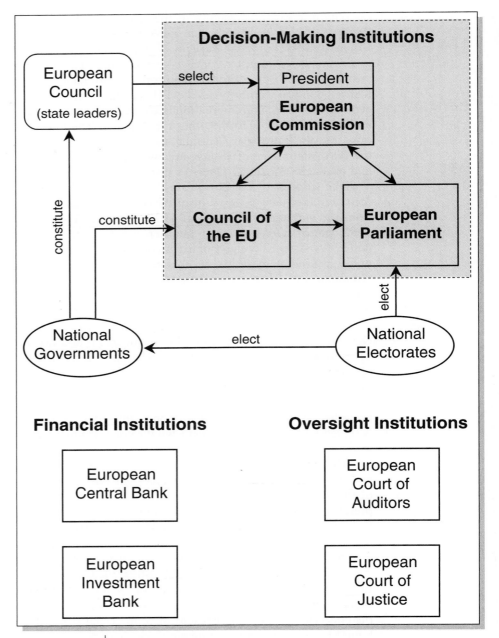

FIGURE 14.1 | MAJOR INSTITUTIONS OF THE EUROPEAN UNION

The citizens of European countries elect their governments, whose leaders assemble as the European Council and whose cabinet-level ministers constitute the Council of the European Union. National electorates also send representatives to the European Parliament. The president of the European Commission, selected by the European Council, chooses the commissioners, who are therefore once-removed from the electorate. This lack of accountability has made the Commission the main target of anti-EU sentiment.

The *European Parliament,* which convenes in Strasbourg, is also involved in the policy-making process. Although its powers have traditionally been quite limited—it does not pass legislation in the manner of national parliaments—the Maastricht treaty and the 1997 Treaty of Amsterdam enhanced the Parliament's role substantially. On many issues, the EU now uses a *codecision* procedure whereby the Parliament may amend Commission proposals to the Council, amend or reject positions taken by the Council, and confer with the Council and Commission in *conciliation committees* when there are lingering differences in draft legislation. A decision-making procedure that does not include parliamentary veto power (called the *cooperation* procedure) still operates in matters relating to economic and monetary union. There are 785 seats in the European Parliament, distributed among member states roughly according to population. Although members of the European Parliament are chosen by national electorates (serving five-year terms), political parties and voting blocs cut across national boundaries. In the 2004–2009 Parliament, the largest blocs of seats were held by the European People's Party (Christian Democrats) and European Democrats (277 seats), followed by the Party of European Socialists (218 seats).

The *European Court of Justice* (ECJ) and the *Court of Auditors* are both located in Luxembourg. Each consists of one official from each EU member state. So that the adjudication of particularly complex cases is not hobbled by expanded EU membership, the ECJ can sit as a "grand chamber" consisting of just thirteen judges; on certain other cases it may sit in chambers of three or five judges. The Court of Auditors can also establish smaller chambers. The ECJ provides authoritative interpretations of the community's treaties and ensures that they are properly applied by EU institutions and member states. Its judgments are binding on member states, and it is therefore another source of supranational authority in the EU.[6] Since 1989, the ECJ has been assisted by the Court of First Instance, which hears complaints brought by individuals and corporate entities (as well as states) against EU institutions. This is in marked contrast to UN's International Court of Justice, which only hears cases brought by nation-states. The Court of Auditors is the EU's financial watchdog. It sees to it that EU expenditures are in accordance with certain budgetary rules and regulations, and its operations are intended to reassure European taxpayers.

Institutionally, the EU is a complex of intergovernmental and supranational institutions—a combination that is sometimes referred to as *pooled sovereignty.* The Commission, the ECJ, and now the Parliament (through the codecision procedure) can take actions that are binding on member states. However, states retain their sovereignty through the European Council, which directs the EU's evolution, and through the institutional powers of the Council of the EU. The distribution of powers among EU institutions has changed with each of the major treaties, but the trend in the balance of authority between the EU and its member states has been moving, ever so gradually, in the direction of supranationalism.

---

[6] Jonas Tallberg, "Supranational Influence in EU Enforcement: The ECJ and the Principle of State Liability," *Journal of European Public Policy* 7 (March 2000), pp. 104–121; Karen J. Alter, *Establishing the Supremacy of European Law: The Making of an International Rule of Law in Europe* (Oxford: Oxford University Press, 2001).

Functionally, today's EU is said to be supported by three "pillars." The first is the European Community pillar, which consists of all arrangements that came before the Maastricht treaty—those established by the Rome treaties, as amended by the SEA—plus post-Maastricht revisions and reforms of the common market and the economic and monetary union (discussed in the next section). This pillar also includes citizenship and immigration policy, social policy, and environmental law. These are generally the areas in which the policies and institutions of the EU are most mature, and where supranationalism is most evident.

The second pillar, the Common Foreign and Security Policy (CFSP), calls on member states to safeguard their common values and independence, to strengthen their individual and collective security, and to promote democratic governance and respect for human rights. With the demise of the Soviet threat, areas of common interests have often been hard to identify, at least for purposes of joint action. At the same time, instabilities in Europe and elsewhere, along with international terrorism and the divisiveness engendered by the U.S.–led war on terror, has made progress on CFSP appear even more urgent. The third pillar, Police and Judicial Cooperation in Criminal Matters (PJCC), is concerned with such things as the illicit trafficking of drugs and weapons, human trafficking, organized crime, and corruption. The second and third pillars involve many areas in which states have not traditionally cooperated and where the EU's institutional arrangements are much less developed. Here the balance tilts toward intergovernmentalism.

Economic and Monetary Union

For those Europeans concerned about the loss of national sovereignty, the move toward monetary union was especially ominous. The idea of monetary union had been seriously contemplated since the late 1960s, and the Maastricht treaty specified a timetable for achieving this by 1999. State leaders were beginning to view a united Europe as a potential counterweight to the United States on global financial issues, especially because U.S. policy was raising questions about the country's ability to sustain its position in the Bretton Woods regime (see Chapter 13). When Bretton Woods collapsed, the rug of stability was torn out from under intra-European exchange rates and thus threatened the stability of their trade relations as well. In an informal arrangement that became known as the "snake," several European countries continued to link their currency values to each other, while together they floated against the dollar.

The snake lasted until 1979, at which time Europe embarked on a more formal procedure for maintaining monetary stability: the European Monetary System (EMS). All member states of the EC (and later EU) were members of the EMS, but membership in the EMS had no practical effect unless the state was a party to the EMS's Exchange Rate Mechanism (ERM). The ERM operated by first constructing a "basket currency," called the European Currency Unit (ECU), defined as the average weighted value of all EC currencies. Most central banks were then required to maintain their currency exchange rates within a couple percentage points of an assigned "par value" relative to the ECU. In addition to their own reserves, central banks could draw from a central resource pool when necessary to comply with the ERM. In essence, this European Monetary Cooperation Fund was the regional equivalent of the IMF under the Bretton Woods regime.

The EMS worked fairly well. European exchange rates remained stable, and the system was flexible enough to permit periodic currency realignments. But in the early 1990s, the EMS began to experience pressures not unlike those that brought down Bretton Woods. German reunification was accompanied by a tight monetary policy that caused an appreciation of the mark (and the ECU). To maintain their currency values, other European central banks were forced to tighten their monetary policies as well. They might have sought currency realignment in the ERM, something that had been done numerous times in the past, but with the target date for monetary union drawing closer, politicians and central bankers wanted to avoid anything that would smack of financial instability. As tight monetary policy worsened, already slow economic growth elsewhere in Europe, Germany was increasingly criticized for putting its own economic health above that of the community—the same sort of complaints that were directed at the United States as the Bretton Woods regime began to unravel.

Despite the difficulties, which included a currency crisis in 1992 and continued economic recession, EU leaders persevered. A single European currency, the euro (€), entered into circulation in 1999, and the *European Central Bank* (ECB), located in Frankfurt, began functioning. At first, the euro served only as an accounting currency, but in January 2002 the euro became legal tender, replacing twelve of the EU's then fifteen national currencies. The ECB conducts European monetary policy in coordination with national central banks within the **Eurozone**: the EU15 minus Britain, Denmark, and Sweden (who at present have opted out), plus Slovenia, Cyprus, and Malta (the only new members to qualify as of 2008). Together they make up the Eurosystem. The European System of Central Banks (ESCB) consists of the Eurosystem plus the central banks of member states outside the Eurozone, whose monetary policies are marginally less constrained. It is expected that all EU members will eventually enter the Eurozone, at which time the Eurosystem will be redundant and presumably absorbed into the ESCB. In addition to having the political will to join, states must satisfy certain economic "convergence criteria," namely, fiscal balance and stable prices, interest rates, and exchange rates. Global trade with the Eurozone is almost twice that with the United States, and the euro is very likely to rival the U.S. dollar as an international reserve currency.

When states adopt a common currency, they are hoping to increase economic efficiency by making it easier to allocate resources to the most productive endeavors, wherever these may be located within a large geographic area. Not having to worry about currency conversion rates allows for an even freer flow of capital and labor across national borders. The downside is that participating in a monetary union involves surrendering policy autonomy to a common monetary authority. When economic shocks—developments that create acute surpluses or deficits in economic resources—tend to affect the entire geographic region uniformly, that is not such a problem; the central authority need not weigh the economic needs of one region against another. Economists call this an *optimum currency area*

(OCA).[7] However, when this is not the case, a state faces the possibility that the central authority will decide to adopt measures that are costly to its national economy while trying to manage the economic health of the larger geographic region.

This is why this latest step in the uniting of Europe is a bold one. By entering into monetary union, European states turn over to the ECB their monetary policies, important tools for correcting cyclical downturns in economic growth. Although European economic performance has converged significantly over the last decade, there are regional differences—between north and south, and now between west and east—which suggests that a one-size-fits-all monetary policy may become problematic. On the other hand, state leaders are often tempted to manipulate monetary policy for political purposes, which is why monetary authority usually resides in a quasi-independent central bank. Locating monetary policy-making responsibility in a supranational institution like the ECB further removes the temptation, introducing monetary discipline while at the same time diminishing national politicians' accountability for the hard economic choices that could cost them votes at election time. Like Odysseus of Greek mythology, who feared the temptation of the Siren song, the interests of national leaders may well be served by having their hands tied.

TOWARD POLITICAL UNION?

Notwithstanding the bumps along the way, the emergence of an economic and monetary union in Europe is one of the truly remarkable developments in world politics over the past half century. Yet many aspire to something even bigger: political union. While there are those who still question the benefits of economic and monetary union, most do not. The benefits of political union, however, are considerably less clear. The early functionalists hoped that the uniting of Europe would finally bring peace to the continent. As we discussed in Chapter 11, war among the EU15 is virtually unthinkable now, and although we might not be quite so confident about the enlarged union, it is fair to say that war among any of the EU27 is extremely unlikely. Peace may not require political union, but the Europeans have nevertheless continued to work toward a post-Westphalian integration of the continent.

The EU's half century of legal and institutional evolution is charted by a series of treaties, agreements, and declarations, the most important of which we have discussed. The Treaty of Nice, in addition to laying the groundwork for EU enlargement in 2004, had attached to it a European Council declaration on the future of the EU that called for a constitutional convention. This European Convention, chaired by former French President Valéry Giscard d'Estaing, drew up a draft constitution. The Treaty establishing a Constitution for Europe was signed in Rome in 2004, but ratification failed after it was rejected by voters in the Netherlands and France—quite a blow to Giscard d'Estaing. Undaunted, European elites forged

---

[7] The classic statement is Robert A. Mundell, "A Theory of Optimum Currency Areas," *American Economic Review* 51 (November 1961), pp. 657–665. In regard to Europe, see Mundell, "A Plan for a European Currency," in Harry G. Johnson and Alexander K. Swoboda, eds., *The Economics of Common Currencies* (London: Allen & Unwin, 1973).

ahead and signed the Treaty of Lisbon in 2007. In lieu of a comprehensive constitution, the treaty seeks to enhance institutional efficiency and transparency within the EU and streamline the three-pillar policy framework. However, even this more limited step forward was uncertain in 2008 after Irish voters said no to the new arrangement.

Although many in Europe do not appear ready for a European constitution, some elements of political unification have been underway for a long time.[8] The most important role of political leaders is to provide for the security of their nations, and the second and third pillars of the EU involve the integration of member states' international and domestic security functions. Earlier we mentioned that the Europeans agreed to form the European Defense Community, but the organization was moribund from the start. In its place the Six plus Britain created the Western European Union (WEU), a defense and security organization with more modest aims. The WEU (which now also includes Portugal, Spain, and Greece) did relatively little from its inception in 1955 until the mid-1980s, when the SEA called for greater European cooperation in foreign and security policy. The Maastricht treaty pledged, even more explicitly, that member states would work toward the objective of a common foreign policy, and the WEU seemed like the logical institutional mechanism for implementing some of the security-related aspects of the CFSP. The subsequent Amsterdam treaty formally assigned to the WEU the duties of peacekeeping, humanitarian rescue, and crisis management (what the WEU had earlier recognized as its "Petersberg tasks").

The civil wars that accompanied the disintegration of Yugoslavia in the 1990s demonstrated the inadequacy of the European security organization. Here were a series of conflicts that any one of the major European states might have been able to handle on an individual basis, but as a collective the EU appeared impotent—although it did mount a WEU naval operation to enforce the UN arms embargo. One approach to addressing this weakness was to develop a Europe-only component within NATO, which would draw on NATO assets to undertake missions in which the United States has little or no interest. However, intra-alliance tensions during the Kosovo crisis and the conduct of the NATO action, not to mention the conspicuous gap between U.S. and European military capabilities, spurred the Europeans to work toward acquiring a joint military capability and doctrine outside of the NATO framework, an endeavor known as the European Security and Defense Policy (ESDP) and falling within the EU's CFSP pillar.[9]

When the European Council met in Helsinki in 1999, EU leaders set for themselves what became known as the Helsinki Headline Goal: to have, by 2003, the

---

[8] On the federalist authority structure emerging in Europe, see R. Daniel Kelemen, "The Structure and Dynamics of EU Federalism," *Comparative Political Studies* 36 (February/March 2003), pp. 184–208. For a critique, see Jack Rakove, Europe's Floundering Fathers, *Foreign Policy* 138 (September/October 2003), pp. 28–38.

[9] See Ingo Peters, "ESDP as a Transatlantic Issue: Problems of Mutual Ambiguity," *International Studies Review* 6 (September 2004), pp. 381–401. On the CFSP and ESDP more generally, see Michael E. Smith, *Europe's Foreign and Security Policy: The Institutionalization of Cooperation* (Cambridge: Cambridge University Press, 2003); Seth G. Jones, *The Rise of European Security Cooperation* (Cambridge: Cambridge University Press, 2007).

capability to deploy within sixty days up to 60,000 troops for peacekeeping or peacemaking tasks, and to sustain them in the field for up to one year. The EU declared that its goal had been met on schedule, although the EU's rapid reaction capabilities have not been tested to the fullest. The European Council established a second Headline Goal for 2010, which includes the capability to deploy highly mobile military forces within two weeks and sustainable for one month (longer if resupplied). By 2007, the EU had fielded fifteen battle groups of about 1,500 combat soldiers, each drawn from a particular lead nation plus a few others, and each reporting to the European Council. In order to link the ESDP's military capability requirements to armaments production, the EU has created the European Defense Agency to coordinate weapons development and procurement.

Among the newer elements of the EU's first pillar are policies concerning the movement of people. The particular rights and responsibilities of citizenship are central elements distinguishing one nation from another, and the ongoing political integration of Europe can be seen in the institutionalization of common standards of personal freedom and justice.[10] European nationals are also EU citizens. The Schengen area—named for the city in Luxembourg where two agreements were signed—is a frontier-free zone. Like travelers inside the United States, residents and visitors in Schengen area may move freely across state borders without routine passport checks. The area includes all the EU states plus Iceland, Norway, Liechtenstein, and Switzerland (some freedoms do not apply in Britain and Denmark). EU residents may also, in principle, settle and work in any EU country, although this prerogative is sometimes hampered by lingering differences in national administrative procedures. Just as a free-trade area makes necessary a customs union, the free movement of people within EU territories requires common citizenship, immigration, and asylum policies, which are key objectives in the Maastricht and Amsterdam treaties.

Fighting domestic and cross-border crime within the EU is still the primary responsibility of the criminal justice authorities of the member states. Intergovernmental cooperation is, however, facilitated by the EU's third pillar. The European Police Office (Europol), for example, serves as a clearinghouse for collection and distribution of intelligence related to international organized crime. The war on terrorism has provided the EU with new incentives for enhancing national and EU–wide capacities for combating terrorism, as well as money laundering, drug trafficking, and other transnational criminal activities often undertaken in support of terrorism.

In all of these areas—foreign and security policy, citizenship and immigration, and crime prevention—Europe has moved beyond the realm of economic and monetary union and into the realm of political integration. The process has been both harder and easier than progress on economic integration. It is harder because the elements of political integration have more profound implications for state sovereignty and thus encounter more resistance from nationalistic segments of the elite

---

[10] John Crowley, "Where Does the State Actually Start? The Contemporary Governance of Work and Migration," in Didier Bigo and Elspeth Guild, eds., *Controlling Frontiers: Free Movement Into and Within Europe* (Burlington, Vt.: Ashgate, 2005).

as well as those they are able to mobilize when agreements are put to the public for approval. In a different way, however, the process of political integration is easier than economic integration. Europe now has more than fifty years of experience with cooperation and institution building. While the functional areas on today's agenda may present greater challenges, the normative and legal frameworks in place relieve some of the burdens confronted by the EU's founders who began building a union from scratch—with economic depression and war, not prosperity and peace, in recent memory.

EMERGING ECONOMIC BLOCS

European integration has been a long and gradual process. In many ways it has conformed to the process imagined by the early functionalists, who were looking for a way to eventually short-circuit the national rivalries that led to two devastating world wars. But contrary to some functionalists' expectations, national sovereignty is not being chiseled away by specialists and technicians behind the backs of state leaders; the EU did not sneak up on the nation-states of Europe. As Ernst Haas and other *neofunctionalists* predicted, the process of integration has required the active involvement of national politicians. Indeed, if the EU has snuck up on anyone, it has been the rank-and-file citizenry of Europe, whose attitudes toward European unification have often oscillated between apathy and resentment.[11]

European state leaders have pushed the process because they see the economic benefits of large integrated markets. But getting there is not easy. In the last chapter we suggested that states often have an incentive to engage in less-than-free trade—to defect, when confronting the prisoner's dilemma—and even when the benefits of free trade are quite clear to all sides, it can be difficult to make the sorts of commitments that economic integration seems to require. As we discuss in greater detail in Box 14.1, international institutions like those of the EU have enabled states to overcome the disincentives to cooperate when there is some uncertainty about others' commitments either now or in the future. The Europeans are not the only ones seeking such solutions.

NORTH AMERICAN FREE TRADE AREA

In 1988, the United States and Canada signed a free-trade agreement that reduced trade and investment barriers and provided guidelines for the trade in services, and in 1992 were joined by Mexico in signing the North American Free Trade Agreement. NAFTA is not nearly as comprehensive as the treaties establishing the EU. And in contrast to European functionalists, its founders were not motivated by a

---

[11] Ernst B. Haas, *The Uniting of Europe: Political, Social, and Economic Forces, 1950–1957* (Stanford, Calif.: Stanford University Press, 1958); see also Haas, *Beyond the Nation-State* (Stanford, Calif.: Stanford University Press, 1964). But neither should we make too much of public opposition; see Lauren M. McLaren, "Opposition to European Integration and Fear of Loss of National Identity: Debunking a Basic Assumption regarding Hostility to the Integration Project," *European Journal of Political Research* 43 (October 2004), pp. 895–911.

IN GREATER DEPTH

BOX 14.1 | TRADE, INSTITUTIONS, AND THE ASSURANCE GAME

Recall from Box 13.1 that international trade can be analyzed as a prisoner's dilemma. According to that model, the optimal outcome for any given state is to protect its own industries from foreign competition while enjoying unfettered access to foreign markets. The prisoner's dilemma does seem to capture states' preferences at certain times in history (like during the Great Depression) and in some industries even today (like production for national defense), but it may not be convincing as a general model of international trade. As most economists are quick to point out, there are costs to protectionism. Exposure to competition, whether domestic or foreign, forces industries to overcome inefficiencies; protectionism undermines those incentives, and ultimately the nation's industrial strength.

Accordingly, erecting barriers to trade, even if these could be maintained unilaterally, is not the optimal outcome for a state. Free trade is; it fosters long-term economic health and prosperity. So instead of a prisoner's dilemma, trade can be depicted in this way:

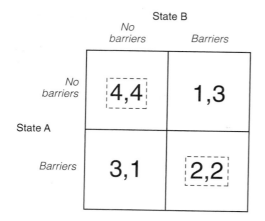

It is easy to see that the outcome in which each state maximizes its own utility (no trade barriers) is the Pareto optimal outcome—the best two trading

states can do jointly. This free-trade outcome is also a Nash equilibrium; if both states are enjoying the benefits of free trade, neither is likely to defect unilaterally from this outcome. But it is not the only equilibrium. If these states find themselves in a situation of mutual protectionism, neither will have an incentive to reduce its own barriers to trade. Thus, although the prospects for free trade are not as bleak as in the prisoner's dilemma, free trade is by no means a foregone conclusion. This model suggests that the players will need some assurances that their cooperative behavior (reducing trade barriers) will be reciprocated, and for this reason it is often called the **assurance game**.

Analysts have sought to understand the impediments to trade and the ways in which institutions help to overcome them. Ronald Coase, a Nobel Prize–winning economist, argued that the firm itself—an institution that organizes the production and marketing of goods—emerged as a means of economizing the costs associated with buying and selling products in the marketplace. These costs, as distinct from the costs of production, are commonly referred to as **transaction costs** and are defined as the expenditure of resources required to negotiate, monitor, and enforce contracts. Transaction costs are incurred in a purchase or exchange of goods when one or both sides to the exchange possess *imperfect information* about the other. In Chinese–American trade, for example, American merchants have been uncertain of the Chinese government's commitment to enforce patent rights and copyrights, which has implications for the profits those merchants can expect from their transactions with Chinese consumers. Chinese merchants, on the other hand, were uncertain about whether the U.S. Congress would renew China's MFN status from one year to the next in light of alleged violations of human rights. This affected the profits they expected from entering the American market.

BOX 14.1 | TRADE, INSTITUTIONS, AND THE ASSURANCE GAME

Coase argued that transaction costs are the costs associated with the establishment and transfer of **property rights**, the ability to freely choose how to use or dispense with a particular good or service. An American film studio wanting to sell DVDs in the Chinese market needs to be confident that its intellectual property rights will be protected when it chooses to transfer motion pictures (property) via DVD to paying Chinese customers. When bootlegged DVDs are also sold in the Chinese marketplace, the American film studio has lost the ability to fully exercise its property rights. When uncertainties exist as to the distribution of property rights, the costs of conducting economic transactions increase and trade is discouraged.

Global and regional institutions like the WTO and the EU help to reduce transaction costs and thereby encourage greater trade among their members. They do this by increasing the information available to economic actors, with the effect of establishing a more clearly defined arrangement of property rights. As a member of the WTO alongside the United States, China need not guess about whether the United States will impose trade-related sanctions in response to China's policies. Procedures for redressing trade-related grievances are well established within

the WTO and are *transparent* to members of the organization. The United States, for its part, need not wonder about China's commitment to protecting intellectual property rights. When joining the WTO, China agreed to adhere to existing rules in that regard, and committed itself to participate in continuing WTO negotiations intended to further clarify and formalize those rules.

International institutions thus help to provide the *assurances* that states and other economic actors need to move from the Pareto suboptimal outcome of protectionism to the Pareto optimal outcome of free and open trade. A large body of economic theory and research—known as the "New Institutional Economics"—has been generated around the basic concepts of transaction costs and property rights. The literature has also had a substantial impact on the way political scientists understand the role and functioning of institutions in both domestic and world politics.

Note: Two seminal articles by Ronald Coase are "The Nature of the Firm," *Economica* 4 (1937), pp. 386–405, and "The Problem of Social Cost," *Journal of Law and Economics* 3 (1960), pp. 1–44. A key contributor to the New Institutional Economics is Douglass C. North, also a Nobel laureate; see, for example, his *Institutions, Institutional Change and Economic Performance* (Cambridge, Cambridge University Press, 1990).

grand vision of continental peace forged out the experience of recent war.[12] There were political motivations, however, especially for the United States. Global trade negotiations under GATT were often less pressing for the Europeans because they could always return home to their own regional free-trade area. It is no coincidence that the arduous Uruguay Round of GATT was successfully concluded shortly after NAFTA was signed; NAFTA enhanced the U.S. bargaining position vis-à-vis the Europeans.

NAFTA created a free-trade area. There is no customs union, no coordination of economic or monetary policy, or anything remotely resembling the EMU in Europe. The economic dominance of the United States in North America and

[12] Robert A. Pastor, *Toward a North American Community: Lessons from the Old World for the New* (Washington, D.C.: Institute for International Economics, 2001). On the repercussions of 9/11, see Peter Andreas and Thomas J. Biersteker, *The Rebordering of North America: Integration and Exclusion in a New Security Context* (New York: Routledge, 2003).

especially the vast economic gulf between Mexico and its two NAFTA partners make the differences among the EU member states look modest by comparison, even after the 2004 enlargement. Instead of economic integration, NAFTA aims at a gradual elimination of tariff and nontariff barriers to trade. There are limited provisions for the movement of capital, but these come with certain exemptions in politically sensitive areas. For instance, Mexico's national oil company, Pemex, a potent symbol of Mexican sovereignty, can still enjoy protection from foreign competition under the terms of the agreement. Similarly, Canada, ever sensitive to American cultural domination, insisted on exemptions for "cultural industries" (film, music, print media, and so on).

Extending the U.S.–Canadian free-trade agreement to include Mexico was a difficult accomplishment. Trade barriers on certain products—most notably automobiles, auto parts, and textiles—have always been touchy issues in U.S.–Mexican relations. NAFTA also brought to the fore issues involving labor practices and environmental degradation. U.S. labor unions were concerned about exploitative labor practices (like sweatshops and child labor) in Mexico and elsewhere, both as a matter of principle and because such inexpensive labor was helping to lure away production facilities at the expense of American workers. Environmental groups were concerned about further environmental damage, which was already bad along the U.S.–Mexican border as a result of the proliferation of loosely regulated industries seeking the advantages of cheap Mexican labor. New provisions regarding these and other issues required painstaking negotiations, but NAFTA was modified in 1993 and then ratified.

Many observers suggest that the economic benefits of NAFTA for the United States are relatively minor. Both Canada and Mexico gain better access to the huge U.S. market, a benefit they cannot quite reciprocate. Mexico also gains credibility in the eyes of foreign investors, who can take some comfort in the fact that the Mexican economy is now more formally linked to the stable U.S. and Canadian economies. The United States, for its part, does stand to gain in certain areas like financial services and intellectual property, but overall the benefits may be more political than economic. In addition to enhancing its bargaining power with the EU, NAFTA is emblematic of the general liberal principles of free trade and deregulation on which the United States has often stood in its international dealings.

OTHER TRADING BLOCS

An important trading bloc that has emerged in Latin America is the Southern Cone Common Market (Mercado Común del Sur, or Mercosur) encompassing Argentina, Brazil, Paraguay, Uruguay, and Venezuela. Mercosur was established in 1991 and is more ambitious than NAFTA in that it is an effort to form a common market and not merely a free-trade area or customs union. Its formation and development have been pushed by the democratic governments that succeeded previous dictatorships. They see economic integration as a protector of democracy as well as an engine of growth. Chile is an associate member of Mercosur, as are the members of the Andean Community (a free-trade area consisting of Bolivia, Colombia, Ecuador, and Peru). In May 2008, these states plus Guyana and Suriname signed a treaty creating the Union of South American Nations (Unión de Naciones

Suramericanas, or UNASUR), which will merge Mercosur and the Andean Community. Like Mercosur, UNASUR aims to achieve a common market and is therefore quite ambitious.

There are also trade arrangements in effect in Central America and the Caribbean. Other agreements found in the Western Hemisphere are nonreciprocal. Through the Caribbean Basin Trade Partnership Act and the Andean Trade Preference Act, the United States gives preferential access to its markets without requiring similar access for U.S. goods, and Canada has a similar arrangement with members of the Caribbean Community (the CARIBCAN program). Lastly, an initiative that has captured the imagination of many is the Free Trade Area of the Americas (FTAA), a plan to bring together all countries of the Western Hemisphere (save perhaps Cuba).[13] Whether or not the hemispheric FTAA succeeds, a web of regional trade agreements already connects virtually every country in the Americas, as we can see from Figure 14.2.

Significant trading blocs exist in Asia and the Pacific as well. Free-trade agreements have been reached by the ASEAN countries, by Australia and New Zealand, and by the countries of South Asia. Other overlapping arrangements include some of these same countries. An increasingly watched development is the Asia Pacific Economic Cooperation (APEC) forum. APEC is an effort to establish a free-trade area comprising countries along the Pacific Rim. If successful—and there are many skeptics—it would be the largest trading bloc by far, accounting for 40 percent of the world's population and more than half of global economic output. There are also several trade arrangements in effect in Africa, the Middle East, and now Central Asia. Some, like the Southern African Customs Union—a subset of the Southern African Development Community—are noteworthy for going beyond free trade to later stages of economic integration. However, many of these agreements have been signed by states that engage in relatively low levels of trade with one another. Although these arrangements could bring about more intrabloc trade in the future, their economic significance may be outweighed by the politically salient fact that agreements, any agreements, require a spirit of regional cooperation, and this is probably reason enough to welcome such developments.

REGIONALISM AND MULTILATERALISM

The proliferation of regional trade blocs is an institutional manifestation of **regionalism**, defined as "the disproportionate concentration of economic flows or the coordination of foreign economic policies among a group of countries in close geographic proximity to one another."[14] The term *disproportionate* seems to imply that the level of intrabloc economic activity exceeds what would be "natural" in

---

[13] Jeffrey J. Schott, *Prospects for Free Trade in the Americas* (Washington, D.C.: Institute for International Economics, 2001). For an analysis of the U.S. role in the FTAA, see Patrick James and Michael Lusztig, "The U.S. Power Cycle, Expected Utility, and the Probable Future of FTAA," *International Political Science Review* 24 (January 2003), pp. 83–96.

[14] Edward D. Mansfield and Helen V. Milner, "The Political Economy of Regionalism: An Overview," in Edward D. Mansfield and Helen V. Milner, eds., *The Political Economy of Regionalism* (New York: Columbia University Press, 1997), p. 3.

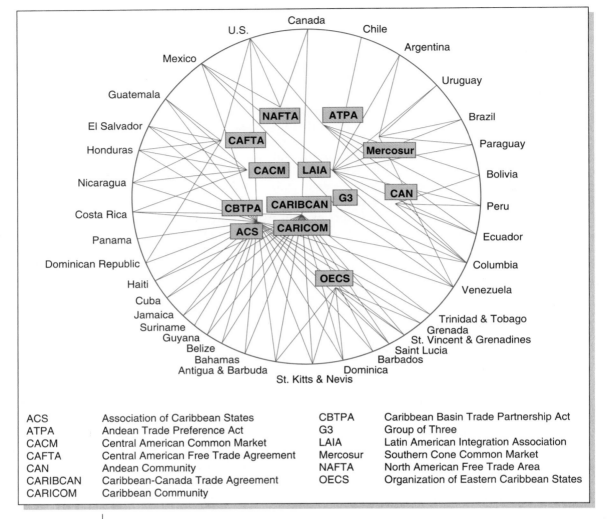

ACS   Association of Caribbean States   CBTPA   Caribbean Basin Trade Partnership Act
ATPA   Andean Trade Preference Act   G3   Group of Three
CACM   Central American Common Market   LAIA   Latin American Integration Association
CAFTA   Central American Free Trade Agreement Mercosur   Southern Cone Common Market
CAN   Andean Community   NAFTA   North American Free Trade Area
CARIBCAN   Caribbean-Canada Trade Agreement   OECS   Organization of Eastern Caribbean States
CARICOM   Caribbean Community

FIGURE 14.2 | WEB OF TRADE AGREEMENTS IN THE WESTERN HEMISPHERE

The global proliferation of regional trading arrangements is well represented by the Western Hemisphere. Although the economic (and political) significance of these arrangements varies greatly, state leaders seem to have seized upon the idea that regionalism can be a means to reap the benefits of free trade. The free-trade area of the Americas would include all countries shown here (except perhaps Cuba).

Source: Updated from Jeffrey A. Frankel, *Regional Trade Blocs in the World Economic System* (Washington, D.C.: Institute for International Economics, 1997), Figure 1.1, p. 10.

an ideal world of perfectly free global trade. Indeed, there is much debate about whether the rise of regionalism comes at the expense of the worldwide, multilateral trading system envisioned by defenders of free trade and pursued by member states of the GATT and WTO.

The period before World War II saw a disintegration of the world trading order into competing economic blocs. The U.S.– and Japan-led blocs were regional, but France and especially Britain increasingly came to confine trade to their far-flung colonial possessions. Somewhat ironically, in an effort to avoid a recurrence of these beggar-thy-neighbor policies that helped push European and other major powers into world war, the founders of the EU sought to replace one form of regionalism with another, this time tying the European powers together in a single economic bloc. Although few suspect that the new and emerging configuration of economic blocs will lead to global war between the EU and NAFTA or APEC, the criticism of regionalism remains. The concern is that agreements that reduce trade barriers within a region may be accompanied by increasing restrictions on trade with states outside the region, and that is not compatible with the global liberalization of trade (and ultimately peace).[15]

The WTO is charged with promoting multilateralism in international trade but does not frown upon regionalism, provided certain criteria are met. Under the terms of the GATT, states notify the WTO of the regional trade agreements they sign. About 200 such agreements are currently in force, and it is the job of the WTO's Committee on Regional Trade Agreements to review them. Article XXIV of the GATT requires that regional trade agreements not include provisions that raise barriers to trade with nonmembers. It also says that regional agreements should eliminate most restrictions on regional trade and that there should be substantial progress toward deeper economic integration. These last two requirements are intended to discourage regional arrangements designed primarily to keep trade out; the WTO applauds "open regionalism" because these agreements help clear the path toward global liberalization.

Recall from the last chapter that the free-trade regime can be understood as a collective good. Collective goods are harder to provide when the number of states in the collective is larger. A single defection from the regime will seem less consequential to a potential defector, giving rise to the free-rider problem as many members of the group make the same calculation. Larger groups also tend to have less in common—deriving from their different economic strengths and weaknesses, for example—making it more difficult to forge trade agreements acceptable to all. By focusing on a smaller collective, regional trade liberalization seems to offer a better chance for success. In effect, free trade ceases to be a pure collective good, one that cannot be denied to noncontributors. Instead, a regional free-trade arrangement is a "club good," because the benefits are limited to those who do contribute by making the formal commitments required of parties to the organization's charter.[16] As long as regionalism does not degenerate into regional protectionism, these efforts are seen in a positive light by proponents of systemwide free trade.

---

[15] For an assessment of the compatibility of regionalism and global free trade, see the World Bank report, *Global Economic Prospects: Trade, Regionalism, and Development 2005* (Washington, D.C.: World Bank, 2004).

[16] Mancur Olson, *The Logic of Collective Action: Public Goods and the Theory of Groups* (Cambridge, Mass.: Harvard University Press, 1965), referred to goods provided by "exclusive groups," which are the same as club goods. See also Arce M., Daniel G., and Todd Sandler, *Regional Public Goods: Typologies, Provision, Financing, and Development Assistance* (Stockholm: Almqvist and Wiksell, 2002).

The current momentum behind regionalism is due to developments in the world economy over the past two decades. One important factor was the new life breathed into the process of European integration with signing of the SEA and then the Maastricht treaty. As it became clear that the EU was actually entering the common-market phase and that the EMU was just around the corner, proponents of regional integration elsewhere had a successful model to follow. Another factor encouraging regionalism, at least in the Americas and the Pacific Rim, has been changing attitudes among U.S. policy makers. After World War II, the United States overcame its traditional aversion to regional trading arrangements in the interest of promoting European unity against Soviet influence. With geopolitics less of an issue today—the peace in Europe is stable, the Soviet threat is gone— one might expect American hostility to regionalism to resurface, but that has not happened. Instead, the United States has embraced it. A liberal interpretation would emphasize that U.S. policy makers came around to the view that regional economic cooperation really can be a stepping-stone to multilateralism. A realist, on the other hand, would find more significance in the American *retreat* from multilateralism, emphasizing instead that U.S. policy makers have concluded that the pursuit of regionalism is the best means of protecting American interests.

GLOBALIZATION

The term **globalization** suggests different things to different people. We will use the term to mean a process whereby economic, political, and cultural transactions are less and less constrained by national boundaries and the sovereign authority of national governments. Two important processes are driving globalization. First, the continuing advancement of technology has made the transnational movement of goods, people, and ideas—both desirable and undesirable—increasingly easy to accomplish. Second, national governments seem to be either less able or less willing to exercise control over the goods, people, and ideas that cross their borders.

This is not to say that national sovereignty is dead. Rather, due to changes in opportunities *and* willingness, governments have become more inclined to surrender some of the control over cross-border transactions they once exercised by virtue of their sovereign authority. In many cases, governments have been forced to surrender; their efforts to control financial and information flows, for example, are often ineffective. In many other cases, however, governments have chosen not to impede the process of globalization, either because they perceive globalization to be in their national interests or because they want to act in accordance with international norms. And in still other cases, states are relatively disconnected from other societies and the global economy, and have remained largely unaffected by the global flow of information and culture.

Interdependence is at the root of globalization. Analysts focus on the extensive new webs of interdependence that are creating a truly global system for the first time. Due to the dismantling of colonial empires and the march of technology, there is much that is new since the end of World War II. Much seems new even since the end of the cold war. We need to acknowledge, however, that a lot of what is being discussed as globalization is not at all new but is just being recognized for the first time.

A New Interdependence?

As our discussion of the EU and other evolving regional trade blocs suggests, expanding and deepening webs of interdependence are nowhere more evident than in global economic affairs. Jeffrey Sachs identifies four areas in which national economies have become increasingly interdependent. The first and perhaps most obvious area is trade. Since World War II, international trade has consistently outpaced global production, and almost all national economies have become more dependent on trade (measured as a share of GDP). However, in a second area, financial flows, the growth in interdependence has been even more pronounced in recent years. More than $3 trillion worth of global currencies are traded every day—up from less than $200 billion in 1986. Foreign direct investment has been steadily climbing since the mid-1980s, while foreign portfolio investment, which is much more mobile than direct investment, surged in the early 1990s (though leveling off thereafter). The activities of MNCs represent a third way in which the global economy is becoming integrated. MNCs are responsible for the growth in foreign investment, and as much as one-third of the total trade in goods worldwide consists of trade between the affiliates of the same corporation. The fourth way, according to Sachs, is through the "harmonization of economic institutions." Not only are more countries adopting free-market approaches to economic development, they are also obligating themselves to this course by signing international treaties on trade, foreign investment, and currency convertibility, as well as on other matters that signal some convergence in economic thinking and practice.[17]

Thus, many of today's conditions are indeed quite new, especially in that some states are much more sensitive and vulnerable than ever before to developments originating beyond their borders. We have suggested that some states, despite their *legal* sovereignty, are so small and poor that they have very limited autonomy; these states are constantly buffeted by systemic economic, political, and cultural forces and are far more vulnerable than most states in the past. Globalization and national sovereignty are not mutually exclusive; state leaders retain a large measure of choice about how to distribute the costs and benefits of the market. Small states, like Iceland or Singapore, may be more socially cohesive than big ones and so better able to mobilize resources to compete for capital and markets. But almost all international actors, big and small, are more interdependent today because of the increasing opportunities for interaction that have been provided by technological advances in communication and transportation—the increasing ability to send ideas and things farther, faster, and at less cost. Transnational linkages have proliferated not only between the governmental elites of nation-states but also between their societies and at multiple levels. These intersocietal linkages have been facilitated by the activities of NGOs, including, of course, multinational corporations.

---

[17] Jeffrey Sachs, "International Economics: Unlocking the Mysteries of Globalization," *Foreign Policy* 110 (Spring 1998), pp. 97–111. For some historical perspective on globalization, see Ian Clark, *Globalization and Fragmentation: International Relations in the Twentieth Century* (Oxford: Oxford University Press, 1997).

TABLE 14.1 | GLOBAL INFORMATION REVOLUTION, 2006

Information Medium	Income Group		
	High	Medium	Low
Personal computers	567	66	14
Internet users	593	141	66
Broadband subscribers	192	33	2
Mobile phones	901	441	143

Note: Each figure is the average, per 1,000 people, for all states in the income group. Number of personal computers is for 2005.

Source: World Bank, *World Development Indicators 2008 CD-ROM* (Washington, D.C.: World Bank, 2008).

Technology has expanded the physical capabilities of people to interact with each other. However, interdependence is also about people's enhanced awareness of such interactions. A major consequence of the "information revolution" is the rapid expansion of analytic capabilities to individual citizens throughout the world. These capabilities come from the ability to access information from radio, television, and the Internet, and to communicate via telephone and electronic mail. The cost of a three-minute telephone call from New York to London has fallen from more than fifty dollars in 1950 to less than twenty cents today (even accounting for inflation). The explosive growth in computer usage, and especially the widespread use of the Internet to disseminate and retrieve information, has added a significant new dimension to the information revolution. Neither the personal computer nor the Internet are new inventions, but their availability to ever-increasing numbers of people from most segments of most societies is a relatively recent development. In 2006, there were more than 100 personal computers and more than 200 Internet users for every 1,000 people worldwide. While these aggregate figures do mask some very real differences between richer and poorer regions of the globe (see Table 14.1), the growth in access to electronic communication and information is a global phenomenon.

Thus, the "new" interdependence is based to a large degree on new patterns of human attention. Individuals can see things that are happening in faraway places, anywhere on the planet—what James Rosenau calls "distant proximities."[18] The democratic revolutions across Eastern Europe were often called the "television revolutions" because people in each country watched and then emulated what had just happened elsewhere in the region. When the Milosevic regime in Yugoslavia began to clamp down on the independent media as the Kosovo crisis came to a head in 1999, Serbian Radio B92 began to rely almost exclusively on the World Wide Web to disseminate its news reports. The tactic had been perfected three years before when Radio B92 was forced off the air for its coverage of

[18] James N. Rosenau, *Distant Proximities: Dynamics Beyond Globalization* (Princeton, N.J.: Princeton University Press, 2003).

antigovernment street demonstrations; it sent audio files via the Internet to the BBC, which then broadcast B92's reports back to Yugoslavia.

The information revolution highlights the psychological dimension of interdependence; people are not only aware that activities are taking place elsewhere but also aware that they are aware. They understand that they belong to some sort of *global village*, to use Marshall McLuhan's famous term, and that they exist as part of some larger world community. Radio, television, and the Internet have brought foreign events into homes all around the world: "For Shakespeare it was a metaphor, but for our generation it has become a reality: the world is now literally a stage, as its actors dance across the TV screen"—and the screens of our computers and personal digital assistants.[19]

Interdependence increases as states become more vulnerable to penetration of various kinds. Interdependence can occur only when the hard shell of the state—its sovereignty—is cracked. Because of both increased interdependence and increased awareness of interdependence, governmental decision makers have to take into account the effects that their domestic policies have on foreign relations with other states. As much as Slobodan Milosevic would have liked Serbian activities in Kosovo to remain an internal Yugoslav affair, the refugee crisis that ensued, and his regime's inability to control information leaving the country, brought about a foreign policy crisis and ultimately a military clash with NATO. Indeed, we have become so accustomed to knowing what is going on across the globe that when information is not forthcoming, as happened after a cyclone hit the closed society of Myanmar in 2008, our need to know (and perhaps to help) can bring pressure to bear on media outlets and even governments. Whether or not actions, events, or policies are meant to cross state boundaries or to affect the peoples and governments of other states, they do.

TRANSNATIONAL RELATIONS

National boundaries, while far from disappearing, are becoming less relevant. Many feel that continuing to view the world in terms of the traditional Westphalian logic is not very useful and may be downright harmful, given the nature of contemporary interdependencies. These observers are implicitly calling for a reversal of the Westphalian trade-off; they feel that if governments continue to look at the world in terms of old images—sovereign nation-states concerned with maintaining their autonomy and enhancing their power—such views will lead to wrongheaded policies that may be disastrous for humankind. This view has been frequently expressed by liberals who see the world in terms of **transnational relations** rather than international relations, but radicals too grapple with the often contradictory implications of transnational exchanges and relationships.[20]

---

[19] Marshall McLuhan, *Understanding Media: The Extensions of Man* (New York: McGraw-Hill, 1964). The quote from James N. Rosenau, *Turbulence in World Politics: A Theory of Change and Continuity* (Princeton, N.J.: Princeton University Press, 1990), p. 344.

[20] James H. Mittelman, *The Globalization Syndrome: Transformation and Resistance* (Princeton, N.J.: Princeton University Press, 2000). For a discussion of different perspectives on globalization, see Mark Rupert, *Ideologies of Globalization: Contending Visions of a New World Order* (New York: Routledge, 2000).

We defined globalization as the increasingly prevalent movement of goods, people, and ideas across national boundaries without significant, direct participation or control by high-level governmental actors. These patterns of penetration and linkage involve heavy participation by various kinds of nonstate actors. NGOs, for example, are "changing societal norms, challenging national governments, and linking up with counterparts in powerful transnational alliances. And they are muscling their way into high politics, such as arms control, banking, and trade, that were previously dominated by the state."[21] This view begins to call into question the importance of sovereignty, of national boundaries; it challenges the realist conception of world politics as consisting primarily of the interactions of governments in an anarchic international system. Because each state has become so permeable, so open to outside influences, domestic and international politics are becoming indistinguishable.

The impact of globalization can be visualized as in Figure 14.3, which contrasts the state-centric view of *international* politics and the transnational view of *world* politics. The main point to note is the multiplicity of interactions that bypass the governments of states and act directly on their domestic environments. In the transnational view, nonstate actors (especially NGOs) are much more important than previously thought, as are the interest groups or subnational actors that exist within states. We have discussed the influence of tribal, ethnic, or separatist groups within states, as well as that of economic interests, MNCs, and parts of the governmental bureaucracy. In accordance with the organizational process model, government bureaucrats often interact directly with their counterparts in other states' bureaucracies, many times without the knowledge of top decision makers. Both NGOs and subnational actors are distinct from state actors and can act independently from states. Some observers even argue that there is no neat hierarchical pattern of influence and authority. States are not necessarily the most powerful actors, nor are subnational actors the least powerful; it depends on both the actors and issues involved under particular circumstances.

Along with states, these transnational actors make up a multicentric world—the groups of many thousands of diverse actors (individuals, groups, organizations, movements) that seek autonomy of action from states. This complex of nongovernmental entities (individuals, groups, and institutions), who interact across state boundaries, is now commonly called **global civil society**.[22] In the multicentric world, nongovernmental (and nonterritorial) actors confront an "autonomy dilemma" quite different from the security dilemma confronted by states. The transnational view holds that nonstate actors can significantly affect the interests and behavior of states. The different needs and vulnerabilities of states, IGOs, NGOs, and transnational social movements provide all actors with some levels of influence. This suggests that the issues that have been central to international interaction are changing, that military and security issues are not always the primary

---

[21] P. J. Simmons, "Learning to Live with NGOs," *Foreign Policy* 112 (Fall 1998), p. 84.

[22] See, for example, John Keane, *Global Civil Society?* (Cambridge University Press, 2003); Mary Kaldor, *Global Civil Society: An Answer to War* (Polity, 2003); Jessica T. Mathews, "Power Shift: The Rise of Global Civil Society," *Foreign Affairs* 76 (January/February 1997), pp. 50–66.

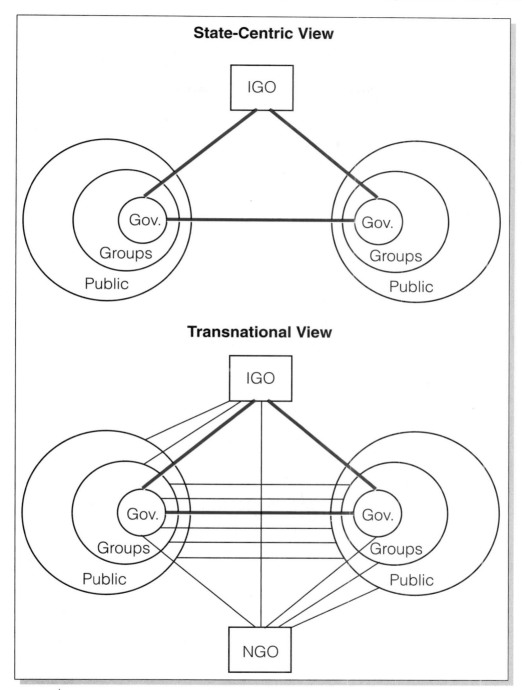

State-Centric View

IGO

Gov. Groups Public

Gov. Groups Public

Transnational View

IGO

Gov. Groups Public

Gov. Groups Public

NGO

FIGURE 14.3 | STATE-CENTRIC AND TRANSNATIONAL VIEWS OF WORLD POLITICS

The state-centric view, with its emphasis on the sovereignty of states, focuses on relations between governments and between governments and IGOs. The transnational view identifies a plethora of interactions that take place between governments and both international and domestic nongovernmental actors, as well as between international and domestic nongovernmental actors themselves. Much of what goes on within global civil society is missed by the state-centric view.

ones, even to nation-states. Indeed, interdependence generates a new set of problems and demands on those with sovereign authority. Traditionally, the power of states has been based in large part on military capability. But military capability is not easily mustered, nor is it appropriate or even effective when dealing with the sorts of economic and social issues that preoccupy the minds of statesmen and citizens in today's interdependent world.

The realists' state-centric view focuses on power and security. Liberals and radicals, by focusing our attention on transnational relations, claim that such matters are no longer central and now compete with economic, cultural, social, and other concerns. As with the phenomenon of regional integration, this perspective presents us with a multitude of anomalies, things that we should not expect to happen (or expect to be very important) if we hold the realist view.

GLOBALIZATION'S DOWNSIDE

One of the main instruments by which economic interdependence has grown is through the activities of multinational business. We noted in Chapter 3 that there are several ways in which MNCs rival states. The global "megacorporation" is transforming the world political economy through its increasing control over three fundamental resources of economic life: the technology of production, finance capital, and marketing. Industry is no longer constrained by geography, as transnational production makes national boundaries decreasingly relevant. Transnational production also makes corporate loyalty to any one state or society somewhat tenuous. Because loyalty is the basis of nationalism, it is not surprising that multinational corporate thinking is wary of such sentiments. In making their business decisions, corporate executives prefer not to be constrained by such noneconomic considerations:

> "For business purposes," says the president of the IBM World Trade Corporation, "the boundaries that separate one nation from another are no more real than the equator. They are merely convenient demarcations of ethnic, linguistic, and cultural entities. They do not define business requirements or consumer trends. Once management understands and accepts this world economy, its view of the marketplace—and its planning—necessarily expand. The world outside the home country is no longer viewed as a series of disconnected customers and prospects for its products, but as an extension of a single market."

This statement was made almost forty years ago, yet public expressions of discontent with this neoliberal economic worldview seem stronger today than ever before.[23]

Globalization's discontents are a motley crew—a "turtles to Teamsters" coalition. The antiglobalization movement is truly transnational and seemingly unorganized, but it draw a large number of NGOs and citizen groups from global civil society, many of them quite well organized and often assembled into overlapping

---

[23] Richard Barnet and Ronald E. Müller, *Global Reach: The Power of the Multinational Corporation* (New York: Simon & Schuster, 1974), pp. 14–15. A more recent analysis of MNCs' global reach is Nathan M. Jensen, *Nation-States and the Multinational Corporation: A Political Economy of Foreign Direct Investment* (Princeton, N.J.: Princeton University Press, 2006).

networks.[24] Some within the movement would like to see the institutions of global economic governance—the WTO, the World Bank, the IMF—dismantled altogether. In their view, these institutions have solidified the power of multinational corporations and seem to legitimize a corporate mentality that has little or no regard for working people or the environment. Some subscribe to a radical economic perspective, which we take up in the next chapter, and would like to see not only the demise of the institutional bulwark of global capitalism but also the retreat (if not defeat) of capitalism itself. The more moderate elements of the antiglobalization movement, many of them political liberals, call instead for substantial reform. For them, the institutions of global governance suffer from a "democratic deficit" and need to be made more accountable to the states and citizens who feel the impact of their actions; this can be accomplished while preserving the many benefits that globalization brings.[25]

It is somewhat ironic that the technological advances that have accompanied and promoted global capitalist development have been so effectively utilized by the opponents of globalization to make their voices heard. The anti-WTO "Battle in Seattle" in 1999 took many by surprise because of its apparent spontaneity and forceful message. But that protest, and many others since, was not spontaneous at all. Information and communications technology has allowed the diverse network of activists to interact, plan their actions, and assemble their "troops" even in the absence of an organizational hierarchy and a single agenda. A transnational social movement with such diversity of membership and mission could not have become such a potent political force in any other context.

The antiglobalization movement has sought to draw attention to the downside of globalization. There are, of course, other transnational actors whose discontent may have little to do with globalization itself, but who also benefit from advances in information and communication technology. As we discussed in Chapter 8, publicity is crucial to the whole concept of terrorism, which is usually aimed at changing the policies of states. The contemporary terrorist has a global audience that can be affected in many ways by a lone act that is geographically distant but that is made psychologically near through communications technology and instantaneous media coverage. Although terrorist groups have adopted loose organizational and networked structures as a means of survival, coordinated action has become easier with the availability of multiple modes of communication.

Transnational crime is another of globalization's downsides. Compared to terrorists, transnational criminal organizations are engaged in the pursuit of wealth rather than political objectives. Their modus operandi is to exploit illicit economic opportunities that the era of globalized capitalism seems to have opened up. The international drug trade is a good example. Although the demand for narcotics is not a new development, the ability of traffickers to get the goods to market is

---

[24] Sanjeev Khagram, Kathryn Sikkink, James V. Riker, eds., *Restructuring World Politics: Transnational Social Movements, Networks, and Norms* (Minneapolis: University of Minnesota Press, 2002); Margaret Keck and Kathryn Sikkink, *Activists Beyond Borders: Advocacy Networks in International Politics* (Ithaca, N.Y.: Cornell University Press, 1998).

[25] Joseph E. Stiglitz, *Globalization and Its Discontents* (New York: Norton, 2003); see also Jagdish Bhagwati, *In Defense of Globalization* (Oxford: Oxford University Press, 2004).

much improved, and this despite an unprecedented effort by states to prevent it. In light of the fact that state borders are better patrolled now than in the past, and that antidrug efforts have increasingly gone to the source, the relentless percolation of illicit drugs is evidence of the capacity of transnational criminal networks to adapt to the methods states have so far employed to disrupt the flow.

Figures on the total value of illicit drug sales are hard to pin down, but a reasonable estimate is between $300 and $500 billion annually, which makes it one of the world's largest commercial industries, with 180 million customers. Cocaine moves from the Andean countries to North America by way of Central America and the Caribbean, to Europe along similar routes as well as by way of Southern and Western Africa, and to Japan and Australia along oceanic routes (See Map 14.2). Heroin and other opiates travel to the same destinations from Afghanistan through Southwest and Central Asian countries, from Myanmar via China and Thailand, and

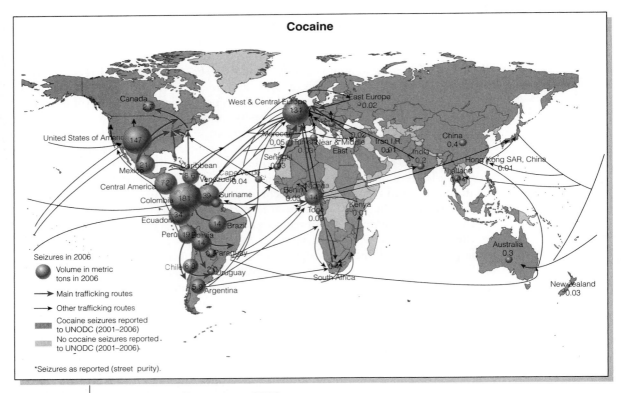

MAP 14.2 | GLOBAL DRUG TRAFFICKING, 2006

One of the downsides of globalization is the illicit drug trade. For different countries, the map shows the volume of seizures of cocaine, concentrated in the Western Hemisphere, and heroine and morphine, concentrated in Asia. The trafficking routes show that illicit drugs generally flow from the less-developed to the more-developed regions of the globe, mainly North America and Europe.
Source: UN Office on Drugs and Crime, *2008 World Drug Report* (Vienna: UNODC, 2008), pp. 12, 15.

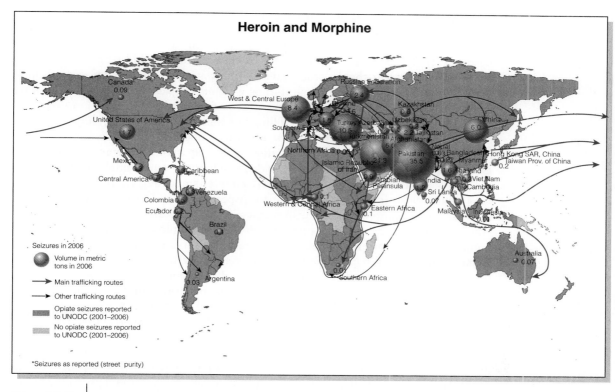

Heroin and Morphine

Seizures in 2006

Volume in metric tons in 2006

→ Main trafficking routes

→ Other trafficking routes

Opiate seizures reported to UNODC (2001–2006)

No opiate seizures reported to UNODC (2001–2006)

*Seizures as reported (street purity)

MAP 14.2 | CONTINUED

now also from Central and South America following familiar cocaine-trafficking routes. Cannabis herb (marijuana) arrives in the United States by way of Mexico; cannabis resin (hashish) travels from Morocco to Spain and then to other European countries and Canada.

Illicit human trafficking—mainly for sexual exploitation and forced labor—is another dimension of transnational criminal activity. The destinations are the same as for illegal narcotics: North America, Western Europe, and East Asia; many go to the Middle East as well. Annually, more than a half million victims are transported from Southeast Asia, South Asia, Latin America, and the Caribbean. The pattern is obvious: The illicit migration is from economically depressed or struggling regions of the globe to the wealthy regions. In 2006, about 800,000 people were trafficked between states—80 percent of them females, 50 percent of them minors—and millions more within states.[26] Human traffickers employ a variety of methods, but

---

[26] U.S. Department of State, *Trafficking in Persons Report: June 2008* (Washington, D.C.: U.S. Department of State, 2008), p. 7. See also Kevin Bales, *Disposable People: New Slavery in the Global Economy* (Berkeley: University of California Press, 1999); Kathryn Farr, *Sex Trafficking: The Global Market in Women and Children* (New York: Worth, 2005).

often women are lured into leaving their countries with assurances of steady employment and a high quality of life; once they arrive at their destination, they may become indentured or even enslaved. Children are typically trafficked using more coercive means—having been sold by their families or kidnapped.

We stated earlier that interdependence is not a new phenomenon in world politics; neither is transnational crime. But as with interdependence, the contemporary era of globalization has brought a transformation of the nature of transnational criminal activity in regard to both willingness and opportunity. Criminal organizations have thrived in the context of economic liberalization. Liberalization and deregulation has provided opportunities to set up front companies and quasi-legitimate businesses for laundering money, while the substantial increase in the volume of goods moving across borders facilitates smuggling contraband. The U.S. Customs Service, for instance, is able to inspect roughly 3 percent of what enters the country, a figure that may drop further in the years ahead. The advent of containerized and intermodal shipping, which allows for the easy transfer of cargo at numerous transshipment points, has been a boon for both international trade and illegal trafficking, and potentially for terrorists as well. The flexibility of modern transportation networks is effectively exploited by criminal organizations in getting their goods to market; the complexity of those networks allows them to conceal origination points in case the goods are intercepted by state authorities.

Transnational criminals have become sophisticated entrepreneurs. Like other international and transnational actors, they take advantage of the opportunities provided by the revolution in information and communications technology. They also employ well-trained specialists—some with impressive university pedigrees—in transportation and logistics, finance and investment, and the law in order to improve the efficiency and global reach of their operations, and to defend themselves against those who would shut them down. Because their menus are less constrained by legal and ethical considerations, transnational criminals can more effectively employ a set of tools that most state actors either do not employ or employ with some reluctance.[27]

Not only have transnational criminal organizations relied heavily on the corruption of politicians and law enforcement officials but also they increasingly ally with each other and with insurgencies and paramilitary groups. As we pointed out in Chapter 8, antigovernment guerrillas have often turned to illicit trafficking to finance their military campaigns, but in the past the overlapping interests of guerrillas and criminal elements were often fleeting. State sponsorship was not always dependable either, but with the end of the cold war many groups have been left out to dry. Thus, guerrilla groups like the Revolutionary Armed Forces of Colombia and the National Liberation Army have become very active in the Colombian cocaine and opium trade, while the Revolutionary United Front in Sierra Leone

---

[27] R. T. Naylor, *Wages of Crime: Black Markets, Illegal Finance, and the Underworld Economy*, rev. ed. (Ithaca, N.Y.: Cornell University Press, 2004); Phil Williams, "Transnational Criminal Networks," in John Arquilla and David Ronfeldt, eds., *Networks and Netwars: The Future of Terror, Crime, and Militancy* (Santa Monica, Calif.: Rand, 2001). On the illicit arms trade, see David Kinsella, "The Black Market in Small Arms: Examining a Social Network," *Contemporary Security Policy* 27 (April 2006), pp. 100–117.

has come to rely heavily on diamond exports. One suspects that the relationships developing between transnational criminal organizations and between them and guerrilla movements are increasingly driven by the same principles of comparative advantage underlying trade between states.

States are not helpless against the onslaught of transnational crime and terrorism; far from it. As the functionalists recognized long ago, interdependence gives rise to new problems that states need to solve, and international cooperation is a proven means for doing so. Governments have acted together to train antiguerrilla and antiterrorist units. They have also acted through IGOs, such as the UN and the Organization of American States, to outlaw and protect against certain acts (for example, by treaties prohibiting offenses against diplomats). National police forces have been coordinated through Interpol and Europol to combat terrorism and transnational crime. Transnational terrorism has even prompted countermeasures from purely transnational NGOs, such as airline pilot associations, which brought direct pressure against governments and IGOs to institute measures against hijackings. Add to all of this the activities of private military companies hired by states to provide strategic assessments, to train government troops, and occasionally to engage in direct combat against guerrillas and international criminal networks.

Globalization and the growth of transnational interactions in the post–World War II era have presented the sovereign state with new problems and new challenges. These challenges also raise doubts about the ability of realism to advance our understanding of world politics in an era of globalization. Such doubts can be summarized with reference to the three elements of Keohane's and Nye's concept of **complex interdependence**. First, complex interdependence refutes the notion that only states count and points to the numerous other consequential actors and interactions that make up world politics. Second, it suggests that there no longer exists a set hierarchy of international issues dominated by the concerns of military security. Finally, complex interdependence seems to preclude the use of military force among states whose societies are linked by a web of transnational relationships, or as a means of settling certain types of issues regardless of the extent of such relationships.[28]

Globalization has rendered the notion of sovereign state autonomy contingent at best, and in some cases illusory. The forward march of technological development, economic transaction, information flows, and the activities of nonstate actors regularly penetrate the state's hard shell. The end of the twentieth century ushered in a period of turbulence characterized both by high levels of complexity and by high degrees of change. There seems to be a willingness to affect a shift in the Westphalian trade-off as states seek to adapt to a changing environment. In adapting to their environments, states do display different combinations of sensitivity and vulnerability. The industrialized countries of the Northern Hemisphere have frequently exhibited a greater measure of sensitivity relative to vulnerability, while the opposite has often been the case for developing states of the Global South. This is a rather crude generalization to be sure, but it is at the center of the so-called North–South development gap, which is the subject of the next chapter.

---

[28] Robert O. Keohane and Joseph S. Nye, *Power and Interdependence,* 3rd ed. (New York: Addison-Wesley, 2001), pp. 24–29.

DEVELOPMENT AND UNDERDEVELOPMENT: THE NORTH–SOUTH GAP

CHAPTER 15

THE DEVELOPMENT GAP

Interdependence binds units within systems, and managing interdependence is a way of dealing with current and future world problems. We ended the last chapter on a somewhat negative note—that there is a downside to interdependence and globalization. But we should not forget the positive aspects of interdependence. Looking at developed Western democracies, we have seen how the various bonds of economic interaction can be productively and positively managed through cooperation; states have learned how to coordinate with each other for the mutual benefit of all. The relationships highlighted in the discussion of the political economy of developed democracies are grounded in open markets and democratic forms of governance. Dominance is missing from these relationships, and even lesser forms of coercion are diminishing.

Nevertheless, we must ask: Do these same mutually beneficial relationships form between developed and developing countries? How about among LDCs themselves? As with transnational crime, some of the dependent relationships between developed and developing countries may be thought of as *pathologies* of interdependence. One-sided relationships of sensitivity and vulnerability create asymmetric interdependencies and thus produce yet another set of problems that need to be managed.

SEVERAL DEVELOPING WORLDS

For large portions of the world's poor, economic development remains an ever-retreating mirage. Reality is a parched existence in the midst of physical misery. Almost 40 percent of the people on Earth (2.4 billion) live in low-income countries. Although the privileged classes in those countries live very well indeed, the average person must survive on an annual per capita GDP of $2,500. Compare this to the 15 percent (992 million people) in high-income countries who have an average per capita GDP of thirteen times that: $33,000. The HIV–AIDS rate in low-income countries is almost seven times that in high-income countries; of the world's 33 million adults and children living with HIV, two-thirds live in sub-Saharan Africa alone. On a per capita basis, citizens in high-income countries consume almost twenty-five times more electricity than their counterparts in low-income countries; together they account for 45 percent of the world's carbon dioxide emissions, whereas citizens in low-income countries account for less than 10 percent. Statistical illustrations of such global inequalities go on and on.[1]

Most of the globe's developing economies are located in the Southern Hemisphere, while industrialized economies are more often found in the north. The discrepancy in development levels, both economic and human, has thus been called the North–South gap. By calling this a *gap*, we are forced to recognize that there is nothing natural or inevitable about the sorry conditions of the world's poor; they can do better, because others do better. How to do better is the subject of great debate among policy makers, academics, and humanitarians, but there can be no question about the possibility of progress in economic and human development. Figure 15.1 shows various indicators of human development—literacy, life expectancy, access to modern sanitation facilities, and child mortality—for both the least-developed countries and the developing world as a whole. These indicators are measured relative to the actual levels of development in the industrialized world (OECD countries), thereby giving a sense of today's North–South gap and the degree of improvement that is in fact possible.

Western social scientists, particularly North Americans, generally did not foresee the persistence of poverty in the developing world. It was clear fifty years ago that economic development in poor countries would be slow and difficult, the result of a long process of accumulating capital investments and human skills. However, most analysts did not expect the gap between the North and South, or between the rich and the poor within countries of the South, to be so great for so long. But the record of development is not uniformly dismal. In some areas the picture is mixed, and even allows for cautious optimism. The last half century has witnessed a remarkable differentiation among countries and regions of the developing world, a differentiation that makes reference to *the* developing world, *the* third world, or *the* South rather misleading. There are areas of growing wealth and development, such as the oil-rich states or the NICs of the Pacific Rim, and some areas caught in perpetual stagnation, such as sub-Saharan Africa. Clearly, East Asia and the Pacific have experienced the highest economic growth rates. In the 1990s, before the Asian financial crisis, the average annual growth rate in GDP per capita for these countries was about 10 percent and had just about returned to

---

[1] Figures are for 2005 or 2006 and come from the UN Development Programme, *Human Development Report 2007/2008: Fighting Climate Change: Human Solidarity in a Divided World* (New York: UNDP, 2007). GDP figures are purchasing power parities and therefore take into account lower costs of living in poorer countries. AIDS and HIV figures, here and in the next section, come from the UN Program on HIV–AIDS, *AIDS Epidemic Update* (Geneva: UNAIDS, 2007).

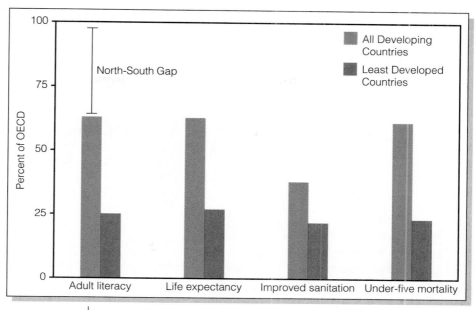

FIGURE 15.1 | NORTH–SOUTH HUMAN DEVELOPMENT GAP, 2005

For each indicator, averages for OECD, all developing, and least-developed countries are indexed relative to the fifth and ninety-fifth percentile countries. The bars represent the indexes for developing and least-developed countries as a percent of the OECD index. The distance between the height of the bar and top of the graph is the development gap, which is very wide indeed for the poorest of the poor.

Source: Calculations by the authors from data in United Nations Development Programme, *Human Development Report 2007/2008.*

that level by 2007. India for almost two decades, and China for three, have also grown very rapidly, and did so right through the Asian crisis.

Countries in Latin America and the Caribbean averaged growth rates less than half that in recent years, but many of those economies that have gradually emerged from their foreign debt problems are attracting substantial foreign investment. Sub-Saharan Africa is quite a different story—very slow (sometimes negative) growth for many years, failure to attract foreign investment, and crumbling economic and social infrastructures with significant health-care problems (especially AIDS), not to mention a breakdown in civil order in a number of countries in East, West, and Central Africa.

Comparing countries and regions in terms of their levels of development is a difficult exercise. There are differing views about what exactly "development" means and therefore different measures of it. One useful indicator is constructed annually by the UN Development Programme (UNDP): the human development index (HDI). The UNDP's view is that while wealth (for example, GDP per capita) is of great importance to development, by itself wealth is not a sufficient measure of human development because it does not always capture *social* progress. The basic purpose of development is to expand human capabilities by expanding

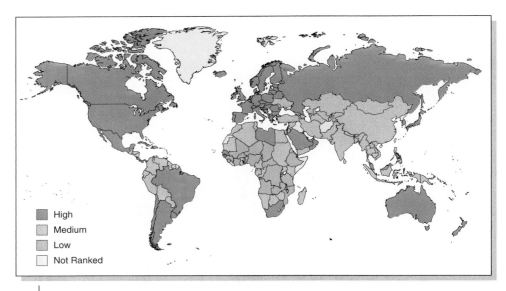

MAP 15.1 | HUMAN DEVELOPMENT IN THE WORLD, 2005

A society's level of human development is a function not only of wealth but also the education and health of its people. The UN's HDI is an attempt to combine all three into a single measure. Human development varies not only between the industrialized OECD, the former Soviet bloc countries, and the developing countries, but also among developing countries themselves. Human development in sub-Saharan Africa is cause for special concern.
Source: Map drawn using data from UN Development Programme, *Human Development Report 2007/2008.* The HDI range for high human development is 0.8 to 1.0; for medium, 0.5 to 0.8; and for low, 0 to 0.5.

the choices that people have to live full and rewarding lives.[2] Some oil-rich countries, like Oman and Saudi Arabia, rank high on per capita GDP but are in the bottom third on literacy (especially female literacy). For other states, like some of the former Soviet republics of Central Asia, the exact opposite is true: They have done well in educating their population but are still relatively poor. These are extreme examples, but they do suggest the need for an indicator of development that measures more than just wealth.

The UNDP's HDI takes into account life expectancy, adult literacy, and school enrollment, as well as GDP per capita. Map 15.1 shows the global distribution of countries classified as having achieved high, medium, and low levels of human development. The North–South gap is readily apparent. The OECD countries are both wealthy and developed in the broader sense. With some exceptions in Latin America and the Middle East (and, of course, Australia and New Zealand), the South has attained intermediate levels of human development at best, and in

---

[2] In addition to the UNDP's annual *Human Development Report,* see Christian Welzel, Ronald Inglehart, and Hans-Dieter Kligemann, "The Theory of Human Development: A Cross-Cultural Analysis,"*European Journal of Political Research* 42 (May 2003), pp. 341–379.

sub-Saharan Africa the picture is bleak. In addition, some countries in what used to be called the *second world* (the former Soviet republics in Central Asia and Eastern Europe, with legacies of communist rule) continue to occupy an intermediate position between the first and third worlds when it comes to economic and social development. Today, the second world countries of the cold war years are often referred to as "emerging market economies."

Some gaps between the North and the South continue to widen—especially differences in wealth and income. Since the early 1990s, LDCs experienced a higher rate of growth in GDP per capita than industrialized countries (on average). However, the growth rate in the least-developed countries was generally lower than in the OECD, and in some sub-Saharan African countries it was actually *negative*. Many indicators of social development have also shown improvement over time for the developing world as a whole while at the same time indicating a substantial lag in progress among the poorest states. For example, the infant mortality rate has dropped almost 50 percent in the developing world since 1970, but for the least-developed countries the decline was only 36 percent. Over the same period, there was a 17 percent increase in life expectancy in the developing world but practically no increase in sub-Saharan Africa. No matter how we group countries for purposes of comparison, it is well to remember that what is often called the *developing world* is, in fact, several worlds, with different problems, prospects, and records of performance.

DEMOGRAPHICS, DISEASE, AND GEOGRAPHY

As we will see in the next chapter, recent population growth in much of the world is extraordinary—with more than 90 percent of the 2.5 billion people added since 1975 living in the developing countries. Over the last thirty years, the average annual population growth rate in the developing world has been 1.9 percent, compared to 0.8 percent for the OECD. The figure for the developing world hides some much higher rates in certain regions. In the Middle East, Northern Africa, and sub-Saharan Africa, the average annual growth in population was almost 3 percent. Greater numbers of people place greater demands on governments for food, housing, health care, and jobs. A basic rule of thumb is that an economy must grow at least as fast as the population just to forestall degradation in economic and social well-being. Economic growth must clearly exceed population growth for conditions to improve. Economic growth rates for the least-developed countries fall drastically short of even matching population growth.

The drag of population is, and will continue to be, a significant obstacle to development in many LDCs. Add the issues of debt and debt servicing, and the obstacles loom even larger. Add additional problems of health care, particularly AIDS, and the task magnifies to daunting proportions. More than 30 million people are HIV-positive, and thus expected to die from AIDS, with 90 percent of the cases in the developing world. Sub-Saharan Africa has been particularly hard hit. In this region there were 1.6 million AIDS deaths and 1.7 million new infections in 2007 alone. One out of every five adults has HIV–AIDS in Zimbabwe, one out of four in Botswana and Lesotho, and one in three in Swaziland. Consequently, since 1990 the life expectancy rate in these four countries has *fallen* by 14 to

20 years for men and 18 to 25 years for women. Economic and social strains are already evident in Africa, with the rising costs of health care, lost workdays by both AIDS victims and caregivers—there are 12 million orphaned children in Africa due to AIDS—and the fact that the disease kills adults during their most productive years. The majority of Africa's new infections have occurred in the 15 to 24 age group.

The AIDS epidemic is truly a case of the poor getting poorer. Robert Kaplan, in a gloomy and controversial portrait of crumbling order in West Africa, sees the region as being isolated by a "wall of disease" that includes AIDS, hepatitis B, tuberculosis, and malaria. The region is for him a microcosm of the way in which "scarcity, crime, overpopulation, tribalism, and disease are rapidly destroying the social fabric of our planet":

> Precisely because much of Africa is set to go over the edge at a time when the Cold War has ended, when environmental and demographic stress in other parts of the globe is becoming critical, and when the post–First World War system of nation-states—not just in the Balkans but perhaps also in the Middle East—is about to be toppled, Africa suggests what war, borders, and ethnic politics will be like a few decades hence.[3]

That is a pessimistic prognosis indeed. Most would like to think that sub-Saharan Africa will narrow the gap with the rest of the developing world, not that the rest of the developing world will eventually experience the problems of development and social disorder currently besetting sub-Saharan Africa.

The developmental stresses of population and disease are also related to geography, which is one reason why the gap between rich and poor is a gap between North and South. The tropical zone is hospitable to many infectious diseases; pathogens carried by mosquitoes and parasitic worms survive at a much lower rate in temperate climates. The prevalence of such diseases weakens the body's immune system and probably accounts for the more rapid progression of HIV infection to AIDS in tropical regions. The natural response of a population to high morbidity and mortality is high fertility, because large families become the best strategy for survival. Large families, in turn, absorb resources—not the least being female labor, which might otherwise be free to enter the paid workforce. The tropical regions of the Global South are also more difficult to farm. Many major food grains (including wheat, corn, and rice) fare better in temperate climates, and tropical agriculture must confront a host of unique difficulties related to soil degradation, highly variable precipitation, and pest infestation. Low agricultural productivity places limits on urbanization as well—urban populations must be fed—and cities tend to provide the social and economic environment most conducive to technological and industrial development.[4]

---

[3] Robert D. Kaplan, "The Coming Anarchy," *Atlantic Monthly* 273 (February 1994): 44–76. See also Kaplan, *The Coming Anarchy: Shattering the Dreams of the Post Cold War* (New York: Vintage, 2001); Dennis C. Pirages, "Nature, Disease, and Globalization: An Evolutionary Perspective," *International Studies Review* 9 (Winter 2007), pp. 616–628.

[4] Jeffrey D. Sachs, Andrew D. Mellinger, and John L. Gallup, "The Geography of Poverty and Wealth," *Scientific American* 284 (March 2001), pp. 70–75; Jared Diamond, *Guns, Germs, and Steel: The Fates of Human Societies* (New York: Norton, 1997).

However, in drawing attention to these and related disadvantages, we must be careful not to engage in geographical determinism. Geography is simply one of the many factors that seem to have conspired against economic and human development in the Global South. History is another factor, and one emphasized by those who believe that the West bears some responsibility for the current North–South gap.

DEPENDENT DEVELOPMENT

The early Western view of development, which came to be known as **modernization theory**, suggested that LDCs would progress along the path of industrialization and economic growth as their societies shed their traditional ways and became more modern. Their argument was that urbanization, secularization, and cultural tolerance encourage an entrepreneurial spirit that was generally missing from traditional societies. Eventually, however, social, cultural, and economic practices in traditional societies would become transformed and LDCs would prosper; after all, this was the sort of transformation experienced by the West as it entered its stage of industrial development.[5]

To some, the failure of Western theories of development to anticipate economic stagnation and political repression in much of the developing world was not surprising. Theorists from Latin America, Africa, and other parts of the world took a view of development that was much more attentive to international and systemic influences on development than was most Western theory. For these people, a crucial flaw in Western theory was its treatment of political and economic development as essentially determined by domestic forces. Instead, critics thought, political and economic structures within LDCs were primarily determined by the role their economies played in the global economy. Understanding the effect of *foreign* penetration of underdeveloped economies and polities and how that penetration helped shape relations between social classes in those countries was essential.

Some of these theories take a historical perspective that extends back to the establishment of a world system in the sixteenth century, and so this body of work is known as **world system theory**. The major powers—Spain and Portugal, and later Britain, Holland, and France—had created a world division of labor between themselves, the "center" of the world system, and their colonial territories in the "periphery." Commerce and manufacturing were established largely in the center, while the periphery provided food and raw minerals for the world market. The populations of the periphery were often subjugated and made to work on big farms or as slave-like labor in the mines. In some areas, especially in the Caribbean, the original populations were largely exterminated and replaced by slaves who were imported from Africa and sometimes worked to death under appalling conditions. Governmental control was exercised from the center or, more commonly in those

---

[5] A classic statement is W. W. Rostow, *The Stages of Economic Growth: A Non-Communist Manifesto* (Cambridge: Cambridge University Press, 1966). On the impact of modernization theory on U.S. foreign policy, see Nils Gilman, *Mandarins of the Future: Modernization Theory in Cold War America* (Baltimore: Johns Hopkins University Press, 2003).

days of slow communication, by the large landowners and urban merchants who sold their products in the world market. Most of the colonial world was thus established as a producer of agricultural products and raw materials for the European center and was ruled by an upper class that imported its manufactured goods from Europe. The local ruling elites had neither the power to resist European penetration nor an interest in doing so because they, too, were profiting from the system.[6]

When countries of the periphery became politically sovereign in the nineteenth and twentieth centuries, their ruling elites maintained close economic links with the world economy. In some instances, their interests coincided closely with those of European capitalists who came to invest in the periphery, and they prospered by providing services and local expertise to the Europeans. In other instances their interests diverged, but still the peripheral states lacked strong central governments that could effectively resist or control European penetration. There were sometimes deep and violent conflicts between landowners and urban entrepreneurs, between domestic and foreign capitalists. Nevertheless, the masses of people in the countryside usually remained poor and powerless. Sharp inequalities in income distribution meant that, except in a few big countries (Argentina, Mexico, Brazil, and much later India), there could be no large mass market for domestically manufactured goods. The result was economic stagnation and relegation to the role of producers and exporters of primary commodities.

In some areas where significant local industry had existed before the colonial era, that industry was stifled. The most famous instance is nineteenth-century India. The British colonial government deliberately destroyed the Indian textile industry; it built a railway system through India with the express purpose of opening up the country so that the textile manufactures of Lancashire could be sold to the Indian population. Another case is that of the Belgian Congo in the late nineteenth century, where the colonial rulers wanted to use the local population as a labor force in the mines. Streams were poisoned so that the Africans could not live from fishing. They were then required to pay taxes, and they could earn money to pay taxes only by working—for very low wages.

There are important differences of interpretation when it comes to the colonial era. In discussing imperialism in Chapter 8, we indicated that although there are conflicting theories about just *how* important economic motives were in promoting imperialism and precisely *what* economic mechanisms were involved—a search for markets, for raw materials, or for outlets for surplus capital—economic motives in general were a major influence. A world division of labor between an industrial center and a periphery producing primary goods (with some states in a "semi-peripheral" status) did arise. Associated with this division of labor were powerful groups and classes in all parts of the world with a great stake in maintaining the

---

[6] The preeminent world system theorist is Immanuel Wallerstein. An early statement is Wallerstein, *The Modern World-System I: Capitalist Agriculture and the Origins of the European World-Economy in the Sixteenth Century* (New York: Academic Press, 1974); see also his *World-Systems Analysis: An Introduction* (Durham, N.C.: Duke University Press, 2004). See also Christopher Chase-Dunn, "World-Systems Theorizing," in Jonathan Turner, ed., *Handbook of Sociological Theory* (New York: Penguin, 2001).

basic structure. However, the importance of these historical circumstances for contemporary patterns of development, the significance of clear exceptions to the general picture, and the prospects for industrial and human development today are issues involving much more controversy.

CONTEMPORARY DEPENDENCE

In the view of some radical theorists, LDCs dependent on the world market face a great many obstacles in developing advanced, diversified economies. Economies dependent on exports of agricultural and raw materials are especially sensitive (and vulnerable) to market forces. Wage rates are suppressed, price inflation is persistent, and the market values of primary exports diminish even as they fluctuate. What is more, their political and financial institutions are often too weak to deal effectively with these deteriorating economic conditions.

The prices of a country's exports relative to the prices of its imports are known as the **terms of trade**. If the terms of trade improve for a commodity-producing country, it can obtain more or better manufactured goods in exchange for a given amount of exports. The problem for many LDCs is that although prices increased sharply in the 1970s (to keep up with rising oil prices) and have maintained roughly the same level since then, when compared to the prices of manufactured goods exported by industrialized countries, commodity prices have fallen. Furthermore, commodity prices have been subject to wide fluctuation. Drops of 25 percent or more from one year to the next for cocoa, rubber, sugar, copper, lead, and zinc have not been rare. When prices fluctuate sharply, producers have a very hard time planning future production and sales. Bad weather may reduce the volume of exports but drive up the price of what is left. Producers who increase their acreage or mining capacity to take advantage of higher prices in future years may go too far, creating an excess supply that lowers prices and earnings instead of raising them. Countries that depend heavily on earnings from commodity exports to provide foreign exchange for development can be hit hard. If export earnings fall, key development plans may have to be eliminated or postponed, or loans may have to be obtained.

Most big, populous countries can have reasonably diversified economies and therefore are not too vulnerable to fluctuations in the prices of particular commodities. In the post-World War II period, a number of big and middle-sized LDCs have become fairly industrialized; South Korea, Taiwan, Mexico, China, and Brazil are examples of states that are no longer overly dependent on commodity exports. But some middle-sized countries and many small ones have been very dependent on commodities, often on just one or two. In the 1970s, when commodity prices were at an all-time high relative to the costs of imported manufactures, the Democratic Republic of Congo (then called Zaire) derived two-thirds of all its export earnings from copper and almost half of Egypt's earnings came from cotton. As real commodity prices fell, these and other countries—for example, Cuba (sugar), Ghana (cocoa), Sri Lanka (tea), Panama (bananas), and Bolivia (tin)—experienced severe economic difficulties.

So that domestic manufactures might eventually replace imports, many LDC governments adopted a strategy of actively promoting industrial development.

This strategy, often called *import substitution industrialization* (ISI), was designed to eliminate the vulnerabilities associated with reliance on commodity exports. For the larger countries with reasonably big domestic markets, this worked for awhile. However, the limits of ISI soon became apparent. These were still relatively poor countries, with an income distribution heavily favoring the rich and therefore without mass markets for consumer goods. ISI policies often meant subsidizing and protecting new domestic industries or required foreign loans and direct investment by multinational corporations.

Radical international political economists who have analyzed these problems are often referred to as **dependency theorists**, and many have hailed from the developing world, especially Latin America, where the problems of underdevelopment were more "real" than for analysts in the industrialized West. Important differences exist among them. Some see LDCs as doomed to stagnation; others see possibilities of "dependent development" that could make possible rapid growth in GDP per capita, albeit in economies that are fundamentally distorted and highly inegalitarian. Writers differ on the relative importance of domestic class relations as contrasted with external forces. While all would qualify as radical theorists, their theories derive from varying mixtures of liberal economics and Marxist analysis. Yet despite their differences, all dependency theorists agree that economic, social, and political conditions in peripheral societies are inextricably linked and that realist emphasis on the nation-state level of analysis often ignores penetration by transnational and international actors in the global system.[7]

Economic penetration of the South by the North can be accomplished by financial or technological means. The foreign subsidiaries of MNCs based in industrialized countries are involved in mining, agriculture, manufacturing, and other forms of extraction and production. Historical and contemporary examples—often the subject of study and criticism—include Kennecott Copper in Chile, British Petroleum in Iran, United Fruit in Guatemala, Firestone Rubber in Liberia, and Volkswagen in Brazil. These subsidiaries typically use technology and production processes originally developed in the industrial economies but have migrated to the periphery to take advantage of cheaper labor and lower taxes, as well as lax environmental and other regulations. By importing much of their technology and capital equipment (computers, transport vehicles, machinery, and so on) from advanced economies, foreign subsidiaries become a conduit for the transfer of manufacturing processes from the center to the periphery. Although liberals have tended to see that as a good thing, radicals point out that it fosters dependence and undercuts the development of indigenous technological and manufacturing capacity.

Social and cultural penetration may come in material or in symbolic "packages"—in books, television programs (reruns or fresh via satellite), newspapers and magazines, and motion pictures. They may also come more abstractly,

---

[7] Early influential studies were Paul A. Baran, *The Political Economy of Growth* (New York: Monthly Review Press, 1957); André Gunder Frank, *Capitalism and Underdevelopment in Latin America: Historical Studies of Chile and Brazil* (New York: Monthly Review Press, 1967). One respected dependency theorist, Fernando Henrique Cardoso, served as president of Brazil from 1995 to 2003; see his *Dependency and Development in Latin America* (Berkeley: University of California Press, 1979), coauthored with Enzo Faletto.

through people who become "carriers" of foreign cultures. Young people are sent to foreign educational institutions and return having adopted elements of Western industrial culture: ways of thinking and behaving, ideologies, values, and appreciation of Western consumer goods. Tourists traveling to developing countries bring with them their cultural values as well. Students may dislike many aspects of the countries in which they study, and tourists may inspire resentment as well as emulation, yet exposure to the cultures of advanced countries can sometimes alter local cultural preferences. People come to want consumer goods that are readily available in advanced industrial economies but unaffordable to a large portion of society in poor countries: automobiles, air conditioners, camcorders, cell phones, laptops.

Indigenous manufacturing enterprises in LDCs may thus turn toward this small market of relatively privileged, Westernized consumers, producing familiar products with well-established technologies, rather than aiming for a working-class market with many potential consumers but limited purchasing power. This means, in effect, that even local industrial and commercial production may end up reinforcing the position of the well-to-do classes rather than promote a more egalitarian distribution of income that would nurture a mass market for basic consumer goods—bread rather than beef, mass transit rather than private cars, village doctors rather than urban medical specialists. By all these means, consumption and cultural values in the global periphery become conditioned by economic dependence on the center. Radical theorists have branded this process *neoimperialism*—or, to emphasize the corrupting influence of Western consumerism, "coca-colonization."

THE DEBT PROBLEM

The effects of foreign penetration and dependence are complex, are often indirect, and vary greatly in different kinds of countries. A country's previous colonial history, its size, its relative level of wealth, and its natural resources all influence its ties with the global economy. In the short run, foreign investment and foreign aid may stimulate growth, but growth will be hindered if foreign subsidiaries ultimately send much of their profits back to the countries where their parent corporations are headquartered. Growth is also reduced through repayment of debts to foreign governments and banks.

At the end of 2007, the foreign debt of all developing and emerging market economies was more than $4 trillion. That was one-quarter of their aggregate GDP and 70 percent of their exports. Much of the ballooning LDC debt burden can be attributed to borrowing by commodity exporters. The so-called third world debt crisis of the 1980s accompanied a sharp fall in world commodity prices. Loans were required to compensate for losses resulting from a deterioration in the terms of trade, a problem that did not affect LDC exporters of manufactured goods. When commodity prices began to stabilize in the 1990s, the debt ratio started to decline. The debt burden has not evaporated, however. Annual debt repayment (interest and amortization) alone laid claim to more than 20 percent of export earnings throughout the 1990s. Since then, the climbing debt burden has leveled off but is still above 10 percent. The 1990s were especially bad in Latin America, where debt payments accounted for 40 to 50 percent of the region's exports (now they are 20 to 25 percent). Some countries, in fact, simply have not been able to make their interest payments. Brazil, for example, has on several occasions negotiated a rescheduling of debt payments in order to avoid defaulting on loans made by international agencies and commercial banks. The emerging market economies are also saddled with high levels of debt. At the end of 2007, Russia and the other former Soviet republics carried debt amounting to almost 40 percent of total GDP, with debt service payments exceeding 20 percent of export earnings. For Eastern European countries, external debt was almost 50 percent of GDP; debt service, 20 percent of export earnings.[8]

The governments of highly indebted countries—there are about fifty of them, according to the World Bank—spend, on average, almost twice as much on servicing their external debt as they do on education, and almost three times what they spend on health care. It is not hard to see why citizens in these countries often feel a great deal of resentment toward foreign lenders. In Chapter 13 we indicated that the IMF is an important player in international finance and development as a lender and as an international agency that confers upon debtors its seal of approval. In making loans, the IMF typically insists on "structural adjustment." The government is usually asked to curb its social spending and adopt other belt-tightening measures designed to control inflation and to otherwise channel government resources away from economically inefficient public projects. When governments agree to IMF conditionality, they also establish their credibility with private foreign lenders, so more is at stake than funding from the IMF itself. Yet the political costs can be severe. Structural adjustment has often bred social unrest as popular programs are scaled back or terminated altogether.[9] As we shall see later in this chapter, economic discipline may require political discipline—that is, state repression.

BEYOND DEPENDENCE: SELF-RELIANCE AND BASIC NEEDS

Dependency theorists and LDC governments have proposed and tried various alternative policies to avoid the worst effects of dependence. The most radical alternative is self-reliance, which implies shifting economic connections from the core countries, the MNCs, and Western aid-giving agencies—in other words, cutting the ties of foreign penetration and dependence. LDCs have tried to build up trade and technical exchange among themselves, especially where domestic markets are too small for economies of scale and where simple labor-intensive technologies seem appropriate for export to other LDCs. Examples include the Central American Common Market or the Caribbean Community.

---

[8] Figures come from International Monetary Fund, *World Economic Outlook Database*, April 2008 Edition; available at <http://www.imf.org/external/pubs/ft/weo/2008/01/weodata/index.aspx>. See also Daniel Marx, Jose Echague, and Guido Sandleris, "Sovereign Debt and the Debt Crisis in Emerging Countries: Experience of the 1990s," in Chris Jochnick and Fraser A. Preston, eds., *Sovereign Debt at the Crossroads: Challenges and Proposals for Resolving the Third World Debt Crisis* (New York: Oxford University Press, 2006).

[9] Randall W. Stone, *Lending Credibility: The International Monetary Fund and the Post-Communist Transition* (Princeton, N.J.: Princeton University Press, 2002); Erik Wibbels, "Dependency Revisited: International Markets, Business Cycles, and Social Spending in the Developing World,"*International Organization* 60 (Spring 2006), pp. 433–468.

Some states took self-reliance to the extreme of a near-total withdrawal from the world market and a reduction of all exports and imports to a bare minimum. From the early 1960s until the late 1980s, the government of Burma (now Myanmar) cut most of its ties with the world economy and even sharply reduced tourism, accepting almost complete economic stagnation as the consequence. China, from its break with the Soviet Union in the late 1950s until its new openings to the West in the mid-1970s, also cut foreign economic and cultural contacts to a minimum. China, however, had some economic advantages in its vast population and the diversity of its natural resources. If self-reliance was to work anywhere and allow economic growth to continue, China offered the best opportunity.

Other countries pursued less extreme versions of self-reliance, attempting to reduce, restructure, and control their contacts with the industrial world rather than cut them sharply or entirely. What all these countries had in common, however, was a desire not to replicate the industrial development of the West or to follow in the footsteps of the many developing countries closely linked with the world capitalist economy. Self-reliance was imposed on the populace by radical socialist leaders, often trying to emulate Soviet development policy during the Stalinist era. Incomes of workers and peasants were kept low to provide a surplus for the government to invest in industry. Being cut off from foreign technology meant backwardness, and being cut off from the competition of the world economy meant inefficiency. Ultimately, self-reliance was a complete economic and political disaster. The failure of the "Burmese Way to Socialism" and other ill-conceived programs probably could have been expected, but China's experience was most disappointing for advocates of self-reliance. After running its economy with a minimum of ties to the world market, and experiencing only modest economic growth, China opened up rapidly; it sought foreign trade and investment and expanded economic ties to the West, especially the United States and Japan.

Advocates for the Global South have sometimes been quite forthright in insisting that rich nations have an *obligation* to help LDCs overcome obstacles to development—through aid, debt forgiveness, and other concessions. Such demands frequently offend residents of developed countries, who respond that they must take care of their own poor citizens before they make giveaways to foreigners. (They could possibly do both; they may in fact do neither.) However, it is important to be aware that the content of these LDC demands is usually not radical but reformist. That is, they still take for granted the existence of an integrated world economy and do not challenge the most fundamental hierarchical characteristics identified by dependency theorists. They wish to reduce their dependence somewhat and to obtain better terms of trade for their products. But they are not seeking to overthrow the existing system of international trade and finance, nor are they seeking to withdraw from that system. They are simply looking to the better positioned members of the system for help.

Some countries have industrialized successfully, in ways not anticipated by dependency theory. The East Asian NICs are the best examples. And in regard to the distribution of income between rich and poor, countries like South Korea and Taiwan have been able to do so in a relatively egalitarian manner. Both countries implemented vast land-reform programs immediately after World War II—Korea under the American occupation, and Taiwan when Chiang Kai-shek, after losing all of mainland China to the communists, fled with his army to the offshore island. In these countries, war and foreign occupation had broken down the traditional sources of resistance to economic reform and equity. Agrarian reforms and redistribution to the poor provided new incentives and a domestic market for simple manufactured goods. Rapid and sustained economic growth followed. Reducing the power of agricultural interests can also lay the basis for independent labor movements and open the possibility of legitimate political challenge to established power, as it did in much of Europe a century ago.[10]

Some development strategies see to it that, along with economic incentives for entrepreneurs, certain essentials are provided for the population. Typically, this means subsidized food production, health care, education, and transportation. Economists sometimes refer to this as a **basic-needs strategy**. This approach to development is not generally concerned with providing consumer goods for immediate use, which might divert scarce resources from investment and leave people no better off when the immediate input of consumer goods has been exhausted. Rather, it tries to build *human capital* that will eventually provide the basis for economic growth. Economists currently studying the impact of equality on growth have shown that investments in such human capital may be as important as investments in industrial facilities. Some governments have attempted to give poor people both the incentives and capabilities to improve earnings through land reform, health measures, and especially access to secondary school education. Amartya Sen, a Nobel Prize–winning economist and pioneer in the study of poverty and inequality, showed that economic crises (like famines) are often not the consequence of shortages but the result of sudden drops in real incomes. Political freedom can help mitigate famine as well; dictatorships often permit a level of starvation that would not be tolerated in democracies with a free flow of information and freedom to protest. Sen has also pointed out the glaring inequalities between men and women in many developing countries. Expanding the social and economic opportunities for women reduces rates of population growth and introduces an otherwise untapped reservoir of talent into the national economy. Thus, gender equality is not only a human rights issue but also part of an effective strategy for economic development.[11]

A NEW ECONOMIC ORDER?

Beginning in the 1970s, developing countries attempted to fashion a program of collective action to allay the conditions of economic dependence. Demands for restructuring world trade and industry on terms more favorable to the South became identified with demands for a **new international economic order** (**NIEO**).

---

[10] On the relevance of the European experience, see Robert H. Bates, *Prosperity and Violence: The Political Economy of Development* (New York: Norton, 2001); Hernando de Soto, *The Mystery of Capital: Why Capitalism Triumphs in the West and Fails Everywhere Else* (New York: Basic Books, 2000).

[11] Amartya Sen, *Poverty and Famines: An Essay on Entitlement and Deprivation* (New York: Oxford University Press, 1981). See also Sen, *Inequality Reexamined* (Cambridge, Mass.: Harvard University Press, 1992); Janet Henshall Momsen, *Gender and Development* (London: Routledge, 2004).

They called for changes in the international market conditions affecting trade in primary commodities, the promotion of industrial development in nonindustrialized countries, and increased developmental assistance and debt relief.

INTERNATIONAL MARKET REFORMS

The LDCs have tried to raise and to stabilize the widely fluctuating prices for their exports of agricultural products and minerals. At meetings of the UN Commission on Trade and Development (UNCTAD), which began in 1964 in Geneva, state leaders pushed for an integrated program for commodity production and trade. This program was advocated by a diverse and sometimes very shaky coalition of developing countries known as the Group of 77 (or G-77, which has in fact grown to include more than 130 members). It called for price and production agreements among producers, the creation of international buffer stocks of commodities financed by a common fund, multilateral long-term supply contracts, and other measures to reduce fluctuations in the price of commodity exports.

Some G-77 members also called for indexing the price of commodities so that they would automatically rise with any increase in the price of manufactured goods (much as wages are often tied to the consumer price index in the United States). This last proposal was opposed, however, by both poor countries and rich countries that were major commodity importers. Although the industrialized countries have become more open-minded about schemes for stabilizing prices, they have vigorously resisted anything that hints of indexing. They argue that price changes are necessary for conveying information about changes in market supply and demand. Indexing would be inefficient, encouraging surplus production (as it has for many agricultural commodities like grain and dairy produced in the EU). Nevertheless, most international markets are, to one degree or another, already quite removed from the idealized model of perfect competition. The clearest example is OPEC, an association of oil-producing countries that for awhile took control of the world oil market and changed the terms of trade markedly in their favor. Through coordinated action—in production and distribution (or nondistribution, in the case of embargo)—this cartel exercised immense influence over the market price of oil throughout the 1970s.

After the success of OPEC in revolutionizing the world oil market, both LDCs and industrialized countries expected similar arrangements to arise for other commodities, as the sellers followed OPEC's example to band together in international commodity cartels. But that did not happen, chiefly because the conditions that favored OPEC largely applied to petroleum products alone. First, there existed cultural and political ties among the Arab members of OPEC. Although the importance of this factor can be exaggerated, these ties did at least facilitate the coordinated action that characterized OPEC policy in the early years. Second, there was a lack of ready substitutes for oil, making it very difficult for buyers to refuse to pay the higher prices dictated by the cartel. Third, the rise of OPEC occurred in the context of high global demand for oil and little excess supply. Those conditions did not apply in all commodity markets. Finally, the hegemonic position of Saudi Arabia, and for awhile Iran, within OPEC helped to overcome the free-rider problem. If these two could agree on price and quantity, they could bring along the rest of the suppliers. Even if one or two small exporters did offer cheaper terms, it did not fundamentally upset the imposed price structure; collective action was not undermined by such defections.[12]

No other major commodity cartel has emerged with anything like OPEC's initial success. Some effort was made in the bauxite industry (bauxite is the principal ore from which aluminum is refined), but the conditions working in OPEC's favor were lacking in this case. Most importantly, other aluminum-bearing ores exist in many of the developed countries and would be brought into production if the price of bauxite were raised too high. Another complication for many commodity producers is the existence of stockpiles in the developed countries. It is not enough for a cartel to control a large share of a commodity's production. To set world prices, it must control the market. Opportunities to manipulate the market are limited when alternatives to a particular commodity are readily available, whether from stockpiles or substitutes controlled by countries outside the cartel. For a commodity cartel to exercise effective influence, target states must be vulnerable, not merely sensitive. The availability of stockpiles and substitutes has thus discouraged the formation of cartels among nonoil commodity producers.

INDUSTRIALIZATION

Even if many new OPEC-like cartels did emerge, they might not serve the interests of member states. These countries would still be specializing in primary commodity production, and therefore denied the potential developmental benefits accompanying a shift to manufacturing. At the least, most LDCs want to move into a stage of refining and processing the raw materials they produce. Otherwise, if the resource is nonrenewable, once the mineral reserves have been exhausted, the country is left with little more than a hole in the ground (and perhaps roads and pipelines leading to the hole). However, if the country shifts to processing or, better, to manufacturing using its raw materials as inputs, it can benefit from "spin-offs" like technical expertise, an infrastructure of communications and transportation, and physical plants and equipment suitable for many uses. The persistent wealth of most developed countries today is based on industry. Processing and industrial diversification seem essential to balanced development, especially in a world where the demand for synthetics has come to replace the demand for so many natural materials.

Exports of technologically advanced manufactured products are typically subjected to low tariffs. But many LDCs that have embarked on a process of industrialization produce simpler manufactured goods and thus do not benefit. Some, for example, export refined or processed raw materials or relatively simple and labor-intensive manufactures like textiles. On such goods, tariffs and other restrictions on imports into the industrialized countries can be very high. LDCs can be effectively shut out of the world market for those exports. Therefore, they lose the

[12] Dag Harald Claes, *The Politics of Oil-Producer Cooperation* (Boulder, Colo.: Westview, 2001); Mark S. LeClair, *International Commodity Markets and the Role of Cartels* (Armonk, N.Y.: M. E. Sharpe, 2000).

revenue from value added by manufacturing and lose the spin-offs that help stimulate wider development.

In negotiations with the developed countries, LDCs have consistently sought to restructure preferences so they could export more simple manufactures to industrial countries. Some improvements have been made. Members of the European Community in 1975 signed the Lomé Convention with most of their former colonies, and at about the same time the United States instituted a Generalized System of Preferences favoring some simple manufactures from LDCs. Regional free-trade areas, such as NAFTA, may also become important. By 2006, low- and middle-income countries accounted for 25 percent of world exports of manufactured goods. The EU imports about 10 percent of its manufactures from these countries; the United States and Japan, about 20 percent. Many potential LDC exports are in industries that are declining in OECD countries, usually because they are low-technology goods requiring labor-intensive production (and labor costs are high in the OECD). The apparel industry, for instance, is endangered in the EU, as well as in the United States and Japan. In times of recession, when unemployment and the number of business bankruptcies are high, resistance to granting preferences to exports from LDCs is especially great. For this reason, many economists say that an essential requirement for rising prosperity in the developing world is continued prosperity in the industrialized countries that serve as their markets. The OECD imports more than 80 percent of the manufactured goods exported by low- and middle-income countries.[13]

Countries following an outward-looking development strategy (South Korea, Singapore, Thailand)—often referred to as *export-oriented industrialization* (EOI)—have typically experienced faster growth rates than inward-oriented LDCs (Argentina, Ghana, India, and Tanzania). As changes in exchange rates began to price some Japanese goods out of the world market, goods from the Asian NICs replaced them—frequently spurred by Japanese capital. The NICs' governments have targeted certain industries for special government assistance, often with great success; the steel and automobile industries in South Korea are good examples.[14]

Governments and businesspeople have devised some very clever strategies to get around developed countries' nontariff barriers to their trade. Yet there remains a question as to whether there is room for many more countries to follow in their path. Could world markets absorb enough manufactures from such vast countries as China and India to make much difference in those countries' large pockets of continuing poverty?

As an alternative or supplement to EOI, some countries are still pursuing policies of limited import substitution. For some larger countries like Brazil, Mexico, India, and Nigeria, this approach has some promise. Their governments have instituted various requirements for *indigenization* by MNCs. For instance, finished

---

[13] Figures computed from World Trade Organization, *International Trade Statistics 2007* (Geneva: WTO Publications, 2007).

[14] Peter Evans, *Embedded Autonomy: States and Industrial Transformation* (Princeton, N.J.: Princeton University Press, 1995); Stephen Haggard, *Pathways from the Periphery: The Politics of Growth in the Newly Industrializing Countries* (Ithaca, N.Y.: Cornell University Press, 1990).

products must consist of locally manufactured components and subsidiaries of foreign firms must be partially managed or owned by nationals of the host country—although MNCs have found ingenious ways to evade indigenization regulations and they can often persuade governments to admit more manufacturers than would be optimal for their small markets. Indigenization requirements, however, do not address questions of whether Western high-technology goods and production processes are appropriate for LDCs. Nor do they do much for small or poor countries that do not have large markets for import-substituting manufactures. Efforts to create larger markets through regional economic integration have had mixed results.

Economic reforms at home became a key part of recent LDC development strategies beginning in the 1990s. Protective tariffs and quotas for domestic industries were dismantled, subjecting local industries to the competitive pressures of the world market. Some industries prove too inefficient to survive competition with imports; others, like the Chilean steel industry, thrive and become efficient exporters of specialty goods. Governments are reducing subsidies to private industry, trimming government regulations, and selling off government-owned corporations. In the early 1990s, the new government of India began reducing government regulation and encouraging private investment, reversing its long-standing preferences for central planning and government ownership. During the administration of Carlos Salinas de Gortari (1988–1994), the Mexican government privatized $20 billion worth of state enterprises. Such reforms reflected the influence of neoclassical theory in development economics and are reminiscent of some of the policies advocated by the previous generation of modernization theorists.

DEBT RELIEF AND DEVELOPMENT ASSISTANCE

Some countries that essentially solved their problems of trade dependence through industrialization have fallen back into another form of dependence: debt. For countries facing international bankruptcy, relief—in the form of debt forgiveness or rescheduling—is essential. The U.S. government's own trade deficits magnify the problem by attracting much foreign capital that might otherwise flow to indebted poor countries. Many LDCs may never repay the principal on their loans; some cannot even afford to keep up payments on the interest. If big countries like Mexico or Brazil should default on their payments, major banks in the developed countries, which have lent large sums to LDCs, could go bankrupt.

The developed countries thus have a direct interest in keeping their debtors afloat financially. The Paris Club, a group consisting of OECD creditor countries plus Russia, provides a multilateral forum for the rescheduling of debt and debt relief for "heavily indebted poor countries" (HIPCs). Under the "Naples terms," the Paris Club allows debt reductions of 67 percent for countries that have debt-to-export ratios exceeding 150 percent and per capita GDPs of less than $755. For the very poorest and the most indebted of the HIPCs—so far, five countries in sub-Saharan Africa have qualified—up to 80 percent of their debt may be cancelled (the "Lyon terms"). Countries in need, but also with a good track record of economic adjustment, are eligible for cancellation of up to 90 percent of the debt (the "Cologne terms"). Commercial creditors, informally organized as the London Club, are also involved in negotiating debt relief.

TABLE 15.1 | TOP RECIPIENTS AND DONORS OF OECD OFFICIAL DEVELOPMENT ASSISTANCE, 2006

Top Recipients

	$ Billions		% GNP
Nigeria	11.4	Solomon Islands	61
Iraq	8.7	Liberia	54
Afghanistan	3.0	Burundi	53
Pakistan	2.1	Micronesia, Fed. States	41
Sudan	2.1	Afghanistan	36

Top Donors

	$ Billions		% GNP
United States	23.5	Sweden	1.02
United Kingdom	12.4	Norway	0.89
Japan	11.2	Luxembourg	0.89
France	10.6	Netherlands	0.81
Germany	10.4	Denmark	0.80

Source: Organization for Economic Co-operation and Development, Development Co-operation Report 2007 (Paris: OECD, 2008).

As the immediate debt crisis is surmounted, the need for long-term development assistance returns to center stage. For some of the poorest countries, foreign aid represents a substantial share of their total income, as shown in Table 15.1. Burundi, Liberia, and the Solomon Islands received aid from the OECD in excess of 50 percent of GNP in 2006. But economic aid can be hard to sell to Western taxpayers far removed from its foreign destinations. Whereas development assistance from the OECD was 0.5 percent of their total GNP in 1960, it had fallen to 0.3 percent by 2006. This has occurred despite an earlier agreement by the developed countries to accept a UN target of economic assistance equal to 0.7 percent of their GNP. As Table 15.1 makes clear, donor countries in the OECD—members of the Development Assistance Committee (DAC)—vary considerably in the absolute amount of aid they give and the burden they are willing to bear. The United States is by far the largest provider of official development assistance (ODA) in dollars, but it is not the most "generous" in terms of aid as a share of GNP; Sweden is. (The U.S. figure of $23.5 billion was 18 percent of its GNP, the lowest share among DAC countries except for Greece.) In response to criticism that the United States is tight-fisted with its development assistance, officials often reply that much American foreign aid comes from the private sector. In terms of private development assistance channeled through NGOs, the United States does indeed rank closer to the top (sixth place in 2006), though many believe this does not justify its light ODA burden.

The problem of promoting development in the South will require creative problem solving by the industrial countries as well as by the LDCs themselves. The situation in the developing world has been exacerbated by the end of the cold war. Whatever advantage some LDCs had in the cold war competition for friends and allies—and thus in extracting aid from both the United States and Soviet

Union—is gone. Instead, LDCs now find themselves in competition with the emerging market economies of Eastern European and the former Soviet republics for Western aid. Russia received $1.2 billion from DAC countries in 2004; only six of the 170 other ODA recipients received more. The geographic proximity of the former communist areas makes them more important to the EU and OECD countries, especially in the movement for European unity and stability. Germany's experience with the ongoing integration of the former East Germany suggests the scope of the effort needed. Not only do some of the former Soviet republics have significant economic problems (including very low GDP growth rates) but also they are states that have moved away from liberalization and in some cases even democracy. The fear that democratic reforms could go the way of some now-scrapped economic reforms has catapulted some of these states to the top of the Western aid agenda.

DEALING WITH FINANCIAL CRISES

The financial crisis that began to unfold in Asia in fall 1997 prompted a reexamination of the global financial system and the types of reforms—international and domestic—that might help the market economies in Asia and elsewhere weather the next financial crisis and the next. Many believe such crises will be increasingly common in the years ahead, especially given some of the transnational economic and financial developments we discussed in the last chapter under the rubric of globalization.

The events in Asia demonstrated that financial crises are difficult to contain. International economists now refer to **contagion** (in 1997 it was the "Asian contagion"), a process of spreading currency crises that may be driven as much by geography and trade patterns as by economic or financial weaknesses in the afflicted countries. Figure 15.2 shows the values of five Asian currencies from July 1996 through January 1999 (relative to their dollar exchange rate at the beginning of the period). Recall from Chapter 1 that the financial crisis hit Thailand first, followed by Indonesia, Malaysia, and the Philippines, and then Korea. If investors' flight from assets denominated in these currencies was prompted by "real" economic conditions, as opposed to speculation, the implication is not only that those conditions were similar across these Asian countries but also that they were changing in unison (or nearly so). That seems implausible.

At the most fundamental level, the problem was a psychological one—*panic*. A herd mentality among investors can provoke an exodus of foreign capital that central bankers in emerging markets may be virtually powerless to prevent:

> The scenario is similar to shouting "fire" in a theater. A small fire may pose no disaster if patrons quietly, calmly, and resolutely leave a crowded theater. But the same small fire may lead to disaster if patrons panic and trample one another to be the first ones out. Thus, if a debtor starts to weaken, a panicked withdrawal of short-term loans by nervous creditors can immediately lead to illiquidity of the debtor and then to bankruptcy, even if the debtor is fundamentally sound.[15]

---

[15] Jeffrey Sachs, "International Economics: Unlocking the Mysteries of Globalization," *Foreign Policy* 110 (Spring 1998): 104–105.

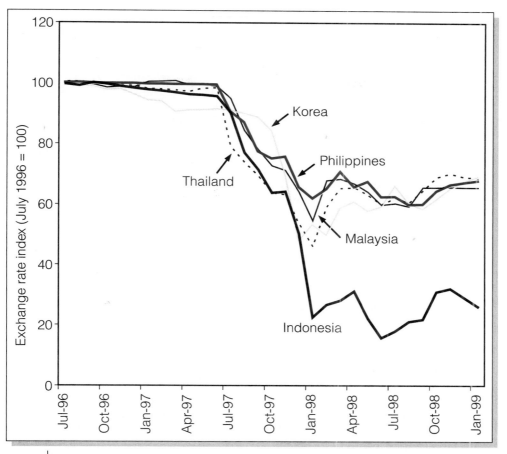

FIGURE 15.2 | ASIAN CONTAGION, 1997–1998

During the period leading up to the Asian financial crisis, the values of Asian currencies were relatively stable. The plunging value of the Thai baht was followed by successive drops in the values of the Indonesian rupiah, the Malaysian ringgit, the Philippine peso, and the Korean won. The financial crisis became known as the *Asian contagion* because it spread like a viral infection to countries in close geographic proximity.

Source: International Monetary Fund, *International Financial Statistics CD-ROM* (Washington, D.C.: IMF, 2005).

LDCs can exhaust their foreign exchange reserves trying to maintain the value of their currencies, but like trying to convince theatergoers that the fire really is a small one, it may not work. Indeed, the fact that an LDC's central bank is making the effort may exacerbate panic among the more jumpy investors.

Dealing with financial crises will depend on how they are ultimately understood, and there is still no consensus on the relative importance of the various factors contributing to the Asian crisis. As we mentioned in Chapter 1, some see the root causes as internal. *Crony capitalism* is the label used to summarize such ills as the loosely regulated banking practices that allowed the accumulation of large amounts of short-term foreign debt and made emerging markets in Asia vulnerable to investor panic. Proposed solutions involve bringing domestic financial practices in line with practices typically adopted in the West. Those who see the causes of financial crises as mostly external point to the rapid liberalization of financial markets in Asia, which led to a flood of foreign investment hoping to profit from the region's impressive economic growth. Their solution is for governments to exercise more control over the capital flowing into and out of emerging markets in order to guard against another mad dash for the exits. Many on both sides of the debate have scrutinized the practices of the IMF as a lender of last resort. Some would like to abolish the IMF altogether, arguing that the availability of IMF-orchestrated bailouts encourages recklessness on the part of investors, or *moral hazard*. Most, however, see a continuing role for the IMF, even if they cannot yet agree on the most appropriate institutional reforms.[16]

The repercussions of financial crises can be severe. The economies of the countries hit by the Asian crisis went into severe recession, with negative GDP growth rates in 1998: contractions of 6 to 8 percent for Hong Kong and South Korea; 10 to 15 percent for Malaysia, Thailand, and Indonesia. Slower growth elsewhere, especially in Latin America, was attributed largely to the Asian crisis (and to subsequent financial turmoil in Brazil), and even where the effects were least felt, in Europe and North America, the decline in industrial production was traceable to withering demand in Asian markets. We shall see in the next section that political stability can be adversely affected by economic downturns. The social upheaval in Indonesia grew out of the Asian crisis, and the financial crisis that engulfed Russia in August 1998 became yet another source of popular resentment directed at the seeming inability of Russian capitalism to deliver on its promises.

DEVELOPMENT AND POLITICAL FREEDOM

Just as the lack of economic rights is common in poor countries, so too is the lack of political rights. Although decolonization resulted in independence for many developing countries in the post-World War II period, liberal democratic governments were the exception, authoritarian regimes the rule. Poverty remains a major characteristic of nonfree countries, especially those that have tasted some measure of freedom and then returned to nondemocratic rule. Government coercion and repression can be part of daily life, especially for anyone who dares to challenge the legitimacy of existing distribution of power and wealth.

DEPENDENCY AND STATE REPRESSION

Analysts of different schools of thought, in both the radical and liberal traditions, have recognized problems of distorted development. Some theorists go further and link foreign penetration and economic distortion with additional distortions in

---

[16] Barry Eichengreen, *Capital Flows and Crises* (Cambridge, Mass.: MIT Press, 2004); Nouriel Roubini and Brad Setser, *Bailouts or Bail-Ins? Responding to Financial Crises in Emerging Economies* (Washington D.C.: Institute for International Economics, 2004).

social and political systems. They believe that economic growth in peripheral countries may lead to the establishment not of liberal democracy but of authoritarian dictatorship. Governments, already in control of substantial state economic enterprises, are often eager to consolidate their political powers. In alliance with foreign interests and domestic capitalists who are positioned to gain from their policies, state bureaucracies have denied their populations basic human rights, both economic rights to decent living conditions and political rights to representation and free speech.[17] Violence, including structural violence (as defined in Chapter 11), is thus seen as being in large part a consequence of economic conditions in the periphery and the linkages with the industrialized core of the world economy.

How does this process play out? Capital-intensive investment reduces the need for large numbers of workers. By limiting employment to a smaller force of skilled workers, even an expanded industrial sector may employ no more industrial laborers than before expansion. Other workers are left unemployed, only partially employed, or working full-time at unskilled jobs for wages that give them a marginal existence. The larger this reserve army of the unemployed, the greater the downward pressure on wage rates for workers in general (workers who demand too much can readily be replaced). In many instances, MNCs will pay relatively high wages, but high wages in MNC subsidiaries may contribute to increasing income inequalities within the working class because they employ only a portion of the workforce. These inequalities, as well as enormous inequalities elsewhere in the economy—between large landowners and peasants, between the business and professional classes and the working classes—may be accompanied by increasing government intervention in the economy. If the government is beholden to either foreign or domestic investors, it will promote their interests by keeping wages down in order to stabilize costs and maximize profits. Whether the state is dominated by capitalists or begins to take on its own major economic role in the public sector, its actions are likely to intensify economic inequalities within society.

We have already encountered the theory that relative deprivation fosters conflict (see Chapter 8). Unequal distributions of the national pie can be a source of resentment, as some groups or classes see others moving ahead rapidly while they themselves gain little or in some instances even slip backward. In highly inegalitarian societies, any appreciable change (either positive or negative) in overall national income will stimulate greater conflict over how the expanded or contracted pie should be divided. This conflict will be especially acute during periods of economic decline.[18]

An example of instability in the context of a contracting pie is Chile in the early 1970s. Under President Salvador Allende, a socialist, Chile experienced economic stagnation and declines in real income in the early 1970s because of mismanagement by Allende's government and economic sabotage by Allende's domestic and foreign

---

[17] An early influential statement is Guillermo A. O'Donnell, *Modernization and Bureaucratic-Authoritarianism: Studies in South American Politics* (Berkeley, Calif.: Institute of International Studies, University of California, 1973).

[18] Robert MacCulloch, "The Impact of Income on the Taste for Revolt," *American Journal of Political Science* 48 (October 2004), pp. 830–848. For a theoretical analysis, see James A. Robinson, "Economic Development and Democracy," *Annual Review of Political Science* 9 (June 2006), pp. 503–527.

enemies (especially the United States) who wanted to see him fail. When Allende tried to pursue policies of redistributing income at a time of overall decline in growth, the result was work stoppages by key groups, riots, demonstrations, and eventually a right-wing military coup against him. The leader of that coup, General Augusto Pinochet, then instituted an extraordinarily repressive and long-lasting dictatorship. By contrast, an example of social upheaval in the context of an expanding pie is Iran under Muhammad Reza Pahlavi, shah (king) from 1941 to 1978. By the late 1970s, Iran had experienced a decade of unprecedented growth in its national income. But these economic rewards were distributed very unequally and left a variety of groups—peasants, urban workers and the urban unemployed, followers of traditional religion, and some intellectuals—very dissatisfied. Many rebelled, culminating in an Islamic revolution and the shah's overthrow.

Foreign economic penetration and coercive government may reinforce each other as local governments become ever more dependent on foreign military assistance—arms transfers, military training, even intervention (overt or covert)—to maintain control over the social unrest that economic developments have created. The condition of peripheral countries in the world economy is therefore quite different from that experienced a century or so ago by Europe and North America or even by Japan. Today's LDCs cannot simply copy the development patterns of the industrialized world. Most European countries already had a stronger tradition of representative government than exists in most LDCs. (There are exceptions; Uruguay, for example, probably had a stronger democratic tradition than did imperial Germany.) Even though European countries experienced periods during which income and wealth were very unequally distributed, most of them ultimately were obliged to make concessions to their peasants and working classes. Those who waited too long, like Czar Nicholas II of Russia, lost everything.

In societies marked by relative equality, economic growth is less likely to foster conflict, as seen in the low levels of violent social conflict in Taiwan. Many economists now argue that the success of the Asian NICs is based in large part on policies that reduce economic inequality, raising the incomes of workers faster than those of economic elites. More generally, some have argued that greater income equality is an important factor in promoting economic and social development. Nevertheless, dependency theory shows us that the achievement of equitable economic and political development is not merely a matter of promoting foreign investment in LDCs. A recipe for trouble is the combination of economic penetration and military dependence. Together, they tend to magnify economic inequalities, and at the same time give the state more power to repress dissent. The ultimate result may well be violent rebellion, with often devastating effects on human development.[19]

---

[19] William J. Dixon and Terry Boswell, "Dependency, Disarticulation, and Denominator Effects: Another Look at Foreign Capital Penetration," *American Journal of Sociology* 102 (September 1996), pp. 543–562; Oksan Bayulgen, "Foreign Capital in Central Asia and the Caucasus: Curse or Blessing?" *Communist and Post-Communist Studies* 38 (March 2005), pp. 49–69.

DEVELOPMENT AND DEMOCRACY

As with economic prosperity, most observers have suspected that the acquisition of political power by the world's poor also would be difficult. According to conventional wisdom in political science, the establishment of stable democratic regimes is possible only when certain prerequisites are met. These prerequisites include enough income and wealth to create a literate population, informed by newspapers, radio and television, and other mass media. They also include an economy healthy enough to ensure that a reasonable position in life can be attained through industry, commerce, agriculture, or intellectual activity—that is, by means other than political power and corruption. Private sources of socioeconomic advancement provide checks on authoritarian government and provide respectable sources of employment and status for defeated politicians, thereby making it possible for them to accept electoral defeat with reasonably good grace. Economic development is thus not only a way to escape the misery of poverty but also a way to promote political liberties.[20]

The strength of this argument identifying the economic prerequisites of democracy lies in the fact that the industrialized countries of the OECD are, without exception, political democracies. Among the OECD, those with the most recent history of military or one-party rule generally have the lowest incomes and levels of human development. Some of the oil-rich Arab OPEC states, which are not democracies, have very high per capita incomes, but typically this wealth has existed alongside a mediocre record in human development; high rates of literacy or markedly improved living conditions for the whole populace (especially women) are still missing. In addition to these exceptions among the richest states, we can point to the fact that some of the worst records on freedom and democracy are to be found among very poor states. Therefore, it seems that there is some validity to the notion that economic underdevelopment is not conducive to political liberalization.

Some analysts have taken the argument a step further, contending that short-term political repression may have to be tolerated for the sake of immediate economic development, after which the prerequisites for democracy will have been established. This is sometimes said to be the basis for economic development in China as well as the Asian Tigers. Weak governments, they claim, cannot satisfy the needs of populations that make major demands on them. Trouble arises from rapid social change and the participation of new groups and classes in politics, coupled with the slower development of political institutions. LDCs typically have large urban centers. Many of their residents have come in from the countryside looking for work, only to remain unemployed or underemployed, living a marginal existence (shantytowns are ubiquitous in São Paulo, Santiago, Bombay, Johannesburg, and many other cities). Nevertheless, in the city they are exposed to the mass media and

---

[20] A classic statement is Seymour Martin Lipset, "Some Social Requisites of Democracy: Economic Development and Political Legitimacy," *American Political Science Review* 53 (March 1959), pp. 69–105. Another, by an economist, is Milton Friedman, *Capitalism and Freedom* (Chicago: University of Chicago Press, 1962), especially chap. 1.

see people in the rich sectors of the city living very well. Their expectations rise but are not fulfilled. In capital cities they can participate in political activity—street demonstrations, riots, and general strikes. The demands of these people, who can be mobilized by activists for political participation, may be nearly impossible for a weak government to meet or repress.

A stable government, the argument goes, requires a strong administrative capacity and political institutions capable of channeling or, if necessary, repressing these popular demands. The institutions of authority might take the form of a mass political party like the Congress party of India, founded in 1885, and the highly capable and well-organized Indian civil service. More commonly, those institutions have not been so clearly associated with democratic rule, more nearly resembling the authoritarian structure of the Ba'ath party in Iraq or a communist party. The coercive arm of an authoritarian political structure is, of course, an efficient internal police force and the military.

It is not a long step from such an analysis to the argument that traditional Western ideas of political rights and liberties must be put aside in the interest of economic development, at least temporarily. In a widely read and controversial study, Samuel Huntington put the argument in these terms:

> Monks and priests can demonstrate, students riot, and workers strike, but no one of these groups has, except in most unusual circumstances, demonstrated any capacity to govern.... The military, in contrast, do possess some capacity for generating at least transitory order.... The coup is the extreme exercise of direct action against political authority, but it is the means of ending other types of action against that authority and potentially the means of reconstituting political authority.... Their job is simply to straighten out the mess and then to get out. Theirs is a temporary dictatorship.

Thus, progress often generates political disorder, but further development cannot occur without the imposition of order. Economic development often requires large-scale sacrifice on the part of the masses; the resources for investment can be obtained only by reducing consumption. However, high incomes and social quiescence must be available as an incentive for wealthy investors at home and abroad. In a very poor country with widespread misery, modernization may require government action to repress discontent—if only to pave the way for a better future.[21]

According to such views, people in poor countries essentially must choose between political liberty and decent material conditions; they cannot have both, at least in the near term, and it is a parochial prejudice to insist on political and civil rights as traditionally defined in the industrialized West. We think these arguments are profoundly wrong. While state capacity is important, for a government to be effective it must be able to generate compliance from its people without the threat of coercion—that is, it must have legitimacy.

---

[21] Samuel P. Huntington, *Political Order in Changing Societies* (New Haven, Conn.: Yale University Press, 1968); quote from pp. 217, 226. Of course, dictatorship may not give way to democracy even after economic conditions improve; see, for example, Bruce Bueno de Mesquita and George W. Downs, "Development and Democracy," *Foreign Affairs* 84 (September/October 2005), pp. 77–86.

NEW PERSPECTIVES ON DEMOCRACY AND DEVELOPMENT

To the extent that the economic prerequisites argument—the notion that economic development comes before democracy—has been accepted as conventional wisdom by political scientists, it has been a grudging acceptance, especially among liberals and radicals. The argument is certainly plausible, and it seems consistent with the experiences of some countries at some times. But much of the social scientific evidence reported in recent years challenges this view, as does recent social science theory. Mancur Olson, for example, has put forth a compelling argument that although dictatorship may provide better conditions for economic development than anarchy and rampant disorder, the economic conditions provided by majority rule are even better.[22] Some degree of social order is necessary for democratic governance to function well, but putting off democratic reforms (or revolutions) until society achieves a standard level of economic prosperity may require a long wait indeed. (We examine Olson's theory in Box 15.1.)

One problem with the economic prerequisites argument is that it only partially fits the facts. In Latin America and parts of East Asia over the past decade or two, many democratic governments have emerged, but usually (as in South American countries) as the result of military dictatorships' *failure* to improve their people's living conditions. Having failed to deliver the economic goods, some military rulers themselves seem to have concluded that the economic prerequisites of democracy are not prerequisites after all. In other areas, while there has been some democratization, a general trend toward an increase in political liberties is harder to discern. Although almost all the former British and French colonies entered their era of independence with governments that were chosen by reasonably free elections and had the forms of parliamentary democracy, today far fewer of them allow competitive elections, free speech, and free assembly. Some have had stagnant economies; others, very dynamic and fast-growing ones. In many of these countries, however, development has typically been skewed sharply in favor of the rich and has had no appreciable effect on the promotion of political liberties. In some countries the suppression of political liberty has brought economic growth, but in many others it has not.

In direct opposition to these theories of economic and political development is a pattern in some of the more prosperous LDCs that culminated in the early 1970s, when a turn away from democratic government to state repression was especially vicious. Uruguay and Chile in the 1960s were relatively prosperous and had long histories of a stable democracy. Chile had had uninterrupted democratic government since 1927, and Uruguay since the 1930s. (Along with Argentina and Venezuela, these countries were the most well-to-do of the twenty Latin American countries.) The Philippines was fairly prosperous compared with other Asian countries and had a high literacy rate. It had developed the institutions and practices of

---

[22] Mancur Olson, *Power and Prosperity: Outgrowing Communist and Capitalist Dictatorships* (New York: Basic Books, 2000). Olson highlights the importance of individual rights, including property rights, for providing the incentives for economic production and exchange (recall Box 14.1). See also Douglass C. North, *Understanding the Process of Economic Change* (Princeton, N.J.: Princeton University Press, 2005).

IN GREATER DEPTH

BOX 15.1 | AUTOCRACY, DEMOCRACY, AND DEVELOPMENT

We have discussed the argument that an environment favorable to economic development requires political stability, and that political stability may require authoritarian government—a discomforting implication for liberals. On the other hand, we have also pointed to the mutually reinforcing relationship between democracy and economic growth and prosperity (in this chapter and in Chapter 11). But what about the causal effects of political democracy on economic prosperity? Economist Mancur Olson offered a theory for this effect, one that is consistent with the empirical evidence but also refutes the notion that democracy is a luxury best postponed until economic development is well under way.

Reasoning by analogy, Olson first asks us to consider the incentives faced by a stationary bandit. Like all bandits, the stationary bandit is motivated by greed and therefore wants to extract as much wealth as possible from his victims. But unlike the roving bandit, the stationary bandit understands that he cannot extract so much from those in his territory that they lose all incentive to engage in production; he does not move on like the roving bandit but stays put and must continue to rely on the same victims into the future. That gives the stationary bandit an "encompassing interest" in the economic productivity of his territory, an interest that the roving bandit does not have. For their part, the stationary bandit's victims aren't exactly pleased with his theft from them, but he is preferred to the roving bandit who, though not a constant presence, robs them blind when she shows up. Furthermore, the stationary bandit is inclined to want to improve the productive capacity of his realm by providing some order—public goods like protection from other bandits, improved roads, and other conditions favorable to profitable economic activity—so that he can increase his take.

The stationary bandit's theft comes in the form of taxation, and the bandit's challenge is to determine what level of taxation will maximize his personal wealth. Of course, his wealth will be limited by the productive potential of the territory—its physical and human resources—but the chosen tax rate can make a big difference in what proportion of the territory's productive potential is actually produced. There is an inverse relationship here: The higher the tax rate, the more it undermines the incentive to produce, and the smaller the ratio of what is produced to what could have been produced. The percentage of potential production that the bandit can take will increase as the tax rate increases, but at some point it will begin to fall as the tax rate becomes so high that it creates severe production disincentives.

The challenge for the autocrat in contemporary society is the same as for the stationary bandit. What tax rate maximizes the autocrat's take? In the figures below, the share of the economy's potential production is shown as a downward sloping function of the tax rate, while the share that the autocrat takes is shown as an inverted U-shaped function of the tax rate. Olson (with one of his colleagues) showed that the ruler maximizes his wealth—the *absolute* amount redistributed from the population to himself—by choosing a tax rate that maximizes the *share* of potential production collected, regardless of how much of that is spent on public goods. At this tax rate, T_A, the population produces P_A percent of the territory's potential, while the autocrat gets R_A percent.

Olson sees no need to abandon the criminal analogy when it comes to democracy. Rulers in democracies are interested in power and wealth just like autocrats (though we don't usually call them bandits). However, in a well-functioning democracy, the rulers are motivated not only by

| BOX 15.1 | AUTOCRACY, DEMOCRACY, AND DEVELOPMENT |

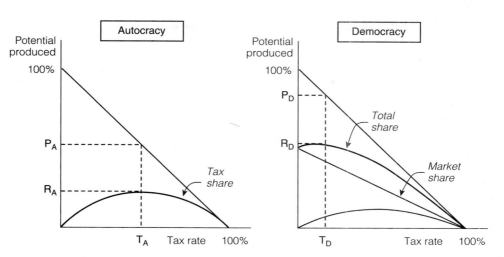

their own greed but also by the greed of the majority, whose support they need to stay in office. So compared to an autocracy, the share of total potential production taken in taxes will be lower at all tax rates (inverted U-shaped curve is flatter); now wealth is being redistributed from only part of the population (the minority) to the rulers and their constituency (the majority). But this is not the ruling interest's only source of wealth. In contrast to an autocrat, the majority is active in the economy; its wealth at a given tax rate consists of what is redistributed from the minority to itself *plus* what it derives from the market. Therefore, the chosen rate of taxation, T_D, will be lower than in an autocracy, because it is at this lower rate that the majority's *total share* of potential production, R_D, is

maximized. We can also see that due to this larger encompassing interest in the productivity of the territory, the chosen tax rate is such that actual production as a share of potential production, P_D, is higher than in the case of an autocracy.

Olson has shown that we need not ascribe noble motives to rulers or majorities in order to conclude that democracy is more conducive to economic development and prosperity than is autocracy. Such motives may be part of the explanation, but it is sufficient to assume nothing more than the rational pursuit of power and wealth to arrive at this conclusion.

Source: Figures adapted from Martin C. McGuire and Mancur Olson, "The Economics of Autocracy and Majority Rule: The Invisible Hand and the Use of Force," *Journal of Economic Literature* 34 (March 1996), pp. 72–96.

political democracy with free elections, first under American colonial rule and then as an independent state after 1946. Following the economic prerequisites view, all these countries should have been able to maintain and deepen their democratic patterns, but they were not. Their democratic governments were overthrown (in 1973 in Chile and Uruguay, and in 1972 in the Philippines) and replaced by repressive, coercive regimes. Argentina, with a highly sophisticated, literate population and sporadic periods of democratic government, similarly slipped back into authoritarian military rule for almost a decade.

What generalizations can we make about the relationship between development and democracy? First, economic development and democracy are strongly correlated. The historical sequence seems to be from development to democracy, rather than in the other direction—and this, at least, is consistent with the economic prerequisites argument. A high level of development has made it easier to sustain democracy. Rich countries tend to be democratic. In many countries, such as Taiwan and South Korea, greater political liberalization and the relaxation of governmental repression followed substantial economic growth.

There are exceptions, however. Some quite rich countries, like Singapore, are still not very democratic; rapid economic growth in China has not yet produced notable political liberalization or a significantly improved record on human rights. And although democracy is rare, it is not unknown in some very poor countries. Even in many countries that are not democratic in the Western sense there are different means and different degrees of enabling the majority of the populace to have some control over their government, at least at the local level. The cases of real democracy in very poor countries show that, in the right social, economic, and cultural circumstances, mass poverty need not prevent the establishment of democracy. We should be careful not to equate the common historical progression from development to democracy with a necessary causal relationship. Nevertheless, the spread of democracy is good news in light of recent social science theory and research suggesting the superior economic conditions associated with political openness.[23]

Second, in contradiction to some variants of the economic prerequisites argument, there is little evidence that authoritarian rule promotes economic development. For every authoritarian government that represses political opposition while promoting growth, there are several dictatorial "kleptocracies"—that is, governments run by a tiny elite far more interested in stealing from the people than in stimulating general economic development. (Mobuto made himself a multibillionaire while impoverishing the rest of Zaire; Suharto did quite well for himself and his family in Indonesia.) The notion that political opposition *must* be repressed in the interest of development, while a convenient justification for authoritarian rule, belies the facts. And even though economic growth may not bring democracy, once democracy has been established in a middle-income country it becomes very hard for dictatorships to overthrow it.

Finally, a vicious cycle operates from political instability to slow economic growth and back again. Poor countries are often socially and politically unstable, with serious ethnic conflicts and weak or arbitrary governments that do not protect property rights. Instability reduces the incentives to save and invest, thereby reducing the capacities for economic growth. Low growth then reinforces the instabilities. Transitions from dictatorial regimes to democratic ones may sometimes

---

[23] See Morton H. Halperin, Joseph T. Siegle, Michael M. Weinstein, *The Democracy Advantage: How Democracies Promote Prosperity and Peace* (New York: Council on Foreign Relations, 2005); Dani Rodrik and Romain Wacziarg, "Do Democratic Transitions Produce Bad Economic Outcomes?" *American Economic Review* 95 (May 2005), pp. 50–55; Adam Przeworski, Michael E. Alvarez, José Antonio Cheibub, and Fernando Limongi, *Democracy and Development: Political Institutions and Well-Being in the World, 1950–1990* (Cambridge: Cambridge University Press, 2000).

produce periods of slow economic growth, ultimately endangering the new and fragile democracy. Wise policies and external assistance can help to ease and shorten the economic pain of transition. A "civic tradition" of respect and tolerance—an underpinning of democracy—encourages political stability and, in turn, enhances the prospects for economic growth.

Economic stagnation brought about the collapse of many authoritarian governments by the end of the twentieth century. They came to power to get the economy moving, and they failed; their people would no longer put up with governments that were politically repressive and at the same time could not deliver prosperity. Throughout the world, authoritarian regimes have been discredited, and both communist and capitalist dictatorships have shared this fate. More are giving democracy a chance. But if LDCs cannot solve their economic problems—the need for growth, with equity—their democratic governments are not likely to be tolerated indefinitely. This reaction can already be seen in some of the former Soviet republics. Without a better life, their people will lose faith in democratic government just as they did in dictatorships. The prospects for growth, equity, and liberty are thus thoroughly intertwined.

The nations of the developing world are enormously diverse in many ways—in their cultural and political systems, as well as in their economic conditions and ties to the rest of the world. Theories of dependence and underdevelopment are important but partial tools for trying to understand what is happening there. The phenomena are complex and defy easy generalization. Governments are concerned not only with gaining a higher standard of living for their people but also with enhancing their own state power. Any theory has to address the effects of different developmental contexts and experiences as well as rapidly changing world resources and social conditions. The menu of choice presented to leaders in the developing world is constrained by the stratified nature of the international political-economic relations, by numerous transnational linkages (political, financial, commercial, and cultural), and by the relative strength of various groups and social classes within those countries.

The body of tested theory to support reliable policy recommendations for LDCs is still relatively small. The lives of billions of people—their hopes for relief from the physical misery of poverty and for the implementation of political liberties—are at stake. Analysts must tread a treacherous line between irresponsibly ignoring the desperate problems of these people and irresponsibly offering ill-conceived "solutions" that others will have to live with. A responsible social scientist in a rich industrialized country cannot become, in the words of the West Indian novelist V. S. Naipaul,

> one of those who continue to simplify the world and reduce other men to a cause, the people who substitute doctrine for knowledge and irritation for concern, the revolutionaries who visit centres of revolution with return air tickets, ... the people who wish themselves on societies more fragile than their own, all those people who in the end do no more than celebrate their own security.[24]

---

[24] V. S. Naipaul, "The Killings in Trinidad: Part Two," *Sunday Times* (London), May 19, 1974, p. 41.

CONCLUSION TO PART III

Part III of this book has examined various topics in international political economy. The three major perspectives that helped to organize the arguments and debates covered in Parts I and II—realism, liberalism, and radicalism—also come into play, whether we are talking about the economics of international politics or the politics of international economics. The political economy of national security has more to do with the former, and here the three perspectives tend to focus our attention on different aspects of world politics, rather than offering different explanations for the same aspect or phenomenon. For realists, economic instruments of influence are among the many tools of statecraft available to leaders pursuing the national interest in a dangerous world. Radicals and liberals pay more attention to the domestic politics and economics of national security. While radicals concentrate on the rise of the military-industrial complex as an imperative of capitalism, liberals have wondered about the adverse economic impact of high levels of military spending and more generally about the misallocation of resources in societies where the military-industrial complex wields disproportionate political influence.

The politics of international economic relations has become an important area of inquiry in the study of world politics, no less central than questions of war and peace. Indeed, distinguishing these two subfields can be difficult. Early liberals like Smith and Ricardo, who theorized about the gains from trade, hoped for additional benefits: the tendency of trading states to remain at peace. The founders of the movement toward European unification had peace and stability very much in mind when they hatched their plans for economic integration among states that had fought repeated and increasingly destructive wars on the European continent. Realists, too, recognize that peace and a thickening web of economic transactions go together, all the more so when there exists in the international system a hegemonic state that can shoulder the extra burden required to encourage or enforce adherence to free-trade practices. The significance of international institutions and regimes—multilateral or regional—and particularly their capacity to constrain the political-economic behavior of member states has and will in all likelihood continue to divide the realist and liberal views.

Perhaps the most significant contribution of the radical perspective in world politics has been to expose the downside of international economic transactions and interdependence—especially for societies of the Global South. The persistence of economic and human underdevelopment owes in part to exploitative transnational linkages connecting the center and periphery of the world economy. There are many doorsteps on which to lay the blame for the North–South gap—state and nonstate actors, foreign and domestic—and there is enough variability in the experiences of LDCs to argue against any single model of development. However, theories of economic dependency have heightened our awareness of the plight of those left behind by the development process and suggest that our obligations to those who are less fortunate should not be delimited by our own national borders. The scourge of global poverty serves to remind us that, in an international system characterized by sovereign equality, some states are indeed more equal than others. Sovereignty has its limits, and we explore a few more of these limits in the next chapter.

This natural inequality of the two powers of population and of production in the earth forms the great difficulty that to me appears insurmountable in the way to the perfectibility of society.

—T. R. Malthus

It is equally impossible to pronounce for or against the future realization of an event which cannot take place but at an era when the human race will have attained improvements.

—Marquis de Condorcet

CHALLENGES FOR THE FUTURE PART 4

Limits of Sovereignty: Humanity and the Commons

CHAPTER **16**

COLLECTIVE GOODS AND COLLECTIVE BADS

Interdependence, in its various forms, generates a set of important problems that shape the menus of national, international, and transnational actors. In this chapter we discuss some of the many ecological issues facing the human race at the global and regional levels. Ecology—the study of the relationships between living things and their physical and biological environments—naturally draws our attention to global interdependencies. Some of these are closely related to matters of economic and human development, as discussed in the last chapter. Others have to do with demography, geology, geography, climatology, and other fields of study outside the immediate expertise of most social scientists. While there is still some debate within various scientific communities regarding the seriousness of the ecological challenges that have accompanied us into the twenty-first century, there is also a widespread feeling that humanity ought not wait for a definitive resolution of these scientific debates before taking action to curb our self-destructive patterns of consumption and waste.

Scholars interested in world order and alternative world futures want to show us why it is important to be aware of global interdependence and emerging transnational ecological problems. To appreciate this, we need to see where we fit in the global system—in effect, where we are located in a set of nested subsystems. As individuals, we tend to give most of our attention to immediate, personal concerns (families, neighborhoods, and local communities); our typical area of awareness is really quite limited. However, to become aware of and concerned with, and then to solve, the sorts of issues discussed in this chapter, we must expand our perspectives both in space (to other regions and the world system as a whole) and in time (at least to the end of the century). More than thirty years ago, Ervin Laszlo, a futurist and student of world order, observed, "World order reform starts at home: with the ideas and values we entertain, the objectives we pursue, the leaders we elect, and the way we talk with and influence those around us."[1]

This observation is even more relevant today with the information revolution and the growth of both interdependence and our awareness of interdependence. With the increased attention to transnational relations and globalization, the desire to rethink security issues, and the growing importance of economic and ecological issues, the interconnectedness of systems and issues has become central. The Club of Rome, a Hamburg-based NGO established in 1968 to raise public awareness, addresses itself to what it calls the *world problematique*: the interconnected set of contemporary global problems that constitute the "predicament of mankind." With the persistence of environmental threats and their appearance in newer and more dangerous forms—acid rain, ozone holes, global warming, soil erosion and degradation, deforestation—interest in the ecological dimension of the world problematique was revitalized in the late 1980s and early 1990s and now has a secure place on the agenda of state leaders, IGOs, and civic groups.

EXTERNALITIES AND "FORCED RIDERS"

In Chapter 13, we introduced the concept of collective goods. Recall that individuals acquire private goods if the "price" is right, based on some calculation of the costs and benefits involved. The market mechanism works pretty well for many goods but not for all; indeed, it can work rather poorly for some goods, such as collective defense or the maintenance of a free-trade regime. In these cases, individual members of the collective (an alliance, a community of trading states) have an incentive to shirk because they believe they can benefit from the collective good without incurring the costs of contribution.

We have seen how the free-rider problem has been overcome in world politics. Free riders are rational actors, and it is not always the case that the group suffers from the self-interested behavior of its members. As an illustration, consider a group composed of two families. Suppose the Smith family gets a cat for the purpose of killing mice on its property. The Smiths have acquired a private good: a rodent-free dwelling. But mice were also infesting the property of the Smiths' neighbors, the Jones family; by controlling the proliferation of mice, the Smiths' cat has produced a benefit for the Joneses as well, and at no cost to them. The benefit for the Jones family is "external" to the private good acquired by the Smiths—it is an **externality**. During the nineteenth century, to protect the security of its colonial possessions and its profitable trade with them, Britain policed the sea lanes of the Western Hemisphere and prevented intervention by other European powers. Like the Smiths' cat, the British navy provided a good for Britain but also positive externalities to the young United States, which also benefited from the conditions of secure trade in the region.

[1] Ervin Laszlo, *A Strategy for the Future: The Systems Approach to World Order* (New York: Braziller, 1974), p. 79. See also Laszlo, *Vision 2020: Reordering Chaos for Global Survival* (London: Routledge, 1994); Edward O. Wilson, *The Future of Life* (New York: Knopf, 2002).

Externalities are not always positive, though. The Smiths' new car, while a private good in the sense that they own it and can use it as they see fit, is also bright red. The Joneses, whose front window looks directly onto the Smiths' driveway, become sick at the sight of bright red. The Jones family thus incurs costs from the Smiths' car and none of the benefits. The Joneses may look out their window and get sick or pull the shades and deprive themselves of the natural sunlight. When a state decides to build a nuclear power plant, it takes into account the benefits and the costs, including the risks of nuclear accidents. In 1986, one of the Soviet Union's nuclear plants at Chernobyl experienced an explosion and gradual meltdown, causing death and disease due to contamination in the surrounding area (the then-Soviet republics of Ukraine, Belarus, and Russia). But the Soviet Union's European neighbors to the west were also exposed to radioactive fallout from the accident. They could not simply pull the shades.

Industrial production usually creates some form of pollution as an externality. Not only is pollution a negative externality, it is jointly supplied, because the foul air that one person breathes is breathed by others as well. It is also nonexcludable; individual residents in a polluted area are not free to lead pollution-free lives unless they uproot their families and permanently move out of the area. Thus, the externality of pollution has the basic characteristics of a collective good, though it seems more appropriate to call it a "collective bad." Many other forms of production and consumption in modern society create negative externalities, some of which we will discuss. They all exhibit collective-action problems, especially as a consequence of nonexcludability. Just as a free rider cannot be excluded from the collective benefits of peace and security or a stable monetary system, neither can a member of the group avoid the costs of pollution, resource depletion, or other collective outcomes that result from the individual pursuit of self-interest. The member is a "forced rider."

Here we are back to the idea of vulnerability in interdependence and the conflicts of interest that negative externalities generate. A system of interaction based on sovereign autonomy does not deal well with the problem of externalities. Unfortunately, the principle of state sovereignty means not only freedom from interference beyond your borders but also freedom from responsibility beyond your borders.

TRAGEDY OF THE COMMONS

As we saw from the prisoner's dilemma, behavior that appears rational from each individual's point of view can lead to an outcome suboptimal for both. This same dilemma manifests as the mistreatment of common property, and we know from Aristotle that such behavior is not unique to modern society: "What is common to the greatest number has the least care bestowed upon it. Everyone thinks chiefly of his own, hardly at all of the common interest." The best example of this form of defection or free riding is what Garrett Hardin has called the **tragedy of the commons.** Hardin's description of the fate of a pasture, the commons, which belongs to all members of a group, is worth quoting at length:

> Picture a pasture open to all. It is to be expected that each herdsman will try to keep as many cattle as possible on the commons. Such an arrangement may work reasonably satisfactorily for centuries because tribal wars, poaching, and disease keep the numbers of both man and beast well below the carrying capacity of the land. Finally, however,

comes the day of reckoning, that is, the day when the long-desired goal of social stability becomes a reality. At this point, the inherent logic of the commons remorselessly generates tragedy.

As a rational being, each herdsman seeks to maximize his gain. Explicitly or implicitly, more or less consciously, he asks, "What is the utility to *me* of adding one more animal to my herd?" This utility has one negative and one positive component. The positive component is a function of the increment of one animal. Since the herdsman receives all the proceeds from the sale of the additional animal, the positive utility is nearly +1. The negative component is a function of the additional overgrazing created by one more animal. Since, however, the effects of overgrazing are shared by all the herdsmen, the negative utility for any particular decision-making herdsman is only a fraction of –1.

Adding together the component partial utilities, the rational herdsman concludes that the only sensible course for him to pursue is to add another animal to his herd. And another; and another…. But this is the conclusion reached by each and every rational herdsman sharing a commons. Therein is the tragedy. Each man is locked into a system that compels him to increase his herd without limit—in a world that is limited. Ruin is the destination toward which all men rush, each pursuing his own best interest in a society that believes in the freedom of the commons. Freedom in a commons brings ruin to all.[2]

The commons is a jointly supplied and nonexcludable good. The tragedy of the commons is the other side of the free-rider problem. When there are free riders, a collective good may not be provided or sustained. In the tragedy of the commons, although individuals follow the logic of rational self-interest, the result is the destruction of a collective good that already exists. The commons remains a collective good as long as usage levels remain low, when the use by an additional member does not reduce its usefulness to others. The tragedy occurs when usage increases so that the good, while still nonexcludable, is no longer jointly supplied. Deterioration of the good means that less and less is available to others; the collective is forced to ride on the destructive behavior of individual members.

The tragedy of the commons may sneak up on us, though it is more often the case that people do see the problem but, as Aristotle noted, do not feel that their behavior is a significant source of the problem. While asserting their right to partake of the common good, people ignore their responsibilities to contribute to maintaining it. And the larger the collective that is served by the good, the more likely we are to encounter free riders. When a violator of a social norm governing the commons can remain anonymous and avoid rebuke from others in the collective, the larger the temptation to defect from those norms. Thus, we have tax evaders and those who cut into long lines at ticket windows or in traffic jams. The goods they exploit *appear* to be indivisible (and infinite), and the costs distributed among the rest of us may be small at first—a minor tax hike, a slightly longer delay—but as socially irresponsible behavior becomes more widespread, those

---

[2] Garrett Hardin, "The Tragedy of the Commons," *Science* 162 (December 1968): 1244. The quote above from Aristotle is from *The Politics*, trans. Sir Ernest Barker, ed. R. F. Stalley (Oxford: Oxford University Press, 1995), book III, chap. 3.

costs increase. The challenge becomes reversing the tide of defection before social norms collapse and the commons are destroyed.

In regard to the global environment, the types of goods most often jeopardized by collective-action problems are **common-pool resources**. These are natural resources that do not belong to any specific state and therefore do not fall under a state's sovereign jurisdiction. They include the deep seabed, the high seas, and their fisheries; outer space; the atmosphere, including the ozone layer; and the electromagnetic frequency spectrum for broadcasting. Many argue that all of the natural resources that exist on Earth, even those within national boundaries (such as rain forests and the species inhabiting them) are part of the "global commons." There are many such examples, including nonrenewable energy resources like oil, natural gas, and coal. But who owns or has jurisdiction over such resources? Who should?

Some feel that coercion is the only way to solve collective-action problems concerning common-pool resources; what is required is a central authority with powers of enforcement. Calls for some form of world government have been made on this basis, although such solutions strike many as extreme. Some issues can be handled by creating international organizations with functional authority over certain matters. For example, according to the UN Convention on the Law of the Sea (UNCLOS), signed in 1982, the common resources of the deep seabed, such as the metal-rich manganese or nickel nodules, were to be "owned" by the newly created International Seabed Authority. The major industrialized countries refused to sign the treaty due to their opposition to this new authority, but the relevant provisions were renegotiated and UNCLOS went into force in 1994; the treaty has now been ratified by nearly 150 countries.[3]

Another way of managing the commons is to foster individual responsibility by converting parts of the commons into enclosed areas. The English enclosure movement of the early nineteenth century, for example, eliminated what remained of the commons pastureland. As an international regime created to help manage common-pool resources, UNCLOS also includes these sorts of provisions. The treaty designates exclusive economic zones (EEZs), which extend coastal jurisdiction to 200 miles for economic purposes. The aim is to undermine the temptation to free ride by giving states an exclusive economic stake in their assigned portion of the commons. Nationals of one state may lawfully navigate but may not fish or extract minerals from the EEZs of other states, and if they plunder their own zones they impose costs primarily on themselves. In this way, 50 million square miles of ocean space (more than one-third of the total) has been put under regulation and restriction.

Such "privatization" of collective goods is directed at the problems arising from jointness of supply. Now coastal states have an incentive to treat their economic zones with care, otherwise they are destroying what is essentially their own property. This is an important way in which international management regimes

---

[3] Robert L. Friedheim, *Negotiating the New Ocean Regime* (Columbia: University of South Carolina Press, 1993). For an analysis of the contention over the provisions establishing the International Seabed Authority, see Thomas Bräuninger and Thomas König, "Making Rules for Governing Global Commons: The Case of Deep-Sea Mining," *Journal of Conflict Resolution* 44 (October 2000): 604–629.

deal with the market failures that bedevil the maintenance of collective goods. By custom and by law, natural resources are usually "owned" by those with legal title to the territory encompassing them; possession, as they say, is nine-tenths of the law. Conflicts of interest arising over common-pool resources—resources to which no state or individual has legal title—can often be resolved by assigning to individuals limited *property rights* to what is otherwise common property.

Managing common property requires resolving several potentially contentious issues. Who is allowed to use the resource? How much exists for consumption ("harvesting capacity"), and at what rate should it be consumed? If there are indirect benefits or costs associated with consumption—technologies developed for deep seabed mining, or pollution from oil spills on the high seas—how are these to be distributed among the members of the collective? Environmental regimes have emerged to deal with these sorts of questions.[4] For example, the North Pacific fur seal regime has developed around a 1957 convention negotiated by the United States, the Soviet Union, Japan, and Canada. To prevent extinction of the seals, the agreement banned open-sea hunting and limited hunting to certain islands, while the North Pacific Fur Seal Commission was charged with setting quotas for maximum annual harvests. Japan and Canada even agreed to abstain from hunting seals altogether in return for being given a share of the profits taken by the United States and Russia.

These examples illustrate the interactions between law, regimes, international organizations, and self-interested states. States have developed sets of governing arrangements for addressing the many issues arising from interdependence. Collaboration and coordination help states and other international actors avoid the temptation to defect or free ride; instead they are steered toward cooperation and, hopefully, socially optimal outcomes. International regimes foster collaboration and coordination by changing the structure of payoffs, making cooperation more beneficial and defection more costly. Regimes can allow for "side payments," as in sharing the fur-seal profits with nonharvesters, and can reduce "transaction costs" by establishing and maintaining an institutional framework for negotiation and conflict resolution. "International regimes do not substitute for reciprocity; rather they reinforce and institutionalize it, ... delegitimizing defection and thereby making it more costly."[5] (We provide a game theoretic illustration in Box 16.1.)

SUSTAINABLE DEVELOPMENT

We now face ecological and environmental problems very different from those in the past. The growth of the world's population and the corresponding expansion

[4] See, for example, Oran R. Young, *The Institutional Dimensions of Environmental Change: Fit, Interplay, and Scale* (Cambridge, Mass.: MIT Press, 2002); Helmut Breitmeier, Oran R. Young, and Michael Zürn, *Analyzing International Environmental Regimes: From Case Study to Database* (Cambridge, Mass.: MIT Press, 2006).

[5] Robert Axelrod and Robert Keohane, "Achieving Cooperation under Anarchy: Strategies and Limitations," in Kenneth A. Oye, ed., *Cooperation under Anarchy* (Princeton, N.J.: Princeton University Press, 1986), p. 250. See also Todd Sandler, *Global Challenges: An Approach to Environmental, Political, and Economic Problems* (Cambridge: Cambridge University Press, 1997).

IN GREATER DEPTH

BOX 16.1 | INDIVIDUAL INCENTIVES, THE COMMONS, AND GOVERNING AUTHORITY

Suppose you have a favorite park where you like to walk your dog. Other people also walk their dogs there, so the park is a collective good. In order for it to remain a collective good, you and others need to clean up after your pets. But what is your incentive to do so? If you simply look away while your dog is doing its business, you know the chances are good that at some point during the day a Good Samaritan will pick it up while cleaning up after her own dog. That is your preferred outcome; you are able to shirk, yet at the same time you enjoy a well-kept park. However, if too many others think like you, the few Good Samaritans will give up and the park will decay into a rather unpleasant place to

outcomes—quantities representing the benefits you derive, minus the costs you incur. Estimating utilities is a much more difficult task than merely ordering preferred outcomes (which is often not easy either), but the utilities we assign below will serve as an illustration. Notice that the game on the left is structured as a prisoner's dilemma. You have an incentive to pollute regardless of what other dog walkers do; and each of them has the same incentive as you. The equilibrium outcome is a polluted park, yet the optimal outcome for the collective is a clean one. Thus, the prisoner's dilemma, generalized to a large group, is a collective-action problem.

No Governing Authority

Others

	Clean up	Pollute
Clean up	10,10	−1,11
Pollute	11,−1	0,0

(You — row label)

With Governing Authority

Others

	Clean up	Pollute
Clean up	10,10	−1,9
Pollute	9,−1	−2,−2

(You — row label)

walk. That's a bad outcome, but it's not the worst; after all, you might have been one of those do-gooders, picking up after others, but all for naught. In hindsight, you wish you had cleaned up after your dog—a small price to pay for a park—but now it's too late.

Maintaining the commons is a collective-action problem, and your incentives resemble those of a prisoner's dilemma in which the other "player" is the collective. Instead of *ordering* the outcomes from 1 to 4 as we have in our previous examples, we can assign *utilities* or *payoffs* to each of the

Now suppose that before the situation gets too bad, the park authorities begin enforcing the rules of dog-walking etiquette. What they need to do is change your incentive structure by imposing an extra cost when you pollute. They can do this by fining you (and others) an amount equivalent to 2 units of utility when you don't follow the rules, as shown in the above game on the right. Your incentives are now different from those of a prisoner's dilemma. Your payoff for defecting has dropped to 9 if you are the only polluter (the park is clean, but you've paid a fine), or to −2 if everyone pollutes

BOX 16.1 | **INDIVIDUAL INCENTIVES, THE COMMONS, AND GOVERNING AUTHORITY**
(Continued)

(you've paid the fine, but the park has been destroyed anyway). Now the equilibrium is the socially optimal outcome of a clean park.

In theory, the imposition of sanctions by a governing authority seems like a good way to prevent collective bads like pollution, and indeed this has been the traditional approach for dealing with such problems. (Economists often call these *Pigouvian taxes* after A. C. Pigou, who proposed the solution early in the twentieth century.) However, there is much debate about whether this is the best solution in all situations. One difficulty is that overcoming the free-rider problem requires effective monitoring and enforcement, which can also be costly. Suppose we assume the park authority does not have perfect information about who's cleaning up after their dogs and who's not, simply because they cannot watch everyone at all times. This means that, as a defector, you (and others) will be fined 2 units of utility not with certainty, but with some probability, p.

1 in 2 that you will be caught polluting the park, you have an incentive to clean up. You can confirm this by substituting for p a value less than 0.5, in which case the game remains a prisoner's dilemma. The governing authority is ineffective in overcoming the collective-action problem.

The persistence of pollution and other problems of the commons have led to efforts to improve the enforcement capacities of governing institutions (at the local, national, and international levels) as well as to very different types of proposals. Most alternative solutions rely on the clarification or assignment of *property rights*, as UNCLOS has done in some areas. The impetus for such efforts rests on the **Coase theorem** (recall Box 14.1), which states that when property rights are well defined, there will be no "market failures"—including failures of the type we associate with tragedies of the commons. In this case, solutions that depend on enforcement by governing authorities will not be superior

Governing Authority with Imperfect Information

		Others	
		Clean up	Pollute
You	Clean up	10, 10	$-1, 11-2(p)$
	Pollute	$11-2(p), -1$	$0-2(p), 0-2(p)$

When do you have an incentive to contribute to the collective good by cleaning up after your dog? When the payoff for cooperation is, on average, greater than the payoff for defecting—that is, when $10 > 11-2(p)$ or when $-1 > 0-2(p)$, depending on what others are doing. In this example, p is the same either way: 0.5. So, if the odds are better than

(and may be inferior) to solutions that rely on market mechanisms. This view is controversial, but it has many proponents in the academic and policy-making communities.

Source: The numerical example is adapted from Elinor Ostrom, *Governing the Commons: The Evolution of Institutions for Collective Action* (Cambridge: Cambridge University Press, 1990).

of economic activity have alerted people to the fact that the Earth's resources are finite and that the limits of its *carrying capacity* can be reached. Resources that were adequate at lower absolute levels of demand are inadequate at higher levels. Such limits challenge our ability to pursue economic and human development while at the same time preserving the ecological systems on which development depends. This sought-after balance has been referred to as **sustainable development**. The UN's World Commission on Environment and Development, in its 1987 report *Our Common Future*—often called the Brundtland Report after commission chair Gro Harlem Brundtland, then prime minister of Norway—defined sustainable development as "development which meets the needs of the present without compromising the ability of future generations to meet their own needs." The Brundtland Report was influential in placing sustainable development on the international agenda, and it led to the 1992 United Nations Conference on Environment and Development in Rio de Janeiro—the Earth Summit.[6]

It is possible that the Earth's carrying capacity is not only limited but also is actually being reduced through the disruption of natural ecosystems that have either been destroyed or are only slowly regenerating. Examples include overfarming in many areas, the southward spread of the Sahara Desert, and the destruction of the Amazon rain forest. In the past, when a tribe exhausted the productive capacity of an area, the people simply moved on or died off. Today, the threatened ecosystem is not local but global; if our global ecosystem is damaged or destroyed, there is nowhere else to go. As both a concept and policy guide, sustainable development has achieved wide popularity. It means different things to different people, but common to all definitions is the notion that we need to address environmental dangers simultaneously with more traditional concerns like economic growth and the alleviation of poverty. If resource utilization and destruction exceed regenerative capacity and ecosystems begin to collapse, progress on other worthwhile developmental goals cannot be sustained.

Many of the major issues identified with the problem of sustainable development were introduced by the Club of Rome in the early 1970s in its limits-to-growth perspective. This often controversial series of books provided an outline of the ecological problematique: (1) the exponential growth of population and human demands on the environment; (2) the finite limits to global resources (even if we cannot agree exactly on what those limits are); (3) the intricate interdependencies among population, capital investment, and the factors that influence growth (such as food, resources, and pollution), including the possibility that working to solve one problem may very well create others; and (4) the long delays between the release of pollutants or creation of other ecological damage and our realization that damage has been done.[7]

---

[6] World Commission on Environment and Development, *Our Common Future* (Oxford: Oxford University Press, 1987).

[7] There have been more than twenty reports sponsored by the Club of Rome, the first and most renowned being Donella H. Meadows, Dennis L. Meadows, Jorgen Randers, and William W. Behrens, *The Limits to Growth* (New York: New American Library, 1972). See also Donella Meadows, Jorgen Randers, and Dennis Meadows, *Limits to Growth: The 30-Year Update* (White River Junction, Vt.: Chelsea Green, 2004).

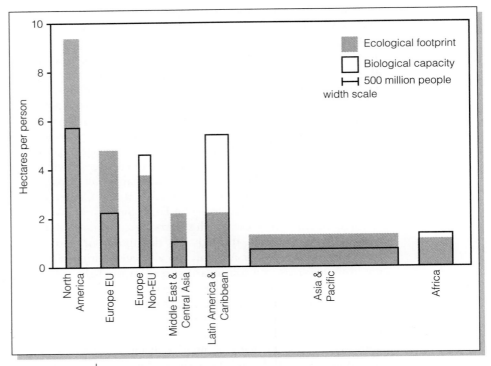

FIGURE 16.1 | ECOLOGICAL FOOTPRINT AND BIOLOGICAL CAPACITY, 2003

The ecological footprint of a population has several components: cropland, grazing land, forest land, and fishing area. The shaded bars in the chart show the composite measure of all these for the populations of different regions, expressed as hectares per person, while the outlined bars shows the actual productive area in these regions. The width of the bars represents each region's population. The total shaded area beyond the outlined bars exceeds the unshaded area within them—Earth's ecological deficit.
Source: World Wide Fund for Nature, *Living Planet Report 2006* (Gland, Switzerland: World Wide Fund for Nature, 2006).

More recently, environmental scholars have developed a measure called an *ecological footprint* designed to give some sense of the land and water area required to sustain a given population indefinitely—that is, to produce what the population consumes and to absorb the waste it generates. Ideally, of course, a community's ecological footprint would correspond to the carrying capacity of the area it occupies, but that is rarely the case. The World Wide Fund for Nature estimates that the ecological footprint of Earth is about 14 billion hectares, but its biological capacity is only 11 billion hectares. That is an *ecological deficit* of 0.5 hectares (1.2 acres) for every person on the planet. Figure 16.1 shows a regional breakdown. The United States and China have large ecological deficits, although in per capita terms the Chinese population is living much closer to its biological capacity than is the American population (with per capita deficits of 0.8 and 4.9 hectares, respectively). Brazil has a large ecological (7.8 hectares), as do other countries in the Amazon region. Nevertheless, the underutilized biological capacity of these and some other large countries (including Russia, Canada, and Australia) is not sufficient to bring about a global balance. Although societies can draw in resources from beyond their territorial confines to cover their ecological deficits, Earth cannot; instead, global overconsumption degrades the planet's carrying capacity.

Sustainable development can be addressed in two ways: restrain the forces of growth or expand the limits to growth. The first approach, which is epitomized by the Club of Rome, is generally pessimistic. Proponents hold that the ecosystem is fragile and therefore difficult to control and manage; when we try to control it, we tend to damage it. This is sometimes called the *Malthusian* perspective, after British economist Thomas Robert Malthus, whose *Essay on the Principle of Population*, written in 1798, warned of a looming demographic disaster if population growth rates continued to outpace the growth in food supplies. Malthusians are "inclusionist" in that they see humankind as an important and integral part of the interdependent global ecological system. In contrast, a more optimistic view maintains that ecological problems are solvable through human ingenuity and technological innovation. Supporters of this view, often called *cornucopians*, have an abiding faith in market mechanisms, which promote the more efficient use of scarce resources and encourage the substitution of more abundant resources (including synthetic ones) before scarcities become too disruptive. This view is "exclusionist" in the sense that humans are effectively outside the confines of the global ecostructure and are able to manipulate its limits through scientific advance and technological development.[8]

Sustainable development, as a goal for humankind, is beyond dispute. The best way to get there, on the other hand, remains the subject of intense debate. How we perceive ecological problems and the urgency of solutions depends, as do most issues raised in this book, on our experiences and worldviews, on our assumptions about human nature and human capacities, and on the way we prioritize the many things we value.

POPULATION AND DEMOGRAPHICS

At the heart of most ecological issues is population. Three central problems arise from the pressures of population growth. The first was highlighted by Malthus: the dwindling of world food supplies. The possibility of starvation is not the only Malthusian outcome. If population growth strains food resources, then malnutrition will continue to limit the mental and physical development of children and the energies and abilities of adults—in other words, the *quality* of the population. The second problem is discontent resulting from deprivation. This pertains to the resentment felt among people who find themselves on the short end of an inequitable distribution of resources (including food) brought about by uneven patterns of population growth. As we discussed in Chapter 8, discontent caused by feelings of

---

[8] See, for example, Julian L. Simon, *The Ultimate Resource 2* (Princeton, N.J.: Princeton University Press, 1996). Bjorn Lomborg, *The Skeptical Environmentalist: Measuring the Real State of the World* (Cambridge: Cambridge University Press, 2001), offers a critique of some of the evidence mustered by Malthusians.

relative deprivation drives various ideological and political movements, especially those seeking revolutionary change. The uneven distribution of population growth in LDCs, especially the tremendous growth of urban populations (and attendant air and water pollution problems), exacerbates this trend and could cause interstate conflicts as well.[9] The third problem, perhaps most emphasized, is ecological. Increases in population inevitably increase the demands for natural resources, thus generating ever greater environmental decay.

HUMAN POPULATION EXPLOSION

The revolutions in industrial production technology, along with the medical and hygienic advances responsible for much of the increase in population, have combined to increase human consumption, and with consumption comes resource depletion and pollution. Statistics abound on the consumption of natural resources (especially nonrenewable resources) and the generation of pollution. But if scientific and technological advance has been more or less continuous throughout human history, what accounts for the fact that the ecological problems we face today seem to have rather suddenly burst into view? One answer is that the problems have always been around, but only recently have we started to take them seriously. However, another answer has to do with the important phenomenon of *exponential growth*, which occurs when some quantity increases at the same rate over a given period of time—when, for example, a population grows by 2 percent every year. This is the principle at work when we deposit money in a savings account so that it will grow through compound interest. It is also a very common process in all sorts of natural biological systems.

Common as it is, exponential growth can provide very surprising results; we do not realize that a problem is brewing until it stands staring us in the face. Two stories presented in the Club of Rome's initial major study, *The Limits to Growth*, illustrate how exponential growth can generate large numbers very quickly:

> There is an old Persian legend about a clever courtier who presented a beautiful chessboard to his king and requested only that the king give him in return 1 grain of rice for the first square on the board, 2 grains for the second square, 4 grains for the third, and so forth. The king readily agreed and ordered rice to be brought from his stores. The fourth square of the chessboard required eight grains, the tenth square 512 grains, the fifteenth required 16,384, and the twenty-first square gave the courtier more than a million grains of rice. By the fortieth square a million million rice grains had to be brought from the storerooms. The king's entire rice supply was exhausted long before he reached the sixty-fourth square.

---

[9] Michael T. Klare, *Resource Wars: The New Landscape of Global Conflict* (New York: Henry Holt, 2001); Philippe Le Billon, "The Political Ecology of War: Natural Resources and Armed Conflicts," *Political Geography* 20 (June 2001), pp. 561–584. For an empirical analysis of civil war in particular, see Michael Ross, "How Do Natural Resources Influence Civil War? Evidence from Thirteen Cases," *International Organization* 58 (Winter 2004), pp. 35–67.

One wonders whether the courtier actually managed to leave with his rice, or with his life. The other story is a French riddle for children, which illustrates the suddenness and surprise of exponential growth:

> Suppose you own a pond on which a water lily is growing. The lily plant doubles in size each day. If the lily were allowed to grow unchecked, it would completely cover the pond in 30 days, choking off the other forms of life in the water. For a long time the lily plant seems small, and so you decide not to worry about cutting it back until it covers half the pond. On what day will that be? On the twenty-ninth day, of course. You have one day to save your pond.[10]

Both these stories demonstrate the explosive effects of 100-percent growth rates; at each interval—the next square on the chessboard, the next day in the life of the pond—the numbers double. Of course, human populations do not exhibit 100-percent growth rates, but analysts have found it useful to think of exponential growth in terms of *doubling time*. From 1990 to 2000 the average annual growth rate of the world's population was 1.4 percent; at that rate the world population will double in just fifty years. If we think we have political, social, and economic problems with the current population of about 6 billion, imagine the problems with a population reaching twice that size by the year 2050. Fortunately, however, demographers do not expect a continuation of current growth rates in population. During the nineteenth century, annual growth rates were around 0.5 percent. They were twice that by the 1930s, and had risen to 2 percent by the 1960s—cutting doubling time in half, then in half again. Growth rates have declined from their peak in the 1960s, but if we are to avoid the disastrous consequences of a doubling of world population by 2050, those growth rates will have to continue to decline.

When will the global population stabilize? Currently, the UN provides multiple projections of the population in the year 2050 based on different assumptions about fertility, mortality (including under different AIDS scenarios), and international migration.[11] Only the most optimistic, low-fertility projection—assuming that all countries converge toward a fertility rate of 1.35 children per woman, and that many reach that during the projection period—has the population stabilizing by mid-century, at about 7.9 billion by 2040. The UN's medium- and high-fertility projections show global populations of 9.2 and 10.8 billion, respectively. Keep in mind that the very idea of population stabilization means rejecting the viability of exponential growth; even the UN's least optimistic, high-fertility projection assumes birthrates decline from current high levels in many countries. At constant birthrates, nothing short of a catastrophe could stop population growth. As economist Kenneth Boulding once observed, "Anyone who believes exponential growth can go on forever in a finite world is either a madman or an economist."

---

[10] Meadows et al., *The Limits to Growth*, pp. 36–37.

[11] UN Department of Economic and Social Affairs, Population Division, *World Population Prospects: The 2006 Revision* (New York: United Nations, 2007); data available at <http://esa.un.org/unpp/>. See also the discussion of population projections in Wolfgang Lutz, Warren C. Anderson, and Sergei Scherbov, eds., *World Population Growth in the 21st Century: New Challenges for Human Capital Formation and Sustainable Development* (London: Earthscan, 2004).

DEMOGRAPHIC TRANSITION

It took from 1800 to 1930 to add 1 billion people to the world's population; the most recent billion arrived in a little more than a decade. The current burst in population is due mostly to the sharp reduction in death rates caused by the public health improvements made over the past two centuries. Developing societies go through a **demographic transition,** as illustrated by Figure 16.2. In the first stage, typified by Europe before the Industrial Revolution, birthrates and death rates are relatively high. Medicine and health care are underdeveloped. Deaths from disease are common, but there are also many births in order to provide enough laborers for what is primarily an agrarian economy. By the middle of the eighteenth century, death rates were dropping in Europe due to advances in medicine and sanitation. At this second stage, birthrates remain high because large families are an asset for agricultural production, which is still central in economies in the early phases of industrialization. This is a period of rapid population growth, given the widening gap between birthrates and death rates. In stage three, industrialization, urbanization, and the entry of women into the workforce decrease the incentives for large families. Birthrates fall and death rates flatten as access to basic health care becomes nearly universal; population growth begins to taper off. The last stage in the transition is marked by the stabilization of birthrates and death rates at fairly low levels.

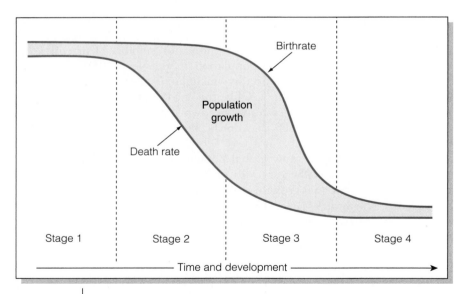

FIGURE 16.2 | DEMOGRAPHIC TRANSITION

Over time, economic development induces changes in the birthrate and death rate in society. It is during the intermediate stages of the demographic transition, when the decline in birthrate lags behind the decline in death rate, that population growth is most pronounced. Many countries are now in these stages of the transition, which accounts for the population explosion during the second half of the twentieth century.

Different countries are at different stages in the demographic transition. The industrialized world as a whole has reached the final stage where both birthrates and death rates are at very low levels and doubling time is high. In many parts of the developing world, however, high birthrates combined with low death rates suggest that these countries are still in transition; they account not only for most of the world's population but also for nearly all the world's population growth. The gap between birthrates and death rates is even higher if China is excluded (it has cut birthrates dramatically, often through draconian measures). In contrast to birthrates, there is much less variability in death rates. This is because advances in medicine, typically achieved in societies further along in the demographic transition, are rather quickly adopted by societies at earlier stages (those with higher birthrates). For an "importer" of medical advances, in effect, the death rate curve in Figure 16.2 turns even more sharply downward in stage two, and when this is not accompanied by commensurate decline in the birthrate, the period of rapid population growth lengthens. Governments, IGOs, and NGOs therefore seek to educate people in these societies about birth control and benefits of smaller family size. The aim is to accelerate the decline in birthrates made necessary by the accelerated decline in death rates.

We need to look at more than birthrates and death rates. To get a true picture of population growth, we have to consider the *population composition* of a country—the numbers of people in different age groups and the fertility rates for those categories. As child and infant mortality rates fall, a country's population becomes younger and a greater proportion of women are of childbearing age. Developing countries, with roughly 800 million females under the age of fifteen, have the potential for much greater population growth in the future. Many girls have yet to reach childbearing age, and in the years ahead a large portion of the populace will be reproducing: the larger group now at childbearing age and those who have yet to reach that age. Although projections for 2025 show a gradual aging of the population in the developing world, there will still be more females of childbearing age than there are today. Even if future parents were to merely replace themselves with two children, so many people have yet to do this that the population of the LDCs will continue to grow for some time.

If the decline in birthrates follows the decline in death rates quickly enough, the demographic transition can serve as an engine of growth, because the economically dependent population (children and seniors) drops relative to the economically productive population in the middle. Chinese economic growth over the last two decades benefited greatly from just this kind of transition; as China's urban working population expanded, the government encouraged private enterprise and free markets. It is especially important that governments adopt good economic policies during the demographic transition, because the opportunity comes only once. What follows is an aging population as life expectancy increases, and a shrinking supply of new young workers entering into the labor force. Without forward-looking policies, societies encounter great difficulties while trying to maintain welfare benefits for growing ranks of elderly. (About 20 percent of the populations in Greece, Italy, and Japan are now more than 65 years old, compared with 13 percent in the United States and 8 percent in China.)

Demographers and policy makers need to look at least fifty years ahead. For example, the longer population control is delayed, the more people of childbearing age will enter the population. In the future, when growth rates are zero and the population has stabilized, the number of people will be much higher; populations continue to grow for decades after control policies are initiated. The uneven rate of population growth is a major factor in the food trade patterns of North America and Latin America. In 1950, both regions had approximately the same population (170 million). However, the rapid increase in the Latin American population and the emphasis on commercial agriculture on exports have forced Latin America to become a net importer of basic foodstuffs, while North America exports food. Countries in Latin America now have almost 70 percent more mouths to feed than those in North America.

RESOURCE DEPLETION

The inclusionist perspective of Malthusians has given rise to a common metaphor in environmental studies: **spaceship Earth**. As Boulding put it more than forty years ago, "the earth has become a single spaceship, without unlimited reservoirs of anything, either for extraction or for pollution, and in which, therefore, man must find his place in a cyclical ecological system, which is capable of continuous reproduction."[12] Population growth, combined with the demands for maintaining high standards of living in the rich countries and demands for development and industrialization in the poor ones, has put great pressures on the world's supply of resources. Moreover, although we have made some initial forays along the "final frontier," it may be quite some time before we come across any supply depots or refuse dumps for spaceship Earth.

FOOD INSECURITY

The UN Food and Agricultural Organization (FAO) estimates that 820 million people in the developing world still suffer from chronic undernutrition. Undernutrition stunts the physical and mental development of one in three children; each year, 5 million children die. While there has been a net decrease in the number (and percent) of undernourished since the early 1990s, this mainly reflects the significant progress made in some large countries like China, Indonesia, Brazil, and Nigeria; most developing countries have seen increases in hunger. There are other, more positive trends, however. Since the late 1960s, world food production has outpaced population growth, and this has helped to bring about a drop in the proportion of undernourished people in the developing world from 37 to 17 percent.[13] Such

---

[12] Kenneth Boulding, "The Economics of the Coming Spaceship Earth," in Henry Jarrett, ed., *Environmental Quality in a Growing Economy* (Baltimore: Johns Hopkins University Press, 1966), p. 9. See also the early statement by R. Buckminster Fuller, *Operating Manual for Spaceship Earth* (New York: E. P. Dutton, 1963).

[13] UN Food and Agriculture Organization, *The State of Food Insecurity in the World 2006* (Rome: FAO, 2006). The figures in the following paragraphs come from this report as well as the FAO's *World Agriculture: Towards 2030/2050*, Interim Report (Rome: FAO, 2006).

improvements are a clear indication that international and transnational efforts are paying off, despite the still unacceptably high number with inadequate diets.

Currently, almost all the globe's best arable land (1.5 billion hectares) is being cultivated; most of the remaining arable land (nearly 3 billion hectares) would be costly to prepare for growing food. The agricultural potential of what remains is open to dispute and partly depends on differing assumptions about our capacity to overcome existing limits with technological advances and other ingenuities. In the meantime, arable land is lost to cultivation every year (5 to 7 million hectares), perhaps permanently, through the expansion of roads and urban areas and, increasingly, through various forms of land degradation. Deforestation contributes to the problem because forests help to prevent topsoil erosion. The expansion of pastures for grazing has been an important cause of deforestation, but pastureland is less productive than arable land in terms of the number of people a plot of a given size can feed. Agricultural scientists try to keep up with loss of arable land by introducing new seeds, fertilizers, and pesticides to raise the productivity of existing land. Nevertheless, it is a hard race, and the new technologies consume a great deal of energy and cause new pollution problems as well.

Part of the problem in assessing the carrying capacity of the world's food resources lies in the definition of "adequate nourishment." Obviously, *adequate* means a certain minimum intake of calories, protein, vitamins, and minerals. It does not require that everyone adopt the eating habits of people living in the industrial countries, where diets are heavy in meat and other animal products (a steer must take in six to eight pounds of grain to produce one pound of beef). The average daily consumption for people in the industrialized world is almost 3,500 calories, while in developing countries it is about 2,800 calories and in sub-Saharan Africa 2,300 calories. Inequalities in levels of "food security" raise serious ethical questions, some of which we explore later.

By the mid-1980s, world food production had reached record levels; indeed, because so much food was produced, prices fell, leading to ever higher subsidies from governments to farmers in the United States, Europe, and even the Soviet Union. During this same period, China became self-sufficient in grain (exporting corn to Japan) and India found itself with a grain surplus. Through improved biotechnology, food production was increased dramatically. American farmers, for instance, get five times the yield of fifty years ago. Because of new frost-resistant breeds of corn, the corn belt in the United States now extends 250 miles farther north than it did in the mid-1970s. The development of aquaculture—the use of fish farms—has been particularly important in China and India. Although agricultural production is likely to grow faster than world population for the next few decades, the growth per person will drop significantly.

Four decades of increasing food production have not eliminated the problems of undernutrition or even starvation. In the short term, yearly harvest fluctuations cause food crises in particular areas. Weather conditions make the world grain crop volatile, and in any one year the grain harvest can drop as much as 5 percent. Still, the larger problem is getting the financial resources needed to produce the food, to pay for the energy needed to produce the food, and to buy the food that is available. The amount of food on the world market may even depress local prices, reducing the money and food available in local areas (as local producers stop producing). Undernutrition and starvation derive *primarily* from political and social factors that affect the distribution of food. Urban growth and the demand for food encourage distributors to direct their supplies to cities where consumption is most concentrated, thereby starving rural areas. Civil war and insurgency (as in Africa) prevent food from getting to certain areas, and governments may punish certain regions or groups, and reward others, by manipulating the distribution system.

In many LDCs, food-distribution facilities are terribly inadequate. Food may rot on the piers of a port city or be eaten by pests on the farms. International food assistance is sometimes diverted by corrupt officials who sell the food for profit. Further, development patterns oriented toward the export market—big commercial crops like cotton, coffee, sugar, fruit, and flowers—may bring in foreign exchange, enabling the rich to buy luxuries or giving governments the finances they want for industrial development. However, when subsistence farms are converted into big commercial establishments raising cash crops, an immediate food deficit is created. Laborers who used to raise their own crops must now use part of their earnings to buy food. Some development programs try to ease this problem by strengthening small farmers, who raise some crops for sale but keep a part of their land for raising their own food.

Land reform and technical assistance to small farmers are receiving increasing attention by international lending organizations like the World Bank, but political and economic resistance to a major reorientation of agricultural development is nevertheless very great. International cooperation has also been channeled through the FAO and other agencies. Agencies such as the World Food Council help keep track of and assist in the deliveries of food, and the Agricultural Development Fund helps developing countries increase production. Yet such activity—a world "food regime"—only begins to meet the problems. Enduring solutions also require an awareness of local political conditions and cultural practices, an effective population policy, and balanced economic development within and among the regions of the world.[14]

The FAO estimates that over the next thirty years, the average annual increase in crop production will be 1.5 percent, down from 2.2 percent during the past thirty years. Partly this will come about because many people already eat as much as they need and want, but there are many others who cannot afford to pay for the food that is produced, especially when prices rise in response to supply disruptions or higher costs of production. From 2006 to 2008, for example, grain prices more than doubled in world markets, triggering food riots in Bangladesh, Egypt, Haiti, and elsewhere. A study by the World Bank estimated that this price increase (and others in food commodities) pushed between 73 million and 105 million more people below the poverty line.[15] Researchers attributed rising food prices to a combination of factors, including record-high oil prices and the use of grains for biofuel production, illustrating the interdependencies among many of today's scarcities and the unintended consequences of policies designed to overcome them.

---

[14] The limits of food aid and development assistance are examined in Alex de Wall, *Famine Crimes: Politics and the Disaster Relief Industry in Africa* (Bloomington: Indiana University Press, 1998). On the difficulties associated with customizing policy solutions to local agricultural practices, see Johan Pottier, *Anthropology of Food: The Social Dynamics of Food Security* (Cambridge: Polity Press, 1999).

[15] World Bank, "Double Jeopardy: Responding to High Food and Fuel Prices," July 2, 2008; prepared for the G8 Hokkaido Toyako Summit and available at <http://www.worldbank.org/html/extdr/foodprices/>.

NATURAL RESOURCES

Some studies indicate that the use of the world's resources is growing exponentially and that in many areas and for many resources it is growing at a rate faster than the growth in population. For example, while world population has increased three and a half times since 1900, industrial energy use per capita has increased more than seven times and total world energy use has grown *fourteen* times. According to World Bank figures, since 1970, energy consumption has doubled worldwide; in low- and middle-income countries, it has almost tripled. Much of this has to do with population growth, but even per capita energy consumption has increased more than 40 percent. This is good news for economic development but bad news for world resources.[16]

Every additional human being and every new item produced for human consumption place demands on the Earth's mineral and energy resources. What is the reserve capacity of the planet? Figures on reserves of minerals and other nonrenewable resources can be deceptive. Reserves are identified resources that are ready for extraction given the existing state of technology. Many known resource deposits are not being tapped, and even where mining and drilling facilities exist, market prices can make it unprofitable to operate them. When prices rise, production may resume, as happened with some petroleum deposits in the United States; oil fields that were no longer profitable once again yielded valuable supplies when market conditions changed. Other resources are known to exist, but are not at present extractable with existing technologies (they are part of the "reserve base"). New technology may be developed for extracting the materials, and thus available resources can be greatly expanded even without discovery of additional reserves. Still other resources are likely to exist given what geologists generally know about the Earth's crust, or based on actual samples or measurements (the "inferred reserve base").

Still, we need to recognize that there are limits. Even with faith that technological advances will allow humans to tap larger portions of the reserve base, technology takes time to develop. In the meantime, the life expectancy of some of the Earth's extractable mineral resources is cause for some concern. Figure 16.3 shows the life expectancy of the oil reserves possessed by OPEC and non-OPEC countries. At today's levels of consumption and production, most significant non-OPEC countries are expected to deplete their reserves by 2025, and most OPEC reserves will not last beyond the end of the century. At some point the planet's petroleum supplies really will be exhausted, even allowing for further exploration and technological advances in extraction.[17] Long before that happens, supplies will become too expensive to use except for very special purposes for which there are no

---

[16] Computed from data in World Bank, *World Development Indicators 2008 CD-ROM* (Washington, D.C.: World Bank, 2008). The figures in the following paragraphs are also based on data from this same source as well as British Petroleum, *BP Statistical Review of World Energy: June 2008*, available at <http://www.bp.com/statisticalreview/>.

[17] See, for example, Kenneth S. Deffeyes, *Hubbert's Peak: The Impending World Oil Shortage* (Princeton, N.J.: Princeton University Press, 2001). The life span of Iraq's reserves is probably overstated in Figure 16.3. At pre–Gulf War production levels, for example, Iraq's reserves will last for about 110 years.

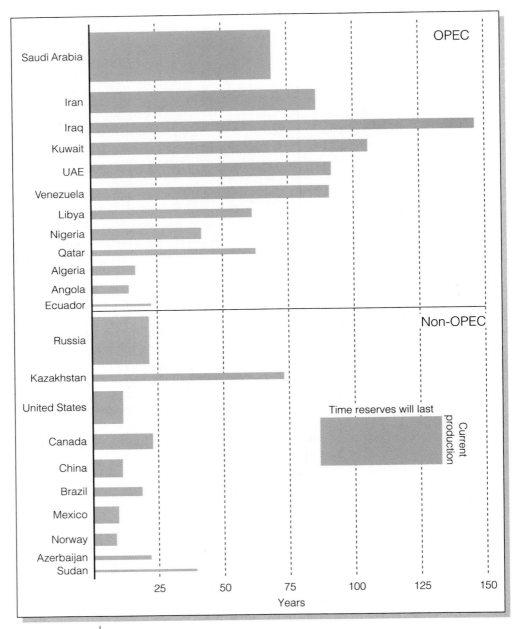

FIGURE 16.3 | OIL RESERVE DEPLETION: OUTLOOK IN 2008

For all OPEC and major non-OPEC oil producers, the length of the bars show the life expectancy of known reserves given rates of production in 2008. Unless there are new discoveries or cutbacks in production, there will be very little non-OPEC oil on world markets in 25 years. OPEC reserves are projected to last longer; exactly how long will depend on whether these countries attempt to make up for shortfalls elsewhere.

Source: Based on data from *BP Statistical Review of World Energy.*

acceptable substitutes. If we extend the life of the Earth's mineral reserves chiefly by making them too expensive to use, we will have made a very dubious bargain.

It is no surprise that industrialized countries consume a disproportionate share of global resources. High-income countries, with about 15 percent of the world's population, accounts for half of all energy consumption, more than ten times what is consumed in low-income countries on a per capita basis. Thus, cutting back resource use in the industrialized world could significantly reduce the projected usage rates of nonrenewable resources and increase the life span of remaining reserves. The United States, with under 5 percent of the world's population, accounts for 20 to 25 percent of the world's consumption of oil and natural gas, as well as disproportionate shares of aluminum, copper, and lead. China, on the other hand, with 20 percent of the world's population, is responsible for less than 10 percent of the world's oil consumption and a little more than 2 percent of natural gas production; the figures for India, with 17 percent of the global population, are a little more than 3 percent and 1 percent, respectively. It is inevitable that these two countries, which are developing rapidly, will consume ever larger shares of the world's resources, putting additional pressure on limited supplies.

Another resource, which is often neglected because it is not strictly nonrenewable, is water. Only about 2 to 3 percent of the world's water is freshwater, and most of that is in the polar ice caps. Less than 1 percent is available for human consumption, directly or indirectly, given current levels of technology: rivers, lakes, water in soil and plants, and vapor in the atmosphere. Though water is a scarce resource, usage is rapidly increasing to meet human consumption and food-production demands. Not all freshwater that is available for human consumption is of sufficiently high quality for drinking, washing, and growing food without treatment. And quality continued to be threatened by a wide range of human-generated pollutants, from sewage to industrial waste to chemical outputs from mining and agriculture. Desalination of seawater might offer some relief and has become more widespread in recent years, but only among countries that can afford it.

Most water consumption takes place in agriculture. Vast quantities of water are needed for opening up new farmland, reclaiming old land, maintaining the land currently in use, and supporting the ongoing "green revolution" in overpopulated areas. To grow 1 pound of corn requires between 100 and 250 gallons of water; growing the grain to produce 1 pound of beef takes 2,000 to 8,500 gallons. Industrial activities also require great quantities of water: 1 ton of steel requires about 1,400 gallons, which is actually a tenfold increase in water-use efficiency compared to World War II–era production.[18] Water consumption grows faster than population—indeed, it has been estimated that water usage triples every time population doubles.

Some analysts call energy the *master resource*. With enough energy, other resources can be mined or otherwise acquired, processed, substituted, or recycled. In other words, the limits to these resources can be relaxed. Increasing food

---

[18] Peter H. Gleick, "Making Every Drop Count," *Scientific American* (February 2001), pp. 28–33; see also Gleick, ed., *The World's Water 2006–2007: The Biennial Report on Freshwater Resources* (Washington, D.C.: Island Press, 2006).

production or cleaning up polluted air and water also requires expending large amounts of energy. Economic development and growing national wealth correlate with the use of energy; consequently, poor countries will require more energy to develop. A vicious cycle emerges here: Birthrates tend to drop and stabilize as countries develop economically, but for this to happen, more energy is needed. Meanwhile, the added population creates demands that devour additional energy and wealth just to maintain the current level of usage. This means that very large amounts of energy must be devoted to the less developed areas.

The drain on the global commons is highly uneven. While population increases in the developing world drive resource consumption, by far the greatest drain occurs in the industrialized countries. Strategies should therefore include changes in lifestyles, as well as changes in the structure of the manufacturing economy: eliminating planned obsolescence, designing longer-lasting and more easily repaired products, recycling, and ending our love affair with disposable products that wind up in rubbish mountains. The current pattern of production and consumption in the industrialized countries probably cannot be maintained even there; an attempt to imitate it worldwide would be an ecological disaster. The *growth* in energy consumption does seem to be leveling off, in part because of effective conservation (especially in Europe and Japan). Given a conducive set of circumstances and incentives, countries can curb (and have curbed) their excessive patterns of resource consumption.

Individual actions and attitudes are important. Many people in the developed countries are slowly changing their habits to reduce consumption and conserve energy. However, the problems of collective goods continue to hamper those efforts when individuals act in accordance with their short-term interests, as most people do most of the time. Preserving the common-pool resources for posterity is certainly not foremost in the minds of individuals inclined to ask, "What has posterity ever done for me?" Altruism alone cannot produce the necessary sacrifices; we still need a combination of raised costs (financial and otherwise) and a heightened awareness of the effects of our actions. Short- and medium-term strategies, including resource substitution, can allow the development not only of new lifestyles, but also of more efficient production technologies and synthetic materials. They can bring us through a difficult period of transition to a point where longer-run thinking has taken root.

ENVIRONMENTAL DECAY

The interaction of population growth, economic development, energy consumption, and pollution emphasized by Malthusians produces a dilemma that has captured the attention of states, IGOs, and NGOs. One way to control population growth is through economic and human development; yet to maintain high standards of living in the developed world and improve standards in LDCs means higher energy usage and the creation of ever higher levels of pollution. Other consequences of economic development we are only beginning to appreciate. Human destruction of the natural habitats of other species obviously represents a negative externality for them, and that may be reason enough to work for their preservation. But it is likely that the extinction of some nonhuman species, whether plant or animal, will also have serious repercussions for human well-being.

POLLUTION

Pollution is always bothersome, but it may also pose a danger to animal, plant, and human life. It can destroy precious food and water resources and make many of the limited resources of the Earth unusable. The increasing use of nonrenewable fuels, as well as the manufacture of chemicals and other industrial products, is producing rising levels of pollution worldwide. Burning fossil fuels produces carbon dioxide, carbon monoxide, sulfur oxides, nitrogen oxides, hydrocarbons, and solid particles, which are emitted into the air and water. Some of these emissions produce acid rain. They settle into or are washed into the soil and are absorbed into the plants and animals that live in polluted areas. Water is also damaged by thermal pollution. Heat from industrial processes and nuclear energy reactors disrupts the ecological balance of rivers, streams, and lakes. Nuclear power produces radioactive wastes, which could become the most dangerous pollutants of all. Many countries simply have no safe disposal sites or viable disposal policies. This is a problem demanding international cooperation.

The spread of pollutants throughout the ecosystem is a byproduct of global interdependence. For example, lead emitted into the air by industrialized countries has been found in the Greenland ice cap. Large deposits of DDT (a chemical pesticide, now banned in the United States and elsewhere) have been found in the bodies of whales that have lived almost entirely in the Antarctic region. Increases in the carbon dioxide content of the atmosphere (resulting especially from the burning of fossil fuels) create the *greenhouse effect*, which traps heat inside the atmosphere. The result is **global warming**, a gradual increase in world temperatures. The UN's Intergovernmental Panel on Climate Change (IPCC) estimates that the average global surface temperature has increased by 0.7 degrees Celsius (1.3 degrees Fahrenheit) since the early 1900s. Based on the available evidence, the rate and duration of this warming trend is greater than any other period in the last 1,000 years, and it is very unlikely that this warming is due to natural climatic variation alone. Human activities are part of what is driving the recent trend in global warming. How big a part is still the subject of scientific debate.

Different climate models use different methodologies and scenarios for forecasting global temperature, but projections for the end of the century show temperature increases between 1.8 to 4.0 degrees Celsius (3.2 to 7.2 degrees Fahrenheit).[19] Climate and topography will change in erratic and unpredictable ways: Forests will move poleward; arid zones in the middle of continents will grow and make grain cultivation uneconomical; the ice caps will melt and the sea level will rise, drowning low-lying coastal areas. The increased frequency and duration of heat waves will claim more lives, as will malaria, dengue, and other diseases carried by

---

[19] Intergovernmental Panel on Climate Change, *Climate Change 2007: The Physical Science Basis* (New York: Cambridge University Press, 2007), chaps. 3, 10. The IPCC won the 2007 Nobel Peace Prize.

mosquitoes and rodents that will proliferate along with warmer and damper climates. Harmful effects will be different at different latitudes and in different regions. Scientists agree on the general outlines, though not the details, of what will happen, but they disagree as to what should be done about it. Energy conservation and, perhaps ironically, greater emphasis on nuclear energy will be required.

The atmospheric concentration of carbon dioxide (CO_2) and methane (CH_4), two of several greenhouse gases, grew exponentially during the twentieth century. These and other trends prompted calls for action. The UN Framework Convention on Climate Change (UNFCC) was signed at the Earth Summit in Rio de Janeiro in 1992, and it adopted as a goal the reduction of greenhouse emissions to 1990 levels by the year 2000. Binding targets for emissions were generally opposed by the United States, but by the end of 1998 it had come around and signed the 1997 Kyoto Protocol to the UNFCC, which obligates contracting parties to reduce greenhouse emissions to 5 percent below 1990 levels no later than 2012. Most parties to the agreement are unlikely to meet their emissions targets.[20]

Critics of the Kyoto Protocol often assert that it does too little to address the problem of global warming. Some climate scientists say that averting the adverse effects of global warming will require cutting greenhouse emissions by 50 percent or more worldwide. Kyoto asks far less of industrialized countries, and asks nothing of developing countries, including big polluters like China and India. Citing such flaws, as well as the costs it would impose on the U.S. economy, the George W. Bush administration rejected the Kyoto accord shortly after taking office in 2001, which placed the entire agreement in jeopardy. Under the terms of the protocol, it could not enter into force until ratified by industrialized states accounting for at least 55 percent of global greenhouse emissions. When the United States opted out, only Russia's ratification would allow that threshold to be met, and for a time it looked as if Kyoto was doomed. However, after some enticements from the EU, Russia did ratify the treaty and it entered into force in 2005.

Whatever its weaknesses, Kyoto is noteworthy because it provides for *emissions trading*. The arrangement grants each country an emission allowance, or "credits," based on their greenhouse emissions in 1990. Countries may sell unused credits to those that have used all of theirs and need more. Thus, the Kyoto arrangement attempts to "privatize" the atmosphere—a collective good—in much the same way that UNCLOS privatized fisheries by creating EEZs. States acquire property rights to a portion of the atmosphere; if they use it up by polluting it, they must purchase more from states willing to sell their surplus. It may seem perverse to buy and sell rights to pollute our common atmosphere, but advocates of "free-market environmentalism" believe that economic incentives are needed to

---

[20] On the difficulties plaguing the Kyoto agreement, see David G. Victor, *The Collapse of the Kyoto Protocol and the Struggle to Slow Global Warming* (Princeton, N.J.: Princeton University Press, 2001); Thomas C. Schelling, "What Makes Greenhouse Sense," *Foreign Affairs* 81 (May/June 2002), pp. 2–9; William D. Nordhaus, "After Kyoto: Alternative Mechanisms to Control Global Warming," *American Economic Review* 96 (May 2006), pp. 31–34.

keep global emissions below an agreed-upon level.[21] Indeed, Russia's ambivalence toward the Kyoto treaty can be explained in part by the loss of a potential customer for its emissions credits. Russia's current greenhouse emissions are far below its 1990 levels, due to the collapse of Soviet-era industrial production, and had the United States become party to the treaty, the demand for pollution rights was likely to remain high.

Atmospheric pollutants are also responsible for the holes that have appeared in the **ozone layer** over Antarctica. Ozone at ground level is a health hazard, but the ozone layer miles above the surface is crucial to life on Earth because it helps to screen out cancer-causing ultraviolet radiation from the sun. The thinning of the ozone layer is partly the result of the use of chlorofluorocarbons (CFCs), now mostly banned from use in spray cans but still widely used in plastics and refrigeration. In 1987, twenty-five major producing countries signed the Montréal Protocol to cut worldwide production of these chemicals by 50 percent by 1998. It was a fairly impressive agreement, given the difficulties: delays caused by vested economic interests, uncertainty about the scientific evidence, and the reluctance of LDCs to pay for more expensive substitutes. In 1990 in London, an agreement was reached to end *all* production of chemicals that destroy the ozone layer by the year 2000. Subsequent amendments moved this date up to 1996 for industrialized countries and back to 2010 for developing countries. The London agreement came about only through compromise, which included the industrial countries setting up a fund to help developing countries pay for phasing in CFC substitutes. By 2004, virtually all states had ratified the Montréal Protocol.

In regard to greenhouse gases, replicating the Montréal Protocol's success in reducing CFC emissions will be difficult. But the impact of the Kyoto accord can and will be seen in other, diffuse ways. Even when Kyoto looked dead in the water, the EU instituted its own emissions trading system designed to push member states toward the Kyoto targets. The continued commitment by industrialized countries, especially Europe and Japan, to address the problem of global warming while some of the world's biggest polluters remain uncommitted is a sign that the *process* leading to Kyoto has gained momentum and may not be easily reversed. Other agreements will follow, and some nonparticipants will come on board. At least this is the hope of those who have pushed the process despite the flaws of particular agreements. It is well to remember that complex regimes and institutions currently serving important functions for states and citizens—the EU and the WTO—emerged in their current form after many years, many rounds of negotiation, and many setbacks.

DEFORESTATION AND THE THREAT TO BIODIVERSITY

Both ozone depletion and global warming are compounded by another form of environmental degradation—**deforestation**. Between 20 and 50 percent of the forest

---

[21] On emissions trading, see Deborah Stowell, *Climate Trading: Development of Greenhouse Gas Markets* (New York: Palgrave Macmillan, 2005); Sonia Labatt and Rodney R. White, *Carbon Finance: The Financial Implications of Climate Change* (Hoboken, N.J.: Wiley & Sons, 2007).

area that covered the Earth in preagricultural times is now gone. Of those large, relatively undisturbed "frontier forests" that remain—mainly in the Amazon Basin, Central Africa, Canada, and Russia—40 percent are now threatened. Large areas of the Amazon and other rain forests are being cleared in the interests of commercial development and of settling new farmers pushed out of their former homes by the South American population explosion. Tropical rain forests, once estimated to have covered more than 15 percent of the world's terrestrial surface, now cover less than half that. Based on data for 2000 to 2005, the FAO reports that global deforestation—the *net* loss of natural forests, as there is some forest expansion, especially in nontropical areas—is occurring at the rate of 7.3 million hectares per year.[22]

When forests are cleared for farming, the ecosystem is damaged in multiple ways. Trees that absorbed carbon dioxide from the atmosphere are eliminated, but also destroyed are the habitats of many other species, in some cases pushing them to the point of extinction. Such a loss represents a reduction in biological diversity, or **biodiversity**—the number and variety of living things on Earth. Again, estimates vary, but scientists believe that between 300 and 350 vertebrates and 400 invertebrates have become extinct over the last four centuries, along with hundreds of plant species. Today 12 percent of all bird species are threatened with extinction; twice that percentage of mammal species are threatened.[23] We ought to appreciate biodiversity as an end in itself, but these extinctions also have implications for economic and social development. All national economies depend on biological resources, and the poor are especially dependent on them. A diversity of life provides greater opportunities for medical discoveries, economic innovations, and adaptive responses to other environmental challenges.

At the 1992 Earth Summit, states signed the Convention on Biological Diversity (CBD), agreeing to safeguard biodiversity within their borders and committing themselves to find ways to share the benefits of biodiversity (like profits from medicines derived from tropical trees) as well as the costs of species protection. Virtually all states had become parties to the convention. The United States did not sign the convention in Rio, the main concern being that intellectual property rights were not adequately protected. The United States has since signed, but remains one of very few states that has not ratified or otherwise acceded to the convention. Many vocal opponents come from the U.S. biotechnology sector, who worry that developing countries will begin to deny them access to protected areas for purposes of "biological prospecting." Worldwide concerns about genetic engineering and other applications of biotechnology led to a supplementary CBD agreement known as the Cartagena Protocol on Biosafety, which entered into force in 2003. It provides for the sharing of sufficient information to allow states to assess the potential impact of genetically modified organisms before they import them in the form of corn and soybean derivatives, pharmaceuticals, and other products. Not surprisingly, the

---

[22] UN Food and Agriculture Organization, *State of the World's Forests 2007* (Rome: FAO, 2007).

[23] Secretariat of the Convention on Biological Diversity, *Global Biodiversity Outlook 2* (Montréal: UN Environment Programme, 2006).

United States has been a strong opponent of the Cartagena Protocol, given the importance of biotechnology and bioengineering to the U.S. economy.

Deforestation and biological extinction, like other forms of environmental degradation, are threats to the global commons resulting from the choices of individuals, often exacerbated by the actions (or inaction) of governments. Restraint at the local level is important, but only by taking a global view can we begin to assess the totality of the damage being wrought by human patterns of production and consumption. Stemming environmental degradation requires negotiation and agreement among nations, as well as changes by international development agencies like the World Bank in the kinds of projects they support and encourage. Education and transnational civic activism, especially as channeled through NGOs, has also been very important in changing the way we think about the environment and our place in the global ecosystem.[24]

DILEMMAS OF DEVELOPMENT

Our discussion of the many ecological challenges facing humanity today has repeatedly pointed to the trade-offs between economic growth and environmental preservation. Although there are ample grounds for pessimism, the international community is beginning to devise ways to get past these dilemmas of development.[25] For example, to prevent even further destruction of tropical rain forests, "debt-for-nature swaps" have been worked out. Governments of developed countries and international organizations have forgiven large portions of some developing countries' foreign debt in return for commitments to give permanent legal protection to large tracts of forest. As with developed countries paying for CFC substitutes, agreements providing for debt relief, trade, and aid in return for protection of tropical forests are examples of using side payments to get actors to cooperate in a tragedy of the commons situation.

Such actions come none too soon. Costa Rica is a case in point. For its size, it has the largest system of protected land and national parks in the world (about half its forest area and one-quarter of its total land area). Yet it also had one of the highest rates of deforestation in the world (four times the global average from 1990 to 2000). In essence, everything that was not protected was being cut at breathtaking speed. Banana growing vividly illustrates the dilemmas of Costa Rican development. The country has long been a major banana producer, and the government hopes to make it the region's foremost banana exporter. MNCs are powerful actors in the domestic politics of this small and not wealthy country.

---

[24] See, for example, Kal Raustiala and David G. Victor, "The Regime Complex for Plant Genetic Resources," *International Organization* 58 (Spring 2004), pp. 277–309; Margaret E. Keck and Kathryn Sikkink, *Activists Beyond Borders: Advocacy Networks in International Politics* (Ithaca, N.Y.: Cornell University Press, 1998).

[25] Paul Collier, *The Bottom Billion: Why the Poorest Countries are Failing and What Can Be Done About It* (New York: Oxford University Press, 2007); Jeffrey D. Sachs, *Common Wealth: Economics for a Crowded Planet* (New York: Penguin, 2008). For a look at different future scenarios, see Barry B. Hughes and Evan E. Hillebrand, *Exploring and Shaping International Futures* (Boulder, Colo.: Paradigm, 2006).

Great plantations provide jobs at good wages, but the environmental effects of clear-cutting forests for cultivation, subsequent exhaustion of the land, and widespread pollution are immense.

Tourism is Costa Rica's third largest industry, thanks to the country's political stability, its great and varied natural beauty, and the park system. But its ecological assets are endangered. The same coral reef that begins far north in Mexico's Yucatan peninsula extends all the way down Costa Rica's east coast and had been a major tourist attraction. Now most of the reef in Costa Rica is dead, a sad remnant of what still remains in the Yucatan and Belize. The runoff of silt and pesticides from coastal banana plantations has killed it. And tourism itself can be a mixed blessing. Costa Rican beaches are not yet carpeted by high-rise hotels, but that may come. Some Costa Ricans are trying to promote "ecotourism" as an alternative. This entails building small-scale units that blend with rather than dominate the natural landscape, employing residents as managers and as guides who can interpret local culture and ecology, and promoting direct and relatively close contact with the indigenous people. A central aim is the education of tourists about ecological problems and possibilities. Tourism of this form is not for everyone, neither visitors nor hosts. It cannot provide anything like the number of jobs that mass tourism provides, and visitors' contacts with the local culture will remain fairly superficial. But perhaps ecotourism can interact with Costa Rica's efforts to preserve large segments of its natural environment. Indeed, the FAO reported that the country had actually *added* to its forest area from 2000 to 2005, the only Central American country to do so.

OBLIGATIONS AND RIGHTS

Resource depletion and environmental degradation are externalities produced by population growth and economic development and are clear examples of collective "bads." Individual states cannot avoid being affected by these ecological developments; individual state action cannot overcome them. Collective action is required but is difficult. Since the late 1980s, some impressive movement toward action on ecological issues has taken place, led by IGOs like the UN Environment Programme and various transnational environmental groups like Greenpeace, the World Resources Institute, and the Sierra Club. Green groups and green thinking have proliferated around the globe, creating the core of a growing environmental regime. This, of course, is what is needed to deal with collective goods problems arising from global interdependence. But sustainable development nevertheless remains a difficult goal. Containing ecological damage must somehow be reconciled with the need for greater global equity and the need to improve living conditions in the poorest countries.

INTERNATIONAL DISTRIBUTIVE JUSTICE

Earlier in this chapter we discussed UNCLOS. In addition to creating exclusive economic zones, UNCLOS established an International Seabed Authority to manage the resources beyond the 200-mile limit in order to preserve the "common heritage of mankind." During the negotiations, industrialized states and LDCs held two different views on how the seabed commons should be regulated. LDCs wanted the Authority (and its operational arm, the Enterprise) to control all exploitation of the seabed. Developed states, the United States in the forefront, desired national control. With their own sophisticated mining industries, the United States, Britain, Germany, and others wanted relatively free access and limited control by the Authority.

The Law of the Sea process illustrates several important issues. As we saw in Chapter 15, differences in wealth and development, past colonial relationships, and dominance or dependence complicate the uneven distribution of resources and the use of those resources around the world. To develop, many countries in the Global South need vast amounts of resources, energy, capital, and aid. In the process of developing they will add considerably to the consumption of nonrenewable resources and will also generate a great deal of environmental degradation. Given Western opposition to the mining and wealth-sharing provisions of the Law of the Sea, and similar positions taken in other contexts, the view that certain states in the North are content to keep the South in an underdeveloped and subordinate position is not altogether unjustified. This view is reinforced when ecologically minded people tell LDCs that they should not aim for similar levels of development as the rich countries in light of the environmental consequences. In short, we have a collective-action problem complicated further by a history of colonialism and exploitation.

It is clear that development strategies based on more equity within nations and modest transfers of wealth between nations could greatly improve the conditions of the world's poor.[26] The relationship between personal income and measures of social health is very strong at the poor end of the spectrum: Small increases in wealth have big positive effects. Figure 16.4 shows the relationship between GDP per capita and undernutrition in 125 developing countries (each country is represented as a dot on the chart). The curve is a way of summarizing the relationship, even though most countries do not fall exactly on the curve. The steepness of the curve at low levels of income per capita suggests that each increment of additional national wealth can substantially reduce the percentage of the population suffering from undernutrition. For instance, an increase in per capita GDP from $300 (the income of Burundi) to $1,000 (Bangladesh) is associated with a 35-point drop in the undernutrition rate. At higher levels of income, the effect of the same increment is much reduced; an increase from, say, $3,100 to $4,000 yields only a one-point decline. This pattern implies that major improvements in health and living conditions for the poor could be brought about at a price not requiring major sacrifices by people in the rich countries, especially if the world's neediest are effectively targeted.

Of course, the calculation of costs and benefits for transferring wealth from rich to poor is much more complicated than this simple illustration suggests. Presumably, any program to bring about a greater degree of international distributive

---

[26] See, for example, Bruce Russett, *Purpose and Policy in the Global Community* (New York: Palgrave Macmillan, 2006), chaps. 3–4; Nora Lustig, ed., *Shielding the Poor: Social Protection in the Developing World* (Washington, D.C.: Brookings, 2001).

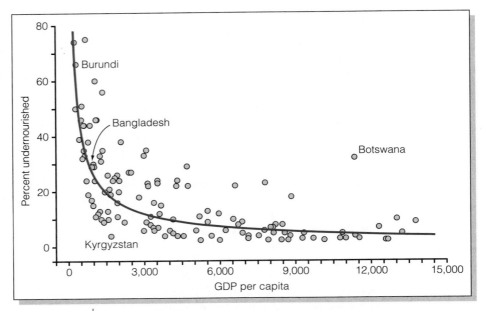

FIGURE 16.4 | UNDERNUTRITION IN RELATION TO INCOME, 2004

The chart locates each of 125 developing countries according to their GDP per capita and rate of undernutrition. The curve is an estimate of the relationship between the two. For the most impoverished nations, increases in GDP per capita have a large effect in bringing undernutrition rates down. Given their incomes, some populations (like Botswana, above the curve) are more undernourished than we would expect; others (like Kyrgyzstan) are less.
Source: Based on data from World Bank, *World Development Indicators.*

justice would not be satisfied with merely lifting the world's poorest out of their desperate circumstances. The expressed goal is usually a more substantial improvement in levels of economic and social development, which brings with it ecological costs. In his controversial "case against helping the poor," Garrett Hardin challenges the popular spaceship Earth analogy:

> The spaceship metaphor can be dangerous when used by misguided idealists to justify suicidal policies for sharing our resources through uncontrolled immigration and foreign aid. In their enthusiastic but unrealistic generosity, they confuse the ethics of a spaceship with those of a lifeboat.... Metaphorically each rich nation can be seen as a lifeboat full of comparatively rich people. In the ocean outside each lifeboat swim the poor of the world, who would like to get in, or at least share some of the wealth.... We must recognize the limited capacity of any lifeboat.

Hardin asks us to imagine that our lifeboats are almost full—there is some room left, but certainly not enough for all those in the water. Obviously, not everyone can be brought aboard, for we would all sink in the process. However, even filling our lifeboats to capacity by helping at least some of those in need is problematic because, says Hardin, we need the extra space as a "safety factor." Our survival demands that we admit no one into the lifeboat. Hardin's **lifeboat ethics** are abhorrent to many, as he recognizes, but they are addressed to the tragedy of the commons. Foreign aid undermines the incentives that would otherwise bring about changes in behavior that are required if the world's resources and environment are to be preserved for posterity. For Hardin, the chief problem is population growth and there may be no better alternative than "population control the crude way"—famine.[27]

Fortunately, most people don't see the trade-off in such stark terms (and perhaps neither does Hardin). The lifeboat may be a reasonable analogy, but we might imagine it as filled with many people, including quite a few first-class passengers with all their luggage. We could bring some more into the boat and still preserve our safety factor, as long as we are willing to toss some of the golf clubs and guns overboard. Those we cannot bring aboard we can help become better swimmers or, better, assist in building their own lifeboats with extra room for emergencies. This is the sort of multitrack approach that seems to best characterize the varied efforts of governments, international agencies, and private groups on behalf of the world's poor.

Such issues raise old and ever-present ethical questions about what responsibility each of us owes others. We typically feel the greatest responsibility for those in our own communities. Our families and close friends get the highest priority; our fellow nationals may occupy some sort of middle ground; and inhabitants farther away, about whom we know little, receive the lowest priority. Yet, given such enormous differences in well-being, to what degree is it just to ignore what could be done?

State Boundaries and Moral Boundaries

The principle of nonintervention precludes our assisting the needy in other countries unless we are invited to do so by their governments. Foreign aid is usually welcomed as long as there are no strings attached, because strings can be an affront to sovereignty. Donors are told that communities in need, or at least their governments, know best how to address those needs. Many do, but sometimes providers of foreign aid watch while their donations are looted from warehouses by warring clans, dictators build themselves lavish presidential palaces, or militaries procure state-of-the-art jet fighters. If sovereignty and the assertion of states' rights have undermined international scrutiny even in such extreme cases (though this is changing), then it is not hard to imagine the difficulties encountered by those who would scrutinize recipients' population control programs or economic development plans.

Nowhere are the limits of sovereignty clearer than in our current ecological predicament—both in the patterns of behavior that have gotten us here and in states' halting efforts to address the problems. The modest success in curbing population growth, hunger, and environmental degradation is really a testament to the

---

[27] Garrett Hardin, "Lifeboat Ethics: The Case against Helping the Poor," *Psychology Today* 8 (September 1974), pp. 38–43, 124–126; excerpt from p. 38. For an early critical response, see Marvin S. Soroos, "The Commons and Lifeboat as Guides for International Ecological Policy," *International Studies Quarterly* 21 (December 1977), pp. 647–674.

efforts of nonstate actors, navigating the inhospitable terrain of sovereign states. But the "limits" of sovereignty has another meaning as well. In Chapter 10 we discussed international human rights and pointed out that civil and political rights require restraint on the part of individuals or governments in a position to deny them; they are "negative" rights that grant *freedoms* from an overbearing government (freedom of speech, religion, association, and so on). We also identified another domain of international human rights: economic and social well-being. These rights, whether defined in terms of basic human needs or a more substantial level of human development, are "positive" rights. When one or more individuals do not possess some minimal level of well-being, their rights imply *obligations* on the part of others, or so it would seem.

Aid to the poor is typically viewed as charitable, even noble if it involves significant sacrifice on the part of the giver. Still, one is obliged to help only by one's own conscience, and although very many people do feel obliged, many others do not. Sometimes our obligations are most strongly felt in regard to those most in need, no matter where they are. When coastal communities in South and Southeast Asia were destroyed by a tsunami in 2004, the outpouring of emergency aid and assistance was instantaneous. When Myanmar was hit by a cyclone in 2008, the only thing preventing a similar effort was the country's xenophobic military government. Such events, brought on when the forces of nature turn violently against us, have a way of reinforcing our perceptions of common humanity. We don't see Indonesians and Burmese in trouble, we see people in trouble, and we want to help—we feel obligated to help. Usually, however, our obligations are most strongly felt toward those closest to home. This seems natural, for home is where our ties to community are "thickest." It is true that most of us feel very little hesitation when our governments and other groups mount relief efforts to prevent foreign populations from dying in large numbers, due to mass starvation or genocide, but these are easy calls to make; our "thin" ties to those far away are normally sufficient to justify their rescue from certain death.[28]

Questions of international distributive justice are harder. In our discussion of human rights we suggested that the communitarian way of thinking is widespread. Obligations to our political communities (our homelands) are normally compatible with the principle of state sovereignty. Indeed, those obligations both reinforce and are reinforced by states' claims to autonomy—and here is the second meaning of the "limits" of sovereignty. National boundaries are more than lines on a map or a string of border checkpoints; they are more than the administrative perimeters of national governments. They also tend to demarcate the outer limits of our most strongly felt obligations to our fellow human beings. They define the collective for whom we are most likely to decline the free ride and contribute our share to the public good. If nothing else, we pay our taxes.

When we adopt the cosmopolitan way of thinking, helping those beyond our borders is not charity, but an obligation. State boundaries are not moral boundaries. If we can help, we should help, by proactively assisting those in need and by

---

[28] Michael Walzer, *Thick and Thin: Moral Argument at Home and Abroad* (Notre Dame, Ind.: University of Notre Dame Press, 1994).

curbing our consumption and other activities that diminish others' prospects for human development. The problem is that the cosmopolitan notion of transnational obligation seems to clash with the communitarian loyalties that form the basis of nationalism, still a powerful force in world politics. The difficulty in coming to terms with a new sense of obligation is perhaps compounded in the West, where the emphasis on freedom and individual liberty is often at odds with the conception of positive rights as entitlements. Yet it is the West that is generally in the best position to help.[29]

Problems of global poverty and the tragedy of the commons amplify the limits of sovereignty manifest in many of the issues we have discussed in this book. All states are not equal; geography and history have seen to that. In confronting the predicaments of humankind, solutions based on individual freedom and liberty will be empty without a more equitable global distribution of opportunity. At minimum, this requires attending to the basic needs and well-being of the least advantaged among us and thus a more pervasive sense of cosmopolitan obligation. And we cannot in the process neglect the rights and well-being of posterity. We live within boundaries of both space and time, and we need to look beyond them. Our obligation is to humanity—ourselves, those who inhabit other parts of the globe, and those still to come. Recognizing that obligation, and translating it into new patterns of individual behavior and creative state policy, is perhaps the most significant challenge we face today.

---

[29] Compare, for example, the views found in John Rawls, *The Law of Peoples* (Cambridge, Mass.: Harvard University Press, 2001), and Onora O'Neill, *Bounds of Justice* (Cambridge: Cambridge University Press, 2000).

WHICH GLOBAL FUTURE?

THREE FUTURES

We study the past in order to understand the present. In the previous chapters we have taken up many important issues in international politics and have shown that social scientists continue to accumulate quite a bit of knowledge about the way state and nonstate actors interact in a complex world system. But we have also tried to convey the different perspectives and understandings that guide the study of world politics, even when the topic of investigation is the same. Thus, military conflict, international norms, globalization, economic development, and the many other topics we consider under the rubric of world politics are accompanied by multiple explanations of cause and effect, and, in some cases, varying ethical judgments about right and wrong, just and unjust. Organizing these competing explanations and judgments using the frameworks of realism, liberalism, and radicalism can be a useful way to keep them all straight.

If there are multiple interpretations of the past and competing explanations of the present, then it follows that there is more than one view of the future. Mindful of that, in this brief closing chapter we will not try to answer the question, "Which global future?" Instead, we present three different visions of the future offered by scholars over the past several years, each of which is obviously speculative. All three are in some ways controversial; those who dare to gaze into the crystal ball, however well informed, almost always invite criticism and quarrel. They are not necessarily realist versus liberal versus radical views of the future, although there are stronger traces of certain perspectives in certain of these global futures. Where we see them, we will try to highlight them, but mostly we want to sketch these alternative futures without much further embellishment. Based on your own understanding of world politics, along with your observation of contemporary world affairs, you will be in a good position to evaluate these scenarios for yourself.

THE WEST HAS WON

In Chapter 11 we discussed the prevalence of peaceful relations among democracies, and we mentioned the argument put forth by Francis Fukuyama regarding the "end of history." Despite the ominous allusions, the "end of history" really is a vision of the future. The argument is that Western ideas about the most appropriate forms of both political and economic interaction—democracy and capitalism—have demonstrated their superiority over all others, and that this is about as good as it gets. Fukuyama's claim is that Western liberalism has triumphed over competing social arrangements; hence the label *triumphalism* has been applied to this argument by many of his detractors.[1]

The concept of the end of history comes from the work of German idealist philosopher G. W. F. Hegel, who wrote that human progress results from the competition of ideas. Ideas condition our behavior, our relationships with each other, our material well-being. There are competing sets of ideas, or ideologies, that purport to outline the best forms of social organization, but the superior ones will emerge to propel societies along the road of human betterment and progress. Eventually we will get to the end of that road—not Armageddon, but the point at which our particular economic and political arrangements can be improved no further. The history of human progress, for Hegel, was the history of these competing ideas and ideologies. That is not to say that someday human progress would come to an abrupt halt, but rather that humankind will have discovered a form of social organization superior to all others for purposes of freeing human potential. That would mark the end of history.

As Fukuyama points out, Hegel actually thought history was coming to an end in the early nineteenth century as Napoléon's armies were conquering Europe and thereby demonstrating the superiority of the French revolutionary ideals of liberty and equality. Although Napoléon was defeated, the ideals of political liberty continued to resonate in Europe and in America. There would be two major challenges to liberalism in the twentieth century: fascism and communism. Fascism was defeated by force of arms during World War II, but its practical and moral bankruptcy was evident in its failure to reemerge after the war as a viable alternative to political and economic liberalism. Communism has been a more serious challenge. As an alternative to Western liberalism, communist—or at least socialist—forms of governance have been more widespread and more durable than fascism ever was. Still, that socialism was in retreat was clear to Fukuyama (and everyone else) when he first presented his view of the future in 1989. Since then socialism has fully collapsed in Russia and Eastern Europe, while market reforms have eaten away at socialist economics in China and elsewhere.

For Fukuyama, the end of the twentieth century was when we truly arrived at the end of history. Western liberalism in the form of free-market capitalism and democracy are on the march globally. Economic and political liberalism as currently implemented in the West are by no means perfect, but the remaining ills of Western society—economic inequality, racism, and so on—can be attended to within a liberal social order; they are not inherent in capitalist democracy. Neither is the end of history signaled by the universal adoption of capitalist democracy

---

[1] Francis Fukuyama, "The End of History?" *National Interest* 16 (Summer 1989), pp. 3–18; see also his *The End of History and the Last Man* (New York: Free Press, 1992). After twenty years, the thesis still generates heated debate; a recent critique is Robert Kagan, *The Return of History and the End of Dreams* (New York: Alfred A. Knopf, 2008).

worldwide. Clearly that is not the case today. What is important, for Fukuyama, is that no other set of ideals currently vie with Western liberalism for the hearts and minds of humanity. Even countries like China that hold tenaciously to certain non-liberal principles (for example, in politics) do not actively promote them as human-kind's destiny. Western liberalism, on the other hand, is understood and promoted in such terms, though more by some states than by others. True, there are many societies "still in history," but political and economic liberalization is the way to human progress and ultimately they too will follow that path. The challengers have been defeated; the West has won.

What Fukuyama and others refer to as Western liberalism is not exactly the same as the term we have used in this book to describe a particular perspective on world politics. Still, there is a great deal of overlap. The liberal approach to world politics does indeed have its roots in political and economic liberalism, as we noted in Chapter 2 (when we introduced the three competing perspectives) and again in Chapter 12 (when we reintroduced them in the context of international political economy). The most obvious affinity between the liberal view of world politics and Fukuyama's vision of the future is that for Fukuyama the end of history brings with it the same sort of peace and stability observed by democratic-peace theorists. As described in Chapter 11, this is a peace among democracies only, reinforced by economic interdependence and international institutions, not among autocratic regimes or between autocracies and democracies. Many of those adopting the liberal perspective would not subscribe to Fukuyama's triumphalism, but there is no denying a common framework that sees domestic politics and society as important influences on foreign affairs.

COMING CULTURE CLASH

Others are far less sanguine about the Western triumph. Rejecting the idea that history has ended, Samuel Huntington instead points to the coming "clash of civilizations." He does not dispute the end of ideological rivalry, as predicted by Fukuyama. Nor is he convinced that geo-economic competition will replace ideological rivalry as a source of conflict, especially among Western powers, as some of Fukuyama's critics have argued. Conflict will indeed be a feature of world politics in the new millennium, but it is civilizations that will come to blows, not ideological or economic blocs. And the main axis of political conflict in the future is likely to be that between "the West and the Rest."[2]

The civilizational entities to which Huntington refers are the Western, Latin American, African, Islamic, Confucian (or Sinic), Hindu, Orthodox, Buddhist, and Japanese civilizations. These will not necessarily replace nation-states as the central actors in world politics, but civilizational identities will increasingly provide the glue that brings some states together and pushes others apart. History, language,

---

[2] Samuel P. Huntington, "The Clash of Civilizations?" *Foreign Affairs* 72 (Summer 1993), pp. 22–49, and his *The Clash of Civilizations and the Remaking of World Order* (New York: Simon & Schuster, 1996). Like Fukuyama's thesis, Huntington's has generated countless critiques. For an empirical analysis that challenges his argument, see Bruce Russett and John Oneal, *Triangulating Peace: Democracy, Interdependence, and International Organizations* (New York: Norton, 2001), chap. 7.

tradition, and especially religion both unite and divide peoples. With the ideological rivalry of the cold war gone, the iron curtain that divided Europe will be replaced by a "velvet curtain" in Europe and elsewhere, and these fault lines between civilizations will be the battlegrounds of the future. In Europe the velvet curtain is actually somewhat east of the old iron curtain, with Finland, the Baltic states, Poland, the Czech and Slovak Republics, Hungary, Slovenia, and Croatia now to the west and the remainder of the former Soviet bloc plus Greece and Turkey to the east. This fault line separates Western Christianity from Orthodox Christianity and Islam.

Huntington also identifies a "crescent-shaped Islamic bloc of nations" from Northern Africa to Central Asia. The struggle between the Western and Islamic civilizations has been going on since the seventh century when the Moors crossed the Strait of Gibraltar and conquered Spain. Conflicts accompanying the rise of Arab nationalism and, more recently, Islamic fundamentalism are simply the most recent manifestations of a long-standing and deep-seated civilizational struggle; both are defined largely in opposition to the legacy of Western colonialism in the Middle East and Northern Africa. There are fault lines dividing the Islamic civilization from non-Western civilizations as well—"Islam has bloody borders," as Huntington puts it—and he implies that the deep historical roots of this struggle ensure that it will continue well into the future.

An Islamic–Confucian connection also figures into this scenario for the future, although for Huntington the connection seems to be restricted more to the realm of power and interests than to cultural affinities. Here he focuses mostly on weapons acquisition, including arms transfers from the East to the Middle East, as well as the Western bias of prevailing approaches to arms control, which are rejected by nations in the Islamic–Confucian bloc. Thus, despite the talk of cultures and civilizations—not central in the vocabulary of realism—this vision of the future does have strong realist overtones. What we can expect in the new millennium, following Huntington, is more power balancing, not so much by interest-maximizing states but by culturally bound states called *civilizations*. An entertaining yet insightful critique of Huntington's thesis, put to verse, includes these apt lines:

> As he explores these culture wars, he seems to be inviting
> What used to be a weakness of the school of "realist" writing,
> Ascribing to a concept, like a culture or a state,
> A physical reality which doesn't quite equate.
> This realist bard from Harvard Yard distorts important factors,
> Converting complex cultures into unitary actors;
> What Morgenthau and Wolfers did with power among nations,
> Huntington has nearly done with full-scale civilizations.[3]

Contemporary events both support and refute Huntington's thesis. Since al Qaeda's attacks on the United States in September 2001 and the start of the U.S. war on terrorism, a generic version of the culture-clash idea seems to be resonating not only in the American public discourse but also elsewhere, including in the Arab

---

[3] Frederick S. Tipson, "Culture Clash-ification: A Verse to Huntington's Curse," FOREIGN AFFAIRS 76, 2, (March/April 1997): p. 168. Reprinted by permission of FOREIGN AFFAIRS, March/April 1997. Copyright 1997 by the Council on Foreign Relations, Inc.

world and especially in the "Arab street." This does not mean that the West versus Islam corollary of the thesis is correct, but there appears to be a kernel of truth in the "microfoundations" of the argument. That is to say, whatever one concludes about the clash of civilizations and the likelihood of global cultural conflict or "fault line wars," there is a social-psychological distance that has more clearly come into view in recent years. Surely that distance has been overstated by some commentators and militants on both sides of the civilizational divide, but it is palpable and very strongly felt by many who are in a position to inflict violence on "the other." For the United States and its friends, the use of military force against the governments of Islamic countries always carries a risk of making the clash of civilizations hypothesis into a self-fulfilling prophecy.

One problem with the civilizational explanation in this and other cases is that intercultural conflict and intracultural cooperation are accompanied by their opposites. In Europe, enthusiasts of NATO expansion have been successful in bringing into the alliance countries east of Europe's cultural fault line, like Romania and Bulgaria, and they want to see others admitted as well (Albania, Macedonia, Georgia, and Ukraine top the list). Romania and Bulgaria are also EU members now, and Macedonia is set to join. If Turkey joins, the EU will have reached well beyond what Huntington delineated as the eastern boundary of Western civilization. In the Balkans, a shared suspicion of the West also has not provided much in the way of cultural affinities between Muslims and Orthodox Christians, while overt military conflicts in the region saw NATO assisting Muslims, not Christians. And in the Arab world, even Islamic fundamentalism, though a potent force for anti-Western sentiment, has neither prevented Saudi Arabia's tilt toward the West nor insulated the Saudi monarchy from fundamentalist-based threats.

Civilizations differ from one another in their political and economic institutions and in the preferences and behavior patterns of their citizens. Huntington suggests that the Western commitment to democracy and market capitalism makes it distinctive from many other civilizations, especially the Islamic one. But institutions and preferences are not immutable, and sometimes they can be changed drastically. After World War II, a "new" Germany and Japan became democratic, and many of their citizens took up pacifist views about international relations. Germany and Japan remained deeply attached to their civilizations, but their behavior in world politics shifted radically. Other countries (like Russia) have radically changed their institutions and shifted their international behavior. Most Islamic countries are not democratic. But can they become so? Many of the sharpest cultural fault lines correspond to democratic–authoritarian fault lines, with sharp breaks in otherwise dense networks of international trade and organizations. Are countries like the Sudan and Iran on the "wrong" side of these fault lines because of a fundamentalist Islamic culture? Was Taliban-ruled Afghanistan? Or is militant fundamentalism more the consequence of isolation from global forces? Perhaps a less confrontational Islam can flourish in a more connected world.

GLOBALIZATION AND FRAGMENTATION

A third global future contains elements of both Fukuyama's end of history and Huntington's clash of civilizations. For Benjamin Barber there are two simultaneous trends in world politics: globalization and fragmentation. Globalization, as we discussed in Chapter 14, involves the declining significance of international borders for the flow of goods, capital, people, and ideas. More to the point, globalization seems to be dominated by the flow of *Western* goods, capital, people, and ideas, which is what Fukuyama finds so compelling. For Barber, the icons of globalization include MTV, Macintosh, and McDonald's, which lend themselves to a convenient shorthand for the process he describes—"McWorld." At the same time, there is a countertendency. This involves fragmentation, a tribalization of nation-states, with new divisions emerging between peoples. Because these divisions, like those identified by Huntington, are defined by cultural and religious differences, Barber uses the term *jihad*—the Arabic word meaning spiritual and religious struggle—to summarize this tendency in world politics. The future, then, will be characterized by the clash of these two trends: "Jihad vs. McWorld."[4]

As does Huntington's culture clash, Barber's jihad conjures up a rather gloomy vision of the future. Unlike Huntington, however, Barber sees this culture clash as a more thoroughly local and fragmenting phenomenon, without the sort of unifying cultural affinities that bring states together into larger civilizational blocs in Huntington's future. The progressive tendencies of Barber's McWorld resemble those that Fukuyama associates with Western liberalism, but Barber sees no end of history in sight. Jihad won't become McWorld; in fact, jihad may be partly brought about by the alienating impact of McWorld, especially among non-Western peoples. Furthermore, Barber fears that neither McWorld nor jihad bode well for the future of democracy. Consumerism supplants participatory politics and human rights on the list of social priorities in McWorld, for democratic ideals cannot be allowed to impede the march toward domestic market reforms, free trade, and foreign investment. Jihad is even more explicitly antidemocratic. Not only is there a willingness to defer to local demagogues, but the exclusion of outsiders from the political community can take on ruthless proportions, as in the case of "ethnic cleansing" in the Balkans. Jihad is not multiculturalism.

"Jihad vs. McWorld" is not exactly a radical vision of the future, as we have characterized the radical view of world politics in this book, but the theme of global capitalism's alienating effects as well as the struggle against its universalizing tendencies is also one found in radical scholarship. However, Barber does not expect that McWorld will come crashing down as a result of its own internal contradictions (nor do many radical scholars, really). Instead, he hopes for a "confederal option," in which democratic ideals can be shored up in the face of antidemocratic trends associated with both globalization and fragmentation. So do we.

A FINAL WORD

In this book we have discussed the different levels at which world politics is analyzed and the variety of interactions and interdependencies that constitute both challenges and opportunities for the new millennium. We have examined the

---

[4] See Benjamin R. Barber, "Jihad vs. McWorld," *Atlantic Monthly* (March 1992): 53–61, and *Jihad vs. McWorld: How Globalism and Tribalism Are Reshaping the World* (New York: Random House, 1995).

behavior of individual states and the consequences of their pursuit of narrowly defined self-interests. These interests derive from political processes in various governments and societies: organizational and bureaucratic dynamics, domestic interest groups like big business or peace activists, and public opinion in general. The outcomes of these political processes help determine whether states will "defect" in the prisoner's dilemma situations that pervade world politics. The outcomes of these political processes may also encourage states to free ride in the context of multilateral efforts at cooperation, expecting to benefit from collective goods like environmental preservation without making any of the sacrifices. While scholars may concentrate on one or another level for purposes of analysis, all the levels are linked. They create a complex set of interrelationships that present each of us—state leaders and ordinary citizens—with a menu for choice.

The three theoretical perspectives that have surfaced throughout this book—realism, liberalism, and radicalism—are not merely worldviews possessed by distant observers. They motivate the policies advocated by domestic groups and pursued by state leaders. These policies not only vary among states but are held variously by the same states over time. Of some periods of history we might say that world politics was marked by a high degree of competition, as highlighted by realists: alliance formation, arms races, frequent crises, and wars deriving from unstable balances of power or economic conflicts. Other periods, often following wars, witness creative challenges to established political practices and ways of thinking. New approaches to conflict resolution or the creation of new international organizations and regimes have often been associated with an increased willingness to apply liberal or radical solutions to recurring problems in world politics. We may not be fully trapped in a realist world where the central principle is the competitive pursuit of power.

Despite numerous challenges to sovereignty, the Westphalian state system is still with us, and nation-states continue to play on center stage. Yet the actions of individuals do have an impact on the future. We each have conceptions of our interests, and the inclusion of the interests of others in our calculations will make a difference. After all, our interests are reflected in the demands we make on our governments. Politics and society—domestic and international—may be slow to change, but they do change, and often for the better.

You may recall the famous opening lines of Charles Dickens's *A Tale of Two Cities:*

> It was the best of times, it was the worst of times, it was the age of wisdom, it was the age of foolishness, it was the epoch of belief, it was the epoch of incredulity, it was the season of Light, it was the season of Darkness, it was the spring of hope, it was the winter of despair, we had everything before us, we had nothing before us.

These lines refer to the social and psychological upheavals associated with revolutionary change at the end of the eighteenth century. Revolutions are periods fraught with problems and the dangers they pose, but also with opportunities for progress if those problems can be solved. We too live in a period of change—some might even say revolutionary change. Ahead of us we see a series of challenges to peace, liberty, and human development in an increasingly interdependent world.

But we also see progress: the erosion of some long-standing global and regional rivalries, the spread of democracy, and an ever rising standard of living for many of the world's people. The challenges are indeed daunting, but the possibilities are enormous. We hope you will close this book with a deeper understanding of what the world looks like and how it works, and a commitment to make it better.

GLOSSARY

absolute gains Shorthand for arrangements that improve the welfare of a state or society, even when those arrangements may be of greater benefit to other states or societies.

alliance States that behave as a coalition, formalized by a written treaty, for purposes of military security.

anarchy An arrangement that lacks a higher authority, and a central feature of the modern international system.

arms control A process that produces agreements either to limit the production or use of weapons or to manage them.

arms race An action–reaction process of acquiring arms in response to the arms acquisitions of an adversary.

assumption A statement that is not evaluated empirically because it is straightforward or because examining its accuracy must be deferred until later.

assurance game A game in which moving from the socially suboptimal to the socially optimal outcome requires some confidence that other players will not defect.

autarky A policy of minimizing trade in favor of domestic production of all goods and services required by society.

balance of power An arrangement, whether bipolar or multipolar, in which capabilities are fairly evenly distributed among the major actors.

balancing Joining the weaker alliance of states in an effort to offset the power of the stronger state or alliance of states.

bandwagoning Joining the stronger alliance of states in the hope of sharing the spoils of victory.

bargaining The process by which two or more parties attempt to settle on the terms of an exchange.

basic needs strategy An approach to development combining local economic incentives with the provision of essentials to the population such as subsidized food, health care, and education.

belief system An integrated set of images and values making up the relevant universe for an individual, encompassing the past, the present, and expectations of the future.

biodiversity Biological diversity, or the number and variety of living things on Earth.

biological weapons Weaponized biological agents—including living organisms, viruses, and toxins derived from them—designed to cause disease and death.

bipolar An international system with exactly two power centers.

brinkmanship A strategy of taking a contest to the point in which both opponents are threatened with great harm or death.

cartel A group of countries often able to exercise influence over the market price of a particular good or commodity through coordinated production and distribution.

chemical weapons Weaponized chemical agents designed to attack the body's nervous system, blood, skin, or lungs.

chicken A game in which each of two opponents threatens the other with great harm or death in an effort to force capitulation.

Coase theorem States that, when property rights are well-defined, there will be no market failures, including failures of the type associated with tragedies of the commons.

cognitive consistency When the mental images held by individuals do not clash with or contradict each other; the opposite of cognitive dissonance.

collective good A good, provided to the collective, that cannot be consumed exclusively by those who pay for it or denied to those who don't; also called *public good*.

collective security An arrangement by which all members of the international community agree to oppose together a threat to the security of any one of them.

common market A grouping of national economies in which barriers to the free movement of labor and capital have been removed.

507

common-pool resources Natural resources that do not fall under any state's sovereign jurisdiction and are therefore available to all.

communitarianism The belief that conceptions of justice emerge from the historical, cultural, and religious experiences shared by the members of a political community.

comparative advantage The benefits of specializing in goods that a state can produce relatively efficiently, even if that state is not the most efficient producer in an absolute sense.

compellence A policy aimed at influencing another state or nonstate actor to stop an action it is already pursuing; also called *coercive diplomacy.*

complex interdependence The idea that interdependence elevates the importance of nonstate actors, international economic issues, and the resolution of conflict using nonmilitary means.

constructivism A perspective that emphasizes the importance of shared meanings in the construction of interests, institutions, and identities in world politics.

contagion A process of spreading currency crises that may be driven as much by geography and trade patterns as by economic or financial weaknesses in the afflicted countries.

cosmopolitanism The belief that conceptions of justice derive from individuals' membership in the community of humankind and should not be particular to political communities.

customary law Customary practice regarded as binding because a majority of states feel a legal obligation to conform.

customs union A grouping of national economies that impose a common set of tariffs on imports from countries outside the group.

decision making The process of evaluating and choosing among alternative courses of action.

defense conversion The process of converting the defense-industrial base to civilian production and attending to accompanying economic and social dislocations.

defense mechanism A mental process protecting an individual from realizations that would otherwise make the individual uncomfortable and anxious.

deforestation The clearing, fragmenting, or degradation of forests.

democratic peace The phenomenon whereby stable democracies are unlikely to engage in militarized disputes with each other or to let any such disputes escalate to war.

demographic transition A process of falling death rates and then falling birthrates experienced by developing societies, in the middle stages of which population growth is at its highest.

dependency theory A perspective that attributes underdevelopment in the Global South to the unequal economic relationships linking industrialized and nonindustrialized countries.

deterrence A policy aimed at influencing another state or nonstate actor to not do something it would otherwise do.

diplomacy Direct, government-to-government interactions between foreign officials in order to communicate desires and accomplish goals.

disarmament A process aimed at reducing in number or totally eliminating weapons.

discrimination In just war doctrine, the requirement that combatants respect the immunity of noncombatants from direct, deliberate attack.

diversionary war International armed conflict intended to divert the public's attention away from domestic problems or unpopular leaders.

dominant strategy In game theory, a move or series of moves that is best for a player no matter what the other players do.

double effect In just war doctrine, the requirement that noncombatant deaths be unintended and proportional to the legitimate end sought through military action.

economic coercion A conflictual form of economic statecraft that can vary in severity from tariffs, quotas, or other restrictions on free trade to economic warfare.

economic integration The process, perhaps slow and incomplete, of amalgamating a group of smaller national economies into a larger one.

economic liberalism Economic principles emphasizing the importance of private ownership, free markets, and the unimpeded flow of goods, capital, and labor.

economic nationalism An appeal designed to decrease demand for foreign goods in an effort to sustain the viability of certain domestic industries, and especially to protect jobs.

embedded liberalism The pursuit of liberal economic policies while cushioning society against the dislocations caused by exposure to international market forces.

empirical theory Theoretical statements about what international actors do, how they do it, and why, with the expectation that they can be evaluated through observation.

equilibrium In game theory, a stable outcome in which all sides have made their best moves in response to each other; also called *Nash equilibrium.*

ethnopolitical conflict Conflict between ethnically and often culturally distinct peoples; also called *communal conflict.*

Eurozone Territory encompassing the twelve European Union states that have adopted the euro as their common currency.

evidence Empirical information collected in order to support an argument or test a hypothesis.

externality The benefits or costs of goods experienced by those who do not own them (private goods) or who have not contributed to them (collective or public goods).

failed state State whose government, if it exists at all, cannot provide citizens with the minimum level of security and well-being expected of a sovereign state.

first-strike capability The ability to launch an initial nuclear attack on an opponent and greatly reduce its ability to retaliate.

fixed exchange rates An aspect of a monetary regime in which foreign currency values are pegged to a common currency such as the U.S. dollar.

floating exchange rates An aspect of a monetary regime in which foreign currency values vary relative to each other in response to supply and demand in currency markets.

foreign policy A guide to action taken beyond the boundaries of a state to further the goals of the state.

formal theory A theory stated in the language of mathematics or formal logic.

free-rider dilemma A situation in which individuals who stand to benefit from a collective good have no incentive to contribute, thus threatening the provision of the good.

free-trade area A grouping of national economies in which there are no tariffs on goods traded among them.

frontier In formal or game theory, the limit of all possible bargains between players.

functionalism The idea that international organizations should aim to solve problems arising in specific functional areas, after which those solutions may be applied in other areas.

game A strategic interaction consisting of moves and countermoves.

game theory A mathematical approach to analyzing strategic interactions between two or more players.

gender gap The observed differences in foreign policy attitudes held by women as compared to men.

geopolitics The conduct of foreign policy with a view to the political-geographic arrangement of states such as physical location, topography, and resource possession.

global civil society Complex of non-governmental entities, including individuals, groups, and institutions, that interact across state boundaries.

global warming A gradual increase in world temperatures, the permanence, effects, and causes of which are debated.

globalization A process whereby economic, political, and sociocultural transactions are decreasingly constrained by national boundaries and the authority of national governments.

governmental politics model A model of decision making that emphasizes the bargaining, compromising, arm twisting, and favor trading going on within bureaucratic organizations.

groupthink A phenomenon often observed in small-group decision making in which individual views tend to conform to group views.

guns versus butter A way to summarize the presumed trade-offs between military preparedness and economic performance during peacetime.

hegemonic stability A theory emphasizing that international stability is brought about by a single state's ability to

establish and enforce the international rules of the game.

hierarchy An arrangement in which formal authority is stratified; sometimes used to describe the stratified distribution of wealth, military capability, or prestige.

human rights Rights possessed by individuals because they are human, not because they are citizens of one state or another.

human security A broad conception of security, including security against violence, the provision of basic human needs, and the protection of human rights.

humanitarian intervention The use of military force, without the consent of the target state, in which the main purpose is to relieve human suffering.

hypothesis A statement that relates a theory to possible observations about the world.

idealism Label applied to the view, popularized during the interwar period, that envisioned the construction of a new and peaceful world order, especially among democratic nations.

idiosyncrasies An individual's values, personality, political style, intellect, and past experience that work together to create a set of images about the world.

IMF conditionality The right of the International Monetary Fund to exercise some supervision over a borrower's economic policies, monetary or fiscal, as a condition for a loan.

import substitution industrialization A strategy of promoting industrial development by substituting domestically manufactured goods for imported ones.

industrial policy A set of arrangements whereby the central government assists certain industries deemed crucial to the nation's economic strength.

intelligence The product of a state's information collection and analysis.

interdependence A relationship in which changes or events in one part of the system produce some reaction or have some significant consequence for other parts of the system.

intergovernmental organization (IGO) An international organization composed of states, in which delegates represent the interests and policies of their home governments.

intergovernmentalism Institutional arrangement whereby authoritative decisions are made by representatives of states acting on behalf of their governments.

international institutions Broadly defined, the formal and informal practices that constitute appropriate behavior in world politics.

international organization Broadly defined, the ways states arrange themselves for purposes of promoting cooperative and collaborative practices in world politics.

international political economy (IPE) The realm of combined political and economic behavior, as well as outcomes, taking place among state and nonstate international actors.

just war tradition A set of principles that identify the circumstances justifying the resort to war (*jus ad bellum*) and, once begun, the requirements for just conduct (*jus in bello*).

legal positivism A viewpoint suggesting that international law consists of nothing more than the customs, agreements, and treaties that states actually make.

levels of analysis A framework for organizing explanations in world politics in terms of the size and complexity of the actors, behavior, and outcomes involved.

liberalism A perspective that emphasizes the importance of institutions and linkages between states for facilitating cooperation, coordination, and nonviolent modes of conflict resolution.

lifeboat ethics A metaphor likening the Earth to a lifeboat and the view that the sharing of resources discourages responsible behavior and thereby threatens to submerge the boat.

maximize utility To select a course of action that will yield the outcome with the greatest benefits relative to costs.

mercantilism Economic doctrine by which states in sixteenth- and seventeenth-century Europe amassed trade surpluses in the form of gold and silver as a means of maximizing wealth and power.

military–industrial complex Sectors of society that benefit from spending on national defense, including the defense industry and professional military establishment.

minimum deterrence A nuclear strategy requiring only a second-strike capability that can be achieved with a relatively small nuclear stockpile.

misperception A mental process in which information is ignored, incorrectly interpreted, or changed to fit existing images.

modern state system Often dated from the Peace of Westphalia in 1648, the system consisting mainly of nation-states, each with sovereign authority over its internal affairs.

modernization theory A perspective that attributes underdevelopment in the Global South to the features of traditional society, which will become transformed over time.

monetary regime An arrangement to help states manage their exchange rates, maintain their reserve currencies, and regulate the movement of international capital.

monetary union A grouping of national economies that have adopted a common currency, central banking system, and monetary policy.

multilateralism An approach to foreign policy that treats international collaboration as a binding norm and not simply as appropriate when it promotes the state's self-interests.

multinational corporation (MNC) An economic enterprise with subsidiaries in one or more countries.

multipolar Describes an international system with multiple power centers.

mutual assured destruction (MAD) A situation in which neither of two states can launch a nuclear attack without suffering enormous damage from a retaliatory attack by the other.

nation A people who feel themselves part of some large identity group.

national missile defense (NMD) A system designed to protect a state's homeland from a ballistic missile strike.

nationalism The set of psychological, cultural, and social forces that drive the formation of a nation and sustain national identity.

nation-state Synonymous with "state" or "country," but with the added implication that the subject population identifies itself as a nation.

natural law Those rights and responsibilities presumed to apply to all members of the community of humankind,

irrespective of their status as citizens of states.

negotiation Bargaining in the form of verbal communication that aims to resolve the parties' incompatible goals.

new international economic order (NIEO) Economic arrangements more favorable to the South, including commodity price stabilization, development assistance, and debt relief.

nonalignment The refusal of a nation to join coalitions or alliances.

nongovernmental organization (NGO) A transnational organization composed of private actors, whether individuals or groups.

nontariff barrier to trade (NTB) A protectionist measure such as a quota, voluntary export restriction, subsidy, boycott, or embargo.

normative theory Theoretical statements about the rightness or wrongness of what international actors do, as well as the justice or injustice of the outcomes.

North–South gap The disparity in development between industrialized countries, located mainly in the Northern Hemisphere, and developing countries, located mainly in the Southern Hemisphere.

nuclear triad A nuclear force structure consisting of bomb-carrying aircraft, land-based missiles, and submarine-basedmissiles.

nuclear weapons Weapons that use massive amounts of energy released by atomic nuclei when split (fission) or combined (fusion).

operational code Mental construct that helps to organize knowledge about other actors or situations.

opportunity Shorthand for the possibilities and constraints that face decision makers.

organizational process model A model of decision making that emphasizes the cautious and incremental remedial approach adopted by bureaucratic organizations.

ozone layer Threatened by carbon dioxide and other emissions, an atmospheric layer that screens out cancer-causing ultraviolet radiation from the sun.

pacifism A viewpoint that rejects in principle the use of force as an instru-

ment of national policy; a philosophical or moral predilection for nonviolence.

Peace of Westphalia Settlement ending the Thirty Years' War in 1648, which reinforced the sovereignty of monarchs and is commonly considered the dawn of the modern state system.

peacekeeping The employment of force for purposes of conflict management or settlement, usually by way of separating warring parties and creating conditions for negotiation.

political openness Extent to which a government is subject to influences from society.

power The ability to overcome obstacles and influence outcomes.

preference ordering The ranking of outcomes for an individual or group.

primacy A term used to describe the predominance (if not hegemony) of U.S. power in the contemporary international system.

principal–agent problem When subordinates' access to information and resources allows them to pursue their own interests at the expense of the interests of their superiors.

prisoner's dilemma A game in which the best strategy for both opponents is to defect but that yields an outcome worse than the one achieved by mutual cooperation.

probabilistic explanation An explanation that is contingent—that is, it holds only under certain conditions.

proliferation The increase in the number of state, and potentially nonstate, actors that possess a certain class of weaponry.

property rights The ability to freely choose how to use or dispense with a particular good or service.

proportionality In just war doctrine, the requirement that the legitimate aims sought by a state resorting to war outweigh the harm resulting from the prosecution of the war.

prospect theory A perspective suggesting that decision makers are willing to take greater risks to protect what they have, and fewer risks to acquire what they want.

protectionism A policy of restricting, but not eliminating, imports in an effort to maintain or nurture the economic viability of domestic industries.

radicalism A perspective that emphasizes the conflicting economic interests of social classes and the injustices experienced by the less advantaged.

rally-'round-the-flag The phenomenon whereby a leader is able to gather popular support for foreign policy initiatives, especially during an international crisis.

rational actor model A model of decision making that emphasizes the process of selecting goals, identifying options, evaluating consequences, and making choices.

rationalism Approach that conceptualizes states and nonstate entities as rational actors pursuing their interests subject to limits imposed by their capabilities and environment.

rationality A characteristic of purposive behavior, or an ability to relate means to ends.

realism A perspective that emphasizes the importance of self-interest, power, and the competitiveness of states in an anarchic international system.

reciprocity A strategy or pattern of behavior in which one actor undertakes similar actions in response to actions directed toward it.

reflectivism A perspective that rejects the idea that a social scientific approach to world politics can be modeled on the natural sciences.

regime The complete set of rules that govern behavior in some specified area of international relations.

regionalism The concentration of economic transactions, as well as the coordination of foreign economic policies, among a group of countries within a geographic region.

relative deprivation A common cause of civil conflict; results when people feel deprived relative to others or relative to their own expectations.

relative gains Shorthand for arrangements that improve the welfare of a state or society to a greater degree than they do for other states or societies.

reprisal An action that is itself unlawful but is taken in response to a previous unlawful act with the intent of persuading the initial law breaker to change its ways.

satisfice To select the first course of action that satisfies a minimal set of requirements, yielding an acceptable outcome.

screening The process by which individuals and organizations filter information about the world.

second-strike capability The capacity to absorb an enemy's initial nuclear attack and have enough weapons remaining to inflict unacceptable damage in retaliation.

security community A group of people who have attained, within a territory, a sense of community, as well as institutions and practices that ensure expectations of peaceful change.

security dilemma A situation in which one state's security is seen as another state's insecurity, leading to a vicious circle of competitive power accumulation.

self-defense In international law, the right that permits a state to use military force to reverse an act of armed aggression.

sensitivity In the context of international interdependence, a condition in which actions or policies undertaken by one state bring about reactions or policy changes by another state.

social choice An action or outcome chosen by society, based on an aggregation of preferences held by groups or individuals within it.

socially optimal An outcome in which no actor does better without another actor doing worse; also called "Pareto optimal."

soft power The ability to exercise influence through attraction rather than coercion or reward.

sovereign immunity The immunity of state leaders from prosecution by other states for their official public actions.

sovereignty Independence from any authority outside one's territory (external sovereignty); supreme authority over all other entities within one's territory (internal sovereignty).

spaceship Earth A metaphor likening the Earth to a spaceship with limited resources, in which humankind must learn to sustain itself without exhausting the ship's reservoirs.

stability Used to describe an international system with infrequent military conflict or minimal volatility in international economic relations.

state A legal entity consisting of a government that manages the affairs of a population in a given territory.

state-sponsored terrorism International terrorist activity conducted by states or with state support through the provision of arms, training, safe haven, or financing.

state terrorism A state's use of terror against its own populations to gain or increase control through fear.

strategic trade A trade policy in which the state promotes certain export industries by providing government subsidies or other forms of assistance.

structural violence Deprivations enforced, often subtly, by repressive social and political systems that are resistant to change.

supranational authority Possessed by an international organization, the authority to overrule the national governments of member states on certain issues.

supranationalism Institutional arrangement whereby authoritative decisions are made by representatives of an international organization and are binding on member states.

sustainable development The pursuit of human, economic, and social development while at the same time preserving the ecological systems on which development depends.

system A set of interacting elements, whether in the physical or the social world.

tariff A tax or duty levied on an imported good in order to raise revenue or to regulate the flow of the good into the country.

technology The application of human skills or techniques to accomplish human purposes.

terms of trade The value of exported goods relative to imported goods, which has generally favored manufactured goods over commodities.

terrorism Shocking acts of violence in which the principal purpose is not destruction itself but the dramatic and psychological effects on populations and governments.

theory An intellectual tool that provides a way of organizing the complexity of the world and helps to show how phenomena are interrelated.

tit for tat A strategy of cooperating after an opponent cooperates and defecting after the opponent defects.

tragedy of the commons The threat to shared resources that comes from individuals having few incentives to curb their destructive behaviors.

transaction costs The expenditure of resources required to negotiate, monitor, and enforce contracts.

transnational relations The multiplicity of interactions that bypass the governments of states and impact directly on their domestic environments.

treaty A formal agreement signed by states that specifies their rights and obligations in some area of international interaction.

unilateralism An approach to statecraft that places a premium on freedom of action and regards cooperation as worthwhile only when it serves the national interest.

unipolar Describes an international system with a single major actor, usually a single state, that possesses a predominant share of capabilities and influence.

universal jurisdiction The claimed authority to try an accused individual whether or not the accused is a national or committed crimes against nationals.

utility For an actor, the net value derived from a chosen course of action or outcome; also called *payoff*.

vulnerability In the context of international interdependence, a condition in which a state must absorb higher costs because it cannot pursue alternative policies.

weapons of mass destruction (WMD) Immensely destructive weapons—including nuclear, chemical, and biological weapons—that are designed to distribute their effects over large areas.

willingness Shorthand for the goals and motivations that lead decision makers to avail themselves of opportunities.

world federalism The idea that permanent peace can be achieved only by establishing a world government.

world system theory A holistic view of the global economy highlighting the relationships of dominance and dependence linking the "center" (North) and the "periphery" (South).

zone of peace An area, comprising most of the industrialized countries of the world, in which war or the expectation of war is absent.

CHRONOLOGY OF WORLD EVENTS

1804	Napoléon becomes emperor of France.
1812	Napoléon invades Russia: Disastrous campaign ultimately leads to French defeat.
1814–1815	Congress of Vienna: Victorious powers reconstitute European order.
1823	Monroe Doctrine: President James Monroe declares the Western Hemisphere off limits to European interference.
1846	Mexican war: The United States defeats Mexico, annexes New Mexico and California (war ends in 1848).
1848	*Communist Manifesto* published by Karl Marx and Friedrich Engels. Antimonarchical liberal revolutions in France, Prussia, Austria-Hungary, and the Italian states.
1852	Napoléon III establishes the Second French Empire.
1853	Japan opened to West by American Commodore Matthew Perry.
1854–1856	Crimean War: France and Britain ally with Turkey against Russia.
1857–1858	Sepoy rebellion: Indian soldiers revolt against British rule in India.
1859	Construction begins on Suez Canal (completed in 1869).
1861	Kingdom of Italy established after process of unification led by Sardinia; emancipation of serfs in Russia; U.S. Civil War (1861–1865).
1864	First International organized by Marx in London.
1864–1870	Lopez War: Argentina, Brazil, and Uruguay virtually destroy Paraguay.
1867	British North America Act creates Canada as a confederation; Marx publishes *Capital*. United States purchases Alaska from Russia.
1870–1871	Franco-Prussian war: German states, led by Prussia, invade and defeat France, completing a process of German unification.
1871	German empire established under leadership of Prussia; Wilhelm I becomes kaiser.
1878	Congress of Berlin: European powers meet to thwart Russia and carve up Ottoman Empire.
1882	Triple Alliance is formed by Germany, Austria-Hungary, and Italy.

1894–1895	Sino-Japanese War: Japan defeats China and becomes an imperial power with acquisition of Taiwan.
1898	Spanish-American War: United States defeats Spain, acquires the Philippines, and becomes a great power.
1899	"Open Door" policy forced on China by the Western powers. Boer War (1899–1902) between British and Dutch settlers begins in South Africa.
1900	Boxer rebellion: Forces of the European powers, Japan, and the United States sent to China to put down revolt against foreign penetration.
1904–1907	Entente Cordiale signed between France and England. (1907: Russia joins and Triple Entente is formed.) Russo-Japanese War: Japan defeats Russia, becomes great power (1904–1905).
1911	Chinese Revolution led by Sun Yat-sen removes emperor and establishes a republic.
1912–1913	First and Second Balkan wars drive Turkey from Europe.
1914	June: Assassination of Archduke Franz Ferdinand of Austria-Hungary. August: World War I breaks out between Triple Entente and Central Powers; Panama Canal opens.
1917	April: United States enters World War I on the side of the Allies. November: Bolshevik Revolution in Russia, led by Vladimir Ilyich Lenin.
1918	March: Treaty of Brest-Litovsk: Bolshevik government of Russia signs separate peace with Germany. November: Armistice signed; World War I ends.
1919	Treaty of Versailles negotiated by victors of World War I (signed by Germans in June).
1920	January: League of Nations, created by Treaty of Versailles, established in Geneva; United States does not join.
1922	October: Benito Mussolini and Fascist party come to power in Italy. December: Union of Soviet Socialist Republics is officially created, the first communist state.
1923	October: Kemal Ataturk's westernized Turkish Republic officially proclaimed.
1924	January: Lenin dies; Joseph Stalin emerges as Soviet leader.
1929	October: Great Depression begins with the collapse of the New York stock market.
1931	September: Japan occupies Manchuria.
1933	January: Adolph Hitler comes to power in Germany.
1934–1935	Mao Zedong leads the Red Army on the Long March in China.
1936	July: Spanish Civil War begins, is a precursor of World War II (Spanish Civil War ends January 1939 with fascist Francisco Franco as ruler of Spain). November: Rome-Berlin-Tokyo Axis formed (formalized in 1937 treaty).
1938	September: Munich agreement—French and British appease Germany over claims to Czechoslovakia.
1939	August: Germany and the Soviet Union sign a nonaggression pact. September: Germany invades Poland, World War II begins.
1941	December: Japan attacks Pearl Harbor, United States enters World War II.
1944	July: Bretton Woods meeting establishes postwar economic system.
1945	February: Yalta Conference—Churchill, Roosevelt, and Stalin plan postwar Europe. May 8: V-E (Victory in Europe) Day marking German surrender. June: United Nations charter signed in San Francisco. August: Hiroshima destroyed by first atomic bomb used in war; August 15, V-J (Victory in Japan) Day, Japanese surrender.

1947	June: Marshall Plan for economic recovery of Europe proposed. August: British leave Indian subcontinent; India and Pakistan separate and become independent.
1948	February: Communists seize power in Czechoslovakia. May: Israel established as an independent state; first Arab–Israeli war (ends January 1949). June: Soviets bar Western access to Berlin, Allies supply city by airlift (blockade ends May 1949).
1949	April: North Atlantic Treaty Organization (NATO) established. August: Soviet Union explodes its first atomic weapon. October: People's Republic of China proclaimed.
1950	June: North Korea invades the South; Korean War begins. October: Communist China enters Korean War.
1951	March: European Coal and Steel Community formed (a founding institution of the European Union).
1952	November: United States explodes the first hydrogen (thermonuclear) bomb.
1953	March: Stalin dies. July: Korean armistice signed.
1954	July: Geneva settlement ends French rule in Indochina; Vietnam divided into North and South.
1955	May: West Germany joins NATO; Warsaw Treaty Organization (Warsaw Pact) established.
1956	July: Gamal Abdal Nasser nationalizes Suez Canal. October: Hungarian revolt against communist rule crushed by Soviet troops. October–November: Britain, France, and Israel invade Egypt (Suez War).
1957	March: European Economic Community (France, West Germany, Belgium, Luxembourg, the Netherlands, and Italy) established by the Treaty of Rome. October: Soviet Union launches Sputnik, first artificial satellite.
1958	July: United States sends troops to Lebanon; Britain sends troops to Jordan to forestall radical takeovers.
1959	January: Fidel Castro leads the overthrow of President Fulgencio Batista in Cuba.
1960	February: France explodes an atomic weapon. July: The Republic of the Congo becomes independent; civil war begins.
1961	April: United States sponsors unsuccessful Bay of Pigs invasion of Cuba. August: East Germany builds the Berlin Wall.
1962	October: Cuban missile crisis. October–November: China and India fight border war.
1963	November: President John F. Kennedy assassinated in Dallas.
1964	October: Nikita Khrushchev deposed by Leonid Brezhnev and Aleksei Kosygin; China explodes its first atomic bomb.
1965	April: U.S. sends troops to Dominican Republic. July: President Lyndon Johnson announces major U.S. buildup in Vietnam. September: War between India and Pakistan over Kashmir begins.
1966	April: Mao-inspired Cultural Revolution begins in China.
1967	May: Biafran civil war begins; Nigerian government ultimately defeats attempt at secession (ends January 1970). June: Six-Day War between Israel and Egypt, Jordan, and Syria.
1968	July: Nonproliferation treaty signed by United States, the Soviet Union, and Britain. September: Soviet and Warsaw Pact troops invade Czechoslovakia.
1969	March: Soviet–Chinese conflict erupts into border fighting at the Ussuri River. July: American Neil Armstrong is first human being to walk on the moon.

1970	September: Socialist Salvador Allende elected president of Chile (killed during a coup to overthrow his government in September 1973).
1971	October: People's Republic of China admitted to United Nations. December: Bangladesh established by breakaway of East Pakistan after civil war and India-Pakistan War.
1972	February: U.S. President Richard Nixon visits People's Republic of China. May: United States and the Soviet Union sign strategic arms limitation treaty (SALT I).
1973	January: Britain, Denmark, and Ireland join European Community. October: Yom Kippur War between Israel and Egypt and Syria. November: Arab members of OPEC embargo oil to U.S.
1974	May: India explodes nuclear device. August: Nixon resigns as president of United States after Watergate affair.
1975	April: Serious fighting begins in civil war in Lebanon; Saigon falls and Indochina War ends with collapse of U.S.–backed South Vietnam and Cambodia.
1976	September: China's Mao Zedong dies.
1977	August: United States and Panama sign treaty to cede Panama Canal to Panama. November: Egyptian president Anwar Sadat makes dramatic trip to Israel.
1978	August: China and Japan sign treaty of peace and friendship. December: United States and People's Republic of China establish full diplomatic relations.
1979	January: Ayatollah Khomeini forms Islamic republic in Iran. March: Egypt and Israel sign peace agreement. June: U.S. and Soviet Union sign SALT II. November: U.S. embassy personnel taken hostage in Iran. December: Soviet troops invade Afghanistan.
1980	September: Iraq attacks Iran. October: Strikes by Polish workers' union (Solidarity) force extensive concessions from government.
1981	January: Greece joins European Community. October: Egypt's President Sadat assassinated by Muslim extremists. December: General Wojciech Jaruzelski declares martial law in Poland.
1982	April: Argentina seizes Falkland Islands; British naval and air forces retake them by June. May: Spain becomes sixteenth member of NATO. December: Final act of the Law of the Sea Convention signed.
1983	September: Korean Airlines civilian passenger plane shot down over Soviet territory. October: Nearly 300 French and U.S. peacekeeping troops killed by terrorist bombs in Lebanon; U.S. invades Grenada.
1984	October: India's Prime Minister Indira Gandhi assassinated.
1985	March: Soviet leader Chernenko dies, is succeeded by Mikhail Gorbachev.
1986	January: Spain and Portugal join European Community; U.S. space shuttle Challenger explodes. May: Nuclear accident at Chernobyl power station in the Soviet Union.
1987	January: Gorbachev calls for glasnost and political reforms. September: Treaty to protect the ozone layer is approved. December: U.S. and the Soviet Union sign INF Treaty to eliminate intermediate range missiles.
1988	May: Soviet troops begin withdrawal from Afghanistan. August: Iran and Iraq agree to cease-fire.
1989	April: Chinese students rally in Beijing, marking onset of democracy movement (in June pro-democracy movement is crushed in Tiananmen Square as troops kill thousands). November: Berlin Wall falls.
1990	February: South African government legalizes the African National Congress and Nelson Mandela is freed from jail. March: Communist party loses its monopoly in the Soviet Union. August: Iraq invades Kuwait. October: East and West Germany unite. November: The UN authorizes the use of force against Iraq.

1991	January: UN coalition, led by the United States, launches air war against Iraq, retakes Kuwait in February. June: South Africa repeals land laws central to apartheid; fighting erupts in Yugoslavia over Slovenian and Croatian secession. July: Warsaw Pact dissolves. December: Union of Soviet Socialist Republics dissolves.
1992	March: Referendum among South African whites endorses new constitution and end to minority rule; Bosnia secedes from Yugoslavia and fighting erupts between Bosnian Muslims, Serbs, and Croats. June: Earth Summit held in Rio de Janeiro. December: United States, Canada and Mexico sign NAFTA treaty.
1993	January: United States and Russia sign START II. September: Israeli Prime Minister Rabin and PLO Chairman Arafat agree to framework for Palestinian self-rule. November: European Community's Maastricht Treaty goes into effect. December: Joint Irish-British framework for peace in Northern Ireland is issued.
1994	April: Civil war and massive ethnic violence breaks out in Rwanda. May: Nelson Mandela and ANC win South Africa's first universal suffrage elections; PLO assumes self-rule in Gaza and parts of the West Bank. July: Israel and Jordan formally end state of war. December: Russian army invades Chechnya.
1995	January: World Trade Organization (WTO) starts functioning. May: Indefinite extension of the NPT approved by over 170 countries; NATO launches air attacks against Bosnian Serb positions. November: Dayton Accord ends fighting in Bosnia, creating a Muslim–Croat federation and a Serb republic.
1996	January: Yasir Arafat is elected president of the Palestinian Authority. November: Pope John Paul II visits Cuba. December: Kofi Annan is named secretary-general of the UN; Guatemalan government and leftist rebels sign agreement to end thirty-six years of civil war.
1997	February: China's Deng Xiaoping dies at age 92. May: Mobutu Sese Seko of Zaire is overthrown, country renamed Democratic Republic of Congo. July: Britain returns Hong Kong to China; Thai currency crisis, later spreads to wider Asian financial crisis. December: 125 countries sign a treaty banning landmines.
1998	April: Britain and Ireland sign peace accord on Northern Ireland to end the 30-year conflict. May: India and then Pakistan explode five underground nuclear devices. July: UN General Assembly votes to create ICC to prosecute crimes against humanity. August: Car bombs explode at U.S. embassies in Kenya and Tanzania. October: Former Chilean dictator Augusto Pinochet is arrested in Britain on a Spanish warrant.
1999	January: Eleven EU currencies tied to the euro. March: Czech Republic, Hungary, and Poland join NATO; NATO begins air assault against Yugoslavia to stop attacks in Kosovo. October: General Pervez Musharraf takes control of Pakistan in coup. November–December: WTO summit in Seattle disrupted by protests; Panama Canal comes under Panamanian control; new government in Northern Ireland begins self-rule.
2000	March: Vladimir Putin elected President of Russia. May: Israel withdraws from Southern Lebanon after twenty-two years. June: Complete map of human genome announced. September: Israeli Likud leader Ariel Sharon visits Temple Mount/Haram al-Sharif, sparking Palestinian rioting. October: Yugoslav President Slobodan Milosevic steps down after nationwide uprising. November: Peruvian President Alberto Fujimori resigns amid corruption scandal, taking refuge in Japan.
2001	February: Ariel Sharon wins Israeli election amid severe Israeli–Palestinian violence. April: U.S. spy plane and Chinese jet collide, triggering diplomatic standoff. June: Slobodan Milosevic delivered to war crimes tribunal in The Hague. September: Al-Qaeda militants crash passenger jets into the World Trade Center and the Pentagon. October: U.S. and British forces begin air

campaign against al-Qaeda and Taliban in Afghanistan (Taliban regime collapses in December). December: China joins WTO.

2002   January: Euro enters circulation. February: Longtime Angolan rebel leader Jonas Savimbi is killed, rebel force enters talks with government. March: Israeli launches large-scale military operations in West Bank. May: U.S. and Russia agree to reduce nuclear arms to low levels; Russia accorded near equal status in NATO decision making. June: United States abandons the ABM Treaty. July: International Criminal Court begins functioning. September: Weapons inspections resume in Iraq.

2003   March: U.S.–led forces invade Iraq (topple Ba'ath regime in April); World Health Organization declares SARS a global health threat. April: North Korea says it possesses nuclear weapons. June: United States announces withdrawal of 14,000 troops from South Korean side of DMZ. July: Iraqi interim government established. August: UN headquarters in Baghdad attacked. December: Libya begins dismantling WMD programs; Iranian earthquake kills 30,000.

2004   March: Al Qaeda attacks train in Madrid, ruling party loses elections; NATO expands eastward, adding seven new members. April: Photos surface showing abuse of Iraqi prisoners by U.S. personnel at Abu Ghraib. May: EU expands eastward, adding ten new members. June: U.S. restores Iraqi sovereignty. November: Yasir Arafat dies; massive protests lead to new Ukrainian elections. December: Earthquake and tsunami kills more than 200,000 in South and Southeast Asian coastal areas.

2005   January: Iraq holds legislative elections. February: Kyoto Protocol enters into force; former Lebanese leader Rafik Hariri assassinated, protests lead to Syrian withdrawal. April: Pope John Paul II dies, succeeded by Benedict XVI. June: Mahmoud Ahmadinejad wins presidential election in Iran. July: Four bombs explode in London, linked to al Qaeda. August: Israeli settlements dismantled in Gaza after 38 years of occupation. October: Earthquake in Pakistan kills 80,000; Iraqis ratify new constitution; trial of Saddam Hussein begins. November: Ariel Sharon quits Israel's Likud Party, forms centrist Kadima.

2006   January: Hamas wins majority in Palestinian legislative elections. March: Slobodan Milosevic dies in Hague jail cell; Basque separatists in Spain lay down arms. April: Iran announces it has enriched uranium. June: Montenegro becomes independent state; U.S. Supreme Court rules Guantánamo military tribunals violate Geneva Conventions. July: Israel launches war against Hezbollah in Lebanon (ends in August). October: North Korea tests nuclear bomb; Muhammad Yunus of Bangladesh wins Nobel Peace Prize for work on microcredit. November: Saddam Hussein convicted of crimes against humanity (hanged in December).

2007   January: EU admits Bulgaria and Romania. February: North Korea agrees to dismantle nuclear program; ICJ rules 1995 Bosnian massacre a genocide. March: Power-sharing agreement signed for Northern Ireland. May: ICC issues arrest warrants for Sudanese politician and militia leader for crimes in Darfur. June: Factional fighting in Gaza leaves Hamas in control, Fatah retains West Bank. Iraq convicts three for 1988 gas attack on Kurds. September: Israel strikes nuclear facilities in Syria. October: IPCC and Al Gore receive Nobel Peace Prize for work on climate change. December: Benazir Bhutto assassinated in Pakistan.

2008   January: Violence sweeps Kenya after disputed presidential election. February: Fidel Castro resigns after 49 years as Cuban leader; Kosovo declares independence from Serbia. March: Vladimir Putin's hand-picked successor wins Russian presidential elections, Putin named prime minister. May: Cyclone hits Myanmar killing more than 100,000; earthquake kills 70,000 in China. August: Russia invades Georgia after Georgian troops attack in South Ossetian separatists. September: U.S. bank failures trigger worst global financial crisis since the Great Depression.

CHARACTERISTICS OF STATES IN THE CONTEMPORARY INTERNATIONAL SYSTEM

Appendix B lists all independent states in the international system as of December 2007, along with some of their key demographic, economic, social, and political characteristics. Except for political freedom, data come from the U.S. Central Intelligence Agency, *The 2008 World Factbook* (Washington, D.C.: U.S. Central Intelligence Agency, 2008), available online at http://www.cia.gov/library/publications/the-world-factbook. Most figures are for the years 2006 or 2007, but in some cases the latest available data are for earlier years. Two dots (..) indicate that recent figures are not available.

1. *Year of Independence.* The year of independence for all states that became independent after the Peace of Westphalia in 1648. If no date is provided, the state was independent before 1648.
2. *Population.* Figures are in millions.
3. *Area.* Area is reported in thousands of square kilometers (1 square kilometer = 0.386 square miles).
4. *GDP.* Gross domestic product represents the sum of all economic activity undertaken within a given country, whether by nationals or non-nationals. Figures are in billions of "international" dollars, calculated using purchasing power parity (PPP) rates.
5. *GDP per capita.* GDP is divided by the country's population and expressed in thousands of international dollars, and is an indicator of average economic well-being.
6. *Trade.* Trade is the value of all exports and imports as a percentage of GDP. Figures can exceed 100 percent.
7. *Military Spending.* This is how much was spent on the military establishment in millions of dollars. Figures generally exclude expenditures on internal policing. Zeros indicate that country maintains no regular military.

8. *Infant Mortality*. Infant mortality is the number of newborn deaths before one year of age for every 1,000 live births. When the figure is divided by 10, it can be interpreted as the probability that a child born in 2007 will die during the year.

9. *Life Expectancy*. This is the expected life span for a child born in 2007.

10. *Internet Users*. Figures show the number of Internet users in the population, in thousands.

11. *Electricity Consumption per capita*. This is the total amount of electricity consumed within the country, expressed as kilowatt hours per person.

12. *Political and Civil Freedom*. States are labeled as free (F), partly free (PF), or not free (NF) based on a number of indicators of political rights and civil liberties. Data are from Freedom House, *Freedom in the World 2008: The Annual Survey of Political Rights and Civil Liberties* (Lanham, Md.: Rowman & Littlefield, 2008); available online at http://www.freedomhouse.org.

Country	Year of Independence	Population (millions)	Area (1,000 km²)	GDP ($ billions, PPP)	GDP per capita ($ thousands)	Trade (% of GDP)	Military Spending ($ millions)	Infant Mortality (per 1,000 live births)	Life Expectancy (years)	Internet Users (thousands)	Electricity Consumption per capita (kW hours)	Status of Freedom
Afghanistan		32.7	648	35	1,069	12	665	155	44	535	24	PF
Albania	1912	3.6	29	20	5,459	22	294	19	78	471	918	PF
Algeria	1962	33.8	2,382	269	7,963	33	8,874	29	74	2,460	815	NF
Andorra		0.1	0.5	3	38,253	73	0	4	84	23	..	F
Angola	1975	12.5	1,247	81	6,460	67	4,614	182	38	85	176	NF
Antigua & Barbuda	1981	0.1	0.4	1	17,024	51	0	18	73	32	1,398	F
Argentina	1816	40.7	2,767	524	12,874	18	6,808	14	77	8,184	2,187	F
Armenia	1991	3.0	30	17	5,669	26	1,094	21	72	173	1,837	PF
Australia	1901	20.6	7,687	767	37,222	38	18,403	5	81	15,300	10,669	F
Austria		8.2	84	320	38,962	99	2,877	4	79	4,200	7,343	F
Azerbaijan	1991	8.2	87	72	8,829	36	1,877	56	66	829	3,363	NF
Bahamas	1973	0.3	14	7	22,524	44	35	24	66	103	5,731	F
Bahrain	1971	0.7	0.7	25	34,261	93	1,107	16	75	157	10,600	PF
Bangladesh	1971	153.5	144	209	1,362	13	3,138	57	63	450	127	PF
Barbados	1966	0.3	0.4	6	19,612	36	28	11	73	160	3,143	F
Belarus	1991	9.7	208	105	10,810	48	1,466	7	70	5,478	3,045	NF
Belgium	1831	10.4	31	379	36,419	171	4,926	5	79	4,800	7,977	F
Belize	1981	0.3	23	2	7,754	47	33	24	68	34	540	F
Benin	1960	8.3	113	12	1,468	14	207	76	54	700	71	F
Bhutan	1949	0.7	47	4	5,134	19	35	52	66	30	557	NF

Country	Year of Independence	Population (millions)	Area (1,000 km²)	GDP ($ billions, PPP)	GDP per capita ($ thousands)	Trade (% of GDP)	Military Spending ($ millions)	Infant Mortality (per 1,000 live births)	Life Expectancy (years)	Internet Users (thousands)	Electricity Consumption per capita (kW hours)	Status of Freedom
Bolivia	1825	9.2	1,099	40	4,302	19	756	49	67	580	366	PF
Bosnia & Herzegovina	1992	4.6	51	30	6,512	44	1,345	9	78	950	1,868	PF
Botswana	1966	1.8	600	24	13,103	31	797	44	50	60	1,412	F
Brazil	1822	191.9	8,512	1,838	9,577	15	47,788	27	73	42,600	1,920	F
Brunei Darussalam	1984	0.4	6	10	25,060	92	430	13	76	166	6,883	NF
Bulgaria	1878	7.3	111	87	11,942	56	2,255	19	73	1,870	5,150	F
Burkina Faso	1960	15.3	274	18	1,146	12	210	86	53	80	31	PF
Burundi	1962	8.7	28	6	735	6	377	61	52	60	19	PF
Cambodia	1953	14.2	181	26	1,811	36	774	57	62	44	15	NF
Cameroon	1960	18.5	475	40	2,166	18	520	65	53	370	186	NF
Canada	1867	33.2	9,985	1,274	38,359	66	14,014	5	81	22,000	16,265	F
Cape Verde	1975	0.4	4	4	8,686	22	26	43	71	29	98	F
Central African Republic	1960	4.4	623	3	699	12	34	82	44	13	23	PF
Chad	1960	10.1	1,284	16	1,577	34	670	100	47	60	9	NF
Chile	1810	16.5	757	234	14,246	46	6,329	8	77	4,156	2,936	F
China		1,330.0	9,597	7,043	5,295	30	302,849	21	73	162,000	2,150	NF
Colombia	1810	45.0	1,139	320	7,118	18	10,894	20	73	6,705	864	PF
Comoros	1975	0.7	2	1	1,725	14	35	69	63	21	25	PF

Country											
Congo, Democratic Rep.	1960	66.5	2,345	19	287	20	477	83	54	180	9	NF
Congo, Rep.	1960	3.9	342	14	3,579	59	433	81	54	70	1,351	NF
Costa Rica	1821	4.2	51	56	13,334	38	224	9	77	1,214	1,853	F
Côte d'Ivoire	1960	18.4	322	33	1,788	72	526	86	49	300	158	NF
Croatia	1991	4.5	57	69	15,460	55	1,660	6	75	1,576	3,333	F
Cuba	1902	11.4	111	51	4,474	28	1,942	6	77	240	1,214	NF
Cyprus	1960	0.8	9	21	27,012	43	814	7	78	357	5,217	F
Czech Republic	1993	10.2	79	249	24,372	89	3,637	4	77	3,541	5,843	F
Denmark		5.5	43	205	37,304	99	3,069	4	78	3,171	6,203	F
Djibouti	1977	0.5	23	2	3,710	101	71	99	43	11	448	PF
Dominica	1978	0.1	0.8	0.5	6,688	80	0	14	75	26	1,026	F
Dominican Republic	1844	9.5	49	85	8,983	23	683	27	73	1,232	925	F
Ecuador	1822	13.9	284	98	7,056	27	2,752	21	77	1,549	636	PF
Egypt	1922	81.7	1,001	432	5,286	16	14,685	28	72	6,000	1,034	NF
El Salvador	1821	7.1	21	36	5,090	35	1,799	22	72	637	753	F
Equatorial Guinea	1968	0.6	28	26	41,673	52	26	84	61	8	42	NF
Eritrea	1993	5.0	121	5	945	12	299	44	60	100	45	NF
Estonia	1991	1.3	45	29	22,446	89	587	7	73	760	5,268	F
Ethiopia		78.3	1,127	55	704	10	1,652	90	49	164	33	PF
Fiji	1970	0.9	18	5	5,451	85	112	12	70	80	789	PF
Finland	1917	5.2	338	186	35,445	100	3,718	4	79	2,925	16,830	F
France		64.1	643	2,067	32,268	56	53,742	3	81	31,295	7,048	F

Country	Year of Independence	Population (millions)	Area (1,000 km²)	GDP ($ billions, PPP)	GDP per capita ($ thousands)	Trade (% of GDP)	Military Spending ($ millions)	Infant Mortality (per 1,000 live births)	Life Expectancy (years)	Internet Users (thousands)	Electricity Consumption per capita (kW hours)	Status of Freedom
Gabon	1960	1.5	268	20	13,521	44	683	53	54	81	835	PF
Gambia	1965	1.7	11	1	771	32	7	69	55	58	78	PF
Georgia	1991	4.6	70	20	4,243	33	116	17	77	332	1,759	PF
Germany	1871	82.4	357	2,833	34,394	88	42,495	4	79	38,600	6,623	F
Ghana	1957	23.4	239	31	1,336	39	250	52	59	610	295	F
Greece	1829	10.7	132	326	30,440	32	14,035	5	80	2,048	5,065	F
Grenada	1974	0.1	0.3	1	10,870	39	0	14	66	19	1,544	F
Guatemala	1821	13.0	109	67	5,188	30	270	29	70	1,320	489	PF
Guinea	1958	10.2	246	10	954	19	166	87	50	50	82	NF
Guinea Bissau	1973	1.5	36	0.9	600	37	28	102	48	37	37	PF
Guyana	1966	0.8	215	4	5,263	33	73	30	66	160	974	F
Haiti	1804	8.9	28	16	1,773	15	63	62	58	650	36	PF
Honduras	1821	7.6	112	25	3,232	43	148	25	69	337	528	PF
Hungary	1944	9.9	93	194	19,555	88	3,399	8	73	3,500	3,623	F
Iceland	1944	0.3	103	12	39,065	87	0	3	81	194	26,783	F
India	1947	1,148.0	3,288	2,965	2,583	12	74,125	32	69	60,000	426	F
Indonesia	1945	237.5	1,919	846	3,560	24	25,368	31	70	16,000	455	F
Iran	1979	65.9	1,648	853	12,943	16	21,315	37	71	18,000	2,068	NF

Country												
Iraq	1932	28.2	437	100	3,543	57	8,600	45	70	36	1,270	NF
Ireland	1921	4.2	70	188	45,114	115	1,688	5	78	1,437	5,796	F
Israel	1948	7.1	21	185	25,997	55	13,498	4	81	1,899	6,085	F
Italy	1861	58.1	301	1,800	30,957	53	32,400	6	80	28,855	5,282	F
Jamaica	1962	2.8	11	13	4,803	59	81	16	74	1,232	2,186	F
Japan		127.3	378	4,417	34,701	28	35,336	3	82	87,540	7,653	F
Jordan	1946	6.2	92	28	4,546	61	2,423	16	79	797	1,370	PF
Kazakhstan	1991	15.3	2,717	162	10,528	46	1,454	27	68	1,247	4,982	NF
Kenya	1963	38.0	583	58	1,519	20	1,614	56	57	2,770	118	PF
Kiribati	1979	0.1	0.8	0.2	2,175	33	0	45	63	2	76	F
Korea, Democratic Rep.	1945	23.5	121	40	1,704	11	5,217	22	72	..	791	NF
Korea, Rep.	1945	49.2	98	1,206	24,496	60	32,562	6	77	34,120	7,487	F
Kuwait	1961	2.6	18	139	53,373	56	7,346	9	78	817	13,971	PF
Kyrgyz Republic	1991	5.4	199	10	1,938	34	145	32	69	298	1,532	PF
Laos	1949	6.7	237	13	1,888	15	63	80	56	25	179	NF
Latvia	1991	2.2	65	40	17,832	53	480	9	72	1,071	2,712	F
Lebanon	1943	4.0	10	41	10,234	32	1,260	23	73	950	2,664	PF
Lesotho	1966	2.1	30	3	1,451	81	80	79	40	52	159	F
Liberia	1847	3.3	111	1	449	557	19	144	41	1	89	PF
Libya	1951	6.2	1,760	79	12,762	66	3,073	22	77	232	2,945	NF
Liechtenstein	1806	0.03	0.2	2	51,771	190	0	5	80	22	..	F
Lithuania	1990	3.6	65	60	16,714	67	715	7	75	1,083	2,607	F

Country	Year of Independence	Population (millions)	Area (1,000 km²)	GDP ($ billions, PPP)	GDP per capita ($ thousands)	Trade (% of GDP)	Military Spending ($ millions)	Infant Mortality (per 1,000 live births)	Life Expectancy (years)	Internet Users (thousands)	Electricity Consumption per capita (kW hours)	Status of Freedom
Luxembourg	1839	0.5	3	39	79,814	120	349	5	79	339	12,994	F
Macedonia	1991	2.1	25	17	8,373	50	1,036	9	74	268	4,197	PF
Madagascar	1960	20.0	587	20	995	15	200	56	63	110	49	PF
Malawi	1964	13.9	118	10	752	15	136	91	43	60	93	PF
Malaysia	1957	25.3	330	358	14,161	85	7,265	16	73	11,292	3,115	PF
Maldives	1965	0.4	0.3	3	7,487	39	156	52	65	20	414	NF
Mali	1960	12.3	1,240	14	1,151	19	269	104	50	70	65	F
Malta	1964	0.4	0.3	9	23,151	82	65	4	79	127	4,855	F
Marshall Islands	1986	0.1	0.2	0.1	1,820	55	0	26	71	2	3,650	F
Mauritania	1960	3.4	1,031	6	1,729	49	320	67	54	100	615	PF
Mauritius	1968	1.3	2	15	11,694	41	45	13	74	182	109	F
Mexico	1810	110.0	1,973	1,353	12,305	40	6,765	19	76	22,000	1,667	F
Micronesia	1986	0.1	0.7	0.3	2,573	53	0	27	71	16	1,659	F
Moldova	1991	4.3	34	10	2,312	50	40	14	71	728	1,284	PF
Monaco		0.0	0.002	1	29,769	167	0	5	80	20	89,645	F
Mongolia	1921	3.0	1,564	8	2,820	47	118	41	67	268	6	F
Montenegro	2006	0.7	14	26	38,898	3	15	..	..	266	..	PF
Morocco	1956	34.3	447	127	3,698	27	6,350	38	72	6,100	602	PF

Mozambique	1975	21.3	802	18	837	32	143	108	178	429	PF
Myanmar	1948	47.8	679	91	1,908	10	1,914	49	32	78	NF
Namibia	1990	2.1	825	11	5,109	53	395	46	81	1,371	F
Nauru	1968	0.01	0.02	0.1	4,357	33	0	9	0.3	2,026	F
Nepal	1768	29.5	147	31	1,039	11	491	62	249	66	PF
Netherlands	1579	16.6	42	639	38,383	136	10,222	5	14,544	6,500	F
New Zealand	1907	4.2	269	113	26,980	51	1,126	5	3,200	8,959	F
Nicaragua	1821	5.8	129	18	3,140	32	109	26	155	506	PF
Niger	1958	13.3	1,267	9	678	14	117	115	40	33	PF
Nigeria	1960	138.3	924	295	2,132	31	4,422	94	8,000	122	PF
Norway	1905	4.6	324	257	55,421	82	4,891	4	4,074	24,524	F
Oman	1970	3.3	212	61	18,483	55	6,978	17	319	2,615	NF
Pakistan	1947	167.8	804	446	2,659	12	14,275	67	12,000	400	NF
Palau	1994	0.02	0.5	0.1	5,902	91	0	14	..	..	F
Panama	1903	3.3	78	29	8,850	75	291	15	220	1,438	F
Papua New Guinea	1975	5.9	463	17	2,792	41	232	47	110	580	PF
Paraguay	1811	6.8	407	27	3,887	52	266	26	260	878	PF
Peru	1821	29.2	1,285	218	7,454	21	3,263	30	6,100	774	F
Philippines	1946	92.7	300	299	3,225	34	2,690	21	4,615	506	PF
Poland	1918	38.5	313	625	16,223	46	10,681	7	11,000	3,127	F
Portugal		10.7	92	232	21,729	53	5,336	5	3,213	4,547	F
Qatar	1971	0.9	11	58	62,123	84	5,769	17	290	13,482	NF

Country	Year of Independence	Population (millions)	Area (1,000 km²)	GDP ($ billions, PPP)	GDP per capita ($ thousands)	Trade (% of GDP)	Military Spending ($ millions)	Infant Mortality (per 1,000 live births)	Life Expectancy (years)	Internet Users (thousands)	Electricity Consumption per capita (kW hours)	Status of Freedom
Romania	1881	22.2	238	247	11,089	42	4,687	24	72	5,063	2,629	F
Russia	1991	140.7	17,075	2,076	14,755	30	80,964	11	66	25,689	7,002	NF
Rwanda	1962	10.2	26	9	842	8	249	83	50	65	19	NF
St. Kitts & Nevis	1983	0.04	0.3	0.7	18,325	64	0	13	73	10	2,935	F
St. Lucia	1979	0.2	0.6	1	6,820	92	0	12	74	55	1,636	F
St. Vincent & Grenadines	1979	0.1	0.4	0.9	7,616	85	0	14	74	..	903	F
Samoa	1962	0.2	3	1	5,611	37	0	25	72	8	450	F
San Marino		0.03	0.1	0.9	28,359	391	0.7	5	82	15	..	F
Sao Tome & Principe	1975	0.2	1	0.3	1,348	28	2	38	68	23	81	F
Saudi Arabia	1932	28.2	2,150	572	20,319	52	57,220	12	76	4,700	5,216	NF
Senegal	1960	12.9	196	21	1,603	26	289	59	57	650	145	F
Serbia		10.2	77	57	5,600	48	1,274	..	75	1,400	..	F
Seychelles	1976	0.1	0.5	2	20,122	70	33	14	73	29	2,634	PF
Sierra Leone	1961	6.3	72	5	776	16	112	156	41	10	36	PF
Singapore	1965	4.6	0.7	223	48,327	380	10,912	2	82	1,717	7,795	PF
Slovakia	1993	5.5	49	108	19,724	104	2,012	7	75	2,256	4,570	F
Slovenia	1991	2.0	20	55	27,290	107	931	4	77	1,251	6,829	F
Solomon Islands	1978	0.6	28	0.8	1,376	62	24	20	73	8	96	PF
Somalia	1960	9.6	638	6	583	20	50	111	49	94	26	NF
South Africa	1910	43.8	1,220	468	10,679	32	7,949	58	42	5,100	5,513	F

Country	Year											Status
Spain		40.5	505	1,362	33,637	45	16,344	4	80	18,578	6,001	F
Sri Lanka	1948	21.1	66	83	3,938	23	2,163	19	75	428	335	PF
Sudan	1956	40.2	2,506	108	2,680	16	3,234	87	50	3,500	82	NF
Suriname	1975	0.5	163	3	7,246	78	21	19	73	32	2,990	F
Swaziland	1968	1.1	17	5	4,805	83	255	70	32	42	1,063	NF
Sweden		9.0	450	333	36,825	100	4,997	3	81	6,981	14,825	F
Switzerland		7.6	41	301	39,689	130	3,009	4	81	4,360	7,684	F
Syria	1946	19.7	185	83	4,203	28	4,897	27	71	1,500	1,722	NF
Taiwan	1949	22.9	36	690	30,108	68	15,182	5	78	13,210	9,642	F
Tajikistan	1991	7.2	143	12	1,646	33	463	42	65	20	2,482	NF
Tanzania	1964	40.2	945	43	1,081	15	87	70	51	384	30	PF
Thailand		65.5	514	520	7,938	51	9,358	18	73	8,466	1,797	PF
Timor-Leste	2002	1.1	15	2	1,998	10	..	42	67	1	..	PF
Togo	1960	5.9	57	5	876	36	82	58	58	320	98	PF
Tonga	1970	0.1	0.7	0.9	7,369	18	8	12	70	3	395	PF
Trinidad & Tobago	1962	1.0	5	23	21,893	90	69	24	67	163	6,763	F
Tunisia	1956	10.4	164	77	7,431	42	1,080	23	76	1,295	1,076	NF
Turkey		71.9	781	668	9,287	40	35,388	37	73	12,284	1,794	PF
Turkmenistan	1991	5.2	488	47	9,146	27	1,611	52	69	65	1,468	NF
Tuvalu	1978	0.01	0.03	0.01	1,227	93	0	19	69	1	..	F
Uganda	1962	31.4	236	31	1,003	13	692	66	52	750	53	PF
Ukraine	1991	46.0	604	321	6,986	31	4,498	9	68	5,545	3,955	PF

Country	Year of Independence	Population (millions)	Area (1,000 km²)	GDP ($ billions, PPP)	GDP per capita ($ thousands)	Trade (% of GDP)	Military Spending ($ millions)	Infant Mortality (per 1,000 live births)	Life Expectancy (years)	Internet Users (thousands)	Electricity Consumption per capita (kW hours)	Status of Freedom
United Arab Emirates	1971	4.6	84	146	31,549	169	4,520	13	76	1,709	11,386	NF
United Kingdom		60.9	245	2,147	35,229	47	51,528	5	79	33,534	5,722	F
United States	1776	303.8	9,827	13,860	45,618	23	562,716	6	78	208,000	12,560	F
Uruguay	1825	3.5	176	37	10,653	27	593	12	76	756	2,021	F
Uzbekistan	1991	28.3	447	62	2,203	18	1,245	68	65	1,700	1,663	PF
Vanuatu	1980	0.2	12	0.7	3,430	27	0	51	64	8	177	F
Venezuela	1811	26.4	912	335	12,682	33	4,020	22	73	4,140	2,777	PF
Vietnam	1945	86.1	330	223	2,584	49	5,563	24	71	17,870	596	NF
Yemen	1918	23.0	528	53	2,286	27	3,472	56	63	270	147	PF
Zambia	1964	11.7	753	16	1,365	44	287	101	39	335	742	PF
Zimbabwe	1980	12.4	391	35	500	64	235	51	40	1,220	991	NF

NAME INDEX

Note: Page numbers followed by n indicate names appearing in footnotes.

A

Abbott, Kenneth W., 69n14
Acheson, Dean, 179
Adams, Gordon, 343, 344n12
Adams, James, 224n36
Adler, Emanuel, 319n19
Ahmadinejad, Mahmoud, 17
Albright, Madeleine, 152
Alexander the Great, 77
Allende, Salvador, 72, 453–454
Allison, Graham, 164, 165n2, 174, 174n8, 239n11
Alperovitz, Gar, 5n3, 265n6
Alston, Philip, 279n20
Alter, Karen J., 405n6
Alvarez, Michael E., 460n23
al-Zawahiri, Ayman, 10
Anderson, Benedict, 54, 54n3
Anderson, Kenneth, 295n28
Anderson, Lisa, 11n9
Anderson, Warren C., 477n11
Andreas, Peter, 413n12
Andropov, Yuri, 6, 189
Annan, Kofi, 130
Aquinas, Thomas, 263
Arafat, Yasser, 127, 154
Arbenz, Jacobo, 72
Arbetman, Marina, 120n12
Arce, M., Daniel G., 417n16
Aristotle, 51, 467, 468
Arquilla, John, 223n35, 224n36, 428n27
Arrow, Kenneth, 140
Asch, S. E., 178n11
Atatürk, Mustafa Kemal, 185
Atef, Mohammed, 11

Augustine of Hippo, 263
Avant, Deborah D., 177n10, 354n25
Axelrod, Robert, 32n6, 247, 248n20, 377n10, 470n5

B

Bahgat, Gawdat, 341n9
Baker, James, 125
Baldwin, David A., 133n27, 337n4, 337n5
Bales, Kevin, 427n26
Ban Ki-moon, 293
Baran, Paul A., 348n18, 440n7
Barber, Benjamin R., 503–504, 504n4
Barber, James David, 187, 187n22
Barbieri, Katherine, 311n9
Barnet, Richard, 424n23
Barnett, Michael, 69n14, 215n26, 274n14, 319n19
Bates, Robert H., 444n10
Bayulgen, Oksan, 454n19
Beck, Robert J., 181n15
Begin, Menachim, 159
Behrens, William W., 473n7
Bellamy, Alex J., 319n19
Ben Gurion, David, 185
Bennett, Andrew, 375n8
Bercovitch, Jacob, 127n22, 211n23, 303n5
Berdal, Mats, 217n29
Bergsten, C. Fred, 380n13
Bernstein, Barton J., 5n3
Betts, Richard K., 122n15
Bhabha, Homi K., 52n2
Bhagwati, Jagdish, 425n25

Bially, Janice, 115n9
Biersteker, Thomas J., 413n12
Bigo, Didier, 410n10
bin Laden, Osama, 10, 109, 119, 157, 219
Bismarck, Otto von, 22, 184
Blair, Bruce G., 253n25
Blanchard, Jean-Marc F., 337n4
Blanton, Shannon Lindsey, 357n27
Boehmer, Charles, 314n13
Boli, John, 70n15
Bonaparte, Napoléon, 22, 61, 112, 131, 209, 323, 500
Bono, 71
Bonturi, Marcos, 10n8
Booth, Ken, 15n12
Bordo, Michael D., 384n17
Boswell, Terry, 454n19
Botea, Roxana, 56n5
Boulding, Kenneth E., 77, 77n2, 301, 301n2, 477, 480, 480n12
Bouton, Marshall, 162n24
Bracken, Paul, 238n10
Bramson, Leon, 195n4
Brauer, Jurgen, 361n29
Brauninger, Thomas, 469n3
Breitmeier, Helmut, 470n4
Bremer, Stuart, 77n1
Brewer, Marilynn B., 320n20
Brezhnev, Leonid, 6, 15, 77, 188, 189
Brody, Reed, 286n24
Bronowski, Jacob, 20, 20n15, 36, 36n11
Brooks, Stephen G., 89n13

SUBJECT INDEX

Note: Page numbers followed by f indicate figures, those followed by t indicate tables, those followed by m indicate maps, and those followed by b indicate boxes.

9/11, 10–13

A

ABM. *See* Antiballistic missile treaty (ABM)
Absolute advantage, 367
Absolute gains, 334
Abu Ghraib prison, 271, 355
Accession, 275
Action-reaction hypothesis, 228
Actors in world politics, 19–21
  intergovernmental organizations, 19
  international actors, 54–64
  international nongovernmental organizations, 19
  nation-states, 19
  nation-states as unitary, 137
  organizations in nation-states, 19
  relations between nation-states and, 15, 18
Acts of aggression, 284
Actual authority, 55
Adequate nourishment, 481
Administrative decisions, 170
Adult literacy, 434
Advanced Research Projects Agency (ARPA), 347
Afghanistan, 5, 6
  al Qaeda and, 10, 11
  economic sanctions and, 337
  external assistance and, 216
  prisoners of war and, 271, 272
  public support for war in, 18
  sanctions against, 337
  Soviet intervention in, 42, 149, 156, 257

  Soviet withdrawal from, 5, 85
  Taliban and, 12, 18, 271
  U.S. invasion of, 267–268
Africa
  disease statistics in, 432, 435–436
  food insecurity in, 481
  human development in, 435
African Postal Union, 70
African Union, 287
Agency for the Prohibition of Nuclear Weapons in Latin America and the Caribbean, 314
Agent Orange, 239
Aggression
  acts of, 284
  relative deprivation and, 196–198
  sociobiological perspective on, 195
Agricultural Development Fund, 482
Agriculture, 481
AIDS. *See* HIV-AIDS rate
Al-Jazeera effect, 270
Alliance portfolios, 86
Alliances, 85–87
Al Qaeda, 67, 219, 221, 267
  bombing of World Trade Center, 10–13
  POW protections and, 272
  training camps in Afghanistan, 11
American primacy
  world order and, 100–103
American Revolution, 218
Amnesty International, 19, 71, 280
Amsterdam treaties, 410
Analysis, levels of. *See* Levels of analysis
Analytical approaches, 27

Anarchist systems, 59, 61, 82, 240–241, 279
Andean Trade Preference Act (ATPA), 415
Angola, 6, 216
Animal Farm (Orwell), 64
Antiballistic missile treaty (ABM), 257
Antiglobalization movement, 424–425
Anti-Personnel Mine Convention, 259
Apartheid, 339
APEC. *See* Asia Pacific Economic Cooperation (APEC) forum
Aquaculture, 481
Arab League, the, 69, 88
Arable land, 481
Arab Street, 502
Arab world
  repression in, 11
  resentment of US, 109
Argentina, 97, 221, 277
  economic development in, 438, 447
Armed forces. *See* Military
Arms control, 32, 150, 227
  disarmament and, 253–260
  minimizing risk of accidents, 256
  negotiations, 172
  nuclear, 156, 234, 254–259
  sovereignty and, 240
Arms races, 228
Arms suppliers, 357–358
Arms transfers, 356–357, 357–360
ARPA. *See* Advanced Research Projects Agency (ARPA)
Arrows impossibility theorem, 140b6.1

OECD. *See* Organization for Economic
Cooperation and Development
(OECD)
Offensive idealism, 102
Offensive realists, 100, 101
American primacy and, 101
Official development assistance (ODA),
449
Offshore balancing, 100
Oil companies, 72
Oil embargoes, 107, 338
Oil resources, 340–342
U.S. invasion of Iraq, 200
Oman
female literacy and, 434
gross domestic product (GDP), 434
Omnibus Trade and Competitiveness
Act, 390
On War (Clausewitz), 131
OPEC. *See* Organization of Oil
Exporting Countries (OPEC)
Openness, 124, 141, 304, 321–322,
393, 460
Open regionalism, 417
Open treaties, 124
Operational codes, 184
Operation Barbarossa, 86
Operation Desert Storm, 155, 270
Operation Iraqi Freedom, 157, 270
Opinio juris, 276
Opinion leaders, 146
Opponent's leadership, stereotyped view
of, 179
Opportunity, 21, 22, 39b2.1
Opportunity costs, 350
Optimism, 248
Optimum currency area (OCA),
407–408
Ordering principles, 95b4.1
Organizational interests, 16
Organizational process model, 174
Organization for Economic Coopera-
tion and Development (OECD),
299–303, 309–314, 320–321,
345, 379–380, 389, 432–435,
447–450, 455
Organization of African Unity (OAU), 67
Organization of American States (OAS),
67, 287
Organization of Oil Exporting Coun-
tries (OPEC), 107, 109, 338,
384, 445–446, 455, 483–484
Organization on Security and Coopera-
tion in Europe (OSCE), 69
OSCE. *See* Organization on Security
and Cooperation in Europe (OSCE)
Oslo Accords, 125, 127
Ottoman Empire, 53
Our Common Future (UN Commission
on Environment and
Development), 473

Outsourcing, 354–355
Overfarming, 473
Ozone layer, 489

P

P5. *See* United Nations Security
Council: permanent members
of (P5)
Pacific Rim, 389, 393
Pacifism, 262
Pacts, 275
Pakistan, 38, 113, 214, 258
assistance to Afghanistan, 216
Bengali secession from, 214, 284
India and, 38, 76–77, 111,
127–128, 238, 253, 284
Islam and, 113
nuclear weapons and,
113, 115, 259, 260
terrorism in, 270
Palestine, 10
Palestine Liberation Organization
(PLO), 127
Palestinian Authority, 73, 125
Panama Canal treaties, 161
Panic, 450
Paquete Habana, 276
Pareto optimal frontier, 128b5.1
Paris Club, the, 448
Parliamentary diplomacy, 125
Partial Test Ban Treaty, 258
Partnership for Peace, 249
Party of European Socialists, 405
Patriot Act, 158
Pax Americana, 101
Pax Britannica, 101
Pax Romana, 315
Peace, 299–320
between democracies, 313–314
democratic, 302–304
dividend, 352
economic growth, 311–315
economic interdependence and,
310–315
enforcement, 295
integration and, 315–320
intergovernmental organization
membership and, 314–315
perpetual, 306–310, 306–315, 322
salaam *vs.* sulah, 301–302
stable, 302
unstable, 301
zone of, 299–301, 303
Peacekeeping, 294–297
Peace of Augsburg, 57
Peace of Westphalia, 57, 59, 279,
366
Pearl Harbor, 121, 173

Peloponnesian League, 92m4.2
Peloponnesian Wars, 91
Pentagon, bombings of, 10–13, 170, 219
Perceptual dilemma, 245
Periphery, the, 437–439
Perpetual peace, 306–315, 322
Persian Gulf War, 269
Personal character, 184–189
Personality disturbances, 186
Personality traits, 186–187
Petersberg tasks, 409
Phillipines, The, 8
Physical location, 112
Physical networks, 220
Pigouvian taxes, 472b16.1
Pirating, 393
PJCC. *See* Police and Judicial Coopera-
tion in Criminal Matters (PJCC)
PLO. *See* Palestine Liberation Organi-
zation (PLO)
Pluralism, 144–146
Poland, 42, 91, 93
democratization of, 327
German invasion of, 86, 181, 200
Polarity, 88–90, 189–190
cold war and, 91–93
international stability and, 95–98
post–cold war, 93–94
Police and Judicial Cooperation in
Criminal Matters (PJCC), 406
Policies, defined, 136
Policy relevance, 44–46
Political analysis, levels of, 13–21,
16f1.1. *See also* Levels of
analysis
Political disorder, 456
Political economy
approaches to, 333–336
defense and, 342–355
defense-industrial policy and,
346–347
global arms transfers, 357–360
guns *vs.* butter, 347–351
international arms market and,
355–357
liberal perspective on, 334–335
military downsizing and outsourcing, 351–355
military-industrial complex,
343–346
national competition and geo-
economics, 340–342
radical perspective on, 335–336
realist perspective on, 334
Political freedom, 452–461
Political-geographic arrangements, 76
Political isolation, 337, 356
Political location, 112
Politically relevant international
environment (PRIE), 77
Political openness, 141